Cambridge studies in medieval life and thought

LITHUANIA ASCENDING

From 1250 to 1795 Lithuania covered a vast area of eastern and central Europe. Until 1387 the country was pagan. How this huge state came to expand, defend itself against western European crusaders and play a conspicuous part in European life are the main subjects of this book.

The emergence of pagan Lithuania is presented against the background of the political and religious crises of fourteenth-century Byzantine and Catholic Christendom. An attempt is made to show how the Lithuanians manipulated their position on the commercial, denominational and colonial frontier to maintain an expanding dominion in the face of Polish, Teutonic and Rus'ian opposition. It questions the mirage of the 'age of faith' as the 'age of totalitarian Christian Europe'.

The book has relevance to the expansion of the Church and Empire between the ninth and eleventh centuries. The rise of the new ruling elites in the fourteenth century, familiar to French and English historians, has its counterpart in Bohemia, Poland, Rus', and in Lithuania, although centralising forces were very weak, thus contributing to the strength of the later Polish–Lithuanian Republic of the Two Nations. Sources are used from across Europe, from Ireland and Spain to the Caucasus. The use of 'literary', 'mythological' chronicles is analysed. Reliance on non-written sources has also proved necessary. The lack of extensive Lithuanian documentation requires a focus on all sides of international affairs: a *desideratum* which is usually missing from western studies.

Cambridge studies in medieval life and thought
Fourth series

General Editor:
D. E. LUSCOMBE
Professor of Medieval History, University of Sheffield

Advisory Editors:
R. B. DOBSON
Professor of Medieval History, University of Cambridge, and Fellow of Christ's College

ROSAMOND MCKITTERICK
Reader in Early Medieval European History, University of Cambridge, and Fellow of Newnham College

The series *Cambridge studies in medieval life and thought* was inaugurated by G. G. Coulton in 1921. Professor D. E. Luscombe now acts as General Editor of the Fourth series, with Professor R. B. Dobson and Dr Rosamond McKitterick as Advisory Editors. The series brings together outstanding work by medieval scholars over a wide range of human endeavour extending from political economy to the history of ideas.

For a list of titles in the series, see end of book.

LITHUANIA ASCENDING

A pagan empire within east-central Europe, 1295–1345

S. C. ROWELL

Centre for West Lithuanian and Prussian History, University of Klaipėda

CAMBRIDGE
UNIVERSITY PRESS

Published by the Press Syndicate of the University of Cambridge
The Pitt Building, Trumpington Street, Cambridge, CB2 1RP
40 West 20th Street, New York, NY 10011-4211, USA
10 Stamford Road, Oakleigh, Melbourne 3166, Australia

First published 1994

Printed in Great Britain at the University Press, Cambridge

A catalogue record for this book is available from the British Library

Library of Congress cataloguing in publication data

Rowell, S. C.
Lithuania Ascending: a pagan empire within east-central Europe.
1295–1345/S. C. Rowell.
p. cm. – (Cambridge studies in medieval life and thought: 4th ser., 25)
Includes bibliographical references and index.
ISBN 0 521 45011 X
1. Lithuania – History – To 1569. I. Title. II. Series.
DK505.7.R68 1994
947'.5 – dc20 92-17442 CIP

ISBN 0 521 45011 X hardback

TAG

In piam memoriam 1991. I. 13

CONTENTS

List of illustrations	page	x
Preface		xiii
List of abbreviations		xix
Glossary of foreign terms		xxiii
Maps		xxiv
Genealogical tables		xxx

1	Central and eastern Europe, 1290–1320	1
2	Sources	26
3	An introduction to Lithuanian political and economic history before 1315	49
4	The expansion of Lithuania	82
5	Political ramifications of the pagan cult	118
6	The metropolitanate of Lithuania	149
7	Pagans, peace and the Pope, 1322–24	189
8	The harshest *Realpolitik*	229
9	1339–45: Endings and beginnings	263
10	Factors contributing to the formation of the Grand Duchy	289

Appendix 1: Russian sources for the Fall of Kiev, 1322–23	305
Appendix 2: List of Orthodox hierarchs, 1283–1461	312
Manuscript sources	315
Bibliography	318
Index	361

ILLUSTRATIONS

FIGURES

MAPS

TABLES

List of illustrations

GENEALOGICAL TABLES

PREFACE

On 6 September 1991 the Bolshevik regime in Moscow formally renounced the Molotov–Ribbentrop Pact and all pretensions to the Baltic states which it had seized in 1940. That same day in Vilnius the Lithuanian Academy of Sciences held an international symposium to commemorate the six hundred and fiftieth anniversary of the death of the founder of Lithuania's medieval power, Grand Duke Gediminas (1315/16–1341/42). Lithuania has a long and distinguished history. In 1386 Grand Duke Jogaila, Gediminas' grandson, married Queen Jadwiga of Poland to become king of a Lithuano-Polish state which stretched from Silesia to Smolensk, from the Baltic to the Black Sea. Lithuania disappeared from the map of Europe as a sovereign state when the last part of the Polish–Lithuanian Commonwealth of the Two Nations was annexed by Russia in 1795. It emerged from the Russian Empire, as did Poland, in 1918.[1]

This study aims to show how Lithuania first came to international prominence. From his citadel in Vilnius, Gediminas governed a state which controlled not only ethnic Lithuania, but also, in the western principalities of Orthodox Rus', more Rus'ian territory than that held by the grand duke of Moscow. The Grand Duchy of Lithuania straddled the major trade routes between the Baltic and the rivers Dvina and Dnepr, between Rus', Poland and the Teutonic Order. Its territory comprised vast Christian lands subject to the Church of Constantinople; its realm promised room for further expansion by the Church of Rome. It *chose* to remain pagan.

There is no detailed account of pagan Lithuania in a Western European language. The present work seeks to remedy this lacuna

[1] For general histories of Lithuania and east-central Europe which are relatively light in their bias see O. Halecki, *The borderlands of western civilisation. A history of East Central Europe* (New York, 1952) and J. Ochmański, *Historia Litwy*, 2nd edn (Wrocław–Warsaw etc., 1982).

in scholarship and add to the achievements of Henryk Paszkiewicz, Zenonas Ivinskis and Vladimir Terentevich Pashuto whose histories of Lithuania (in Polish, Lithuanian and Russian) show some signs of wear and are, in any case, unavailable to an English readership.[2] This monograph gives full treatment to Gediminas, the most prominent of the secondary figures in John Fennell's excellent study of the rise of Moscow.[3] It aims to recount events from all sides and especially from Vilnius rather than from Warsaw, Moscow or Königsberg, by dealing with the Grand Duchy in its own right not merely as an aspect of Teutonic, Polish or Russian territorial expansion. In the process an attempt will be made to counter those pernicious western approaches to eastern and central European history which marginalise, from ignorance, Slavonic and Baltic contributions to European culture. For too long medieval Lithuanian history has been treated as a *tabula rasa* awaiting the inscription of the glories of its neighbours as the powers which 'civilised' the Grand Duchy.

We shall examine Lithuania's rise to prominence under Gediminas with reference to the achievements of his predecessor and brother Vytenis (1295–1315) and his chosen heir Jaunutis (1342–45). Our major concerns will be the Grand Duchy's exploitation of its neighbours' military and political weaknesses, its manipulation of the confessional frontier between Baltic Catholic Christendom and Orthodox Rus', and its diplomatic skill in dealing with foreign princes who were as ready to connive with pagan Lithuanians (and seek pagan princesses in marriage) as they were to maintain a crusade against them. Such a study questions presuppositions of the place of a pagan polity within Christendom and the 'necessity' of conversion as a condition of participating actively in the affairs of the international community in the later Middle Ages.

This approach requires us to examine the tensions in European history in the fourteenth century. The sparsity of native sources available to the student of Lithuania encourages this recourse to the wider context, the European wheel of which Lithuania forms a hub and diverse regional ambitions the spokes: the conflicts

[2] H. Paszkiewicz, *Jagiellonowie a Moskwa I: Litwa a Moskwa w XIII i XIV wieku* (Warsaw, 1933); Z. Ivinskis, *Lietuvos Istorija iki Vytauto Didžiojo mirties* (Rome, 1978; Vilnius, 1991, 2nd edn); V. T. Pashuto, *Obrazovanie Litovskogo Gosudarstva* (Moscow, 1959).

[3] J. L. I. Fennell, *The emergence of Moscow 1304–1359* (London, 1968).

between Rus'ians and Germans and Tatars; Moscow and her rivals for power in Rus'; Poland and Rus', the Holy Roman Empire, the Teutonic Ordensstaat and the Baltic pagans; the Papacy and the Empire; Byzantium and her Commonwealth and the Papacy. Hence a survey of Lithuania's immediate neighbours is given in the first chapter. The confines imposed on students of medieval Lithuania by the exiguity of many sources are discussed before a general introduction to the pagan realm is provided in chapter 3. Studies of Lithuanian expansion in Rus', the pagan cult, the Orthodox hierarchy and the Catholic Mission of 1323–24 ensue before chapters devoted to military diplomacy, the last years of Gediminas' reign, and the dynastic and military problems which bedevilled the reign of Grand Duke Jaunutis.

In this account the terms Lettovia and Lettovian have been adapted from medieval Latin usage (for Lithuania) to provide a general term for the Grand Duchy of Lithuania as a whole. They are used sparingly for clarity and stylistic ease. Lithuania proper (roughly the equivalent of the modern Republic) controlled vast territories whose inhabitants were Slavs. Since the revival of Lithuanian national sentiment in the nineteenth century, 'Lithuanian' has come to refer almost exclusively in an ethnic sense to speakers of that Baltic language, rather than being used as a political term for those subject to Lithuanian rule. Given the sensibilities of the descendants of these peoples (the modern Belorussians and Ukrainians) to that term, we have decided to invent a shorthand term to distinguish actions involving the Grand Duchy which are primarily Slavonic rather than Baltic. The days when a poet born in Belorussian Novgorodok and writing entirely in Polish would refer to himself as a Lithuanian have faded like good health and we appreciate how good they were only now that we have lost them.

Non-specialist readers may be confounded momentarily by the use of the name Rus' to refer to the land inhabited by the eastern Slavs. This is a harmless scholarly convention which denotes an area of common political, religious and literary culture before the rise of the Great Russians (that is the Muscovites) over their brother Rus'ians of Ukraine and Belorussia.

On occasion reference to medieval Rus'ian customs of chronology cannot be avoided. The reader may find it helpful to note that Rus'ian and other Orthodox chroniclers date events from the creation of the world (*annus mundi*) in 5508 BC. The year was held to begin on 1 March, a day which falls usually after our 1 January but sometimes before it. Thus AM 6808 is the equivalent of 1 March 1299/29 February 1300 or 1 March 1300/28 February 1301. The translation to our system depends largely on a comparison of the record with events occurring outside Rus'.

Foreign names are given for the most part in their native forms, except where they are well known (such as popes, writers or rulers) in English. Given the international nature of previous studies of Lithuanian history, the names of rulers of the Grand Duchy are known under a confusing variety of forms. Thus Gediminas appears as Gedimin (Russian and German), Giedymin (Polish) and Gedeminne (Latin); his son Algirdas (Olgerd, Olgierd) likewise has a number of disguises. Lithuanian names are given according to established Lithuanian custom. Non-Lithuanian variants of the names of major figures may be found in brackets in the index. Orthodox Christian names have not been Lithuanised. Cyrillic texts are transcribed, where common sense does not rebel, according to the system used by the Library of Congress (the ligatures i͡a and i͡u are disregarded). The use of patronymics for Lithuanian and Russian characters helps concise reference. Thus the forms *-aitis/-aitė* (son/daughter of; plural *-aičiai/-aitės*) and *-ovich/-ovna* (plural *-ovichi/-ovny*) appear regularly throughout the text. Hence we meet (in Lithuanian) Aigusta Gediminaitė, the wife of Semën Ivanovich (in Russian).

The author readily acknowledges the assistance of many individuals and institutions in Great Britain, Lithuania, Poland, Latvia, Estonia, Russia, Germany, the United States of America, Canada and Rome which have lightened his burden: Mr and Mrs C. Rowell, the Grabowski Fund, the University of Warsaw and the British Academy, Magdalene and Clare College, Cambridge. Valuable assistance has been rendered by the directors and staff of: Archivio Segreto Vaticano; Geheimes Staatsarchiv, Preussischer Kulturbesitz, (Königsberg Archive), Berlin; the libraries of the Universities of Warsaw and Kraków; the Polish Academy of Sciences and the Czartoryski Library (Kraków); the City Archives of Riga and Tallinn; the Central Library of the Lithuanian Academy of Sciences (Vilnius) and the City Museum of Pskov.

The unnodding supervision of Dr J. E. B. Shepard, the advice of Mr M. Giedroyć and consistent encouragement from Dr R. J.

Mažeika, heated discussion with Dr A. Nikžentaitis and the support of the Revd Professor P. Rabikauskas have rendered a complex task pleasant.

Clare College, Cambridge
Solemnity of Mary, Mother of God, 1993

ABBREVIATIONS

Acta Ioannis	*Acta Ioannis PP XXII (1317–1334)*, ed. A. L. Tautu (Vatican, 1952)
AE	*Arkheograficheskii Ezhegodnik* (Moscow, 1957–)
AIuZR	*Akty, otnosiashchiesia k istorii iuzhnoi i zapadnoi Rossii*, ed. N. Kostomarov, I (1361–1598) (St Petersburg, 1863)
AO	*Arkheologicheskie Otkrytia* (Moscow, 1965–)
AW	*Ateneum Wileńskie*, 14 vols. (Vilnius, 1923–39)
AZR	*Akty, otnosiashchiesia k istorii Zapadnoi Rossii*, ed. I. Grigorovich, I (1340–1506) (St Petersburg, 1846); II (1506–1544) (St Petersburg, 1848)
ChOIDR	*Chtenia v obshchestve istorii i drevnostei rossiiskikh pri Moskovskom Universitete* (Moscow, 1846–1918)
CDP	*Codex Diplomaticus Prussicus*, ed. J. Voigt, 6 vols. (Königsberg, 1836–61)
CEV	*Codex Epistolaris Vitoldi magni ducis Lithuaniae (1376–1430)*, ed. A. Prochaska (Kraków, 1882)
Długosz	*Ioannis Dlugossi Annales seu cronicae incliti regni Poloniae* ed. J. Dąbrowski, D. Turkowska *et al.* (Warsaw, 1964–)
EpG	*Epitome Gestorum Prussiae (Canonici Sambiensis)*, *SRP*, I , 272–90
FRB	*Fontes Rerum Bohemicarum*, ed. J. Emler *et al.* 6 vols. (Prague, 1871–1907)
GL	*Gedimino Laiškai*, ed. V. T. Pashuto and I. Štal (Vilnius, 1966)
GVNiP	*Gramoty Velikogo Novgoroda i Pskova*, ed. S. N. Valk (Moscow–Leningrad, 1949)
HW	Hermann of Wartberge, *Chronicon Livoniae*, *SRP*, II, 21–116

IORIaS	*Izvestia otdelenia russkogo iazyka i slovesnosti Imperatorskoi Akademii Nauk* (St Petersburg, 1896–1927)
ILKI	*Iš Lietuvių Kultūros Istorijos* (Vilnius, 1958–)
JBS	*Journal of Baltic Studies* (1972–) [Published by the Association for the Advancement of Baltic Studies]
KDKDW	*Kodeks dyplomatyczny Katedry i diecezji wileńskiej*, ed. J. Fijałek and W. Semkowicz (Kraków, 1948)
KDWP	*Kodeks dyplomatyczny Wielkopolski*, 5 vols. ed. F. Piekosiński (Poznań, 1877–1908)
KH	*Kwartalnik Historyczny* (Lwów–Warsaw, 1887–)
KSIIMK	*Kratkie Soobshchenia Instituta istorii materialnoi kultury* (Moscow, 1939–)
LAMMDI	*Lietuvos TSR Aukštųjų Mokyklų Mokslo Darbai: Istorija* (Vilnius, 1958–). [Usually abbreviated to *Istorija*]
LMADA	*Lietuvos TSR Mokslų Akademijos Darbai. Serija A* (Vilnius, 1955–). [now *Lituanistica*]
L1, *L2*, *L3*	Redactions of the Lithuanian Chronicle, *PSRL*, XXXV (Moscow, 1980) and XXXII (Moscow, 1975)
LR	*Livländische Reimchronik* ed. L. Meyer (Paderborn, 1876). English translation by J. C. Smith and W. L. Urban, *The Livonian Rhymed Chronicle, Indiana University Publications: Uralic and Altaic Series*, CXXVIII (1977)
LU	*Liv- Esth- und Kurländisches Urkundenbuch, nebst Regesten*, ed. F. G. von Bunge, 6 vols. (Reval–Riga, 1853–71; Aalen, 1967–74)
MM	*Acta Patriarchatus Constantinopolitani*, ed. F. Miklosich and J. Müller, 2 vols. (Vienna, 1862)
MGH SRG	*Monumenta Germaniae Historica. Scriptores Rerum Germanicarum* 32 vols. (Hanover–Leipzig–Hahn, 1826–1934); new series 12 vols. (Berlin–Weimar, 1922–)
MPH	*Monumenta Poloniae Historica: Pomniki dziejowe Polski* ed. A. Bielowski *et al.*, 6 vols. (Lwów, 1864–93); new series (Kraków–Warsaw, 1946–)

MPV	*Analecta Vaticana (1202–1306)*, ed. J. Ptaśnik, *Monumenta Poloniae Vaticana*, III (Kraków, 1914)
NL	*Novgorodskaia Pervaia Letopis', starshego i mladshego izvodov*, ed. A. N. Nasonov (Moscow–Leningrad, 1950)
OF	*Ordens Folianten*, manuscripts in the Teutonic Order's Königsberg Secret Archive now in PKKA, Berlin
OSP	*Oxford Slavonic Papers* (Oxford, 1950–).
PD	Peter of Dusburg, *Chronica terrae Prussiae*, *SRP*, I, 3–219
PG and PL	*Patrologiae cursus completus ... series graecus*, ed. J. P. Migne, 161 vols. (Paris, 1857–66) and *... series latina*, ed. J. P. Migne, 217 vols. (Paris, 1844–55)
PG	*Polotskie Gramoty XIII – nachalo XVIvv.*, ed. A. L. Khoroshkevich, 3 vols. (Moscow, 1977–80)
PH	*Przegląd Historyczny* (Warsaw, 1905–)
PKKA	Geheimes Staatsarchiv, Preussischer Kulturbesitz, Königsberg Archive, now in Berlin
PL	*Pskovskie Letopisi*, ed. A. N. Nasonov, 2 vols. (Moscow–Leningrad, 1941–55)
PSRL	*Polnoe Sobranie Russkikh Letopisei* (St Petersburg–Moscow, 1841–)
PU	*Preussisches Urkundenbuch*, 6 vols. ed. M. Hein, E. Maschke, K. Conrad *et al.* (Königsberg–Marburg, 1882–1986)
PVL	*Povest' vremennykh let*, ed. D. S. Likhachev, 2 vols. (Moscow–Leningrad, 1950)
RAU	*Rozprawy Akademii Umiejętności. Wydział historyczno-filozoficzny*, 25 + 47 vols. (Kraków, 1866–1952)
RIB	*Pamiatniki drevnerusskogo kanonicheskogo prava*, ed. A. S. Pavlov, *Russkaia Istoricheskaia Biblioteka*, VI (St Petersburg, 1880)
RLA	*Russko-Livonskie Akty*, ed. K. E. Napiersky (St Petersburg, 1868)
Sof.	*Sofiiskaia Pervaia Letopis'*, *PSRL*, V (St Petersburg, 1851)

SRP	*Scriptores Rerum Prussicarum*, ed. T. Hirsch, M. Töppen and E. Strehlke, 5 vols. (Leipzig, 1861–74; 2nd edn, Frankfurt-am-Main, 1965, vol. VI added)
TrRHS	*Transactions of the Royal Historical Society*, 6 series (London, 1873–)
TL	*Troitskaia Letopis': rekonstruktsia teksta*, ed. M. D. Priselkov (Moscow, 1950)
TODRL	*Trudy Otdela Drevnerusskoi Literatury* (Moscow, 1934–)
VMPL	*Vetera Monumenta Poloniae et Lithuaniae gentiumque finitimarum historiam illustrantia*, ed. A. Theiner, I (Rome, 1860)
Wig.	Wigand of Marburg, *Cronica nova Prutenica*, *SRP*, II, 429–662
ZH	*Zapiski Historyczne* (Toruń, 1908–)
ZfO	*Zeitschrift für Ostforschung: Länder und Völker im östlichen Mitteleuropa* (Marburg/Lahn, 1952–)
ZhMNP	*Zhurnal Ministerstva Narodnogo Prosveshchenia*, 362+72 vols. (St Petersburg, 1834–1917)

FOREIGN TERMS

Basqaq – Tatar official, tax collector
Bajor-as/-ai; boiar – nobleman/-men
Druzhina – princely retinue
Grivna – silver ingot
Iarlyk – charter, patent to throne or diocese issued by the Tatar khan
Kunigaikštis – Lithuanian prince, analogous with Russian *kniaz'*
Kunigas – Lithuanian priest, originally also a political leader
Namestnik – governor, lieutenant (representing a prince or bishop)
Posadnik – mayor (Novgorod, Pskov)
Prigorod – defensive outpost of city; town dependent on a larger town
Reise – military campaign led by Teutonic Knights usually with the assistance of Catholic princes and knights from western Europe
Svod – chronicle compilation
Tysiatskii – militia commander, police chief
Veche – popular assembly of a largely oligarchic nature

PRONUNCIATION CHART FOR CENTRAL EUROPEAN LANGUAGES

Most letters can be pronounced more or less in the English fashion. Some combinations of consonants however may cause the reader to stumble. The strangest are listed below:

ą (Polish) = French *on*	ė = eh (as in *care*)
ai = eye	ë = yo
au = ow	ł = w
c = ts	ř = rsh
cz/č = ch	rz/ž/ż/ź = zh
ę (Polish) = French *un*	sz/š = sh

Map 1. Central and eastern Europe *c.* 1340.

Map 2. Expansion of Lithuania *c.* 1248–1342.

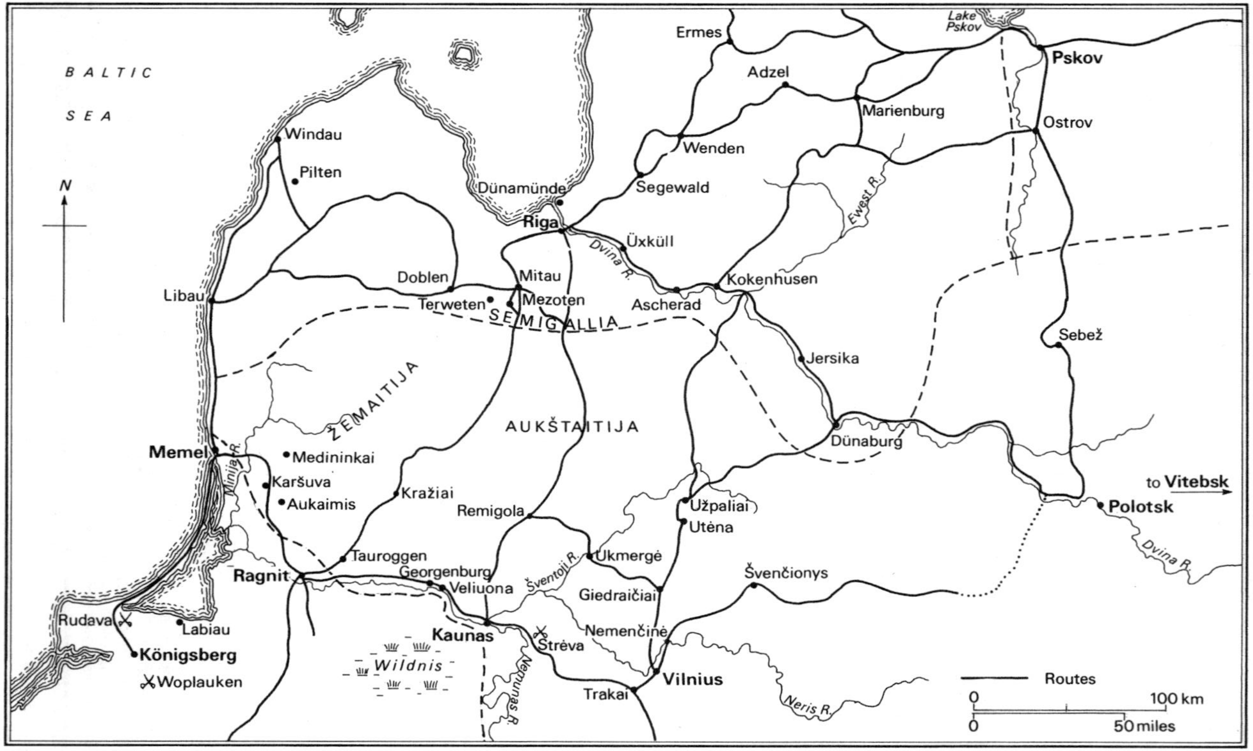

Map 3. Trade routes in the Grand Duchy of Lithuania.

Map 4. Map of Lithuanian forts.

Map 5(a). The Teutonic *Ordensstaat* in Prussia.

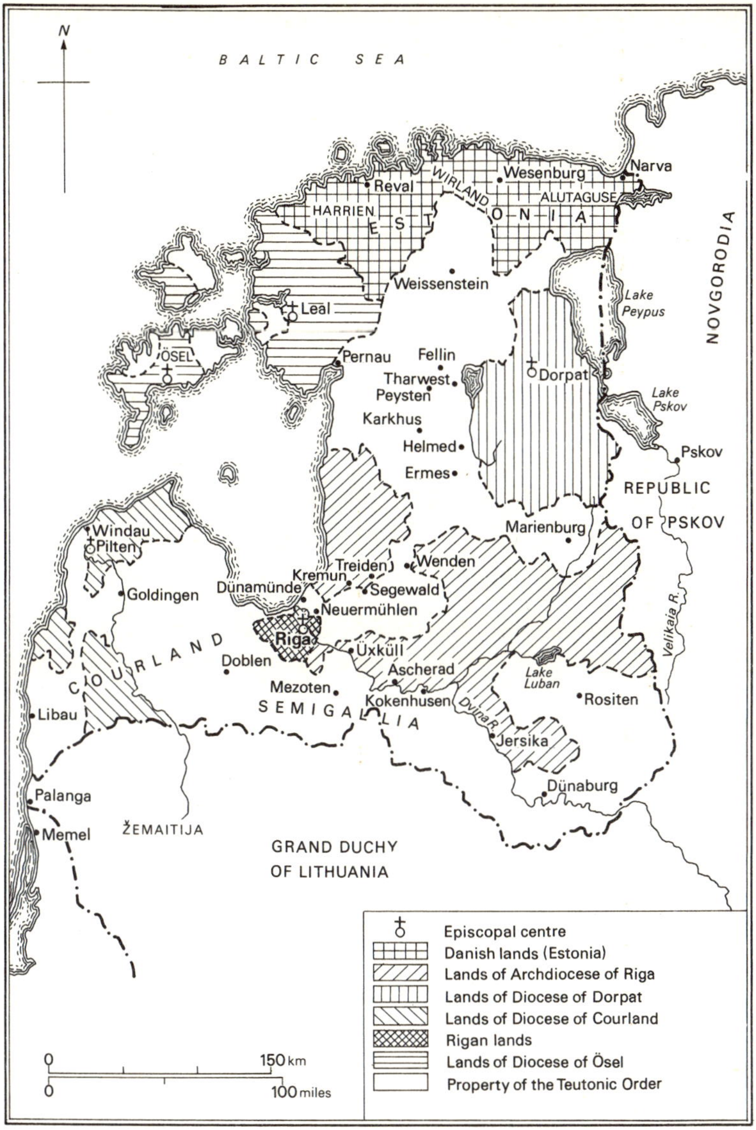

Map 5(b). The Teutonic *Ordensstaat* in Livonia.

Genealogical table 1. Central European monarchies

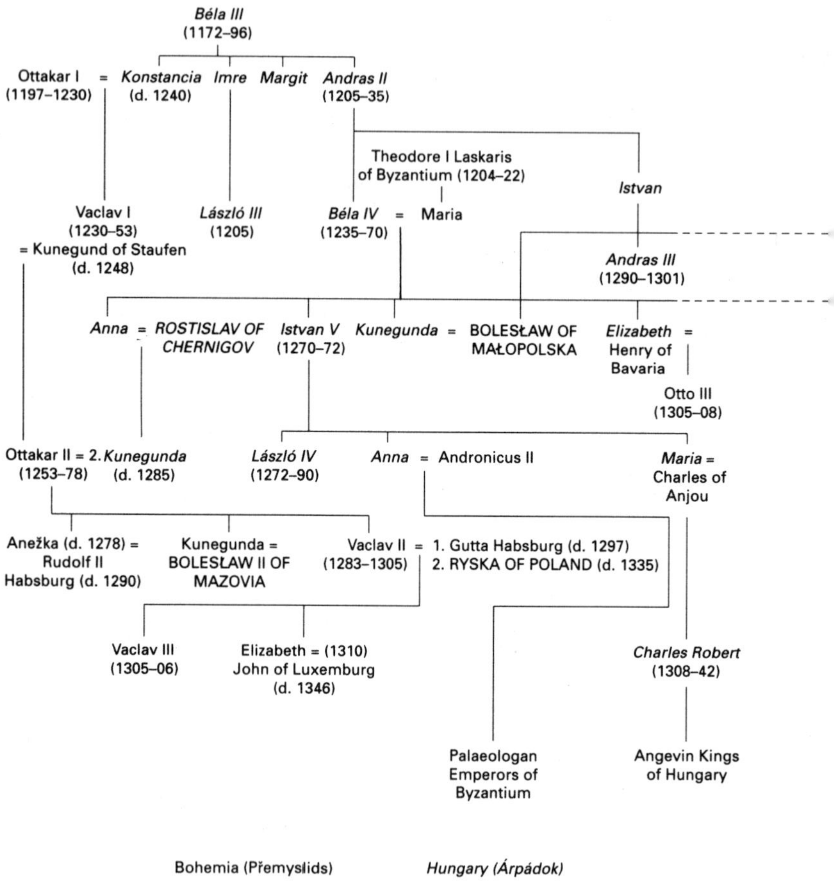
Béla III
(1172–96)
Ottakar I (1197–1230) = Konstancia (d. 1240)
Imre
Margit
Andras II
(1205–35)
Theodore I Laskaris
of Byzantium (1204–22)
Istvan
Vaclav I
(1230–53)
= Kunegund of Staufen
(d. 1248)
László III
(1205)
Béla IV = Maria
(1235–70)
Andras III
(1290–1301)
Anna = ROSTISLAV OF CHERNIGOV
Istvan V
(1270–72)
Kunegunda = BOLESŁAW OF MAŁOPOLSKA
Elizabeth = Henry of Bavaria
Otto III
(1305–08)
Ottakar II = 2. Kunegunda
(1253–78) (d. 1285)
László IV
(1272–90)
Anna = Andronicus II
Maria = Charles of Anjou
Anežka (d. 1278) = Rudolf II Habsburg (d. 1290)
Kunegunda = BOLESŁAW II OF MAZOVIA
Vaclav II = 1. Gutta Habsburg (d. 1297)
(1283–1305) 2. RYSKA OF POLAND (d. 1335)
Vaclav III
(1305–06)
Elizabeth = (1310) John of Luxemburg
(d. 1346)
Charles Robert
(1308–42)
Palaeologan Emperors of Byzantium
Angevin Kings of Hungary
Bohemia (Přemyslids)
Hungary (Árpádok)

Dates given are regnal; those after '=' refer to date of marriage.
d. 1300 – died in 1300
d.a. 1300 – died before 1300
d.p. 1300 – died after 1300
♀ – daughter, female
♀ Boris – daughter of Boris
♂ son

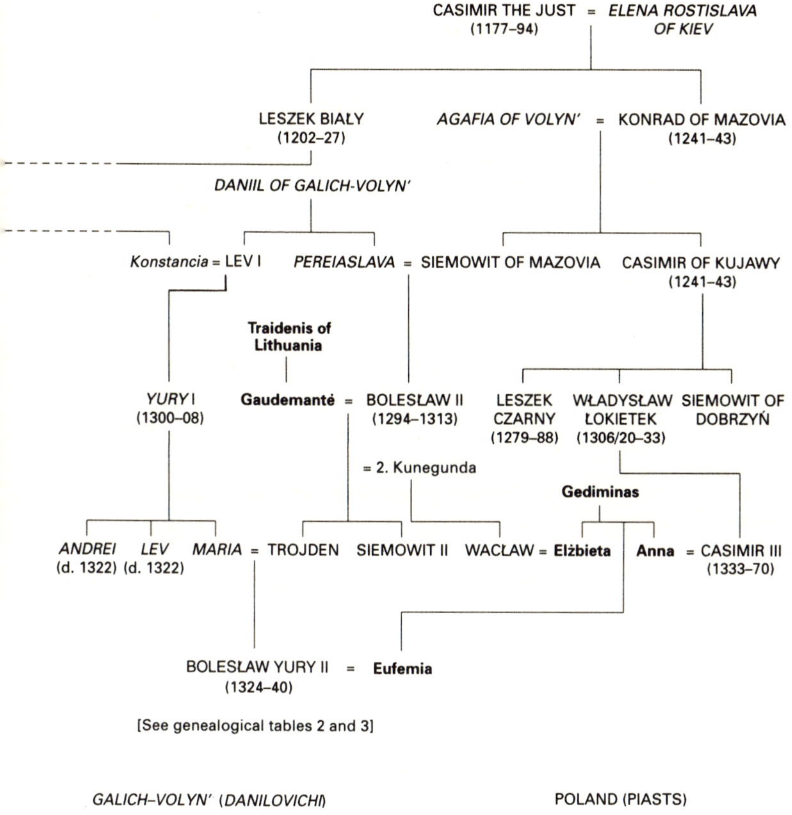
CASIMIR THE JUST (1177–94) = ELENA ROSTISLAVA OF KIEV
LESZEK BIAŁY (1202–27)
AGAFIA OF VOLYN' = KONRAD OF MAZOVIA (1241–43)
DANIIL OF GALICH-VOLYN'
Konstancia = LEV I
PEREIASLAVA = SIEMOWIT OF MAZOVIA
CASIMIR OF KUJAWY (1241–43)
Traidenis of Lithuania
YURY I (1300–08)
Gaudemantė = BOLESŁAW II (1294–1313)
= 2. Kunegunda
LESZEK CZARNY (1279–88)
WŁADYSŁAW ŁOKIETEK (1306/20–33)
SIEMOWIT OF DOBRZYŃ
Gediminas
ANDREI (d. 1322)
LEV (d. 1322)
MARIA = TROJDEN
SIEMOWIT II
WACŁAW = Elżbieta
Anna = CASIMIR III (1333–70)
BOLESŁAW YURY II (1324–40) = Eufemia
[See genealogical tables 2 and 3]
GALICH–VOLYN' (DANILOVICHI)
POLAND (PIASTS)

Genealogical table 2. The Gediminids

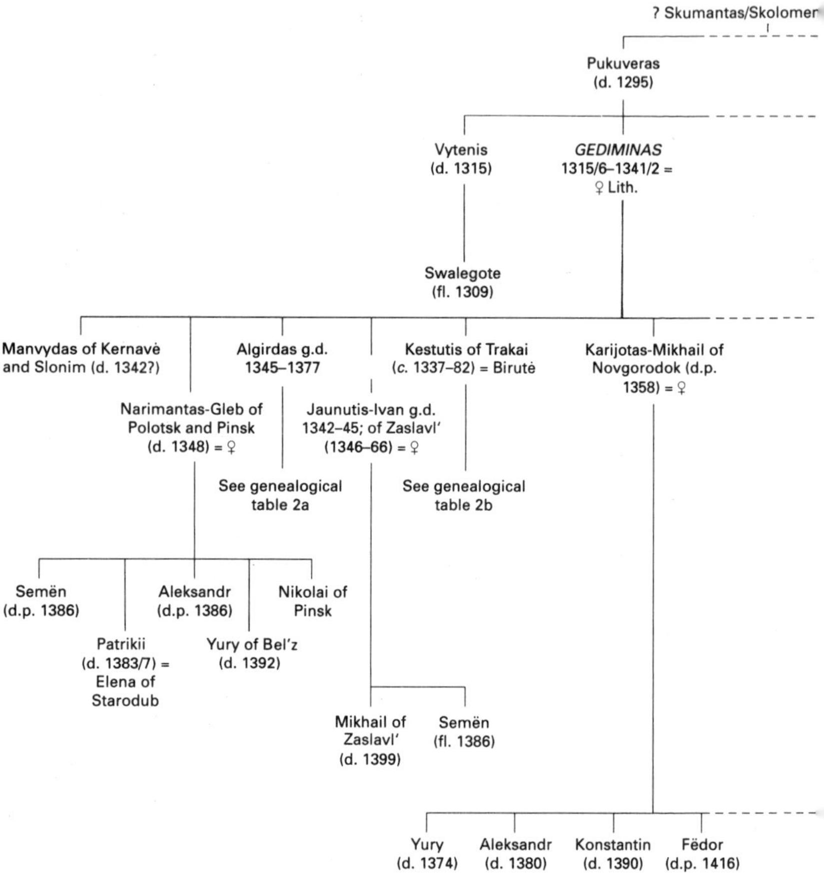

Dates given are regnal; those after '=' refer to date of marriage.
d. 1300 – died in 1300
d.a. 1300 – died before 1300
d.p. 1300 – died after 1300
♀ – daughter, female
♀ Boris – daughter of Boris
♂ son

Butigeidas
(fl. 1289)

Voin of Polotsk (fl. 1326) — Liubko (d. 1342)

Fëdor of Kiev (fl. 1331–62)

♀

Liubartas-Dmitry of Vladimir (d. 1384) = 1. ♀ Andrei Yurevich of Vladimir = 2. (1349) ♀ Konstantin of Rostov

Fëdor (d. 1431)

Semën

Lazar

Maria (d. 1349) = (1320) Dmitry Mikhailovich of Tver' (d. 1325)

(see genealogical table 4)

Elżbieta (d. 1364) = (1316?) Wacław of Płock

Bolesław III of Płock (d. 1351)

Anna (d. 1363) = (1337) Henry V of Żagań (d. 1369)

Jadwiga (d. 1390) = (1365) Casimir III of Poland (d. 1370)

(see genealogical table 3)

Aldona-Anna (d. 1339) = (1325) Casimir III of Poland

Eufemia (d. 1342) = (1331) Bolesław-Yury of Galich-Volyn'

Aigusta-Anastasia (d. 1345) = (1333) Semën Ivanovich of Moscow

(see genealogical table 4)

♀ = Andrei Mstislavich of Kozel'sk

Dmitry (d. 1399) = (1356) Liubov' Ivanovna of Moscow

Anastasia (fl. 1401) = Vasily Mikhailovich of Tver' (d.p. 1426)

The interrelationship of princely clans in Lithuania before Pukuveras

Ringaudas (I) (d.a. 1219)

Živinbudas (II) (fl. 1219)

Traidenis (VIII) (*c.* 1270–82)

Gaudemantė (d. 1288) = Bolesław II of Płock (d. 1313)

Dausprungas (III) (d.*c.* 1238)

♀

Daumantas (IX) (d. 1285)

Švarnas (VII) (d. 1268/9)

Mindaugas (IV) (*c.* 1238–63)

Vaišvilkas (VI) (1265–67)

♀

Treniota (V) (1263–65)

Daujotas Vilikaila (fl. 1219)

2(a). Algirdaičiai

Algirdas = 1. ♀ (Maria?) of Vitebsk (= 1318?, d.a. 1349)
- Andrei of Polotsk (d. 1399)
- Dmitry of Briansk (d. 1399) = Anna
- Konstantin of Czartorysk (d. 1390)
- Vladimir of Kiev (d. 1398)
- Fëdor of Ratno (d. 1400)
- Fëdora = Sviatoslav of Karachev
- ♀ = Ivan of Novosil'
- Agrafena = (1354) Boris of Suzdal'

= 2. Ul'iana Aleksandrovna of Tver' (= 1350, d. 1392)
- JOGAILA, Władysław II KING OF POLAND, 1386–1434
- Skirgaila-Ivan of Polotsk (d. 1397)
- Lengvenis-Semën = 1. Maria Dmitrievna of Moscow (d. 1399); = 2. ♀ of Moscow
- Korigaila-Casimir of Mstislav (d. 1390)
- Wigand-Aleksandr of Kernavė (d. 1392 = Jadwiga of Opole
- Koributas-Dmitry of Novgorod Seversky = Anastasia Olegovna of Riazan'
- Švitrigaila-Bolesław g.d. 1430–32 (d. 1452); = Anna Sofia Ivanovna of Tver'
- Kenna-Joanna (d. 1368) = (*c.* 1359) Kaźko of Słupsk
- Elena = (1372) Vladimir Khrobry of Serpukhov
- Maria = 1. Vaidila (d. 1380); = 2. David of Gorodetsk
- Wilheida-Katarzyna = (1388) Jan of Schwerin
- Aleksandra (d. 1434) = (1387) Siemowit IV of Mazovia (d. 1426)
- Jadwiga = (1394) Jan II of Oświęcim (d. 1405)
- ♀ =Oleg Ivanovich of Riazan' (1st wife)

2(b). Kestutaičiai

Kestutis = Birutė of Palanga
(d. 1382) (d. 1382)

- Vaidotas-Butautas [Christian name: Henry, d. Prague, 1380]
- Vytautas (g.d. 1392–1430)
- Tautvilas (d. 1390)
- Žygimantas (g.d. 1432–1440)
- Miklausė-Maria = (1375) Ivan of Tver'
- Danutė = (*c.* 1370) Janusz of Mazovia
- Ringailė (d. 1433) = (1390) 1. Henryk of Mazovia
2. Aleksandr of Moldavia

Note The number of wives and children attributable to Kestutis varies. Tradition holds that a pagan priestess, Birutė of Palanga, mother of Grand Duke Vytautas, was the prince's second wife. This supposition is based on the erroneous attribution to Kestutis of certain boiars and other Gediminid princes (Patrikii Narimantaitis) as sons who were active much earlier than Vaidotas or Vytautas – see Kučinskas, *Kęstutis*, 196–7 for a discussion of this matter. It seems justifiable to accept that Kestutis married once and that 'Birutė' was the mother of the seven children known from verifiable sources. The religious legend surrounding this princess and her name remain plausible, albeit unproven. Vaidotas is sometimes considered to be the name of another son, but it seems legitimate to agree with the editor of *Wig.* (*SRP*, II, 550 n. 759), that the name is a dialect variant of Butautas.

Genealogical table 3. Gediminid Catholic marriages

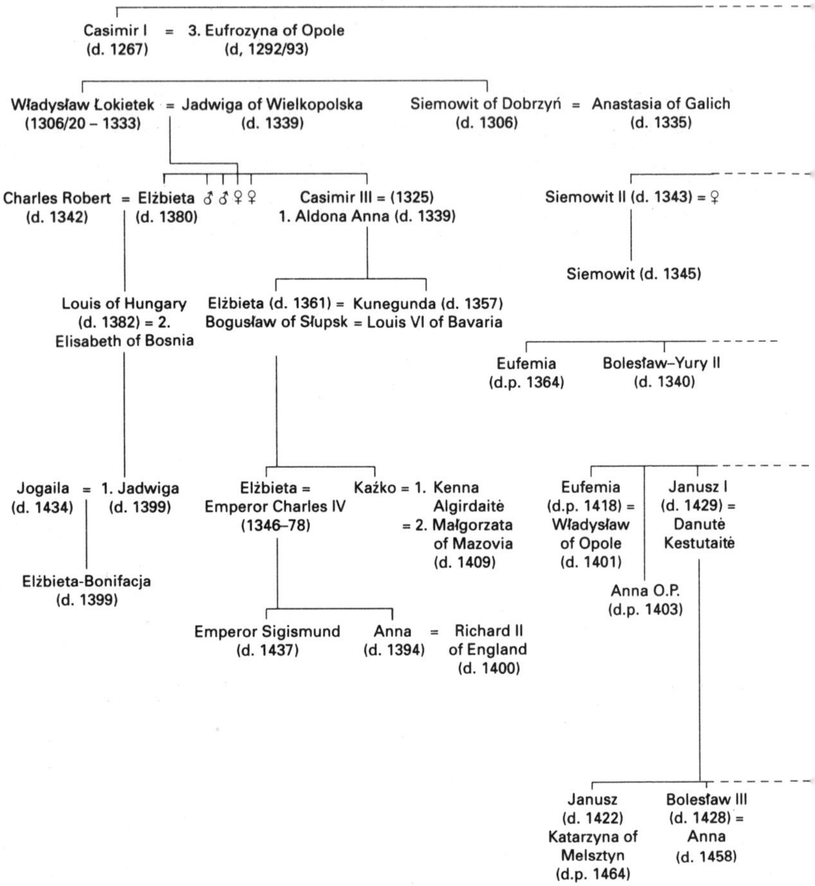

Dates given are regnal; those after '=' refer to date of marriage.
d. 1300 – died in 1300
d.a. 1300 – died before 1300
d.p. 1300 – died after 1300
♀ – daughter, female
♀ Boris – daughter of Boris
♂ son

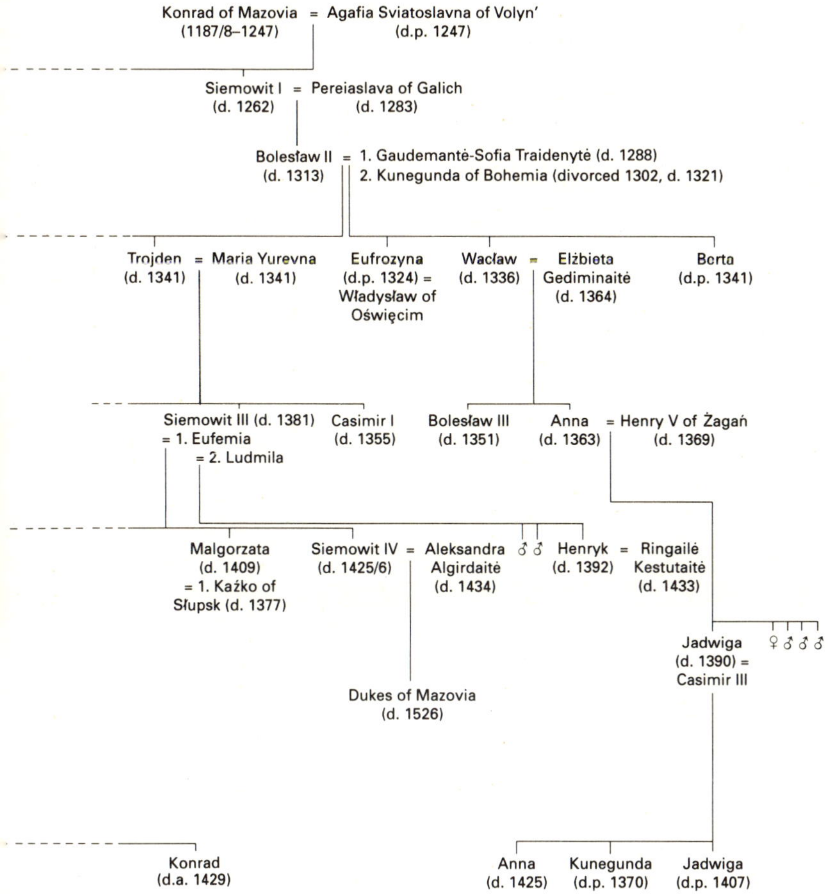
Konrad of Mazovia (1187/8–1247) = Agafia Sviatoslavna of Volyn' (d.p. 1247)
Siemowit I (d. 1262) = Pereiaslava of Galich (d. 1283)
Bolesław II (d. 1313) = 1. Gaudemantė-Sofia Traidenytė (d. 1288)
2. Kunegunda of Bohemia (divorced 1302, d. 1321)
Trojden (d. 1341) = Maria Yurevna (d. 1341)
Eufrozyna (d.p. 1324) = Władysław of Oświęcim
Wacław (d. 1336) = Elżbieta Gediminaitė (d. 1364)
Berta (d.p. 1341)
Siemowit III (d. 1381) = 1. Eufemia = 2. Ludmila
Casimir I (d. 1355)
Bolesław III (d. 1351)
Anna (d. 1363) = Henry V of Żagań (d. 1369)
Malgorzata (d. 1409) = 1. Kaźko of Słupsk (d. 1377)
Siemowit IV (d. 1425/6) = Aleksandra Algirdaitė (d. 1434)
♂ ♂
Henryk (d. 1392) = Ringailė Kestutaitė (d. 1433)
Jadwiga (d. 1390) = Casimir III
♀ ♂ ♂ ♂
Dukes of Mazovia (d. 1526)
Konrad (d.a. 1429)
Anna (d. 1425)
Kunegunda (d.p. 1370)
Jadwiga (d.p. 1407)

Genealogical table 4. Gediminid Orthodox marriages

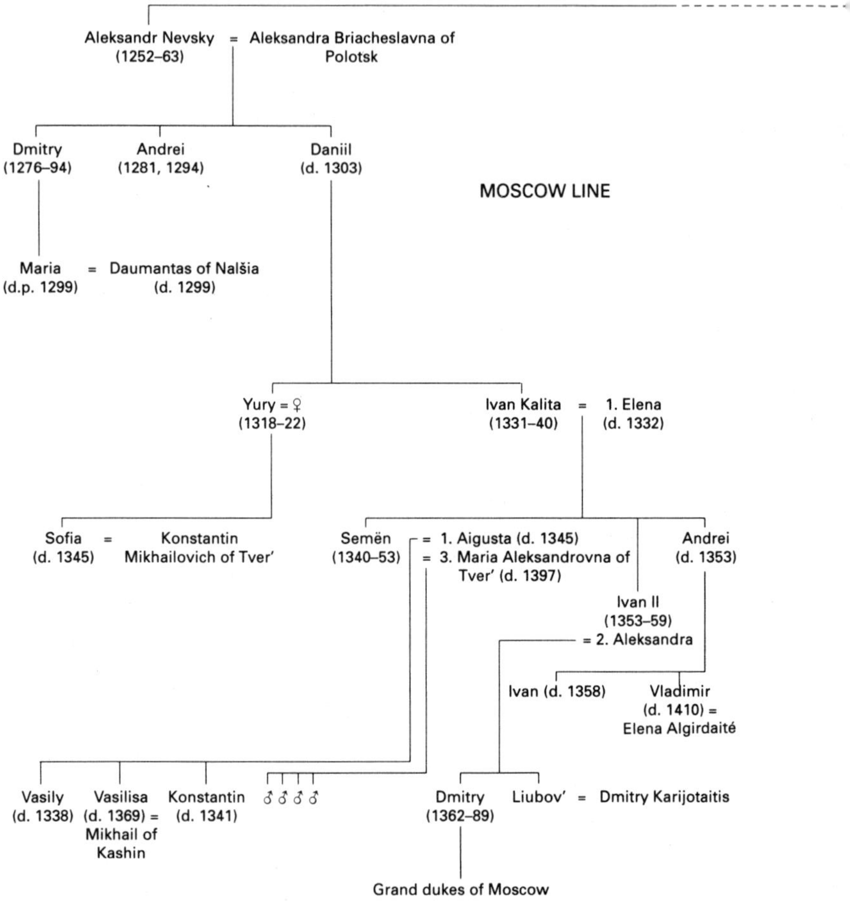

Dates given are regnal; those after '=' refer to date of marriage.
d. 1300 – died in 1300
d.a. 1300 – died before 1300
d.p. 1300 – died after 1300
♀ – daughter, female
♀ Boris – daughter of Boris
♂ son

Yaroslav Vsevolodovich (1238–46) = 3. Feodosia Igorevna of Riazan' (d. 1244)

Yaroslav (1263–71) = 2. Ksenia Yurevna (from Novgorod) (d. 1313)

Mikhail (d. 1319) = Anna Dmitrevna of Rostov (d. 1368)

TVER' LINE

Dmitry (1322–25) = Maria Gediminaitė (d. 1349)

Fedora

Aleksandr (1326–7, d. 1339) = Anastasia (d. 1365)

Konstantin (d. 1345) = Sofia Yurevna

Vasily of Kashin (d. 1368) = Elena Ivanovna of Briansk (d.p. 1373)

Vsevolod of Kholm (d. 1364) = Sofia of Riazan'

Maria (d. 1397) = Semën of Moscow

Ul'iana

See genealogical table 2a

Mikhail = Evdokia* of Mikulin

Mikhail of Kashin (d. 1373) = Vasilisa of Moscow

Ivan (d. 1402) = ♀ Boris Konstantinovich and Agrafena Algirdaitė of Suzdal (d. 1393)*

Ivan (d. 1425) = 1. Maria Kestutaitė (d. 1405)

Vasily (d.p. 1426) = 1. ♀ Vladimir Algirdaitis (d. 1397) 2. Anastasia Karijotaitė (fl. 1401

Aleksandr (d. 1425) = ♀ Fëdor Mikhailovich of Mologa

Boris (d. 1461) = Anastasia Aleksandrovna Shuiskaia of Suzdal' (d. 1486)

Mikhail (d.a. 1505) = Sofia Olelkova (d. 1483)

Konstantin Vasilievich of Suzdal' (d. 1355)

Agrafena Algirdaitė (d. 1393) = Boris (d. 1394)

Evdokia (d. 1404) = Mikhail Aleksandrovich of Mikulin (d. 1399)

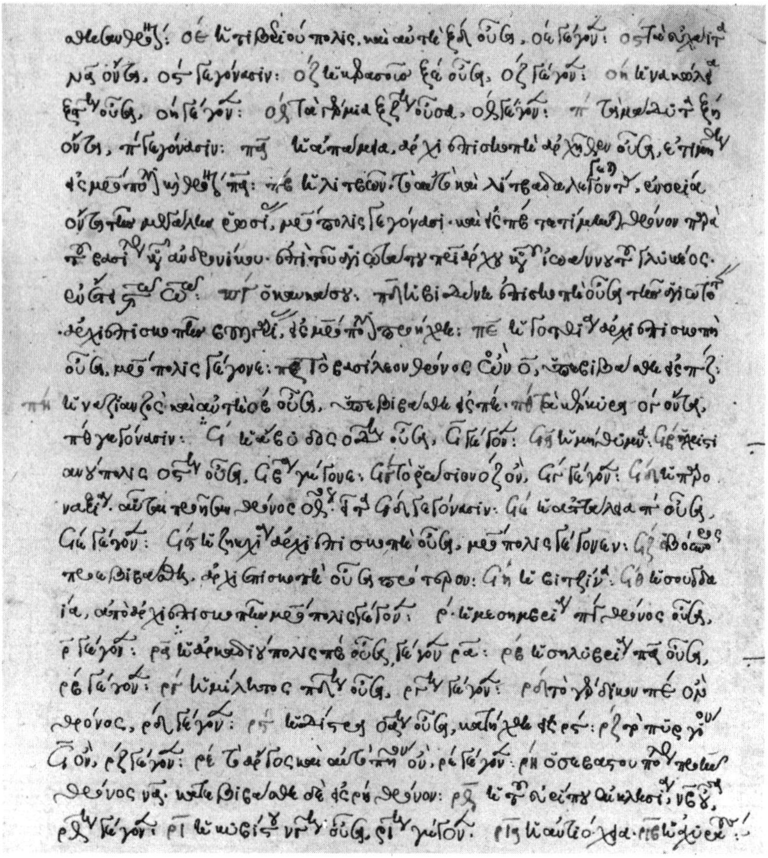

Notitiae Episcopatuum eccles. constantinop. 17. Cambridge, University Library, MS. Dd.II.51 fol. 187r. (in 4°, paper, fourteenth-century). Photo: by permission of the Syndics of Cambridge University Library.

Chapter 1

CENTRAL AND EASTERN EUROPE, 1290–1320

Conflict and change and the cladding of new regimes in the cast-off finery of the old establishment characterise every age. As the new century dawned in 1300 the dynasties and nations which had dominated Europe, many since before the turn of the second Christian millennium, underwent massive restructuring. One of the new leaders of central and eastern Europe, Gediminid Lithuania, whose ruling house would govern Poland, Rus', Bohemia and Hungary before 1500, was emerging slowly from isolation. Before we turn to examine more closely the development of the pagan Gediminid state and the ways in which it succeeded in interweaving itself into the nexus of competing economic, religious, military and political ambitions in central and eastern Europe, we must acquaint ourselves a little with the world of Lithuania's closest neighbours, lying in the shadow of the Empire and the Papacy: the kingdom of Poland, the duchy of Mazovia, the Teutonic Ordensstaat in Prussia and Livonia and the Baltic sphere of German and Danish migration. The Byzantine 'Commonwealth' and Rus' met Catholic Christendom on the territories of the Grand Duchy (see map 1).

THE CONFLICT OF POPE AND EMPEROR

At moments of crisis in the relations of two powerful supranational institutions it may be considered fortunate should the leader of one or other party die. When both major protagonists die, chaos rather than calm ensues. Such a scenario faced western Christendom in the second decade of the fourteenth century. In 1313 Emperor Henry VII passed away as his conflict with Pope Clement V over temporal dominion in Italy reached its peak. The Pope had reiterated earlier the 'superiority with regard to the Empire which we indubitably hold'[1] and stressed his right to govern the Empire during any interregnum, but within a year of Henry's death Clement too lay in the tomb. Far from subsiding, the conflict of authority between the Papacy and the Empire flourished as other rival princes chose sides. Henry's son John of Luxemburg, king of Bohemia, resigned his claim to succeed his father as emperor and lent his support instead to a Bavarian duke, Louis Wittelsbach. Louis was preferable to the other major pretender, Frederick of Habsburg, since his landholdings were small and his own kin favoured the Habsburg's election. He was expected to be malleable; he was misjudged. Louis IV assumed power in 1314 despite continued Habsburg opposition and without regard to the Holy See which remained vacant for two further years.

The new Pope, John XXII (1316–34) was a brittle man 'of fiery temperament' who jealously guarded papal prerogatives and, as is the wont of too many schoolmen, he idolised regulation. Time and again, in his correspondence with non-Catholic princes, John stressed almost inordinately the supreme position of St Peter's heirs, who held the power to loose and bind, to arbitrate between temporal rulers.[2] During the opening months of his pontificate, he declared his neutrality between the two German candidates, requiring them both to submit to papal scrutiny. As far as John was concerned, the empire was vacant and his were the rights to administer it. Louis of Bavaria however stood by the legitimacy of his own disputed election and refused to submit his claims to papal approval. Louis and the Pope attracted support from princes involved in disputes all across Christendom, from Scotland to Poland and Prussia. John of Bohemia supported Louis at first and hoped, as a result, for rewards in Silesia and the Polish kingdom. The Polish duke Władysław Łokietek chose to support the Papacy. The other major Catholic power on the eastern frontier of Catholic Christendom, the Order of Knights of the Hospital of the German House of St Mary in Jerusalem (more familiarly, the

[1] *Corpus Iuris Canonici*, ed. E. L. Richter and E. Friedberg, II (Leipzig, 1881), col. 1153. A. Black, *Political thought in Europe* 1250–1450 (Cambridge, 1992), 85–116.

[2] 'Vita Iohannis PP XXII auctore Heinrico Dapifero de Dissenhoven', *Vitae paparum avenionensium*, ed. E. Baluze and G. Mollat, I (Paris, 1914), 172–7. Letters to rulers of Serbia, the Golden Horde, Armenia and Russia see *Acta Ioannis*, 138, 145, 39 and 1. For Gediminas of Lithuania see *VMPL*, no. 293, p. 194. On pope as international arbitrator see J. Gaudemet, 'Le rôle de la papauté dans le règlement des conflits entre états aux XIIIe et XIVe siècles', *Recueil de la Société Jean Bodin XV*: *La paix* (Brussels, 1961), 79–106.

Teutonic Order or Knights), became increasingly, but not always definitely associated with Louis.[3] In disputes arbitrated by John XXII a deciding factor became how a prince interacted with the German Emperor. This was the case with Poland, whose crown was contested by Łokietek and John of Bohemia.

THE KINGDOM OF POLAND

For much of the twelfth and thirteenth centuries the kingdom of Poland had existed only in the hearts and memories of various Polish prelates and dukes. These years witnessed the disintegration of the kingdom into a group of five squabbling duchies each ruled by a different line of the royal house of Piast. In the west and north, duchies fell increasingly under the influence of their German and Bohemian neighbours, especially in Silesia. As a result of a complex network of dynastic marriages, the Bohemian kings of the House of Přemysl regarded themselves as rightful rulers in Poland. This ambition was realised temporarily by Vaclav II who occupied the Polish throne between 1300 and 1305. When the Přemyslid dynasty died out in the male line with Vaclav III in 1306, its successors, especially John of Luxemburg who ruled in Prague from 1310, inherited pretensions to the Polish crown. Meanwhile the duchy of Lubusz fell away completely into the hands of the German Ascanian clan and became part of the imperial New Mark of Brandenburg. Even so the ideal of the united *Regnum Polonie* did not die altogether among the Piast dukes.[4]

Władysław Łokietek, duke of Łęczyca in south-eastern or Little Poland (Małopolska) eventually made this dream a reality. After outlasting the rival claims of his kinsmen from Silesia and Greater Poland and six years of Bohemian rule, Łokietek was, by 1306 the most powerful prince in Poland. His power, nevertheless, was far

[3] A. Gerlich, *Habsburg--Luxemburg--Wittelsbach in Kampf um die deutsche Königskrone. Studium zur Vorgeschichte des Königtums Ruprechts von der Pfalz* (Wiesbaden, 1960). H. S. Offler, 'Empire and Papacy: the last struggle', *TrRHS* 5th series 6 (1956), 47. For Louis and the Teutonic Order see below pp. 218, 220–1.

[4] O. Pustejovsky, *Schlesiens Ubergang an die Böhmische Krone* (Cologne–Vienna, 1975) and J. Szymczak, 'Genealogia Przemyślidów z przełomu XIII i XIV wieku spokrewnionych z Piastami', *Acta Universitatis Nicolai Copernici. Historia*, 8 (1973), 39–54 and B. Nowacki, *Czeskie roszczenia do korony w Polsce w latach* 1290–1335 (Poznań, 1987), 74–81, 88f. For the New Mark see J. Walachowicz, *Geneza i ustrój polityczny Nowej Marchii do początku XIV wieku* (Poznań, 1980), 10–21.

from universally acknowledged. When the city of Gdańsk rebelled against Łokietek in 1308 and the Ascanians invaded Pomorze (see map 5a), in desperation the Polish pretender enlisted the aid of an external power: the Teutonic Order. Although the Knights succeeded in raising the siege of the Gdańsk garrison in September, they never found time to evacuate the city. By the end of 1311 they held not only Gdańsk but also the whole of Eastern Pomorze and the long and bitter conflict between Poles and Germans for control of the Baltic littoral had begun.[5]

By 1314 all the major territories of fourteenth-century Poland lay in the hands of Łokietek or of kinsmen who approved his ambition. With most noble and clerical support won, all Łokietek needed to become king was papal blessing. It seems likely that Polish arguments in 1316 for the Pope's granting a crown to Łokietek, particularly the assertion that Łokietek provided protection for Christendom against the schismatic Rus'ians and pagan Lithuanians, prompted John XXII to write to the princes of Rus' and Lithuania on 3 February 1317, suggesting they convert to Catholicism.[6] In other words the Pope was attempting to solve Poland's eastern problem without following the policy Łokietek's men proposed. The bull he issued to Łokietek as late as 1319 stresses that the Holy See not only understands the pagan and schismatic threat but also takes account of the Bohemian claim to the Polish crown.[7] This scrupulous hesitation to choose between the conflicting claims of princes, each of whom was of different service to the Holy See is typical of Johannine policy. We might recall his slowness to recognise Robert Bruce as king of Scotland, despite the Declaration of Arbroath, because he was loth to displease Edward I of England.[8]

Łokietek did not relent, neither did his rival retire. In 1318 Bishop Gerward of Włocławek bore a petition from the whole kingdom, clergy, burgesses and nobles to Avignon begging the Pope to recognise Łokietek as king, reminding him of the fight

[5] On Gdańsk and Pomorze see P. Knoll, *The rise of the Polish monarchy. Piast Poland in East Central Europe, 1320–1370* (Chicago–London, 1972), 28–32.

[6] *MPV*, III, nos. 137–9, pp. 203–5.

[7] For 1319 letter to Łokietek see below n. 9. In 1317 the Teutonic Knights exhorted King John not to allow the Polish duke to swindle him of his throne – *Długosz*, IX, 96–7. On link between 1317 letters and the Polish case see *Historia dyplomacji polskiej*, ed. M. Biskup, I (Warsaw, 1982), 232–3.

[8] On Arbroath see *Annales Ecclesiastici*, ed. C. Baronius *et al.*, XXIV (Paris–Freiburg–Bar-le-Duc, 1872), 134–7, 376–7.

against the schismatic Rus'ians, the Tatars and the pagan Lithuanians and the safe collection of papal taxes. In an open reply to the Polish request issued on 20 August 1319, the Pope acknowledged, as he had before, the virtues of the *duke* of Poland alongside the rights of John of Bohemia. On 11 September the Pope granted Duke Łokietek a year's indulgence for those fighting the pagans and schismatics.[9] The Pope remained unmoved, hoping that the rules would be obeyed and the problem disentangle itself. However it seems that the Bohemian's ever-closer connections with Louis of Bavaria in 1318 and 1319 prompted the Pope to choose.[10] Secret letters lay in Bishop Gerward's pouch as he travelled home late in September, informing both Łokietek and the bishops of Poland that the Pope condescended to agree to the matter which Bishop Gerward had brought before him from the bishops, clergy and nobles of Poland. In the letter John refrained from specifying the exact nature of the *negocium* which he had considered 'with diligent deliberation'.[11] All soon became clear. On 20 January 1320 Łokietek was crowned King Władysław I of Poland in the Wawel Cathedral in Kraków. Thenceforth Avignon addressed Łokietek as *Rex Polonie*.

It would be mistaken to view the triumph of the coronation in Kraków as the end of Łokietek's twenty-two years' struggle to restore the *Regnum Polonie*. Both on the battlefield and before papal tribunals the new king continued to press for the return of Pomorze, 'land which has belonged to the kingdom of Poland

[9] *Kodeks dyplomatyczny Małopolski*, ed. F. Piekosiński, II (Kraków, 1886) nos. 573–4, pp. 241–3 and Knoll, *Rise*, 36–7. Papal reply – *VMPL*, no. 224.

[10] *FRB*, IV, 392–3.

[11] Knoll, *Rise*, 38–9. The 'secret letter' preserved in the papal register now in Cambrai, *Bibliothèque Municipale*, Ms. 538 f. 140 reads: '...Hec autem in te, fili, beneuolentia sincera perquirimus et ad hec te pii patris more intentis affectibus exhortamur, ut preter multifarias laudes quas tua nobilitas ex premissorum obseruatione commendabili consequetur, Ille, cui nunquam sine remuneratione seruitur, adaugeat in benedictionibus dies tuos et post presentis mortalitatis excursum tibi coronam inmarcessibilis glorie largiatur. Preterea negocio, pro quo prelati et clerus ac nonnulli nobiles Polonie venerabilem fratrem nostrum G[erwardum] episcopum Wladislauiensem exhibitorem presentium ad sedem apostolicam destinarunt, diligenter inspecto, post deliberationem quam super illo habuimus diligentem, cura ipsius expeditionem quantum cum Deo potuimus uotis condescendimus corde prout in his apostolicis archiepiscopo et suffraganeis eisdem directis poteris intueri.' The full text is published in an edition more difficult to see than the manuscript: W. Abraham, 'Stanowisko kurii papieskiej wobec koronacji Łokietka', *Księga pamiątkowa wydana przez Uniwersytet lwowski ku uczczeniu 500-letniego jubileuszu Uniwersytetu krakowskiego* (Lwów, 1900), 1–34. See also A. Liedtke, 'Stanowisko papieża Jana XXII wobec koronacji Władysława Łokietka', *Nasza Przeszłość*, 36 (1971), 91–107.

from antiquity' (as the court records of the Polono-Teutonic dispute proclaim).[12] On 11 September 1319 John XXII instructed papal investigators to provide redress for Łokietek against the Teutonic Order which had not complied with the findings of previous investigations into Polish and Rigan claims against the Knights. In March 1320 he went on to find in favour of Poland in the Polono-Teutonic dispute over Pomorze. The Knights ignored the command to return Pomorze and Gdańsk to the Polish crown. Łokietek never tired of working for the reincorporation into the *Regnum* of the duchies which still remained outside his control.[13] Through a policy of marriage and shared military action with Charles Robert of Hungary and eventually John of Bohemia too, Łokietek maintained pressure on the Knights and the Empire whilst joining forces on occasion with Denmark and the eastern imperial duchies. His heir Casimir formed a quadruple alliance with Bohemia, Hungary and south-west Rus' in 1337.[14] In compensation for his losses to the Germans in the north and west, Łokietek sought to expand Polish dominion eastwards into south-west Rus'. It was in these ambitions that he came face to face with Grand Duke Gediminas with whom, in the fulness of time, he formed an anti-Teutonic alliance.

As both duke and king, Łokietek set about opening the trade routes of his realm to German and Rus'ian merchants and settlers while establishing new towns and villages, especially in the south but also in Greater Poland.[15] These measures which have their counterparts throughout central Europe, especially in Bohemia and Hungary, helped counter the dreadful effects of the famine which hit Poland (and the whole continent) between 1316 and

[12] *Lites ac res gestae inter Polonos Ordinemque cruciferorum*, ed. H. Chłopocka, I (Wrocław–Warsaw–Kraków, 1970), 31.

[13] Knoll, *Rise*, 50; B. Włodarski, *Polska i Ruś* 1194–1340 (Warsaw, 1966), 264–5; H. Chłopocka, *Procesy Polski z Zakonem krzyżackim w XIV wieku. Studium źródłoznawcze* (Poznań, 1967), 9–29.

[14] Marriages of Łokietek's daughter Elżbieta to Charles Robert of Hungary in 1320 – *Długosz*, IX, 113; proposed marriage of Casimir to John of Bohemia's daughter Jutta in 1322 – *FRB*, IV, 314. Treaty of 27 June 1315 with Denmark see *Diplomatarium Danicum* II.7 (Copenhagen, 1956), no. 286, pp. 211–12. For Congresses of Visegrád see below pp. 255–6.

[15] *KDWP*, II, nos. 970, 971, 976, 979, 981, 999; Toruń charter – *Zbiór dokumentów małopolskich*, ed. S. Kuraś and I. Sułkowska-Kuraś, IV (Wrocław–Warsaw–Kraków, 1969), no. 892 pp. 35–6. T. Ładogorski, *Studia nad zaludnieniem Polski XIV wieku* (Wrocław, 1958), 50. For a general study of colonisation in Poland see B. Zientara, '*Melioratio terrae*: the thirteenth-century breakthrough in Polish history', in *A republic of nobles. Studies in Polish history to 1864*, ed. J. K. Fedorowicz (Cambridge, 1982), 28–48.

1319. The princes of south-west Rus' granted privileges for Kraków merchants in 1320 and for some time before that as documents issuing from the courts of Andrei and Lev Yurevich make clear.[16]

MAZOVIA

In eastern Poland, the duchy of Mazovia attempted to follow its own way outside the restored Polish kingdom. It occupied a very important geo-commercial position between the lands of the Teutonic Order and those of southern Poland and western Rus'. Its dukes encouraged trade and urban settlement within their realm. In 1311 and 1313, they invited German and Polish merchants to their lands, granting charters of German law to new settlements. Mazovia acted as a possible route for merchants from Toruń and Chełmno en route for Kraków and for Saxons wishing to trade with Lithuania.[17] This intermediate position created a need or at least an opportunity to foster good relations with both the Knights and the princes of western Rus'. Links between the Mazovian house and the Rurikid rulers of south-west Rus' formed the basis of Polish claims to the principalities of Galich and Volyn' when the local line was exterminated by the Lithuanians in 1323.[18]

To further the strength and independence of their own duchy, the Mazovian Piasts came to favour close relations with the nascent power on their eastern borders. In 1279 Bolesław II of Mazovia married Gaudemantė (baptised Sofia), the daughter of Grand Duke Traidenis of Lithuania. This union encouraged a decline in Lithuanian raids on Mazovian territory and fostered trade.[19] In 1295 Bolesław's town of Wizna was rased by the Knights in order to prevent its being abused as a base for pagan incursions into

[16] For Bohemia – P. Bolina, 'K problematice kolonizace a počátků hradů na severo-východni Moravě ve 13 století', *Československý Časopis Historický*, 34 (1986), 565. J. Spěváček, *Král diplomat/Jan Lucemburský 1296–1346* (Prague, 1982), 96–246. For Hungary – E. Fügedi, 'Das mittelalterliche Königreich Ungarn als Gastland', *Vorträge und Forschungen*, 18 (1974), 471–507 and A. Kubinyi, 'Urbanisation in the east-central part of medieval Hungary', in *Towns in medieval Hungary*, ed. L. Gerevich (Boulder, CO, 1990), 103–49. Lev's charters – *Zbiór dokumentów*, nos. 895, 898 and 904; Andrei Yurevich – see below n. 80.

[17] Mazovian charters – E. Suchodolska, *Regesty dokumentów mazowieckich z lat 1248–1345* (Warsaw–Łódz, 1980) nos. 77, 78; 86, 92; 76, 81, 82, 84, 87–91, 93–100, 102–6. For Lithuanian trade see below p. 205, n. 93.

[18] See below pp. 98–9.

[19] *Długosz*, VIII, 209, 225, 288. Bolesław endowed memorial masses for Gaudemantė in the ducal Benedictine house at Jeżów in 1313 – Suchodolska, *Regesty*, no. 85. See B. Ulanowski, 'O dacie przywileju Bolesława Mazowieckiego rzekomo z r. 1278 wydanego dla klasztoru w Jeżowie', *RAU*, 17 (1884), 71.

Prussia.[20] After Bolesław died in 1313, the alliance, like the duchy, did not survive intact. The duchy was divided between his three sons: Siemowit II received Rawa (in the south) and his brother Trojden was endowed with the eastern region of Czersk. Their half-brother Wacław, born of Bolesław's second marriage to Kunegunda of Bohemia, gained Płock which lay on the western border with the Knights. Trojden, who had married Maria Yurevna of Galich in 1308, and Siemowit chose to ally themselves with Rus' and the Teutonic Order against the Lithuanians whose western ambitions all three parties feared.[21] One suspects that during the Mazovian civil war of 1316 Gediminas sided with Wacław of Płock against the elder brothers in an attempt to rebuild Traidenis' policy with Mazovia. The marriage between Wacław and Gediminas' daughter Elżbieta may have taken place at this time. Certainly Lithuanian forces aided Wacław in internal Polish disputes in the 1320s, especially against the duke of Dobrzyń.[22] The pagans did not touch Płock when the lands of Siemowit II, Trojden and Bishop Florian were ravaged in 1324. When these princes joined the Knights in a denunciation of Lithuanian perfidy in 1324 Wacław took no part in the affair.[23] It is often noted that in 1321 Wacław signed a treaty with the Order promising not to hinder the Knights as they marched through his lands to attack Lithuania and to inform the Order of any pagan plans to attack Prussia via Płock. Nevertheless this treaty is not specifically anti-Lithuanian, neither is another alliance made in 1326. Indeed, the 1321 arrangement seems to have been directed against Łokietek as Wacław sought an ally who also objected to the king's attempt to spread the new rate of Peter's Pence into his territory.[24] Włodarski is right to suggest that this treaty did little to change Lithuano-Płockian relations and may even have been concluded with Gediminas' knowledge. It is less

[20] *Długosz*, VIII, 288.

[21] Włodarski, *Polska*, 240, 241; 244–7.

[22] Wacław marries – below pp. 91–3; civil war in Mazovia – *MPH*, II, 886. On the disputes between the Piasts of Dobrzyń and Mazovia see Z. Guldon and J. Powierski, *Podziały administracyjne Kujaw i ziemi dobrzyńskiej w XIII i XIV wieku* (Warsaw–Poznań, 1974) and below, p. 210. On Mazovia in general at this time see K. Pacuski, 'Mazowsze wobec walk o władze w Polsce na przełomie XIII/XIV w.', *KH*, 85 (1978), 585–603.

[23] *CDP*, II, no. 114, p. 152 not signed by Wacław; Gediminas burns the lands of Siemowit and Trojden and the bishop of Płock in Pułtusk – *PD*, 191.

[24] 1321 and 1326 treaties – *PU*, II, nos. 335, 541. Peter's Pence in Mazovia and Teutonic Poland is discussed in E. Maschke, *Der Peterspfennig in Polen und dem Deutschen Orden* (Leipzig, 1933), 155–8.

well advertised that in 1320, before the papal hearing against the Knights at Inowrocław, Wacław gave evidence on behalf of Łokietek against the Teutonic Order.[25] The untidy truth is that Wacław found it convenient to use several mutually hostile allies in his struggle to maintain control of his lands. Historians generally fail to distinguish clearly enough the differences in policy (especially towards Lithuania) of the three sons of Bolesław II. Every realm in eastern and central Europe, Catholic, pagan or Orthodox had to hedge its bets by seeking out those who shared its interests not its friends. In their ambitions the Mazovians hung between the Polish Crown and equally dangerous non-Polish enemies. Some bolstered their power through German and Rus'ian alliances, others through cooperation with Lithuania (and unwillingly, even Bohemia). Diplomatic tension was maintained by all factions in central and eastern Europe at that time. There was no monolithic balance of 'great' powers. Lithuania survived because she too learnt to play the game.

In their policy of rapprochement with the Knights, Bolesław's elder sons were supported by Bishop Florian of Płock whose see covered the whole of Mazovia. Needless to say, this provoked the ire of the Lithuanians who attacked the bishop's lands and his cathedral repeatedly. An assault on the diocese of Płock did not necessarily involve any danger to Wacław for the cathedral stood in Pułtusk outside his recently created duchy. Diocesan lands in Pomezania and Michałowo, areas closely controlled by the Knights, were exchanged in 1312 and 1316 for villages on the Mazovian border with Chełmno. This exchange which should be viewed perhaps as the tidying up of church lands by two important local ecclesiastical institutions suited the Knights particularly well, consolidating their holdings on the southern borders of Prussia.[26]

THE TEUTONIC ORDENSSTAAT

The Teutonic Knights were newly established in the Baltic region, where they owed their first possessions to Mazovian policy. These

[25] Wacław's testimony of 1320 – Chłopocka, *Lites ac res gestae*, 30–1. Włodarski, *Polska*, 252.

[26] Mazovian bishop swaps land – Suchodolska, *Regesty*, nos. 83, 97, 101, 116. Lithuanian attacks in 1324 and 1327 – *PD*, 191; *Nowy kodeks dyplomatyczny Mazowsza. Część druga*, ed. I. Sułkowska-Kuraś, S. Kuraś *et al.* (Wrocław–Warsaw-etc., 1989), no. 188, pp. 187–8.

Knights of the Cross were invited to Prussia in 1230 by Duke Konrad of Mazovia who had been unable to destroy the threat of pagan incursions into his lands in the 1220s.[27] The Order had houses throughout northern and central Germany and the Low Countries in addition to fortresses in Northern Syria. By 1237 it had captured most of western Prussia and subsumed the land and the brethren of another military order, the Sword Brothers of Livonia. Thus the Teutonic Order came to comprise two parts, the Livonian Order governed by its own Landmarshall and the Prussian Order which was separated from its counterpart by a corridor of Lithuanian and Semigallian land (see map 5). From 1309 the Grand Master presided over both branches of the Order from his residence at Marienburg in Prussia rather than Venice, a development which reflects both the increase in the Order's commitment in the Baltic after the seizure of Pomorze and fear of secular power in the West in the wake of the depredation of the Templar trials in France.[28]

The history of Livonia and Prussia in the thirteenth century is dominated by the eradication or enforced translocation of Baltic tribes, who were neither Slavs nor Teutons, at the hands of armed monks.[29] The Germans found it easy to divide and rule their conquered enemies. The Estonians submitted to Denmark in the 1220s. By 1283 when the Jatwings or Sudavians surrendered to the Knights, most of Prussia and Livonia were under the Order's sway and attention focussed on converting the Lithuanians and the Semigallians by force of arms. In 1290 half the Semigallians whose lands formed the bridge between Prussia and Livonia accepted Teutonic overlordship, whilst half their number followed the example of other tribes and fled into exile in Lithuania, whence they continued the struggle to eject the crusaders from their

[27] M. Biskup and G. Labuda, *Dzieje Zakonu Krzyżackiego w Prusach* (Gdańsk, 1986), 96–121. H. Boockmann, *Der Deutsche Orden* (Munich, 1981).

[28] Spread of the Order in central and southern Europe see R. Schmidt, *Die Deutschordenskommenden Trier und Beckingen 1242–1794* (Marburg, 1979), 273–320, 418–55 and K. Forstreuter, *Der Deutsche Orden am Mittelmeer* (Bonn, 1967). The Sword Brothers are assessed in F. Benninghoven, *Der Orden der Schwertbruder. Fratres Milicie Christi de Livonia* (Cologne, 1965). See also *PD*, 65–6, 175. Grand Master moves to Marienburg – *PD*, 175. For the significance of 1309 see A. Forey, *The Military Orders. From the twelfth to the early fourteenth centuries* (London, 1992), 223.

[29] Biskup and Labuda, *Dzieje Zakonu*, 93–5, 129–33, 169–201; Boockmann, *Der Deutsche Orden*, 66–112; M. Hellmann, *Studien über die Anfänge der Mission in Livland, Vorträge und Forschungen. Sonnerband* XXXVII (1989). *PD*, 91–2; *SRP*, II, 4.

lands.[30] The Knights' chronicler, Peter of Dusburg, records of 1283 that after 'fifty-three years had flowed since the war was begun against the Prussian nation, and all nations in the said land had been beaten and exterminated so that not one survived which did not humbly bend the neck to the holy Roman Church, the aforesaid brethren of the German House initiated the war against that mighty people, most hard of neck and well-versed in war, which is neighbour to the land of Prussia dwelling beyond the Nemunas river in the land of Lithuania'.[31]

That they might maintain the military mission to the Lithuanians, the Knights devoted themselves to bringing in settlers to exploit their new lands as well as granting fees to Prussian tribesmen who had proved their loyalty. The Knights themselves dwelt in fortress monasteries which were spread strategically across their lands but the brethren were few, numbering perhaps no more than two hundred at any given time. The community of Knights in a single monastery was usually thirteen or so.[32] These relied on laybrethren to swell their ranks along with hosts of west-European knights from Germany, France, Flanders, England, Scotland and Holland who came to Prussia almost every summer and winter on campaign or *Reise* during the fourteenth century. The Knights led recruiting drives for the Crusade from their houses all over Europe and as in the Order's Syrian campaigns much reliance was placed on paid troops.[33]

The colonisation of Livonia and Prussia with foreign artisans, retired laybrethren and re-settled natives must rank among the major achievements of the Order. In Prussia the Order settled the wastelands on the Lithuanian border (the so-called *Wildnis*) with colonists who enjoyed privileges of German Law. The Knights expanded existing towns such as the Polish cities of Toruń and Gdańsk and established new ones under German Law.[34] For the years between 1283 and 1341 almost 500 charters survive which

[30] *PD*, 96–103, 137–46. Cf. 132, 136, 148. For the continued Semigallian war see below p. 190.

[31] *PD*, 146.

[32] See below p. 246, n. 83 and Forey, *Military Orders*, 69–70, 82.

[33] W. Paravicini, 'Die Preussenreisen des europäischen Adels', *Historische Zeitschrift*, 232 (1981), 25–38 and more fully in his *Die Preussenreisen des europäischen Adels*, I (Sigmaringen, 1989).

[34] *PU*, II, nos. 104, 481, 869. A general portrait of the Order's settlement policy is given in C. Higounet, *Die deutsche Ostsiedlung im Mittelalter* (Munich, 1990), 218–47, 282–305. Biskup and Labuda, *Dzieje Zakonu*, 196–8, 318–21. See also H. Wunder, 'Siedlung und Bevölkerung im Ordensstaat, Herzogtum und Königreich Preussen 13–18 Jahrhundert', *Studien zum Deutschtum im Osten*, 19:2 (1987), 67–98.

were issued in rural districts by masters of the Order in Prussia and local ordinaries such as the Bishop of Pomezania.[35] In return for land the settlers were often expected to provide men, horses and arms for the Knights in the war against the pagans. Prussian 'light armaments', the *platendyst* and *brunie*, were required of native colonists, whilst a German might provide geldings or breast plates.[36] The farmers were to maintain defences, build bridges and take care of the roadways.[37] These people were generally of German stock, although Polish and even Rus'ian settlers were not uncommon. In the East in the Sambian district (Labiau, Sambia, Elbing) many Prussian tribesmen were granted lands.[38]

The Balts were not alone in resenting the growing power of the Order. Catholic princes, especially Łokietek looked askance at the expansion of the Knights. However it should be emphasised that their geographical position also gained them allies. Ensconced between Denmark and Sweden who did not enjoy papal favour and Poland, and between Rus' and Poland and the Empire, the Knights were able to exploit difficulties between competing authorities in the West. Thus John XXII feared to alienate them lest they abandon his interests to the papacy's enemies, especially Louis IV. They did in fact enjoy the full support of the Wittelsbach emperor. When the Pope failed to find in the Order's favour in its dispute with Riga in 1332, Louis granted full rights in Livonia to the Order.[39] Louis found in the Order his only constant ally in international politics and at times the emperor was, as he claimed himself, the Knights' truest friend.

Consideration should be given to the political, economic and ecclesiastical rivalries of the German and Danish colonists with the Order too. In his dealings with the Teutonic Knights and the Danish colonies of Estonia, Eric VI of Denmark instructed his colonists to aid the Knights against the Lithuanians but insisted that their neutrality in the Order's dispute with the Archbishop of Riga be respected. The irregularities discernible in Danish dealings with

[35] *PU*, I.2-III.1 passim. See lists given for particular years below pp. 231, n. 7 and 260, n. 156.

[36] *PU*, II, nos. 21, 556, 758, 775, 780–1.

[37] *PU*, I.2, nos. 530, 557, 559, 690, 765; II, nos. 43, 77, 177, 404, 659, 838; III.1, nos. 175, 178, 228, 288.

[38] Polish – *PU*, II, nos. 569, 447, 858; Russian – *PU*, II, no. 485; Prussians – Labiau *PU*, II, nos. 57, 125, 126, 222, 425, 598, 758; III, nos. 50, 51, 249, 251. – Elbing *PU*, II, nos. 358, 481; – Sambia *PU*, III, nos. 72, 73, 109, 122, 123, 176, 188, 189, 199, 250, 253. See also R. Wenskus, 'Der Deutsche Orden und die nichtdeutsche Bevölkerung des Preussenlandes', *Studien zum Deutschtum im Osten*, 8 (1971), 86–106.

[39] *LU*, II, no. 749, col. 267–8 and below p. 243.

the bishopric of Reval were overlooked by the Holy See as acceptable from a defender of the faith from the pagan Balts and Schismatic Rus'ians.[40]

Although the Estonian bishopric of Reval was controlled by Denmark, it seems that the Knights attempted to infiltrate the Reval chapter with their own men long before the grand master purchased the whole territory from the Danish king in 1346. In Livonia territorial ambitions were more bitter and shameless. Only a part of the land in Livonia was controlled by the Livonian branch of the Order; considerable regions and some very prosperous commercial towns were controlled by the local bishop and his chapter under the jurisdiction of the local metropolitan, the archbishop of Riga.[41] Gradually the Knights took control of the sees and chapters in both their Livonian and Prussian territories. They attempted from an early date to influence the bishops of Prussia: of Sambia, Pomezania and Warmia. These bishoprics lay within the province of Riga. Two thirds of the territory of each of them were under Teutonic control by 1300.[42] The Knights consolidated their grip on their territory by buying out lords from other areas.[43] The Knights acted in Livonia as they acted in Prussia and in the northern territories seized from Poland, pressurising their fellow clerics, the lord bishops of Ösel, Courland and Dorpat into following pro-Teutonic policies. They bought up lands from secular dukes who were only too keen to mortgage them. They purchased property which other religious were desperate to sell. In this way in 1305 they gained from the Cistercians of Dünamünde a monastery which guarded river access between Riga and the

[40] N. Skyum-Nielsen, 'Estonia under Danish rule', in *Danish medieval history. New currents*, ed. N. Skyum-Nielsen and N. Lund (Copenhagen, 1981), 112–16, 120–3. *Annales Danici Medii Aevi*, ed. E. Jørgensen (Copenhagen, 1920); P. P. Rebane, 'Denmark, the Papacy and the christianization of Estonia', *Gli inizi del Cristianesimo in Livonia--Lettonia* (Vatican City, 1989), 171–201.

[41] F. Benninghoven, *Rigas Entstehung und der frühhansische Kaufmann* (Hamburg, 1961). E. Gudavičius, 'Ryges recht ir ius civile Rigensis civitatis Gedimino aktuose', *Lietuvos Istorijos Metraštis* (1986), 79–85. The Teutonic Order's Königsberg Archive in Berlin has a copy of Rigan Law from the fourteenth century – PKKA, *OF*, 293, f. 50–97^{v} (*Das Gemeine Recht des stichtiches Ryge*) and f. 155–182 (*Rigisch Recht anno* 1370). On Gediminas and Rigan Law see below pp. 204, 211–12. Riga, which became a Hansa city in 1282, was governed by an elected council of consuls, a pro-consul and the mayor. However the archbishop retained his right to confirm the elected chief justice.

[42] *Chronicon de vitis episcoporum – Scriptores Rerum Warmiensium*, ed. K. P. Woelky and Y. M. Saage, I (Braunsberg, 1866), 47, and B. Poschmann, 'Bistümer und Deutsche Orden in Preussen 1243–1525', *Zeitschrift für die Geschichte und Altertumskunde Ermlands*, 30 (1962).

[43] See above n. 26; for Michałowo mortgage, 1317 – *PU*, II, no. 187, pp. 128–30.

coast. This they converted into one of their own forts.[44] We can see how interested the author of *Execrabilis*, the bull which condemned the holding of more than one benefice and the interference of princes in ecclesiastical appointments, must have been in these allegations of foul play in the election of northern bishops and canons. Between 1318 and 1323 John XXII examined all episcopal elections to Livonian sees (and found them valid).[45] Similarly the Knights sought to control the governing bodies of local regular chapters, as was the case with Chełmno from the 1250s.[46] Thus when accusations are laid against the order by the archbishop of Riga or Baltic secular lords, the Knights call upon defenders from the Prussian Franciscans, Dominicans and Cistercians and these coordinate their apologies for the Order with the Prussian bishops. Such is the case in the inquiries of 1310 and 1323–24 into atrocities allegedly committed by the Teutonic brethren.[47]

From the turn of the fourteenth century as the Knights sought to control Riga itself, this advocacy became increasingly important. Territorial concessions were required, chapter elections were interfered with and the representatives of the archbishop were assaulted. Claims were made by the archbishops that the Knights prevented other regular clergy from preaching to the pagans and that they obstructed trade between Riga and Lithuania whilst selling weapons and food to the pagans. When war broke out between the Knights and the citizens of Riga in 1298, the Rigans accepted an offer from Lithuania to establish a pagan garrison within the city walls.[48]

After the Moravian Franciscan, Frederick von Pernstein, formerly a papal confessor, became archbishop, he spent more time in exile in Avignon suing the Knights before the Pope than he ever dared spend in Riga. When he attempted to enter his

[44] *PU*, II, no. 13, p. 9.

[45] *Execrabilis* – G. Mollat, *The Popes at Avignon*, tr. J. Love (London, 1963), 9–25; for the Livonian investigations see below pp. 218–19 n. 166.

[46] K. Górski, *Studia i szkice z dziejów państwa krzyżackiego* (Olsztyn, 1986), 115–21.

[47] Prussian Dominicans write 7.10.1310 – *PU*, II, no. 19, pp. 12–13; the bishops of Prussia did so 18.10.1310 – *ibid.*, no. 20, pp. 13–15; for the campaign of 1323–24 see below pp. 212–13.

[48] *Das Zeugenverhör des Franciscus de Moliano (1312). Quellen zur Geschichte des Deutschen Ordens*, ed. A. Seraphim (Königsberg, 1912), 26, 157 and U. Niess, *Hochmeister Karl von Trier (1311–1324). Stationen einer Karriere im Deutschen Orden.* (*Quellen und Studien zur Geschichte des Deutschen Ordens* XLVII) (Marburg, 1992), 77–86. Riga details given below, pp. 57–9.

province in 1305 he was warned by the Knights that he had no protector but the Pope and that for them the sword was pope enough.[49] Accusations against the Order were laid before the Pope almost continually from 1305. Clement V found in Riga's favour in 1310 and sent a papal commission to the Baltic in 1312 under the leadership of Francis of Moliano. As a result of this enquiry into Rigan and Polish charges against the Knights, the Order was excommunicated – but to no avail.[50] In 1317 John XXII asked the two parties to live in peace and not scandalise the pagans by their bad example; Frederick continued to bring witnesses to Avignon to denounce the Knights.[51] Gediminas used the Rigan complaints to boost his own denunciations of the Knights, although soon he would come to realise that he had made a serious miscalculation in choosing an ally 'who cannot even defend himself for he spent twelve good years in the Roman Curia on his affairs and still could not conclude them'.[52]

THE BYZANTINE COMMONWEALTH

The picture we have sketched of Catholic Christendom is one of a mass of petty rivalries between kings and dukes and monks in lands where political boundaries are contentious. In eastern Christendom similar conditions prevail, especially in the Balkan empires and in Rus'. While the western patriarch and emperor quarrelled over their relative jurisdictions, the fourteenth century in the eastern Christian Empire saw reconciliation between Church and state in Constantinople and chaos in Asia Minor and the Balkans. Life in Byzantium and her *oikumene* was neither calm nor easy as the Ottoman gazis rode ever closer.

Andronicus II Palaeologus (1282–1332) faced increasingly strong demands from former provinces of the Empire in the Balkans for recognition as imperial powers endowed with

[49] K. Forstreuter, 'Erzbischof Friedrich von Riga (1304–1341). Ein Beitrag zur seiner Charakteristik', *ZfO*, 19 (1970), 652–65; V. Gidžiunas, 'De missionibus fratrum minorum in Lituania', *Archivum Franciscanum Historicum* 42 (1949), 22–35 and R. Mažeika and S. C. Rowell, '*Zelatores maximi*: Pope John XXII, Archbishop Frederick of Riga and the Baltic Mission, 1305–1340', *Archivum Historiae Pontificiae* 31 (1993); see also below pp. 225 n. 199 and 278f.

[50] *PU*, II, no. 69, pp. 44–5. For Moliano see above n. 48.

[51] *LU*, II, nos. 659–60, col. 98–102; *HW*, 58. Accusations were still being collected by Frederick in 1318 – *VMPL*, no. 208. He maintained his quarrel with the Knights until his death in 1341 – see below pp. 190, 197–8, 216–18, 278–9.

[52] *GL*, 141. On Gediminas see below p. 189f.

churches independent of Constantinople. The Second Bulgarian Empire under the control of the Shishman dynasty enlisted Byzantine support against the growing power of Serbia before succumbing to that realm in 1330. The Bulgars had been able to exploit the civil war between Andronicus II and his grandson Andronicus III which erupted in the 1320s to gain concessions from the Empire. The Bulgarian Church operated independently of Constantinople under its own patriarch in Trnovo.[53] In Serbia the Nemanjid clan sought to create its own empire and patriarchate. The local rulers invited German settlers to their land to build towns and mines. Some of them, especially Stefan Uroš III (1321–31) entertained conversion to Catholicism in order to gain foreign recognition and a high-ranking prelate. In 1346 King Stefan Dušan declared himself emperor of the Serbs, Greeks, Bulgars and Albanians and was solemnly crowned as such by the archbishop of Peč whom the 'emperor' promoted to rank of patriarch.[54] The authority and the example of these self-declared patriarchates came to bear an influence on Lithuanian ecclesiastical pretensions and on the Byzantine response to pagan demands.

In the 1320s Andronicus II toyed with the idea of reuniting the Byzantine Church with Rome as he faced the possibility of invasion from Venetian and Genoese forces and other crusaders. Andronicus exploited papal hopes for reunion under the shadow of a western mission. When special papal delegates arrived in Constantinople to discuss these matters with the emperor face to face in 1327, Andronicus declared disingenuously that he had never expressed any desire to be converted to the Roman faith. While Andronicus understood the need to dupe Catholic princes and prelates, he was devoted to his own Church.[55]

Although the Byzantine Church enjoyed Andronicus' patronage, the patriarchs of the first third of the fourteenth century were generally weak men, weakened further by the dire nature of the problems facing them. Lengthy investigations of simoniacal abuse

[53] D. M. Nicol, *The last centuries of Byzantium 1261–1453* (London, 1979), 23–62, 146–7. J. V. A. Fine jun., *The late medieval Balkans: A critical survey from the late twelfth century to the Ottoman Conquest* (Ann Arbor, 1987), 224–8, 269–75; A. Burmov, *Istoria na B'lgaria prez vremeto na Shishmanovtsi (1323–1396)*, in *Izbrani Proizvedenia*, I (Sofia, 1968), 229–63.

[54] G. C. Soulis, *The Serbs and Byzantium during the reign of Tsar Stephen Dušan (1331–1355) and his successors* (Washington, 1984), 60–85.

[55] A. E. Laiou, *Constantinople and the Latins. The foreign policy of Andronicus II 1282–1328* (Cambridge, MA, 1972), 249–60. R. P. T. Kaeppeli, 'Deux nouveaux ouvrages de Philippe de Péra', *Archivum fratrum praedicatorum*, 23 (1953), 172–4.

of office which dominate synodal proceedings in Patriarch Niphon's day (1310–14) touched on Rus' and ended with the deposition of the patriarch for the very same crime.[56] More generally too the hierarchy underwent much restructuring as bishops of once mighty provinces were stripped of their lands by Ottoman advances. Andronicus caused a table of episcopal rank to be set down for the first time in two centuries. These *Notitiae* reflect the growing significance of some metropolitan sees and the collapse of others into nonentity. The list of 112 metropolitans include 15 which were newly created. The surviving sees such as Brusa, Ioannina and Apamaeia were granted metropolitan rank to reflect their loyalty to the emperor or their outliving previous prelacies.[57] The granting of such status was also intended (as in the case of Brusa) to shore up morale in areas subject to Ottoman incursion. In Monemvasia the new ecclesiastical status reflected the naval services provided by this city in defence of the Empire.[58] In Rus', the largest, wealthiest and on the whole most loyal ecclesiastical province, the patriarchs Athanasius I, Niphon and John XIII Glykys were required to contend with interference in church affairs from nascent secular powers in the north-east (Vladimir–Moscow), south-west (Galich–Volyn') and north-west (Lithuania).[59]

RUS'

The metropolitanate of Kiev and All Rus' was Byzantium's prize. In the twelfth and thirteenth centuries, the land of Rus' which was united under one metropolitan became a patchwork of separate principalities under the aegis of the senior member of the Rurikid clan. This prince assumed the title and rights of grand duke of Kiev. The disarray and internecine dynastic competition which typifies Rus'ian political life between 1125 and 1359 mirrors similar chaos in Poland. By the time the Tatars invaded Rus' from

[56] V. Laurent, 'Notes de chronologie et d'histoire byzantine de la fin du XIIIe siècle', *Revue des études byzantines*, 27 (1969), 209–28 esp. 219–28. See also *Codex Vaticanus Graecus*, 847, f. 260v-271v. A good example of what amounts to an obsession with simony is given in I. Ševchenko, 'Nicolas Cabasilas' "anti-zealot" discourse: A reinterpretation', *Dumbarton Oaks Papers*, 11 (1957), 81–171, esp. 135–6.

[57] J. Darrouzès, *Notitiae Episcopatuum ecclesiae constantinopolitanae. Texte critique, introduction et notes* (Paris, 1981), 180–4.

[58] H. A. Kalligas, *Byzantine Monemvasia. The sources* (Monemvasia, 1990), 107–15.

[59] J. Meyendorff, *Byzantium and the rise of Russia. A study of Byzantino-Russian relations in the fourteenth century* (Cambridge, 1981), 48–72 and M. Giedroyć, 'The Ruthenian–Lithuanian metropolitanates and the progress of Christianisation (1300–1458)', *Nuovi studi storici*, 17 (1992), 315–42 and below pp. 155–72.

the eastern steppes between 1237 and 1240 and devastated an already weakened Kievan region, the central authority had resided in the north-eastern city of Vladimir 'beyond the forests' for over a century, rather than in the south. Thanks to the cooperation shown the Tatar khans by Prince Aleksandr Nevsky in the 1250s, the Grand Duchy of Vladimir remained the political centre of Rus'.[60] The southern principalities of Galich and Volyn', more or less cut off from Vladimir by both the Tatars and the northern forests, developed in the thirteenth century as a separate realm known to Catholics as the *regnum* (*Galicie et*) *Ladomerie*. In 1299 the head of the Russian Church, Metropolitan Maksim transferred his residence to Vladimir from Kiev, whose economy could no longer support a high prelate.

The Tatars did not rule Rus' directly. Instead they used the local princes to gather tribute under the supervision of Tatar officials. The Khan granted the senior prince of the Rurikid line his patent to rule (*iarlyk*) without the possession of which the grand duke of Vladimir and All Rus' could not stand at the head of the Rus'ian princes. Under Khan Uzbek (1312–42) the Golden Horde reached its zenith, transferred its central administration to Sarai Berke on the banks of the Volga and converted to Mohammedanism.[61] In Lithuania, however, there were no Tatar settlements. The first reliable evidence we have of Tatars' settling in Lithuania is the case of Tokhtamysh's allies who sought asylum with Vytautas in 1398. The legend of Tatar settlement in Lithuania in 1324 is false.[62]

When the last son of Aleksandr Nevsky, Andrei, died in 1304 the princes of Moscow and Tver', grandsons respectively of

[60] J. L. I. Fennell, *The crisis of medieval Russia 1200–1304* (London–New York, 1983), 114–21.

[61] C. J. Halperin, *Russia and the Golden Horde. The Mongol impact on Russian history* (London, 1987), 33–40.

[62] Tokhtamysh – F. M. Shabul'do, *Zemli iugo-zapadnoi Rusi v sostave velikogo kniazhestva litovskogo* (Kiev, 1987), 145f. On Lithuania – P. Borawksi, 'Za dziejów kolonizacji tatarskiej w Wielkim Księstwie Litewskim i w Polsce (XIV–XVIIw.)', *Przegląd Orientalistyczny* 104 (1977/4), 291–2; and, *Tatarzy w dawnej Rzeczypospolitej* (Warsaw, 1986), 35. The error persists - J. Tyszkiewicz, *Tatarzy na Litwie i w Polsce. Studia z dziejów XIII–XVIIIw.* (Warsaw, 1989), 145–6, based on A. Mukhlinskii, *Issledovania o proiskhozhdenii i sostoanii litovskikh Tatar'* (Odessa, 1902), 52. Here Mukhlinskii allegedly cites L. Wadding, *Annales Minorum*, I (Lyons, 1672), 459 to the effect that friars travelling to Lithuania in 1324 came across Scythians from the land of a certain Khan who worshipped God in an Asiatic tongue. The quotation is bogus. The information is in neither the Lyons edition of 1636 (*AM*, III) nor the second Roman edition of 1732 (*AM*, VII) which is supplemented by Melissanus' notes. Mukhlinskii was followed by S. Kryczyński in *Tatarzy litewscy*: *Próba monografii historyczno-etnograficznej*, *Rocznik Tatarski-Tatar Yili*, III (1938), 4.

Nevsky and his brother Yaroslav, competed for the throne of grand duke of Vladimir.[63] Although Mikhail Yaroslavich of Tver' held the traditional right of succession by male seniority within the Rurikid clan, his cousin Yury Danilovich of Moscow challenged him for the throne. During his reign as grand duke from 1304 to 1318 Mikhail was unwise enough to alienate several important sections of Rus'ian society including the Metropolitan of All Rus', Pëtr, who found it difficult to reside within Mikhail's patrimony.

It appears that Mikhail sought support for his power from neighbouring lands. When he was put to death by the Khan in 1318, one of the charges laid against him was that he intended to hand over his treasury to the Germans. This accusation is not supported by extant sources but it is not incredible that the grand duke might wish, like the south Rus'ian princes, to consort with the Teutonic Knights against the Tatars.[64] He seems certainly to have encouraged close relations with the Lithuanians and may have been instrumental in the establishment in Lithuanian Novgorodok of an Orthodox hierarchy separate from Metropolitan Pëtr. In 1320 Mikhail's son Dmitry married Gediminas' daughter Maria, a policy in keeping with his attempt to regain the *iarlyk* from Moscow.[65] The Lithuano-Tverite alliance against Moscow dominated Russian political life well into the fifteenth century.

When Mikhail was murdered by Khan Uzbek with Muscovite connivance, Yury Danilovich of Moscow (*d.* 1325), who had married the Khan's sister, became grand duke of Vladimir (1318–22). Although Mikhail Yaroslavich's sons Dmitry and Aleksandr regained the *iarlyk* from their Muscovite cousins in 1322 and 1326, Tverite chances of retaining the patent were severely curtailed by an uprising in Tver' in 1327, in the course of which the Khan's cousin and lieutenant, Chol-Khan and all the Tatars in the city were murdered. Ivan Danilovich, Yury's brother portrayed the citizens' retaliation for Tatar excesses in Tver' to the Khan as the infidelity of Mikhail's son Grand Duke Aleksandr.[66] Ivan, surnamed Kalita ('Moneybags') for his charity (or his efficiency as a Tatar *rentier*), persuaded the Khan to grant him the full *iarlyk* in 1331. For the previous three years he had held half of the Grand Duchy on probation. Ivan (grand duke from 1331 to his death in 1340) was the first consolidator of the north-eastern

[63] Fennell, *Emergence*, 60–110.
[64] *PSRL*, XV(ii), 410–11 s.a. 6826.
[65] See below pp. 89–90.
[66] Fennell, *Emergence*, 105–9.

principalities of Rus' around Moscow.[67] However to the west lay principalities which lay outside Moscow's control or, in the case of Novgorodia, exercised a choice of higher political allegiance.

The western principalities flourished during the twelfth and early thirteenth centuries as the Rus'ian windows (and doors) to Catholic Christendom. In the course of the thirteenth century, the cities of Black Rus', Grodno and Novgorodok came under Lithuanian control as their native dynasties weakened and died out. Polotsk was the centre of the major west Rus'ian principality which included other urban centres of note such as Minsk, Iziaslavl and Vitebsk. The region covered the conjunction of three major river routes: the Dnepr route south to Kiev and Constantinople, the Lovat' link to Novgorod, the major northern commercial centre, and the Dvina (Düna, Dauguva) route into the developing Baltic and German markets of Livonia and Saxony. The princes of this region established trading posts among the Lettish tribesmen on the Dvina at Kokenhusen and Jersika. These were taken over by the German merchants in 1208 and 1214 respectively. The local prince, Konstantin gave the Livonian settlers possession of the lands around Lake Luban. The buoyant southern trade is reflected in the large finds of cheap imported goods of Byzantine origin (glass-ware, small portable icons and the like) and in the architecture of churches and cathedrals in Polotsk, Vitebsk and Novgorodok.[68] These cities and their lands gradually fell victim to Lithuanian expansionism from the mid-thirteenth century. When King Mindaugas of Lithuania first converted to Catholicism, he asked the Pope in 1253 to grant him rights to any (west) Rus'ian lands his subjects might conquer.[69]

The history of thirteenth-century Polotsk is only partially known and the circumstances of the Lithuanian invasions remain obscure. The Prince Konstantin who donated the Luban region to the Order is unknown but may be the son of David of Smolensk. Certainly he is not the prince Konstantin (Rostislavich) mentioned in the Novgorodian Chronicle s.a. 1264, whom some historians

[67] *Ibid.*, 111–95.

[68] Surrender of Livonian lands to the Germans by Polotsk *c.* 1214 – Henry the Latvian (Henricus Lettus), *Chronicon Livoniae*, ed. L. Arbusow and A. Bauer (Darmstadt, 1959), 172. The growth of trade and artistic contacts between Western Rus' and Byzantium is discussed by F. D. Gurevich, 'Zapadnaia Rus' i Vizantia v XII–XIIIvv.', *Sovetskaia Arkheologia* (1988/3), 130–44.

[69] Mindaugas' expansion – *PSRL*, II, 858, 860–1; papal support – *VMPL*, no. 123, pp. 60–1.

have mistakenly claimed was the son of Prince Tautvilas, the Lithuanian who ruled Polotsk between *c.* 1250 and 1263. It seems highly probable that Tautvilas' son was the Prince Aigust whom the Novgorodians sent to Pskov in 1271.[70] From 1264 to 1267, following the murder of Tautvilas and the flight of his son to Novgorod, Duke Gerdenis of Nalšia, the Lithuanian territory which bordered Polotian land, ruled the city. After Gerdenis' death in 1267 the rulers of Polotsk are known only vaguely, although it seems that after 1307 the principality was almost continually under Lithuanian control. The lack of a stable local dynasty in the second half of the thirteenth century encouraged the local bishop and boiars to increase their authority before the prince, a situation which continued under Lithuanian rule.[71]

Vitebsk which also experienced Lithuanian rule in the mid-thirteenth century and traded with the pagans, especially in slaves, in the 1280s during the reign of Prince Mikhail Konstantinovich, fluctuated in allegiance between Polotsk and Smolensk. Several trade agreements originating in the latter cities but including Vitebsk, Riga and Lübeck survive from the second half of the thirteenth century. Smolensk from 1229 was also home to a German mercantile community. Its position on the Dnepr

[70] Konstantin Davidovich (*d.* 1218) may have been involved with Polotsk when Smolensk influence in the city was strong. His donation may be referred to by the Lithuanian prince Gerdenis in a charter of 1264 (*RLA*, no. 25a, p. 13) which mentions a Konstantin. Lithuania ruled the cities in the 1250s through Prince Tautvilas (*PSRL*, II, 858). This Konstantin was not the unnamed son of Tautvilas who fled to Novgorod from Polotsk when Gerdenis arrived in 1263. A theory arose that the Konstantin (?Rostislavich of Smolensk), son-in-law of Aleksandr Nevsky mentioned in *NL*, 83, 86 was Tautvilas' son (Fennell, *Crisis*, 132–3) but there is no connection between these two men in the text. It seems highly probable that this unnamed Tautvilaitis is the Prince Aigust sent to Pskov from Novgorod in 1271 (*NL*, p. 89). The prince of Pskov, a Lithuanian named Daumantas, was an ally of Tautvilas in the 1260s (S. C. Rowell, 'Between Lithuania and Rus': Dovmont–Timofey of Pskov, his life and cult', *OSP* n.s. 25 (1992), 5–6). Gerdenis ruled Polotsk 1263–67. Around this time a Rus'ian prince, Iziaslav was also in Polotsk (*RLA*, no. 25b). Of him no more is known. In the 1280s we find Mikhail Konstantinovich in Vitebsk (not Polotsk). Who his father was is unknown. Mikhail is either the father or grandfather of Algirdas Gediminaitis' first wife: see below p. 88. Vitebsk relations with Polotsk remain unclear. These various strands of Konstantins and Polotsk–Vitebsk–Smolensk have been woven together into bad cloth – Konstantin 'the Donor' is not the same as Konstantin of *NL*, 83, Nevsky's son-in-law and neither is the son of Tautvilas. Wasilewski's attractive but completely erroneous theory that Algirdas married a granddaughter of Tautvilas and thus linked him with the grand dukes of the thirteenth century cannot hold: see below p. 88, n. 27.

[71] For Gerdenis' rule in Polotsk in 1264 see *RLA*, nos. 25a and 25b. Polotsk seized for good by Lithuania in 1307 (*PSRL*, XXXV, 192). See also below pp. 83–4, 180–2.

enhanced its trade with Livonia via Polotsk, with Kiev and the south and with the wealthy lands of north-eastern Rus'. The Lithuanians occasionally took advantage of dynastic struggles within Smolensk to expand their trade and military influence further east. In the early fourteenth century members of one branch of the ruling family, the descendants of Prince Aleksandr, allied themselves with Gediminas.[72]

In the north-west the dominant economic and political power was the archdiocese of Novgorod which comprised the principalities of Novgorod and Pskov and the minor towns of Ladoga and Staraia Rus'. Novgorod also held colonies in the far north on the White Sea and to the east in Permia where the land was rich in furs. From the 1150s the citizenry of Novgorod elected their own prince to defend them from outside attack without allowing him to reside in the city or establish a dynastic hold on the region. At the *veche* or oligarchic council of citizens the *posadnik* (mayor) and militia captain (*tysiatskii*) were elected. The *veche* maintained the right to elect the nominal head of state, the archbishop. Despite close early links between Novgorod and its junior colleague Pskov, the Pskovites were jealous of their independence. In the fourteenth century the citizenry of both towns often looked independently towards Lithuania to provide for the military defence of the cities against Swedes,[73] Teutonic crusaders and the ravages of other Rus'ian princes. Pskov became a virtual client of the grand duke of Lithuania from 1322 until around 1400. The grand duke of Moscow envied Novgorod's wealth and tried always to establish a Muscovite presence in the city. The local boiars created factions which favoured Lithuanian or Muscovite alliances as the best means to safeguard their trade routes. Novgorod was the most important trading post in northern Europe with a resident community of German merchants in the

[72] For Vitebsk–Lithuania trade see *RLA*, 26–8. For Smolensk, *Smolenskie Gramoty XIII–XIV vekov*, ed. R. I. Avanesov (Moscow, 1963); and below pp. 85, 258. Also Fennell, *Crisis*, 6–7, 102–3.

[73] On Novgorod see H. Birnbaum, *Lord Novgorod the Great. Essays in the history and culture of a medieval city state. Part One: the historical background* (Los Angeles, 1981), 40–54, 82–100; Pskov – S. I. Kolotilova, 'K voprosu o polozhenii Pskova v sostave Novgorodskoi feodal'noi respubliki', *Istoria SSSR* (1975/2), 145–6; *GVNiP*, no. 38, pp. 67–8; V. L. Ianin, *Novgorodskie Akty XII–XVvv. Khronologicheskie kommentarii* (Moscow, 1991), 88–9. See also G. Pickhan, *Gospodin Pskov. Entstehung und Entwicklung eines städtischen Herrschaftszentrums in Altrussland, Forschungen zur osteuropäischen Geschichte*, XLVII (Berlin, 1992), 104–60 and J. Gallen, *Nöteborgsfreden och Finlands medeltide östgräns* (Helsingfors, 1968), 39–40.

Court of St Peter. Under the guidance of powerful archbishops such as Vasily Kaleka (1331–52), Novgorod used her powerful neighbours for her own interests. Muscovite historians who relate the seemingly 'inevitable' rise of Moscow overlook this balance of tension.[74]

The southern Rus'ian kingdom of Galich–Volyn' which, as we have seen, was cut off from the influence of the grand dukes of Vladimir by the Mongol invasion, looked to central Europe for leadership, especially as a result of several twelfth- and thirteenth-century marriages between the Rus'ians and the Hungarian royal house (see genealogical table 1). A political rapprochement with the Papacy was essayed by Daniil Romanovich for two years between 1254 and 1256 in order to gain a royal crown. Daniil was invested with a Latin crown and sceptre but he refused to convert to Catholicism. Even so he styled himself *korol'* (king) a term reserved for western rulers in Rus'ian chronography, rather than *kniaz'* (prince). In 1309 Yury L'vovich, Daniil's grandson, rejected a papal mission to his lands, after having initiated it, because he had already succeeded in gaining a hierarch for his Church from Constantinople to circumvent the influence of the metropolitan of Kiev who now lived in Vladimir.[75]

The princes of the south-west allowed themselves to become embroiled in the political troubles of their Polish neighbours. Lev Danilovich (1264/69–1300) intervened militarily in eastern Poland in 1290 to help Łokietek and Bolesław of Mazovia resist Bohemian rule in Kraków. His grandsons, Andrei and Lev Yurevichi (1309–23) enjoyed close relations with Poland and the Teutonic Order. The Knight Sieghard von Schwarzburg, who appears as *consanguineus noster dilectus* in treaties concluded by Lev and Andrei (and later by Bolesław-Yury II), was a cousin of the princes'

[74] Foreign merchants – E. A. Rybina, *Inozemnye dvory v Novgorode XII–XVIIvv.* (Moscow, 1986), 15–46. The power of Kaleka is illustrated below, p. 248–50.

[75] Yury, Daniil and West: Meyendorff, *Byzantium*, 39–45, 92, 94. The style *korol'* is used in Russian of Swedish kings (*NL*, 360, s.a. 6856) and Polish ones (*PL*, I, s.a. 6918). In the Ipat'evskaia Chronicle from Galich–Volyn' it comes to be used of native princes first in connection with the *korol'* of Hungary (*PSRL*, II, s.a. 6658, col. 405; 6739 col. 764; 6763, cols. 830–1) and Rus'ian princes of Magyar descent. In official documents Mstislav Danilevich calls himself a *syn' korolev'*, the king's son (*PSRL*, II, s.a. 6797, cols. 928, 932). This seems to be connected with Daniil Romanovich who received royal title and insignia (*korolevskii san'*) from Pope Alexander IV in 1255 (*PSRL*, II, 826–7). The *rex* and *regnum Galicie* appear in Latin sources. However the last Rurikid rulers of south-west Rus' reverted to the normal title of prince (*kniaz'/dux*) (*PU*, II, no. 157). See also S. A. Bol'shakova, 'Papskie poslania galitskomu kniaziu kak istoricheskii istochnik', *Drevneishie gosudarstva na territorii SSSR* (1976), 122–9.

father. He acted as a go-between for the Order and the princes of south-west Rus' on more than one occasion.[76] Their throne was coveted by the successors of distant kinsmen in Hungary who traced a claim back through the siblings of Konstancia of Hungary, the grandmother of Lev and Andrei. Their aunt Anastasia was married to Siemowit of Dobrzyń and their sister was the wife of Trojden of Mazovia.[77] This latter marriage related them to Traidenis, the last mighty grand duke of Lithuania who was not of Gediminas' line,[78] and provided the last independent prince of Galich–Volyn'. Bolesław-Yury II acceded to power in 1324 as a result of Polish, Mazovian and Lithuanian agreement over the fate of the southern neighbour.

German and Polish craftsmen (farmers, fletchers, blacksmiths and silversmiths) were invited to the *Regnum Galicie et Ladomerie* in 1259 to the new town of Kholm to rescue the south-west Rus'ian economy from the after effects of the Mongol invasion.[79] The privileges of living under German Law and gaining recompense for mistreatment at the hands of tax officials were established in Andrei Yurevich's charters for Kraków and Toruń merchants and artisans in 1320. Similar privileges adorn the charter for the new town of Sanok which Bolesław-Yury II issued in 1339. These compare well with their equivalents in Hungary, Serbia or Bohemia. By 1320 the Prague groat was in circulation in south-west Rus' as it was in neighbouring Poland.[80]

In the early fourteenth century Europe was a patchwork of new ecclesiastical and princely polities struggling in a general power vacuum to assert their desires – be they on the outer fringes of the continent or in its heartlands. Of great importance was the ability to exploit differences between the German Emperor and the Pope,

[76] Włodarski, *Polska*, 244–7. Łokietek also used Sieghard to treat with the Order over Pomorze, *ibid.*, 271. See also K. Forstreuter, *Preussen und Russland im Mittelalter. Die Entwicklung ihrer Beziehungen vom 13 bis 17 Jahrhundert, Osteuropäische Forschungen*, n.s. 25 (1938), 14f.

[77] The connections between the Hungarians and Daniil of Galich are discussed in T. Senga 'Béla királyfi Bolgár, halicsi és osztrák Hadjárataihoz', *Századok*, 122 (1988), 36–51. See also J. Dąbrowski, 'Z czasów Łokietka. Studya nad stosunkami polsko-węgierskimi w XIVw. Część I', *RAU*, 2nd series 24 (1916), 318–22. Dobrzyń – Włodarski, *Polska*, 264–6.

[78] Włodarski, *Polska*, 192.

[79] *PSRL*, III, 842–3; M. Hrushevsky, *Istoria Ukraini-Rusi*, II (New York, 1954), 471–2.

[80] Andrei Yurevich's charters of 27 August 1320 to merchants of Toruń and Kraków and that of Bolesław-Yury II for Sanok are given in *Boleslav' Iurii*, 77–9; 150–1. In his Kraków charter Andrei speaks of *ubi prius tres grossi solvebantur* – for the groat see E. Nohejlová-Prátová, 'A propos de la période du gros pragois', *Nummus et Historia. Pieniądz Europy średniowiecznej* (Warsaw, 1985), 237–44.

the Papacy and the Patriarchate of Constantinople and imperial contestants in central Europe and Byzantium. The economies of almost every European state required resuscitation after the plague and famine which struck the continent in the second decade of the century. As in more recent times the solution to those problems appeared to be German technology and manpower. In central Europe the old families of Přemysl and Árpád died out, bequeathing territorial ambitions to newcomers whose position was threatened at home by noble discontent and abroad by their neighbours' ambitions. Compromises had to be drawn with the newly re-established Piast monarchy in Poland to settle disputes between Hungary and Poland over south-west Rus' and between Poland and Bohemia over Polish territories. Into a web of dynastic and political alliances on the borders of Poland and Mazovia, the Teutonic Ordensstaat and Rus', for and against the Wittelsbach Empire and the Teutonic Order, the pagan Lithuanian Empire gradually allowed herself to be ever more closely drawn. Meanwhile the eastern Empire suffered economic hardship and alien occupation. The Venetians, Genoese and the Ottomans threatened the queen of cities, Constantinople. In the richest province of the Byzantine Church the princes of Moscow, Tver', Galich–Volyn' and Lithuania sought to rebuild the lands occupied by the Tatars. The chaos rampant in the interbred monarchies of central Europe is by no means irrelevant to our subject. The divisions within the Christian houses weakened the chance of any concerted and united attack on Lithuania. Sitting on the frontiers of warring states, the Lithuanians could choose their allies and pick off their enemies. It is no coincidence that from this welter of political and economic struggle within and between both halves of Christendom there emerged a strong pagan polity at exactly the time Lithuania learned to overcome internal dissension and exploit the disunity of her enemies.

Chapter 2

SOURCES

There are several reasons why the history of medieval Lithuania has not received the attention it is due, given the Grand Duchy's power, size and influence. The most striking academic problem has been a perceived lack of sources and the real linguistic demands which the diversity of the evidence make of the scholar. Indeed, the corpus of data relevant to a study of the Grand Duchy of Lithuania under Gediminas may be complex but often it lacks depth. The spread of sources throughout Europe and the languages in which they are written makes the surviving material more difficult to sift than it might have been. It may be helpful simply to list the main countries whence our sources emanate: Lithuania, Livonia, Russia, Poland and Prussia; the Holy See, Byzantium, the Low Countries and France. We have data from Hungary and Bohemia, Switzerland and Spain, Ireland and England. The main advantage of this documentary diaspora lies in the need it creates for the historian to observe Lithuania from all sides rather than myopically from domestic records alone. Completely independent sources often corroborate one another. Russian chronicles can be used to fix the chronology of imprecisely dated Livonian diplomatic texts and on occasion a Polish Latin chronicle clarifies corrupt readings in a Lithuanian Russian genealogy.[1] A closer bibliographical analysis of all the major sources country by country is given elsewhere.[2] It is our intention here to note the types of material we have available, the problems which some of them present and the types of history they allow us to write.

Chronicles and annals survive from across central and eastern Europe although chronography within Lithuania itself developed only in the early fifteenth century. Chronicles, a resource

[1] See below p. 195, n. 37 and p. 280, n. 63. *Bilgeny frater* (*PSRL*, XXXV, 117) is a mistranslation of *byl iny brat*.

[2] S. C. Rowell, 'Of men and monsters. Sources for the history of Lithuania in the time of Gediminas (*c.* 1315–42)', *JBS*, 24:1 (1993), 73–112.

unjustly despised by scholars who have access to sheaves of bureaucratic records, form the mainstay of research on Lithuanian, Russian and, to a lesser extent, Polish history. By and large these records are annalistic rather than discursive and the best were kept at the courts of princes, bishops, grand masters and burgher institutions throughout Rus', Poland and Prussia–Livonia. They deal with the Lithuanians as these impinge on domestic affairs. In Catholic realms we also reap the benefits of records kept by individual religious orders. The single most important of these for our purposes, the *Chronica terrae Prussiae* of Peter of Dusburg acts not only as a history of the Teutonic settlement in Prussia but also as an explanation and justification of the Teutonic Knights.[3] Lithuanian relations with Livonia where power was shared between the Teutonic Order and the local bishops are provided by the Westphalian priest Hermann of Wartberge.[4] We benefit greatly from the work of Jan Długosz, the fifteenth-century Polish chronicler, not only because it holds information gleaned from annals which have since been lost but also because in gathering his material from Prussia and Lithuania as well as Poland, Długosz caused several texts to be translated into Latin.[5] These translations often survive in better condition than the originals. Wigand of Marburg's *Cronica nova Prutenica* is a case in point.[6]

The broadest set of sources comes from one group of authors: Franciscan friars. The records of the Franciscans reflect the nature of their authors: a group of preachers spread across the whole of

[3] U. Arnold, 'Deutschordenshistoriographie in Deutschen Reich', in *Die Rolle der Ritterorden in der mittelalterlichen Kultur*, ed. Z. H. Nowak (Toruń, 1985), 65–87. *SRP*, ed. T. Hirsch *et al.*, 5 vols. (Leipzig, 1861–74; Frankfurt am Main, 1965 [vol. VI added]). Peter of Dusburg, *Chronica Terrae Prussiae*, *SRP*, I, 3–219. Lithuanian translation and commentary in R. Batūra, *Petras Dusburgietis Prūsijos žemės Kronika* (Vilnius, 1985). On the author's origins see *ibid.*, 25–31. The *SRP* text has been reprinted with a modern German translation, *Die Peters von Dusburg Chronik des Preussenlandes*, ed. and tr. K. Scholz and D. Wojtecki, *Ausgewählte Quellen zur deutschen Geschichte des Mittelalters*, XXV (Darmstadt, 1984). Of Polish sources, see J. Wyrozumski, *Kazimierz Wielki* 2nd edn (Wrocław–Warsaw–Kraków–Gdańsk–Łódź, 1986), 222. Further details in Rowell, 'Of men and monsters', 79–80, 82–3.

[4] Hermann wrote his chronicle between 1356 and 1378. Published in *SRP*, II, 9–116. For early fourteenth century see pp. 58–68. A modern Lithuanian translation is available: Henrikas Latvis, Hermanas Vartbergė, *Livonijos Kronikos*, ed. and tr. J. Jurginis (Vilnius, 1991), 154–208.

[5] *Długosz*, IX, ed. D. Turkowska *et al.* (Warsaw, 1978), 91–222. J. Dąbrowski, *Dawne dziejopisarstwo polskie (do roku 1480)* (Wrocław–Warsaw–Kraków, 1964), 189–211, 233–40. On his sources see *ibid.*, 222–32.

[6] *Cronica*, *SRP*, II, 429–662. See K. Helm and W. Ziesemer, *Die Literatur des Deutschen Ritterordens*, *Giessener Beiträge zur deutschen Philologie* 94 (1951), 165–7.

Christendom who used their own history as justification in the face of accusations of heresy, and as exempla in preaching. This is in sharp contrast with their fellow mendicants, the Dominicans who have left no chronicles or documents relevant to the Lithuanian mission, despite the friars' presence in Vilnius. An eyewitness account of events in Lithuania in 1323 is recorded by a Franciscan in Switzerland in the 1340s; friars in Spain and Ireland include Lithuania in geographic treatises and the English Franciscans Roger Bacon and Bartholomew use Baltic examples in their crusade theory and universal histories respectively. In Lithuania itself Franciscans acted as grand-ducal scribes and secretaries throughout the fourteenth century. Polish and German friars compiled annals of some worth especially in Lübeck, Gniezno and Toruń.[7]

Much of the chronicle data composed by Prussian priests and the mendicants is derived from diplomatic sources. The value of Dusburg's chronicle derives from the access he was permitted to the grand masters' archive in Marienburg as official chronicler. It is tempting to see some of his starkest errors and most convincing descriptions of pagan custom as a result of consulting documents such as the Lithuano-Livonian Peace of 1323 and the Christburg Treaty of 1249 in the archive.[8] The modern historian has access to the remnants of the same archive and the same documents – the Secret Archive of the Order which once was in Königsberg now lies in Berlin. Its riches have been published for the most part in the codices and *Urkundenbücher* of Dogiel and Voigt, von Bunge, Maschke, Hein and Conrad.[9]

[7] On the prevalence of Franciscan sources in Poland and central Europe, see Dąbrowski, *Dawne*, 63–8 and Rowell, 'Of men and monsters', 80, 82, 91–3. For a general comparison of Franciscan historiography with the work of the Dominicans, see A. G. Little, *Franciscan papers, lists and documents* (Manchester, 1943), 25–41. For John of Winterthur, see below p. 266; for the Spanish friars and the Irish source, see below n. 23 and p. 51, n. 10. Bartholomew is cited on p. 49. For Roger Bacon see R. Bacon, *Opus Maius*, ed. J. H. Bridges, 3 vols (Oxford, 1897; III London–Edinburgh–Oxford, 1900), *Pars Septima*, IV: vol. II, 377 and *Pars Tertia*, XIII: vol. III, 121–2.

[8] Peter's confusion in documentary sources is evident from his reference in 1323 to two kings of Lithuania where he means Gediminas known in the Treaty of Vilnius as *Lithuanorum Ruthenorumque rex* – *PD*, 191. His accurate use of the Treaty of Christburg (1249) is noted below, p. 124.

[9] *Codex Diplomaticus regni Poloniae et Magni Ducatus Lithuaniae*, ed. M. Dogiel, I, IV, V (Vilnius, 1758–64); *Codex Diplomaticus Prussicus*, ed. J. Voigt, 6 vols, (Königsberg, 1836–61); *Liv- Esth- und Kurländisches Urkundenbuch nebst Regesten*, ed. F. G. von Bunge, 6 vols. (Riga–Reval, 1853–71) [reprint of all twelve vols. of Erster Abtheilung, Aalen, 1967–81]; *Preussisches Urkundenbuch* (*Politisches Abtheilung*) I.1-III, ed. K. P. Woelky,

It is in the sphere of diplomatics that one of the most tenacious pseudo-problems of Lithuanian history resides. The documentary records of Gediminas' reign are the richest Lithuania possesses for the period before 1387. We have contemporary copies of half a dozen letters sent by Gediminas to his neighbours in north-eastern Europe and the Papacy along with a handful of letters addressed to the grand duke which deal with Lithuanian policy in the 1320s. Gediminas sought skilled colonists from Saxony, promising a safe home for Catholics and their clergy and complaining vigorously against the Teutonic crusade. He creates an impression that he is willing to be baptised although he takes great pains never to say so explicitly. A report composed by the emissaries of the papal legates to Vilnius which discusses Gediminas' reaction to the news of a mission to baptise the pagans is invaluable for the information it reveals of the grand duke's persona, the internal confrontations within court factions and between competing missionaries, and the influence of the Franciscans within the grand duchess' household. It is clear that the grand duchess, like her predecessor Queen Morta (fl. 1250–63) patronised the foreign clergy who worked as scribes for her husband. Two treaties, one military, the other commercial, also survive from 1323 and 1338.[10]

In the eighteenth century Prussian scholars first began to publish their doubts concerning the authenticity of Gediminas' letters, claiming that the charges the grand duke makes against the Teutonic Order, especially that its 'barbarous' methods were responsible for the Lithuanian rejection of Catholicism, were not genuine. Poles and Russians cited these charges as proof of Prussian perfidy.[11] The pseudo-*Quellenkritik* of Prussian scholars which was

M. Hein *et al.* (Königsberg, 1882–1944) [now under Conrad reaches 1366 in vol. VI (1986)]; *Russko-Livonskie Atky*, ed. K. E. Napiersky (St Petersburg, 1868).

[10] *Gedimino Laiškai*, ed. V. T. Pashuto and I. Štal (Vilnius, 1966) and *Codex Diplomaticus Lithuaniae*, ed. E. Raczyński (Wrocław, 1845). A new edition of documents dating from 1251 to 1428 and emanating from Lithuania, Livonia, the Papacy, Byzantium, Rus', and Prussia is being prepared for publication in Vilnius in 1994–5. A preliminary list of corrections to and a description of the manuscripts of the published texts of Gediminas' letters is given in S. C. Rowell, 'The Letters of Gediminas: *Gemachte Lüge*? Notes on a controversy', *Jahrbücher für Geschichte Osteuropas*, 41: 3 (1993).

[11] On Prussian objections to the letters see K. Forstreuter, 'Die Bekehrung Gedimins und der Deutschen Orden', *Altpreussische Forschungen*, 5 (1928), 239–61; and 'Die Bekehrung des Litauerkönigs Gedimin: eine Streitfrage', *Jahrbuch der Albertus Universität Königsberg*, 6 (1955), 142–58. Refutation of Forstreuter's claims in Rowell, 'Letters'. A different solution to Forstreuter's dilemma is given by A. Nikžentaitis, 'Dėl Gedimino laiškų autentiškumo (1. Gedimino laiškai Hanzos miestams)', *LMADA*,

intended to defend their national honour was based on a serious misunderstanding of fourteenth-century Lithuania which is shared by their opponents in Poland, Lithuania and Russia. All sides fail to recognise how Gediminas manipulates the truth in his letters.[12] The correspondence is authenticated by references to it in contemporary records. Indeed it survives only in copies made at the behest of foreign potentates during careful investigation or rebuttal of Gediminas' promises and accusations. Repeated independent enquiries into its authenticity and the sincerity of Gediminas' proposed settlement grants were made in 1323 and 1324 by the Order, the Burghers of Livonia, the Papacy and even the envoys of the papal legates to Vilnius. Only once is there an attempt to call the letters a Rigan invention and this comes as part of a clearly coordinated propaganda campaign, by which the Order sought to discredit Gediminas and the Peace of Vilnius after the treaty of 1323 had been signed. In 1409 the episode was used by the Order's lawyers as proof of Lithuanian deceit but deception is merely diplomacy unveiled, not forgery.[13]

The letters are genuine. They were produced at the new royal court in Vilnius by Franciscan friars of the Saxon province who performed the services of scribes, advisers and translators for the Lithuanian ruler in his dealing with Catholic Christendom. We even know the names of the friars who penned the correspondence of 1323. Gediminas employed foreign scribes for correspondence with eastern and western Christendom much in the way that the early Bulgars had used Greek slaves to record their history and communicate with foreign potentates.[14] The texts of this correspondence survive in contemporary transcripts in the archives of the Holy See, the archbishopric of Riga and the Teutonic Order. No pre-conversion Lithuanian documents issued by Gediminas or his sons Algirdas and Kestutis exist in Lithuanian copies. These certainly existed once (since reference is made to them in other documents) but they were probably lost in the fires which struck

101 (1987/4), 92–9 and 'Dėl ... (2. Gedimino laiškai popiežiui ir krikščonybės įvedimo Lietuvoje klausimas 1323–1324m.', *LMADA*, 103 (1988/2), 66–76.

[12] See below p. 197.

[13] On the confidence trick, see below pp. 212f.; 1409 case published in *Codex Epistolaris Vitoldi magni ducis Lithuaniae, 1376–1430*, ed. A. Prochaska, *Monumenta medii aevi historica*, VI (Kraków, 1882), 997.

[14] For Gediminas' scribes see *GL*, 133–5. The Bulgar system is noted in S. Runciman, *A history of the First Bulgarian Empire* (London, 1930), 278.

the grand-ducal archives in the fifteenth and sixteenth centuries.[15] It is also possible that they were deliberately overlooked by the archivists of the new Catholic regime as relicts of Lithuania's dark past. The records of the Saxon Franciscans in Vilnius do not survive and the earliest *acta* of the Polish friars who replaced them in 1387 are known to us largely from sixteenth century résumés. The *Lithuanian Metrica* or court records which survive begin in the mid-fifteenth century.[16]

The documents shed light on more aspects of the Grand Duchy than simply the major themes which dominate them. We see the development of the grand ducal title: the description of Gediminas' seal reflects his preoccupation with his royal honour and the language which the Franciscan scribes use imitates the Aristotelian and evangelical claims of the Papacy to primacy in Christendom. The letters present an impressive mixture of fashionable Catholic political jargon which runs through contemporary treatises on papal and imperial power, and native Lithuanian wit. Gediminas claims to be as a slave in a household; this slave also proclaims his power to loose and bind. The appropriation of papal rhetoric is more subtle in the reference his scribes make to the Aristotelian image of the ruler as *forma in materia*.[17] The voice of Gediminas surely lies behind certain of the phrases incorporated into the letters, as we read wry commentary on Christian reaction to earlier Lithuanian overtures 'to which not even a dog replied'.[18] Indeed although Gediminas did not write the letters himself (any more than a Christian prince would have done), he did dictate them to known Franciscan scribes and interpreters. This brief glimpse of grand-ducal personality has no equivalent in Moscow.

[15] Gediminas' version of the treaty was copied for John XXII – *MPV*, No. 168, pp. 226–7. Parchments were not preserved in the grand-ducal records or Lithuanian Metrica which survive from the early fifteenth century – P. K. Grimsted, 'The archival legacy of the Grand Duchy of Lithuania: The fate of early historical archives in Vilnius', *Slavonic and East European Review*, 57 (1979), 552–71.

[16] Confirmation of privileges given to the Franciscans of the friary of St Mary in Arena by Zygmunt Stary, 3.12.1522 – Kraków, Biblioteka P. A. N., dok. 481. For the Metrica see *The 'Lithuanian Metrica' in Moscow and Warsaw: Reconstructing the archives of the Grand Duchy of Lithuania*, ed. P. K. Grimsted and I. Sułkowska-Kurasiowa (Cambridge, MA, 1984).

[17] *GL*, 37; cf. the language of Marsiglio of Padua in *Defensor pacis, Fontes iuris germanici antiqui*, ed. R. Scholz (Hanover, 1932), 34f. or H-X. Arquillière, *Le plus ancien traité de l'Eglise. Jacques de Viterbe, De Regimine Christiano (1301–1302). Etude des sources et édition critique* (Paris, 1926), 233.

[18] *GL*, 39.

Although Lithuania is only beginning to interest modern researchers, the pagans of north-eastern Europe were very attractive to medieval scholars. They provided fertile ground for theorising about crusade methods and deciding explanations of why they worshipped as they did. Pope Pius II devoted several folios to explaining that the Balts worshipped the sun because they lived in a cold land.[19] They were used as examples of the remains of classical civilisation. Setting aside the fifteenth-century linguistic comparisons of Lithuanian with Latin which lent convenient support to theories of the Roman origins of the Lithuanians,[20] we see much earlier how a chronicler's knowledge of 'his' pagans helped to explain references in classical authors. The Russian translator of John Malalas' Chronicle equates the Lithuanians with the Hellenes and describes how they came to practise cremation. His account of the old man, Sovii, reeks of pagan legend. The translation was revised around 1261 in south-western Rus', a period which coincides with the growth of Lithuanian reportage in the local *Ipat'evskaia Chronicle*. The two texts seem to be intimately connected.[21] Indeed the Chronicle appears to have incorporated records from the Lithuanian-held city of Novgorodok which deals with the reigns of several Lithuanian rulers from 1219 to 1290. A Catholic author, Petrarch, compares what he learned from the Teutonic Order with what he reads of the Latins in the Aeneid. He notes how ancient Latin customs of sacrificing an animal during the striking of a treaty survive in Lithuania.[22] Scholars of heraldry and geo-

[19] Piccolomini, *De Europa*, cap. 26 in: *Aeneae Sylvii Piccolominei Senensis ... Opera quae extant omnia ...* (Basle, 1551), 417–19. Bacon cites the crusade in the Baltic as an example of how not to treat pagans – see above n. 7.

[20] Roman origins – E. Kulicka, 'Legenda o pochodzeniu litwinów', *PH*, 71 (1980), 8f.; J. Suchocki, 'Geneza litewskiej legendy etnogenetycznej', *ZH*, 52 (1987), 27–66. Compare these with western origin-legends – S. Reynolds, 'Medieval *origines gentium* and the community of the realm', *History*, 68 (1983), 375–90. See also *Państwo, naród, stany w świadomości wieków średnich. Pamięci Benedykta Zientary* (Warsaw, 1991), esp. 130–47.

[21] *PSRL*, II (Moscow, 1962). The text is discussed in A. I. Gen'sors'ky, *Halyts'ko-Volyns'kyi Litopys: Protses skladannia redaktsii i redaktory* (Kiev, 1958). Of Malalas, three mss. survive in Vilnius, Moscow and Warsaw. The relevant sections of the first two have been published: see W. Mannhardt, *Letto-Preussische Götterlehre, Magazin der Lettisch Litterärischen Gesellschaft*, XXI (Riga, 1936; Hanover-Döhren, 1971), 56–68 and E. Wolter, 'Mythologische Skizzen', *Archiv für slavische Philologie* 9 (1887), 636–7. The Warsaw text (Biblioteka Narodowa, BOZ IV 83) is a recent discovery. On the Slavonic Malalas see S. C. Franklin, 'Malalas in Slavonic', *Studies in John Malalas*, ed. E. Jeffreys, B. Croke and R. Scott, *Byzantina Australiensia*, VI (1990), 276–87, esp. 278.

[22] For Petrarch see Rowell, 'A pagan's word: Lithuanian diplomatic procedure 1200–1385' *Journal of Medieval History*, 18 (1992), 159–60.

graphy incorporated Lithuania into their works, describing a Lithuanian banner which bears a striking resemblance to a star of David. It is unclear whether this is an accurate representation of Lithuanian heraldry or the attribution of one non-Christian symbol to a pagan community.[23] Western European perceptions of the exotic eastern regions of our continent exhibit a certain constancy.

While serious scholars used references to the pagans so did the poets and romancers. Accounts of the crusade appear in chivalric propaganda for John of Bohemia and in rather flowery chronicles such as that of the Fleming Jean des Preïs. These contain important extra details which do not survive in straightforward chronology – in Machaut we get a list of five towns destroyed by John of Bohemia in 1329 while in Peter of Dusburg we must be satisfied with the bare statistic. Jean gives a romanticised account of King Marger which can be analysed effectively. His account of a king who promises to open his lands to German merchants if he loses a battle smacks of truth. Even the strange city he names as Ycône, which commentators have taken as Iconium, may be located more accurately at Jūkainiai in north-western Lithuania.[24]

A great deal of Orthodox liturgical material survives from the fourteenth century. The famous chasuble or *sakkos* which bears the images of the Lithuanian Martyrs of 1370 and the Serbian *vita* of those saints are not the only ecclesiastical records of the Grand Duchy in pagan times.[25] In western Rus' several codices of canon law, the *Ustavy* survive. These refer to areas 'where Christianity is' and the insistence on the eastern understanding of the Eucharist and the Holy Trinity reflect life in an area open to Catholic infiltration.[26] The *sinodiki* or books where the names of those to be

[23] *Libro des conoscimiento de todos los reynos* ..., ed. and tr. C. Markham, *Hakluyt Society*, 2nd series 29 (London, 1912). See also A. Gieysztor, 'Polska w "El libro des conoscimiento" z połowy XIV wieku', *PH*, 56 (1965), 397–412.

[24] Jean d'Outremeuse des Preïs, *Chronique et geste*, ed. A. Borgnet, VI (Brussels, 1880), 412–16; the historical use of this chronicle is indicated by A. Nikžentaitis, 'Trapėnų žemė', *Žemaičių praeitis*, I (1990), 93–9. Guillaume de Machaut, *Confort d'Ami*, in *Oeuvres complètes de Guillaume de Machaut*, ed. E. Hoepffner, III (Paris, 1921), 106–7. Machaut also mentions Lithuania in his *Dit dou Lyon*, in *Oeuvres complètes*, II, 210, line 1450.

[25] E. Plitz, *Trois sakkoi byzantins: analyse iconographique*, *Acta universitatis upsaliensis*, n.s. 17 (1976); vita in M. N. Speranskii 'Serbskoe zhitie litovskikh muchenikov', *ChOIDR* (1909/4), 26–31. Based on Greek original of 1374 – D. Ogizki, 'Blutzeugenisse für Christus im Litauen des 14 Jahrhunderts', *Stimme der Orthodoxie*, 8 (1984), 42–3.

[26] Ia. N. Shchapov, *Drevnerusskie kniazheskie ustavy XI–XVvv.* (Moscow, 1976); *Kniazheskie ustavy i tserkov' v drevnei Rusi XI–XIVvv.* (Moscow, 1972) and 'Turovskie Ustavy XIV veka o desiatine', *AE* (1964), 252–73.

remembered in the liturgy are recorded are very useful for establishing genealogies and the full names of princes in addition to marking the spread of devotion to certain saints, one of whom in Pskov was of Lithuanian birth.[27]

Papal records and the *acta* of the Byzantine patriarchate reflect the prominent position of Lithuania in ecclesiastical ambitions. Letters from a fifteenth-century Byzantine cleric in the Peloponnese even use the creation of the Lithuanian metropolitanate as a precedent for their own ambitions for status within the hierarchy.[28] Other princes of Church and state, especially the kings of Poland and the archbishops of Riga cite Lithuania in their legal cases against the Teutonic Order. These cases reveal the extent of trade between the crusaders and the pagans in addition to the nature of the complaint. The Rigans do not object to the Knights' trading with Lithuania; they are furious that the Knights prevent them from full participation in the same enterprises, for 'the Brethren conduct special deals with the pagans once they have driven away our citizens and certain other Christians'.[29]

In the fifteenth century the increasing growth of noble ambitions and royal power led to a jockeying for position within

[27] I. V. Dergacheva, 'K literaturnoi istorii drevnerusskogo sinodika XV–XVIIvv.', in *Literatura drevnei Rusi. Istochnikovedenie*, ed. D. S. Likhachev (Leningrad, 1988), 63–73; *Slovar' knizhnikov ... vtoraia polovina XIV–XVIv. chast'* 2 (Leningrad, 1989), 339–44. For use of Liubech *sinodik* see below p. 102; of Pskov see Rowell, 'Between Lithuania and Rus'', 17, 32–3.

[28] *VMPL*, nos. 290–301, pp. 190–9. On papal documents preserved in the Archive of the Teutonic Knights in Königsberg see W. Hubatsch and E. Joachim, *Regesta historico-diplomatica Ordinis S. Mariae Theutonicorum 1198–1525*, I.2 (Göttingen, 1948). MPV; A. Tautu, *Acta Ioannis PP XXII (1317–1334)* (Vatican City, 1952) and *Lettres communes du pape Jean XXII analysées d'après les registres dits d'Avignon et du Vatican*, ed. G. Mollat, *Bibliothèque des Ecoles françaises d'Athènes et de Rome*, 3rd series, 16 vols. (Paris, 1904–47). See also *Bullarium Poloniae* I, ed. I. Sułkowska-Kuraś and S. Kuraś (Rome, 1982). Patriarchal sources available in: F. Miklosich and J. Müller, *Acta Patriarchatus Constantinopolitani*, I (Vienna, 1862), nos. 39, 65 and 67. New edition with a German translation – *Das Register des Patriarchats von Konstantinopel II: Edition und Übersetzung der Urkunden aus den Jahren 1315–1331*, ed. H. Hunger and O. Kresten (Vienna, 1981). Darrouzès, *Notitiae. Codex Vaticanus Graecus*, 840, ff. 9–10 and 244 were written in Rus' between 1320 and 1340. The list of episcopal consecrations (ff. 9–10) was published in W. Regel, *Analecta byzantino-russica* (St Petersburg, 1891).

[29] 1312 – Seraphim, *Das Zeugenverhör*, 157. 1320–21 – Chłopocka, *Lites ac res gestae*. 1330–31 – *PU*, II, no. 747, pp. 494–6. 1339 – *Lites ac res gestae ...*, ed. T. Działyński, I.1 (Poznań, 1855). 1366 – *Die Berichte der Generalprokuratoren des Deutschen Ordens an der Kurie*, I, ed. K. Forstreuter (Göttingen, 1961), 316–21 and *SRP*, II, 149f. 1409 – See above n. 13. On trade, see R. Varakauskas, *Lietuvos ir Livonijos santykiai XIII–XVIa.* (Vilnius, 1982), 55–119 and R. Mažeika, '"Nenorim kad jie kovotų prieš mus mūsų pačių ginklais ..." – Popiežių bandymai reguliuoti prekybą su Pabaltijo pagonimis', *Lituanistica* (1990/4), 11–18.

Poland, Lithuania and Rus' which involved the production of genealogies as proof of claims to precedence. From these which eventually come to appear in chronicles we can establish the family tree of Gediminas' line. These undervalued sources provide important evidence for the age of the legends in the Lithuanian Chronicles. The grand dukes of Moscow sought to establish early Gediminid dependence on Rus'ian princes or even the grand dukes of Rus' and the existence of Orthodoxy within Lithuania as proof of Moscow's imperial right to rule Lettovia.[30] It is necessary to look behind the outer appearance of such documents. All too often Baltic historians jib at the use of literary and linguistic analysis.

Quite apart from these written sources we have much help from art and archaeology. The depiction of grand dukes on their seals shows much of how the rulers of Lithuania regarded themselves and whom they sought to imitate. It is worthy of note that on his seal Gediminas calls himself *rex* but refrains from depicting himself wearing a royal crown. Instead he sits bearing a diadem in his right hand, master of the Christian symbol of royalty. The use of 'Lithuanian' symbolism, the horseman or *vytis* on seals shows the spread of Lithuanian influence in western Rus'.[31] In the case of Daumantas of Nalšia (alias St Dovmont-Timofei) we see the spread of devotion to a Lithuanian-born prince-saint through the Pskov region.[32]

Archaeology is essential if we are to show the pagan coinage system, Lithuanian trade networks or the increase in the prosperity of Novgorodok when this city became the centre of the Lithuanian metropolitanate.[33] The archaeological evidence of variety in pagan death customs supports literary clues as to the decentralised nature of the pagan cult which changes over time and place. Lithuanian farming techniques and crops are discernible only from archaeological surveys.[34] The cult of the horse is attested by grave finds. Most important of all, perhaps, was the uncovering of a

[30] Texts in R. P. Dmitrieva, *Skazanie o Kniaziakh Vladimirskikh* (Moscow–Leningrad, 1955), 159–213. On their importance for establishing Gediminas' conquest of Kiev and revealing Muscovite propaganda, see below pp. 108–11. Shilovskii genealogy from *c.* 1457 is given in *Akty sotsial'no-ekonomicheskoi istorii severo-vostochnoi Rusi kontsa XIV–nachala XVIv.* (Moscow, 1964), no. 352, pp. 376–8. A Kraków manuscript containing two Lithuanian grand-ducal genealogies is worthy of note; see below pp. 54, 282, n. 70.

[31] Seal of Gediminas, p. 64; of Aleksandr Mikhailovich, p. 173, n. 94.

[32] See below pp. 177–9.

[33] See below p. 83, n. 3.

[34] R. Volkaitė-Kulikauskienė, 'Nauji duomenys apie žemdirbystę ir gyvulininkystę rytų Lietuvoje', *LMADA*, 48 (1974), 51–65. See also below p. 227, n. 203. Much valuable information in the series *AO*, *LMADA* and *Lietuvos archeologija* (Vilnius, 1979–).

thirteenth-century church beneath the cathedral in Vilnius. This building seems to have been partly demolished after Mindaugas' apostasy in 1261 and used in the fourteenth century as a pagan shrine.[35]

Having outlined the types of sources, we might consider certain of the problems which face the scholar who uses them. Although they date from the thirteenth century to the seventeenth, by far the majority of our written data come from the fourteenth century and are contemporary with Gediminas or his sons. Some unique but verifiable records such as the fourteenth-century Ronneburg Annals or the accounts of Lithuanian expansion into south-western Rus' survive only because they were incorporated into fifteenth- and sixteenth-century texts.[36] As always, the provenance and age of data must be established carefully. Age neither renders the obviously old accurate, nor the brand new unavoidably dubious.

Scholars often forget the obvious fact that records are not written for their convenience. Given that both the Teutonic Order and Gediminas needed to enlist foreign aid to continue their war, the propagandistic intentions of certain sources, especially legal cases and diplomatic démarches should not be overlooked as much as is generally the case. In their depiction of the Knights, the letters of Gediminas are aimed at convincing a papal court that the brethren deserve severe punishment. The Knights, for their part, encouraged dismal stories about the Lithuanians in western Europe.[37]

The boundaries between propaganda and bias can be blurred, especially when a source's primary bias is not anti-Lithuanian. The Lithuanians can appear on the Guelf side in a Ghibbeline text. Christian authors were quite capable of writing fair assessments of their pagan neighbours. The pagan–Christian conflict is described in our sources as objectively as it could be. Making allowances for genre (poetry, propaganda, plain reportage), the truth appears almost always to be told albeit not always in its entirety. The success of John of Bohemia's *Reise* of 1329 (Machaut) was in fact short-lived (Peter of Dusburg).[38] We cannot dismiss a source out

[35] See below pp. 134–7.

[36] 'Chronik von Dünamünde', *SRP*, II, 139–42; 'Die Danziger Ordenschronik' *SRP*, IV, 371; 'Kurze Preussische Annalen 1190–1337', *SRP* III, 4; *Ronneburg Annals* survive only in Polish translation – *Stryjkowski* I, 283. See Helm and Ziesemer, *Die Literatur*, 147.

[37] See below pp. 195–6, 212–13.

[38] See below pp. 239–41.

of hand merely because it emanates from a power inimical, or indeed, friendly to Lithuania.

The mind-set which can depict the pagans as beasts of some satanic field has no trouble in portraying a Lithuanian serf as a northern monster with a dog's head. This is called poetry; John of Wurzburg (fl. 1314) was a poet with a taste for the exotic.[39] The noble savages portrayed by Dusburg as obedient to their pope are meant to shame the Teutonic Order, not give a bland account of the enemy's religious life. The ideological baggage which surrounds Christian tales of the Lithuanian Crusade needs to be borne in mind by researchers much more than the simplistic equation of Christian with anti-pagan. Recent work by the Russian historian, Matuzova, and the Austrian, Birkhan, suffice to alert the reader to the subtler hidden agenda behind the chroniclers.[40]

When the scholar is confronted by a relative sparsity of material, he is tempted to take in all and believe all. It takes some determination to reject rare material even though it is wrong. The best approach to the sources imitates St Augustine who, in dealing with the problem of holy legends, declared that rather than call the stories false or invented by the overcredulous, he would prefer to say that the accounts were too difficult for him to comprehend. The legendary clothes of the Lithuanian Chronicles are a motley which disguises more sober facts. The coat of Peter of Dusburg is much more subtle and can disguise brilliant fancy. Some historians mistake those parts of his chronicles which are ideological tracts for plain reportage, especially when a useful, but nonetheless imaginary construct such as the pagan papacy hints at an established centralised religion akin to Christianity. In approaching the early parts of the Lithuanian Chronicles we should not reject a more straightforward reading of 'mythological' accounts out of hand. Sixteenth-century versions of thirteenth- and fourteenth-

[39] Johann von Wurzburg, *Wilhelm von Österreich aus der Gothaer Handschrift*, ed. E. Regel, *Deutsche Texte des Mittelalters*, III (1906) lines 7771–7775, p. 107. See V. Straub, *Entstehung und Entwicklung des frühneuhochdeutschen Prosaromans*, *Amsterdamer Publikationen zur Sprache und Literatur*, XVI (1974) with excellent bibliography, pp. 151–8. Discussed in context by H. Birkhan, 'Les croisades contre les païens de Lituanie et de Prusse. Idéologie et réalité', in *La Croisade: réalités et fictions. Actes du colloque d'Amiens 18–22 mars 1987*, ed. D. Buschinger (Göppingen, 1989), 40–3.

[40] Birkhan, 'Les croisades', 36–9. See also V. I. Matuzova, 'Ideino-teologicheskaia osnova "Khroniki Zemli prusskoi" Petra iz Dusberga', *Drevneishie gosudarstva na territorii SSSR* (1982), 152–69.

century events which are garbled or encrusted with late boiar propaganda have been over-criticised in the past.[41] It is possible to salvage material from the Lithuanian record. Sixteenth-century language should put the historian of the fourteenth-century on his mettle; it should not frighten him from closer textual analysis. Many written sources which were available four hundred and more years ago have since disappeared; the oral memory of a pagan state where remembrance was more common a record than parchment has faded, as though it had never been.

In this study we shall approach two of the main Prussian and Lithuano-Russian texts in a way that is different from the traditional one. Historians usually fall eagerly on the necks of Peter of Dusburg and the authors of the fifteenth- and sixteenth-century Lithuanian Chronicles. Peter they embrace as an omniscient fellow-scholar; the Lithuanians they yearn to throttle for squandering an historical opportunity on fancy.

Peter was a Netherlandish priest of the Teutonic Order. He composed his chronicle in 1326, drawing on information from earlier *Ordenschroniken*, the Grand Masters' archive in Marienburg, hagiography and oral records. The ideological content of the prologue to the chronicle is self-evident. Peter provides a lengthy apologia for the Baltic Crusade, the crusaders and their methods but this does not encroach upon the main text. The non-apologetic account of the Lithuanian War is the first extensive description of the Order's battles with the Lithuanians that we have and it appears to be unimpeded by irrational prejudice. It became a major source for later chroniclers and historians.[42]

In an early chapter of Part Three of his chronicle, Peter refers to the pagan system of religion, headed by a pagan pope whom everyone obeys. He lives in a place in Nadruvia called Romowe (Romuva) which is named after Rome. This account has always been taken literally rather than as the moral exemplum which it is. It is a means of explaining to Christians at war with the pagans and in disobedience to the real Pope of Rome how the pagans worship

[41] On the hypercritical tendencies of nineteenth-century scholarship see M. Giedroyć, 'The rulers of thirteenth-century Lithuania: a search for the origins of Grand Duke Traidenis and his kin', *OSP*, n.s. 17 (1984), 11–12 and below pp. 100–6.

[42] As in Nicolaus von Jeroschin's translation, *Di Kronike von Pruzinlant*, *SRP*, I, 291–624 and 'Epitome Gestorum Prussiae (Canonici Sambiensis)', *SRP*, I, 272–90. On these see respectively Helm and Ziesemer, *Die Literatur*, 151–61 and G. Labuda, 'Zu den Quellen der 'Preussische Chronik' Peters von Dusburg', *Quellen und Studien zur Geschichte des Deutschen Ordens*, 30 (1982), 147–9.

and how they are pious in their own way.[43] Parts of the story can be traced to treaties and earlier chronicles kept by the Order. Historians leap on this tale because it provides a structure for a religion which has one main characteristic – decentralised variety.[44] Scholars love models. The fact that the pagan pope never appears in the annalistic parts of the chronicle and that the closest Peter gets to recording a holy place is a reference to *Romene* in an area far from Nadruvia, is never noted. Why Krivė, the 'pope', is never shown in action is a question no one bothers to ask. Like the author of the *Chanson de Roland* (to whose work Peter refers obliquely), our chronicler explains paganism as an inverted Christianity.[45] This is how all historians work, relating their discoveries to a form which the reader can understand. Added to this, Peter acts as preacher, holding up the pagan paradigm to his disobedient brethren rather as Tacitus used the idealised ancient Germans to shame the decadence of Rome.[46] A poet writing in the 1360s tells of a pagan prince who is converted after he sees a vision of the Blessed Sacrament transformed into three giant warriors and given to Knights to grant them strength. This poem is intended as propaganda for devotion to the feast of Corpus Christi.[47]

Dusburg's chronicle is a very valuable work and deserves to be trusted as an account of the wars between the Order and numerous pagan tribes. However the discursive parts of the chronicle, in one of which we read the information on Krivė, are not of the same genre as the accounts of the crusades. The anthropological narrative seeks to understand the Baltic Crusade, explain what the Crusade meant and idealise the Christian knights who took part in it. This ideological aspect of Peter's writing is discussed fully by Matuzova in two recent articles and Pollakówna in her study of

[43] *PD*, 53 and below pp. 125–8.

[44] E. Christiansen, *The northern crusades: The Baltic and the Catholic frontier 1100–1525* (London, 1980), 137.

[45] Inverted Trinity invented for the Saracens in *La Chanson de Roland*, ed. F. Whitehead (Oxford, 1965), 79, lines 2696–2697. For Baligant the Saracen king, see *ibid.*, 76, lines 2614f. and *passim*. Peter notes this ruler, *PD*, 76.

[46] Tacitus, *Germania*, XVII. The text is analysed in J. M. Wallace-Hadrill, *Early Germanic kingship in England and on the continent* (Oxford, 1971), 2.

[47] Birkhan, 'Les croisades', 42 and 'Der Littauer', *Schondochs Gedichte* ed. H. Heintz, *Germanistische Abhandlungen*, 30 (Breslau, 1908), 42–55. See *Die Geschichte der Deutschen Literatur von den Anfängen bis zur Gegenwart* [*GDL*], ed. H. de Boor *et al.*, III/1 (Munich, 1962), 551–2.

the chronicle.[48] Peter was an ardent supporter of the Papacy and a chider of moral backsliders at a time when the Order was beginning to lend aid to the Emperor in his struggle against John XXII. It was in sore need of moral reform. With Krivė Peter gives a morally uplifting lesson.

The account Peter gives of pagan customs bears the hallmarks of Christian preconceptions of 'heathen' behaviour. The detail of their polygamy is little more than a topos. Jurginis argued convincingly three decades ago that the Lithuanians did not take more than one wife at a time or trade in spouses.[49] Apart from this imagined flaw, the pagans as portrayed by Peter are almost perfect. They do not covet costly apparel, nor do they sleep in feather beds or dine on dainty foods. They drink pure water, mead or milk and show their guests 'all the humanity they can'. No one is allowed to go begging but the poor and needy are welcomed from home to home to dine without shame. Murder is punished in accordance with *lex talionis*. They even have a pope whom they obey unreservedly and whose messengers are treated with utmost courtesy. One might wish the Christians were similar. Indeed the recommendations Bishop Siegfried of Sambia set down for the conduct of his priests in the first decade of the century are remarkably similar to the virtues of the pagans.[50] As Tacitus exalted the Germans, so Peter idealises his exotic northerners. In Constantinople the chronicler Nicephoras Gregoras also used the Lithuanians as a moral exemplar.[51] While we cannot say that Peter's description of the behaviour of the pagan Balts here is pure invention – in some cases such as funeral practice, his sources can be detected – he marshals his facts very carefully. Krivė appears here more as a way of shaming the Knights and other Christian readers who may be in rebellion against the Pope (as the emperor was in 1326 when the chronicle was composed) than a real phenomenon.

Just as Peter is generally admired, so are the sixteenth-century Lithuanian Chronicles despised. The sixteenth-century language

[48] See above n. 40 and V. I. Matuzova, '"Khronika zemli prusskoi" Petra iz Dusberga v kul'turno-istoricheskim kontekste', *Balto-Slavianskie Issledovania* (1985), 102–18. M. Pollakówna, *Kronika Piotra z Dusburga* (Wrocław–Warsaw–Kraków, 1968), 172f.

[49] J. Jurginis, 'Lietuvių šeima XIII–XIV amžiais', *ILKI*, 1 (1958), 248–59.

[50] *PD*, 53–5. Cf. Bishop Siegfried of Sambia's letter of instruction for his clergy (4 August [1302–10]) in *Nova Alamanniae*, I, ed. E. E. Stengel (Berlin, 1921), no. 75, pp. 31–4.

[51] The Gregoras is given in R. Mažeika, 'Was Grand Prince Algirdas a Greek Orthodox Christian?', *Lituanus*, 33:4 (1987), 55.

of these texts and the clear interpolations into what was once an austere annal form compel the 'knowing' scholar to reject the evidence. At least the 'scientific' historians of the 1880s used the new methodology to destroy the simplistic faith of previous scholars in the Chronicles' absolute reliability.[52]

The First Lithuanian Chronicle (*L1*) was composed some time after 1446 near Smolensk in the eastern marches of the Grand Duchy. It covers Lithuanian history from the death of Gediminas to 1430 and Rus' from the ninth century to 1446. It is based in part on late fourteenth-century accounts of Gediminas' sons and a general Rus'ian chronicle from Smolensk. The Lithuanian component known in its Latin early variant as *Origo regis Jagyelo et Wytholdi ducum Lithuanie* also betrays the cleaning up of unsavoury details in the dynasty's past.[53] It is clear for example that the account of the boiar Vaidila who was an important supporter of Grand Duke Jogaila against his uncle Kestutis has been written so as to remove all recognition of the incident of noble domination of the grand-ducal line.[54] When *L1* was revised in the third decade of the sixteenth century it became a truly Lithuanian text with less dependence on a Rus'ian account. The Second Redaction (*L2*) begins with the Incarnation and sketches Lithuanian history from its legendary Roman origins to the death of Gediminas after which comes a revised version of the First Redaction. The major versions of this text have been printed in two volumes of *Polnoe Sobranie Russkikh Letopisei*.[55] The early parts of the text have been dismissed as useless except as evidence of political ideology in Lithuania in the sixteenth century. However the early parts are not homogeneous in style as some scholars claim. A classicising myth merges with native proto-history and princely and boiar genealogy. The

[52] See above n. 41 and below pp. 101–6.

[53] For *Origo* and date of *Letopisets velikikh kniazei litovskikh*, see V. A. Chamiarytski, *Belaruskia letapisy iak pomniki literatury* (Minsk, 1969), 97–118. Joined to *svod* of 1446 to form *L1*, *ibid.*, 119–34. Surviving redactions were published in *PSRL*, XXXV: *Nikiforovskaia*, 19–35; *Akademicheskaia*, 103–14; *Suprasl'skaia*, 36–67; *Slutskaia*, 68–84. See also N. N. Ulashchik, *Vvedenie v izuchenie Belorussko-Litovskogo letopisania* (Moscow, 1985), 29–50.

[54] Vaidila removed – *PSRL*, XXXV, 115–16. For his background see S. C. Rowell, 'Gediminid dynastic diplomacy in Žemaitija 1350–1430', *Žemaičių Praeitis*, 3 (1993).

[55] Date of composition of *L2* – Chamiarytski, *Belaruskia*, 156ff. Seven redactions of *L2* have been published viz: 1. *Letopis' Krasinskogo* – *PSRL*, XXXV, 128–44; 2. *Letopis' Arkheologicheskogo Obshchestva* – *PSRL*, XXXV, 91–102; 3. *Letopis' Rachinskogo* – *PSRL*, XXXV, 145–72; 4. *Ol'shevskaia Letopis'* – *PSRL*, XXXV, 173–92; 5. *Rumiantsevskaia Letopis'* – *PSRL*, XXXV, 193–213; 6. *Evreinovskaia Letopis'* – *PSRL*, XXXV, 214–38; 7. *Patriarshii Spisok* – *PSRL*, XVII, 247–93 (in variant readings).

garbling of Rus'ian chronicle records and Polotsk hagiography points to an oral transmission of evidence which the authors of the third redaction supplement with reference to the written tradition. The material which deals with Gediminas is patently a late addition to the text which is clearly joined to the fourteenth-century account of the grand duke's will and the sixteenth-century linking passage which joins Gediminas via Vytenis to the late thirteenth century.[56]

Some of the Gediminas details can be traced to tradition – the campaigns in Žemaitija fit in with Prussian chronicles. The account of the wizard Lizdeika and the founding of the city of Vilnius are legends with a dash of accuracy when we consider the possibilities of a temple being built in Vilnius for the first time by Gediminas and the latter's establishment of this city as the major grand-ducal curial centre. The account of how the Lithuanians conquered south-western Rus' in the 1320s can also be substantiated in essence if not in all its detail.[57]

Careful examination of the textual history of *L2* reveals that the legend of Gediminas' invasion of Kiev is at least fifty years older than the Second Redaction itself. Separate traditions can be unravelled in western Rus' (that is the Grand Duchy of Lithuania) and eastern Rus' (Moscow and Tver'). Gediminas' exploits are related under the alias Gegimenik in Muscovite political propaganda of the late fifteenth century which was hardly designed to further Lithuanian claims on Kiev. The Kievan chronicle tradition of the seventeenth century seems to be independent of the Lithuanian stories. The confusion of the names of princes involved in this war is explicable and the most peculiar, Stanislav of Kiev, seems to be justified by genuine genealogical records of Ioann Stanislavich who flourished in the second third of the fourteenth century. When nineteenth-century scholars found it ridiculous that a Lithuanian could be the Fëdor who appears as prince of Kiev in the 1350s, they had no knowledge of a Greek inventory from

[56] 1. Classical tale of Prince Palemon and his arrival with two companions in Lithuania – *PSRL*, XXXV, 144^{1-37}. 2. Three sons of Palemon found towns and name rivers which bear their names. Foundation of Lithuania-*Litus-tuba*. Genealogies of princes known from Rus'ian sources as alive in 1219 – Erdvilas and Vykintas (*PSRL*, II, 735–6) – 145^{38} – 146^{31}. 3. Vykintas and Erdvilas, contemporaries of Khan Baty – 146^{32} – 147^{10}. 4. Polotsk history and garbled hagiography 147^{11-36}. 5. Skirmont, Treniota, Sventaragis, Utenis, Roman, Narymont–Dovmont quarrel – 147^{37}–151^{4}. 6. Traidenis – 151^{4-35}. 7. Vytenis as introduction to Gediminas; reign of Gediminas – 151^{36}–154^{17}.

[57] See below p. 96f.

Metropolitan Feognost's chancery which records property belonging to a Lithuanian prelate of *c.* 1331. The record shows that the dead metropolitan's patron was Gediminas' brother Fëdor. When one strips away interpolations in the text which are clearly marked by changes in syntax the reader is faced with a stark account of a march on Kiev by the pagans which is told from a Kievan point of view, lamenting the fall of the Mother of Rus'ian cities.[58]

There is much that is dross in the pre-1340 data of the Lithuanian chronicles. Dross, that is, from the point of view of a political researcher interested in the fourteenth century. However as a literary monument the chronicle is fascinating. One can trace genealogical strands through it; recognise garbled Russian chronicles from Lithuanian Rus' and an attempt in the Third Redaction to reorder material. Indeed the Orthodox nature of *L2* is in sharp contrast with the chronologically sharper organisation of a Third Redaction, the *Bychowiec Chronicle* (*L3*) which was composed in tandem with *L2* but over a much longer timespan. It appears to have been completed around 1574. *L3* concentrates on Catholic institutions much more. Indeed in *L3* one can trace the development of a Franciscan martyrology which began with two groups of martyred friars numbering seven in all (in an Italian chronicle) through a Lithuanian story of fourteen martyrs to the thirty-six of the Irish friar Wadding's *Annales*. Each record bred more martyrs from a confusion of numbers and texts which was not aided by later writers adding various fictitious names to the accounts. The constituent parts of *L2* must be read for what they are rather than treated as an ugly and untenable whole. The seams of the narrative are clearly visible; it is foolishness to ignore the key they can sometimes provide to unlock earlier data. There are occasions where the historical imagination should be permitted to hypothesise on *L2* material within confines established by a critique of external sources. The cases of Kiev and the Franciscan martyrs are just such occasions. However the genealogical stories of the earlier parts of *L2* have as yet no such boundaries and encourage far too many equally (im)plausible theories.[59]

[58] See below p. 107.

[59] J. Ochmański, 'Nad Kroniką Bychowca' *Studia Źródłoznawcze*, 12 (1967), 155–63. Text in *PSRL*, XXXII (Moscow, 1975), 128–73. See also M. Jučas, *Lietuvos Metraščiai* (Vilnius, 1968). Palemon moved to Attila's time – *PSRL*, XXXII, 128. Garbled version of Mindaugas (Narymont) in *L2* – *PSRL*, XXXV, 149–50; same in *L3* – *PSRL*,

Less unsightly but equally complex are the records we depend on from Rus'. Most of our knowledge of Lithuania's battles and alliances with the eastern Slavs comes from the chronicles of northern Rus', both to the west (Novgorod and Pskov) and the east (Moscow and Tver'). These records often contain the same matter, for almost all were manipulated by the grand-ducal secretariat in Moscow when that principality established itself as the centre of re-united northern and eastern Rus' in the course of the fifteenth century. Some local traditions were severely curtailed in order to fit in with Muscovite understanding of its past and present roles in Rus'. The chronicles of its major Slavonic competitor (as opposed to Lithuania), Tver', have almost all disappeared with two notable but shorn exceptions.[60] The records of Pskov which was Lithuania's strongest ally in Rus' in the fourteenth century were rewritten in the mid-sixteenth century.

The process of chronicle adjustment is particularly well shown by the case of Novgorod, where in 1331 Gediminas won the role of captain of the Republic's northern frontier for his son Narimantas and his progeny. This contract was to last as long as the Republic was independent of Moscow. The Novgorodian chronicles relate Lithuanian activities in Pskov and the struggle between Vilnius and Moscow for greater influence in Rus'ian affairs. Contemporary with Gediminas' Novgorodian ambitions is the *Novgorod First Chronicle* (*NL*) which survives in two redactions. The older redaction is preserved in a defective manuscript of great value, the *Sinodal'ny spisok* (*NLs*). This

XXXII, 135–6 but prefaced (pp. 132–4) with a section based on *PSRL*, II, 815f. On Algirdas' *gesta* and the Martyrs see S. C. Rowell, 'Lithuania and the West 1337–1341 – A question of sources', *JBS*, 20 (1989), 332 and n. 86. The story of Peter Gostautas and the Franciscan martyrs was intended to show how Catholicism came to Lithuania without Polish intervention – Rowell, 'Lithuania and the West', 311.

60 Tver' – *PSRL*, XV (i), 41, 42 – *Rogozhsky Letopisets*; (ii), 414, 415 – *Tver'skaia Letopis'* (Moscow, 1965). Moscow–Novgorod – *Sofiiskaia Pervaia Letopis'*, *PSRL*, V (St Petersburg, 1853) – Ia. S. Lur'e, *Obshcherusskie Letopisi XIV–XVvv.* (Leningrad, 1976), 67–121. Moscow – Moscow *Svod* of 1479 – *PSRL*, XXV (Moscow, 1949). Connected with *Vologodsko-Permskaia Letopis'* (*c.* 1502), *PSRL*, XXVI (Moscow–Leningrad, 1959) and *Nikanorovskaia Letopis'*, *PSRL*, XXVII (Moscow–Leningrad, 1962) – Lur'e, *Obshcherusskie*, 122–50. Of less importance for our purposes is the 1408 Moscow compilation, *Troitskaia Letopis'* reconstructed by M. D. Priselkov (Moscow–Leningrad, 1950) from *Semeonovskaia Letopis'* – *PSRL*, XVII (St Petersburg, 1913). *Ermolinskii svod* – *PSRL*, XXIII (1910). Pskov – *Pskovskie Letopisi*, ed. A. N. Nasonov, 2 vols. (Moscow–Leningrad, 1941–55) and H-J. Grabmüller, *Die Pskover Chroniken. Untersuchungen zur russischen Regionalchronistik im 13–15 Jahrhundert* (Wiesbaden, 1975). See *PL*, I, 12, 16; II, 22, 23

manuscript is written in hands of the thirteenth, fourteenth and possibly fifteenth centuries and deals with events between 1016 and 1352.[61] It was kept at the archbishop's court and its condition reveals the extent to which someone has tampered with it. The later redaction survives in several fifteenth-century manuscripts (of which the *Kommissionny spisok* (*NLk*) is the best) and represents a revision and a continuation of the older *svod*.[62] *NLs* was kept at the court of the archbishop in Novgorod and reflects the official record of events in the first half of the fourteenth century.

Greater detail of events, especially of Gediminas' treaty with Archbishop Vasily Kaleka in 1331 are given in the *Novgorod Fourth Chronicle* (*NL4*) which is a fifteenth-century compilation. *NL* and *NL4* highlight conveniently how a Rus'ian chronicle tradition manipulated Lithuanian data to suit later political taste not crudely from anti-Lithuanian prejudice but from the needs of domestic policy. The manuscript of *NLs* and the texts of *NLk* and *NL4* betray the manipulation: curtailed texts, obvious erasures and rewriting and most tellingly of all, several folios missing from the original quiring.[63] The contemporary accounts of Vasily's prelacy have been shorn of all material which might be considered by later generations as detrimental to his honour.[64] It seems likely that scribes promoting the veneration of Vasily in Novgorod around 1440 are responsible for the changes in the text of *NLs* and the incomplete change of *NLk*, the manuscripts of which are all fifteenth-century.[65]

61 *NL*. German translation in *Die Erste Novgoroder Chronik nach ihrer ältesten Redaktion* (*Synodalhandschrift*) 1016–1333/1352, ed. J. Dietze (Leipzig, 1971). Date of manuscript given in *NL*, 5 (*NLs*) and text of *NLs* – pp. 15–100.

62 *NLk*, 101–427; date of manuscripts, *ibid.*, pp. 7–8.

63 *PSRL*, IV(i) (St Petersburg, 1848). This Chronicle is analysed in Lur'e, *Obshcherusskie*, 67–121. Editing of *NL* – the change in hands is obvious from the manuscript as reproduced photographically in *Novgorodskaia Kharateinaia Letopis'*, ed. M. N. Tikhomirov (Moscow, 1964), 338–9. The manuscript is made up of 169 folios in 21 quires of 8 folios, from which two are missing. To these 166 folios are added 3 extra leaves – *NL*, 5–6. The difference in ligatures used on f. 167 from those on 166 is as obvious as the change of hand and ink – on f. 167r we read *TOGO*^{ZHE} *LE*^{T} as opposed to *TO*^{GO}*ZHE LE*^{T}. Fuller details in Rowell, 'Of men and monsters', 85–7.

64 Cf. *NLs* s.a. 1331, 1332, 1333, 1337, 1345, 1352 (*NL*, 99–100) with *NLk* pp. 343, 344–6, 347–8, 357–8, 362–3 and especially *NLs*, 100 for Pskov visitation in 1352 which is missing from other sources.

65 A. S. Khoroshev, *Tserkov' v sotsial'no-politicheskoi sisteme Novgorodskoi feodal'noi respubliki* (Moscow, 1980), 93–5 for plan to canonise Vasily. The background to Novgorodian 'independent' politics in the fifteenth century is given in J. Raba, 'Evfimij II Erzbischof von Gross-Novgorod und Pskov. Ein Kirchenfürst als Leiter

These sources dictate the subject matter of this book. We can manage a good deal of the high, mainly diplomatic politics of the Grand Duchy, but not a deep survey of politicians other than the grand dukes or of social conditions, except in the very broadest terms. As we have already seen, the letters of Gediminas give an insight into grand ducal diction and diplomatic brinkmanship. The Christian propaganda imagery which Gediminas approved for use in dealing with Catholic powers is also recorded.

The next best attested area is the military scene. Details of battles, tactics and equipment are available from chronicles, letters, muster-lists (an indication of the price of war), treaties and the tombs of warriors. The Prussian record of routes into Lithuania reveals not only the roads through pagan territory favoured by the crusaders, but also illustrates the spread of noble and royal vills, the settlement of non-Lithuanian Balts, Rus'ians and even Catholics in the western marches of the Grand Duchy.

The religious diplomacy of the Grand Duchy between Rome and Byzantium is adequately attested and the pagan cult can be reconstructed through chronicle accounts, treaties, travel notes and archaeology. Social history is much more difficult. The structure of society from slaves to grand dukes can be sketched broadly but there is little room for detail. It is very tempting to indulge in comparative history. Traditionally this has taken Tacitus as its starting point for a methodology as misguided as it is racialist. Some think they compare fourteenth-century Lithuania with second-century Germania when they merely deduce the first from the second on the grounds that all north European pagans are the same and certainly never change until they convert to Christianity eleven hundred years later. It also grossly over-estimates Tacitus' value and is attractive to the well-read who fear no one will ever be quite so chic as even a Silver Latin author. Tacitus never saw the Baltic, although nineteenth-century German histories produce lithographic evidence of the scene! He used an ideal based on hearsay and a report, which was already a century old when he read it, as a preaching exemplum.

The economic history of Lithuania can be reconstructed meagrely from debt-books, hoards of silver ingots and treaties which describe safe routes through the war zone. The debt-books

einer weltlichen Republik', *Jahrbücher für Geschichte Osteuropas*, n.s. 25 (1977), 161–73. For date of mss. of *NLk* see *NL*, 7–9.

give a glimpse of women traders who stand surety alongside their spouse.[66]

The role of female protagonists in the creation of the Grand Duchy is difficult to describe precisely, although it cannot be denied. This study will not seek to isolate women from the main argument but specifically female experiences are recorded even more rarely than others. The distaff diplomacy of the Gediminids which gave Lithuanian dowagers in Mazovia and Tver' considerable wealth and power has been ignored on the whole until recently. The wills of foreign princes often give indications of the large size of Lithuanian dowries and the implications this has for Lithuanian status and wealth can be sketched. A concentration on the experience of women in Lithuania shows how they shared much of the male experience: women acted as priestesses and seers, they killed their own warriors to save them from falling prisoner to the crusaders. Their tombs are no less well endowed with funerary goods than those of their male counterparts. A comparison with Viking society immediately suggests itself, although for this to be useful more gender-specific reports are required from the archaeologists. Looking at female Christianity requires a change of focus from concentration on successful institutions (of which there were none before 1387) to the survival of belief and patronage on a smaller and more private scale – women patrons of the Franciscans who remained in Vilnius but without an official religious role for Lithuanians; princesses who were nuns; captive Rus'ian wetnurses who acted, according to a Franciscan report of Mindaugas' coronation, as the earliest proselytisers. However those vast areas of social history where accounts of female contributions might be expected to dominate are almost as unknowable as they have been unmentioned for the Lithuanian medieval historian. It is only after the Conversion that documentation begins slowly to proliferate.[67]

The sources for fourteenth-century Lithuania call to mind those data available for an earlier military society, ducal Normandy in

[66] *Das Rigische Schuldbuch (1285–1352)*, ed. H. Hildebrand (St Petersburg, 1872) and *LU*, III, nos. 1044a/b, col. 182f. See E. von Lehe, 'Die Schuldbücher von Lübeck, Riga und Hamburg', in *Städtwesen und Bürgertum als geschichtliche Kräfte. Gedächtnisschrift Fritz Rörig*, ed. A. von Brandt and W. Koppe (Lübeck, 1953), 165–77. On Lithuanian goods in the possession of Archbishop Frederick of Riga as recorded in inventories of his property made in Lyons in 1324 and 1325 see L. Arbusow, 'Römischer Arbeitsbericht', *Latvijas Ūniversitātes Raksti*, 17 (1928), 378.

[67] See below especially pp. 89–94, 282–3, 297–9.

the tenth century. The earliest local chronicle, *L1*, like the account of Dudo of St Quentin, was written a century after many of the events it describes in order to propagate the glory of a new power. Much of these chronicles is bombastic and highly fictionalised. Even so, the historian must attempt to pick his way through the rampant verbiage to the very well concealed facts. It is unfortunate that, unlike the Normans who invaded a literary society that has preserved certain of its impressions of the newcomers and recorded the practical effects of the imposition of the new regime, the Lithuanians came to dominate an area now stripped of its records. Polotsk and the duchies of western Rus' certainly produced charters, treaties (and chronicles), for several survive in the Rigan Archive and in later annals, but too few remain for us to establish in great detail the practicalities of the Lithuanian annexation. By the time extant records increase in number the local Lithuanian princes have become absorbed into Rus'ian society and become ready to mythologise their past.[68]

From this broad base of sources we may proceed with caution to examine several major aspects of life in the Grand Duchy of Lithuania. The material we have is not perhaps what we might choose. It cannot compare in quantity or variety with the records of an English county in the fourteenth century. Nevertheless its quality presents a challenge and rewards the researcher. What is not in the record is often as interesting as what is present. The editing of the Novgorodian record to fit in with the fifteenth century's perceptions of what a sainted archbishop should do is fascinating in itself. It also stands as a stark reminder of the gaps which are everywhere in the sources.

[68] Dudo of St Quentin, *De moribus et actis primorum Normanniae ducum*, ed. J. Lair (Caen, 1865). See also D. Bates, *Normandy before 1066* (London, 1982), xi–xix. On the destruction of Polotsk libraries in 1579, a far from unique disaster, see Ia. N. Shchapov, 'Biblioteka polotskogo Sofiiskogo sobora i Biblioteka Akademii Zamoiskoi', in *Kul'turnye sviazi narodov vostochnoi evropy v XVIv. Problemy vzaimootnoshenii Pol'shi, Rossii, Ukraini, Belorussii i Litvy v epokhu Vozrozhdenia*, ed. B. A. Rybakov (Moscow, 1976), 272–3. Surviving documents are gathered in *PG*, I–III.

Chapter 3

AN INTRODUCTION TO LITHUANIAN POLITICAL AND ECONOMIC HISTORY BEFORE 1315

Outside the territories of western Rus' which had submitted to Lithuanian princes in the second half of the previous century, Lithuania in 1300 covered an area roughly two thirds the size of England to the north-east of the Nemunas (Niemen, Neman, Memel) in the watersheds of the Nevežis and Neris rivers. The land abounded with myriad lakes and rivers hidden under a dense canopy of forest. Here one might travel for days through wilderness without sight or sound of another man. The tracks which snaked between isolated farming settlements and the castles of the nobility were often no broader than an arm's length. Access from Order domains to the fertile glebe of the Lithuanian heartland was possible only during the winter when, as the English bishop and world-historian Bartholomew records, 'water and ryuers ben yfrore',[1] and in summer when the sun dried out the morass and the harvest preoccupied the natives.[2] The forts with which the banks of the Nemunas bristled (see map 4) controlled merchant shipping and hindered the passage of military vessels.[3] The ferocity of the aurochs, boar and wolf which roamed the forests was matched only by the stubborn resistance of the human population to the unwelcome attentions of neighbouring Christian armies.[4]

Lithuania was the home of a largely agricultural society focussed on the farms and castles of a warrior elite, the *bajorai* (or noble servitors whose title is borrowed from Rus') and dukes (*kunigai*,

[1] *On the properties of things. John Trevisa's translation of Bartholomaeus Anglicus, De proprietatibus rerum. A critical text*, ed. M. C. Seymour, II (Oxford, 1975), 777.

[2] The Knights' routes make chilling reading – *SRP*, II, 662–711.

[3] Nemunas forts – see below n. 26 and p. 244; river battle on Nemunas – *PD*, 179–80.

[4] 'Lithuaniam, terram vastam, palustrem, nemorosam in qua populus terrae similis, nimirum silvestris et crudus, ac ferus potius quam ferox', Johannes Dubrawius, *Historia Bohemica*, I (Frankfurt, 1687), 540. Although Dubrawius' text is not devoid of prejudice (see below n. 95) in this case his description neatly summarises other accounts of Lithuania.

kunigaikščiai). We shall follow Giedroyć in defining as dukes rulers 'of an independent polity ... with an allegiance to a higher regnal power' and call prince 'any person related by blood to a ruler'.[5] The head of this hierarchy is the grand duke (in Lithuanian *didysis kunigaikštis* and in Russian *velikii kniaz'*). In the early thirteenth century powerful dukes still ruled several regions or *terrae*: Nalšia, Deltuva and Upitė in Aukštaitija (Upper Lithuania) and Ceklis, Karšuva and Kretuva in Žemaitija (Lower, that is north western, Lithuania; called Samogitia in Latin and sometimes in English).

In 1219 one duchess and twenty princes and dukes concluded a treaty with the Romanovichi of Galich–Volyn', making peace between Lithuania and her Rus'ian neighbours to the south-west. This is the earliest agreement involving Lithuanian leaders which survives, albeit only in the text of a Rus'ian chronicle. Five leaders of the clans from Aukštaitija who struck this agreement were recognised as senior by the other Lithuanian dukes.[6] The clans to which these princes – Živinbudas, the brothers Daujotas and Vilikaila and the sons of Ringaudas – belonged, created the grand-ducal office.[7] Well before the dawn of the fourteenth century, Aukštaitija (namely Lithuania) was governed by one ruler, the grand duke. The dukes of the remaining thirteenth-century families such as the Alšeniškiai and the Radvilai became important noble counsellors and acted as the lieutenants (*capitanei* in Latin, in Russian *namestniki*) of the ruling clan, but for the most part they entertained no pretensions to supreme power for themselves. Those noblemen who did seek to gain princely power were usually executed by the grand duke for their presumption.[8] Žemaitija, by contrast, remained parcelled out among many nobles although, in theory, these acknowledged the overlordship of the grand duke of Lithuania, the *Rex de Owsteiten*. The alliance between Aukštaitija and Žemaitija was a marriage of convenience between tribes who spoke similar dialects and faced a common foe. It did not become an indissoluble union until after 1422.[9] The

[5] Giedroyć, 'Rulers', 3.

[6] *PSRL*, II, 735.

[7] E. Gudavičius, '1219 metų sutarties dalyviai ir jų vaidmuo suvienijant Lietuvą', *LAMMDI*, 22 (1982), 33–46; Giedroyć, 'Rulers', 3. Following the Giedroyć analysis of grand-ducal families we can devise a stemma of the three clans of 1219, see genealogical table 2.

[8] Giedroyć, 'Rulers', 15–16. For dukes killed when they sought to equate themselves with Gediminid royal status see *PSRL*, XXXV, 115–16; *HW*, 73.

[9] *Austechiam terram regis Lethowie* – *PD*, 159. *Rex de Owsteiten* is a term the Knights apply to the grand duke of Lithuania – *PU*, II, p. 381. See also Bartholomaeus Hoeneke, *Liivimaa noorem riimkroonika (1315–1348)* (Tallinn, 1960), 62. Aukštaitija seems to have

achievements of these early grand dukes is worth examining before we assess the political institutions and the economy of Lithuania and the rise of the Gediminids.

THE HOUSES OF RINGAUDAS AND ŽIVINBUDAS

Around 1238 Prince Mindaugas assumed, although not without challenge, supreme power in Lithuania. By the familiar processes of marriage, murder and military conquest he consolidated the influence his father, Ringaudas, and his brother, Dausprungas, had earlier established in a similar fashion over the dukes. In 1251 with the hope of gaining support from the Teutonic Order for his military campaigns in Žemaitija and with an eye to attracting western merchants to his lands, Mindaugas was baptised a Catholic through the good offices of the Grand Master of the Order, Andreas von Stirland. Two years later, he was crowned king by Bishop Heinrich, the papal representative.[10] The princes whom the king did not defeat in battle or whose relatives he did not marry, were despatched to Rus' to carve out patrimonial domains of their own to replace those confiscated by Mindaugas in Lithuania.[11] This policy of exporting potential troublemakers was common to many warrior societies. The example of Julius Caesar's conquest of Gaul springs to mind. Indeed Mindaugas' control of the other leaders was not so complete even as Caesar's command of Rome. Several princes and dukes from Nalšia, Lithuanian Rus' and Žemaitija joined forces against him and his Christian advisers. Despite Mindaugas' subsequent apostasy and his expulsion of Christians from Lithuania, the king was murdered in 1263 by Daumantas of Nalšia acting on behalf of Mindaugas' ambitious

been the cradle of Lithuanian monarchy; its *kunigai* annexed the once independent territories of Nalšia and Deltuva in the thirteenth century. On the difficulties of controlling Žemaitija which led Vytautas to surrender the land temporarily to the Order in the 1390s see P. Rabikauskas, 'La cristianizzazione della Samogizia', *La Cristianizzazione della Lituania, Atti e Documenti*, II (Vatican City, 1989) 219–331.

[10] Mindaugas' reign is described well in Paszkiewicz, *Jagiellonowie*, 49–104 and E. Gudavičius, *Kryžiaus karai Pabaltijyje ir Lietuva XIII amžiuje* (Vilnius, 1989), 92–110. The coronation was discussed recently in M. Hellmann, 'Der Deutsche Orden und die Königskrönung des Mindaugas', *ZfO*, 3 (1954), 387–96, Z. Ivinskis, 'Mindaugas und seine Krone', *ZfO*, 3 (1954), 360–86. A new source in M. L. Colker, 'America rediscovered in the thirteenth century?', *Speculum*, 54 (1979), 716–26. See also K. Stopka, 'Próby Chrystianizacji Litwy w latach 1248–1263', *Analecta Cracoviensia*, 19 (1987), 1–65.

[11] See pp. 82f.

nephew, Treniota.[12] Seven years of civil strife and the assassination of Mindaugas' three immediate successors, Treniota, Vaišvilkas and Švarnas, ensued. Out of this chaos that effectively put an end to the Ringaudas clan arose Traidenis: a scion of the House of Kentauras which had given Lithuania her second grand duke, Živinbudas.[13]

Traidenis, who acceded to power *c.* 1270 and ruled Lithuania for twelve years, was firmly pagan. He governed with a strong arm, repulsing the Teutonic Order and trading with both Rus' and Livonia. It could be argued that in these respects Traidenis revived the main aims of Mindaugas minus the ill-fated attempt to convert the pagans. Contrary to the view of traditional historiography, he enjoyed the friendship, or at least the cooperation, of Mindaugas' assassin, Daumantas of Nalšia after the latter fled to Pskov in 1265.[14] He sought Polish and Rus'ian allies to counter the threat posed to his realm by the Order which turned its attention more constantly towards Lithuania as the other Baltic tribes submitted to its hegemony. Traidenis established friendly relations with Bolesław II of Mazovia when that duke harboured ambitions to wear the Polish crown. This Mazovian alliance survived under various guises for several centuries. When Traidenis died of natural causes in 1281 or 1282, he was succeeded by another Daumantas of whom we know only that he died on campaign in north-east Rus' in 1285.[15]

THE HOUSE OF PUKUVERAS: THE 'GEDIMINIDS'

Before 1289 there emerged what appears to have been a new ruling dynasty led by the brothers Butigeidas and Pukuveras (*alias* Budividas). The ancestors of these princes are shaded in a mystery whose penumbra is likely to remain impenetrable until a new light can be found to illuminate the Lithuanian chronicles or a new source emerges. They appear to have had no close blood relationship with Traidenis, for a blood kinship with such a powerful leader would surely have been claimed by their most

[12] Rowell, 'Between Lithuania and Rus'', 5–6. [13] Giedroyć, 'Rulers', 19–20.

[14] On Traidenis' religious policy see M. Giedroyć, 'The arrival of Christianity in Lithuania: early contacts (thirteenth century)', *OSP*, n.s. 18 (1985), 26–9 and Paszkiewicz, *Jagiellonowie*, 124–42. On Lithuano-Pskov relations during Traidenis' reign see Rowell, 'Between Lithuania and Rus'', 12–13. [15] *PSRL*, I, 483.

illustrious offspring, Gediminas, *nominatim*.[16] There is certainly no evidence that Traidenis produced any sons, although it is clear that he did father a daughter. The marriage of his great-grandson Bolesław-Yury of Galich with Gediminas' daughter Eufemia in 1331 would have been contrary to canon law had Gediminas been Traidenis' grandson. Although the pagan ruler was not constrained by canon law of course, his Christian ally most certainly was. Such dynastic alliances were reviewed constantly by the popes in the thirteenth and fourteenth centuries, not least when rival princes delated those unions to the Curia.[17] Whatever the status of this legalistic finery as evidence in this matter, *L2* indicates that Vytenis (or rather, his father) was not directly related to Traidenis.

Two manuscripts of the fourteenth-century Russian prose-poem *Zadonshchina* which refer to the grandsons of Gediminas as the great-grandsons (*pravnuki*) of Skolomend/ Skoldimer may be more trustworthy. The term *pravnuk* also means 'distant descendant' and it is very probable, as Ochmański has argued, that Skolomend comes from a generation before Pukuveras. Unfortunately the name appears in no other record, although Giedroyć may be correct to follow Tikhomirov and associate it with the duke recorded rather fancifully in *L2* as Skirmont (Giermantas).[18] Even so this suggestion remains nothing more than a hypothesis. It may be that Skolomend is none other than Skumantas, the powerful Sudavian warrior who flourished in the 1240s and that the Gediminids are descended from him in the maternal line. There is no evidence that the Sudavians, a large group of whom

[16] For Budividas/Pukuveras and Butigeidas see Paszkiewicz, *Jagiellonowie*, 151–2. Traidenis' family bore the Centaur arms; Pukuveras' clan bore the 'Columns of Gediminas' blazon. No details are given anywhere of Pukuveras' parentage. Giedroyć considers that despite the difference in arms Pukuveras was the son of one of Traidenis' Orthodox siblings. There is no evidence for this theory – M. Giedroyć, 'The arrival of Christianity in Lithuania: between Rome and Byzantium (1281-1341)', *OSP*, n.s. 20 (1987), 6–7 and n. 49.

[17] Marriage policy discussed below pp. 87–94. On problems of consanguinity within the fourth degree in 1324 and 1365, the latter case being provoked by Louis of Hungary who wished to prevent the marriage of Casimir of Poland and Jadwiga of Żagań, see *Bullarium Poloniae*, II, nos. 1002, p. 161 and 1515, p. 252.

[18] Skolomend appears in the Kirillo-Belozerskii and Undol'skii mss. of *Zadonshchina – Povesti o Kulikovskoi Bitve*, ed. M. N. Tikhomirov (Moscow, 1959), 11. The text is discussed in J. Ochmański, 'Gediminovichi – "pravnuki Skolomendovye"', *Pol'sha i Rus'* (Moscow, 1974), 358–64. Giedroyć considers Skolomend to have been Giermantas, an uncle of Traidenis – Giedroyć, 'Arrival ... (1281–1341)', 7, n. 49 – and Nikžentaitis that he was Traidenis' brother, *Gediminas* (Vilnius, 1989), 8.

fled to Lithuania rather than submit to the Knights in the 1280s, were isolated from the Grand Duchy. A marriage between Gediminas' family and the powerful clan of Skumantas is not entirely fanciful.[19] Given that all previous grand dukes and pretenders belonged to two clans which were acknowledged as senior in 1219, it is possible that Pukuveras was related to the family of Daujotas and Vilikaila, the other 'senior' princes of the Galich Treaty.[20] It is not completely beyond the realm of possibility that the clan was descended from Vilikaila and that it originated in Ukmergė (Vilkmergė, Wilkomierz), as a sixteenth-century genealogy alleges. Ukmergė was a major fortified centre in eastern Lithuania which was often held in the later fourteenth century by senior members of the Gediminid clan and was one of the first grand-ducal possessions to be adorned with a Catholic church after 1387.[21]

Hypothesis breeds ever more fanciful hypothesis. Let us be content to limit ourselves to that little of which we may be certain: Pukuveras fathered at least four sons: Vytenis who became grand duke *c.* 1295; Gediminas, who succeeded his brother *c.* 1315; Voin of Polotsk; and Fëdor of Kiev. These are the earliest reasonably well-known members of the family which ruled Lithuania and later, Poland until 1572. The Gediminids certainly came from Aukštaitija, as did the clans of 1219. The theory fashionable in Polish scholarship in the 1930s, which taught that the Gediminids came from Žemaitija, has been proven erroneous, based as it was on a misunderstanding of a Prussian document of 1290. The fifteenth-century Prussian legend that Gediminas was a stable-boy who murdered Vytenis before usurping his master's throne has long been debunked by scholarship. Another claim, made by the compiler of *L2*, that Gediminas was the son of Vytenis is

[19] Skumantas of Sudavia is recorded as a prince-priest in 1250s – see p. 138. Although Skumantas converted to Catholicism and fled to Prussia with his sons, he did return briefly to Lithuania (*PD*, 127, 128, 137, 142, 143, 147; *PU*, I.2, no. 464, pp. 297–8). No record of a daughter is available, but this is hardly a rare omission. The authors of *Zadonshchina* may have borrowed the exotic name from the *Ipat'evskaia Chronicle*.

[20] See above n. 7.

[21] Kraków, Biblioteka Czartoryskich Ms. 2211, p. 100, *Rod litowskich kniazeÿ*: A Wilkus postawil horod na toy sze reky na swiatoy y narek jeho wo swoie ymia Wolkomir ... a u Wilkusa syn, Kedimin y Wilkusow wnuk byl. Ukmergė was always an important strategic post – *HW*, 67, 84, 104, 116; *Wig.*, 626, 633, 645; *SRP* II, 695, W67, W68. First church – *KDKDW*, no. 4 p. 10. Gudavičius says it was in centre of Gediminid lands – *Miestų atsiradimas Lietuvoje* (Vilnius, 1991), 49–50. It lies in the Deltuva region (connected with Daujotas).

unfounded rationalisation on the part of the chronicler. Incontrovertible evidence has since emerged that Gediminas was Vytenis' brother.[22]

The reign of Grand Duke Vytenis spans approximately twenty years and is reasonably well-documented in comparison with that of his predecessors, yet the exact dates of his accession *c.* 1295 and his death *c.* 1315 cannot be given. He appears in the Prussian chronicle record for the first time in 1292 when his father Pukuveras sent him on campaign against the Teutonic Knights. He is mentioned for the last time in Dusburg's account of a Lithuanian raid in Prussia in September 1315, in the course of which the pagans suffered many casualties.[23] Sixteenth-century chronicles use him as a link between his brother Gediminas and his most illustrious predecessor, Traidenis.[24] His reign is almost as long as that of his younger brother but he can be passed over in a brief paragraph. Modern historians are wont to imitate their Renaissance forbears. We and the chroniclers have been duped by Gediminas' greater success and his descendants' control of the written record. Contemporary foreign accounts portray Vytenis as a much more vigorous character than even his successor. In the early fourteenth century his reputation outshone that of Gediminas who is referred to by Vytenis' name on several occasions. Gediminas himself was proud to refer to his predecessor's achievements in relations with Christian merchants and prelates. The elder brother's mistake was to die without a large number of children.

Vytenis is a useful connection between the revival of Lithuanian foreign relations under Traidenis and Pukuveras and the powerful diplomacy of Gediminas. The chroniclers were right, if only for the wrong reason. Vytenis was the first grand duke of the House of Pukuveras whose rule over Aukštaitija lasted for a considerable number of years; his father, by contrast, appears to have governed

[22] Žemaitijan theory based on misreading of a letter of the Master of Prussia – *PU*, I.2, no. 568, p. 355. It is questioned in Paszkiewicz, *Jagiellonowie*, 152–6 and dismissed effectively in J. Jakštas, 'Naujasi Gedimino dynastijos kilmės tyrinėjimas', *Lietuvos Praeitis*, 1940 (1), 29–56. Rigans refer to Vytenis as Gediminas' *frater et antecessor* – *GL*, 59. For Gediminas as *stabularius* or *koniushii* in fifteenth-century propaganda, see *SRP*, V, 223, *PSRL*, XVII, 593. Cf. Algirdas' insult of a rival – *HW*, 72.

[23] *PD*, 156. Vytenis appears for the last time in the sources in September–October 1315 – *PD*, 181–2. It appears that his only known son, Swalegote (fl. 1309), died before him. Swalegote is recorded in the Rigan Annals – Paszkiewicz, *Jagiellonowie*, 165, n. 11.

[24] *PSRL*, XXXV, 151 is typical.

for only five. In Žemaitija, Vytenis relied on local nobles for influence in the province. Those nobles were not averse to opposing grand-ducal policy when it suited them to do so, as frequent rebellions illustrate. Gediminas seems to have exercised influence on his brother's behalf in the north-west from his castle of Gedimin-Burg in Pograuden. We first hear of this fort's coming under enemy attack in 1305 from Peter of Dusburg.[25] It is during Vytenis' reign that the two networks of castles along the Nemunas and Jūra river frontiers became established. These were matched by Teutonic forts on the opposite river bank.[26] The war between the Teutonic Order and Lithuania intensified in the 1290s after the Prussian and Livonian tribes had capitulated or been rendered extinct.

Despite his appearing in Teutonic sources primarily as a great war leader marching armies into Livonia, Prussia and Poland, the grand duke also understood the need to foster military alliances with his neighbours against a common foe: the Teutonic Order. He maintained pressure on the Knights in both Livonia and Prussia throughout his reign. His attacks seem to have been particularly fierce in Warmia, an area which the Knights and the local bishop had used as a major site for the relocation of Baltic tribesmen from other regions.[27] The settlement of Balts, including disaffected Lithuanian nobles, increased in the early years of the fourteenth century, especially as Žemaitijan leaders drifted towards compromise rather than conflict with the crusaders when neither party could win outright victory. In 1301 Pope Boniface VIII permitted the see of Reval in Estonia to escape the interdict because of the large number of neophytes which had been settled there. These were under constant pressure to recant from frequent Rus'ian, Karelian, Ingrian and Lithuanian raids on their settlements.[28]

[25] *PD*, 153, 159, 173, 177; Gedimin-Burg 1305 – *PD*, 170–1, 183; the exact location of this fort is unknown – E. Gudavičius, 'Gedimino pilies (Žemaitijoje), Pagraudės srities ir Paragaudžio vietovės problematika', *LMADA*, 100 (1987/3), 59–66; 101 (1987/4), 82–91.

[26] R. Batūra, 'Oborona pravoberezh'ia Nizhego Nemana protiv agressii Tevtonskogo Ordena (XIII–nachalo XIVv.)', *Drevneishie gosudarstva na territorii SSSR* (1985), 184–93; A. Nikžentaitis, 'Rašytiniai šaltiniai apie Lietuvių pilių systemą XIIIa. pabaigoje – XIVa. pradžioje', *LMADA*, 96 (1986/3), 51–62.

[27] Pressure on the Order in Warmia – *PD*, 165. Attacks on Christburg (1300) and Löbau (1302) – *PD*, 166, 169.

[28] Settlement of Balts – *PU*, I.2, nos. 464, 718, 838–9; II, nos. 77, 142; *PD*, 145–6. When the bishop of Warmia granted land to two Lithuanians in 1307, the charter was witnessed by Lithuanians – *Codex Diplomaticus Warmiensis*, I, no. 139, pp. 242–3. The

On the advice of Bolesław II of Mazovia, Vytenis intervened in Łokietek's struggle for the Polish crown by supporting the pretender. Bolesław's first wife had been a Lithuanian princess: Gaudemantė. Even after the Mazovian duke had surrendered his claim to the throne to Łokietek, he maintained close contacts with his pagan allies. In 1295 and 1306 Vytenis campaigned in Poland for the benefit of Bolesław and the Polish pretender.[29]

However Poland was not the scene of Vytenis' greatest diplomatic triumph. In 1297 the Knights and the citizens of Riga came to blows over the Order's presence in Riga. The following year, at a period of increasing commercial traffic between Lithuania and the city of Riga, Vytenis offered the archbishop of Riga, John II, the services of a Lithuanian garrison to fend off the unwelcome attentions of the Prussian Knights. Thus the greatest danger to Lithuanian commerce in Livonia, the closure of Riga to pagan merchants was averted. Vytenis offered vaguely to adopt Catholicism (or the archbishop suggested this course of action) in order to sugar the pill for the Rigans of having a pagan army encamped within their city to fight off a crusading religious order. As matters turned out, the grand duke never submitted to baptism. Nevertheless, the alliance was accepted and Lithuanians fought in the Livonian civil war against the Knights, inflicting a series of defeats on the Knights both in Livonia and in Prussia.[30] In 1298 the Knights were defeated at Karkhus, Treiden, and Neuermühlen (see map 5), reducing their power in the vicinity of Riga. The momentum of the attack on the Order could not be maintained indefinitely but the pagans more than matched the Knights.[31] Ironically it was probably the success of the Lithuanian fortress in Riga which made the Knights so eager to buy and hold on to the Cistercian convent at Dünamünde in 1305 to use it as a military base controlling river access to and from Riga.[32] Each side seems to

grand master gave land to Lithuanians near Tilsit that same year – G. Mortensen, *Beiträge zu Nationalitäten und Siedlungsverhältnissen von Pr. Litauen* (Konigsberg, 1927), 32 based on a manuscript now in Berlin, PKKA, *OF*, 112. For the letter of Boniface VIII to Reval, see *VMPL*, no. 200, p. 114. The frequent Lithuanian attacks on Dorpat and Ösel *c.* 1303–4 are noted in *LU*, II, no. 608, cols. 7–12.

[29] 1295 alliance – *PD*, 156–7, 158–9, 160; 1306 – *PD*, 172. See J. Bieniak, *Wielkopolska, Kujawy, ziemie Łęczycka i sieradzka wobec problemu zjednoczenia państwowego w latach 1300–1306* (Toruń, 1969), 150.

[30] *LU*, I, no. 570; Albert von Bardewik, 'Aufzeichnungen', *Chroniken der deutschen Städte*, XXVI (Leipzig, 1899), 313–15; *PD*, 163f.

[31] *PD*, 163; Albert von Bardewik, 315; *LU*, I, nos. 584–6, VI, no. 3207.

[32] *PU*, II, no. 13, p. 9; *Diplomatarium Danicum*, II.7, no. 126, p. 86–7.

have balanced the power of the other and, for the next decade or so, armed truce alternates with intense but inconclusive warfare. The pagan garrison remained in Riga in the *castrum Lethowinorum* until 1313 when the citizens were prevailed upon by the Knights, after several similar demands had proved fruitless, to send the pagans away. During these fifteen years several attempts were made to break the Rigan–Lithuanian alliance. These failed since successive archbishops found it useful to employ the pagans to defend their interests against the growing influence of the Knights in Livonian ecclesiastical affairs. The citizenry benefited too from increased trade with the Lithuanians.[33]

The close contacts from 1305 between Vytenis and the new archbishop, Frederick von Pernstein built on the alliance of 1298. The grand duke permitted the archbishop to continue his policy of gathering friars for the Lithuanian Mission. In 1310 Frederick persuaded Clement V to permit the expansion of the Franciscans throughout the Archdiocese of Riga to the greater benefit of the faithful 'and that the infidels might be converted more swiftly'. The Pope granted such permission in February 1311.[34] A year later, in an act which Gediminas imitated in the 1320s, Vytenis invited two Franciscans to man a Catholic church for German merchants in the trading centre of Novgorodok in Lithuanian Rus'. The lapse in Lithuanian association with Catholic prelates which had followed on from Mindaugas' expulsion of all clergy and the death of the last titular bishop of Lithuania in western Germany in the early 1290s was remedied.[35] However lest the (pagan) world gain the impression that the grand duke had abandoned the gods of his fathers, Vytenis is recorded in 1311 as having blasphemed Christ during a raid in Prussia: the balance between native paganism and mercantile Christianity was struck.[36] Certainly he could not look to Frederick for reliable assistance, since the archbishop returned to his exile in France soon after

[33] *LU*, II, nos. 694–5, cols. 78–81; for consequences see table 2, p. 75 and Hildebrand, *Rigische Schuldbuch*.

[34] For Frederick see above p. 14–15 and below p. 190; 1311 bull – *VMPL*, no. 207, p. 123.

[35] 1312 Franciscans – *GL*, 25; last bishop of Lithuania, John, a suffragan of the bishop of Constance, first mentioned in 1271 and for the last time in 1291. Active in Alsace–Burgundy and Speyer; see H. Paszkiewicz, *Regesta Lithuaniae ab origine usque ad Magni Ducatus cum regno Poloniae unionem*, I (Warsaw, 1930), nos. 489, 498, 517–19, 535, 550, 574, 585, 590–1, 596, 601, 606–9, 619, 622–3, 625–7, 629, 638, 641–2, 656, 662–6, 669–70, 677, 678, 701, 509a; also *Chartularium Sangallense*, ed. O. P. Clavadetscher (St Gallen, 1985), no. 2265, p. 375; *Bündner Urkundenbuch*, ed. E. Meyer-Marthaler and F. Perret, III (Chur, 1985), no. 1194, pp. 141–2.

[36] *PD*, 176.

Francis of Moliano left Livonia in 1313. Vytenis' experiences of the Teutonic crusade were reported by the papal legate in 1312.[37] Vytenis also sets the pattern for Gediminas' balance between east and west. The groundwork for the creation of an Orthodox metropolitanate in the Grand Duchy in the early years of Gediminas' reign appears to have been established by Vytenis' achievements in western Rus' and his enlistment of such clerics as the bishop of Polotsk.[38]

It seems that under Vytenis the Rus'ian territories of the Grand Duchy were the more important. At least more attacks were made against Rus'ian towns under Lithuanian control by the Knights. Grodno, a frontier city which all dealing with Lithuania have to endure at least once, was regularly attacked by the Knights as a major trading centre close to Prussia and Mazovia. The Lithuanians and the Rus'ians became closely connected in Prussian complaints against foreign attacks. Rus'ian archers feature prominently in the 1305 invasion of Sambia as they had in similar attacks in the 1270s.[39]

When Grand Duke Vytenis died without heirs some time after October 1315, Gediminas assumed supreme power. During his reign which lasted from the winter of 1315/16 to the winter of 1341/42 the Grand Duchy became firmly established as a major diplomatic and military power of eastern Christendom rather than a mere piratical irritation on the borders of Poland and Rus'. It is legitimate to pause now to ask what grand-ducal power governed and how it referred to itself; where its administrative centre was and how the grand dukes financed their policies are questions which need consideration.

LITHUANIAN POLITICAL INSTITUTIONS

According to his own analysis Gediminas was 'by the providence of God', the mightiest prince in Lithuania where he enjoyed the right 'to instruct and rule, to lose and to save, to close and to open'.[40] Even allowing for the echoes of papal rhetoric in this

[37] Moliano – see below p. 190, n. 3.

[38] See below pp. 150, 180–1.

[39] Grodno *PD*, 147, 162, 163, 170–2, 175; *PD*, 172. See also Rowell, 'Between Lithuania and Rus'', 13.

[40] 'in quibus habemus precipere et imperare, perdere et salvare, claudere et reserare', *GL*, 37. The papal overtones of this declaration are noted below p. 205.

declaration which Gediminas made to Saxon merchants in 1323, the grand duke was very powerful indeed. He was very probably the high priest of the Lithuanian cult.[41] He concluded binding agreements with foreign powers and granted rights to settle in Lithuania and live under specified codes of Teutonic law. He released new colonists from certain taxes on trade and tithes on land which he was otherwise capable of collecting. He collected revenue in silver (*srzebrzczysna*) and in kind (*dakla*).[42] He had authority to summon men-at-arms from the vills of the boiarate, order boiars to build and maintain castles, bridges and military highways and call upon the services of Rus'ian forces.[43] The grand duke enjoyed the power of granting hereditary property rights to his subjects while reserving the privilege of disregarding the rules of inheritance, if he so chose. In this way he placed his own son Narimantas on the throne of Polotsk, despite the presence in the city of his brother's heir who might have expected to succeed his father.[44] The grand-ducal office which had originally been contested by the leading dukes of Aukštaitija, became in the fourteenth century the undisputed patrimony of Gediminas' own line and none outside that family ever openly contested it. Despite the presence of powerful local nobles, the grand duke held strategic estates, especially studs of warhorses and forts on the country's frontiers in the west and north- and south-east. The grand dukes appear to have established networks of kindred with the nobility in these important frontier zones. The *dvory* are the equivalent of the *villae regis* of the Anglo-Saxon kingdoms in

[41] See p. 138.

[42] Peace Treaty of 1323 – see pp. 217f. For taxation and exemptions see below, p. 77. *Srzebrzczysna*, as its name suggests was a tax collected in silver; *dakla* (Polish: *dziaklo*) was *avene, feni dacio*. Jogaila released the canons of Vilnius Cathedral from payment of these taxes on their land in February 1387 – *KDKDW*, no. 6, p. 14. The beginnings of the Lithuanian legal system are discussed with reference to merchants in V. Andriūlis, 'Gedimino diplomatijos dokumentai kaip šaltinis teisės istorijai pažinti', in *Teisinių Institutų raida Lietuvoje XVI–XIXa.*, ed. P. Dičius *et al.* (Vilnius, 1981), 33–43.

[43] Summons to boiars to defend routes into Lithuania – *Wig.*, 548; participation of Rus'ian troops in Lithuanian battles against the Order – *HW*, 75, 107; *Wig.*, 511, 518 and numerous occasions cited in H. Paszkiewicz, *The origin of Russia* (London, 1954), 222. Exemption from these duties and command to build roads, castles and bridges was granted to the canons of Vilnius in 1387 – *KDKDW*, I, no. 6, p. 14.

[44] See pp. 83–4; a claim to patrimonial rights supported by grand-ducal charter was made in 1385 by Andrei of Polotsk – 'regnum Plescoviense quod pater noster Algirde quondam rex Littovie nobis in vita sua assignavit et dedit et post patris nostri obitum fratres nostri nobis dederunt et assignaverunt, sicut in eorundem fratrum nostrorum patentibus litteris clarius apparet', *LU*, III, no. 1226, cols. 456–7.

England which Bede describes. These settlements were not restricted until Grand Duke Alexander promised not to build new vills in Žemaitija in 1492.[45]

Judging from the charters which Jogaila issued in the 1380s, princes, dukes and nobles often acted as grand-ducal *namestniki* in their own regions. They owed their ruler, the grand duke, loyalty which they swore at his installation ritual, and military service in return for his recognition of their rights to their estates.[46] Those who ruled duchies in Lithuanian Rus' were usually of grand-ducal blood and enjoyed princely rights under the grand duke. When Gediminas made a treaty with the Livonian cities in 1338 which involved safeguarding the commercial routes from Livonia to Lithuania, Polotsk and Vitebsk, he ensured that his sons Algirdas and Narimantas, the rulers of those towns, also signed the agreement along with the local bishops. During the reigns of Gediminas' sons, Jaunutis and Algirdas, several princes and dukes added their names to treaties with Poland and Prussia alongside, or in lieu of the grand duke.[47] However the grand dukes shied away wherever possible from allowing noblemen to marry into the ruling dynasty. A balance had to be maintained between the grand duke and his underlings and while a powerful man ruled his country and his kin, this precarious balance was maintained.[48]

Before embarking on major campaigns, Vytenis would gather a council of his *bojarai*, a body of advisers which Dusburg calls *parlamentum*. On occasion Gediminas, like Mindaugas before him and Jogaila after him, decided certain matters of foreign policy

[45] *Tres villae regis*, near Memel, 1306 – *PD*, 171–2; *koninghes hoff bis czu*: Lepone, Ponnau, Allyten, Nampnaythen, Rudemyn (W79, *SRP*, II, p. 698); Cannewa (W79, p. 699); Asmen, Thudenisken (W81, p. 699); Bytisken (W81, p. 700); Perwalken (W83, p. 701); Aysora (W89, p. 703); Wentishken (W97, p. 707); Essera (W98, p. 707); Astrynen (W88, p. 702; W89, p. 703; W91, p. 703; W98, p. 707); Dolletitsch (Novgorodok area, W91, p. 704; W97, pp. 706, 707). In the north-east, fifteen leagues from Dünaburg lay Court le Roy – *Oeuvres de Guillebert de Lannoy*, 38. Promise to build no more vills – *AZR*, I, no. 103, p. 121, §18. Cf. T. Charles-Edwards, 'Early medieval kingships in the British Isles', in *The origins of Anglo-Saxon kingdoms*, ed. S. Bassett (Leicester, 1989), 28–9.

[46] Jogaila issued charters to his kinsmen in Rus' in 1388 – *Pam'iatki ukraïn'skoi movi. Gramoti XIVst.*, ed. M. M. Peshchak (Kiev, 1974), nos. 44, 47, 48, 59, 81, pp. 84, 98, 99–101, 113–15, 146–7.

[47] See below pp. 256–8. and *AZR*, I, no. 1; 1358 agreement with Mazovia survives in original manuscript, Kraków, Biblioteka Czartoryskich, 307 – copy published in *Iura Masoviae*, I, no. 16, pp. 19–20. It names *Helgerdus supremus princeps*, three of his brothers and the other *seniores duces*; *LU*, II, no. 1041, cols. 772–3, dated 1367 includes the nobles Stirpeyke and Waysewist whose lands are prominent in the treaty.

[48] Rowell, 'Gediminid dynastic diplomacy'.

'with the agreement of his sons and all his boiars'.[49] This is more than a formulaic nicety; it reflects political reality. Peter records with some relish the outcome of disputes between Vytenis and his Žemaitijan noblemen. When Gediminas achieved the diplomatic coup of his reign in 1324 by persuading a papal legation to uphold a truce without first effecting his baptism, he had to take into consideration the anti-Catholic feeling of his counsellors who attended the legation's audience.[50] Gediminas could not afford to alienate Žemaitijan and Rus'ian nobles by changing his religious status and it seems that he was almost compelled to deal harshly with Catholic missionaries who disturbed the Vilnius population with their preaching. The same necessary sensitivity to non-familial feeling lies partly behind Algirdas' execution of three non-conforming Orthodox courtiers in 1370.[51] This regard for the opinion of his subjects reflects the finesse of Gediminas' political control, tying hands by consultation rather than naked command. It is surely not without significance that the terms employed in several foreign texts for certain members of the Lithuanian nobility carry overtones of service and counsel. Although the term *bajoras* is sometimes glossed as *armiger* (armed man in both military and heraldic senses) in late fourteenth-century texts, its Rus'ian equivalent refers to one who supports his prince in a political as much as in a military way. Other noble titles occurring in foreign references to Lithuanian leaders also bear a more political interpretation. *Satrapa* in Latin is a noble who serves and advises his lord; the German *wittinc* similarly means wiseman or counsellor.[52]

Careful attention to the views of his powerful underlings benefited Gediminas. There were no major defections from Lithuania to Prussia or Rus' between 1315 and 1342. A handful of

[49] Vytenis and his *parlamentum* – *PD*, 171–2; sons and boiars – 'van vulbort ... siner kindere unde alle siner boyarlen', *GL*, 195; cf. Mindaugas' charter for Bishop Christian, 1254 – *GL*, 21; the example of Jogaila is illustrated in *LU*, III, no. 1186, col. 395. [50] See pp. 214, 222. [51] See below pp. 184, n. 157, 275, n. 48.

[52] Jogaila's 1387 charter for the class of *armiger sive bojarin* is given in *Zbiór praw litewskich*, ed. V. Działyński (Poznań, 1849), no. 1, p. 1. References to boiars are made in *Wig.*, 533, 552, 579; *HW* prefers the term *satrapa* – *HW*, 80, 88, 92. Boiar estates appear in the *Wegeberichte*: Gastowtendorf, W92 (*SRP*, II, 704–5); Iwanendorf, W81 and *Wig.*, 552; Kymundsdorf, W95, 98; Manstendorf, W78; Manewidendorf, W92; Mikullendorf, W87; Sangailsdorf, W99; Sodimptendorf, W82; Surwillendorf, W97 and *Wig.*, 550, 597; curia ... baioris Wyrduk, *Wig.*, 579; Wissegirdendorf, W82. For boiar families who took part in the Treaty of Horodło in 1413 see W. Semkowicz, 'O litewskich rodach bojarskich zbratanych ze szlachtą polską w Horodle roku 1413', *Lituano-Slavica Posnaniensia Studia Historica*, 3 (1989), 7–139.

boiars did change sides and accept land in Prussia in return for aiding the Knights in their war against Lithuania. Some of these were landless malcontents; some had hereditary possessions which they intended to regain in northern Lithuania after the Knights' victory.[53] Be that as it may no major princeling like Suxe who went over to the Knights in the 1260s, or the castellan of Aukaimis who deserted Vytenis, abandoned Gediminas. Vytenis seems to have been particularly badly served by the nobles 'through whom Žemaitija was governed in those times', but only when these were exhausted by the Knights' onslaughts and seriously considered resettlement in Prussia as vassals of the Order.[54] Certainly no brother or cousin betrayed Gediminas. This contrasts sharply with events after his death when Jaunutis fled briefly to Moscow after Kestutis and Algirdas seized power. In the 1380s Vytautas Kestutaitis plotted from Marienburg against his cousin Jogaila.[55] Quite simply Gediminas had no sibling rivals for his power. His two surviving brothers, Voin and Fëdor, were content to rule territories in Lithuanian Rus' on Gediminas' behalf.[56]

It is self-evident that in any polity the title a ruler adopts to describe himself is a major statement of how he views his power. In his correspondence Gediminas styles himself with variation as *Gedeminne (Dei Gratia) Letwinorum et (multorum) Ruthenorum Rex* ('Gediminas, by the grace of God, of the Lithuanians and many Rus'ians King') or simply 'King of Lithuania' (*Rex Lethowye, Koningh van Lettowen*).[57] This reflects the growth of Lithuanian

[53] In the first four decades of the century the Knights issued charters to several Lithuanian renegades. Those who held no estates in Lithuania are recorded in *PU*, II, nos. 125, 126, 336, 781; *PU*, III.1, no. 321; those with patrimonies include:

Gygale, Byenken	(20.02.03) from Aukaimis – *PU*, I.2, nos. 791–2, cf. *PD*, 167.
Leppe	(29.08.33) from Laukuva – *PU*, II, no. 798.
Rusteyko	(2.07.39) from Siaudine – *PU*, III.1, no. 249.
Welot	(4.07.39) from Kulva – *PU*, III.1, no. 250.
Wissegal	(4.07.39) from Kulva – *PU*, III.1, no. 251.
Sipe	(19.11.39) from Gaydyn – *PU*, III.1, no. 277.

[54] Suxe bequeathed his lands to the archbishop of Riga on 5 April 1268 – M. Perlbach, 'Urkunden des Rigischen Capitel – Archivs in der fürstlich Czartoryskischen Bibliothek zu Krakau', *Mitteilungen aus dem Gebiete der Geschichte Liv-Est und Kurlands*, 13 (1886), 1–23.

[55] Jaunutis was deposed in 1345 – see pp. 285–6; Vytautas in Prussia – *Wig.*, 621–33 s.a. 1383–85.

[56] See pp. 83, 100.

[57] Long version in *GL*, 23, 29, 37, 47, 51, 59, 85, 91, 113, 167, 175. *Rex Lethowie* – *GL*, 117, 147; *Koningh van Lethowen* – *GL*, 65, 187. See also J. Adamus, 'O tytule panującego i państwa litewskiego parę spostrzeżeń', *KH* 44 (1930), 313–32. Hoeneke, *Liivimaa*, 60–2 records the title *koninge van Ansteiten und Sameiten*.

dominion in the first quarter of the fourteenth century. His seal of 1323 read + *S. Dei gratia Gedeminni Lethwinor et Rutkenor Reg.*[58] The variation between citing people and country is common enough practice and no legitimate cause for suspecting the document's authenticity.[59] On certain occasions, as in his letters to the Papacy in 1322 and 1323, when it was apposite to make territorial claims, Gediminas added *princeps et dux Semigallie* ('prince and duke of Semigallia') to his style.[60] This distinguishes his role as protector of the Semigallians, whose own princes had been killed by the Knights, from his royal status as grand duke of Lithuania. Some Catholic correspondents referred to Gediminas as *rex sive dux* and the Pope seems to point out the illegality of the appellation *rex* (which *he* had not sanctioned), when he calls the Lithuanian, in a letter to the king of France, 'one who styles himself king'. This pope, as we recall from the case of Louis IV, was particularly sensitive to the unauthorised assumption of the royal title. Nevertheless in direct communications with Gediminas, John XXII does use *rex*.[61]

Mindaugas is the only ruler of Lithuania to have borne this title in the full legal sense. His crown was sent to Vilnius in 1253 by Pope Innocent IV. The Papacy continually regarded the attribution of royal status as a major incentive for pagans to convert (although pagan rulers did not always share this preconception!). In October 1350 Clement VI promised to adorn Kestutis and Algirdas and their progeny with the 'royal title and regalia'.[62] The pagan grand duke's adoption of the theological reference (*DG*) may be an imitation of Mindaugas' title (*Myndowe Dei gratia rex Lettowie*) or a borrowing from the titles of the Catholic princes with whom he corresponded, as was the habit of the princes of Galich–Volyn' and Novgorod. Gediminas was the equal of any Christian prince. It seems more probable that the use of the style *DG* was a deliberate reference to the grand-ducal power which is no longer ordained by social agreement but by a supernal power. Gediminas is ruler by God appointed. This makes sense of the

58 Raczyński, *Codex*, 32.

59 Cf. *rex Anglorum* and *rex Anglie* – *Treaty Rolls preserved in the Public Record Office*, ed. P. Chaplais, I (1234–1325) (London, 1955), nos. 362, p. 137; 368, pp. 145–6; 376, p. 149. Forstreuter cited the variety in royal style as proof of forgery – 'Die Bekehrung des Litauerkönigs', 154f.

60 *GL*, 29–57; *PD*, 191. On Semigallia see below pp. 194–5.

61 Letter of John XXII – *GL*, 85; *regem sive ducem* – *CDP*, II, no. 114, p. 152.

62 Letter of Clement VI 20 October 1350 – *VMPL*, no. 691, p. 526.

theological reference and the use of rhetoric in his correspondence which refers to divine providence and imitates papal claims to holding supreme authority. Gediminas mimics papal humility by referring to himself as the least of all princes but the greatest in Lithuania. It is intriguing that in his letters to western burghers, bishops and mendicants Gediminas uses the same rhetoric of power (Aristotelian images of form and material, evangelical references to servant status) as John XXII and Louis IV employ in their rivalry, or at least his Franciscan scribes choose those translated images on Gediminas' behalf, knowing the resonance they hold for a Christian reader.[63] The grand duke alone of all Lithuanian princes titles himself by grace of God. The other princes, his brothers and sons bear their titles from the grand duke. Kestutis is prince of western Lithuania but he never calls himself ruler *dei gratia*. Similarly on seals only the grand duke styles himself in this way. Indeed it is tempting to speculate whether the famous depiction of Gediminas on his seal as bearing the crown in his hand is not a further statement that he holds and bestows the diadem. It is not sitting on his head, placed there by another human being. Gediminas does not imitate the seal of Mindaugas whom a bishop crowned as representative of an earthly dominion higher than the 'king' of Lithuania. Indeed there seems to have been no coronation in the inauguration ritual of the grand dukes.[64]

It would appear that even as *rex* of the Lithuanians and the Rus'ians, Gediminas did not consistently imitate the grander eastern Rus'ian style of *velikii kniaz'* (grand duke) which had been used by the most senior prince of Rus' since the late twelfth century.[65] This title was first adopted in Lithuanian *diplomata* by

[63] Black, *Political thought*, 51. Note papal fury in March 1324 over Louis IV's assumption of the style 'by the grace of God, ever august King of the Romans' – *MGH, Constitutiones*, IV.5, pp. 695–7. Mindaugas' *DG* – *GL*, 21; cf. *Andreas van Godes Gnaden der van Nowarden koning*, 1301 – *GVNiP*, no. 33, p. 62; *DG* employed in Galich–Volyn by Lev and Andrei Yurevichi in 1316 – *PU*, II, no. 157, p. 108; and Bolesław-Yury II in 1325 – *Ibid.*, no. 537, p. 362.

[64] For inauguration rituals distinct from coronation see below pp. 140–2 and cf. E. Vestergaard, 'A note on Viking Age inaugurations', in *Coronations. Medieval and early modern monarchic ritual*, ed. J. M. Bak (Berkeley–Los Angeles–Oxford, 1990), 119–24. For Mindaugas' seal see W. Kętrzyński, 'O dokumentach Mendoga', *RAU*, n.s. 25 (1907), 200 and plate II.

[65] *Kniaz' litovski* – *NL*, 98, 341, 343. On eastern Rus'ian styles see A. Poppe, 'Words that serve the authority. On the title of "Grand Prince" in Kievan Rus'', *Acta Poloniae Historica* 60 (1959), 159–84. See also M. Szeftel, 'The title of the Muscovite monarch up to the end of the seventeenth century', *Canadian–American Slavic Studies*, 13 : 1–2 (1979), 59–61.

Algirdas who called himself *magnus rex*, *supremus princeps*, *velikii kniaz'*. In Greek he assumed the imperial title of *basileus*, although Byzantine authors and imperial scribes call him *reks* or *megas reks*, an adaptation of the title usually bestowed on Catholic princes.[66] Algirdas' Rus'ian ambitions were based firmly on his father's achievements and it seems that his desire to be ruler of all Rus' led to the Lithuanian rulers' imitation of the *velikii kniaz'* style of their Muscovite rivals. This provoked the appearance of various Lithuanian styles in Catholic records: *Furst*, *herczog*, *rex* and *dux* bearing the qualifications of *gross*, *obirster*, *supremus* and *magnus*.[67] We are faced with a complex problem of translated terminology. *Rex* in many chronicles is used as 'one who rules' rather than 'king' and in that sense is often the same as *dux*. Historians must be wary of mechanical translation from their own minds and dictionaries: *reks*, *kniaz*, *dux* and *rex* are points on an ever rolling circle. Further confusion is possible from an equation of the Lithuanian *kunigas* (originally a prince, but later meaning priest) with the German cognate, *König* and through this with *rex*. It would be of considerable interest if the *reges* of Lithuania were better known so that a comparison with the kings of seventh-century England or Ireland could be made, but this is to be tantalised by unreachable sources.[68] However, setting these caveats aside and although Gediminas appears not to have used the epithet 'grand', we shall continue to attribute the title 'grand duke' to him retrospectively in accordance with historiographical tradition.

Even though Gediminas' sons cooperated in governing Lettovia after their father's death, the office of grand duke maintained its uniqueness. Kestutis and Algirdas, who alone of seven brothers controlled considerable lands in Lithuania, enjoyed more authority than their siblings. Kestutis controlled western Lithuania (including Žemaitija) from his castle at Trakai, but even he regarded Algirdas who resided in Vilnius as the only holder of grand-ducal

[66] *Velikii kniaz'* – *AZR*, I, no. 1, p. 1; *supremus princeps*, 1358 – see above n. 47; *basileus*, 1371 – *RIB*, Appendix no. 24, p. 136; *megas reks*, *ibid.*, nos. 20, p. 119; 25, p. 145. Gregoras refers to Algirdas as *tou khedetou rēgos* whilst terming Rus'ian princes *hēgemones* – Nicephoras Gregoras, *Historiae Byzantinae* [*HB*], PG, CXLIX, 457–8.

[67] Paszkiewicz, *Origin*, 198, n. 6. Thirteenth-century references to the Lithuanian ruler do not include honorifics such as 'great' – *PSRL*, II, 933; *GL*, 21; *LR*, *passim*. The authors of *Ipat'evskaia* prefer to use the verb *kniazhiti* rather than add a title to Mindaugas' or Traidenis' name. The exception to this is a memorial note on Mindaugas where the dead monarch is eulogised as *kniaz' velikii* and *samoderzhech'* – *PSRL*, II, 858 s.a. 6770.

[68] E. James, 'The origins of barbarian kingdoms: the continental evidence', in *The origins of Anglo-Saxon kingdoms*, 40–52.

authority.[69] The titulature of Lithuanian grand dukes and princes reflects the uniqueness of the grand-ducal office, as will become apparent.

The division of Lithuania between the duchies of Vilnius and Trakai seems to have been an innovation of Gediminas' based on his appreciation of the rivalry which divided his sons into two main camps. It was a means of satisfying his heirs' ambitions. The theory that it emerged from Gediminas' experience of equal power-sharing with his brother during Vytenis' reign remains an unproven hypothesis. More credibly it arose from a need, growing continually from the 1290s onwards, to concentrate fully on policies to counter the impetus of the Knights' attacks in the west, whilst actively pursuing a policy of eastern expansion into Rus'.[70] Certainly this rough division of territory and spheres of interest is described for the first time in *L1* in an account of Gediminas' last acts. The earliest reference to a duke of Trakai comes in 1337. Archaeologists date the major fortifications at Trakai to the early fourteenth century.[71] Had the unnamed *rex de Tracken* who died in 1337 held joint power alongside Gediminas, we would surely find references to him in Gediminas' earliest wars and treaties with the Order. Even if he were the unnamed envoy *quasi secundus post regem* whom Gediminas dispatched to Riga to negotiate on his behalf in 1324, as Gudavičius has suggested, he was no more than 'second *after* the grand duke'. The duke of Trakai must have been a member of Gediminas' family.[72]

The cooperation of Kestutis with Algirdas in the governance of Lithuania has come to be misrepresented by some scholars as a shared and equal kingship known as diarchy. Recently Gudavičius

[69] See pp. 280–2, 285–6. Two other brothers inherited land in Lithuania in addition to cities in Rus'. However after their deaths Kernavė and Krėva fell to the lot of the heirs of Lithuania.

[70] The war on two fronts is analysed on pp. 229–62.

[71] Gediminas' division of Lithuania – see pp. 280–1; *rex de Tracken* – *Wig.*, 493–4. Borders of the duchy of Trakai as they were in 1387 are described in J. Jakubowski, 'Opis księstwa trockiego z roku 1387', *PH*, 5 (1907), 44–6. In the fifteenth century the duchies of Vilnius and Trakai were transformed into *województwa* under the control of noble administrators.

[72] *PD*, 192; J. Deveike, 'The Lithuanian diarchies', *Slavonic and East European Review*, 28 (1949–50), 392–405. E. Gudavičius, 'Po povodu tak nazyvaemoi 'diarkhii' v Velikom Kniazhestve Litovskim', *Feodālisms Baltijas reģionā. Zinātisko Rakstu krājums* (Riga, 1985), 35. The Vytautas who was father to the otherwise unknown Yury Vitovtovich of Pskov (*PL*, I, 18) cannot have been Gediminas' grandson. Historians therefore have argued that Gediminas must have had another son who does not appear in *L1* because he predeceased Gediminas; see A. Nikžentaitis, 'Dar kartą apie tai 'Kas žuvo prie Bajerburgo?'', *LMADA*, 98 (1987), 35–6.

has claimed that throughout late medieval Lithuanian history it was not unusual for two brothers to cooperate in this way: Dausprungas and Mindaugas; Pukuveras and Butigeidas; Vytenis and Gediminas; Jaunutis and Kestutis; Algirdas and Kestutis; Jogaila and Vytautas.[73] However, Gediminas does not appear in the sources at Vytenis' side in any undertaking. We may deduce from attacks on a Žemaitijan castle called Gedimin-Burg that Gediminas kept an eye on the northern and western marches for Vytenis, but this is not diarchy, it is normal service from a junior sibling to his kinsman and leader. One presumes that the other brothers, Voin and Fëdor did likewise elsewhere for Vytenis as later they did for Gediminas. Close cooperation is documented adequately only for the cases of Algirdas, Kestutis, Jogaila and Vytautas, and this reflects political expediency; it certainly does not meet the formal definition of diarchy as 'rule by two independent authorities'. Algirdas and Kestutis collaborated in the coup which removed Jaunutis from power; Jogaila and Vytautas were cousins who each sought supremacy for himself but withdrew from outright internecine conflict when the Knights threatened Lithuanian independence. The authorities in the Grand Duchy were often superficially more than two and they were certainly interdependent. We have noted how several princes might collaborate in such matters as the conclusion of treaties, even though special deference was made to the two princes who held Lithuanian rather than Rus'ian patrimonies. Furthermore even those two leaders were not equal: the grand duke in Vilnius was supreme. After Jogaila became king of Poland in 1386 and Vytautas, who had been *dux Trocensis*, styled himself *magnus dux Lithuanie*, the king retained his seniority in the clan over his cousin. Indeed close cooperation with the supreme ruler was the lot of many of his kin rather than of one special brother as the treaties contracted between Lithuania and powers in Prussia, Poland and Rus' throughout the fourteenth century show.[74] Far from being a diarchy, Lithuanian government was ever the collaborative exercise of power by several blood-related princes under the acknowledged seniority of one ruler and as such it finds parallels in other developing polities: Anglo-Saxon England, Visigothic

[73] Gudavičius, 'Po povodu', 35–42.

[74] On the relationship between Vytautas, grand duke of Lithuania and his cousin Jogaila, king of Poland see Paszkiewicz, *Jagiellonowie*, 438–46. For the participants of treaties see *AZR*, I, no. 1, *Iura Masoviae*, no. 16, *LU*, II, no. 1041; Raczyński, *Codex*, 58.

Spain, Burgundy, Hungary, Poland or Rus'.[75] The sharing of power between two princes of the same family is not restricted to pagan or even early monarchies in western and central Europe. The example of Bohemia springs immediately to mind. Here in 1331 King John created his son Charles Margrave of Moravia after the youth had returned from training in the royal court of France, and bestowed many royal duties upon him lest, depriving the young prince of these, Charles might form a centre of noble discontent within Bohemia as a whole. This rule through two men, the junior subject to the senior, effected good government in a land where the new dynasty was repeatedly challenged by the native aristocracy. Since Gudavičius acknowledges that the alleged diarchy of Dausprungas and Mindaugas differed from that of Pukuveras and his brother or Algirdas and Kestutis, this misleading terminology should be banished from historiography.[76] Lithuania was governed by the Gediminid clan. The heirs of Kestutis and Algirdas disputed the leadership of the clan well into the fifteenth century. The Jagiellonian line did not restrict the grand-ducal title to its own members until after the death of Žygimantas Kestutaitis (Vytautas' brother) and the accession of Kazimierz Jagiellończyk (Jogaila's son) in 1440. The main effect of clan rule was to strengthen the power of Lithuanian nobles, some of whom belonged to the family of Gediminas (but never sought grand-ducal office, like the Czartoryscy and Alšeniškiai) and some did not, like the Giedraičiai.[77]

However he may be styled, a prince holds court and in time this becomes associated with a particular place. The association of the grand duke with Vilnius is a constant feature of Lithuanian politics from the reign of Gediminas onwards. It is unclear when the grand-ducal court first settled in one place. Several towns formed in thirteenth-century Lithuania among which the most prominent were Vilnius, Kernavė, Aukaimis and Lida, Punia and Maisiagola.

[75] I. N. Wood, 'Kings, kingdoms and consent', in *Early medieval kingship*, ed. P. H. Sawyer and I. N. Wood (Leeds, 1977), 17–23 and D. Dumville, 'Essex, Middle Anglia and the expansion of Mercia in the south-east Midlands', in *The origins of Anglo-Saxon kingdoms*, ed. S. Bassett, 136–9.

[76] For the Bohemian example see *FRB*, IV, 318. Gudavičius, 'Po povodu', 42 notes the variety of 'diarchies' in Lithuanian history.

[77] On the civil war in Lithuania between Švitrigaila and Jogaila Algirdaičiai and Žygimantas Kestutaitis in the 1430s which almost destroyed the union of Lithuania with Poland see *PSRL*, XXXV, 163–5 and L. Kolankowski, *Dzieje Wielkiego Księstwa Litewskiego za Jagiellonów*, I (Warsaw, 1930), 145–226. The strife ended with the election of Jogaila's son Kazimierz as grand duke in 1440 and king in 1447.

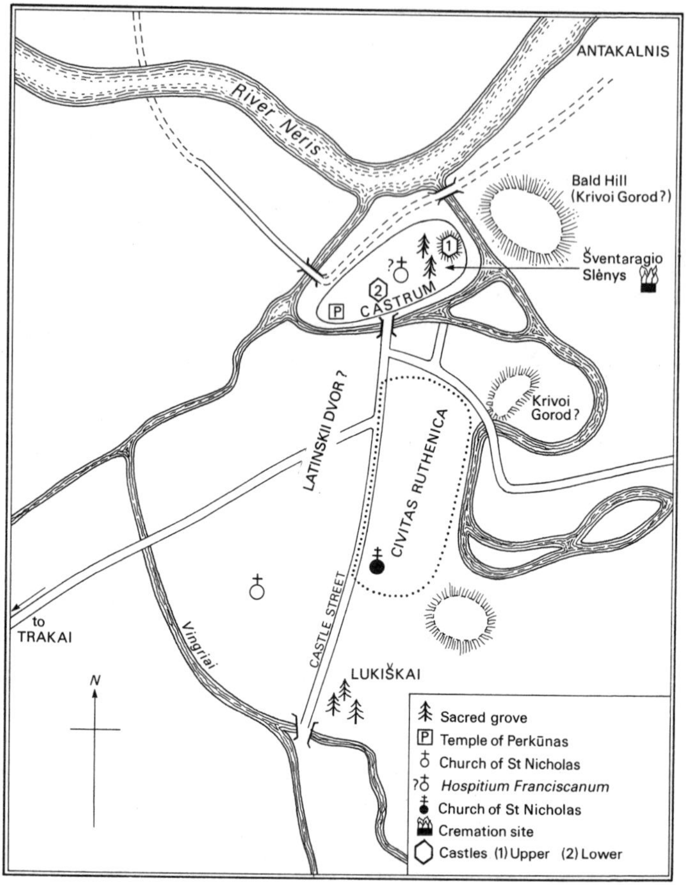

Fig. 2. Map of Vilnius *c.* 1342, based on Ochmański *Historia Litwy*, 65.

The grand duke appears, like all other medieval rulers as *rex ambulans*. He progressed among his people (*na poliude*), collecting dues and inspecting defences in the *villae regis*. In Rus' certain towns were set aside for Lithuanian princes for food-rendering (*kormlenie*), thereby performing a similar function to these royal vills (or manors) in Lithuania. In the fifteenth century Jogaila progressed regularly around Poland and the Grand Duchy.[78] The

[78] Town formation – A. B. Lukhtan and V. A. Ušinskas, 'Ranee srednevekov'e i epokh feodalizma. K probleme stanovlenia litovskoi zemli v svete arkheologicheskikh dannykh', in *Drevnosti Litvy i Belorussii*, ed. L. D. Pobol' and A. Z. Tautavičius

civitas regia was often wherever the *rex* happened to be. Nevertheless this does not preclude the existence of a preferred residence.

Mindaugas refers to his court as *curia nostra*, *voruta* or *burg*, all of which appear to be common rather than proper nouns. Consequently the precise location of Mindaugas' residence has been the subject of considerable debate.[79] It seems most probable that he held court in Vilnius, the site of a major settlement since well before the year 1000. Archaeological evidence indicates that it was the most strongly fortified site in thirteenth-century Lithuania.[80] According to the Knights' records, Mindaugas built a cathedral in Vilnius and recently the remains of what is presumed to have been this church have been excavated.[81] The centre of the new religion must have been established hard by the political heart of the new kingdom, as was the case in Canterbury, Gniezno and Kiev. The scholarly tradition that Mindaugas was crowned in and therefore presumably ruled from Novgorodok has no basis in any text. It is known too that Mindaugas' son was prince of that Rus'ian city during his father's reign. Paszkiewicz proposed locating Mindaugas' court in Kernavė, but the geographical data which form the sole basis of this theory fit Vilnius equally well.[82] Traidenis on the other hand did have some connection with Kernavė, a city

(Vilnius, 1988), 100; for *poliude*, a phrase used in the *L2* account of Gediminas' arrival in Vilnius (see below, p. 72, n. 85) – see *The modern encyclopedia of Russian and Soviet history*, ed. J. L. Wieczyński, XXVIII (Gulf Breeze, 1982), 235–6. Jogaila's progresses are described and analysed in A. Gąsiorowski, *Itinerarium króla Władysława Jagiełły 1386–1434* (Warsaw, 1972).

79 Paszkiewicz, *Origin*, 197; R. Batūra, 'XIIIa. Lietuvos sostinės klausimų', *LMADA*, 20 (1966), 141–65; E. Gudavičius, 'Dėl Lietuvos valstybės kūrimosi centro ir laiko', *LMADA*, 83 (1983), 61–70; A. B. Lukhtan and V. A. Ušinskas, 'K voprosu o stolitse Litvy do 1323g.', *Trudy V mezhdunarodnogo kongressa slavianskoi arkheologii (Kiev 18–25 sentiabria 1985) III.1b.Sektsia V: Goroda, ikh kul'turnye i torgovye sviazi* (Moscow, 1987), 5–13; J. Jurginis, 'Vilniaus miesto ikūrimo klausimų', *LMADA*, 6 (1959), 103–13. Jurginis' conclusion that Vilnius was created from nothing in 1323 is false.

80 Lukhtan and Ušinskas, 'Ranee srednevekov'e', 89–104.

81 On religious significance of Vilnius see pp. 132f. Gudavičius objected to Vilnius as a pagan shrine and as the site of Mindaugas' cathedral – Gudavičius, 'Dėl Lietuvos', 63–4. He wrote before the discovery of the cathedral and a temple in the city. He is also mistaken in his conclusion that Canterbury and Gniezno were not political centres when they became the religious capitals of Kent and Poland (and therefore Vilnius was not a 'capital' settlement when the Church established herself there). All three cities were royal residences.

82 A summary of the Novgorodok arguments is given in Paszkiewicz, *Origin*, 197–8. Paszkiewicz's geographical evidence for Kernavė as *voruta* (cf. *tvirtovė*: fort, *castrum*) are also given there. One must also ask whether a grand duke would readily instal a foreign prince in his residence. Vaišvilkas handed Novgorodok over to Shvarno of Galich in 1253 while Mindaugas lived – *PSRL*, II, 837–8.

which grew considerably after Mindaugas' assassination.[83] Kernavė and Novgorodok both seem to have been favoured by Vytenis who built a Catholic church in the Rus'ian city.

In January 1323, Vilnius appears for the first time in a text as a grand-ducal residence and it is described as a *civitas regia* or *hovestat* from this date forth.[84] According to *L2*, Gediminas moved his government from Trakai the twenty-eight kilometres eastwards to Vilnius where he built two castles. 'He built one castle (*gorod*) on the Lower Shvintorog hill and a second on Crooked Hill which is now called Bald Hill and he called those castles Vilnia'.[85] Gediminas perhaps had resided at Trakai during Vytenis' reign. It is credible that as grand duke, Gediminas transferred his seat to a site which was better equipped by nature and his own industry as a fortress and trading post. The phraseology of *L2* has been taken in the past to mean that Gediminas founded the city (also *gorod* in Russian) of Vilnius and this imputed meaning was then used to prove that the text was unreliable in the face of archaeological evidence illustrating the great antiquity of the site. When *L2* was written down in the sixteenth century *gorod* still retained its original meaning of citadel.[86]

There is no reason to doubt Gediminas' construction of a castle in Vilnius. There Gediminas lived in a strong wooden keep (not the brick tower which now bears his name) behind stone defences with a Franciscan house (*hospitium* or *locus fratrum*) nearby which provided secretaries, scribes and interpreters for the pagan court. The religious significance of Vilnius for the pagan cult was increased by the creation of a temple amid the ruins of Mindaugas' cathedral. Gediminas built Catholic and Orthodox churches in Vilnius to serve foreign merchants and artisans. The city had wooden houses built in the same manner as the dwellings of Polish, Livonian and Rus'ian cities along rudimentary, wood-

[83] *LR*, 8347, tr. p. 102; Lukhtan and Ušinskas, 'K voprosu', 12.

[84] *GL*, 35; Hoeneke, *Liivimaa*, 62 s.a. 1334.

[85] *PSRL*, XXXV, 96, 153, 180, 201, 222.

[86] The data are mixed into a mythological narrative which involves the wizard Lizdeika. However the wording of the foundation information is clearly distinguishable from the sixteenth-century myth which surrounds it and bristles with polonicisms (*zbudovavshi gorody*). On the meaning of *gorod* see A. M. Sakharov, 'O termine 'gorod' v istochnikakh XVIv.', *Obshchestvo i Gosudarstvo feodal'noi Rossii. Sbornik statei posviashchennykh 70-letiiu Akademika L. V. Cherepnina* (Moscow, 1975), 62–6. A Polish version of the *L2* account, the Olszewski text replaces a transcription of *gorod* with the Polish word for a castle, *zamek* – *PSRL*, XXXV, 180.

paved streets.[87] In the fourteenth century Vilnius acquired trading districts along the lines of the German court (*Hoffe*) in Novgorod and the Polotsk *Contur* in Riga. Rus'ian merchants lived together in a *civitas ruthenica* (*rouskii konets*), which Wigand of Marburg cites in 1383.[88] The Rus'ian Quarter was in the eastern part of Vilnius near the Krivoi Gorod ('Crooked Hill') fortifications. Here in Gediminas' day stood the merchant church of St Nikolai.[89] A German (Latin) Quarter, the so-called *Latinskii dvor* stood near the road which led south out of the royal castle. A Catholic church, also dedicated to St Nicholas, provided spiritual support for Rigan and Saxon merchants during Gediminas' reign. By 1382 the chief of the Rigan merchants, Hanul was acting as adviser and ambassador for Grand Duke Jogaila, before whom he represented the commercial interests of the Hansa.[90]

THE PAGAN ECONOMY

Having examined the trappings of Gediminid power, we might consider briefly how the grand duke financed his government. Lithuania in the fourteenth century was, as she remains, largely an agricultural society, producing grain and linen. The 'glebe of the cuntrey of Lectonia ... bereth wele corne and fruyte'.[91] Most of her population were peasants (*smerdy, cmethones, gebuwer*) whose lives centred on the farms and vills of the *bajorai* and dukes. Much labour was provided by slaves, especially in the houses of the nobles and in their fields. The terms used for them all refer to domestic, manorial employment: *famuli obnoxi, drelle*.[92] However Lithuania's natural resources and geographical position near a

[87] A. Tautavičius, 'Vilniaus žemutinės pilies mediniai pastatai XIII–XIV amžiais', *ILKI*, 4 (1964), 171–87; and, 'Iš XIVa. Vilniaus gyventojų buities', *ILKI*, 1 (1958), 94–103. For Franciscan *hospitium* see pp. 228, 275.

[88] *Wig.*, 623; *rouskii konets* escaped the worst of the Fire of Vilnius, 1471 – *PL3*, *PL*, II, 179. The Quarter was located tentatively in J. Ochmański, 'Krzywy gród wileński. Próba lokalizacji', *ZH*, 36 (1971), 57–66.

[89] See p. 207 and K. Blaschke, 'Nikolaikirchen und Stadtentstehung im pommerschen Raum', *Greifswald-Stralsunder Jahrbuch*, 9 (1970), 21–40.

[90] The term appears for the first time in the *PL3* account of the 1471 Fire – *PL*, II, 179 – but the existence of such an area is clear from Gediminas' reign. For Hanul see M. Kosman, 'Rzekoma działalność pisarka Hanula', *Studia Źródłoznawcze*, 12 (1967), 149–53.

[91] See above n. 1.

[92] *GL*, 73, 171; *PU*, II, no. 675; *MPV*, no. 168, p. 227; on this type of economy cf. T. Reuter, 'Plunder and tribute in the Carolingian Empire', *TrRHS*, 5th series 35 (1985), 75–94. For details of slaving see table 1, p. 74.

Table 1. *Lithuanian slave raids, 1277–1377*

Date	Number	Provenance	Source
1277	1000	Łęczyca	*PD*, 138; *Długosz*, VII, 197–8.
1278	Many	Chełmno	*Długosz*, VII, 205.
1282	Maximus Numerus	Lublin	*Długosz*, VII, 217.
1287	3000	—	*Długosz*, VII, 243.
1290	Many	Prussia	*PD*, 153.
1291	—	Kujawy	*Długosz*, VII, 268.
1294	—	Łęczyca	*Długosz*, VII, 279.
1298	—	Chełmno	*Długosz*, VIII, 301.
1306	Many 1000s	Kalisz, Stawiszyn	*Długosz*, IX, 39.
1311	500	Sambia	*PD*, 175; *Wig.*, 455.
1311	1200	—	*PD*, 176.
1322	5000	Dorpat	*PD*, 186; *EpG*, 284.
1323	Very Many	Reval	*PD*, 197.
	5000	Prussia	*Długosz*, IX, 126.
	c. 70	Memel	*PD*, 187.
	—	Dobrzyń	*Długosz*, IX, 126.
1324	4000	Mazovia	*Długosz*, IX, 130.
1336	1200	Mazovia	*Długosz*, IX, 191.
1345	—	Rastenburg	*Wig.*, 508.
1346	1000	Sambia	*Długosz*, IX, 243.
1348	700	Prussia	*Długosz*, IX, 251.
1350	—	Radomir Sandomir	*Długosz*, IX, 258–9.
1351	—	Lviv, Bel'z	*Długosz*, IX, 261.
1352	1600	Prussia	*Wig.*, 517–18.
1353	500	Prussia	*Wig.*, 520; *Długosz*, IX, 267–8.
1370	—	Prussia	*Długosz*, IX, 352–3.
1376	580	—	*Wig.*, 580.

crossroads of the Baltic–Black Sea and west European–Rus'ian–central Asian trade routes encouraged the growth of commerce. Lithuania, *pace* Paszkiewicz, has a long trading history and not only in Vilnius.[93] Evidence of luxury goods (necklaces, buckles, stirrups and spears) imported by sea from western Europe and

[93] 'Lithuania did not take part in international trade', Paszkiewicz, *Origin*, 192. ' ... did not take *a large part* in international trade' may be more accurate a description of the period before the thirteenth century.

Table 2. *Table of Lithuanian debts in Riga*

Year	Money		Wax			Other
	Silver Marks	Farthings	Scippunt	Lîspunt	Punt	
1286	6					
1287	15					3 *timmer* of *varia*
1288	6	1				
1289	21	1				
1290	5	5		6	3	
1292	17.5		1	4		
1294		3		4		
1295		7				
1296	16			4		
1297	10					
1298					10	
1302	7	1				
1303				3		
1319	30	2				
1320–23	79	1				
Total	212.5	1	21	13	3	

Notes:
1 scippunt = 20 lîspunt. 1 lîspunt = 16 punt.
1 scippunt = 164 kg. 1 lîspunt = 8.2 kg. 1 punt = 0.5 kg.
Source – Hildebrand, *Schuldbuch* nos. 1312; 216; 1725; 549; 20; 1284; 1533; 663; 682; 251; 1255; 760; 1364; 1764; 76; 1267; 1167; 1374; 1885; 1884; 1886; 1887; 1889–93.

overland from Rus' (glass beads, ceramics, metal locks) is available from the tenth century onwards.[94] Contrary to sixteenth-century historiography, pagan Lithuania was not a destitute country bereft of metals and other precious commodities. Her pagan princes enjoyed wealth enough to ransom captives to and from the Teutonic Order with gold, silver and horses, and bribe the Knights and uncooperative Žemaitijan warriors.[95]

[94] O. Navickaitė-Kuncienė, 'Senosios Rusios importas X–XIII amžių Lietuvoje', *LMADA*, 16 (1964), 115–34; and 'Vakarų Europos importas Lietuvoje IX–XII amžiais', *LMADA*, 22 (1966), 85–103.

[95] Dubrawius' claim that 'nullum in Lithuania metallum', *Historia Bohemica* I, 540 is typical of sixteenth-century historiography. The statement is made to explain why the Lithuanians should wish to make war on the crusaders. Ransoms and bribes are

The settlement of Hanseatic merchants in Livonia and economically active crusaders in Prussia, combined with Lithuanian expansion into the major trading centres of western Rus', encouraged more reliable commercial relations from the 1250s. Money and imported goods were essential to the defence of Lithuania from the well-organised and well-provisioned campaigns of the Teutonic Order, as the grand duke's Rus'ian allies understood.[96] When the forts of Medininkai, Lida and Krėva were rebuilt in stone in the mid-fourteenth century, huge quantities of stone and bricks were required in addition to a skilled labour force.[97] The Gediminid use of dynastic marriage as the mainstay of Lithuania's alliances with Mazovia, Poland and Rus' also demanded the outlay of considerable dowries as the cases of three of Gediminas' daughters whose dowries amounted to the income of a whole Polish duchy make clear.[98] Clearly slave raids and war booty alone could not support the Lithuanian economy, nor could the ransom of important German prisoners of war.[99] A programme of colonisation with skilled artisans, rather than captives as in thirteenth-century Poland or Prussia, was required. Under Gediminas we get the first attempt to change the balance of the Lithuanian economy from a peasant- and slave-based one to one built on skilled immigration; from plunder and slavery to commerce and settlement.[100]

Lithuanian merchants traded with the Knights and the burghers of Livonia, especially Riga, throughout the crusades. As a Catholic king, Mindaugas granted commercial privileges to the merchants of Riga in 1253. In the same decade the pagan Žemaitijans concluded a two-year truce with the Order during which we may presume trade with the enemy to have been common.[101] Trade between Riga and Lithuania continued even after Mindaugas'

described in *LR*, 3074, tr. p. 43; *PSRL*, II, 816, 820. Silver has been wrought in Lithuania since the third century; goldsmithery is a more recent phenomenon. Gediminas' father employed a smith in 1292 – L. Nakaitė, 'Auksakalystės Lietuvoje iki XIIIa. klausimų (1. Technika, ornamentika)', *LMADA*, 22 (1966), 67–84.

96 For Pskovite provisioning of the Lithuanian war effort in the 1270s see Rowell, 'Between Lithuania and Rus'', 13.

97 For the repair of these forts an estimated 37,500 m^3 of stone and 12,900 m^3 of bricks were required – *Istoria Litovskoi SSR (s drevneishikh vremen do nashikh dnei)* (Vilnius, 1978), 45.

98 Dowry prices – see below pp. 91–2.

99 *Wig.*, 494–6.

100 Skilled immigration under Gediminas, see below pp. 202–3, 226–7. For slave settlements in Poland see Zientara, '*Melioratio terrae*', 32.

101 Mindaugas' treaty is published in *LU*, I, no. 243, cols. 312–13; the Žemaitijan truce is described in *LR*, 4629, tr. p. 60.

apostasy. Traidenis agreed terms with the Livonians some time between 1275 and 1277 and by 1313 Lithuano-Rigan commerce was regarded as acceptably ancient trading (*mercatio antiqua*) to the Knights who still disapproved strongly of military cooperation between Riga and the pagans, denouncing the allies of Lithuania and Rus' as pariahs.[102] According to the debt-register of Riga, mercantile ventures in Lithuania were particularly frequent between 1287 and 1303,[103] reaching a peak in the years before the Rigans decided to invite the pagans to establish a garrison within their city. When the Rigans accused the Knights in 1312 of trading illegally with the Lithuanians and selling them weapons, fruit, cabbages, onions and radishes, their main objection was directed against the exclusion of Rigan merchants from this lucrative trade rather than the commerce *per se*.[104] The Order exploited papal privileges which permitted them to trade with the pagans. Both the Knights and the Rigans sold swords and spurs to the Lithuanians in violation of a papal embargo on the sale of military hardware to dangerous infidels.[105]

For their part, the Lithuanians sold timber, furs and grain to the Christians besides wax, honey and linen. Gediminas encouraged trade by removing the burden of commercial taxation. Import dues and tolls such as *theolonium*, *angariae*, *perangariae* and *poshlina* were reduced in the 1320s in an attempt to attract Hanseatic merchants to Vilnius after the economic depression of the previous

[102] Traidenis' agreement with Bishop John I of Riga and Master Ernest of Livonia is referred to in a letter of Bishop John II, dated 1286 (*LU*, I, no. 507, col. 627). John I was bishop from November 1274 to 1285; Ernest was elected in 1273 and killed in 1279. The treaty was violated by the Lithuanians in 1277 (*Lübeckisches Urkundenbuch*, I (Lübeck, 1843), no. 388, pp. 357–8; cf. *LU*, I, no. 507). It must therefore have been concluded between 1275 and early 1277. *Mercatio antiqua* – *LU*, II, no. 645, col. 81.

[103] Hildebrand, *Rigische Schuldbuch*; V. Pavulāns, *Satiksmes ceļi Latvijā XIII–XVIIgs.* (Riga, 1971), 87–92. A tabulated list of entries in the debt-book, which of course does not list all trading ventures between Riga and Lithuania, is given in table 2. See also Benninghoven, *Rigas Entstehung*, 161.

[104] Seraphim, *Das Zeugenverhör*, XX, 11, p. 111; Appendix IX, 278, p. 205; Appendix II, 47, p. 159; VII, 11, p. 26. See also R. Varakauskas, *Lietuvos ir Livonijos santykiai XIII–XVIa.* (Vilnius, 1982), 255–64 and R. Mažeika, 'Prekyba ir taika mirties zonoje: Prekybinės taikos sutartys tarp kryžiuočių ir Lietuvių XIVa.', *Lietuvių Katalikų Mokslo Akademijos XIV suvažiavimo darbai* (Rome), forthcoming.

[105] Indulgences – Seraphim, *Zeugenverhör*, Appendix IX, 280; weapons sold by Knights – *ibid.*, XX, 11, p. 111. Rigans sell spurs – *Kämmerei-Register der Stadt Riga 1348–1361 und 1405–1474*, ed. A. von Bulmerincq, I (Leipzig, 1909), 49. This refers to events of December 1355. On the course of German trade with the Baltic Pagans see R. Mažeika, 'Of cabbages and knights: Trade and trade treaties with the Infidel on the Northern Frontier, 1200–1390' *Journal of Medieval History* (forthcoming).

decade.[106] There is no information to tell for sure whether the grand duke was a major trader in Vilnius, as the grand duke of Moscow was in his domains. Nevertheless the cumulative effect of the evidence hints that such was the case. The grand dukes maintained vills (centres of production in addition to defence outposts) and encouraged the settlement of foreign merchants in markets which were established in major Lettovian cities. They took pains to safeguard access to these markets.

The trade between Lithuania and Livonia increased in importance not simply because Lithuanian produce became more desirable and the grand duke patronised friars who would serve German merchants, but also because the Lithuanians increased their hold on the mercantile towns of western Rus'. From 1307 the major trading post of Polotsk was under Lithuanian control. Its bishop who interceded in trade matters with the citizenry of Riga regarded Vytenis as 'his son'. The nearby city of Vitebsk, which entered the Grand Duchy finally through marriage *c.* 1318, had close connections with Vytenis' Lithuania too, as a letter of the Rigan council to Prince Mikhail Konstantinovich makes clear. The Rigans report the fate of one of their merchants, complaining that 'when the Lithuanian army was below your town [Vitebsk], he wished to go out and buy slave girls from the troops, but as he passed by a monastery three monks and another man leaped out and seized him, beating and assaulting him'.[107] Gediminas held Novgorodok and enjoyed close relations with Pskov, Smolensk and Novgorod. Gediminas' son Narimantas reacted to Livonian complaints about the quality of wax sent from Polotsk to Riga by offering compensation to merchants who bought contaminated wax and threatening traders who sold goods with false measure with prosecution.[108] By the end of the fourteenth century the main Polotsk–Riga trade route passed regularly through Vilnius.

In 1333 when the Lithuanians took charge of the defence of Novgorodia's northern frontier, the prince who commanded the mercenary garrison received Kopor'e and Karelia as part of his

[106] *Theolonium, angariae etc.* – *GL*, 41. These dues were major sources of revenue in Merovingian France – J. M. Wallace-Hadrill, *The long-haired kings* (London, 1962), 9; 206, n. 2. *Poshlina* and its removal is a feature of Rus'ian treaties with Lithuania – *GVNiP*, no. 335, p. 322. Colonisation attempts of Gediminas – see pp. 203f., 227.

[107] *RLA*, 26–8

[108] For the expansion of Lithuania see pp. 82–7. The Order's complaints of shoddy Lettovian merchandise (*HU*, II, no. 569 §6, p. 250) made in 1335 were assuaged by Narimantas-Gleb's wax declaration – *RLA*, no. 74, pp. 54–5.

patrimony. These possessions which were intended to finance the prince's actions, provided valuable contributions from Novgorod's lucrative fur trade. It seems probable that the Lithuanians also benefited from the area's natural wealth. By the second half of the century, Novgorodian furs from further east were regularly exported to Lithuania.[109]

Under Gediminas' agreements with the Livonians of 1323 and 1338, pagan and Christian merchants were guaranteed free access to and from Lithuania and Livonia along recognised routes or *vredelant*. Gediminas took pains to provide a 'clear path' to his markets where the brigandry of Lithuanian and Teutonic bandits might be controlled. It seems that the pagans respected the safe passage of merchants rather more than the Pskovites did.[110] It is perhaps no exaggeration to speak in terms of a *pax lithuanica* which protected trade routes in western Rus' and Lithuania from Gediminas' reign onwards.

Lithuanian merchants traded on equal terms with Christians; they were not benighted savages to be exploited by sophisticated foreigners. They travelled to Hanseatic markets, borrowed money from Christian merchants, exchanged silver for goods and carried their own weights and measures.[111]

Gediminas' Lithuania did not produce its own minted currency; neither for that matter did Rus'. From the mid-twelfth century, the Lithuanians traded with locally produced silver ingots, triangular in cross-section which weighed 108 g or 196.2 g. These differed in shape and size from Novgorodian *grivny* and by 1350

[109] The Permians told their Bishop that 'не нашеа ли ловля и в Орду посылаются … но и в Царьград и в Немци и в Литву' 'Are not our furs sent to the Horde … and even to Constantinople, Germany and Lithuania?', Epifany Premudry, *Povest' o Stefane episkope Permskom*, in *Sokrovishcha drevnerusskoi literatury – Drevnerusskie predania* (*XI–XVIvv*), ed. V. V. Kuskov *et al.* (Moscow, 1982), 177.

[110] Main Hanseatic route from Novgorod to Gotland passed through Lettovian territory (Pskov, Polotsk) in the 1330s – *HU*, III, nos. 69, 586, 590, pp. 34–7, 364, 366–7. This was noted by Gediminas in his letters to Saxony in 1323 – *GL*, 38–9. Dangers of travel along these routes highlighted in Seraphim, *Zeugenverhör*, Appendix IX, 279, 290, 291; Teutonic brigands attacked Lithuanian merchants too – *GL*, 180–3. Gediminas strove to make the routes safer, see below pp. 257–8. In 1298 the Knights complained that after a Lithuano-Pskovite raid on Order merchants the pagans returned the booty but the Pskovites refused to respect the rights of merchants to travel freely – *HU*, II, no. 569, p. 251; *HU*, III, no. 626, p. 424.

[111] 'Be he heathen or Christian' – *GL*, 189; possible that a Lithuanian merchant might be slain during a pagan attack on a Livonian town – *GL*, 191; on the Lithuanian systems of weights and measures see O. Navickaitė-Kuncienė, 'Seniausios (X–XIII amžių) svorio matų sistemos Lietuvoje klausimų', *LMADA*, 21 (1966), 143–59. See also Gudavičius, *Miestų*, 66–80.

had a value of thirty Prague groats. The Prague coins made their first appearance in Lithuania in the second half of the fourteenth century although they were known in south-west Rus' before 1320. If Fedorov's dating of the silver ingots is accurate, the weight of these *slitki* became standardised after the turn of the fourteenth century, reflecting perhaps grand-ducal interest in their production.[112]

From these divers aspects of Lithuanian history, we may conclude that the Grand Duchy was divisible into three major parts: Aukštaitija, the patrimony of the Gediminid grand duke; Žemaitija, the western borderland held by nobles which he took pains to keep under his control with a network of border settlements and dynastic marriages; and the territories of western Rus'. Setting the latter to one side, Lithuania in the fourteenth century was a small, fertile and largely agricultural country, relatively inaccessible to enemy troops. She enjoyed a growing economy and effective government under the tutelage of a grand duke whose power was based not only on military strength and the fruits of commerce but also on his subjects' respect for the authority he had inherited from his ancestors and predecessors. This respect was earned partly by Gediminas' appreciation of boiar opinion, especially where negotiations for conversion to Christianity were concerned. Princes of Gediminas' line had ruled Lithuania only since around 1289 but they appear to have been related to the Aukštaitijan clans which had dominated the country since the late twelfth century. The grand duke's authority was monarchical although by no means absolute. Noble counsellors retained an important function at court. The fact that the grand-ducal clan was more sacrosanct than its leader cannot be overemphasised. The description of the consolidated Lithuanian polity as diarchical is too vague to have any historiographical value.

Urban development took place in Gediminid Lithuania which fits characteristics acknowledged by historians of western develop-

[112] G. B. Fedorov, 'Klassifikatsia litovskikh slitkov i monet', *KSIIMK*, 29 (1949), 64–75. Fedorov has three classes of ingot with average weights: (a) 112.5 g (tenth to twelfth centuries); (b) 104.8 g (tenth to beginning of fourteenth centuries) and (c) 104.475 g (tenth to beginning of fifteenth centuries). The range of weights 112–196 g is given in Lukhtan and Ušinskas, 'K voprosu', 11; A. Tautavičius, 'Papildomi duomenys apie naujus sidabro lydinių ir XIVa II pusės–XVa pradžios Lietuvos moneta radinius Lietuvos TSR teritorijoje', *LMADA*, 28 (1965), 67–84; Sh. I. Bektineev, 'Prazhskii grosh v denezhnom obrashchenii Velikogo Kniazhestva Litovskogo (XIVv.)', in *Drevnosti Litvy i Belorussii*, 130–4; N. A. Soboleva, 'K voprosu o monetakh Vladimira Ol'gerdovicha', *Numizmatika i Epigrafika*, 8 (1970), 81–7.

ing states. Vilnius possessed defences, artisan settlement, monumental architecture (one stone temple, a castle and two wooden churches), a rough network of streets, markets and even a mendicant friary. It functioned as a central place where the grand duke resided with his scribes and counsellors.[113] Gediminas strengthened Vilnius as a major trading town. By 1387 there were several stone towns within the pagan realm.[114] Far from being an economic and political wilderness, fourteenth-century Lithuania was open to the benign influence of her neighbours and capable of defending herself against unwelcome intrusion. The pagan Grand Duchy was thus a realm capable of fitting relatively smoothly into (a certain circumscribed part of) the life of Christendom.

[113] For the conditions held necessary for medieval urban development see R. Hodges, *Dark Age economics: The origins of towns and trade AD 600–1000*, 2nd edn (London, 1989), 20–5.

[114] *Spisok russkikh gorodov dal'nikh i blizhnikh*, ed. M. N. Tikhomirov, *Istoricheskie Zapiski* 40 (1952), 236–42, esp. 238. This list of Rus'ian and Lettovian cities was composed in Smolensk between 1380 and 1390 – A. V. Podosinov, 'O printsipakh postroenia i mesta sozdania 'Spiska russkikh gorodov dal'nikh i blizhnikh'', *Vostochnaia Evropa v drevnosti i srednevekov'e. Sbornik statei*, ed. L. V. Cherepnin (Moscow, 1978), 40–8. The Lithuanian cities listed among the Lettovian ones (with stone-walled towns in italic) are: Kernavė, Maisiagola, Ukmergė, *Vilnius*, Old Trakai, *Krėva*, *New Trakai*, *Medininkai*, Loshesk, Alšenai, Merkinė, Puniai, Lida, Kaunas, Shumesk, Perelai. The most convenient text is included in *NL*, 475–7; Lithuanian cities appear on p. 476. On Lithuanian towns in general see Gudavičius, *Miestų*, 38–63.

Chapter 4

THE EXPANSION OF LITHUANIA

When Grand Duke Jogaila enforced the baptism of the Aukštaitijan pagans in 1387, he governed a realm ten times as large as that which Mindaugas had inherited 150 years earlier. How far and by what means the Grand Duchy penetrated Rus' and built up a network of western alliances during the reign of Gediminas are questions which bear serious investigation. The examples of Galich–Volyn' and Kiev show how a large band of south-western Rus' was brought within the Lithuanian sphere of influence in the 1320s by main force and held more loosely thereafter by means of complex diplomacy and dynastic marriage. The Gediminids learned to coexist in Rus' with their fellow 'outsiders', the Tatars whose hegemony never stretched as far as Lithuania. However before looking at these questions we might first tour the Rus'ian lands of the Lithuanian dynasty.

Lithuania's growing interest in Rus'ian trade and a pressing need to find new patrimonies for land-hungry Lithuanian princes, as Mindaugas established his control of the Aukštaitijan duchies, had led to the conquest of Black, or western, Rus' in the mid-thirteenth century.[1] By Gediminas' day Lithuania's strongest grip on Rus' was in these areas which she had held longest. Grodno, a major trading city, had been in Lithuanian hands since the 1250s. It was the seat of Gediminas' military commander, *namestnik* and close noble ally (*amicus specialis*) David, who in 1322 was also elected prince, that is military commandant of Pskov. The assertion made by Stryjkowski that David was the son-in-law of Gediminas has no support from the sources extant today. Grodno retained its commercial, military and religious significance throughout the Middle Ages, being the seat of an important prelate. The city was frequently ransacked by the Knights because of its position on Lithuania's western border with Mazovia and

[1] *PSRL*, II, 816.

Prussia which at this point lay two leagues from the Grand Duchy. Merchants on the trade route (*cupenpint*) were not spared the ravages of war. In the 1350s the region was controlled by Prince Kestutis as part of his territories defending the western frontier.[2] Further east lay Novgorodok, another important mercantile and cultural centre which after 1316 enjoyed the added distinction of being the cathedral city of the newly created Lithuanian Orthodox metropolitanate. The city which had been the patrimony of Mindaugas' heir Vaišvilkas may even have been a favoured residence of the Lithuanian grand dukes[3] and, like the cities of Volkovysk and Slonim, it lay in the personal gift of the ruler. According to the account of Gediminas' final division of lands among his sons as it is given in the Lithuanian chronicles, these three were the only towns outside Lithuania bequeathed by Gediminas to his heirs. The inheritance of Algirdas (Vitebsk) and Liubartas (Vladimir) was gained by war and rendered loyal by those princes through marriage.[4]

The cities of White Rus' were no less attractive a prize for Lithuanian princes. Lithuanians had been connected with Polotsk since the 1250s and it was from there that they had taken control of the western Dvina trade route.[5] Little is known of Polotsk after the death of the Lithuanian prince Gerdenis in 1267. However forty years later the city was more firmly in the hands of the Lithuanian ruler. In 1326 Gediminas' brother Voin was prince of Polotsk.[6] He was succeeded there some time after 1333 and

[2] Paszkiewicz, *Origin*, 204–5 and above p. 59, n.39. Grodno was two leagues from the border and on 15 November 1325 seven visitors arrived in Zinten, looking for relatives who had been captured on the *cupenpint* by the Knights in Grodno the previous autumn. Six were Rus'ians from Vladimir, the seventh came from Wizna, Siemowit of Mazovia's seat. Grodno was rebuilt in 1325 – *PU*, II, no. 528, p. 356. David of Grodno became prince of Pskov in 1322, see below pp. 195, 237–8. The appointment of Gediminas' *amicus specialis* is recorded by the Rigans – *GL*, 63. Only *Stryjkowski*, I, 380 says he married a Gediminaitė. He died in 1326 – *PD*, 194. His military exploits are described in *PD*, 181, 185, 187, 191, 194. Kestutis as prince of Grodno – *Iura Masoviae*, I, no. 16, p. 19.

[3] F. D. Gurevich, 'Detinets i okol'nyi gorod drevnerusskogo Novogrudka v svete arkheologicheskikh rabot 1956–1977', *Sovetskaia Arkheologia* (1980/4), 87–8. Vaišvilkas and Novgorodok – see Giedroyć, 'Arrival ... (thirteenth century)', 15. Metropolitanate of Lithuania – see below pp. 149–88.

[4] *PSRL*, XXXV, 61.

[5] See above pp. 20–1.

[6] Vytenis and Polotsk – *Polotskie Gramoty XIII–nachala XVIvv.*, ed. A. L. Khoroshkevich, I (Moscow, 1977), no. 3, pp. 36–8; III (Moscow, 1980), 123–6. The *Olszewski Chronicle* includes an abbreviated Lithuanian chronicle which recalls the Lithuanian seizure of Polotsk s.a. 1307 – *PSRL*, XXXV, 192. For Konstantin of Polotsk see p. 21. On Voin – *NL*, 98, 341.

probably in 1335, not by his own son Liubko but by Narimantas-Gleb Gediminaitis.[7]

The neighbouring principality of Vitebsk was won and lost by the pagans in the thirteenth century. After 1318 when Algirdas married the only daughter of the town's last Rus'ian prince, Vitebsk was a permanent, albeit far from always a stable Lithuanian possession.[8] It is known from *NL* that in 1326 Minsk was subject to Gediminas. In that year Vasily of Minsk accompanied Voin of Polotsk and one Fëdor Sviatoslavich to Novgorod to make peace with the Republic and the Teutonic Order.[9] Turov and Pinsk became provinces of the Grand Duchy some time before Gediminas died,[10] while Brest passed back and forth between Galich–Volyn' and Lithuania. It was seized by Gediminas around 1316 and held but briefly. In 1322–23 Brest was perhaps a part of the Grand Duchy again as it was undoubtedly in the 1340s.[11] It still distinguishes itself from other cities of the same name with the soubriquet of *Litovsk*, 'Lithuanian'.

In the cities of western Rus' outside this central territorial band Lithuanian influence was strong but far from imperial. Novgorod bought protection from the pagans when need arose, but it never became a Lithuanian possession. The city looked to Lithuania as a source of mercenary defence when accepting Muscovite troops for the same purpose might encourage the princes of Moscow to interfere in the Republic's internal affairs. The ever-changing nature of Lithuano-Novgorodian relations is best exemplified by treaties struck in 1323 and 1326. In the first of these the Teutonic Order and Novgorod allied themselves against Lithuania and Pskov; the second agreement made peace between the pagans and the allies of 1323. Following on from an agreement which Gediminas wrought with Archbishop Vasily Kaleka in 1331, Gediminas despatched military forces in 1333 to defend the northern garrisons of Novgorodia from the threat of Swedish attack.[12]

By contrast Pskov on the Rus'ian border with Livonia was

[7] *PG*, I, no. 4; *GL*, 187–95 (Treaty of 1338). These two treaties mention Gleb of Polotsk, who in the Smolensk–Livonia treaty of 1339 is called Gediminas' son – Ivanesov, *Smolenskie Gramoty*, 70. Narimantas was baptised Gleb in 1333 – *NL*, 345.

[8] Fennell, *Emergence*, 122 and below n. 27.

[9] *NL*, 98, 341 and Paszkiewicz, *Origin*, 210–11.

[10] Paszkiewicz, *Origin*, 209–10.

[11] Shabul'do, *Zemli*, 10.

[12] Fennell, *Emergence*, 98, 104. On the dating of the treaty and the reasons behind Novgorod's apparent volte-face see below pp. 215, 238–9, 248–51.

much more clearly and constantly an ally and semi-dependent client of Lithuania. The Pskovites regarded the Lithuanians as necessary to their struggle for full independence from Novgorod and security from the forces of the Teutonic Knights in Livonia. Their relations with Lithuania, friendly or otherwise, go back at least to 1265, when the renegade Lithuanian prince Daumantas arrived in the city, and continue far into the fifteenth century with a whole (but not uninterrupted) line of princes of similar origin. In 1323 Gediminas referred to the Pskovites as a part of Rus' which was subject to his rule (through David of Grodno). Between 1329 and 1337, the city was governed by Gediminas' protégé, the refugee prince of Tver' and former grand duke of Vladimir, Aleksandr Mikhailovich.[13]

The principality of Smolensk which lay on the eastern frontiers of Novgorodia and enjoyed close mercantile links with Riga was a faithful ally of Lithuania during the reign of Ivan Aleksandrovich (1313–59). His loyalty was presumably encouraged by the fact that the western Dvina trade routes which ensured his city's prosperity were in Lithuanian hands. In 1339 Ivan referred to Gediminas as his 'elder brother' in a trade treaty with the Teutonic Order which complemented a similar agreement struck in November 1338 between the Knights and Gediminas, Polotsk and Vitebsk. Lithuania surely helped Ivan fend off enemy raids from the Tatars and Briansk in 1333 and 1339–40.[14]

The Grand Duchy's own eastern border was guarded by the fortresses of Riasna and Osechen, as *NL* informs us.[15] Viaz'ma, despite being a Smolensk *udel* (appanage), probably did not form a Lettovian line of defence along with these two towns. Paszkiewicz deduced that Viaz'ma was under Lithuanian control because he regarded its prince, Fëdor Sviatoslavich, who in 1345 married his daughter to Semën Ivanovich of Moscow, as the same Fëdor who was part of the embassy Gediminas sent to Novgorod in 1326. Fennell was probably nearer the mark in considering this to be unlikely. The Fëdor of 1326 is more likely a son of Sviatoslav Glebovich of Briansk, the prince who was murdered in 1310 because of his Lithuanian sympathies.[16] Some scholars consider that neighbouring Murom too was a Lithuanian satellite. However,

[13] *GL*, 69; See pp. 172–3.
[14] See map 2 and below pp. 257–8.
[15] *NL*, 347; *PSRL*, IV (i), 266; Fennell, *Emergence*, 50.
[16] Paszkiewicz, *Origin*, 212 and n. 3. On Fëdor Sviatoslavich see Fennell, *Emergence*, 104 and n. 1, 173 and 206.

the fact that the metropolitan of Lithuania who died *c.* 1330 left money there cannot alone justify calling the city Lithuanian as Paszkiewicz does.[17]

We can be more confident of calling Novosil and Kozel'sk, the minor principalities which lay to the south-east of Smolensk (see map 2), Lithuanian allies. In 1326 Aleksandr Novosilsky was killed in the Horde alongside Gediminas' son-in-law and ally Dmitry Mikhailovch of Tver'. Andrei Mstislavich of Kozel'sk who in 1330–31 held fifteen *grivny* belonging to the dead metropolitan of Lithuania was another son-in-law of Gediminas.[18]

Briansk, like Novgorod, changed its alliance between Moscow and Lithuania on the basis of local factional interests. Sviatoslav Glebovich supported a Lithuanian alliance but he was killed in 1310 as a result of this policy. He was succeeded by Ivan and Dmitry Romanovichi, of whom the latter was a particularly staunch supporter of Moscow. It was not until another *coup* late in 1333, that a prince sympathetic to Lithuanian ambitions was restored to Briansk in the person of Gleb Sviatoslavich. However his reign was short; he too fell victim to a violent power struggle seven years later.[19]

Our knowledge of other southern Rus'ian principalties in the first four decades of the fourteenth century is rather more scant. Novgorod, Seversky and Chernigov appear to have been Lithuania-oriented and Lithuanians appear to have travelled there without hindrance.[20] Neighbouring Riazan', however, appears to have been very loosely associated with Moscow. In the 1330s Riazanite troops took part in Moscow's campaigns against Lithuania's allies. Later in the century the city chose Jogaila as an ally against Moscow.[21]

Galich–Volyn', as we shall see, was conquered in the early 1320s by Lithuania and then handed over to Bolesław of Mazovia who took the name of his grandfather Yury and was joined by

[17] Paszkiewicz, *Origin*, 211. See also Priselkov and Vasmer, 'Otryvki', 50. Here we read that Prince Yaroslav held fifteen *grivny* which belonged to the metropolitan. The money may well have been a bribe – see p. 161. Murom was incorporated into Moscow in 1392 – *PSRL*, XXV, 219 and *NL4*, 99.

[18] Fennell, *Emergence*, 120; S. Kuczyński, *Ziemie Czernihowsko-Siewierskie pod rządami Litwy* (Warsaw, 1936), 111. Kozel'sk marriage noted in R. V. Zotov, *O Chernigovskikh kniaziakh po Liubetskomu sinodiku i o Chernigovskom kniazhestve v tatarskoe vremia* (St Petersburg, 1892), 292. For *grivny*, see Priselkov and Vasmer, 'Otryvki', 58.

[19] Fennell, *Emergence*, 170–2.

[20] Kuczyński, *Ziemie*, 111.

[21] Fennell, *Emergence*, 174–6.

marriage to Gediminas' family. It is not impossible that Liubartas Gediminaitis was allowed to rule in parts of Volyn' which he claimed through his wife who appears to have been a daughter of Andrei Yurevich of Volyn'.[22] As for Kiev, the mother of Rus'ian cities, it was captured and given a Lithuanian prince in 1323.

DYNASTIC DIPLOMACY

Military force is not, however, the only means of acquiring lands and allies. Gediminas very shrewdly married his children into the leading dynasties of eastern Europe in an attempt to bring prosperity and security to his realm. The establishment of dynastic ties in eastern Rus' and Poland illustrates the skill of Gediminas in using peaceful means to build alliances with neighbours who shared the main aims of Lithuanian foreign policy: to contain or destroy the Teutonic Order and the growing power of Moscow and to keep Poland at bay. The pagan rulers of Lithuania had appreciated the value of dynastic inter-marriage in the early thirteenth century when the clans competing for grand-ducal rank were careful to ally themselves to one another through marriage.[23] The tradition also highlights a neglected aspect of Lithuanian history: the role of princesses in Gediminid diplomacy. A Lithuanian princess was a prize coveted by the Polish and Rus'ian princes on Lithuania's southern, eastern and western borders.[24] Marriage into an established dynasty also brings some legitimisation of a new royal family. We must not overlook the role of the Lithuanian ruler in providing a veneer of legitimacy to the new dynasties of Poland and Rus'. The House of Pukuveras had wielded power in Lithuania since 1289. The Tverite grand dukes of Vladimir first gained prominence in 1304; Łokietek was crowned king of Poland in 1320.

From the scant evidence available to us it seems that the grand dukes themselves married within Lithuania at least until Algirdas and, as we have seen, even his first wife came from within the ambit of the Grand Duchy. Vytenis' wife was probably a pagan

[22] Shabul'do, *Zemli*, 10–11 and n. 21. Paszkiewicz produces evidence that Liubartas once held Geranony (north of Novgorodok) – Paszkiewicz, *Origin*, 210 and n. 3. There is no telling, however, when or for how long Liubartas held this town.

[23] Giedroyć, 'Rulers', 9.

[24] S. C. Rowell, 'Pious princesses or the daughters of Belial: pagan Lithuanian dynastic diplomacy 1279–1423', *Medieval Prosopography*, 15: 1 (1994).

and the same is true of Gediminas' grand duchess. It is unclear whether Gediminas married twice but we should perhaps listen to the voice which pleads that genealogists multiply spouses and children only in cases of dire necessity.[25] Whatever our arithmetic, an important marriage between Gediminas and a Rus'ian or Polish princess would have been noted. It is not, and here perhaps we may be sure that silence speaks. Most sons of grand dukes married within the Grand Duchy in order to strengthen dynastic control of Rus'ian territories. Kestutis took the daughter of an important Žemaitijan duke to wife for the same reason, as did Vytautas when he wed two Lithuanian noblewomen.[26]

The marriage of Algirdas to the daughter of the last prince of Vitebsk around 1318 established Lithuanian princely and later grand-ducal rights over this major mercantile centre which for some time had been indirectly controlled through an alliance with the local princes of the line of Konstantin. Another of Gediminas' sons, Liubartas married the heiress of Volyn' around 1320 to increase Lithuanian influence in south-west Rus'. We shall see that eventually war, rather than the marriage bed, gained the territory for Lithuania.[27]

[25] Vytenis' wife, the mother of Swalegote is unknown. A reference to Narimantas as the half-brother of Algirdas and Kestutis in the *Jüngere Hochmeisterchronik* (*SRP*, V, 120) and the enmity between him and Algirdas suggest that they were born of different mothers. However the chronicle source is late fifteenth-century and is not supported by many references to the princes as brothers. Fraternal violence is hardly unknown. The tradition that Gediminas had two wives, one of whom was Orthodox (Eva mother of Evnuty-Jaunutis) has no solid basis – Paszkiewicz, *Jagiellonowie*, 359.

[26] Legend of Birutė the priestess – *PSRL*, XXXV, 154; death in *Wig*., 614; *CEV*, 1026. On fortifications of Palanga, Birutė's birthplace see V. Žulkus, 'Birutės kalnas ir gyvenvietė Palangoje', *Lietuvos Istorijos Metraštis* (1985), 21–35. For discussion of this marriage see Rowell, 'Gediminid dynastic diplomacy in Žemaitija'.

[27] Algirdas married twice; in Vitebsk *c*. 1318 a princess whom later, probably erroneous tradition names Maria. Earliest extant reference to Algirdas' marriage is *L1*, not the hypothetical Rus'ian *svod* of 1408. Second wife (from 1350) was Ul'iana of Tver' – *PSRL*, XXXV, 115; *TL*, 370. Recently Wasilewski has argued for three wives but his reasons (that a Christian mother cannot bear pagan childen) are spurious, his conclusions defective – 'Trzy małżeństwa wielkiego księcia Litwy Olgierda. Przyczynek do genealogii Giedyminowiczów', *Kultura średniowieczna i staropolska. Studia ofiarowane Aleksandrowi Gieysztorowi w pięćdziesięciolecie pracy naukowej* (Warsaw, 1991), 673–82 and 'Daty urodzin Jagiełły i Witolda', *Przegląd Wschodni*, 1:1 (1991), 15–34. On Liubartas – the date of the marriage is unsure. It is recorded only in *L1* (*PSRL* XXXV, 61, 85, 110, 115). Liubartas was born after 1300; he was Gediminas' youngest son. Andrei Yurevich was born of a marriage contracted in 1290–91 (Włodarski, *Polska*, 237; he was born of Yury I's second wife) and would not have fathered a child until *c*. 1308. It is likely that Liubartas was betrothed to the child after 1316. These details show that the choice in 1324–25 between Liubartas and Bolesław for honour in Rus' involved young men of similar age. Liubartas did not have the power to object to

By contrast with Gediminas' sons whose marriages tend towards the consolidation of Lithuanian power within the Rus'ian territories of the Grand Duchy, his daughters were sent abroad to marry as players in a diplomatic game aimed at strengthening foreign alliances and weakening the possibilities of internal competition between the Gediminid clan and Lithuanian noble affines. There are even occasional hints in Rus'ian chronicles that some Lithuanian princesses were educated in the east in preparation for their role later in life.[28] The reasons for such an exogamous marriage policy are obvious: foreign alliance and the prevention of contamination of the ruling house with the ambitions of ducal outsiders. When Lithuanian chronicles were composed in the fifteenth century the idea that only the Gediminids had the experience and the charisma to rule was well established. The memory of ducal interlopers into the royal line was almost entirely (but certainly not completely) suppressed. The marriages were particularly successful in cases where the ally was of similar standing to the Gediminids and where, as is understandable, both sides had equal need of cooperation.

In 1320 Maria Gediminaitė was married to Dmitry Mikhailovich of Tver', a competitor with Yury of Moscow for the throne of Vladimir and All Rus'.[29] His father, Grand Duke Mikhail Yaroslavich had supported the creation of a Lithuanian Orthodox metropolitanate. The marriage built on a tradition of Tverite interest in Lithuania which dated back to the second half of the thirteenth century. It was arranged soon after the murder of Mikhail Yaroslavich at a time when all of his three sons were seeking foreign support for Dmitry's claim to the *iarlyk* for All Rus'.[30] After Grand Duke Dmitry was killed in 1325, his widow Maria lived for another twenty-four years. Although almost all of Maria's widowhood was spent in a Tverite convent, it is likely that she exercised considerable political and financial influence over her

Gediminas' plans for south-west Rus'. Hrushevsky's theory that Liubartas married a daughter of Bolesław Yury seems unlikely. Bolesław could scarcely have fathered a nubile daughter before his death – Hrushevsky, *Istoria*, IV, 506. Liubartas' first wife died before 1349, when the prince married an unnamed princess of Rostov – *PSRL*, VII, 215; XVIII, 96–7.

28 Education in Rus' in the family of her mother may be hinted in a reference to pagan daughter of Algirdas taken to Tver' in 1364 – *PSRL*, XV(i), 76; X, 13.

29 *PSRL*, XV(i), 41.

30 Dmitry, Aleksandr and Konstantin married in 1319–20 (*PSRL*, XV (ii), 413–14). Part of the agreement with Moscow over the latter includes a promise not to undermine Dmitry's position as grand duke – Paszkiewicz, *Jagiellonowie*, 298–9.

Rus'ian kinsmen if she is anything like later Lithuanian dowagers in Rus'. Meanwhile the Gediminid political connection with Tver' was maintained through Dmitry's brother and heir Aleksandr who governed Pskov in collusion with Gediminas in the 1330s after Aleksandr had been expelled from Tver' and stripped of the grand-ducal *iarlyk* for Vladimir.[31] The next generation saw her niece Ul'iana married to her brother Algirdas. In 1375 Ul'iana's nephew, Ivan Mikhailovich, married Gediminas' granddaughter, Maria Kestutaitė. Given the scope of Lithuania's growing connections in Tver', it would have been impossible to walk around the cathedral of the Saviour in Tver' by 1380 without feeling the ghosts of the Lithuanian bishop and several princesses who were buried there. Despite interludes when pro-Muscovite princes held Tver', that principality maintained strong links with Lithuania well into the fifteenth century.[32] This relationship owed much of its strength to the influence in both states of Tverite and Lithuanian princesses.

An alliance with Moscow in 1333 had similar potential, but less lasting repercussions. That year a truce was won in Lithuano-Muscovite relations by the wedding of Aigusta-Anastasia Gediminaitė to Ivan Kalita's heir Semën. Although fighting broke out again in 1335, Aigusta did spread Lithuanian influence among her father's strongest rivals. The rivalry between Moscow and Vilnius was too strong for war between them to be averted. It is impossible to tell what would have happened had Aigusta's sons survived infancy and lived to become grand dukes of Moscow; her only daughter, Vasilisa, married a Tverite prince who opposed Lithuania, Mikhail of Kashin. When the Grand Duchess Aigusta died in 1345 she left money and instructions for the painting of icons by foreign masters in the Kremlin church of *Spas na Boru*, the grand-ducal mausoleum. It is probable that when Grand Duke Jaunutis fled Vilnius in the wake of the coup of 1345, he was hoping to take refuge with his sister and her husband. At any rate

[31] Fennell, *Emergence*, 134–5. Widowhood of Maria – *PSRL*, X, 190, 221. Her niece Elena Algirdaitė, wife of Andrei Vladimirovich of Serpukhov had full rights over her lands after the death of her husband – *Sobranie gosudarstvennykh gramot i dogovorov khraniashchikhsia v gosudarstvennoi kollegii inostrannykh del'*, I (Moscow, 1813), no. 40, pp. 74–9 and no. 82, pp. 189–91 (under incorrect date of 1452, really 1437).

[32] Ul'iana – *PSRL*, XXV, 177, 219. On political influence in 1380s see M. Giedroyć, 'Lithuanian options prior to Kreva (1385)', *La Cristianizzazione*, 98; Maria Kestutaitė – *PSRL*, XV (ii), 435; XI, 24, 166, 191. On the Lithuanian tombs in the Cathedral of the Saviour, see N. N. Voronin, 'Tverskoe zodchestvo XIII–XIV vekov', *Izvestia Akademii Nauk, seria istorii i filosofii*, 5 (1945), 375–9. See genealogical table 4.

he arrived in the chief city of eastern Rus' and was baptised there later that year.[33]

To the west, new alliances were made and more ancient ones restored by Gediminas. He revived Traidenis' link with Mazovia after it had fallen into disarray following the death of Bolesław II by marrying his daughter Elżbieta to Bolesław's third son Wacław. He also supported Łokietek's hold on Kraków by uniting Aldona-Anna with the Polish heir Casimir in 1325. A third daughter married the Mazovian prince of south-west Rus'.[34]

Bolesław's first wife had been a Lithuanian, Gaudemantė, and her memory was green in Mazovia, yet it was not one of her sons, but the son of Bolesław's Bohemian marriage who became Gediminas' son-in-law. Trojden and Siemowit preferred to ally themselves with the Order and south-west Rus' against Lithuania. It seems very likely that Gediminas sided with Wacław during the Mazovian civil war of 1316 and it is to this date that we might revise the marriage of Wacław and Elżbieta from the traditional supposition of 1321. The Lithuanian marriage meant as much to Wacław as to Gediminas, perhaps more, for he needed to bolster his position in the divided duchy of Mazovia *vis-à-vis* his half brothers and their Teutonic allies. There is a charter of 6 December 1320 granted at Wyszgród wherein the duke refers to his wife and children. This would put the marriage back to 1318 at the very least and probably to 1316.[35]

This marriage was a major affair. Elżbieta's dowry was three times the size of an ordinary Polish duchess' – 720 Kraków silver marks and nine marks of gold. She had a considerable sum, *dotalicium*, from her husband to use, the equivalent of the income of the castellany of Wyszgród. It is on a par with the holdings of her niece Elena of Serpukhov almost a century later.[36] As

[33] Aigusta marries Semën in 1333 – *TL*, 361–2. Some including Fennell (*Emergence*, 144) call her Gediminas' granddaughter for no good reason. Died 11 March 1345: *PSRL*, XV (i), 60. Sons Vasily (1337–38): *PSRL*, XXV, 171; Konstantin (1341); *TL*, 365. Vasilisa – *PSRL*, XV (i), 60; XI, 12. *Spas na boru* painted on the orders and from the treasury of Aigusta – *PSRL* XV (i), 60, XXV, 175, *TL*, 367. See G. V. Zhidkov, *Moskovskaia zhivopis' srediny XIV veka* (Moscow, 1928), 64–7. Jaunutis flees – see below p. 286.

[34] Aldona and Eufemia – see below pp. 232–3, 224.

[35] Gaudemantė – see above pp. 7–8. Wacław date usually 1321, Włodarski, *Polska*, 252. Reference to wife and children in document of December 1320 in *Kodeks dyplomatyczny Małopolski*, II, no. 580, pp. 249–50.

[36] Dowries – for Eufemia of Wrocław, Pacuski, 'Mazowsze', 593, n. 41; for Aleksandra Algirdaitė (5000 grossi and 500 marks per annum from specified villages – *Kodeks dyplomatyczny Małopolski*, IV, no. 1038, pp. 54–5; *Kodeks dyplomatyczny Księstwa*

duchess, Elżbieta was also *princeps Masovie* alongside her husband. When Wacław died in 1336, Elżbieta controlled not only her own wealth but also, one suspects, much of her son Bolko's power. Elżbieta argued for her rights as castellan of Wyszgród before the King of Poland against her brother-in-law Siemowit's claims to feudal dues from her lands.[37] The dowager played a major part in arranging the marriage of her daughter Anna (named after her aunt of Poland?) to Henry of Żagań in 1337, thereby strengthening an alliance with the Piasts of Silesia and forming a balance of power with Casimir – a very useful balance when one considers Lithuano-Polish relations at that time, as Casimir allied himself with Hungary and Bohemia.[38] Elżbieta's father was still alive at the time of this union. The most surprising result of Anna's marriage was the union she engineered in 1365 for her daughter Jadwiga who became Casimir's fourth wife, the second to have Lithuanian blood. It is tempting to speculate on Elżbieta's involvement with the marriage of her sister Eufemia to Wacław's nephew, Bolesław-Yury of Galich in Płock in 1331.[39]

Elżbieta Gediminaitė maintained her relations with her pagan

Mazowieckiego, ed. T. Lubomirski (Warsaw, 1863), no. 115, pp. 106–7; no. 196, pp. 215–16 from Władysław of Mazovia – 3,000 sexagenarum grossorum. The sum of 720 marks was accepted by Maria of Cieszyń as her part of the inheritance from her father, Trojden of Mazovia – *Iura Masoviae*, I, no. 12, pp. 14–15. [In this case Maria renounced her inheritance rights in return for this sum – *abrenuntiatio mulieris* – see M. Koczerska, *Rodzina szlachecka w Polsce późnego średniowiecza* (Warsaw, 1975), 50–1.] See also S. Roman, 'Stanowisko majątkowe wdowy w średniowiecznym prawie polskim', *Czasopismo prawno-historyczne*, 5 (1953), 80–5; Koczerska, *Rodzina*, 52. *Dotalicium* – sum given to wife by husband upon receipt of dowry, usually the monetary equivalent of dowry property; called *wiano* in Polish. See Koczerska, *Rodzina*, 55–6 and *Iura Masoviae*, I, no. 66, section 1. Casimir took a much larger dowry for Aldona-Anna and for his second wife, Adelheid of Hesse – K. Jasiński, 'Małżeństwa i koligacje polityczne Kazimierza Wielkiego', *Studia Źródłoznawcze*, 32–3 (1990), 69.

[37] Cf. *Iura Masoviae*, I, no. 17, p. 21 with no. 12, p. 14; on power after Wacław (and Bolko) died: no. 17, p. 21.

[38] Jasiński, 'Małżeństwa', 67–76. Casimir married Jadwiga of Żagań in 1365. She was the granddaughter of his first wife's sister. In 1366 Louis of Hungary accused this marriage of being illegal on grounds of consanguinity – *Bullarium Poloniae*, II, no. 1515, p. 252. Kenna – *ibid.*, no. 1002, p. 161 – Kaźko's great-grandfather was Kenna's grandfather, Gediminas; R. J. Mažeika, 'The role of pagan Lithuania in Roman Catholic and Greek Orthodox religious diplomacy in east-central Europe (1345–1377)' (Unpublished Ph.D. Thesis, Fordham University, New York, 1987; Ann Arbor: University Microfilms International, 1987), 162 and n. 182. This marriage was contracted in the aftermath of a failed mission sponsored by Casimir. It established Lithuanian support for the succession of Kaźko to the Polish throne after his grandfather's death.

[39] Jasiński, 'Małżenstwa', 73. Eufemia, we recall, married Bolesław not in Rus' but in Płock – see below p. 224.

siblings. In 1361 her brother Kestutis took refuge with her as he fled from captivity in Prussia. Her lands remained important routes for arms and trade between Lithuania and northern Germany. The influence of such princesses is generally severely underestimated. They did not cut themselves off from political affairs in Lithuania and even acted as providers of refuge for their brothers in time of need. It is not completely flippant to note that Lithuanian princesses were blessed with such strong characters that after their husband's death some were murdered in order to remove them from possible succession struggles. The case of Eufemia Gediminaitė who was drowned beneath the ice of the river Vistula in 1342 comes to mind. There are vague suggestions that Gediminas' own widow was active in the government of Lithuania during the brief reign of Jaunutis.[40]

The growth of Lithuania's territorial holdings and diplomatic alliances exhibits many features. Certain Polish and Rus'ian lands were allied to Lithuania through marriage. These alliances were formed in periods of uncertainty against a common enemy (with Mazovia and Poland against the Teutonic Order, with Tver' against Moscow). Sometimes marriage brought land into the Grand Duchy as in the cases of Liubartas' Volynian union, although when Algirdas took the Vitebsk heiress to wife, he was consummating Lithuanian control of the principality rather than annexing it for the first time. In the case of Polotsk or Smolensk, economic advantages encouraged ever closer cooperation with Lithuania as the pagan empire encroached further upon the Dvina–Baltic trade arteries. Sometimes flight to Lithuania saved an individual prince from Tatar punishment and Rus'ian knavery, as was the case with Aleksandr Mikhailovich. Certain towns, however, were captured by force of arms. It is necessary to balance the rather starry-eyed notion that Lithuanian expansion was almost thrust upon the grand duke by Rus'ian cities which preferred incorporation into the Grand Duchy to independence. Surely it was in Smolensk's interest to resist Muscovite pressure and join the power which influenced the principality's trade relations, but Galich–Volyn' had no cause to abandon her long-cherished independence for Lithuanian suzerainty without a fight. And fight there was. Adhesion to Lithuania did not even provide

[40] For 1361 flight of Kestutis to Elżbieta see *Wig.*, 528, *Długosz*, IX, 308–9; murder of Eufemia – see below p. 267. Gediminas' widow is discussed below p. 282.

an escape from the Tatars, although it did provide military support on certain specific occasions.[41] The theory that Lithuania expanded thanks to the good will of Rus'ian princes is a Russian fallacy as old as Ivan the Terrible. It is a subtle anti-Lithuanian myth popular in nineteenth-century historiography which portrays the Lithuanians as benefactors from Muscovite direction (Ivan's propagandists depict Gediminas' expansion into Kiev as a task set by Ivan Kalita of Moscow) or Rus'ian preference to govern the pagans apparently from below rather than submit to the Mongols. Some Lithuanians find the myth flattering as evidence of a peaceful imperialism to contrast with Russian aggression. Nevertheless, in the 1360s it was well known in Byzantium that the 'Lithuanian people ... are numerous and very brave ... Their ruler surpasses immensely all the Christian princes of northern Rus' in power and the martial skill of his army'. The worldly poet of *Beowulf* reminds us in his description of the marriage of Hrothgar's daughter to Ingeld of the Heathobards how few wars have been put to rest in a prince's bed, for 'a bride can bring a little peace, make spears silent for a while, but not for long'.[42]

GEDIMINAS AND THE FALL OF KIEV

Now that we are more familiar with the general scope of Lithuanian expansion up to and during Gediminas' reign, let us consider more closely the Lithuanian invasion of south-west Rus'. Soon after his accession to the grand-ducal throne or even shortly before, in 1315, Gediminas led an attack on Brest. As a result of this attack the local princes Andrei Yurevich of Volyn' and his brother Lev of Galich drew up a treaty of mutual defence with the Teutonic Order.[43] It may be that these two events led Gediminas to marry his son Liubartas to the daughter of Prince Andrei.

The united principalities of Galich and Volyn' were eyed greedily by the princes' neighbours and relatives: the Piasts of Mazovia, Dobrzyń and the kingdom of Poland, the king of

[41] See p. 113 and n. 137.

[42] Peaceful expansion – Fennell, *Emergence*, 124; 145; Giedroyć, 'Arrival ... (1281–1341)', 30. Gregoras, *HB*, XXXVI, cap. 6 and 8; PG, CXLIX, 456, 457 and *Beowulf*, lines 2,026–2,031.

[43] Shabul'do, *Zemli*, 10 and A. M. Andriiashov, *Ocherki istorii Volynskoi zemli do kontsa XIV stoletia* (Kiev, 1887), 200–2. *PU*, II, no. 157, p. 108. The link between this treaty and the activity of Gediminas is suggested in Włodarski, *Polska*, 247–8.

Hungary and the grand duke of Lithuania. The lands were rich and controlled the eastern borders of both Poland and Hungary. They offered access south to Moldavia and eastwards to Kiev. What would happen if the two brothers were to die without male issue?

A trustworthy manuscript colophon reveals that the two brothers were alive in May 1321; by May 1323 however they were both dead, as Łokietek told the Pope in a letter, dated 21 May.[44] How they died is a matter of some importance for our reconstruction of subsequent events.

In his letter Łokietek uses the word *interitus* to describe their demise. It is a general word for death which may simply imply some degree of violence but Łokietek mentions none, except the increased danger for Poland of attacks from the Tatars. A Swiss Chronicler, John of Winterthur says that they were poisoned by their Rus'ian subjects but it is by no means clear that John was not ascribing their death simply to the same cause as that which in 1340 put an abrupt end to the life of their successor, Bolesław-Yury.[45] He was poisoned, as John and other chroniclers report. Some historians have claimed that the princes died in battle with the Tatars but there is no evidence available for such a patriotic assumption.[46] However one group of sources plainly states how the princes died: the Lithuanians led by Gediminas invaded Volyn' and killed them. This version is found in *L2*,[47] *L3*,[48] two Ukrainian chronicles of the early seventeenth century[49] and the *Kronika* of Stryjkowski.[50] We shall follow this group of inter-related sources as represented by *L2*. What follows is a re-

[44] A. Sobolevskii, 'Russkoe izvestie o poslednikh galitskikh Riurikovichakh', *Sbornik statei v chest' Matveia Kuz'micha Liubavskogo* (Petrograd, 1917), 214–15. See also *MPV*, no. 83. [45] See below pp. 266f. [46] Shabul'do, *Zemli*, 22–3.

[47] *PSRL*, XXXV, 95–6; 152–3; 179–80; 200–1; 221–2. See also Appendix 1, pp. 305–8. Date of redaction – Giedroyć, 'Rulers', 12–13.

[48] *PSRL*, XXXII, 136–7. See also Ochmański, 'Nad Kroniką', 155–63.

[49] *Gustynskaia Letopis'*, *PSRL*, II (Moscow, 1843 *only*), 348, survives in a copy from 1670. Its reputation for unreliability is not altogether deserved, at least for the later Middle Ages. Textual history is given in M. I. Marchenko, *Ukrains'ka istoriografia (z davnikh chasiv do seredini XIXst.* (Kiev, 1959), 35 and E. M. Apanovich, *Rukopisnaia svetskaia kniga XVIIIv. na Ukraine. Istoricheskie sborniki* (Kiev, 1983), 66–77. The *Mezhigorskaia Letopis'* dates from *c.* 1620 – Marchenko, *Ukrains'ka*, 53. The text has not been published in full and thus its place in Russian and Polish historiography is very difficult to establish. Extracts relating to the siege of Kiev were given in N. Dashkevich, *Zametki po istorii litovsko-russkogo gosudarstva* (Kiev, 1885), 55–7. The arguments for and against *Mezhigorskaia* are summed up in P. G. Klepatskii, *Ocherki po istorii Kievskoi zemli I: Litovskii period* (Odessa, 1912), 2–17. [50] *Stryjkowski*, I, 364–8.

Fig. 3. Map to show the Lithuanian campaign in southern Rus', 1322–23

construction of events according to the Raczyński Codex text of that chronicle, interpreted in the light of information from other sources. My interpolations are signalled by square brackets. The Russian text is printed with a full translation in Appendix 1.

Having made peace with the Teutonic Knights in Žemaitija, Gediminas marched against Volyn' [in the second half of 1322. This period of peace on Lithuania's western borders which was probably facilitated by discord within the Order and between the Order and Poland is attested by German sources. These list no Teutonic attacks on Lithuania between July 1320 and March 1322[51]]. In the attack on Vladimir Volynsky the local prince,

[51] *PD*, 185–6.

Andrei [mistakenly called Vladimir in the text] was killed. [From the early 1320s, Andrei and his brother Lev had been consolidating their alliance with the Teutonic Order. In 1320 Andrei had extended trading privileges to the merchants of Toruń and had even sent troops against Lithuania, while Gediminas was at war with the Order].[52] Gediminas subdued Volyn' and left his *namestniki* in charge. Lev fled to his brother-in-law (?) Dmitry Romanovich [in *L2*, Roman] of Briansk. The Lithuanians meanwhile wintered in Brest before launching an attack on Kievan cities in the second week after Easter, [that is around 10 April 1323]. After capturing Ovruch and Zhytomir' on the route south, the Lithuanians met Stanislav of Kiev, Oleg of Pereiaslavl, Dmitry Romanovich of Briansk and Lev of Galich in a battle on the river Irpen' at Belgorod, 23 km south-west of Kiev. During the encounter Lev and Oleg were slain and Dmitry and Stanislav fled to Briansk.

Gediminas captured Belgorod, which was one of Kiev's major defence outposts, and laid siege to Kiev for a month. [By early June 1323] Kiev and Pereiaslavl were in Lithuanian hands. Kiev was placed in the care of [Gediminas' brother Fëdor and] a *namestnik*, Algimantas Mindaugaitis Alšeniškis. As the Lithuanians set about consolidating their gains Stanislav of Kiev fled to Riazan' where, according to the Chronicle, he married the local prince's daughter and succeeded to the throne. Over this detail I shall argue against the *L2*.[53] Here the chronicle story ends.

During the south-western campaign, Gediminas opened negotiations with western cities for peace and better trade relations. The letters of January and May 1323 sent to the Papacy, Hansa towns and the Baltic Germans may very well not be meant as a prelude to Lithuanian expansion into Volyn', as much as a preservation of the uneasy truce of 1320–22 which had allowed Gediminas to move against his rivals in south-west Rus' in the first instance. It is interesting to note the similarities between the commercial policies of the Yurevichi in 1320–21 and Gediminas in 1323. It is not impossible that commercial rivalry contributed to the attack on Rus'.[54]

The death of the Rus'ian princes, I suggest, should be dated to

[52] *Boleslav'-Iurii*, 114; 151. *Stryjkowski*, I, 363; Shabul'do, *Zemli*, 10,

[53] See p. 103.

[54] Compare the Rus'ian accord with the Knights in 1320, *Boleslav'-Iurii*, 150–1 with *GL*, nos. 3–6.

the winter of 1322–23. The immediacy of Łokietek's report to the Pope breeds doubt that a year or so had passed since the death of Lev and Andrei, and both were alive in May 1321.[55] An exceptionally cold winter in Prussia in 1322 prevented the Knights from setting out on *Reise* and hence Gediminas could concentrate his forces on his southern border without fear of Teutonic attack.[56] This period of uneasy peace with the Order was combined with distraction for the Tatars who were heavily involved in campaigns in Egypt, Iran and Azerbaidjan. The Tatars turned their attention to Lithuanian expansion only in 1324 and 1325.[57] Other historians have chosen to date the campaign to different years. Rogov argues for 1322, Batūra for 1325 and Shabul'do for 1324.[58] A century ago, Dashkevich preferred some time after 1332 when, he believed, Gediminas was freer from other cares.[59] It must have happened before 1331 when Gediminas' brother is known to have been in Kiev. Rogov, Batūra and Shabul'do take pains to avoid 1323 when Gediminas turned one eye to the west. Nevertheless Gediminas' truce with Catholic Christendom need not preclude his waging war in the south. Batūra and Shabul'do take account of the Tatar attacks on Lithuania in 1325 as an immediate reaction to Lithuanian expansion, ignoring the fact that the Horde was busy outside Rus' for several years before 1324–25. The winter of 1322–23 remains the most probable date for the campaign.

Galich–Volyn' was subject to too much outside interest for Gediminas to divide his spoils in peace. Anastasia of Dobrzyń was looking to see one of her sons enthroned in south-west Rus' and in this ambition she enjoyed the support of Łokietek, *tutor nepotum suorum*.[60] As the boys' uncle and 'guardian', he was their most senior male relative. A claim that Łokietek's rivals for power in Poland, Henryk and Jan of Głogów, were also pretenders to the Rus'ian throne has been disproved. The *dux Halecie* in a printed

[55] See above n. 44. The dates of 1321, 1322 and 1323 are given by an eighteenth-century version of *L2* for the capture of Galich–Volyn' and Kiev – *PSRL*, XXXII, 37–9.

[56] *PD*, 186–7.

[57] Chronicle of Ibn Duqmaq in V. G. Tiesenhausen, *Sbornik materialov, otnosiashchikhsia k istorii Zolotoi Ordy* (St Petersburg, 1884), 321–9. See also Chronicle of Rashid-ad-Din in Tiesenhausen, *Sbornik*, ed. A. A. Romashkevich and S. L. Volin, II (Moscow–Leningrad, 1941), 142–3. For the relevance of these data to the Horde's policy in Rus' see R. Batūra, *Lietuva tautų kovoje prieš Aukso Ordą: Nuo Batu antplūdžio iki mūšio prie Mėlynųjų Vandenų* (Vilnius, 1975), 204–6.

[58] Rogov, *Russko-pol'skie*, 156. Batūra, *Lietuva*, 201–2. Shabul'do, *Zemli*, 28.

[59] Dashkevich, *Zametki*, 56; 59.

[60] H. Paszkiewicz, *Polityka ruska Kazimierza Wielkiego* (Warsaw, 1925), 19, n. 5.

copy of a letter of Henryk's is a misreading of the style *dux Slezie*.[61]

In 1323 the Lithuanian attack on Dobrzyń which was instigated by Wacław of Płock, may well have been connected with the Rus'ian succession.[62] Wacław supported the claim of his own nephew, Bolesław of Mazovia, to the throne of Galich–Volyn'.[63] This boy's maternal uncles were Andrei and Lev Yurevich. Gediminas seems to have been unable to place his own son Liubartas on the throne of Volyn' because of Polish opposition, although as son-in-law of Andrei and son of the conqueror, Liubartas perhaps had the strongest claim to the throne. The stripling Bolesław was chosen as a candidate acceptable to all interested parties. The Rus'ian boiars chose him as their prince 'unanimously'.[64] He was probably elected in late 1323 or early 1324. Bolesław adopted the name and seal of his grandfather Yury I when he became prince.[65] He was nephew to Wacław of Płock, the grandson of Łokietek and within a relatively short space of time he became son-in-law to Gediminas. In 1331 Bolesław-Yury II married Eufemia Gediminaitė in Płock Cathedral when the prince had reached the age of twenty-one, neatly entwining all parties in the hymeneal bond. The marriage may have been planned in 1323–24 as part of the succession agreement. Certainly the marriage of two Orthodox Christians in a Catholic church in Płock is hardly commonplace. At that very time, the metropolitan of All Rus' was visiting the church in Galich–Volyn'; he was ignored by the prince. All this points to the complex political settlement of the Rus'ian Question involving Poland, Mazovia, Lithuania and Rus' and the limited nature of Lithuanian gains in south-west Rus'.[66]

The new prince maintained the old Galich alliance with the Order and remained on good terms with Poland and Lithuania. No attempt was made to abandon the Teutonic alliance until 1338–39 when Bolesław joined the kings of Hungary, Bohemia and Poland in opposition to the Order.[67] It is impossible to tell whether Liubartas was granted lands on the Kiev–Volyn' border

61 *MPV*, no. 84.
62 *PD*, 188; *GL*, 158–61.
63 He was not only Bolesław's uncle but also the sponsor of his marriage – see n. 66.
64 *MPH*, II, 629. In 1340 the *namestnik* Dmitry D'iadko led the politicking to find a successor to Bolesław – Shabul'do, *Zemli*, 37f.
65 Seal in *Boleslav'-Iurii*, 4–5; 77–8; 153–5.
66 *Długosz*, IX, 173; Włodarski, *Polska*, 278.
67 *PU*, II, no. 537, pp. 361–2; Włodarski, *Polska*, 278f.

in compensation for the loss of his wife's inheritance. Certainly by 1340, he was in a position to take control of Volyn' after Bolesław's assassination. Paszkiewicz's theory that Liubartas held Geranony in Black Rus' does not preclude his ruling in south-west Rus' some time in the period 1323–40.[68]

The position of Kiev, the other prize of Gediminas' campaign, in Lithuanian affairs has long been a subject of enquiry. The involvement of a Kievan prince named Fëdor in a Lithuano-Novgorodian imbroglio of 1331 has caused much argument over who controlled Kiev: the Kievans, the Tatars or the Lithuanians.[69]

On 25 August 1331, Vasily Kaleka, Gediminas' ally, was consecrated by Metropolitan Feognost in Vladimir Volynsky as archbishop of Novgorod. A week or so later, Kaleka set off home along a route 'between Kiev and Lithuania'. He and his party were intercepted *en route* by Prince Fëdor of Kiev, a Tatar *basqaq* and fifty Lettovian warriors. The significance of Kaleka's journey is discussed in fuller detail elsewhere.[70] Our interest here is who Fëdor of Kiev was and what importance if any can be attached to the presence of a Tatar tax collector in his entourage.

Nineteenth-century scholars thought that Fëdor, given his Christian name, must have been a Rurikid prince of unknown lineage, most probably one of the Chernigov Olgovichi. The *basqaq* meant that Kiev could not have been subject to Lithuania since it was still paying Tatar tribute.[71] However in 1916, new evidence came to light which refers to a brother of Gediminas named Fëdor who gave the metropolitan of Lithuania two silver cups. This evidence is the list of property belonging to a dead metropolitan which was written in Feognost's chancery in the 1330s.[72] Modern scholars accept that this Fëdor is the same man who appears in Kiev in 1331 and who is replaced, according to the *Gustynskaia Chronicle*, in 1362 by Algirdas' son Vladimir.[73] The *basqaq* was in Kiev because the Kievans were still paying tribute to the Tatars and this was a duty which not even subjection to Lithuanian or Polish control could remove, as we shall see. The Lithuanians did exercise some control over Kiev in the 1330s.

After this rather lengthy digression let us look a little more

[68] Shabul'do, *Zemli*, 34 and n. 131; for Paszkiewicz see above n. 22.
[69] Summary in Batūra, *Lietuva*, 176–210.
[70] See pp. 174–7.
[71] Klepatskii, *Ocherki*, 16, n. 1; Batūra, *Lietuva*, 189 and n. 58.
[72] See p. 160.
[73] Fennell, *Emergence*, 122, n. 1. Vladimir Algirdaitis – *PSRL*, II (1843), 350.

closely at the chronicle texts which recount Gediminas' exploits in south-west Rus' (see Appendix 1, pp. 305–11) and the doubts scholars have entertained over their authenticity. The main objections against the accounts arise from the unjustifiably low opinion which is held of *L2*, *L3* and the Ukrainian chronicles of the early seventeenth century. This overhasty hypercritical approach to the texts dates from the nineteenth century and fails to take into account new evidence which has emerged since Antonovich first questioned the reliability of the chronicles in the 1880s.[74] His approach was a reaction against the unquestioning acceptance of all the chronicles' data which typifies earlier scholarship. Antonovich's criticisms have been followed more or less unquestioningly ever since.

Antonovich was familiar with references to Yury/Georgius and Boleslaus as princes of south-west Rus' in the 1320s and 1330s. He also reasoned that since Yury II was a Rurikid prince (only a Rurikid could be called Yury) and reigned until 1335 (the date of the last document signed *Georgius*)[75], there was obviously no successful Lithuanian invasion of Galich–Volyn'. Bolesław, whose name appears in texts after 1335 was clearly not a Lithuanian. Antonovich did not know that Bolesław and Yury II were one and the same *Mazovian* prince, the affine of Gediminas. The history of the prince was unravelled by Řežabek only in 1883.[76] One of Antonovich's basic premises is clearly erroneous.

A study of the names of the princes listed as having taken part in the battles for south-west Rus' confirmed Antonovich's belief that the story was untenable. The chronicle speaks of Vladimir, prince of Vladimir and there was no prince of Vladimir Volynsky of that name during Gediminas' reign. The last such was Vladimir Vasil'kovich who died in 1289.[77] It may be however that an uncertain chronicler transferred the name of the city to its prince and Andrei Yurevich is probably meant here. Lev Lutskii (or

[74] For example Antonovich dwells on the reigns of Bolesław and Yury in south-west Rus'. The first realisation that Bolesław-Yury was one man came in J. Řežabek, 'Jiři II, posledni kniže veškevé Malé Rusi', *Časopis Musea Královstvi Českého*, 57 (1883), 120–41. Antonovich wrote two years after Řežabek – V. B. Antonovich, *Monografii po istorii zapadnoi i iugo-zapadnoi Rossii*, I (Kiev, 1885), 50–8 and V. B. Antonovich and D. Ilovaiskii, *Istoria velikogo kniazhestva litovskogo* (Ternopol', 1887), 37–48.

[75] Antonovich, *Monografii*, 51; 53–4.

[76] See n. 74.

[77] Vladimir Vladimirskii, Lev Lutskii, Roman Brianskii, Oleg Pereiaslavlskii, Stanislav Kievskii, Olgimunt Mendovgovich Olshanskii, Ivan Riazanskii. For objections to these names see Antonovich, *Monografii*, 50f.

accuratius Galitskii – a misreading is not impossible) was indeed his brother.[78]

Roman of Briansk was a thirteenth-century prince who was long dead by 1322. Dmitry Romanovich of Briansk on the other hand was a very live enemy of Lithuania in the 1320s and 1330s.[79] There is no evidence to prove or disprove kinship between him and Lev. According to *L2*, they were brothers-in-law. Mistaking Dmitry Romanovich for his illustrious thirteenth-century namesake is not an incomprehensible error. It must be conceded that in 1274 Vladimir of Vladimir, Lev Danilovich of Galich and Roman of Chernigov fought against the Lithuanians at Dorogichin[80] and it would appear reasonable to conclude that this battle lies behind the *L2* story. However there are two important reasons for doubting such an interpretation: the outcome of the battle was completely different (none of the Rus'ian princes was killed) and the text has no echo in *L2*, even though there are elsewhere in *L2* clear borrowings from the *Ipat'evskaia Chronicle* which deals with the 1274 episode.[81]

The strangest name in the *L2* story is that of Stanislav of Kiev. We can be forgiven for wondering whether this western-Slavonic name could be connected with Kiev and Riazan'. Certainly Stanislav is not a common name among the eastern Slavs. A Kievan boiar of the twelfth century bore that name as did a late fourteenth-century boiar of Riazan'.[82] Nonetheless the *Liubech Sinodik* edited by Zotov records a prince Ioann Stanislavich who belonged to a generation of the mid- to late fourteenth century. Since he must have had a father, we may deduce that that parent was Stanislav of Kiev. Ioann is listed among the Viaz'ma princes – Simeon of Kroshinesk and Simeon Viazemskii[83] – and thus it is tempting to view him as a prince of Viaz'ma, perhaps even the Ivan Viazemskii who attacked Algirdas in 1370.[84] Perhaps

[78] Shabul'do, *Zemli*, 157, n. 90.

[79] Fennell, *Emergence*, 70, n. 1; 135; 171–2; 202–4.

[80] *PSRL*, II, 871–4. The compiler of *Gustynskaia* does in fact make this rationalisation by calling Vladimir, Vasilkovich (see Appendix 1) but without echoing *PSRL*, II. No other chronicle except this late one makes this connection.

[81] Cf. references to *Antiokh sirskii* and *Irod* in *PSRL*, II, 869 and *PSRL*, XXXV, 93.

[82] *Russkaia Pravda – prostrannaia redaktsia* in *Pamiatniki Russkogo prava I: Pamiatniki prava kievskogo gosudarstva X–XIIvv.*, ed. A. A. Zimin (Moscow, 1952), 113. Stanislav the Riazanite was active in 1389 – *PSRL*, XI, 95. Galich Stanislav of 1229 – *PSRL*, II, 756.

[83] Zotov, *O Chernigovskikh*, 29. Kroshinesk is a small district of the Viaz'ma principality. Zotov mistook Kroshinskii for the Polish name *Krasiński* – *ibid.*, 166–7.

[84] *RIB*, 135–40.

Stanislav passed through Riazan' to become prince of Viaz'ma – the difference in the manuscript ligatures of *Viazemskii* and *Riazanskii* might be confused by a careless scribe.

The flight from Kiev to Riazan' could not have ended in Stanislav's being adopted by Ivan of Riazan and his institution as prince of that city. The historicity of Ivan of Riazan' is unassailable. He undoubtedly existed in 1322–23 but so did his son Ivan, who succeeded him in 1327.[85] A brief stay by Stanislav in Riazan' before moving on elsewhere, perhaps to a Riazan' district (if not Viaz'ma) is not, however, impossible.[86] Stanislav also appears in the genealogy of the Shilovskiis, a Riazan' boiar family. The genealogy may have been composed in the first half of the fifteenth century, although it survives only in a sixteenth-century copy.[87] In it the Shilovskis claim to have fled from Kiev to Riazan' with Stanislav. Even if the Stanislav reference is intrinsically erroneous, if the *rodopis* itself is from the period 1427–56, it is proof that the *legend* of Stanislav and Gediminas is much older than the *L2* account. It may be pertinent to note that another boiar family, the Kvashniny, also claimed to have fled from Kiev in the early years of Lithuanian dominion (1332).[88]

Oleg of Pereiaslavl', unlike Ivan Riazanskii is another character shrouded in mystery. We know nothing of Pereiaslavl' princes after the Tatar invasion of 1240. It is not impossible though that a minor branch of a royal line survived there. The capture of the city and its incorporation into the Grand Duchy as *L2* claims may be corroborated purely circumstantially by the visit there of the metropolitan of Lithuania. At the very least, someone worth visiting must have lived there.[89]

The only Lithuanian mentioned in this part of *L2*, with the

[85] Fennell, *Emergence*, 219–20.

[86] A. G. Kuz'min, *Riazanskoe Letopisanie* (Moscow, 1965), 200.

[87] *Akty sotsial'no-ekonomicheskoi istorii Severo-vostochnoi Rusi kontsa XIV–nachala XVIv.*, III (Moscow, 1964), no. 352, pp. 376–8. See also A. A. Zimin, *Formirovanie boiarskoi aristokratii v Rossii vo vtoroi polovine XV–pervoi treti XVIv.* (Moscow, 1988), 269.

[88] The Kvashniny claim to have left Kiev for Moscow in 1332 – *Rostovskaia Letopis'* (1539), cited in N. M. Karamzin, *Istoria gosudarstva rossiiskogo*, I.4 (St Petersburg, 1842; Moscow, 1988), cols. 123–4, n. 324. A Kvashnin letter of 1576 repeats the text of the Chronicle – N. P. Likhachev, *Razriadnye d'iaki XVI veka: Opyt istoricheskogo issledovania* (St Petersburg, 1888), Appendix II, p. 7. These texts are discussed in A. N. Nasonov, *Istoria russkogo letopisania XI–nachalo XVIII veka: Ocherki i issledovania* (Moscow, 1969), 354–6. Kvashnin estates in Muscovy are described in S. B. Veselovskii, *Feodal'noe zemlevladenie z severo-vostochnoi Rusi*, I (Moscow–Leningrad, 1947), 192–202.

[89] Priselkov and Vasmer, 'Otryvki', 58. The palaeographical evidence of the texts has been examined recently in B. L. Fonkich, 'Paleograficheskie zametki o grecheskikh

exception of Gediminas, is Algimantas Mindaugaitis Alšeniškis. His name is not Mendovg Olgimuntovich, as Antonovich misnames him in order to dismiss him as an [inaccurate] anachronism for Mindaugas.[90] He may have been active in Kiev in 1320s and 1330s as a *namestnik* for Gediminas' brother Fëdor. His son Ivan, who was first recorded in a Lithuanian treaty with the Teutonic Order in September 1379,[91] was appointed regent in Kiev in 1399 by Vytautas.[92] The longevity of Ivan, implied by this explanation is not incredible. Jogaila for instance was born *c.* 1356, ruled in Lithuania in 1377 and died in Poland in 1434. His father, Grand Duke Algirdas (*d.* 1377) flourished as early as 1318. Batūra in his excellent study of the Kiev problem followed Kuczyński to suggest that Fëdor may have been Algimantas' Christian name, thereby reconciling the *L2* references with the 1331 Novgorodian account.[93] Shabul'do recently showed this hypothesis to be mistaken.[94] A list of Alšeniškiai in a manuscript of the Kievan Pechory Monastery which dates from the end of the fifteenth to the early sixteenth century refers to one 'Prince Olgimont (Algimantas) called Mikhail in holy baptism and in religion Evfimy'.[95] To call him Fëdor too would be prodigal. Antonovich, needless to say, was unaware of this source which was published in 1892. He was also unaware of Fëdor's possible relationship to Gediminas since the Feognost chancery records were not published until 1916.[96]

Antonovich was also suspicious of the cities mentioned in *L2*. He was unwilling to believe that Zhytomir' existed in the 1320s, although the city had been an important military site from the tenth century onwards.[97] He considered that Vyshgorod and

rukopisiakh ital'ianskikh bibliotek', *Vizantiiskie Ocherki*: *Trudy sovetskikh uchenykh k XVI mezhdunarodnomu kongressu vizantinistov* (Moscow, 1982), 254–62.

[90] Antonovich, *Monografii*, 54. The text reads *i posadil na nikh kniazia Mindovgova syna Olkgimunta* which some historians misinterpret as *Mindovg syn Olkgimunta*. The clear meaning is surely *Olkgimunt Mindovgov-syn*.

[91] *CDP*, III, 134. In 1390 he accompanied Sofia Vytautaitė to Moscow to marry Vasily I Dmitrievich and is last referred to in the Treaty of Vilnius, 18 January 1401. See also Rowell, 'Gediminid dynastic diplomacy in Žemaitija'.

[92] Shabul'do, *Zemli*, 29 and n. 94.

[93] Batūra, *Lietuva*, 198; Kuczyński, *Ziemie*, 107–8.

[94] Shabul'do, *Zemli*, 29 and n. 94.

[95] S. T. Golubtsev, 'Drevnii pomiannik Kievo-Pecherskoi Lavry (kontsa XV–nachala XVI stoletia)', *Chtenia v istoricheskom obshchestve Nestora Letopistsa*, 6 (1892), 7.

[96] See above n. 89.

[97] *Istoria mist i sil ukrains'koi SSR v dvadtsati shesti tomakh*: *Zhitomirs'ka Oblast'* (Kiev, 1973), 86.

Belgorod had lost their significance as the defensive outposts of Kiev by the mid-thirteenth century.[98] This is difficult to substantiate. He may be correct, however, to doubt that Gediminas took Putivl', Cherkasy and Kanev. This episode seems to be an interpolation in the text and may well refer to Vytautas' Rus'ian campaign of 1392.[99] The discrete nature of this dubious episode cannot *ipso facto* validate the remaining text but it does show how the text can be analysed. The excision of this part of *L2* does not damage the sense or the importance of the remainder of the text. On the whole, Antonovich seems happy to date the Lithuanian seizure of Kiev to 1362 and Algirdas' activity following his victory over the Tatars at Siny Vody.[100]

The *L2* account is not perfect. It bears no date and those dates given by other accounts are at odds with one another.[101] The text appears to be littered with interpolations: explanatory clauses to make clear where a prince came from, the use of two different relative pronouns in reported speech (*izh*, *shto*: 'how, that'), and it may even mix in information from other campaigns.[102] Despite such blemishes the text deserves serious attention. The accounts of the pacification of Žemaitija at the beginning of Gediminas' reign as we read them in *L2* do, in fact, concur with Latin sources.[103] The

98 Antonovich, *Monografii*, 55.

99 See n. 102. The 1392 campaign is described in *PSRL*, XXXV, 65, 101–2, 159, 186, 206, 228. See Shabul'do, *Zemli*, 138–40.

100 Antonovich, *Monografii*, 229–30; Rowell, 'Lithuania', 311 and n. 88.

101 *Gustynskaia*, 1304–5 – *PSRL*, II (1843), 348–9. *Stryjkowski*, I, 364, 368 settles on 1320/21. It should be noted that references to the text of *L2* also apply to *L3* and *Stryjkowski*.

102 See Appendix 1. Explanatory clauses which read like interpolations come in lines 8–11; different relative pronouns used in same verbal construction – lines 8–9, 46, 56–8, 63–4. It is quite likely that the list of *prigorody* seized by Gediminas (Cherkasy, Kanev, Putivl', Slepovrod) is an insertion to explain which towns were Pereiaslavlian. The insertion is fitted in with *И переяславлене слышали, иж*. This construction and *и въслышали тое... што* are different from the *въслышали тое, иж* used in line 46. This difference in construction is common to all redactions of this section (*PSRL*, XXXV, 96, 153, 180, 200, 221).

103 *PSRL*, XXXV, 152–3. The Gostautas mentioned here is probably the one who was killed at Veliuona in 1364 – *Wig*., 540; 547. The ransom of a Gostautas is probably an echo of a fifteenth-century case. In 1431 Peter Gostautas rebelled against Jogaila and was fined 2000 marks – *Codex Epistolaris saeculi decimi quinti*, ed. A. Lewicki, I (Kraków, 1876), no.73. The battle with the Order at Žeimyla (Žeimys) [here Zheimy] near the Akmiana river in Žemaitija is quite plausible as an action of 1315–20 (see *PD*, 180–6) and it is possible that Gostautas was included in this account because of his clan's estates at the homonymous Oszmiana (south-eastern Lithuania). *Oshmene* is the Russian form of both places. *PD*, 181 records a Lithuanian campaign against Ragnit and Tilsit (Schalauenberg).

story of the high priest Lizdeika and Gediminas' temple in Vilnius is vaguely corroborated by Polish documentary sources and recent archaeological discoveries in Vilnius of a pagan temple sandwiched between the Catholic cathedrals of *c.* 1253 and 1387.[104] Small scraps of circumstantial evidence from Polish chronicles, Order records and eastern European diplomacy support a reasonable amount of confidence in the Kiev–Volyn' section of *L2*.

Approached without prejudice against its authenticity and the presumption that it could not possibly be true, the *L2* account reads true. The march south via Ovruch and Zhytomir' is logical and was used later in the century by Vytautas. The specification of time (the second week after Easter) and the placing of Belgorod near Kiev do not appear to be the invention of a fraudulent scribe. The account mentions two princes in Galich–Volyn' where we might expect an inventive author of a later period to name but one. Indeed why should *force majeure* be made the Lithuanian claim to rule in south-west Rus' when the dynastic rights of Liubartas might have been stressed by a later propagandist? The author of *L1* knew that Liubartas was married to the Volyn' heiress.[105]

The textual imperfections cited by Antonovich which mark all versions of the account, whether in *L2*, *L3*, Stryjkowski or the Ukrainian Chronicles, are at best inconclusive. The apparently late date of the story's composition also worried Antonovich and continues to worry sceptical historians. *L2* in its earliest redactions goes back only to 1520–30 and the Kiev–Volyn' account does not figure at all in *L1* which dates from the mid-fifteenth century.[106] The story is repeated in *L3* (in the section composed *c.* 1516–42)[107] and with some additions in the work of Stryjkowski, whose *Kronika* was published first in 1582.[108] However, the Polish historian was not the originator of the story as Antonovich imagined.[109]

The *Gustynskaia Chronicle* was composed between 1623 and 1627 near Poltava.[110] It gives a much briefer account of the campaign than any of the earlier chronicles and mixes it with information about Mazovian and Prussian battles which are relevant to 1323–24. Since no manuscripts of *L2* are known from the Ukraine, it is difficult to pinpoint *Gustynskaia*'s source. It is

104 See pp. 134–7. 105 *PSRL*, XXXV, 61, 85, 110. 106 See p. 41.
107 *PSRL*, XXXII, 136–7; Ochmański, 'Nad Kroniką', 157–9.
108 See n. 50 and Rogov, *Russko-Pol'skie*, 155–61.
109 Antonovich, *Monografii*, 47. 110 See n. 49. The text is given in Appendix 1.

probably not Stryjkowski but may be another Polish historian such as Decius.[111] It is not impossible that a Ukrainian tradition informed the compiler of *Gustynskaia*. The account reads as a Kievan source might. It laments the capture of the city and seeks to explain why the former Rus'ian capital fell to the Lithuanians. Glorifying Gediminas' achievement is not the aim of the narrative. Of course, monastic chronicles or simply annalistic records are very likely to have been kept in Kiev in the fourteenth century. They have simply not survived. The compiler of *L2* mentions having found other accounts (of thirteenth-century Lithuanian history) in one such Rus'ian source. We know that the Royal Library in Vilnius in 1510 owned a Kievan Chronicle which has not survived to our day.[112]

The *Mezhigorskaia Chronicle* (post 1620) has not been published in full and thus it is difficult to assess its independence from Polish and Lithuanian sources. Its compiler did have recourse to authors other than Stryjkowski, if Antonovich is correct. Its Kiev account is more laconic even than *Gustynskaia* but it includes several references to the siege under other accounts dated 1340.[113]

The account of the campaigns in south-west Rus' appears then in several late redactions whose interrelationship is difficult to establish exactly. Lateness of redaction, however, does not signify irredeemable unreliability. The story was not necessarily created *a nihilo* two centuries after the events it purports to relate. Its authors may have had recourse to works which are now irretrievably lost or hidden in Russian archives. Can it really be that no records were

[111] All manuscripts of *L1* and *L2* originate in Belorussia, not the Ukraine. Stryjkowski became an important source for Ukrainian historians in the mid-seventeenth century when the *Sinopsis* was composed – Rogov, *Russko-Pol'skie*, 259f. and *Sinopsis, Kiev* 1681. *Facsimile mit einer Einleitung*, ed. H. Rothe, *Bausteine zur Geschichte der Literatur bei den Slaven*, XVII (Cologne--Vienna, 1983). F. Sielecki wrote in 1966 that the compiler of *Gustynskaia* borrowed much from Bielski – 'Kronikarze polscy', 160. Bielski did not describe the south-west Rus'ian campaigns of Gediminas. One other Polish historian does mention the battles – J. L. Decius, *De vetustatibus Polonorum*, printed in Kraków in 1555. The text is most easily available in *Poloniae Historicae Corpus*, ed. Pistorius (Basle, 1582), 386–9. Whether Decius is the source behind *Gustynskaia* is difficult to tell. He took *L2* or *L3* as his source.

[112] *U ruskoi kroinitse*, *PSRL*, XXXV, 150. On royal manuscript see Shchapov, 'Biblioteka polotskogo sofiiskogo sobora', 268–9.

[113] Rogov, *Russko-Pol'skie*, 159–60 and Dashevich, *Zametki*, 56–7 (text below in Appendix 1). The compiler gives 1341 as the date of Gediminas' death (correctly) and says that by Jogaila's day (1377–1434) Kiev had been in Lithuanian hands for fifty years. Klepatskii, *Ocherki*, 8 considers that *Mezhigorskaia* is a shortened version of *L3*. Only Kiev, not Volyn', is mentioned.

kept in Novgorodok, Polotsk or Kiev in the fourteenth and fifteenth centuries and that these may not have spoken of the fate of Kiev and Volyn' in the first quarter of the fourteenth century?

To take a parallel case, scholarship has accepted that Algirdas attacked Kiev *c.* 1362, removed the ruling prince, Fëdor, and replaced him with his own son, Vladimir.[114] This is based mainly on an entry in *Gustynskaia* which is corroborated vaguely by references in the Rogozhsky Chronicle to the Lithuanian capture of the Belobrezhie in 1361–62 and in the Nikon Chronicle which s.a. 1377 tells how Algirdas gave Kiev to Vladimir.[115] If the 1362 section of *Gustynskaia* is acceptable – and given the events of 1360–80 it seems much more probable than not – where did it originate? The capture of Kiev by Algirdas is not in *L1*, *L2*, *L3* or Stryjkowski. *Gustynskaia*'s compiler must have had another source to hand. It may be that this source did not also deal with events of 1322–23 and that *Gustynskaia* took the earlier siege story from *L2*, *L3* or Stryjkowski. We cannot be certain however that the compiler of *Gustynskaia* did not have before him a source similar to that which the compiler of *L2* beheld a century earlier. If the Shilovskii genealogy is truly a fifteenth-century document, information of some sort was available about Stanislav of Kiev and Gediminas before *L2* was compiled.

There is another source entirely unconnected with *L2* which recounts Lithuanian activity in Volyn' in the 1320s: the *Rodoslovie Kniazei Litovskikh* ('The Genealogy of the Lithuanian Princes'). This forms a part of both the *Poslanie Spiridona Savvy* ('The Epistle of Spiridon-Savva')[116] and 'the Tale of the Princes of Vladimir' (*Skazanie o Kniaziakh Vladimirskikh*).[117]

Spiridon-Savva wrote his *Poslanie*, a glorification of the Tverite dukes, at the end of the fifteenth century[118] soon after his defection from Lithuania to Moscow. He was a Tverite cleric who in 1476 had been appointed Metropolitan of Lithuania. Apart from tracing the lineage of the Rurikids from Augustus, Spiridon also tells how Aleksandr Mikhailovich of Tver' sent out two vassals, Boreiko to Volyn' and Kiev, and Gegimenik to the Nemunas river, to collect

[114] Shabul'do, *Zemli*, 58, 60; Batūra, *Lietuva*, 294–8; Knoll, *Rise*, 163.

[115] *PSRL*, II (1843), 350; *PSRL*, XV (i), 75; *PSRL*, XI, 26.

[116] Dmitrieva, *Skazanie*, 159–70.

[117] *Ibid.*, 171–91.

[118] Ia. S. Lur'e, review of Dmitrieva's book in *Izvestia Akademii Nauk SSSR – Otdelenie literatury i iazyka*, 15 (1956), 176 (Lur'e, *OLIa*); and *Ideologicheskaia bor'ba v russkoi publitsistike kontsa XV–nachala XVI veka* (Moscow–Leningrad, 1960), 386–91. A. A. Zimin, *Rossia na rubezhe XV–XVI stoletii* (Moscow, 1982), 153f.

tribute.[119] Gegimenik is a derogatory form of Gediminas suitable in a piece which refers to the legend about Gediminas' origin as Vytenis' groom or, perhaps, constable (*koniushii*, *stabularius*). This particular legend gained credence in Prussian circles in 1412–13.[120] As for Boreiko, he seems to have been a Žemaitijan nobleman who enjoyed Gediminas' protection and may have been one of Gediminas' *namestniki* in Volyn' in 1322. In later versions of the story which are incorporated into the *Skazanie*, Gegimenik goes to Volyn' before he becomes the first grand duke of Lithuania.[121] This version dates to 1520–30. The story gives a verifiable list of Gediminas' sons and traces the Lithuanian dynasty up to the fifteenth century.[122] The story is not intended as a justification for Lithuanian claims to Rus'ian lands but simply a glorification of the grand duke of Vladimir. In the earliest redactions, Aleksandr Mikhailovich of Tver' is that grand duke while in later ones Yury Danilovich of Moscow is the guiding force. Especially interesting is the reversal of roles in the use of the Tverite: Aleksandr was Gediminas' client and not vice versa. The later Rus'ian propagandist, aware of the true subsidiary relationship of Aleksandr to the Lithuanian grand duke, chose to recast this role in order to glorify the Rus'ian prince and support the claims of sixteenth-century Muscovite grand dukes to rule Lithuania and Kiev (then still in Lithuanian hands). An equally clouded version of the truth is the reference to Narimantas Gediminaitis' being ransomed from the Khan by Ivan Kalita. This is a (con)fusion of two real incidents: in 1345 Narimantas fled to the Horde when Algirdas seized power in Vilnius. He later returned to Lithuania. In 1348, Algirdas sent his brother Karijotas to the Khan to seek assistance against the Order. The Khan promptly handed the Lithuanian over to Semën Ivanovich of Moscow who forced Algirdas to pay a ransom for his

119 *Poslanie Spiridona-Savvy* in Dmitrieva, *Skazanie*, 167. Text given in Appendix 1.

120 Chamiarytski, *Belaruskia*, 128–9.

121 See Stryjkowski's verse chronicle, *O początkach, wywodach, dzielnościach, sprawach rycerskich i domowych sławnego narodu litewskiego i ruskiego, przedtym nigdy od żadnego ani kuszone, ani opisane, z natchnienia Bożego a uprzejmie pilnego doświadczenia*, ed. J. Radziszewska (Warsaw, 1978), 239, 241–3. He was claimed as an ancestor by the Chodkiewicz family – Z. L. Radzimiński, 'Sprawa odrębnego pochodzenia Chodkiewiczów litewskich i białoruskich (z tablicami genealogicznymi)', *Rocznik polskiego towarzystwa heraldycznego we Lwowie*, 8 (1926–27), 111–13. Boreikovs appear in *L2* but not with Gediminas – *PSRL*, XXXV, 30, 51, 72, 73, 89, 102, 138, 159, 186, 207, 228. Cf. Dmitrieva, *Skazanie*, 179–80 (text in Appendix 1, pp. 310–11).

122 For genealogy see Dmitrieva, *Skazanie*, 179–81. The date is given in Zimin, *Rossia*, 150–1.

return.[123] The events described in the *Skazanie* version of the *Rodoslovie* are not pure invention. From the Gegimenik episode we might conclude that in the first third of the fourteenth century the Lithuanians were in Volyn' and Kiev.

There are literary connections between the late fifteenth-century *Poslanie* and Tverite literature of the late fourteenth and mid-fifteenth centuries. Although scholars dispute the precise date of the *Poslanie* and *Skazanie*, Lur'e, Dmitrieva, Zimin and Gol'dberg are all agreed that they have their origin in Tverite literature about Lithuania and Tverite grand dukes which existed by the mid-fifteenth century – seventy-five years or so before the *L2* Kiev and Volyn' tales.[124]

This eastern Rus'ian source has no discernible connection with the west Rus'ian legend about the capture of Volyn' and Kiev and it predates the earliest *L2* version by at least a generation, although in fact, its source may go back another 30–50 years before that. If the link between the two versions is Spiridon-Savva himself, the western legend must have existed before 1482, the date of Spiridon's flight eastwards.[125] Perhaps a lost chronicle tradition provided a common source. It is difficult to believe that two legends about south-west Rus' in the 1320s (Yury of Moscow died in 1325 and Aleksandr Mikhailovich ceased to be grand duke in 1327 and both appear in different redactions of the *Skazanie*) were invented *a nihilo* within a century in both east and west Rus'.

This is as much as can be said of the sources for Gediminas' invasion of Volyn': the legend is older than *L2* and exists in an eastern and western variant. Both variants are confused: *L2* took information from other sources to fill up gaps in *L1*; in the Shilovskii genealogy and the *Rodoslovie* tradition the prime intention is not a glorification or justification of Lithuania but family self-glorification. The illustrious lineage of a Riazan' family or the political pretentions of the Moscow dynasty (the *Skazanie* is part of Ivan the Great's claims to be Lithuania's overlord) have no need to invent a specifically south and west Rus'ian campaign.

[123] See below p. 114.

[124] Lur'e, *OLIa*, 176; Zimin, *Rossia*, 154; Zimin, 'Antichnye momenty v russkoi publitsistike kontsa XV veka', in *Feodal'naia Rossia vo vsemirno-istoricheskom protsesse. Sbornik statei posviashchennykh L'vu Vladimirovichu Cherepninu* (Moscow, 1972), 136–7. A. L. Gol'dberg, 'K istorii rasskaza o potomkakh Avgusta i o darakh Monomakha', *TODRL*, 30 (1976), 209. Dmitrieva, *Skazanie*, 74–90; and 'O nekotorykh istochnikakh 'Poslania' Spridona-Savvy', *TODRL*, 31 (1959), 440–5.

[125] Zimin, *Rossia*, 150.

It must be conceded that the evidence adduced here is largely circumstantial but there is no other. The arguments against the validity of the story as given by Antonovich and his sceptical disciples do not stand in the face of critical analysis with the exception of the doubts over the 'Kanev list' and this list is very probably an interpolation into the text. The text is not perfect but it is all we have and more than prejudice is needed to dismiss it. The idea behind Antonovich's scepticism, that Lithuania was incapable of building such an empire in the early fourteenth century has been dismissed by the scholarship of the past eighty years.[126]

GEDIMINAS AND THE TATARS

The Lithuanians were not the only non-Christian power operating in Rus'. We might wonder what the Tatars made of Lithuanian imperialism and the changes it wrought in the political balance of Rus'. Lithuanian expansion into Rus' of necessity increased the contact the grand duke had with the Tatars. In the thirteenth century this contact was generally hostile and was caused by Lithuania's wars in southern Rus'. The princes of Galich–Volyn' were not loath to call upon Tatar aid to fend off Lithuanian attacks.[127] However when the Rus'ians and Tatars were in conflict with the Poles, the Lithuanians joined forces with the enemy to raid Poland.[128] It is likely that traditionally the Tatars and Lithuanians coexisted in an uneasy peace when Lithuanian ambitions did not bring them to battle. The same might be said of Gediminas' relations with the khan of the Golden Horde. References to Lithuano-Tatar relations in the first four decades of the fourteenth century are as scant as they are laconic. We have some eleven references to encounters between the two outsider nations of Rus' between 1315 and 1340.[129] They are of varying degrees of credibility. The account of Tatar damage to Bisenė in 1315, recorded in the Sambian *Epitome Gestorum* is of very dubious authority.[130] In 1933 Paszkiewicz raised doubts over the Tatar attack on that fortress, suggesting that the reading *multa dampna*

[126] See summary of thirteenth century, pp. 50f.

[127] 1258–59 – *NL*, 82; *PSRL*, II, 847. 1274 – *PSRL*, II, 871–2.

[128] *MPH*, II, 879, 953. *MPH*, III, 188–9.

[129] 1315 – *SRP*, I, 285–6. [*falsissime*]; 1318 – *PSRL*, X, 184; 1319 – *Stryjkowski*, I, 360; 1320 – *Stryjkowski*, I, 363, 365; 1324 – *GL*, 137; 1325 – *PSRL*, X, 189; 1331 – See below p. 112; 1333 – *PSRL*, X, 206; XV(i), 47; 1338 – *PSRL*, X, 208; 1339 – *TL*, 63; *PSRL*, X, 211, XV(i), 51–2; 1340 – *CDP*, III, no. 21, p.34.

[130] See n. 129.

illata a Tartaris ('much damage caused by the Tatars') should be *illata a fratribus* ('caused by the [Teutonic] Brethren').[131] This suggestion is almost certainly correct. The Knights did attack Bisenė several times between 1313 and 1316 as other Teutonic sources which do not mention the Tatars reveal.[132] Paszkiewicz also questioned the value of certain entries in the Nikon Chronicle which refer to Tatar raids in 1325 and 1338. He was unhappy with the formulaic nature of these one line accounts[133] but it is perhaps unwise to quarrel with the Chronicle's laconic style and obsession with *topoi*. The same bare phrases are used of other undoubtedly genuine military campaigns: *воеваше Литву*, 'they made war on Lithuania'; 'and they came to the Horde with many prisoners', *и со многимъ полономъ приидоша въ Орду*.[134] Although the chronicler may have known no more details or even have chosen to suppress tales of these Tatar offensives, his barebones style does not mean he invented the battles.

Stryjkowski mentions Lithuano-Tatar relations twice: in 1319 the Tatars helped Gediminas in his war with the Order but in 1320 (*sic*) they fought alongside the Rus'ians of Galich–Volyn' against Lithuania.[135] This is a common pattern in Tataro-Lithuanian affairs.

The papal legates' envoys who came to Vilnius in November 1324 report that they were unable to gain a private audience with Gediminas because he was 'occupied with the Tatars': *cum Tartaris erat impeditus*.[136] It seems logical to assume that Tatar envoys had come to Vilnius to seek an explanation for Gediminas' seizure of Kiev and settle a *modus vivendi* with the new power in southern Rus'. The military expedition sent in 1325 was presumably a response to Gediminas' alliance with Poland and the institution of Bolesław of Mazovia as prince of Galich–Volyn'.

The khan seems to have accustomed himself to the status quo fairly promptly. A period of peaceful coexistence with Lithuania began. In 1331 we read of a Tatar *basqaq* who accompanied Gediminas' brother Fëdor on a Lithuanian expedition to intercept Archbishop Kaleka. Normal Rus'ian life under Tatar hegemony

131 Paszkiewicz, *Jagiellonowie*, 334, n.1. *EpG*, 285 dates the 'Tatar' attack on Bisenė to *post palmarum* of *eodem anno*; no date is specified in the text. *PD*, 183 dates a Teutonic attack on Bisenė to 4 April 1316. In that year 4 April was Palm Sunday. It is reasonable to deduce that these two accounts describe the same event of 1316. Paszkiewicz did not note this chronological coincidence.

132 *PD*, 179–83.

133 See n. 131.

134 *PSRL*, X, 211.

135 See n. 129.

136 *GL*, 137.

seems to have continued in Kiev under the new regime. The *basqaq* was no doubt present to oversee the payment of tribute to the khan.

Although Lithuania did not pay tribute to the Golden Horde, some of the Rus'ian lands within the Grand Duchy, especially those in the south-west, were subject to Tatar demands for money or military service. This is evident not only from the presence of a *basqaq* in Kiev but also from *iarlyks* (patents to rule) granted to later grand dukes by the khans for Kiev, Vladimir and Smolensk and treaties such as that between Casimir of Poland and the Gediminaičiai where Liubartas of Volyn' promises not to join Tatar expeditions against Poland.[137]

When Lithuania became too powerful, the Tatars sustained Rus'ian opposition to Gediminas. In the winter of 1333, that year when Lithuanian troops guarded the Novgorodian frontier against Sweden and Kalita was reduced to seeking a marriage alliance with Lithuania, the khan set about chivvying Lithuanian towns in eastern Rus'. Dmitry Romanovich of Briansk, the same who fought Gediminas in 1323, attacked the client city of Smolensk. He was aided by the Tatars Kolontai and Chiricha and many generals but he was forced to make peace with Ivan Aleksandrovich of Smolensk, presumably because Gediminas defended his 'younger brother'.[138]

The attack on Lithuania so tersely reported in the Nikon Chronicle s.a. 1338 seems similarly to be connected with Lithuanian policy in Rus'. Following the sequence of events recorded for 1338, it is noticeable that Kalita came from Moscow to the Horde; the Tatars attacked the Grand Duchy; malicious reports about Aleksandr Mikhailovich of Tver', Gediminas' former vassal, caused the khan to summon Aleksandr to the Horde where he was murdered in 1339.[139] We may deduce that the raid on the Grand Duchy was a warning to Gediminas not to interfere in Rus'.

In the winter of 1339–40, after Ivan Aleksandrovich of Smolensk had made an agreement with the Order which complemented the trade treaty signed by Gediminas and the

137 B. N. Floria, 'Litva i Rus' pered bitvoi na Kulikovskom Pole', *Kulikovskaia Bitva: Sbornik statei* (Moscow, 1980), 145–8. Also *AZR*, I, no. 1, p. 1.

138 See n. 129 and Fennell, *Emergence*, 171.

139 Especially Gediminas' support for Aleksandr Mikhailovich after Aleksandr returned to Tver' in 1337 – Fennell, *Emergence*, 163. Also *PSRL*, X, 208.

Livonians in 1338, the khan sent an envoy named Tovluby and a warrior called Mengutash to attack Smolensk. They were accompanied by a Rus'ian army from Riazan' (again mentioned as an opponent of Lithuania in 1333), Moscow, Suzdal', Rostov and Yur'ev, but as in 1333 the attack failed.[140] The villages surrounding Smolensk were ravaged and many captives were taken but Smolensk itself did not fall. Again Gediminas seems to have supported Ivan Aleksandrovich in the defence of his city.

Despite the enmity of 1339, by December 1340 the Tatars were allied with Lithuania. In that month Prussian bishops complained that recently the 'emperor of the Tatars together with his princes, especially the rulers of the Lithuanians and the Rus'ians' were disrupting trade with Prussia.[141] Meanwhile Casimir of Poland had begun the struggle with Lithuania for control of south-west Rus'.[142]

In purely Rus'ian terms, Lithuania, after 1327 was slowly replacing Tver' as Moscow's chief rival for supremacy in Rus'. When Tver' sought prominence later in the century, that prominence rested upon alliance with Lithuania.[143] However for the Tatars perhaps, Lithuania was a second Galich–Volyn': a western buffer against Poland and the Order, which as ruler of Kiev and ally of Bolesław-Yury, it in fact was. When Lithuanian power was too strong in Rus', the khan retaliated with violent warnings; when Lithuanian princes sought aid against Poland they received it, if it was not dangerous to Rus' to grant it them.

This friendship could not be presumed by Lithuanian rulers. When Narimantas-Gleb fled Lithuania in 1345 in the wake of Algirdas and Kestutis' coup d'état, he was welcomed by the khan.[144] However when Karijotas, another brother, was sent east by Algirdas in 1348 to request aid against the Order, he was handed over to the Muscovites for ransom.[145] The khan had no doubt viewed support for Moscow against Lithuania as a more urgent priority in 1348 than Lithuania's need for help from the Horde against the Teutonic Knights. When Moscow and Lithuania were at peace after 1349 the khan, Jani Beg, was ready to help

[140] See p. 258. and above n. 129.
[141] See n. 129.
[142] Shabul'do, *Zemli*, 39f.
[143] Fennell, *Emergence*, 106–9, 234f.
[144] *NL*, 358. The garbled version is in Dmitrieva, *Skazanie*, 180. The legend that Narimantas married a Tatar princess lacks a serious basis in our sources despite the protestations of the Rożyński clan – K. Niesiecki, *Herbarz Polski*, VIII (Leipzig, 1841; 2nd edn, Warsaw, 1979), 168.
[145] *TL*, 370; *PSRL*, XV (i), 59.

Lithuania by raiding Podolia and Galich which were under Polish control.[146]

We may conclude that a re-evaluation of *L2* and the west Rus'ian historiographical tradition has proved necessary to develop a fuller picture of Lithuanian power in the early fourteenth century. The hypercritical approach to sixteenth-century texts established in the late nineteenth century in reaction to the uncritical methods of earlier scholars, must itself be revised in the light of discoveries made since Antonovich wrote his monographs on Ukrainian history. A more sympathetic but no less rigorous analysis of these texts reveals valuable, albeit vague information about the expansion of Lithuania.

This expansion, begun in the thirteenth century, continued at a greater rate throughout the reign of Gediminas. The boundaries of the state were spread by means of diplomatic marriage, close political alliances based on trade or fear of a mutual enemy and not least, by war. The role of Lithuanian princesses who were sent abroad as the wives of foreign princes should not be neglected. Their control of considerable financial resources, especially when widowed and their choice of spouse for their own offspring made them a formidable fifth column in Poland and Rus' familiarising Christian peoples with the daughters 'of Belial'.

Historians have long remarked on the broad scope and peaceful nature of Lithuanian expansion.[147] In this they are abetted by the lack of records from the cities which were so 'peacefully' annexed. Silent screams become cries of joy. Later in the century, Algirdas found it necessary to regain by force of arms the cities of Kiev, Smolensk and Polotsk. Lithuania would be the only power in history to which peoples have willingly bent the knee. The Lithuanians, skilled as they were in diplomacy, did not shirk the use of main force when such proved necessary to the growth of their dominion. Relations with Rus' in the thirteenth century were largely bellicose, although war often alternated with alliance. In the fourteenth and fifteenth centuries grand-ducal authority needed to reassert itself several times in western Rus' through force of arms. The capture and partial surrender of Galich–Volyn' illustrates the complexity of the growth of the Grand Duchy and may shed light on what is generally perceived as the peaceful annexation of western Rus'.

[146] Fennell, *Emergence*, 201.
[147] Fennell, *Emergence*, 124, 145; Giedroyć, 'Arrival ... (1281–1341)', 30.

Despite the need to balance the 'peaceful expansion' thesis of Russian historiography, it must be stated that the Rus'ian cities under Lithuanian hegemony were not disadvantaged by their incorporation into the Grand Duchy. Lithuanian domination meant the rule of a strong prince, usually of Lithuanian stock, who swore allegiance and paid revenues to the grand duke. This allegiance also entailed the provision of troops for the Lithuanian army serving on the Livonian border. It did not mean slavery. The Lithuanians had been familiar to the inhabitants of western Rus' for centuries. In return the Slavs enjoyed the *pax lithuanica* which protected their trade routes to the Hansa and defended them from the depredations of the grand dukes of Moscow. They were not freed from Tatar tribute, but this could hardly be expected. The Lithuanians respected local religious and political practices. If the declarations of fifteenth-century grand dukes made to vassals in Rus' reflect the attitude of fourteenth-century Lithuanian rulers, then in return for loyalty and the provision of service the grand duke promised to introduce no new laws and to respect the status quo: *my novin' ne uvodim', a starin' ne rukhaem'*.[148] This is not the mark of a primitive regime but a sophisticated recognition of how best to exploit alien subjects.

It is all too easy to concentrate on the size of Gediminas' conquests. Such an achievement would be remarkable enough for a prince of Poland or Moscow. Lithuania was a pagan state which carved out a Christian empire but not as the Mongols did. The Tatars ruled over Rus' but pressurised its princes from the outside; the Lithuanians insinuated themselves into the system of eastern Christendom.

As for Mongol reaction to the Grand Duchy, the Tatars accepted Lithuanian expansion while it did not interfere with their hegemony in Rus'. Violence and diplomacy were used to temper Lithuanian power while always an eye scanned the political usefulness of the Grand Duchy as a bulwark against the Poles.[149] The Poles in their turn regarded Lithuania as a shield against the Tatars.

Lithuano-Tatar relations were practical. When the Tatars got in

[148] Grand Duke Alexander endows Mikhail Zheslavsky as *namestnik* in Vitebsk with these words, 11.04.1495 – *AZR*, I, no. 127, p. 151. Cf. *ibid*., no. 90, p. 110 (*c*. 1486) and *AZR*, II, no. 204, p. 368 (19.02.1540). This style is mirrored in Vytautas' dealing with the Orthodox Church, see p. 186.

[149] Violence was used against Smolensk in 1333 and 1339; diplomacy persuaded Novgorod not to abandon Moscow in 1334 – see pp. 250, 258.

Gediminas' way, he fought them but he did not go out of his way to arouse their displeasure. Tatar power in Rus' was respected. Gediminas certainly did not ally himself with Moscow or even Tver' against the khan. Lithuanian conflict and cooperation with the Tatars increased sharply in Algirdas' time when Lithuania was more clearly a Rus'-oriented state.

Chapter 5

POLITICAL RAMIFICATIONS OF THE PAGAN CULT

Muted horror and ignorance typify the reaction of learned Rus'ians to the arrival of the Tatar hordes in Kiev in 1240. How differently did the monks regard the horsemen who descended on their land from the west! When Lithuanian warriors first appropriated Polotsk and Novgorodok around 1250, the natives were curious to learn what the invaders believed. They were familiar with Lithuanians, for the two peoples had been at daggers drawn since the early eleventh century. In the 1260s the compiler of a Rus'ian version of a Byzantine chronicle saw fit to describe the religious practices of 'our Lithuanians' in an aside from his main text.[1] Those who wish to assess the influence of Christendom on the Grand Duchy might imitate the translator and investigate Lithuanian paganism, especially since one might easily presume that a non-Christian state was altogether alien to a Christian one. Who were the Lithuanian deities, how was the pagan cult practised and most pertinently, what was the relevance of the latter to the government of the Grand Duchy?

For answers to these questions we must turn to written accounts[2] and the discoveries of archaeologists, and to a lesser degree, to surviving Lithuanian folklore and the hypotheses of linguists. Through Christian eyes we see Balts who usually conform to Christian models of paganism, although sometimes the pagans and their practices are noted as dispassionately as an antiquary might describe a curious shard. The records of Gediminas' dealings with Catholics between 1322 and 1324 and the record of his reaction to the very thought that he might be baptised allow us to glimpse through a very dark mirror the heathens' own world view.

In the thirteenth and fourteenth centuries the Lithuanians

[1] See below pp. 129–30.

[2] Most of these sources have been collated in: A. Mierzyński, *Źródła do mytologii litewskiej*, I–II (Warsaw, 1892–96); Mannhardt, *Götterlehre*.

appear to have venerated a particularly holy triad of deities.[3] Whether or not these three gods – Perkūnas, the Lithuanian version of the Slavonic Perun and the Norse Thorr, Andai/Andojas and the smith-god Teliavel/Kalevelis – represent the patrons of the ruling house remains unclear.[4] The popularity of the sky god, Perkūnas, who sometimes appears under the title *Diviriks* (interpreted either as 'chief of the gods' – *Dievų Rikys* – or *Dievų Rykste* – 'scourge of the gods') long outlived the official conversion of Lithuania to Catholicism (1387–1417), but it seems that in Žemaitija he yielded first place in the pantheon to a god of the earth. The cult of Perkūnas was condemned, as in the first extant Lithuanian text – Mažvydas' Catechism of 1547 – almost as often as the god was invoked.[5] Thus from the outset we should be aware that our somewhat partial evidence is subject to biases of time and place. There is no reason to expect that pagan religion should have a canonical pantheon where the same hierarchy of gods is maintained throughout long periods or across wide areas of terrain. A strong written culture is necessary to overcome the tendency to localised devotion to a divine patron. We shall see that cult practices also varied from district to district and from one time to another.

All manner of spirits populated the air and the Underworld.[6]

[3] Mannhardt, *Götterlehre*, 341–401. A table of fourteen gods is given in V. N. Toporov, 'Zametki po baltiiskoi mifologii', *Balto-Slavianskii Sbornik* (1972), 289–314, esp. pp. 293 and 312.

[4] Perun – A. Brückner, *Mitologia słowiańska i polska*, ed. S. Urbańczyk (Warsaw, 1985), 81f. According to A. J. Greimas, *Des Dieux et des hommes* (Paris, 1985), 131–3. The Triad evolves as:

Malalas (Mannhardt, *Götterlehre*, 58)	Andai	Perkūnas	Teliavel	
Ipat'evskaia, 1252 (*PSRL*, II, 817)	Andai	Diviriks	Teliavel	Meidein
Ipat'evskaia, 1258 (*PSRL*, II, 839)	Andai	Diviriks	-	

Greimas calls Andai a water-god (Greimas, *Des Dieux*, 132) but Toporov considers him to have been a chief god (Toporov, 'Zametki', 310, 313). On the lack of any well-defined system of pagan gods and beliefs among the Germanic peoples see H. R. Ellis Davidson, *Myths and symbols in pagan Europe. Early Scandinavian and Celtic religions* (Manchester, 1988), 198.

[5] Toporov, 'Zametki', 310. See *Litauische und Lettische Drucke des 16 Jahrhunderts herausgegeben von Adalbert Bezzenberger*, I: *Der Litauische Katechismus von Jahre* 1547 (Göttingen, 1874), 3.

[6] Greimas, *Des Dieux*, 29–78. For 'Qui ad malas artes adiiciunt animum Eithuaros et Caucos deos profitentur suos' – *Litauische Katechismus*, *1547*, 3. For *veles*, the spirits of the dead see M. Gimbutas, *The Balts* (London, 1963), 189f.

The natural world seems to have been god-sated and thanks to this plethora of deities the pagans did not appreciate the exclusivity of Christian belief. There is no reason why they should have. Even after King Mindaugas became a Catholic, he did not cease sacrificing to his old gods, a practice which led the Rus'ian chronicler to view the whole conversion as an act of deceit. A similar interpretation was put on Mindaugas' actions by a witness to the commission of inquiry headed by the papal legate, Francis of Moliano, in 1312 who recalled that 'the said king was a christian and kept clergy but he still maintained his earlier errors'.[7] The Church could not acknowledge that in the case of many newly converted peoples, baptism did not represent so much the desired continual *metanoia* as a practical change of name which could be merely temporary. In effect, this meant simply the addition of Christ to the established pantheon. Lithuanian paganism was in essence utilitarian. There was no danger in accepting a new god, but for the superstitious pagan there lurked potential peril in the rejection of an old one.

Pagan survivals in neophyte countries are almost too numerous to merit note. The Swedes and Goths kept their pagan deities in reserve for times of trouble, while Raedwald of Kent, Samaritan-like, kept one altar for Christ and a smaller *arulam* 'for offerings to demons'.[8] The syncretism of the Lithuanians is by no means unique to that people; it is a type of conversion which Nock classifies as 'adhesion'.[9] On more than one occasion even syncretism could not take root. After John of Bohemia had defeated the Lithuanians at Medvegalis in February 1329 and forced 6,000 to submit to baptism, the neophytes returned to their vomit almost as soon as the Bohemian's back was turned.[10]

How then did the preferred native religion function? The ways in which the pagan Lithuanians revered the divine were many and varied. A witness to the coronation of Mindaugas in 1253 summed

[7] *PSRL*, II, 817, and Seraphim, *Das Zeugenverhör*, V, 16, p. 8.

[8] *Aelnothus monachus Cantuarensis, De vita et passione S. Canuti regis Daniae. Item anonymous, De passione S. Caroli comitis Flandriae eius filius*, ed. J. Meursius (Copenhagen, 1631), 9 (chapter 1 of *Canute*). On Raedwald see Bede, *Historia Ecclesiastica*, II, 15.

[9] M. Kosman, *Drogi zaniku pogaństwa u Baltów*, (Wrocław etc., 1976); and 'Pogaństwo, Chrześcijaństwo i synkretizm na Litwie w dobie Przedreformacyjnej', *Komunikaty Mazuro-Warmińskie*, 115 (1972), 103–36. On 'adhesion', see A. D. Nock, *Conversion: the Old and the New in religion from Alexander the Great to Augustine of Hippo* (Oxford, 1933), 6–7.

[10] See pp. 239–40.

up pagan practices in Lithuania as the worhip of special trees as gods and the following of many auguries. 'They burned their dead with their horses and weapons and better apparel because they believe they may use these and the other things they burn in the next world.'[11]

Whether or not the Lithuanians held woods and trees to be gods, they certainly regarded them as holy.[12] In the *Ipat'evskaia Chronicle* we read that when Mindaugas rode out into a field and a hare crossed his path he would not enter the grove which lay across his route nor even dare to break a twig.[13] Like the pagan Irish *bíle*, certain groves were held to be sacred and not to be profaned. Apart from sites in Vilnius, notably the area which Algirdas handed over to the Orthodox Church to build the monastery of the Holy Trinity[14] and the unnamed grove where a Franciscan friar was martyred in 1341,[15] there were several holy groves or *al̃kos* in northern Lithuania, many of which are recorded in the Teutonic Knights' handbook of routes, the *Wegeberichte*.[16] According to Toporov, the term *al̃ka* denotes a sacred grove or hill of sacrifice and occurs in numerous Lithuanian toponyms and hydronyms, especially in Žemaitija and Semigallia. These are the 'holy pine woods (as they call them), where they burn the bodies of their dead and render them as a sacrifice' which are mentioned by the French chronicler, Jean Cabaret d'Orville. This author mentions how the Knights were willing to respect the sanctity of these shrines.[17] Žemaitija was both rich and stubborn in pagan beliefs and holy sites, and her tribesmen were to prove the most

[11] Colker, 'America', 722.

[12] *Opusculum contra canciones adversum regem Albertum confictas*, lines 7–8 in T. Tyc, 'Inwekty na Litwinów i Polaków z XV wieku', *AW*, 4 (1927), 459.

[13] *PSRL*, II, 817. Cf. the western superstition, 'Leporis timebis occursum' – John of Salisbury, *Polycraticus*, PL, CXCIX (Paris, 1855), 412.

[14] For *bíle* see F. J. Byrne, *Irish Kings and High Kings* (London, 1973), 27. On Lithuanian groves – *Długosz* X, 168. Tradition relates that Algirdas built the Holy Trinity Monastery on the site of a sacred grove – F. Dobrianskii, *Staraia i novaia Vil'na*, 3rd edn (Vilnius, 1904), 128; see figure 2, p. 70.

[15] The Franciscan was punished 'in quodam nemore iuxta ripam Vilnensis fluminis' – 'Passio fratrum Ulrici de Adlechonwitz et Martini de Ahd', *Analecta Franciscana*, 3 (Quaracchi, 1910), 536. See below pp. 275–7.

[16] See *al̃ka* in *Encyclopedia Lituanica*, I (Boston, 1970), 76. *SRP*, II, 662–708 or *Kraštas ir žmonės. Lietuvos geografiniai ir etnografiniai aprašymai* (*XIV–XIXa.*), ed. J. Jurginis and A. Sidlauskas (Vilnius, 1983), 8–42.

[17] V. N. Toporov, *Prusskii Iazyk. Slovar' A-D* (Moscow, 1975), 72–4. Jean Cabaret d'Orville, *La chronique du bon duc Loys de Bourbon*, ed. A. M. Chazaud (Paris, 1876), 65: 'saints bois (que ainsi ils appellent) des pins, ou ils consumoient les corps de leurs morts par feu, et en faisoient sacrifice'.

staunch in their defence of the old ways as Christianity gained the upper hand in Lithuania.[18]

Springs, rivers and rocks were also accounted holy by the heathens. Hallowed rainwater was stored in the hollows of sacrificial stones. In Poland too springs and trees were honoured by the people, while in Rus', we read, the Poliane 'are pagans who sacrifice to lakes and springs and groves like other heathens do'.[19] The whole world of nature was highly valued by the Lithuanians and their Scandinavian and Slavonic neighbours. Rus'ians were constantly chided by canon-lawyers for praying in groves or by the water's edge.[20] In a predominantly rural society like that of Lithuania or Rus', it is no surprise to find natural sites used as places of worship. Religion develops everywhere out of local needs and expresses itself in images and practices which arise from local conditions.

Favoured ways of discovering the will of the gods included reading omens from the behaviour of certain animals, especially snakes and horses which were particularly revered. The green snake or *žaltys* was not to be harmed by anyone because he gives omens of good and bad fortune. He was kept in the byre and treated with great respect. The pig represented a harbinger of life in the Other World and was regarded as a particular servant of water gods such as Upinis. The pig or boar appears in stories of life after death.[21] The horse too was venerated by the pagans.

The cult of the horse extended from the totemistic use of horse-skulls as protection from evil spirits to the carving of twin horses (*žirgẽlis*) on the gables of houses and the burial of the remains of the dead (burned or unburned) with horses (dead or alive).[22] The horse was a major piece of battle equipment for the pagan warriors

[18] E. Sturms, 'Baltische Alkhügel', *Conventus primus historicorum Balticorum* (Riga, 1938), 116–32 and 23 plates.

[19] Gimbutas, *Balts*, 195–6. B. Gierlach, 'Wczesnośredniowieczne ośrodki kultu pogańskiego w Polsce', *Euhemer-Przegląd Religioznawczy* (1979/2), 19–24. *NL*, 105.

[20] Shchapov, *Ustavy*, 47. For an account of similar worship see 'Povest' o vodvorenii Khristianstva v' Murome', *Pamiatniki Starinnoi russkoi literatury*, ed. N. Kostomarov (St Petersburg, 1860), 235.

[21] *Opusculum*, lines 23–24, Tyc, 'Inwekty', 459. On pigs see N. Vėlius, *The world outlook of the Ancient Balts* (Vilnius, 1989), 107 and below p. 130.

[22] Gimbutas, *Symbolism*, 43, 113–14. More often than not the horse is to be found in the graves of wealthy men where it was placed alongside other grave goods to help the deceased on his journey to the next world. The account given by Ibn Fadlan of a Rus' burial on the banks of the Volga in 922 comes to mind as one reads in Peter of Dusburg of a horse which is ridden to exhaustion before its consignment to eternity alongside its master – cf. *PD*, 54 with Ibn Fadlan in J.Brønsted, *The Vikings* (London, 1980), 303.

and as such it acquired great value. It was not in itself sacred but was hallowed by its role as a servant of the gods. In some areas a black horse could not be ridden, in others a white mount was not permitted to carry mortals, for such animals belonged to the gods.[23] Perkūnas had his own fiery steed named Lieponotas and Dievas owned a whole stable of mounts caparisoned in silver and furbished with gold.[24] As a means of divining the will of the gods, the horse was used by Lithuanian and Slav alike. Bishop Theodoric was no doubt relieved that the horse of the Livs at Thoreyda put forward its 'foot of life' and saved him from being sacrificed to the gods to make it rain. The sacrifice of horses (and riders) as thanksgiving for success in battle is far from uncommon in Scandinavian and Baltic religion.[25]

Farmers supervised religious practice in their communities. This practice involved harvest sacrifices and prayers in the corn stores where sacred stones were buried.[26] What else would we expect from an agricultural society attuned to magic in the natural world? Even so the farmers and their wives were by no means the only ministers of the pagan cult. Both priests and priestesses existed in pagan Lithuania and indeed the patron of *matresfamilias*, Dimstapatis, was served by leading women of the community. *Vetulae* ('witches') and *prophetissae* enjoyed honour as did their male counterparts, just as female soothsayers had been revered by the Slavs at Arkona or the Vikings in Iceland.[27] The role of women should not be underestimated in a cult which still revered a pantheon of goddesses even older than Perkūnas and his fellow male deities. Similar religious functions were performed by

[23] *PD*, 55. For the white horse of Swantowit at Arkona see Saxo Grammaticus, *Historia Danica*, ed. P. E. Müller and J. M. Velochow, II (Copenhagen, 1839), 826–7. The account here of the Arkona temple (*Historia*, Book XIV) is now regarded as authentic. See Saxo Grammaticus, *Danorum Regum Heroumque Historia Books X–XVI. The text of the first edition with translation and commentary in three volumes by E.Christiansen, II: Books XIV, XV and XVI, British Archaeological Reports*, International Series CXVIII(ii) (1981), 835–6 and 838, nn. 476 and 486 respectively.

[24] Gimbutas, *Balts*, 199 and P. Dundulienė, 'Arklys Lietuvių liaudies pasaulėjautoje', *LAMMDI*, 17:1 (1977), 83–102.

[25] Z. A. Rajewski, 'Koń w wierzeniach u Słowiań wczesnośredniowiecznych', *Wiadomości Archeologiczne*, 30:4 (1975), 516–21. Henry, *Chronicon*, I, 10, p.6. See also Ellis-Davidson, *Myths and symbols*, 54.

[26] *Annuae Litterae Societatis Jesu, 1600*, quoted by Greimas, *Des Dieux*, 169–70. Greimas discusses the term *horreum* here.

[27] *Annuae Litterae Societatis Jesu, 1604* (Douai, 1618), 746. Z. A. Rajewski, 'Pogańscy kapłani-czarodzieje w walce klasowej słowiań we wczesnym średniowieczu', *Wiadomości Archeologiczne*, 39:4 (1975), 503–9.

women in pagan Scandinavia before the end of the first Christian millennium.[28]

Holy men lived in the *Wildnis* in remote places which may or may not have been connected with the *sacrae villae*, manors in the wilderness which acted as places of refuge in war and cultic centres in times of peace,[29] but the most important priests, beside the princes were the priests of sacrifice, the *blûtekirl*. These were responsible for making offerings to the gods in return for victory in war (a third of the spoils was stipulated in thirteenth century treaties and chronicle records as a fit holocaust for the gods). They would cast lots before a battle and address encouragement to the warriors after the prince had done likewise.[30] The Lithuanians made sacrifices of objects and animals (cocks, pigs and oxen) and on very rare occasions, after an elaborate process of divination, they offered human victims to their gods. The Knights Gerard Rude and Nicholas Cassow were burned on horseback after the auguries had shown that such an offering would be efficacious.[31]

Lesser augurs called *tulissones* and *ligaschones* are known to us from the Treaty of Christburg which was concluded by the Prussians and the Teutonic Knights in 1249. Their titles are difficult to interpret etymologically but they were referred to as 'most deceitful actors who like heathen priests observe the torments of the damned in hell during funeral rites'.[32] They claimed the ability to see the souls of the dead ascending and descending and were employed to deliver funeral orations in their memory.

[28] On the earlier matriarchal religion of the Balts see M. Gimbutas, 'The pre-Christian religion of Lithuania', *La Cristianizzazione*, 16–19. On women and farm-centred cults in Scandinavia see G. Steinsland, in 'Kvinner og kult in Vikingtid', *Kvinnearbeid i Norden fra vikingtiden til reformasjonen*, ed. Andersen, Randi *et al.* (Bergen, 1985), 31–42.

[29] For *quendam sanctum virum* see *Wig.*, 542.

[30] *PD*, 54; *LR*, lines 4680–4683, p. 108, tr., p. 60 and lines 4653f., p. 107, tr., p. 60. *PD*, 153 is a case in point.

[31] Mažeika, 'Role', 119–20. Gerard Rude, *Vogt* of Sambia was captured in July 1320 and was sacrificed fully armed in a pyre – *PD*, 185; sixty years later the commandant of Memel suffered the same fate after lots had been cast. Like Gerard he was fully armed and mounted on a charger when he was burned to death – *Wig.*, 638, s.a. 1389. These are the only two examples of such a sacrifice that have survived in records. Perhaps this suggests that the elaborate ritual was not a frequent occurrence.

[32] Treaty of Christburg, 1249. Text in Pashuto, *Obrazovanie*, 494–507. Here see p. 500, §3: 'mendacissimos histriones qui quasi gentilium sacerdotes in exequiis defunctorum vae tormentorum infernalium promerentur'. On divination from the smoke of funeral pyres see also the record of Ghillebert de Lannoy who visited Lithuania in the early fifteenth century (1412): 'ilz se font ardoir en lieu de sépulture ... et croyent se la fumière va droit ou ciel que l'âme est sauvée, mais s'elle va soufflant de costé, que l'âme est périe', *Oeuvres de Ghillebert de Lannoy*, 30.

A theory that the pagan cult was controlled by a high priest has held attractions for scholars since the 1320s. Historians particularly like to institutionalise life so as to make it clean for lofty theories. According to an early chapter of Part Three of Dusburg's Chronicle, there was to be found 'in the midst of a perverse nation' (the Prutheni), in Nadruvia, a 'certain place' called Romowe. Peter derives the name of this place explicitly from the papal city of Rome. There lived in Romowe (Romuva) a 'certain man' called Krivė, whom the people revered as pope, 'for just as the Lord Pope rules the universal church of the faithful, so not only the aforesaid peoples but also the Lithuanians and other nations of Livonia are ruled at his behest or command'.[33] Such was his authority, that when he or a member of his clan spoke or he sent his messenger 'with his rod or other recognised insignia' to any of the heathen territories, he was held in reverence by noble and commoner alike. He guarded the sacred flame; he was sought out by relatives of the dead to find out whether he had seen portents concerning their deceased kinsfolk. He received one third of any booty won by warriors in battle.

Such is the tale. There is no other account like it. The story was embellished considerably by sixteenth-century historians such as Simon Grunau.[34] Grunau's contemporaries in Lithuania wrote down the legend of one Lizdeika who appears to have been a soothsayer-prince (like Skumantas or Oleg) and Gediminas' *vorozhbit* ('sorcerer, fortune-teller'). He appears to have been a *pop poganskii*, a 'pagan priest' (but not a pagan pope). The Radvilas clan which produced several chancellors and bishops for Lithuania in the sixteenth century claimed descent from this wizard.[35] In the hands of Stryjkowski the pagan pope was equated with Lizdeika and the modern scholar Kosman continues the tradition, calling Lizdeika 'the last Krivė'.[36] Maciej of Miechów tried to make sense of the story by claiming that Krivė was mentioned in the *Life of St Adalbert*. He was not.[37]

33 *PD*, 53–4.

34 For Grunau's treatment of 'Kriwe-Kriwaito', see Mannhardt, *Götterlehre*, 190–227, esp. 205f.

35 *Letopis' Pantsyrnogo i Averki*, *PSRL*, XXXII, 194. For Lizdeika's connections with Kernavė and the Radvilai, see Semkowicz, 'O litewskich rodach', 61 and K. Aścik, 'O pochodzeniu rodu Ościków (legendy i rzeczywistość)', *Acta Baltico-Slavica*, 11 (1977), 317–29.

36 *Stryjkowski*, I, 371–2; Kosman, *Drogi*, 257.

37 Maciej z Miechowa, *Opis Sarmacji azjatyckiej i europejskiej*, ed. H. Barycz and T. Bieńkowski (Warsaw etc., 1972), 71: 'about Krivė and the place called Romuva we read in the Life of St Adalbert'. It is true that the Life of St Adalbert (*MGH. Scriptores*,

Elements of the story of Krivė ring true. The Treaty of Christburg, available to Peter as he wrote from the Order's Marienburg Archives, tells how the *tulissones* and *ligaschones* claimed to be able to see the souls of the dead mount to paradise. The Order's own *Livländische Reimchronik* speaks of the *blûtekirl* who collected a third part of the booty from Žemaitijan raiders as an offering to the gods.[38] Peter may even have heard of the temple in Vilnius (or of Lizdeika, if he lived).

However Romowe, the alleged cult-centre of all the Baltic tribes, this *locus quidam* (not a very specific term) is never mentioned anywhere else including the main text of Peter's own chronicle. Surely had Romowe existed and been so important, at least one narrative source would have mentioned it. The site has never been discovered, either by the Knights in the Middle Ages (despite the fact that they controlled the whole of Nadruvia) or modern archaeologists. The man who allegedly wielded supreme power over the whole Baltic region (*quidam*, *obriste*[39] – again very bland, unprovable terms translating 'a certain', although 'an uncertain' comes more readily to mind) has never been described in action by accounts of life in Lithuania or anywhere else. A century ago Brückner remarked that 'Krivė did not exist nor were there any statues in Romowe; we suppose that *Krivė* was not the name of a man or any ruling chief priest but of the rod, *krzywula* which priests sent to the people to gather them together for the annual temple sacrifice'.[40]

Krivė the pope did not exist. He was Peter's creation designed to make the Baltic religion appear like the 'counter-church' which Christiansen, to cite but one example, dutifully deduces from it.[41] In describing pagan belief Peter had to work according to his own model of how religion was run. His evidence was written, oral and perhaps even empirical and had to make sense from a Christian point of view. He is rather like the author of the *Chanson de Roland*

IV (Hanover, 1841), 593) speaks of a *sacerdos ydolarum* but there is no way of linking this priest with Krivė or *Romuva*. 38 See above p. 124.

39 Jeroschin, 348f. The translation of Peter's section on the customs of Prussia begins at line 3983. Jeroschin introduces Krivė thus: [4020] 'Dî stat dî hîz Rômowe/ und was nâch Rôme genant,/ want dar was wonende irkant/ der *obriste* êwarte/ nâch heidenischir arte/ Criwe was genant sîn name'.

40 A. Brückner, *Starożytna Litwa*: *Ludy i bogi. Szkice historyczne i mitologiczne*, ed. J. Jaskanis (Olsztyn, 1985), 22. Brückner's conclusion has been ignored by scholars since who prefer the romance of Krivė the Pope. See M. Kosman, 'Polskie, rosyjskie i radzieckie badania nad religią Bałtów', *Euhemer-Przegląd Religioznawczy* (1976/1), 45–7. 41 Christiansen, *Northern crusades*, 137.

who tried to make the Saracen enemy of another crusade comprehensible to his French audience by inventing for the heathen a devilish 'trinity' of their own.[42] It is fitting that Peter refers to Baligant the villain of the *Chanson* elsewhere in his work. It seems never to have struck scholars as oddly convenient that in a place named after Rome there lived a man whom his neighbours treated as a pope. He even appears to field *legati a latere* who bear insignia and are obeyed as the Pope would be.[43] Efforts have been made to find Romuva (the root *Rom* is quite common)[44] but it has remained elusive. Perhaps in the wilds of Nadruvia there was a holy grove called Romowe but it would be unlikely that the centre of a pagan cult remained in a war-zone controlled by the Knights, when pagans who wished to save their religion had already taken to fleeing to Lithuania, since in Vilnius there flourished a strong and secure pagan cult. Even if Romuva did exist, there was no pope. The *sacra villa* of Romene in Aukštaitija which Peter notes s.a. 1294 was not the residence of a high-priest.[45]

When Laurenz Blumenau wrote his *Historia de Ordine Theutonicorum Cruciferorum* in 1457, he condensed Peter's introduction into his own text but he replaced the name Krivė with the plain noun *augur* or *aruspex* ('seer') when he described pagan rites.[46] As for any papal equivalents in Lithuania, he ignored the idea completely, as he did the 'Roman' Romowe.

The search for Krivė has become so desperate that wholly ingenious false logic has been employed in exegesis. Toporov is very keen on linking Krivė with the existence in Vilnius of a *castrum curvum*, called in Russian *Krivoi gorod*.[47] This was a large fort capable of defending thousands of refugees which Ochmański locates across the river from Gediminas' castle.[48] The name means 'crooked' castle and refers either to the castle or the hill on which it stood that was not level. If *castrum curvum* is to mean 'Krivė's

[42] *La Chanson de Roland*, ed. F. Whitehead (Oxford, 1965), 79, lines 2696–2697.

[43] Baligant – *PD*, 76. For Krivė's *baculus* see Brückner, *Starożytna*, 45 and A. Mierzyński, 'Nuncius cum baculo', *Wisła*, 9:2 (1895), 361–95. On the insignia of papal legates (representatives of whom visited Vilnius in 1324 – see below p. 222), see R. A. Schmutz, 'Medieval papal representatives: legates, nuncios and judges-delegate', *Studia Gratiana*, 15 (1972), 455–6 and n. 44.

[44] Batūra, *PD*, 355f.

[45] *PD*, 159.

[46] Laurenz Blumenau, *Historia de Ordine Theutonicorum Cruciferorum*, *SRP*, IV, 35–73.

[47] V. N. Toporov, 'Vilnius, Wilno, Vil'na: Gorod i mif', *Balto-Slavianskie Etnoiazykovye kontakty*, ed. T. M. Sudnik (Moscow, 1980), 64; and *Prusskii Iazyk. K-L* (Moscow, 1984), 196–205. On *Krivoi Gorod*, see Ochmański, 'Krzywy Gród', 57–66.

[48] *CEV*, 1009–10, §XXII.

castle' it should read *castrum Criwe* (as Gediminas' fort is called by the chroniclers *castrum Gedeminne*). *Krivoi Gorod* in Vilnius has no more to do with the putative Krivė than a winding street in Warsaw's Stare Miasto (*Krzywy*) was the man's second home. At best it could be a confusion of a real place with a fictional man. If Krivė was the Vilnius high priest, why did Peter, who was writing at the time the temple was functioning in Vilnius place his 'pope' in a dangerous provincial backwater? Brückner's attempt to salvage a literal interpretation of Peter's text by inventing a crooked wand is similarly futile.

We have already noted how Peter marshals his material very carefully in an attempt to make pagan society understood by his Christian readers while, at the same time, using the Order's achievements in the north as a means of reforming the Knights.[49] The idea of a central priesthood whose leader is obeyed was particularly attractive to a priest dealing with conflict between the various Christian peoples, the German emperor and the Roman pontiff. However from what we see of pagan cult practices in sources other than and including Peter, the lack of uniformity of practice and belief is striking. However a similar picture emerges from studies of Germanic and Scandinavian religion. It is easy to forget that religion is a dynamic and mutable force which is governed by physical, geographic and political needs within a changing society.

Of all religious ceremonies, those which surround death reveal most about a society. An investigation of elaborate Lithuanian burial customs shows that the Baltic peoples had no fixed method of despatching their loved ones. Some peoples at some times preferred cremation to inhumation as the quickest way to paradise; others chose the opposite. The text of the Christburg Treaty is a more accurate guide to pagan funerary custom than the emphasis laid on cremation alone by the unnamed witness of Mindaugas' coronation. The treaty seeks to forbid natives from cremating the dead or burying them with horses and men (slaves) or weapons and raiment.[50] There are stories of pagan apostates who threw off the new religion and exhumed their wives and loved ones from Christian graves to reconsign them to paradise by fire in the holy places.[51]

Archaeological studies of Lithuanian tombs reflect the het-

[49] See above pp. 38–40.

[50] Pashuto, *Obrazovanie*, 500, §1.

[51] Henry, *Chronicon* XXVI, 8, p. 286–8.

erogeneity of pagan practice. Urbanavičius, who has devoted much time to pagan history, notes that in certain parts of Lithuania (mostly the north) corpses were always inhumed rather than cremated while in other areas (notably the west) the burning of the dead long survived the conversion to Catholicism which forbids this practice. The end of pagan cremation in Uliūnai can be dated to the mid-sixteenth century.[52] In some areas burials continued in pagan cemeteries with festal clothing (*įkapės*) and grave goods (including a horse or a bull) well into the seventeenth century.[53] It is apparent that pagan burial practices were subject to regional diversity. This variety of custom reflects the decentralised nature of the cult and, as we shall see, the attempt to centralise the cult in a temple was late and circumscribed.

Cremation was so deeply embedded in the Lithuanian mind that by the thirteenth century there already existed a legend about how the custom had come to be invented. Given the prevalence of cremation in the eastern regions of Lithuania, it is not surprising to find this story in a Rus'ian text. It is inserted into a west Rus'ian translation of the sixth-century Byzantine *Chronicle of John Malalas* which was compiled in 1261. A supplementary chapter entitled 'A tale of how there is pagan deceit in our Lithuania' was added to the chronicle text by an unknown compiler.[54] Similarities between the triad of gods in this translation and the accounts of Mindaugas' reign given in the *Ipat'evskaia Chronicle* in a section of that work which was composed in the 1260s, encourages a suspicion that the two texts may be related.[55]

[52] V. F. Urbanavičius, 'K voprosu o pogrebeniakh s trupopolozheniem XIVv. v Litve', *LMADA*, 21 (1966/2), 183–90. Uliūnai is a village in central Lithuania. For its burial customs see Urbanavičius, 'Senųjų tikėjimu reliktai Lietuvoje XV–XVII amžiais (3. Laidojimo papročiai Uliūnuose XVI–XVII amž.)', *LMADA*, 50 (1975/1), 51–62.

[53] V. F. Urbanavičius, 'Laidosena Lietuvoje XIV–XVII amžiais', *LMADA*, 22 (1966/3), 105–19. For grave-goods at Biačiai in the sixteenth century see G. Zabiela's report in *AO* (1985), 480. In 1985 K. Rickievičiutė unearthed a tomb with a horse among grave-goods – *ibid*, 485–6.

[54] Mannhardt, *Götterlehre*, 56–68 and Wolter, 'Mythologische Skizzen', 636–7. The tradition of the tale is discussed in V. N. Toporov, 'Ob odnoi 'iatviazhskoi' mifolegme v sviazi so slavianskoi parallel'iu', *Acta Baltico-Slavica*, 3 (1966), 143–9. See also above p. 32. On eastern Lithuanian aspects of the tale, see Vėlius, *World outlook*, 266.

[55] Compare texts mentioned above n. 4. The 'triad' of gods in these two texts is identical. There is in the *Ipat'evskaia Chronicle* s.a. 1114 (*PSRL*, II, 277–9) an interpolation into the *PVL* text which forms the basis of the early part of the chronicle. This interpolation, an account of certain pagan practices, is based on the *Chronicle of Malalas* (*PVL*, II, 480). On the possible connection between the chronicle *svod* of the 1260s and the Malalas text of 1261 (Mannhardt, *Götterlehre*, 56) see Rowell, 'Of men and monsters', 77. Cf. problems with transmission of Norse texts – Ellis-Davidson, *Myths and symbols*, 218.

The Malalas interpolation recounts how, after a certain man named Sovii died, a wild boar was sacrificed (we have already noted the connection between the pig and the Underworld), but instead of burning the spleens of the animal, his sons ate them. Sovii could not rest in peace and one of his sons had to try three ways of despatching the corpse. When Sovii was buried in a coffin, he was tormented by slugs and worms. When the son laid out his father in a tree, Sovii's soul was tormented as though stung by bees. Eventually the son built a pyre and burned his father's body, after which Sovii rested in peace 'like a babe in its cradle'. From that time on, says the legend, the bodies of deceased pagans were burned rather than interred. In this way 'the great devilish deceit was introduced among the Lithuanian people and the Jatwings, Prussians, Yem and Livonians and the many other heathens who are called *Sovitsa*'.[56] This *Sovitsa* or 'Sovidom' is almost an inverse of Christendom. Toporov derives both *Sovii* and *Sovitsa* from a common Baltic root associated with fire and the oven: *šauti*. Whether these various ways of dealing with the dead reflect the practices of different social groups so that only princes were cremated and priests interred, as seems to have been the case in Germanic and Scandinavian cults, is unclear.[57]

The grand dukes of Lithuania were certainly princes of this Sovidom. Elaborate cremation rituals followed their deaths until Lithuania was brought to the font in 1387. The last princely pyre was lit in 1382 for Kestutis, prince of Trakai and regent of western Lithuania, as one had been in 1342 for his father Gediminas and in 1377 for his brother Algirdas. The corpses of all three leaders were brought to Vilnius for cremation amid great panoply. Horses (in Algirdas' case, eighteen destriers), hounds and hawks accompanied their master to the flames beside a trusted servant.[58]

The French diplomat Philippe de Mézières who came to Lithuania on *Reise* in 1364 describes the funeral of a grand duke. Not too long before Philippe's arrival, a rite had taken place during which the corpse of the grand duke equipped with weapons and arrayed in splendour, was cremated on horseback on

[56] Mannhardt, *Götterlehre*, 58.

[57] V. N. Toporov, 'Zametki po pokhoronnoi obriadnosti', *Balto-Slavianskie Issledovania* (1985), 10–52. Sovii is dealt with on pp. 24–8. For a list of Toporov's latest work, see *ibid.*, 24, n. 8. See also G. Beresnevičius, *Dausos* (Klaipėda, 1990), 72–85. On reflection of social status, see Vėlius, *World outlook*, 267.

[58] Gediminas' funeral is described in *Stryjkowski*, I, 385–6. Algirdas' cremation given in *HW*, 113. Kestutis' death is recalled by *Wig.*, 620 and *Stryjkowski*, II, 65.

a mass of pine branches, constructed like a *messangiere* (bird trap). His *bon amy*, a faithful servant was burned with him.[59] The grand duke's noblemen had wished to burn a Catholic captive who had become a favourite of the late prince alongside his master. However the wily Knight persuaded the pagans that since he had only one eye, he would not be a suitable offering, and he was allowed to return to Prussia.[60] Since the last grand-ducal funeral before 1377 was that of Gediminas in 1342 and de Mézières came to Lithuania in 1364, it seems prudent to agree with Nikžentaitis that the grand duke of Philippe's story was Gediminas.[61] This grand duke is known to have had a German favourite who escaped from captivity,[62] and the details of the cremation (the horse, apparel, pine pyre, sacrificial servant and German slaves) fit the data given by Stryjkowski for Gediminas' funeral. Stryjkowski did not know of de Mézières' account.

The funeral rite was presided over by Gediminas' sons who also used the occasion to decide upon the implementation of their father's will. Only princes directed the ceremonial of a grand duke's funeral. Kestutis, who cremated his brother Grand Duke Algirdas in 1377, was himself consigned to the flames five years later by Skirgaila, his would-be successor as duke of Trakai.[63] Skirgaila had transported the corpse of Kestutis from Krėva to Vilnius. The importance of this city in the ceremonies which involved the grand dukes (both inaugural and funerary) deserves closer attention.

Vilnius had been the resting place of princes from at least the thirteenth century. Cremation there cannot be separated from the legend of Šventaragis, a mythical (which is not a synonym for non-existent) thirteenth-century prince. He is associated with the keeping of the sacred flame in the Vilnius valley which bears his name: *Šventaragio slėnys* to the west of the castle on the other side of the Vilnia river forming a symbolic 'world beyond the waters'.[64]

[59] V. Kiparsky, 'Philippe de Mézières sur les rives de la Baltique', *Neuphilologischen Mitteilungen*, 41 (1940), 65, n. 1; de Mézières, *Songe*, I, 235–7. On the death of Gediminas, see below, pp. 270f. The details of weaponry, clothing, the faithful servant, German captives and the *pine* pyre are given in *Stryjkowski*, I, 385–6.

[60] de Mézières, *Songe*, I, 237.

[61] Nikžentaitis, 'Dar kartą', 37.

[62] *Wig.*, 494–5. This knight escaped from Vilnius four years before Gediminas died but confusion between the story of a knight's escape and the funeral sacrifice is not impossible.

[63] *Stryjkowski*, II, 65.

[64] For Šventaragis see Kosman, *Drogi*, 13, 20, 36 and Giedroyć, 'Rulers', 14. Toporov, 'Zametki po pokhoronnoi', 28–30 investigates the legend. The Balts were widely renowned as 'fire-worshippers' – see the patriarchal bull appointing Kiprian as

It was here that Gediminas is said by the authors of *L2* to have established his citadel of Vilnius.[65]

Long before Gediminas built his citadel in Vilnius, the site enjoyed political and religious significance. Mindaugas had built his Catholic cathedral there in the 1250s and before that the valley of Šventaragis and the grove of Lukiškai had been important cult sites, *pace* Gudavičius.[66] These sites were a major focus of pagan worship in a city where a temple probably did not exist before Gediminas' day.

In northern Europe in general and Lithuania in particular the temple seems to have been a late development, an attempt to centralise pagan religious practice alongside the growth of royal power. The temple at Uppsala described by Adam of Bremen was not an ancient construction and the rites which so fascinated the chronicler were conducted in a nearby grove rather than the temple itself. It appears that the role of the temple had not yet been fully established. Contact with the gods took place in the open in Germanic societies, as it did among the Balts in their *al̃kos* and the Celts in the groves termed *nemeton*.[67] The Uppsala, Lejre and Arkona temples of the Swedes, Danes and Wends may even have been built as a result of the pagans' contacts with Christianity. Such was probably the case in Vilnius where (it seems) Gediminas built or rather adapted a temple on the site of a former Catholic cathedral in a city which boasted at least three Christian churches.[68] In the mid-eleventh century the Polish pagans at Gniezno seem to have wished to use the cathedral for their own rites in imitation of the Catholics whom they had temporarily evicted.[69]

metropolitan of Kiev in 1380 – *RIB*, 168 and the description by Gregoras published in V. Parisot, 'Notice sur le livre XXXVII de Nicéphore Grégoras avec une traduction française et des notes', *Notices et extraits des manuscrits de la Bibliothèque Nationale*, 17:2 (1851), 70. The sacred flame is in *Długosz* X, 165 and *Stryjkowski*, I, 373.

65 See p. 72.

66 Gudavičius argues that Romuva, not Vilnius was the Lithuanian cult centre – Gudavičius, 'Dėl Lietuvos', 61–70. For Vilnius as centre of cult for other Balts, see letter of Urban VI, below n. 82.

67 O. Olsen, *Hørg Hov og Kirke. Historiske og Arkaeologiske Vikingetidsstudier* (Copenhagen, 1966), 280, 282–3 and Ellis Davidson, *Myths and symbols*, 15, 24.

68 A Franciscan and a Dominican Church for Catholic merchants – see pp. 203–4 and an Orthodox church in the Rus'ian merchant quarter – p. 159. On the Wendic temple at Arkona and the temples of Uppsala and Lejre see Olsen, *Hørg*, 280f., and 'Vorchristliche Heiligtümer in Nord Europa', *Abhandlungen der Akademie der Wissenschaften in Göttingen. Phil.-Hist. Klasse*, 74 (1970), 259–78.

69 J. Burchardt, 'Dlaczego pogańscy Polanie w XIw. nie zniszczyli katedry Gnieźnieńskiej', *Literatura Ludowa* (1986/1), 33–40.

Neither the Lithuanian nor the south Germanic languages have a native word for 'temple'. *Kunigas*, 'priest' and *auka*, 'sacrifice' are of Baltic origin but the Lithuanian words for 'temple', *šventnyčia*, *šventykla* derive from Slavonic roots.[70] Temples were not necessary for cult purposes *ab initio*. Lithuanian society was centred on the farms and castles of the nobles and dukes. The latter had once been the religious leaders of the tribes (of which the Sudavian Skumantas is an excellent example).[71] It may be that Lithuanians in their farm communities, like the Scandinavians in theirs, came to use farm buildings in addition to groves and rivers as cult sites. Perhaps the *sanctas domos* and *edes sacras*[72] mentioned by Teutonic chroniclers throughout the fourteenth century and whose function is none too clear are loosely analogous with the Norse *hof*. Olsen has defined this as a 'farm where cult meetings were regularly held for more people than those living on the farm'.[73] The descriptions we have of the pagan cult, its ministers and its holy creatures (the snake in the byre, and the pig) indicate a farm-centred cult. It is known that in the seventeenth century religious festivals took place on farms under the supervision of the farmer or his wife for the benefit of the workforce after the harvest had been gathered in. There is no reason to believe that this practice was innovative.[74]

The terms *hof* and *sacra domus* are not quite synonyms but they seem to indicate the way in which Scandinavian and Lithuanian alike had recourse to domestic religious observances for the community at a time when temples, that is, 'buildings constructed for the express purpose of performing religious rites' were not widely known. The construction of cult buildings in Scandinavia and Lithuania was a late development.

Among many sacrificial stones, countless tombs and even streets and domestic buildings, not one temple (other than the Vilnius adytum) has been found. When sacrificial stones have been uncovered, they have been found in remote woods held sacred by

[70] No native words – see Olsen, *Hørg*, 279. For Lithuanian religious terms, see E. Fraenkel, *Litauisches Etymologisches Wörterbuch* 2 vols. (Heidelberg–Göttingen, 1962–65) – *šventnyčia* – II, 1042; *auka* – I, 25. See also P. Skardžius, *Die slawischen Lehnwörter im Altlitauischen* (Kaunas, 1931), 219.

[71] See pp. 54, 138.

[72] Knights encountered Lithuanians standing in front of *edes sacras* whither they fled for shelter when the enemy approached – *Wig.*, 623–4. The 'holy buildings' may have been fortified farmsteads.

[73] Olsen, *Hørg*, 280.

[74] *Annuae Litterae Societatis Jesu, 1605* (Douai, 1618), 944.

the pagans whither bishops could not penetrate.[75] We should not build temples where the pagans did not. The exception to this rule is provided at the foot of Castle Hill in Vilnius.

Gediminas, who revitalised Vilnius as a political centre between 1316 and 1320, after fifty years during which grand-ducal power had had no permanent home, was particularly sensitive to Lithuania's history both pagan and Christian.[76] He took care to associate his dynasty with policies and practices from the Lithuanian past, aware of the need to graft the new scion onto the ancient stock.[77] He was also familiar with how the Christian Church functioned from his cooperation with Orthodox hierarchs and his use of Catholic friars as scribes and merchants. He built churches for the use of Catholic traders and settlers in his realm.[78] If any structure were to be imposed upon his native religion it would probably bear the impression of these Christian influences. An analogy might be drawn between Gediminas' Vilnius in the fourteenth century and the Kiev of Vladimir Sviatoslavich in the tenth, where Christian enclaves existed in a predominantly pagan town. When Vladimir had taken power from his half-brother Yaropolk in 980, he set about consolidating his power by imposing his own gods on the Kievan populace with the construction of a large shrine on the hill outside his palace.[79] There is, as we shall see, evidence that Gediminas did likewise. However the Lithuanian was more successful than Vladimir, who eventually strengthened his power by introducing Christianity to Rus'.

Stryjkowski and the eighteenth-century version of *L2*, *Khronika Litovskaia i Zhmoitskaia* credit Gediminas with having built a temple for the sacred flame and his god Perkūnas in an oak grove in Vilnius.[80] It was built, according to Stryjkowski, in the Lower Castle 'in that place where today the church of St Stanislaus stands'.[81] This site, hallowed by the flame which Długosz says 'was believed falsely to be everlasting', was chosen by King Jogaila as the place for the Cathedral of Vilnius in 1387.[82] Rivius,

75 *Relationes status diocesium in Magno Ducatu Lithuaniae, I: Diocesis Vilnensis et Samogitiae* ed. P. Rabikauskas (Rome, 1971), 238–9. This is a report of an episcopal visitation in Žemaitija in 1625.

76 On Gediminas' sensitivity to Lithuania's past experience of Catholicism, see pp. 195–6.

77 Pukuveras – see pp. 52–3.

78 See p. 203.

79 *PVL*, I, 56 and V. V. Sedov, 'Pagan sanctuaries and idols of the Eastern Slavs', *Slavica Gandensia*, 7–8 (1980–81), 72.

80 *PSRL*, XXXII, 41.

81 *Stryjkowski*, I, 373.

82 *Długosz*, X, 163. Cf. 'In quodam loco populoso Wilna nuncupato, in quo tam ipse rex [Jogaila] ... quam Litwani *et alii infideles* in quodam fano vana deorum et ydolorum

a late seventeenth-century chronicler who based his account on the (lost) work of Augustus Rotundus, describes a square roofless temple with an entrance from the river Neris.[83] At the back of this stone building was a wooden idol of Perkūnas which stood behind a square altar erected on twelve steps. This, he says, was built in 1285. The nineteenth-century historians Daukantas, Narbutt, Balinski and Kraszewski give similar descriptions but they date the temple twenty years earlier than Rivius.[84] However all these accounts are late and the sceptical historian has long doubted the existence of such a sanctuary.

New evidence came to light in 1984, when archaeologists began to excavate the remains of the 1387 cathedral which had been unearthed during repair works to the modern (eighteenth-century) building damaged by the Neris floods of 1931.[85] The excavators discovered the remains of a thirteenth-century 'Gothic' church. This square church built of brick and stone was 22.7 m long and 22.4 m wide with a nave divided into three parts by two rows of pillars. An apse and presbytery were constructed on the east side and two chapels adjoin the north wall of the presbytery.[86] This discovery corroborates the fifteenth-century Prussian evidence that after his baptism Mindaugas 'founded a cathedral church in a certain city which is called Vilnius (Wille)'.[87] The subsequent fate of Mindaugas' cathedral holds the key to the mystery of what we shall call Gediminas' temple.

Sometime after the cathedral was built, presumably after Mindaugas' apostasy and murder, the glazed brick floor of this square church was strewn with sand and the upper parts of the building were burned. Some time later, attempts were made to restore the ruins. On the Neris side in the middle of the northern wall a breach was made, at either side of which a staircase 1.6 m wide was built (see *fig.* 4). The ghat was built of brick similar to that used in the former cathedral belfry. This staircase formed a

supersticiose colebant ... in eodem loco quandam ecclesiam in honorem sancte et individue Trinitatis ac Gloriose Dei Genetricis Virginis Marie et beati Stanislai martiris erigi fecit ... ' Letter of Pope Urban VI to Bishop Dobrogost of Poznań, 12 March 1388. *KDKDW*, no. 10, pp. 20–1. If Urban's terminology and information is precise, it appears that the Vilnius *fanum* was a centre of piety for more than just the Lithuanians.

[83] A. Kajačkas, 'History and recent archaeological investigations of Vilnius Cathedral', *La Cristianizzazione*, 263–84. This is in effect an English summary of findings reported most extensively in N. Kitkauskas, *Vilniaus pilys. Statyba ir architektūra* (Vilnius, 1989). For the Rivius and Rotundus information, see Kitkauskas, 16, 17.

[84] *Ibid.*

[85] *Ibid.*, 89–91, 123.

[86] Kajačkas, 'History', 268–9. See fig. 4.

[87] *Pamiętnik Zakonu Krzyżackiego o wypadach zaszłych na Żmudzi w 1409r. CEV*, 966.

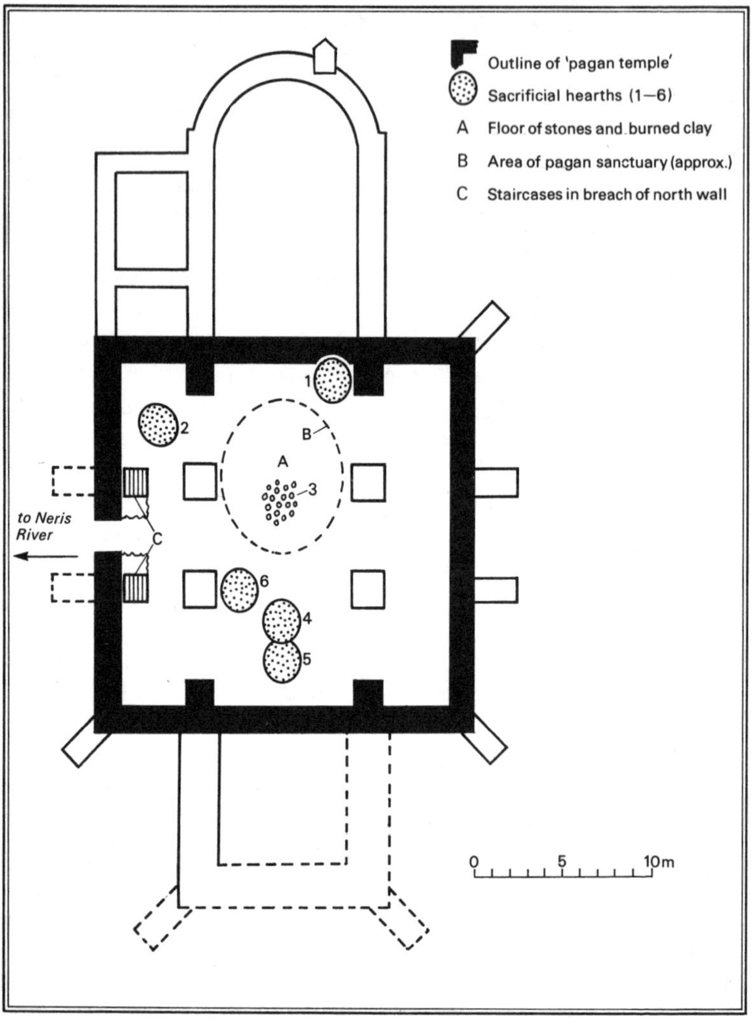

Fig. 4. Plan of the archaeological investigation of Vilnius cathedral, based on Kitkauskas, *Vilniaus pilys*, 139

large part of the northern wall of the square edifice and its six remaining steps were not worn down. It would not have been possible to enter this square building by these stairs. Entrance was gained through a five metres' gap in the centre of the northern wall.[88] It seems sensible to assume that this strange square

[88] Kitkauskas, *Vilniaus pilys*, 91–134.

construction salvaged from the former cathedral is identifiable with the pagan sanctuary (square with twelve stone steps facing the Neris) which was described in detail by Rivius and in part by Długosz and Stryjkowski.[89] The dates given by Rivius and nineteenth-century historians for this temple are however a debatable issue.

The 1265 date (given by Daukantas *et al.*) seems to have been influenced by the apostasy of Mindaugas (1261), so that he who had given the temple site to the Church took it back again. There is no evidence, however, that Mindaugas reacted violently against the religion he adopted for just ten years. The political troubles which dominated his last two years and his struggle for survival as grand duke do not seem to be the ideal time for building a new temple. The 1285 date (of Rivius) fits in with another power vacuum: the decline of the House of Kentauras and the ascendancy of the Gediminid clan. Why should a new temple be built at a time of confusion in a city no longer associated (so far as we can tell) with government?

It seems more reasonable to associate the temple with the religious programme of Gediminas, a stable, powerful grand duke ensconced in Vilnius who is credited by literary sources with the erection of an idol of Perkūnas in a temple built on the site of the cathedral. Gediminas' name, not that of Traidenis or Mindaugas, is associated with religious reform and temple-building by Stryjkowski and the Lithuanian Chronicles.[90] The archaeological evidence is at least compatible with such an association for it dates the square temple to the second half of the thirteenth or the first half of the fourteenth century.[91] Gediminas, who from his patronage of Christians (for purely non-religious reasons such as trade with the west and the governance of Orthodox Rus') was familiar with the building of centres for cult practices, was very probably influenced by church-building in his ordering of the pagan cult. It appears to be an attempt to focus the decentralised cult for the benefit of the new ruling clan.

Having looked at the general background of Lithuanian paganism, let us look more closely now at the role of the grand duke and his family in the pagan cult and distinguish the political implications of the heathen religion. The development of a central

[89] *Ibid.*, 117f.

[90] *Stryjkowski*, I, 373; *PSRL*, XXXII, 41.

[91] N. Kitkauskas, A. Lisanka and S. Lasavickas, 'Perkūno šventyklos liekanos Vilniaus žemutinėje pilyje', *Kultūros Barai* (1987/2), 56.

temple at a time when grand-ducal power was being firmly established and concentrated in Vilnius should not surprise us, for of all the types of priest known to the Lithuanians the most important was the prince or *kunigas*. Chief among these was the grand duke himself.

The *kunigas* was originally the chief military and religious leader of the small tribal units which were spread throughout Lithuania. The title means 'priest' today. The prince-priest functioned like his counterpart in many other originally acephalous pagan societies, such as the Irish *ri* or the Icelandic *goþi*. The *goþi* was the chief of one of sixteen *goþorþs* or districts of Iceland and functioned as both *goþi* ('priest') and *þegn* ('leader') of the *liþ* ('troop').[92] As an example of the *kunigas* in action, as it were, we might take the case of the thirteenth-century Sudavian leader, Skumantas. The *Ipat'evskaia Chronicle* calls him a *vol''khv'* ('wizard') and a fortune-teller (*kobnik''*) who, swift as a wild beast, was a great fighter.[93]

As chief of the warrior princes, the grand duke was the nation's high priest. The title demanded that its holder be a pagan in order to retain the loyalty of the heathen tribesmen of Lithuania, above all, of the Žemaitijans. It may be that the townsfolk of Vilnius were as staunch in their paganism as the Žemaitijans. There is some evidence of this.[94] However surviving sources, which are by no means of Žemaitijan origin, say little of Aukštaitijan devotion. The northerners were especially staunch adherents of the pagan cult, perhaps because they faced the brunt of Teutonic attempts to convert Lithuania. In order to maintain their loyalty it seems that Mindaugas renounced the Catholicism he had adopted earlier partly in the vain hope of quelling Žemaitija by force with the help of the Teutonic Order.[95] The province of Žemaitija was too strong and too strategically important for the grand duke to ignore. When Gediminas seemed to be considering Catholic baptism in 1323, the Knights are said to have bribed the

[92] For the function of the *ri*, see Byrne, *Kings*, 23; the *gothi* is given in M. Stein-Wilkeshuis, 'Laws in medieval Iceland', *Journal of Medieval History*, 12:1 (1986), 40 and G. Karlsson, '*Goþar* and *höfþingar* in Iceland', *Saga Book of the Viking Society*, 19:4 (1977), 358–70. For the case of Alli the Dane, see E. Moltke, *Runerne i Danmark og deres oprindelse* (Copenhagen, 1976), 182 and photograph of rune referring to Alli as *þegn* and *goþi*, p. 183. Commentary in E. Roesdahl, *Viking Age Denmark* (London, 1982), 26.

[93] *PD*, 127–8, 137, 142, 143, 147. *PSRL*, II, 799–800, cf. *PVL*, I, 20–30.

[94] On Vilnian reactions to anti-pagan preaching see below p. 276.

[95] *LR*, line 6357f. p. 145, tr. p. 79f.. His rival for power, Treniota, is said to have declared: 'Samogithians, have no worry. We will hurry to Mindaugas and implore and threaten him until all his Christianity becomes hateful to him.' On Mindaugas, see above, p. 51.

Žemaitijans to threaten the grand duke with the result that the Žemaitijans 'rose up against the king, saying that if *he* received that faith, they would attack him, his sons and all his supporters and in company with the Teutonic Brethren they would drive him from his kingdom and completely destroy him'.[96]

The Žemaitijans must have been well aware that several of Gediminas' sons and daughters were already Christian. It was not to the conversion of junior members of the dynasty that the Žemaitijans objected. The disgruntled pagans baulked at Gediminas' receiving the faith ('*si ipse reciperet*'). This is an interesting inversion of the situation in neophyte Anglo-Saxon England where the sons of a Christian king might be pagan in order to protect the dynasty against pagan reaction after the Christian king was no more.[97] The conversion of Gediminas would not so much have deprived the Žemaitijans of a prince as of a priest. They could always have broken away from the rest of Lithuania as they had in 1251, when Mindaugas converted and they did again in 1387, when Jogaila was baptised.[98] Kestutis, the son to whom Gediminas bequeathed western Lithuania, was particularly devoted to the practice of the pagan cult.

When Christiansen wrote that in the fourteenth century the grand duke became high priest of a reorganised kind of paganism that would fulfil the social and political functions of the Christian churches,[99] he missed the main issue. With Gediminas the grand dukes became firmly established and could develop the traditional pagan role of cult king. When Gediminas spoke of 'loosing and binding' in his own kingdom, he was adopting papal terminology because it fitted his situation, not because he was merely imitating the Pope.[100] The only trappings which Gediminas borrowed from the Christians seem to have been the temple and its concomitant idea of central control.

Having established that the fourteenth century witnessed a major development in Lithuanian religious organisation (the

[96] *GL*, 139. On Žemaitijan opposition to Gediminas' apparent plans to accept Catholic baptism in 1323–24, see pp. 214, 222.

[97] A. Angenendt, 'The conversion of the Anglo-Saxons considered against the background of the early medieval mission', *Settimane di studio del Centro Italiano di Studi sull'alto medioevo XXXII: Angli e Sassoni al di qua e al di là del mare*, II (Spoleto, 1986), 754.

[98] On Žemaitijan discontent in the 1250s see above p. 138; on their reaction to Jogaila's conversion in 1387 and the eventual conversion of the Žemaitijans, see Rabikauskas, 'La cristianizzazione', 225–7.

[99] Christiansen, *Northern crusades*, 137.

[100] See pp. 59, 64–5.

Vilnius Temple), even if there was no 'pope', is it possible to discern any rituals which have a bearing on the central figure of the grand duke?

Public rites were as essential to the stability of political power six hundred years ago as they are today.[101] The Lithuanian grand dukes were familiar with the trappings of Christian kingship and adopted the style of ruler by 'the grace of God'.[102] In 1253 Vilnius had witnessed a Catholic coronation during which Mindaugas had been invested with a crown from the Pope by a Catholic bishop. However Mindaugas proved unable to establish his family on the grand-ducal throne and the chaos which followed his murder did not allow this ceremony to be repeated. When Mindaugas' son Vaišvilkas managed to regain supreme power in 1265, he was acclaimed as ruler and sworn allegiance. The grand master's ambassador wrote that 'he is now reunited with his people and they have sworn allegiance to him, according to the pagan custom'.[103]

The basis of this 'pagan custom' was the oath, whether a contract was made between king and people or nation and nation. Nothing is known of how Traidenis or Vytenis made their accession publicly known and accepted but presumably some type of acclamation and oath of allegiance was forthcoming from the other dukes and the general populace. After Gediminas' reign the ritual seems to have been made more formal.

Stryjkowski gives two accounts of *podniesienie* (*sublimatio*: elevation) as distinct from the *koronacja* of Mindaugas, of princes who ruled after 1342. These are the inaugurations of Jaunutis (1342) and Jogaila (1377).[104] It must be admitted that Stryjkowski is a late source but he does not employ excessive descriptions of the inauguration rites and he links them (in Jaunutis' case at least) with minor figures. Complete invention would be more probable if the subjects were 'big names' like

[101] M. Kosman, 'Podniesienie książąt litewskich', *Acta Baltico-Slavica*, 10 (1976), 15–36. Kosman has since qualified his views although he accepts that a rite of sacrifice was performed – Kosman, *Litwa pierwotna. Mity, legendy, fakty* (Warsaw, 1989), 244–82. See also Z. Piech, 'Mitra książęca w swietle przekazów ikonograficznych od czasów rozbica dzielnicowegeo do końca epoki Jagiellońskiej', *Kwartalnik Historii Kultury Materialnej*, 35 (1987), 3–48.

[102] See pp. 64–5.

[103] *LR*, lines 7204–7206, p. 165, tr., p. 89.

[104] *Stryjkowski*, I, 288–9; II, 2 and 60. The same term (*vozvodiat*: *elevant*) is used of Daumantas of Pskov's inauguration in 1266 – V. I. Okhotnikova, *Povest' o Dovmonte* (Leningrad, 1985), 200.

Gediminas (already linked with strange legends) rather than if the description concerned relative failures like Jaunutis. A Silesian account from 1381 (a report of Kestutis' coup d'état compiled for the grand master) indicates an acclamation in Vilnius similar to that described by Stryjkowski for Jaunutis.[105] This is an adequate corroboration of the Polish author's basic theme, although of course it is not evidence to support his detailed description.

In the castle in Vilnius, Jaunutis was invested by his brothers with a sword and other regalia including a princely cap and garb. He was acclaimed 'with the usual pagan rites ... according to the old custom'.[106] This reads as textual padding. Nevertheless a crown and sceptre were depicted on Gediminas' seal as we have from a description made in 1323[107] and the cap (*czapka*) was traditionally worn by Rus'ian grand dukes. This influence from Rus' where the grand duke wielded great power, and where his own kinsmen must have been invested with a cap upon assumption of power in the Lettovian principalities is hardly surprising. The location of the ceremony, Vilnius, is also to be expected since that is where grand-ducal power was concentrated by Gediminas during his lifetime. The city was stipulated in his will as the seat of future grand dukes.[108] The Lower Castle in Vilnius (not specified by Stryjkowski) was the site where Mindaugas was crowned in the Catholic cathedral in 1253. It was by 1341 presumably the site of a (Gediminas') pagan temple. Whether this building played a part in the ritual is impossible to tell but it is probable that it did.

It appears from the scant evidence we have that Gediminas staged his own power-rite in Vilnius long after his accession to the grand-ducal throne. Delay between accession and installation was not uncommon, for example, in Anglo-Saxon England.[109] Ac-

[105] Compare *mos et ritus*, described below p. 142 with the *starodawni zwyczaj* of *Stryjkowski*, II, 2. For background to 1381 Coup, see *Wig.*, 608.

[106] *Stryjkowski*, II, 2.

[107] Seal described in a Lübeck transcription of Gediminas' Saxon Letters of May 1323, the only surviving copy of which is now in Berlin, PKKA L. S. Schieblade XI.17. Published with errors in Raczyński, *Codex*, 32. For detailed discussion of this seal see Rowell, 'Letters'.

[108] Gediminas' will is narrated in all redactions of the Lithuanian Chronicle – *PSRL*, XXXV, 61, 97 etc. Gediminas bequeathed the title of grand duke to Jaunutis: 'А тых двух сынов своих посадил на великих князствах: Евнутя на столцы своем на Вилни и на великом князстве литовском, а Кестутя на Троцех и всеи земли жомоитскои', *PSRL*, XXXV, 97.

[109] G. Garnett, 'Coronation and propaganda: Some implications of the Norman claim to the throne of England in 1066', *TrRHS*, 5th series 36 (1986), 92.

cording to the *Ronneburg Annals*, Gediminas was 'acclaimed grand duke' in 1323.[110] Since Gediminas had taken power in 1315–16 but by 1323 was resident in Vilnius, it seems possible that he created a rite for himself associated with his new *civitas regia*, which had been Mindaugas' city, as he knew.[111] This rite based firmly on earlier practices of acclamation, sacrifice and oath swearing he bequeathed to his sons.

Oaths, however, can be broken. Pagan rites make a man no more or less honest than Christian ones. In 1381, in accordance with a plan elaborated by Kestutis, Grand Duke Jogaila was removed from power in a coup d'état. Kestutis gathered his army and made as if to attack the Knights but he doubled back from the Žemaitijan border and entered Vilnius, where he 'extracted homage from his vassals who gave it willingly. He bound them to their word with the sprinkling of blood from a slaughtered animal according to their rite and custom'.[112] It is evident from this description of the Lithuanian *mos et ritus* that there was a well-established inauguration complex in Lithuania by the late fourteenth century which involved oaths of fealty and blood sacrifice and was possibly rooted in a location in Vilnius. The grand duke often performed this rite himself, especially the blood sacrifice. A similar practice is recorded for ninth-century Hungary where the duke Almos was acclaimed by his nobles with a blood-

[110] The *Ronneburg Annals* survive only in a Polish translation placed arbitrarily into *Stryjkowski*, I, 282–4. The material given therein about Prussian and Lithuanian history is verifiable from other Teutonic chronicles and is accurate. Under the year 1323, we read: 'Pskowiane Litwy na pomoc wezwawszy, ziemie króla Duńskiego [Reval] zwojowali i pięc tysięcy ludu w polon wywiedli. Tegoź roku Litwa Memel spaliła. *Tegoź roku król litewski byl obwołany*', *Stryjkowski*, I, 283. ('The Pskovites called on Lithuania for assistance and attacked the lands of the King of Denmark, taking 5,000 captive. The same year Lithuania burned Memel. That year the Lithuanian king was acclaimed'). The Lithuanian campaigns of 1323 are all accurately described, see pp. 209–10. The remark 'that year the King of Lithuania was acclaimed (*obwołany*)' is intriguing. This acclamation is mentioned in no other source. It deserves serious consideration as an aspect of Gediminas' statecraft at a time when he was anchoring his power in a new city and was approaching Catholic powers to gain recognition for his own position and for Lithuania's international boundaries: see below pp. 189–228.

[111] That Gediminas was aware of Mindaugas' example is indicated by his correspondence with the West, see pp. 195–6.

[112] From the Formulary of the Königsberg Schlossbibliothek, document no. 101 published in *CDP*, VI, no. 2, pp. 2–3, under the wrong date: '... castrum Wille dictum, fugatis suis patruis de eodem cum matre, cepit, et a Litwanis dictorum patruorum suorum vasallis congregatis in unum fidelitatis extorsit omagium, et ex eis quibusdam sponte hoc sibi prestantibus iuxta morem et ritum suum cum aspersione sangwinis animalis mactati constrinxit eosdem ... quo devenit rex precipuus'.

smearing rite and the swearing of an oath.[113] More than this we cannot say.

Rites which involve blood sacrifice and oaths feature prominently in Lithuania's forging of ties with foreign powers. The ceremonies of the heathen cult were not only effective in support of the Gediminid rule at home, they were also accepted by those Christian rulers who sought Gediminas as an ally. An agreement must be sanctioned by a promise made in a form which is meaningful to the party which swears. Despite their paganism, if not because of it, for a pagan could do unspeakable deeds on a Christian prince's behalf, which the Christian could not do himself, the Lithuanians were welcome allies throughout the thirteenth and fourteenth centuries. Agreements with settlers in the Baltic,[114] the Order,[115] the Empire,[116] Poland[117] and Rus'[118] were several, if not many. In these agreements, if the Christians were bound by oaths sworn in Christ's name, an oath bound the pagans to the accord. In 1338 a trade agreement between the German Baltic settlements and the Grand Duchy of Lithuania was confirmed with oaths: the kissing of the Cross for Catholic and Orthodox signatories and 'their own rites' (*ere hilligh*) for the ethnic Lithuanians.[119] If Dusburg speaks from experience when he notes how illiterate pagans marvelled at how men can communicate by letter, he was completely out of date where the Lithuanians are concerned. From the thirteenth century onwards Lithuanian rulers made written agreements and understood the eastern Christian practice of returning written oaths before renouncing a peace treaty well enough to abuse it subtly.[120]

[113] *Magistri P. Belae Regis notarii Gesta Hungarorum, Historiae hungaricae fontes domestici*, ed. M. Florianus, II (Leipzig, 1863), 6.

[114] 1180 – *LR*, line 201, p. 5. tr., p. 3; 1201 – Henry, *Chronicon* V, 3 and VI, 5, pp. 22, 24 (treaties involving Curonians, Rigans, Semigallians and the Order); 1275–76 – Traidenis' Livonian treaty, see p. 77; 1298 – Vytenis petitioned the Rigans to make peace 'sensibilibus argumentis ac *sacramentis secundum eorum morem* ac pactis in concussae servandis coram nobis' – *LU*, I, no. 570, col. 715.

[115] The Žemaitijans and Teutonic Knights made peace in 1257 'in the proper manner' – *LR*, lines 4543–4628, pp. 104–6, tr., p. 59. For the Treaty of Vilnius 1323, see pp. 211–12. The Trade Accord of 1338 is discussed below pp. 257–8.

[116] Notably in 1358, see Mažeika, 'Role', 130–65.

[117] For the 1325 alliance between Poland and Lithuania, see pp. 223–5, 232–7. For Gediminas' Mazovian alliance see pp. 8–9, 91–2.

[118] The Lithuano-Rus'ian Treaty of 1219 is discussed in M. Kosman, 'Forma umów międzynarodowych Litwy w pierwszej ćwierci XIII wieku', *PH*, 57 (1966), 221–9. For details of the Lithuano-Pskov alliance of 1322/3, see pp. 237–8 and for the Novgorodian treaty of 1331, see pp. 248–9.

[119] *GL*, 194–5. See p. 257.

[120] Rowell, 'A pagan's word', 148–57.

Like the Ancient Kievans, the Lithuanians depended upon the oath as the basis for confirming agreements, as they did for acclaiming their prince. Both Christian and pagan alike had something they owned dear by which they could swear. The pagans could be trusted; their *hilligh*, or *sanctio spiritualis* as Mikucki would call it, was considered binding.[121] When the Žemaitijans came to make peace with the grand master in 1257, both parties shook hands 'for it is the custom of the land that if one gives his hand to another, even if in a third land, he has made an honourable peace, binding on the pain of death'.[122] Oaths were uttered just as the Kievans swore to the Greeks in the tenth century.[123] The Lithuanians invoked their deities, as the Kievans had sworn by Perun and Volos more than three centuries earlier.[124] When it was necessary to give the impression that he was willing to embrace Christianity such as in his letters to western Catholics in 1323, Gediminas would couch promises in terms which evade the need to swear by any deity: 'iron will turn to wax and water change into steel before we will withdraw a word issued from our lips'.[125]

By contrast, in 1351 Kestutis invoked the Lithuanian god during an elaborate ceremony intended to confirm his pact with the king of Hungary. The Lithuanians swore to keep a treaty and followed this with the sacrifice of an animal and a threat to the effect that he who broke the treaty should suffer the same fate as the sacrificial victim.[126] This agreement provides a convenient summary of fourteenth-century custom (including the perverting of it).

When a Hungaro-Polish army led by Louis of Hungary appeared on the Lithuanian border in 1351, Kestutis sent messengers to the king to sue for peace, demanding in return for the

[121] *PVL*, I, 52. Mikucki refers to such threats as *sanctio spiritualis*: S. Mikucki, 'Etudes sur la diplomatie russe la plus ancienne', *Bulletin International de l'Académie polonaise des sciences et des lettres. Classe de philologie–Classe d'histoire et de philosophie, Numéro supplémentaire*, 7 (1953), 26. Cf. Ellis-Davidson, *Myths and symbols*, 53.

[122] *LR*, lines 4616–4620, p. 106, tr. p. 60.

[123] *PVL*, I, 25, 28–9, 38–9, 52, 59. See A. N. Sakharov, *Diplomatia Drevnei Rusi IX–pervaia polovina Xv*. (Moscow, 1980), esp. pp. 254–8.

[124] In the 1351 Treaty with Hungary and Poland the Lithuanian prince called upon an unspecified *Deus* – *Chronicon Dubnicense* in *Historiae Hungariae fontes domestici*, ed. M. Florianus, III (Leipzig, 1884), 160–1. The other chronicler of this treaty regards the sacrifice itself as an oath: Henry of Diessenhoffen, *Chronica*, *SRP*, III, 420.

[125] *GL*, 51. For this letter to the Dominicans see pp. 206–7. Let the readers of lips beware.

[126] For animal sacrifice and *sanguinis aspersio/effusio* see Henry, *Chronicon*, V, 3, p. 22 and the 1351 Treaty – see above n. 124.

baptism of Lithuania *inter alia* the release of his brother Liubartas from Polish captivity, a royal crown from the Pope and military aid in recovering lands occupied by the Teutonic Knights. Two eye-witness accounts and several later reports survive of the manner in which Kestutis, prince of Trakai and closest ally of Grand Duke Algirdas, made this agreement with the Poles and Hungarians. These were incorporated into the Hungarian *Chronicon Dubnicense* and the *Chronica* of Henry of Diessenhoffen.[127] The striking of the treaty involved a most exuberant *tour de force* from one who claimed that he intended to accept baptism.

On the feast of the Assumption, Kestutis came to the pavilion of the king of Hungary and, in plain view of all, swore a Lithuanian oath to abide by the treaty which had been devised. By way of confirmation of his good faith, he (not a lower priest) then performed a sacrificial rite as he had at his acclamation in Vilnius. A ruddy ox was brought forth and secured to two posts. Kestutis then plunged a Lithuanian dagger into the beast's jugular and blood spurted out *largissime*. He and all the Lithuanians next anointed their hands and faces with the blood and cried out in Lithuanian (in fact in west Russian, perhaps as a means of invalidating the oath from the beginning by using the 'wrong' language): *Rogachina roznenachy gospanany* which was interpreted as meaning: 'O God, regard us, our souls and this horned one and the oath we have made today'. According to Henry they were to share the fate of the animal if they broke the oath. The head was then cut from the carcase and the men walked three times through the remains. The ritual made a deep impression on the Christians present and on those to whom it was reported. Petrarch found it useful as a commentary on the practice of the Ancient Latins in the *Aeneid* and the Austrian poet Suchenvirt recorded it in his chivalric verse.[128]

The smearing of blood during the ritual had a long pedigree in Lithuania. In Mindaugas' reign when the Žemaitijans attacked the

[127] See above n. 124. The sacrifice was also described by the fourteenth-century German poet Peter Suchenvirt – 'Von hern Puppily von Elrwach', 93 and 'Von chunik Ludwig von Ungerland', 106–11, given in *SRP*, II, 158–9. On Suchenvirt's use of this episode see S. Cain Van D'Elden, *Peter Suchenwirt and heraldic poetry*, *Wiener Arbeiten zur Germanischen Altertumskunde und Philologie*, IX (Vienna, 1976), 185–6.

[128] *Dubnicense*, 161. In a marginal note to *Aeneid*, VIII, 641 in his manuscript of Virgil, Petrarch comments of the Latins' swearing an oath over the carcase of a dead pig, 'Comperi hunc morem feriendi federis et easdem imprecationes in caput frangentis fidem apud Lutuinos et id genus hominum etiam nunc servari' – *Petrarcae Vergilianus Codex*, f.174. The oath was made in *Russian*, not Lithuanian. Given Hungarian

Order in Courland, their *blûtekirl* drew lots in accordance with tradition and sacrificed *ein quek, als er wol wiste*.[129] The Knights were certainly impressed by Kestutis' performance. Teutonic chroniclers of the thirteenth century had written of blood-smearing many times but never in the same detail as the witnesses of the 1351 treaty. Nevertheless it was an act of insolent confidence on Kestutis' part to ratify a treaty which promised the conversion of the Lithuanians with such flamboyant heathen ceremonial. The display was vain, for as soon as Kestutis learned that his brother Liubartas had been freed and that the Christian army had withdrawn from Lithuanian borders, he abandoned all pretence of intention to convert. It also acts as a warning to any romantic notion that pagans could not abuse their religion as Christians do.[130]

What are we to conclude about a religion which gave one of its chief adherents such flamboyance in the face of Catholic princes who seemed to have forced him to abandon it? Above all Lithuanian paganism was diverse and the sparse sources cannot be constrained sensibly into the creation of a monolithic, unchanging cult. The natural world was sated with deities and their angels and many were the ways of serving them and gaining their assistance. In the whole of Lithuania pagan beliefs were held no more strongly than in the marcher provinces of the north and west. Here the onslaught of the Teutonic *Reisen* was felt most keenly and the difficulty of the terrain hindered enemies in their attempts to reach secluded settlements. As we might expect from what is known of Lithuanian society in general, the religion of the realm was particularly suited to an agricultural and martial culture; that is the milieu whence it sprang.

The local prince-priests of Lithuania had always been involved with the direction of the pagan cults. Such is common among politically acephalous and predominantly agricultural societies such as Lithuania in the early Middle Ages.[131] The cults were even

pronunciation and orthography the text may have been (with lacunae) *рогатыи назри и неначникъ господи на ны – ad cornutum respice et non servantes, Deus, et ad nos*. The text, despite its faults, reads as an incantation. The use of Russian here and its description in the chronicle as *lithwanice* provide curious information about both the rite itself and foreign understanding of what was Lithuanian/Lettovian.

129 *LR*, lines 4683–4684, p. 108, tr. p. 60.

130 *Dubnicense*, 162. See also Ellis-Davidson, *Myths and symbols*, 224–6.

131 Cf. F. Fugelstad, 'Earth-priests, 'priest-chiefs' and sacred kings in ancient Norway, Iceland and West Africa. A comparative study', *Scandinavian Journal of History*, 4 (1979), 47–74.

more decentralised than the political control of the Gediminids. There was no single ritual of the dead; the sacred horse of Perkūnas might be black in one region and white in another. Perkūnas the sky deity was the chief god in some areas but in others he had to surrender primacy to the earth god. There was no papal figure in Lithuanian religion. No pagan pope lived in a heathen Rom(e)uva; nowhere in the Nadruvian wilds did there pontificate a respected *pagan* John XXII. Indeed we should not expect such a priest to exist in a polytheistic cult. Until the reign of Gediminas there was probably no special cult building in the land, although Vilnius appears to have been closely associated with holy sites, if only that so many dead dukes lay round.

As political power gradually comes to be concentrated in one centre and around one dynasty, we might expect the political significance of religious practice to increase. Such practice may serve to unite a people. King Mindaugas sought to make his power more secure (mostly from external attack) by importing Catholicism as a strong centralised cult in the 1250s and failed. Gediminas and his sons show that religious pluralism within strict confines can unite a people, as we shall see from an analysis of pagan Lithuania's experience of Christianity. In Lithuania Gediminas attempted to strengthen his dynasty's control by revitalising the native religion. He was keen to associate himself and his family with the old ways. What appears to have been his temple was built close to his residence in the Lower Castle in Vilnius and it was in this long-hallowed vicinity that state ceremonies took place. The accession and funerary rites of Gediminas and his family served to focus attention on the new grand-ducal dynasty. Prince Kestutis directed major state ceremonies (inaugurations, funerals, diplomatic agreements) in person rather than relying on a lesser *kunigas* or *blûtekirl*.

Despite the close connections of the Gediminids with the heathen cult, the sons of Gediminas never claimed descent from Perkūnas or any other of the pagan gods. In the fourteenth century such a claim of kinship could not credibly be arrogated and in the fifteenth, the dynasty drew national prestige from myths of Roman ancestry.

The heterogeneous, non-doctrinal and decentralised nature of paganism in Lithuania was perfectly suited to the loose-knit structure of the Grand Duchy in the fourteenth century. Rather than impose a powerful centralised cult on the whole of the country, which was patently impossible and out of keeping with the grand duke's political authority (Orthodox Rus' could hardly be forced back into official idolatry and pagan Lithuania would not abandon Perkūnas and his fellow gods without a fight) Gediminas permitted all religions, pagan, Catholic and Orthodox to operate freely within their respective spheres of influence. He said as much to the envoys of the papal legates in November 1324 when he 'declared that he desired ... Christians to worship their god according to their own custom, Rus'ians according to their rite and Poles according to their own custom. For we all worship one god'.[132] I say that Gediminas permitted this circumscribed freedom of religious practice, for it is clear that he knew what he was doing. It is no accident that a Catholic friar was welcome to serve the Catholic enclave in Vilnius or Novgorodok and he did so under grand-ducal patronage, but let him step a-preaching into a pagan grove and the implicit threat he had made thereby to the religio-political balance of the Grand Duchy by insulting the local gods and stubbornly disobeying the grand duke could cost him his life.[133] When an Orthodox hierarchy in Lithuania had been established, the grand duke regarded it as his patronal right to ensure that the Church had a pastor, even though he was never himself Orthodox. This fits in with the Lithuanian political maxim of 'introduce nothing new, change nothing old'.[134]

Gediminas took as much as he wanted from Christendom without failing to maintain control of a reformed native tradition. On occasion the Christian God was invited to take His place in the pantheon, for it would have been inauspicious to reject Him. In no way did the Lithuanians feel their religion (or their polity) to be inferior to that of the Christians. It would take more than merchantable commodities such as gold, silk and incense and the inestimable glories of the liturgy to defeat Lithuanian paganism. At a time when, as we shall see, Christian alliances were easily bought and Lithuania's enemies were in disarray it was possible for the pagan state to march alone. By 1342 the choice of alliance with east or west was possible but it was not the necessary union of 1385.[135]

[132] *GL*, 126–9. [133] See below p. 276. [134] See p. 116.
[135] Giedroyć, 'Lithuanian options', 85–103.

Chapter 6

THE METROPOLITANATE OF LITHUANIA

Until 1387 when Lithuania received Christianity via Catholic Poland, the native pagan cults which the Gediminids attempted to manipulate for their own ends, remained the religion of the Lithuanian populace. Despite the fact that officially Catholicism has been the national religion of the Lithuanians for six centuries, when we examine Lithuanian Christian terminology – nouns for ecclesiastical institutions and practices such as 'church', 'baptism', 'Christmas' or 'fast' – we discover that it comprises mostly loanwords from Russian rather than Polish.[1] The relationship between Russian Orthodoxy and pagan Lithuania which is reflected in this vocabulary is an important factor in both the formation of the Grand Duchy of Lithuania and the development of the Church of Rus'.

Lithuania's longlasting connection with Orthodoxy began in the thirteenth century as Lithuanian princelings began to seize and retain land in western Rus'. As they settled there these princes commonly, but not necessarily, adopted the Orthodox faith of their subjects.[2] By 1254 King Mindaugas' own son Vaišvilkas had taken Novgorodok. He was baptised, became a monk and later founded a convent outside this city which traditionally has been identified with the Lavrashev Monastery, where future senior

[1] *Bažnyčia – bozh'nitsa*: church; *krikštas – kr"st'*: baptism; *kalėdos – koliada*: Christmas; *gavėnia – goven'e*: fast. See N. Borowska, 'Wpływy słowiańskie na litewską terminologię koscielną', *Studia z filologii polskiej i słowiańskiej*, II (Warsaw, 1957), 320–65; Z. Zinkiavičius, 'K istorii litovskoi khristianskoi terminologii vostochno-slavianskogo proiskhozhdenia' *Balto-Slavianskie Issledovania* (1980), 131–9.

[2] As was the case with Vaišvilkas or many of the Gediminids: Karijotas-Mikhail who governed Novgorodok (*PSRL*, XXXV, 46); Liubartas-Dmitry of Volyn' (*AZR*, I, no. 1) or Narimantas-Gleb of Polotsk. However, Algirdas, despite having once ruled Vitebsk, remained a pagan – Mažeika, 'Was Grand Prince', 35–55. Recently it has been argued that Algirdas became a catechumen in order to consort with Christians but was never baptised – T. Wasilewski, 'Prawosławne imiona Jagiełły i Witolda', *Analecta Cracoviensia*, 19 (1987), 109.

Lithuanian hierarchs were to take up residence.[3] In 1263 Mindaugas was murdered and Vaišvilkas abandoned the religious life to avenge his father. His fiercest opponent in the ensuing struggle for power in Lithuania was Daumantas of Nalšia (known to Russians as Dovmont of Pskov) who fled into exile in Pskov in 1265. In north-west Rus' Daumantas embraced Orthodoxy, became prince of Pskov and an ally of the Nevsky clan and finally came to be revered as the celestial patron of his adopted city.[4]

In the second half of the thirteenth century the brothers of Traidenis were faithful Christians.[5] The influence of Orthodoxy on princely families was fostered further by the use of Rus'ian slaves as wetnurses.[6] As Lithuania began to tighten her control of Polotsk and the cities of Black Rus', the local Orthodox clergy came to regard their Lithuanian rulers and eventually their princes' pagan overlord as ecclesiastical patrons. Bishop Iakov of Polotsk (fl. 1309) even acted as an intermediary between his 'son' Vytenis and the archbishop of Riga in a matter of commercial discipline.[7]

In eastern Rus', the grand duke of Vladimir, Prince Mikhail Yaroslavich of Tver' (1304–18), was served by Andrei, a bishop of princely Lithuanian parentage whom Daumantas had brought to Rus' as a child captive.[8] The alliance of this prelate and his political master with the Lithuanian grand-ducal family in petty rivalry with a south Rus'ian Metropolitan of Kiev was to have important consequences for the Church under Lithuanian control. How the Church functioned in Lithuania and how the political power attempted to manipulate the ecclesiastical authorities will be our concern here. We shall distinguish between grand-ducal relations with the princes of the Church (the patriarch and the metropolitans) and collaboration with the local bishops and note the mutual

[3] On Vaišvilkas' reign see Giedroyć, 'Arrival ... (thirteenth Century)', 16–19. The site of Vaišvilkas' monastery is discussed in D. M. Goldfrank, 'The Lithuanian prince-monk Vojšelk: A study in competing legends', *Harvard Ukrainian Studies*, 11:1–2 (1987), 60 and n. 82. On the residence of later Lithuanian hierarchs see K. Chodynicki, *Kościół prawosławny a Rzeczpospolita Polska. Zarys historyczny* 1370–1632 (Warsaw, 1934), 129, 146, 163.

[4] On Daumantas see below pp. 177–9. and Rowell, 'Between Lithuania and Rus'', 22–32.

[5] Sirputis, Svilkenis, Borza and Lesis were Christian but Traidenis was a resolute pagan – *PSRL*, II, 869 s.a. 6778.

[6] Giedroyć, 'Arrival ... (thirteenth Century)', 11.

[7] *PG*, I, no. 3, p. 36.

[8] That Andrei was the son of the Lithuanian Duke Gerdenis, see *TL*, 345; the wife and children of Gerdenis were captured in 1267 by Daumantas of Pskov – *PL*, II, 16, 83.

exploitation of the spiritual and temporal powers. Before examining the Orthodox Church in the regions under the control of Gediminas and his successors, we must first sketch out the state of the Church in Rus' in the early fourteenth century. The Lithuanian metropolitanate cannot be understood outside the Byzantine struggle to maintain the unity of the Rus'ian province and its financial contributions to Constantinople at a time when the political rivalries enmeshing Tver', Moscow, Galich and Lithuania disrupted Rus'ian life. Whatever the rulers of these lands wanted, they were given what the patriarch thought was best for the Church. It is sometimes too easy to forget that the medieval Church, even the Byzantine part, was a formidable maker of its own policy.

In 1299 Maksim, metropolitan of Kiev and All Rus' formally abandoned his cathedral city of Kiev and followed the major secular power in Rus', which had long since migrated north-eastwards, to Vladimir.[9] As a result of the abandonment of Kiev, Yury L'vovich, Prince of Galich–Volyn' made efforts to gain a metropolitan of his own to govern the Church in south-west Rus'. In 1303 Patriarch Athanasius I and Emperor Andronicus II acceded to the southerner's request and appointed a metropolitan of Galich with jurisdiction over the sees of Vladimir Volynsky, Lutsk, Kholm, Peremyshl' and Turov.[10] The success of this request to break the unity of the metropolitanate of All Rus' probably depended on several factors, including simple bribery or the provision of Rus'ian aid at the turn of the century when Ottoman attacks on the Byzantine borderlands increased.[11] The patriarch may even have been threatened with the conversion of Galich–Volyn' to Catholicism if he refused Yury's request. The interest shown by the Papacy in Galich since the days of Daniil Romanovich (1221–64) had not declined.[12]

However it came about, this split in the Church of Rus' did not

[9] *PSRL*, I, 485 s.a. 6808.

[10] Until the metropolitans began to move to Vladimir, the princes of Galich–Volyn' exercised influence over the hierarchy. Kirill (1242–81) was Daniil Romanovich's appointment – Meyendorff, *Byzantium*, 40–6. On the metropolitanate of Galich see Darrouzès, *Notitiae*, no. 17, p. $403^{157-163}$. Date of foundation discussed in A. S. Pavlov, 'O nachale galitskoi i litovskoi mitropolii i o pervykh tamoshnikh mitropolitakh po vizantiiskim dokumental'nym istochnikom XIV veka', *Russkoe Obozrenie* (1894/3, May), 216.

[11] Bribery was common practice in Byzantium – Meyendorff, *Byzantium*, 80. On Byzantine difficulties *c.* 1300 see Gregoras, *HB*, VI, cap. 10–11; VII, cap. 1; PG, CXLVIII, 361–76.

[12] Meyendorff, *Byzantium*, 41–2.

last long. In 1305 Metropolitan Maksim died; shortly afterwards the first metropolitan of Galich, Nifon, also passed away.[13] As a result of these two deaths Patriarch Athanasius found himself confronted with two Rus'ian monks, one sent from Galich (Pëtr) and the other from Vladimir (Geronty), both seeking ordination to the metropolitanates of Rus'.[14] It may even be that Pëtr presented himself as a candidate for the province of All Rus'.[15] Athanasius made use of a delay in Geronty's arrival in Constantinople to ordain Pëtr as metropolitan of Kiev and All Rus' in May or June 1308, thereby reuniting the Rus'ian province in the person of Pëtr. The election of the Galician candidate at a time when Yury L'vovich was in correspondence with Pope Clement V was doubly attractive.[16] It countered the independence of the Galich clergy, whilst allowing Athanasius to ordain a man to Kiev and All Rus' who was not a creature of the grand duke of Vladimir. Pëtr was to be no prince's puppet after he returned to Rus' in the autumn of 1308 or spring 1309.[17]

Grand Duke Mikhail Yaroslavich was furious at the failure of his candidate to win the metropolitan throne. So presumably was Bishop Andrei of Tver' who, as the prelate serving the grand duke's personal patrimony, might expect a monk he had selected to find favour in Constantinople. Almost as soon as Pëtr arrived in Rus', Mikhail and Andrei showered accusations of an unknown nature upon the new metropolitan and indicted him before the patriarch in Constantinople. In 1309, Athanasius sent a personal envoy to preside over a conciliar trial of Pëtr in Pereiaslavl'.[18] In the

13 On the name of first metropolitan, Nifon see *ibid.*, 93. On the death of the Rus'ian hierarchs see Fennell, *Emergence*, 125–6.

14 Metropolitan Kiprian, *Zhitie sviatogo Petra Mitropolita* in B. S. Angelov, *Iz starata b''lgarska, ruska i sr'bska literatura* (Sofia, 1958), 166–9 [henceforth: *ZhP*].

15 Fennell, *Emergence*, 68–9, n. 5. Such a hypothesis is in keeping with Kiprian's account of Yury's sending of Pëtr to Constantinople – *ZhP*, 167.

16 In a letter to the Apostolic Delegates in Hungary in 1307 Clement V refers to Franciscans who seek the reunion of Galich and Volyn' with Rome – A. L. Tautů, *Acta Clementis PP V* (Vatican, 1955), no. 18, p. 31. For Yury's dismissal of Clement's envoys in 1309 (i.e. after Pëtr's consecration) – *Długosz*, IX, 56.

17 Pëtr came to Kiev in 1308 and moved on to Suzdal' in Spring 1309 – *TL*, 352–3.

18 *ZhP*, 170–1 where the charges are not specified. Athanasius is named in the 1327 life of Pëtr by Bishop Prokhor, see Makary, *Istoria russkoi tserkvi*, IV.1 (St Petersburg, 1886), 314. The dating of events concerning Metropolitan Pëtr and Bishop Andrei is very confused. Fennell, following Russian tradition, places the trial in late 1310 or early 1311 (*Emergence*, 71, 72, n. 4). This is incorrect. In nineteenth-century scholarship the second patriarchate of Athanasius was held to have ended in 1310. It is now known that Athanasius resigned in September 1309 – V. Grumel, *La Chronologie* (Paris,

presence of the patriarch's representative and the clergy and princes of Rus', Bishop Simeon of Rostov defended Pëtr against the charges Bishop Andrei laid before the court.[19] Pëtr was vindicated and attempted to reconcile the Tverite faction, but to no avail.[20] In Spring 1310, the grand duke and his bishop sent the Tverite monk Akindin to Constantinople to investigate the laws against simony. That autumn, after a new patriarch, Niphon, had presided over a council in Constantinople in October to legislate on the ubiquitous malpractice of simony, Akindin reported back to Mikhail Yaroslavich on the council's verdict: not even half a hyperperon, the traditional fee covering the ordination of a cleric, was legal revenue.[21] It appears that after the grand duke learnt this, new evidence was sent to Niphon accusing Pëtr of trading the gifts of the Holy Ghost and sanctioning marriages within forbidden degrees of kindred.[22]

Meanwhile Pëtr continued to progress around his province intervening in political crises in Briansk (September 1310) and north-eastern Rus' (1311) and cautioning the princes of Tver' or their allies not to provoke the wrath of the Tatars or split the

1958), 437. Since the trial was conducted in the presence of Athanasius' envoy it probably took place in the summer or autumn of 1309. This would have given Andrei enough time from the arrival of Pëtr in Rus' to present his complaints to Constantinople.

[19] Fennell, *Emergence*, 71 n. 3 views Simeon as an ally of Andrei of Tver'. However, Simeon, unlike Andrei, is referred to respectfully in *ZhP*, 171 as *bogoliubivyi* and Pëtr's companion in Pereiaslavl', Prokhor was his successor as bishop of Rostov in 1312. The suggestion that Simeon was replaced in 1312 at Pëtr's request is unfounded. It seems from the description of the trial that Andrei was prosecutor, Athanasius' man was judge and Simeon was Pëtr's counsel as is clearer in the *Velikie Minei Chitei* version of Pëtr's life cited in V. A. Kuchkin, 'Skazanie o smerti mitropolita Petra', *TODRL*, 18 (1962), 68, n. 54.

[20] *ZhP*, 171–2.

[21] Akindin appears to have been sent to Constantinople after Pereiaslavl' because his report gives details of a synod held by Patriarch Niphon, Patriarch Athanasius III of Jerusalem and thirty-six metropolitans in October 1310 where simony was condemned. The unpublished report of the Council (*Cod. Vat. Gr.*, 847, ff. 260v-271v) as described in J. Darrouzès, *Les Regestes du Patriarcat de Constantinople I: Les actes des patriarches* 5, *Les regestes de 1310 à 1376* (Paris, 1977) no. 2005, 6–7 fits closely if not exactly the details of the text of *Napisanie Akindina*, *RIB*, no. 16-ii, pp. 150–8. Akindin urged Mikhail to prosecute Pëtr further. The payment of a small charge at ordination which had become established practice in Byzantium and Rus' (*RIB*, no. 6, p. 92) was condemned by Niphon and this may have been the basis of Pëtr's prosecution. Ironically Niphon was forced to resign in 1314 because of his own much graver simoniacal misdemeanours – Meyendorff, *Byzantium*, 149–50.

[22] Undated letter of Niphon to Mikhail – *RIB*, no. 16-i, p. 148. Because Niphon discusses accusations that Pëtr sanctioned unlawful marriages but Akindin does not, it seems likely that this is the patriarch's response to Mikhail's following of Akindin's advice to continue the case against Pëtr.

armies of Rus' by waging war on their rivals.[23] Such eirenic counsel no doubt appeared to Mikhail as anti-Tverite agitation even though it was no such thing. Briansk suffered greatly at the hands of the Tatars in 1310 as a result of ignoring Pëtr's advice, and for Tver' to fight Moscow in 1311 was foolishness. Pëtr found it impossible to reside in his cathedral city of Vladimir when faced with the open hostility of the grand duke. He travelled throughout Rus' before eventually (that is after more than five years) settling in Moscow where the local prince was still relatively powerless to interfere in metropolitan affairs whilst remaining powerful enough to defend the Church.[24] It is misleading to label Pëtr 'pro-Muscovite' simply because Moscow provided a secure, unhostile and unthreatening home for a prelate who did not enjoy the support of the grand duke. Only after Kalita and his clan hijacked Pëtr's corpse and made Moscow the famous shrine of a celebrated saint did Pëtr belong to Moscow rather than to the see of All Rus'.[25]

Some time around 1312, Patriarch Niphon made known to the grand duke his willingness to re-try Pëtr or ordain a metropolitan of Mikhail's choice.[26] What came of this is not known for sure. In March 1312, when Simeon of Rostov was replaced as bishop of that city by Prokhor, another cleric who was favourable to Pëtr,

[23] Fennell, *Emergence*, 70, 73. In 1310 when Sviatoslav died in the Briansk uprising against the Tatars, Pëtr sheltered in a church in that city – *PSRL*, XXV, 159.

[24] *ZhP*, 172 – 'Якоже убо прихождаша места и грады, бжии члвкъ Пётръ прииде во славныи град зовомыи Москва, еще же тогда малоу сущоу емоу и не многоу народу' – 'For he visited places and cities and Pëtr, the man of god came to the glorious city called Moscow which then was still small and had not many people ...'

[25] There is a strange tendency to label prelates politically without regard to the needs of the Church. Thus Moisei of Novgorod is pro-Muscovite in 1329 and anti-Muscovite in 1352 when in fact he is pro-Novgorodian always. On the development of the cult of Pëtr see *ZhP*, 175–6 and Meyendorff, *Byzantium*, 270. On Feognost's referral of the cult for patriarchal approval in 1339 see Darrouzès, *Regestes*, no. 2192, p.148. Despite the constant repetition of Muscovite hagiographical topoi in ecclesiastical historiography there is no evidence of Pëtr's 'pro-Muscovite' activities. The apparition of Pëtr to Kalita in a dream is an innovation of the early sixteenth-century – I. A. Kochetkov, 'Ikonopisets kak illiustrator zhitii', *TODRL*, 36 (1981), 314. N. S. Borisov is the first historian to publish his scepticism about the links between Church and state in Moscow – *Russkaia tserkov' v politicheskoi bor'be XIV–XV vekov* (Moscow, 1986), 45, 55–6.

[26] 'Егда придетъ митрополитъ или исправитися тотъ, или другого поставимъ, кого всхочеть боголюбьство твое' – 'If the metropolitan comes he will be corrected or we will create another whom Your Piety wishes' – *RIB*, no. 16-i, p. 149. The date 1312 suggests itself because Akindin wrote to Mikhail *after* October 1310. The prince then wrote to the patriarch, receiving this letter in response.

the bishop of Tver' assisted at his consecration.[27] Whether Andrei's presence at this ceremony indicates a reconciliation between Tver' and the metropolitan is unclear. It was in Tver' that same year that Pëtr consecrated Bishop Kharalampy to an unspecified see. Four years later, however, in March 1316 Andrei vacated his see and retired to a monastery.[28] It is unlikely that this retirement was voluntary, given Andrei's former antagonism towards Pëtr and the interest he continued to show in political matters. In 1321 he emerged from retirement to treat in a dispute between Moscow and Tver'.[29]

It is against this background of discord in Rus' that in August 1317 we come across a metropolitan of Lithuania for the first time. He appears unnamed in the records of the patriarch of Constantinople as present at a synodal discussion of the boundaries of certain Byzantine metropolitanates.[30] When exactly a Lithuanian hierarch was first ordained we do not know. According to the Constantinopolitan *Notitiae Episcopatuum* and a report of one Metropolitan Cyril of Monemvasia, the metropolitanate was established by Andronicus II (1282–1328) and a prelate was ordained to it by Patriarch John XIII Glykys who ascended the patriarchal throne in May 1315.[31] These dates do not refer of course to the time when the idea of such an ordination was first considered by the Byzantine authorities or proposed by a grand duke of Lithuania (Vytenis or Gediminas). Some historians have suggested that the metropolitanate was created (rather than merely mooted) as early as 1300, when John XII Kosmas was patriarch, in accordance with a date given in two manuscripts of the second redaction of the *Notitiae*. However this date is a later, erroneous addition to the *Notitiae* which in their original form bear no date whatsoever.[32] It also

[27] *PSRL*, XV (i), 36.

[28] *Ibid.*, 42.

[29] *NL*, 96; *NL4*, 258; *PSRL*, XV (ii), 414. Readiness of Andrei to retire unlikely – V. S. Borzakovsky, *Istoria tverskogo kniazhestva* (St Petersburg, 1876; reprinted The Hague, 1969), 97–8 and P. Sokolov, *Russkii arkhierei iz Vizantii i pravo ego naznachenia do nachala XV veka* (Kiev, 1913; reprinted Gregg International, 1970), 249.

[30] Darrouzès, *Regestes*, no. 2080, p. 57; *MM*, I, no. 39, pp. 71–3. The most recent edition of these texts with a German translation is Hunger and Kresten, *Register*, no. 50, pp. 332–7.

[31] Darrouzès, *Notitiae*, no. 17, p. 399; no. 18, p. 409. For Cyril's report of 1428, see S. Lampros, 'Duo anaforai mētropolitou Monemvasias pros ton patriarkhēn', *Neos Hellēnomnēmōn*, 12 (1915), 298. Discussed more fully in Kalligas, *Byzantine Monemvasia*, 250–3. For dates of John Glykys see Grumel, *Chronologie*, 437.

[32] The thirteen manuscripts of *Recensio*, I of Notitia 17 bear no date except for *Taurinensis*, B, IV, 16 and *Genevensis*, 23 which give 1291/2 (*sō*), probably in imitation of the date

seems likely that the Lithuanian metropolitanate holding eighty-second rank was created after the Galich province which held eighty-first and was created, as we have seen, in 1303.[33] Although the *Notitiae* are not strictly records of ecclesiastical precedence, Darrouzès has noted how the fourteenth-century metropolitanates are listed in a rough order of their creation. We must adduce therefore a date between May 1315 and August 1317 for the creation of a metropolitanate of Lithuania separate from that of Kiev and All Rus'. The primate was probably ordained *c.* 1316 very soon after Glykys became patriarch.

Novgorodok, the city associated with grand-ducal power in the thirteenth century, was chosen as the seat of the new metropolitan, whose suffragans were the bishops of Turov and Polotsk.[34] The city had been part of the diocese of Turov and hence subject in 1303 to the metropolitan of Galich, whilst the see of Polotsk, the other major acquisition of the Lithuanians in Rus', had remained in the care of the metropolitan of Kiev [, Vladimir and all Rus'].[35] Therefore the Lithuanians must have been aware of the division of the Church of Rus'. Similarly as allies of the princes of Tver', the grand dukes of Lithuania were almost certainly aware of Mikhail Yaroslavich's troubles with Metropolitan Pëtr who since 1308 had governed the Church throughout the Grand Duchy. Bishop Andrei of Tver' was himself a Lithuanian of a family related

which all manuscripts give for the creation of Galich. Of the twenty-one manuscripts of *Recensio*, II of Notitia 17 (including Cambridge University Library, Dd.II.51 f.187, see fig. 1) all but two give the date 1291/2; *Parisinus*, 1362 and *Patmensis*, 376 give 1299/1300 (*sōē*) – Darrouzès, *Notitiae*, no. 17, p. 399. The text of Notitia 18 (*ibid.*, 409) gives no date. Since all manuscripts of all redactions say that the metropolitanate appeared during the patriarchate of John *Glykys* there can be no doubt that this was so. The date *sōē* appears as a secondary attempt to fit a date with the name of the patriarch and implies that John XII *Kosmas* (1.01.1294 – 21.06.1303) was responsible for the ordination. However the soubriquet *glykys* is always present. This second and late attempt does not deserve the faith Giedroyć places in it as the 'outcome of two successive attempts at establishing an accurate record of events' – Giedroyć, 'Arrival ... (1281–1341)', 16–17. For earlier scholars who debated between 1300 and 1317 as the date of foundation see *ibid.*

33 Darrouzès, *Notitiae*, no. 17, p. 399. Although the *Notitiae* are not generally reliable for chronological deductions, the order of metropolitanates created between 1300 and 1323 is accepted as accurate – *ibid.*, 182–3.

34 On the position of Novgorodok, see p. 83; in 1356 Turov and Polotsk were described as the 'two bishoprics of the eparchy of the Lithuanians' and there is no reason to doubt that this was the case in 1316 – *MM*, I, 426[19]–427[1].

35 Lithuanian territorial acquisitions by Gediminas – see pp. 82–7; on suffragans of Galich, see above p. 151. Novgorodok paid tithes to the see of Turov in the 1330s – Shchapov, 'Turovskie ustavy', 255–6.

distantly to that of Gediminas and Vytenis and he too perhaps strengthened the connections between Lithuania and Tver'. As Vytenis and Gediminas took greater control of western Rus' (and it seems that in 1315 Gediminas seized Podlasie from Yury L'vovich) they must have appreciated the possibility of influencing the governance of the Church.[36] The control Gediminas enjoyed over the dry trade route from the Baltic to Constantinople would have benefited from the offices of a clerical intermediary in Byzantium. Gediminas may even have been supported in his pretensions by the Tverites as Algirdas would be in the 1350s.[37] By removing Polotsk and Turov from Pëtr's control, Gediminas not only reduced the income of the metropolitan of Kiev but also provided a base for a potential rival to Pëtr for supremacy in the Church of All Rus'. Mikhail of Tver' had spent many years seeking to undermine Pëtr's position. Since Pëtr had been ordained to heal the rift between the Churches of north and south Rus', it was not likely that the independent metropolitanate of Galich could be revived. Lithuania was a powerful land, friendly to Tver' and capable of purchasing Byzantine favour. Perhaps this type of connivance between Lithuania, Tver' and Byzantium (where Niphon had exhibited patriarchal willingness to ordain another prelate for Rus') was connected with Andrei's 'retirement' in 1316. The coincidence of the two events is curious. Pëtr could not but resent the diminution of his power, especially if one of his own suffragans had had a share in it. We learn from the list of princes included in the Sinodal manuscript of *NL* that it was in 1316 that Pëtr moved from the south to Suzdalia and Moscow.[38]

For their part, the Byzantines probably regarded the appointment of a metropolitan of Lithuania as a means of reducing temporarily pressure on the metropolitan of Rus'. The Byzantines always claimed that the division of the Rus'ian province had been permitted as a temporary measure 'in a time of trouble'. In this period of uncertainty and dread of the Ottoman incursion, it is possible that the Byzantines may have sought military or financial

[36] Seizure of Podlasie (the Brest region) – see p. 84; on the friendship of Lithuania and Tver', see Fennell, *Emergence*, 69.

[37] Trade routes described in M. N. Tikhomirov, 'Puti iz Rossii v Vizantiiu v XIV–XVvv.', *Vizantiiskie Ocherki* (Moscow, 1961), 3f. The Mongols used the bishop of Sarai in their political and commercial dealings with Constantinople – A. N. Nasonov, *Mongoly i Rus'* (Moscow–Leningrad, 1940), 45. On Tverite support for Algirdas in the 1350s and 1360s, see below pp. 165–6.

[38] *NL*, 469.

aid from Gediminas or Vytenis during the Turkish War of 1315.[39] Indeed, we should not overlook the contribution of Vytenis to this policy, given the number of years which must have been involved in the negotiations over the church province. Contemporary Byzantine sources emphasise how Emperor Andronicus II liked to establish new ecclesiastical provinces *peri filotimia*, through a generosity which was no doubt prompted by foreign gold. Lithuania was known in Constantinople as a rich and populous land on the Rus'ian border which produced very brave and invincible armies.[40] This very secular usefulness should have evoked a response from the emperor who is credited with the creation of the metropolitanate of Lithuania.

Having attempted an explanation of when and how the province came to be created, let us turn now to examine more closely what was established *c.* 1316. The Turovian parish (ενορια) of Novgorodok was elevated by Andronicus to the status of metropolitan cathedral city of the Lithuanian province. The new 'bishop of the Lithuanians' who enjoyed metropolitan title and assumed responsibility for Christians within pagan Lithuania, resided in Black Rus'. From there he controlled his suffragans in Turov and Polotsk, the sees which covered the whole of Lithuania's Rus'ian territories.[41] Novgorodok became a centre of

[39] Gregoras, *HB*, VII, cap. 10; PG, CXLVIII, 433–42. In 1315 the Turks ravaged Thrace and the emperor suffered from an acute financial deficit. The patriarch always claimed the metropolitanate of Lithuania was an anomaly and closed it as soon as its incumbent died.

[40] ἅπαξ γεγονότα τῇ τοῦ βασιλέως ... περὶ τὰ τοιαῦτα φιλοτιμία – Darrouzès, *Notitiae*, no. 18, p. 409[7]. Andronicus created many metropolitanates in the early fourteenth century – see above p. 17. On the power of bribes see Meyendorff, *Byzantium*, 80. Impressions of the pagans in Byzantium were respectful – πολυανθρωπότατον τε ὀν μαχιμωτατον – Gregoras, *HB*, XXXVI, cap.6; PG, CXLIX, 456 and *HB*, XXXVI, cap. 8, PG, CXLIX p. 457 – μάχιμον ἔθνος ὡς τα πολλα καὶ ὀυ πόρρω που γίνομαι λέγειν ἀνανταγωνιστον.

[41] 'Now perhaps you will cite the canon "It is possible for the Emperor to ordain concerning ecclesiastical parishes and privileges". This has not only been decreed, it has also been practised. Leaving aside the majority of very ancient cases, did not the blessed late Emperor the Lord Andronicus Palaeologus promote to the rank of metropolitanate of the eighty-second throne a mere parish of the metropolitanate of Rus' which had not even been a bishopric? And did not the most holy Patriarch the late lord John Glykys appoint a metropolitan to this province and after him another and others for many years, even if the irregularity of affairs does not permit this to happen now [1438]?' – Lampros, 'Duo', 298. It seems clear that Novgorodok was made the centre of a bishopric of Lithuania (φθάνει μὲν ἡ ἁγιωτάτη ἐπισκοπὴ τῶν Λιτβῶν ... *MM*, I, no. 270, p. 525) and that later this bishopric fell vacant. On the vacancy of the bishopric, see n. 57. Certainly the bishop of Turov or Polotsk was not raised to metropolitan rank – unlike the bishop of Galich. The Lithuanian metropolitanate was an entirely new creation. The reference to many metropolitans probably includes Feodorit, Roman and Kiprian,

ecclesiastical art and architecture worthy of its new hierarch and in this respect it benefited directly from the economic decline of Kiev.[42] It is likely that the metropolitan sent a *namestnik* or vicar to serve the Orthodox merchants of Vilnius once that city became established as the centre of grand-ducal power in the 1320s. A merchant church of St Nikolai flourished in the *civitas Ruthenica* or Rus'ian Quarter in Vilnius, just as Christian churches had served alien believers in the Podol' area of Kiev before the conversion of Rus'.[43] The metropolitan of All Rus' also retained *namestniki* in Grodno, Novgorodok and Vilnius to look after his affairs in the Grand Duchy at times when there was no Lithuanian prelate.[44] Orthodoxy made very little headway in Lithuania outside the grand-ducal commercial centre of Vilnius and this very paucity of native converts was used as an excuse later to close down the province.[45] The metropolitan of the Lithuanians, despite his title and care of souls in Lithuania, was a Lettovian hierarch with his eyes set on becoming the metropolitan of All Rus'. He remained in Novgorodok long after Vilnius became the undisputed political centre of the Grand Duchy.

We do not know how many metropolitans were ordained for Gediminas between 1316 and 1330 nor do we know their provenance. It seems likely that only one was ordained and that he was a Rus'ian. Feofil, the metropolitan of Lithuania who is named in a synodal decree of 1329, enjoyed great influence from Novgorodok in the west to Murom in the east, from Moscow to Vladimir Volynsky and Surozh.[46] He was known not only in

not all of whom were ordained in Constantinople or restricted to Lithuania. When Cyril of Monemvasia was writing the letter cited above in English, the metropolitanate of All Rus' had been united for thirty-eight years. On the date of the letter see V. Laurent, 'Isidore de Kiev et la métropole de Monembasie', *Revue des Etudes Byzantines*, 17 (1959), 150. On Lithuanian converts see Giedroyć, 'Arrival ... (1281–1341)', 19.

[42] Novgorodok became a centre of craftsmanship and a new cathedral was built there after the abandonment of Kiev: see Gurevich, 'Novogrudok 1956–1977', 97–8 and M. V. Malevskaia and E. V. Sholokhova, 'Raskopi tserkovnykh postroek na detintse Novogrudka', *AO* (1974), 391–2.

[43] *Civitas ruthenica* – see p. 73; the church of St Ilia in Kiev is mentioned in *PVL*, I, 38 s.a. 945. On the church of St Nikolai in Vilnius in Gediminas' day see Dobrianskii, *Staraia*, 152.

[44] For a letter of Metropolitan Iona dated 9 February 1451 referring to ancient practice of *namestnich'stvo* – *Russkii Feodal'nyi Arkhiv XIV–pervoi treti XVI veka*, ed. V. I. Buganov (Moscow, 1986), I, no. 44, p. 172. See also Makary, *Istoria*, V, 2 (St Petersburg, 1886), 92–5.

[45] Darrouzès, *Notitiae*, no. 18, p. 409^{8-10}.

[46] *MM*, I, no. 67, 146–8 (Hunger and Kresten, *Register*, no. 98, 552–7). N. D. Tikhomirov, *Galitskaia Mitropolia*: *Tserkovno-istoricheskoe issledovanie* (St Petersburg, 1896), 170 argues that the metropolitan who was in Constantinople in January 1327 (see below

Table 3. *The spread of Metropolitan Feofil's property throughout Rus'*

North-west	North-east
Novgorodok – 20 gr.[a]	Moscow – the monk Fëdor – 20 gr. – ? – 2 *kaukia*
Drutsk – Prince Mikhail – 1 silver *kaukion*	Kostroma – 20 gr.
Smolensk – Bishop Ivan – 1 silver paten	Kozel'sk – Prince Andrei, Gediminas' son-in-law – 15 gr.
Minsk – erased from record	Murom – Yaroslav owes 15 gr.
Pskov[b] – Aleksandr Mikhailovich – 1 silver *kaukion*	Yuriev – 2 *kaukia*
South-west	**South-east**
Galich – 10 gr.	Surozh – Yury holds 1 *kaukion*
Pereiaslavl' – 3 *kaukia*	Briansk[c] – silken sakkos; epigonation; embroidered epigonation; pearl-studded epimanika embroidered chalice veil; 2 deacon's mandulia; alb and stole of Arseny; seamless garment; calfskin garment; 2 garments of which one decorated
Kiev – Fëdor, brother of Gediminas – 2 silver *kaukia*	
Liubartas-Dmitry took 39 gr. from Stolsk, a golden cross, 29 horses and 5 mares	
Vladimir – princess – 2 *kaukia* – boiarin – 2 *kaukia*	
Provenance uncertain	
A bishop – 1 *kaukion*; monk Antonii – 1 *kaukion*; Artemy – 2 *kaukia*; 1 gr. Iakov – 3 golden gr.; 1 silver gr. from G.; 2 sable garments; 500 squirrel skins; 3 marten coats and 1 marten pelt (*doknostai*); 3 broadcloth garments, 1 lighter robe; 28 golden *kaukia*; 6 silver *kaukia*	

Notes:

[a] The sums referred to as gr. (*grivny*) above are σωμια in the manuscript. This word derives from the Arabic *sawma* and refers to silver ingots mined in Rus' – M. F. Hendy, *Studies in the Byzantine monetary economy c. 300–1450* (Cambridge, 1985), 547–51.

[b] The reference to Pskov is deduced from the name Aleksandr. The only prince of that name in Rus'ian Chronicles for 1330–31 is Mikhailovich of Pskov.

[c] From the quantity of vestments Feofil left in Briansk it seems that he was particularly active or interested in that city.

Source: Notes from Feognost's chancery preserved on f. 244v of Codex Vaticanus Graecus 840, published in Priselkov and Vasmer, 'Otryvki', 49–50, 58–9.

Vladimir, Galich and Lithuania but even in the Golden Horde. He left property and gifts – gold and silver cups, furs, liturgical vestments and money – throughout Rus' as is clear from an inventory of his goods which was made after his death. A summary of these artefacts is given in table 3. Some historians have used Feofil's property to illustrate the extensive political influence of the grand dukes of Lithuania.[47] However this is questionable since Gediminas had no political influence in Moscow where Feofil left twenty *grivny*, even if Andrei of Kozel'sk, Gediminas' son-in-law, received fifteen *grivny* from the metropolitan.[48] The evidence illustrates Feofil's influence and that is not quite the same thing. We may deduce from this evidence that Feofil travelled widely in Pëtr's province or at least scattered gifts broadly, perhaps to win support for his ambitions to become hierarch of All Rus'. After 1323 he was the chief prelate of the power which held Kiev.[49] It is certainly not surprising to see him in Constantinople in January 1327 before Pëtr had lain a month in the grave.[50] It is likely that he had travelled south whilst Pëtr was still alive in order to pursue his case with the patriarch before the Muscovite candidate to succeed Pëtr, Abbot Fëdor, had been dispatched to Byzantium. This is a pattern which would be followed several times later in the century as a metropolitan of Kiev, Vladimir and All Rus' ailed.[51] The cups or *kaukia* which Feofil distributed throughout Rus' were bribes which formerly a Byzantine consul might have showered legitimately upon his electorate.[52]

If bribery to gain high office did lie behind Feofil's gifts it availed him nought. In summer 1327 the patriarch rejected both Feofil and Fëdor, presumably on the grounds that they were both

n. 50) was not Feofil because in 1328 Feognost controlled the bishop of Turov. This presumes that Feognost was acting legally in 1328. There is no reason to suppose Feofil was not Gediminas' only metropolitan. On Turov, see below n. 54.

47 Giedroyć, 'Arrival ... (1281–1341)', 29; Fennell, *Emergence*, 123.

48 See table 3. For Andrei of Kozel'sk see p. 86.

49 See pp. 94–111.

50 Pëtr died in winter 1326 – *NL*, 97–8; on 20 December according to the life written by Prokhor in 1327 – Makary, *Istoria*, IV, 1, 315. Feofil was in Constantinople in January 1327 – *MM*, I, no. 65, 143–4 – Hunger and Kresten, *Register*, no. 96, pp. 542–5.

51 As with Feodorit in 1352 (Feognost had been ill since 1350), Aleksei in 1354 and Kiprian in 1378, see below pp. 164–5, 167.

52 *Legum Iustiniani imperatoris vocabularium. Novellae pars graeca*, ed. G. G. Archi, IV (Milan, 1988), 1508 refers to *Novellae*, 105.2.1; 105.2.3. It is difficult to imagine how so many cups came to be spread throughout Rus' and why Feognost was so keen to collect them all if they had served merely a potatory purpose.

too closely associated with princes in Rus', and appointed a Greek, Feognost, as metropolitan of Kiev and All Rus'. The latter's first loyalty would be to the Church and his appointment was a prerogative the Byzantines often chose to presume for themselves in the fourteenth century.[53] When Feognost came to Rus' in May or June 1328, he spent the greater part of his first years of office in south-west Rus' ordaining bishops and commanding the attendance of other prelates thereat, especially those who earlier had been suffragans of the metropolitans of Galich, and Fëdor of Turov who was still subject officially to Feofil.[54] Feognost was clearly emphasising his power in Rus'. Complaints about such interference in the affairs of another metropolitan (a charge with which Feognost was familiar) may explain Feofil's continued presence in Constantinople where he appears to have died in 1330, and the embassy of Metropolitan Matthew of Ephesus to Rus' in 1330–31.[55]

After Feofil died, Feognost began assiduously to clear up the dead metropolitan's belongings and leave his own mark in southern Rus' and the Grand Duchy.[56] The patriarch helped restore the unity of the Rus'ian province by using the excuse that there were too few Christians in Lithuania and that those there were could be served best by the metropolitan of All Rus', to

[53] Feognost was ordained 'certainement avant la fin de l'automne 1327' – Darrouzès, *Regestes*, no. 2136, pp. 102–3. On Fëdor see Prokhor's life of Pëtr, 315 (as n. 50). The alternation of Greek and Rus'ian metropolitans of Rus' in the late thirteenth and fourteenth centuries, proposed respectively by the patriarch and the church of Rus' is discussed in Meyendorff, *Byzantium*, 88.

[54] In May 1328 he was in Galich to ordain bishops for Vladimir and Galich in the presence of the bishops of Peremyshl', Kholm, Lutsk and Turov as we see from election notices in *Cod.Vat.Gr.*, 840ff., 9v-10r, published in Regel, *Analecta*, 52–6.

[55] That Feognost was aware that charges could be brought against a metropolitan who interfered in the province of another prelate is clear from notes which survive from his chancery in *Cod.Vat.Gr.*, 840f., 243 citing the twenty-first canon of the Council of Antioch – Priselkov and Vasmer, 'Otryvki', 56. Feofil was in Constantinople in 1329 as we have seen – n. 46. For the *ante quem* dating of Feofil's death to 1331 see *ibid.*, 64–6. On the embassy of Matthew of Ephesus to Rus' see Reinsch, *Briefe*, no. 41, p. 320[32–35]; commentary in S. I. Kourouses, *Manouēl Gabalas eita Matthaios Mētropolitēs Efesou (1271/2–1355/60) A-Ta biografika* (Athens, 1972), 247–52.

[56] See above, p. 160 and Fennell, *Emergence*, 130, n.1. In Kiev behind the altar of St Sofia there is a graffito bearing Feognost's full title. It must have been carved there when the city was a Lithuanian possession: *Гресщому/митрополит/Феогносту/всея/ Роуси/мно/лет*: 'Long live the sinful Metropolitan of All Rus', Feognost – S. A. Vysotsky, *Drevnerusskie nadpisi Sofii kievskoi XI–XIVvv* (Kiev, 1966), 102–3 and tables lxi, 1; lxii, 1. This is an early example of the style *Mitropolit vseia Rusi*. Cf. A. Pliguzov, 'On the title "Metropolitan of Kiev and all Rus'"', *Harvard Ukrainian Studies*, 15:3–4 (1991), 340–53.

reduce Novgorodok to episcopal rank. This bishopric was left vacant (*scholasas*) but it was not suppressed: should a metropolitan of Lithuania prove necessary in the future one could be appointed.[57] Feognost now controlled all Rus' and Lithuania too.

The preservation of the unity of the metropolitanate of Rus' was the main aim of the patriarchate which exercised considerable power within and gained most wealth from the 'very populous' lands of Rus'. A parcelling out of the metropolitanate would increase the power of local princes over the Church in their realms. The Byzantines feared the removal of ecclesiastical provinces from the domain of emperor and patriarch by ambitious local rulers, as had happened in Bulgaria in 1235 and would happen again in Serbia in 1346.[58] The Byzantine authorities regarded a split in the metropolitanate of Rus' when it happened as an 'anomaly' or the result of 'confusion' during a 'time of trouble'.[59] For their part, the princes of Rus' and Lithuania regarded an attempt to control the metropolitanate as an important part of their political ambitions. Clearly Feognost's united province would always be coveted or challenged. Although he visited the faithful throughout Rus', Feognost settled in Moscow where Pëtr's relics were venerated and where the strongest contender for the grand-ducal *iarlyk* held court. When the new metropolitan arrived in Rus' in 1328, Tver' was subject to Tatar retaliation for the uprising of 1327 and so he had little choice but to go where his predecessor had died.

In the 1330s, as Bolesław-Yury II of Galich–Volyn' edged ever closer towards a western alliance and perhaps reconversion to

[57] Darrouzès, *Notitiae*, no. 18, 409[8]. These excuses may have been furnished by Feognost. *Scholasas* refers to a see which has no bishop rather than one which has been completely suppressed – *Greek Lexicon of the Roman and Byzantine Periods* (*from B.C. 146 to A.D. 1100*), ed. E. A. Sophocles (New York, 1900), 1064. Note that Novgorodok was not reduced to its earlier status as a parish.

[58] On the re-establishment of the patriarchate of Bulgaria at T'rnovo in 1235 and the creation of the patriarchate of Serbia by Stefan Dušan in 1346 at Peč, see Soulis, *The Serbs*, 30–2 and D. Boko Slijepchevich, *Istorija srpske pravoslavne tsrkve*, I (Munich, 1962), 172–89. Byzantine interest in Rus'ian money is explained in Meyendorff, *Byzantium*, 80.

[59] Of the creation of Galich according to a patriarchal letter of 1347 καιρὸς τῆς συγχύσεως καὶ τὴν τοιαύτην τοῦ ἔθνους κατάστασιν ἀνέτρεψε καὶ συνέχεε ... ἀλλὰ βουλομένους ἀσάλευτον καὶ ἀμετακίνητον μένειν τὴν, ἣν εἶχον ἐκ παλαιοῦ συνήθειαν, ὡς δεδήλωται, καὶ πάντα τρόπον κινοῦντας εἰς τὴν τῆς τοιαύτης καινοτομίας κατάλυσιν – *MM*, I, no. 120, pp. 267, 268. In 1370 when Lithuania was suppressed, the patriarch commented that it had been created of great necessity and had provoked numerous problems – ἐπεὶ ἅπαξ γεγονὸς τοῦτο ὄχλησιν προεξένησε καὶ ἄτοπα πολλὰ, καὶ ταῦτα δι'ἀνάγχας μεγάλας, ὡς ἔδοξε, γεγονος – *MM*, I, no. 270, p. 527.

Catholicism, the patriarch was borne upon to restore the metropolitanate of Galich.[60] Bolesław's success was emulated by Gediminas' son Liubartas (baptised as Dmitry) when he ruled Vladimir Volynsky in the 1340s. He took advantage of the political crisis in Byzantium between 1342 and 1347 to obtain metropolitan rank for Bishop Fëdor of Galich.[61] When that crisis was resolved by the coronation of Emperor John VI Kantakuzenos in 1347, the metropolitan of Galich was duly relegated to episcopal rank. The emperor addresses Liubartas, as he does Semën Ivanovich of Moscow, as 'nephew', revealing the imperial acceptance of the Lithuanian prince within the Orthodox family of princes.[62]

Within five years of the closure of the Galich province, Algirdas of Lithuania, regarding the whole of Rus' as his domain sent out a protégé, Feodorit, to Constantinople for ordination as metropolitan of All Rus' in succession to Feognost, who (it seemed) was dying.[63] We note that Feodorit sought ordination to the whole Rus'ian province, not merely its Lithuanian eparchy. However in 1352 Feognost was still alive and the patriarch refused to ordain Feodorit. The monk promptly set off for Bulgaria where the schismatic patriarch of T'rnovo ordained him as 'metropolitan of Rus''.[64] Metropolitan Feodorit returned to the Grand Duchy and took up residence in Kiev, the original centre of the metropolitanate of All Rus'. It is clear that the Byzantines feared that Feodorit's influence would spread into the areas of Rus' which bordered on the Grand Duchy and that Rus' might join Bulgaria in schism. In 1353 the patriarch granted Archbishop Moisei of Novgorod the right to wear the *polystavrion*. The wearing of this special vestment, which symbolised autocephalous status for a prelate, had been denied him by Metropolitan Feognost. In July 1354 Patriarch Philotheos warned Moisei against recognising

[60] There was perhaps a metropolitan of Galich in 1331 (*MM*, I, no. 73, 164–7 – Hunger and Kresten, *Register*, no. 106, 604–15) but this could be an error – see Meyendorff, *Byzantium*, 154 and n. 26. There was certainly a metropolitan in 1336 – *MM*, I, no. 75, 168–71.

[61] In 1342 Bishop Fëdor of Galich was granted metropolitan rank – Darrouzès, *Regestes*, no. 2224, pp. 175–7.

[62] In September 1347 it was suppressed – *MM*, I, nos. 120–1, pp. 267–71. On the connection of this appointment with Byzantine politics see Meyendorff, *Byzantium*, 55. Liubartas as *anepsios*: *MM*, I, 265.

[63] *MM*, I, 350. See J. Meyendorff, 'Alexis and Roman: A study in Byzantino-Russian relations (1352–54)', *Byzantino-Slavica*, 28 (1967), 278–88. Feognost had been ill since 1350 – *TL*, 371.

[64] *MM*, I, 350.

Feodorit.[65] The concession and the admonition do not appear unconnected. Defection to Feodorit's jurisdiction was not to be countenanced. Meanwhile Bishop Aleksei of Vladimir, the son of a Muscovite boiar and godson of Kalita was ordained, after a year of careful scrutiny, as metropolitan of Kiev, Vladimir and All Rus' in accordance with the wishes of the late Metropolitan Feognost (d. 1353).[66] As it became obvious that the Byzantines, who had declared Algirdas' actions with regard to Feodorit to be 'very irregular and most unlawful',[67] would never accept the accession of a Bulgarian appointee to the metropolitanate of All Rus', Algirdas abandoned Feodorit and adopted a new candidate to fulfil his purposes. Late in 1354 a monk from Tver' named Roman who, significantly, was a relative of Algirdas' wife Ul'iana (as Aleksei was a spiritual kinsman of the Muscovite prince), was sent to Constantinople to challenge Aleksei for his metropolitanate. In 1316 a prince of Tver' had supported Gediminas in his attempt to wrest the Lettovian sees from the control of a prelate in eastern Rus'. Similarly thirty-eight years later Mikhail Aleksandrovich of Tver', the son of Gediminas' vassal in Pskov, provided Algirdas with support in his ecclesiastical pretentions. Algirdas promised to convert to Orthodoxy in return for Roman's ordination.[68] The situation became dramatic when late in 1354 a new patriarch, Callistos took office. Now Algirdas seized his chance.

Faced with insurmountable rivalry for the Rus'ian primacy, Patriarch Callistos appointed Roman metropolitan of the Lithuanians in 1355. That same year, the new hierarch acted as a witness to the reconciliation of Byzantium and Bulgaria (where Feodorit

[65] After Feodorit in Kiev (*MM*, I, 352), the patriarch granted Vladimir official status as a metropolitan residence on the condition that Kiev would always be the cathedral city of the province whither one day wealth and power would return – *ibid.* Philotheos' letters to Moisei are published in *RIB*, Appendix nos. 10, 11, pp. 51–64. Moisei coveted the chasuble with four crosses (*polystavrion*) which was worn by autocephalous prelates, as the archbishop of Novgorod was in theory if never in practice. Feognost had granted the right to wear it to Kaleka but he refused Moisei – Meyendorff, *Byzantium*, 84–5, 169, 277.

[66] *MM*, I, no. 183, 425–30. For Aleksei's background see 'Rasskaz o Aleksei Mitropolite', G. M. Prokhorov, *Povest' o Mitiae: Rus' i Vizantia v epokhu kulikovskoi bitvy* (Leningrad, 1978), 216–18. He was not of Lithuanian descent despite the claim made to that effect in *PSRL*, XVIII, 120. On Feognost's patronage of Aleksei and the year of scrutiny see Meyendorff, *Byzantium*, 166–8.

[67] παραλογώτατον καὶ παρανομώτατον – *MM*, I, 350.

[68] On Roman's origins and the attempt to ordain him, see Meyendorff, *Byzantium*, 169–70. Algirdas' promise of conversion is recorded by Gregoras – *HB*, XXXVI, cap. 34; PG, CXLIX, 458.

had been ordained).[69] However, Roman and his grand duke were not satisfied with Lettovia alone. Roman regarded himself as metropolitan of All Rus' and attempted to interfere in those parts of Aleksei's province which lay under Lithuanian control: Kiev and Briansk. In 1356, after a good deal of horsetrading in Constantinople and the soliciting of financial assistance from Tver', the two rivals were brought to a truce. Callistos combined the formerly separate metropolitanates of Galich and Lithuania and presented them to Roman whilst Aleksei retained his title of metropolitan of all Rus'.[70] Nevertheless this rivalry continued until Roman died in 1362, at which point the metropolitanate of Lithuania–Galich returned to the control of the Muscovite. In June 1370 Lithuania was formally reduced once more to the rank of bishopric and placed officially under 'Kievan', that is Muscovite, control.[71]

In 1371 the metropolitanate of Galich was revived and redefined to cover those territories of south-west Rus' which had been captured by Poland. Casimir the Great had threatened the patriarch that he would rebaptise his Rus'ian subjects Catholic if an Orthodox prelate could not be found to govern them. Patriarch Philotheos readily acceded to Casimir's demand.[72] The hegemony of Catholic Poland now cut off Galich ecclesiastically from Rus', whilst the Grand Duchy of Lithuania, being under the control of

[69] In 1354 John VI and Patriarch Philotheos were replaced by Emperor John V and Patriarch Callistos; Callistos held office until 1364 when Philotheos was reinstated – see Meyendorff, *Byzantium*, 168, 175. On recreation of Lithuania – *MM*, I, no. 183, pp. 425–30. On 17 August 1355 the Bulgarians were reconciled with Constantinople and a treaty was made to which Roman was a witness – *MM*, I, no. 185, p. 433.

[70] *MM*, I, no. 183, pp. 425–30; Meyendorff, 'Alexis', 284–5. In 1356 both Aleksei and Roman sought financial aid from Bishop Fëdor the Good of Tver' to give money to the Patriarch – *PSRL*, XV (i), 63, 65. In 1355 Roman tried to win popular support in Kiev to force the Patriarch's hand – *PSRL*, XXXV, 47.

[71] *MM*, I, no. 270, pp. 525–7. Aleksei promoted the cult of the Three Martyrs of Vilnius in order to denigrate Algirdas in Byzantine eyes – Meyendorff, *Byzantium*, 181. Martyrs described below p. 184 and n. 157. For Aleksei's neglect of Lettovian sees, see Meyendorff, *Byzantium*, 195–7 and Kiprian's letter to Sergii Radonezhsky – Prokhorov, *Povest'*, 199.

[72] Casimir wrote to Philotheos in 1370 that 'we will be forced to baptise the Russians in the faith of the Latins if there is no metropolitan in Russia, for the land cannot remain without a law' – *MM*, I, p. 578, tr. Meyendorff, *Byzantium*, 287. The patriarch realised that the king was a Catholic capable of fulfilling his threat – 'he is not one of ours but a Latin; how could we refuse his request?' – *MM*, I, p. 583. Casimir had resumed Polish attacks on south-west Rus' in 1340 – see below pp. 266f. Suffragans of Metropolitan Antonii were the bishops of Kholm, Peremyshl' and Vladimir – *MM*, I, p. 589. One document includes Turov in this list but it is very unlikely that this bishopric was given to a Polish metropolitan – Meyendorff, *Byzantium*, 192.

a potential convert and a dedicated competitor for power in the whole of Rus', was still regarded by Byzantium as a part of the metropolitanate and polity of All Rus'.[73]

At this very time, Algirdas was leading his armies against Moscow. He also began to demand once more the ordination of a metropolitan for his realm, claiming that Aleksei was neglecting Lithuania. In 1373 Philotheos replied by sending a Bulgarian monk, Kiprian by name, to negotiate with Algirdas, Aleksei and Grand Duke Dmitry Donskoi of Moscow.[74] Algirdas would not be refused and threatened, like Casimir, to introduce Catholicism to his realm. On 2 December 1375 Kiprian was appointed by Philotheos to be metropolitan of Kiev, Lithuania and Rus'. He was ordained thus while Aleksei still lived so that after the metropolitan of All Rus' died Kiprian could govern the Church throughout Rus' and the Grand Duchy. By this means Algirdas could have his hierarch before Aleksei died without formally breaking the unity of Rus'.[75] Kiprian was not a prelate intended for Lettovia alone. However his first successful years in the Grand Duchy (1375–78) caused Dmitry Donskoi to reject him in 1378. Dmitry regarded Kiprian as a creature of Algirdas and attempted to gain the ordination of his own candidates Mitiai and Pimen after Aleksei's death. He accused the patriarch, the emperor and the *Synod Endemousa* of being 'Lithuanian'. It took twelve years and the death of Dmitry for Kiprian to establish himself in Moscow.[76]

[73] A metropolitan continued to be appointed to Galich until Jogaila, as king of Poland, was persuaded to accept Kiprian and reject his own man, Ioann of Lutsk – Pavlov, 'O nachale', 235–6.

[74] Algirdas attacked Moscow three times, in 1368, 1370 and 1372. On the last occasion his forces were beaten back at Lubutsk – L. V. Cherepnin, *Obrazovanie russkogo tsentralizovannogo gosudarstva v XIV–XV vekakh* (Moscow, 1960), 560–72. In 1371 he wrote to the patriarch demanding 'another metropolitan for Kiev, Smolensk, Tver', Little Russia, Novosil' and Nizhny Novgorod' – *MM*, I, p. 581. There is no mention of Lithuania here. As Meyendorff points out (*Byzantium*, 194–5) this metropolitanate would have been much more 'All Rus'ian' than the province controlled by Aleksei.The patriarch consented to Algirdas' demand lest 'such a numerous nation were abandoned without episcopal supervision and were in danger of utter catastrophe and spiritual perdition by being united to another church' – *MM*, II, p. 120, translated in Meyendorff, *Byzantium*, 201. Algirdas claimed that Aleksei neglected Lithuania – Meyendorff, *Byzantium*, 196–7.

[75] On Algirdas' dealings with Avignon see Giedroyć, 'Arrival ... (1341–1387)', 48–52. On Kiprian's mission, see Prokhorov, *Povest'*, 25–31 and Meyendorff, *Byzantium*, 193–9; Kiprian as metropolitan – *ibid.*, 200f.

[76] Kiprian wrote to St Sergii Radonezhsky on 23 June 1378 that: 'Кладет на мене вины, что был есмь в Литве первое ... Аще был есмь в Литве, много христиан

Kiprian was succeeded in 1406 by Fotii who took up residence in Moscow. In 1415, Vytautas of Lithuania summoned a Lettovian church council in Novgorodok, led by Archbishop Feodosy of Polotsk to elect a metropolitan of Lithuania in opposition to Fotii. Although the grand duke was a Catholic, he reserved the right as the local prince to appoint clergy to vacant offices.[77] Thus he revived a practice which had been known in Kiev in the twelfth century and which had been recommended to Mikhail Yaroslavich by Patriarch Niphon.[78] However Metropolitan Fotii denounced Vytautas' man, the Bulgar Grigor Tsamblak, and Patriarch Joseph saw fit to excommunicate him. Fotii intensified his visits to his flock in the Grand Duchy and, as it became clear that Byzantium would never recognise Grigor's position, Vytautas abandoned the Novgorodok candidate who, like Feodorit half a century earlier, then disappears from the record.[79]

After Fotii died in 1431, the Grand Duke of Moscow imitated Vytautas' attempt at appointing his own hierarch. A council of Rus'ian bishops was called to elect Iona of Riazan' as metropolitan of Vladimir and All Rus'. The patriarch objected to this use of a local council to elect a metropolitan and in 1434 ordained Bishop Gerasim of Smolensk, a protégé of Švitrigaila of Lithuania, to the

горькаго пленениа освободил есмь. Мнозе от невидящих Бога познали наши истиннаго Бога и к православнои вере святым крещением пришли.' – 'He heaps guilt on me because I went to Lithuania first ... When I was in Lithuania I released many Christians from bitter servitude. Many who did not believe in God came to know our true God and entered the orthodox faith with holy baptism', Prokhorov, *Povest'*, 199–200. Dmitry Donskoi called all Constantinople 'Lithuanian' because Church policy did not favour Moscow exclusively – 'Патриарха литвином назвали, царя тако же, и всечестный сбор вселенжскии' – *ibid.*, 201. On Mitiai and Pimen (1378–79; 1380, 1382–89) and Kiprian's brief rule in Moscow in 1381 see Meyendorff, *Byzantium*, 214–19, 228–41.

77 The Lettovian bishops were those of Chernigov, Lutsk, Vladimir, Peremyshl', Smolensk, Kholm and Turov, all under the guidance of the archbishop of Polotsk. See *Vitoldiana: Codex privilegiorum Vitoldi Magni Ducis Lithuaniae* 1386–1430, ed. J. Ochmański (Warsaw–Poznań, 1986), no. 207, pp.183–4 – 'но мы хотячи, чтобы ваша вера не меншала, ни угыбала и церквам вашим бы строение было, учинли есмо так митрополита по правилом нам годитися митрополита збором поставити' 'But we, wishing that your faith should not decrease or die and that your churches should be built, have seen fit to appoint a metropolitan by council according to the canons'.

78 Niphon promised to ordain a metropolitan chosen by Mikhail – *RIB*, 150. Akindin reminded Mikhail that 'Царь еси, господине княже, вь своей земли – 'You are emperor, lord prince, in your own lands' – *ibid.*, 158. This is an equivalent to the claim of Catholic princes to be *imperator in regno suo*. On the Kievan precedent of Kliment Smoliatich and Iziaslav, see Meyendorff, *Byzantium*, 265 and n. 18.

79 Mezendorff, *Byzantium.*, 266–7.

province of All Rus'.[80] Švitrigaila, whose political control of Lithuania was by no means secure and whose rivals Jogaila and Žygimantas had granted privileges to his Orthodox subjects to enable them to hold political offices that were open to Catholics, appeared to the Byzantines as less likely to dominate the metropolitan than the Grand Duke of Moscow was. Indeed Gerasim was burned in Vitebsk in 1435, after having been implicated in a rebellion against the Lithuanian ruler.[81] He was succeeded by a Greek cleric, Isidore, despite Moscow's renewed attempts to ordain Iona of Riazan'. In 1441, after he had returned to Rus' from the Ecumenical Council of Florence (1438–39) at which he had supported the reunion of the Byzantine Church with Rome, Isidore had to fly for his life from Moscow. Grand Duke Vasily II Vasilievich strenuously opposed his unionist metropolitan and the unionist patriarch of Constantinople. In 1448 Iona was successfully elected metropolitan of Moscow and All Rus' against Byzantine wishes. Constantinople fell to the Turks before the discord between Rus' and Byzantium could be harmonised. Moscow regarded herself as the home of pure Orthodoxy and continued to appoint her own hierarchs. In the Grand Duchy of Lithuania, Isidore became the first in a line of unionist metropolitans of Kiev. The competition between Vilnius and Moscow for influence over the hierarch of the single province of Rus' ended effectively in 1448.[82]

The grand dukes of Lithuania and Moscow sought to manipulate the metropolitan of Rus' (or the pretender to All Rus' in Lithuania) as a means of extending their own power throughout Rus'. This had been tried in Vladimir in the twelfth century.[83] From the time of Gediminas onwards, especially after the fall of Kiev in 1323 and Algirdas' penetration of eastern Rus' in the 1350s

[80] Election of Iona – *ibid.*, 267; on Gerasim see *NL*, 417; *PL*, I, 40–3. (*RIB*, 521, 578).

[81] *PSRL*, XXXV, 57–8; *PL*, I, 43. See J. Matusas, *Švitrigaila Lietuvos didysis kunigaikštis*, 2nd edn (Vilnius, 1991), 120–3. On concessions to the Orthodox from Jogaila and Žygimantas during the Lithuanian civil war, see *Codex epistolaris saeculi decimi quinti*, III, Appendix, no. 17, pp. 523–4 (Jogaila, Lviv, 15.10.1432), no. 22, pp. 529–31 (Žygimantas, Trakai, 06.06.1434) and *Arkhiv iugo-zapadnoi Rossii*, V.1 (Kiev, 1869), no. 1, pp. 1–2 (Jogaila, Lutsk, 31.10.1432).

[82] On Isidore and the aftermath of Ferrara–Florence, see E. E. Golubinsky, *Istoria russkoi tserkvi*, II, 1 (Moscow, 1900), 421–68. For Metropolitan Iona of Moscow (1448–61), see *ibid.*, 469–515.

[83] See S. Franklin, 'Diplomacy and ideology: Byzantium and the Russian church in the mid-twelfth century', *Byzantine Diplomacy*, ed. J. Shepard and S. Franklin (London, 1992), 145–50.

and 1360s, the grand dukes of Lithuania came to regard themselves increasingly as lords of All Rus'. Byzantine sources state explicitly that Algirdas sought the ordination of Roman that he might control all Rus' through the metropolitan.[84] For their part, the Byzantines feared lest Algirdas or any other prince gain control of the Church. The patriarch was worried with good reason by Feodorit's consecration in Bulgaria in 1352. Algirdas was not afraid of finding an ecclesiastical power outside Constantinople to do his will. The Bulgarian model of ecclesiastical policy was studied by Vytautas in the early fifteenth century when a history of the patriarchates of Serbia and Bulgaria was composed for him.[85]

The maintenance of the unity of the Rus'ian ecclesiastical province and its loyalty to Constantinople were the main concerns of the Byzantine patriarch in his dealings with the Rus'ian Church in areas under Muscovite and Lithuanian control. A hierarch was appointed to Lithuania or Galich only if such a division of the province was unavoidable, given the threats or promises of the grand dukes. An independent metropolitan of Lithuania never took office when there was a metropolitan of Galich.[86] Although on occasion these two sees were united as in the case of Roman, Galich and Lithuania were not the same.[87] Nevertheless they did perform a similar function by providing a temporary means to resolve the conflict over the office of metropolitan of All Rus'. The more the patriarchate strengthened the unity of the politically-unaligned ecclesiastical power in the divided realm of Rus', the more the rival princes sought to dominate and appropriate that ecclesiastical unity to improve their own status as if by sympathetic magic. This rivalry meant that the ecclesiastical power had to be

[84] Patriarch Neilos remarked in 1380 that Algirdas 'had him [Roman] consecrated … under the pretext that the Lord Aleksei was not acceptable as metropolitan in the nation which was under his rule, but his real goal was to find a means with Roman's help of ruling Great Russia', *MM*, II, 12–13, tr. Meyendorff, *Byzantium*, 169. In 1358 Algirdas expressed his desire to rule the whole of Rus' to Catholic envoys with whom he was discussing Roman conversion – *sed omnis Russia ad Letwinos deberet simpliciter pertinere* – *HW*, 80. On Algirdas' expansion into Rus' see Giedroyć, 'Arrival … (1341–1387)', 38–40.

[85] Ia. N. Shchapov, 'Iuzhnoslavianskii politicheskii opyt na sluzhbe u russkikh ideologov XVv.', *Byzantino-Bulgarica*, 2 (1966), 209.

[86] See Appendix 2.

[87] Golubinsky argued that there was in fact only one metropolitanate, of south-west Rus', which included both Galich and Lithuania – *Istoria*, 126, n. 1. Pavlov opposed this conclusion vigorously although he had given rise to it first. His opposition was justified – Pavlov, 'O nachale', 241–2.

divided at certain times. However, from the beginning the metropolitan of the Lithuanians was a Rus'ian hierarch (especially with the probable Tverite involvement in Feofil's elevation and the certain Tverite connivance with the ordination of Roman and Kiprian), not a local prelate for Lithuania alone or even the Grand Duchy as a whole. Local puppets like Feodorit were not acceptable to Constantinople nor were they attractive to their grand duke once it became obvious that they would not gain all Rus'.

Ironically even when the political power appeared to win over the metropolitan, it discovered that the former bishop who had been a willing ally became a stubborn prelate whose chief concern lay in protecting the best interests of the Church. At his consecration he swore not to obey his prince.[88] Gerasim of Smolensk did not share all the priorities of Gerasim of All Rus' nor was Pëtr the Galich abbot quite the same as Metropolitan Pëtr. This does not mean that the metropolitan would not serve his prince loyally, if such loyalty was consonant with the interests of the Church. Feognost and Kiprian served Moscow well but they also met the needs of the Lettovian faithful. When Feognost interfered in Novgorod in 1352 and annoyed Archbishop Moisei such that the patriarch feared Moisei would recognise the claims of Feodorit, he did so not as a pawn of Moscow but as a prelate jealous of his own status.[89] Historians of the Middle Ages appear to forget that truly consistent Russian erastianism began with the Holy Synod of Peter the Great not with the metropolitans and later, the patriarchs of Moscow.

Attempting to effect control of the Church or the curtailment of its potential to be hostile to the secular power was as important an adjunct of Gediminas' plans for expansion into Rus' as it was of Kalita's ambitions to centralise power in Rus' around Moscow. A metropolitan could show his displeasure with political machinations for quite non-partisan political or moral reasons, as in 1311 Pëtr refused to sanction a Tverite attack on a Muscovite army in Nizhny Novgorod.[90] Even the patriarch was not averse to condemning Rus'ian princes who refused to side with Dmitry Donskoi against Algirdas, when Dmitry's position was parlous and Algirdas' plans for the Rus'ian Church undesirable.[91] More

[88] As specified by a formulary of the 1460s – *Russkii Feodal'nyi Arkhiv*, no. 15, pp. 95–6.
[89] See above p. 165 and n. 65. [90] See above, p. 154.
[91] Philotheos condemned Algirdas' Rus'ian allies in 1370 when the pagans marched on Moscow – *MM*, I, p. 524; Meyendorff, *Byzantium*, 285–6.

often than not a boon for the Church in Moscow was viewed in Vilnius as an attack on the Lithuanian polity and *mutatis mutandis* the same view was held in Moscow.

Let us now examine Gediminas' relations with Metropolitan Feognost and the archbishop of Novgorod, as the grand duke sought to extend his influence over Pskov, and consider his reaction to the political clout of the non-Lettovian hierarchy. Gediminas appears to have accepted Metropolitan Feognost quite readily after the death of Feofil. In 1331 he attempted to have a bishop ordained for his protectorate of Pskov to remove the city from the direct ecclesiastical control of the archbishop of Novgorod, whose *namestnik* governed the church in Pskov.

In 1327 as a result of a failed uprising against the Tatars in Tver', the grand duke of Vladimir, Prince Aleksandr Mikhailovich of Tver', the brother-in-law of Gediminas' daughter Maria, was forced to abandon his home and crown and fly to Pskov where he was welcomed by the citizenry.[92] In March 1329 Ivan Kalita of Moscow, prince of Novgorod and pretender to Aleksandr's grand-ducal throne, Metropolitan Feognost and Archbishop Moisei of Novgorod joined forces against Aleksandr and urged him to surrender to the Tatars. This united action represents a symphony of motives: Kalita's desire to deprive Aleksandr of his grand-ducal *iarlyk*; Feognost's desire to punish a rebel and therefore assuage the wrath of the Tatar Khan on whose kindness the Church relied for exemption from duties to the Horde;[93] and Moisei's hope to prevent Aleksandr from establishing himself in Pskov and diminishing archiepiscopal authority in that city further. In order to dislodge Aleksandr from Pskov, Moisei and Feognost threatened the Pskovites with ecclesiastical sanction for harbouring an enemy of the state. To ease this pressure on the Pskovites, Aleksandr fled to Lithuania where he stayed for eighteen months, returning to his wife in Pskov in 1330 to govern the city as Gediminas' close ally. Aleksandr alone was excommunicated. He remained in Pskov until 1337 when the khan permitted him to return to Tver'. Even his seal as prince of Pskov betrays

[92] Fennell, *Emergence*, 112–19.

[93] Metropolitans of All Rus' were granted privileges by the Khan – M. D. Priselkov, 'Khanskie iarlyki russkim mitropolitam', *Zapiski istoriko-filologicheskogo fakul'teta imperatorskogo S-Peterburgskogo universiteta*, 133 (1916); and Meyendorff, *Byzantium*, 161.

Gediminas' influence over him.[94] In his first year in Pskov, he was to witness and comply with Gediminas' grand plan to diminish the archbishop of Novgorod's power in Pskov which had seemed so formidable in March 1329. Gediminas seized his chance when the political conditions in Novgorod changed dramatically.

In Spring 1330, Archbishop Moisei retired, probably under pressure from factional disturbances in Novgorod between those who objected to his alliance with Kalita and those who viewed Moscow as a better friend than Lithuania.[95] His retirement seems to have been as voluntary as that of Andrei of Tver'. For eight months Novgorod was without an archbishop (and thus head of state) while discussions over a suitable replacement for Moisei continued.[96]

An election was held between three candidates to succeed Moisei, as specified by canon law: Arseny, Grigory (Kaleka) and Lavrenty.[97] Lavrenty was archimandrite of the Yuriev Monastery and appears to have been a supporter of friendship with Lithuania; Grigory was priest in charge of the Smiths' Church of SS Kosma and Damian. As for Arseny, nothing further is known of him, although it seems highly likely that he was the same Arseny whom Gediminas would attempt to see created bishop of Pskov in 1331.[98] It seems, however, that Arseny was the favoured candidate

94 Aleksandr Mikhailovich lost the *iarlyk* in 1327 and the Grand Duchy was divided in 1328 between Aleksandr Vasilievich of Suzdal' (Vladimir and eastern principalities) and Kalita (Novgorod and Kostroma) – Fennell, *Emergence*, 112–13. For the whole Tverite fiasco see *ibid.*, 116–19. Aleksandr's seal as prince of Pskov is of the *vytis* or horseman type used in Lithuania and is markedly different from the seal he had used when grand duke of Tver' – S. V. Beletsky, 'Pechati 'Kniazha Oleksandrova'', *Sovetskaia Arkheologia* (1985), 231–40.

95 Fennell, *Emergence*, 137–8.

96 *Ibid.*

97 On the regulations for the election of a bishop see F. T[itov], 'Postavlenie v diakona i sviashchennika i izbranie episkopa v drevnei zapadno-russkoi tserkvi ili kievskoi mitropolii v XIV–XVIvv.', *Trudy Kievskoi Dukhovnoi Akademii* (1902, May), pp. 134–45. See also Meyendorff, *Byzantium*, 82–5. Three candidates were presented for election in the presence of at least two or three bishops – Meyendorff, 192, n. 57. On the Novgorod list of candidates, see Regel, *Analecta*, no. 12, p. 56. The election of an archbishop of Novgorod is very different from that of an ordinary bishop in that he was chosen from three candidates in *Novgorod* and not in the presence of the metropolitan – Meyendorff, *Byzantium*, 83–4. On the origins of this electoral right of the Novgorod *veche* see Ia. N. Shchapov, *Gosudarstvo i tserkov' drevnei Rusi X–XIIIvv.* (Moscow, 1989), 62–9.

98 Lavrenty's political tendencies are not known for certain although we know that he was expelled from office in 1333 when Kalita rejected his embassy to Moscow – *NL*, 99–100. His place was taken by Iosif who collaborated with Kalita and was removed in 1337 after the prince increased the hardship of monastery peasants in the Archimandrite's name – *GVNiP*, no. 86, p. 143 and Cherepnin, *Obrazovanie*, 505. Grigory – *NL*, 342. Arseny is discussed below pp. 175–6.

for Novgorod. He is mentioned first on the list of candidates. From a list of thirteen episcopal elections between 1328 and 1347 which survives from Feognost's chancery, we see that in seven cases the first-named candidate was consecrated by the metropolitan, in four cases full details are not available and only twice was a candidate who was named second, ordained. These two occasions involve the politically sensitive sees of Novgorod (1331) and Tver' (1335).[99]

On 1 January 1331, Grigory was chosen by God in the cathedral of St Sofia and adopted the name Vasily. He appears to have been a compromise between the old order and two candidates who were inclined to favour Lithuania. He turned out to be an excellent archbishop for Novgorod who used both Lithuania and Moscow to benefit his archdiocese. Uniquely among the bishops of Rus', the Novgorodian hierarch was elected from a list of three local candidates by the city *veche*. The metropolitan merely invited the city's 'God-chosen' man to consecration; he took no part in his election.[100] In Holy Week 1331, Vasily was summoned to Vladimir Volynsky for consecration by Feognost. Before he set out for the south in June, Vasily set about building up the stone defences of the Novgorod kremlin, perhaps in some anticipation of Muscovite displeasure.[101]

On the feast of St John the Baptist, Vasily set out for Volyn' taking with him the boiars Kuz'ma Tverdislavich and Val''fromei Evstaf'evich.[102] The party travelled to Lithuania where Gediminas met them and concluded an agreement with the archbishop-elect. The Novgorodians agreed to grant Gediminas' son Narimantas patrimonial control of the northern defence outposts of Novgorodian land. To this they swore a solemn oath.[103] Those chronicles which narrate these events in detail (for in some chronicles all reference to the conclusion of this treaty have been excised) claim that the agreement was struck *въ таковои тяготе*, 'under great duress'.[104] This is a common excuse of both Catholic and Rus'ian

[99] Regel, *Analecta*, no. 11, p. 55; no. 12. p. 56. First named candidate elected in Vladimir and Galich (1328), Rostov (1329), Suzdal' (1330), Lutsk (1331), Chernigov (1332; 1335) – *ibid.*, 52–6. [100] *NL*, 342–3. On electoral practice see above n. 97.

[101] *NL*, 343. Fortifications discussed below pp. 248–9.

[102] Kuz'ma treated with the Teutonic Order (1338, *NL*, 349), Sweden in Karelia (1339, *NL*, 350), at Torzhok in 1340 (*NL*, 352) and was ambassador to Sweden in 1348 and the Order in 1350 (*NL*, 359–60; 362). Val''fromei was the son of the military commander of Novgorod and was himself a soldier – *NL*, 352. [103] *NL4*, 52; *Sof.*, 219.

[104] *Ibid.* On the manipulation of the texts which describe these agreements see above pp. 44–5.

chroniclers when they have to record Christian dalliances with heathen princes which embarrass their readers.[105]

It seems that Vasily's actions were intentional; he was accompanied by boiars who were fit to conclude a military treaty. He found an intelligent solution to the problem of defending his northern borders without relying on Kalita who had been contracted to defend the city itself against attack.[106] That the agreement was both binding and welcome is confirmed by the fact that in 1333 Narimantas Gediminaitis was baptised Gleb and settled in northern Novgorodia to begin a tradition of Lithuanian mercenary service on the Swedish border which lasted intermittently until Novgorod fell to Moscow in 1477.[107]

After making this agreement, the archbishop-elect moved on to Vladimir Volynsky where he was consecrated on 25 August 1331 in the presence of four south-western bishops.[108] At this very time messengers arrived in Vladimir from Pskov, sent by Aleksandr Mikhailovich, Gediminas and 'all the Lithuanian princes'.[109] The messengers were accompanied by one Arseny whom Gediminas desired to see appointed as the first bishop of Pskov. He may very well be the same man whose vestments were found among the belongings of Metropolitan Feofil and who was named first on the list of candidates for Novgorod.[110] The name is not such a common one and no other Arsenies appear in the Rus'ian chronicles at this time. Whoever this man was, Feognost refused to ordain him and he was sent away *posramlen*, 'shamed'.[111] That Arseny fully expected to be appointed to the lesser half of the see of Novgorod which was Pskov is indicated perhaps by the strength of this word. One cannot be 'shamed' by a chance refusal. *Posramlen* is the term used by the author of the Life of Metropolitan

[105] In October 1323 Gediminas made a treaty with the Catholic powers of Livonia (see pp. 211–12) which was voluntary. One Livonian chronicler notes however that 'fratres cum nunciis episcoporum perduxerunt ad regem ... compulit igitur eos rex taliter ad perpetuam pacem' – *HW*, 61–2.

[106] Kalita was prince of Novgorod from 1328 – see above n. 94.

[107] See pp. 250–2.

[108] *NL4*, 52; *Sof.*, 219; *NL*, 343; Regel, *Analecta*, no. 12, p. 56. According to the chronicle accounts, Grigory of Polotsk was also present but his name does not appear in the metropolitan's record. If he was present then the effectiveness of Feognost's assumption of Feofil's rights was even more complete than when he ordained bishops in the presence of Fëdor of Turov in 1328.

[109] *NL4*, 52; *Sof.*, 219; *NL*, 343.

[110] *NL4*, 52; *Sof.*, 219; *NL*, 344. On Arseny's stole which was found amongst Feofil's property see Priselkov and Vasmer, 'Otryvki', 50.

[111] *NL4*, 52; *Sof.*, 219; *NL*, 344.

Pëtr to describe Bishop Andrei after his plot to remove Pëtr from office was thwarted.[112]

Although Gediminas alone could not have expected the metropolitan to comply readily with the wishes of one who had given succour to the man Feognost had threatened to excommunicate in Pskov in 1329 and who had very recently maintained his own primate, he may have hoped to succeed in his plan, provided that he enjoyed Vasily's support. Perhaps this plan was also discussed by Vasily and Gediminas when they concluded their defence contract. Golubinsky's claim that Feognost refused Arseny because he 'had set Novgorod at nought' can only be partially correct. *NL4* expressly states that the metropolitan refused to ordain because the Pskovites had received Aleksandr Mikhailovich 'from Lithuanian hands'.[113]

After his 'shaming', Arseny left Vladimir for Kiev. On 1 September Vasily too left Feognost's court to return home, taking a route 'between Kiev and Lithuania'.[114] He went quickly and his haste is explained by the First Sofiisky Chronicle as caused by 'fear of Lithuania'.[115] And yet Vasily's route sweeps through territory where Lithuanians were free to travel. The fear mentioned by the chronicler may simply be an invented explanation continuing the theme of Lithuanian threat which is used in some accounts of Gediminas' defence treaty with Vasily.[116] Vasily's return to Novgorod is an extremely murky affair which the chroniclers' sensibilities have left virtually incomprehensible. Be that as it may, Feognost sent a messenger after the archbishop to warn him that Gediminas had despatched three hundred soldiers in pursuit of him.[117] In fact Gediminas' brother Fëdor of Kiev, prompted perhaps by Arseny's arrival in his city, set out with a Tatar *basqaq* and fifty men to intercept the Novgorodians on the outskirts of Chernigov. The archbishop paid a ransom and sent Rostislav, the metropolitan's man back to Feognost via Kiev. The archbishop

112 *ZhP*, 171.

113 Golubinsky, *Istoria*, 154; *NL*, 343 – Нь Богъ и святая Софея низлагаеть всегда же высокыя мысли, зане Плесковици измениле крестъное целование к Новураду, посадиле собе князя Александра из литовъскыя руки' – 'But God and Saint Sofia always bring low haughty thoughts, for the Pskovites betrayed their oath to Novgorod and installed Prince Aleksandr from Lithuanian hands'.

114 *NL4*, 52; *Sof.*, 219.

115 'Оттуде поеха на Киевь, бояся Литвы, и еха вборзе' – *Sof.*, 219. Other chronicles (i.e. *NL4*, 52) omit this explanation of Vasily's speed.

116 See *NL4*, 52. For a full discussion of the manipulation of this text see Rowell, 'Of men and monsters', 85–7.

117 *NL4*, 52; *Sof.*, 219.

then continued on his way to Briansk and may have explained to a representative of the Lithuanians what had gone wrong in Vladimir.[118] The metropolitan's man was safely out of the way. Vasily did not arrive in Torzhok until 3 November and by the time he saw Novgorod on 8 December, a *lozhnaia rech'* or dismal story (a lie!) that the Lithuanians had killed him and his retinue was gaining currency in Novgorod.[119] It is tempting to see Kalita behind the rumours of Vasily's demise. He was certainly in the city before Vasily returned and may even have taken the opportunity to persuade the Novgorodians to restore Moisei to the archi-episcopacy.[120]

Vasily continued his friendship with Lithuania. In 1333 he baptised Aleksandr Mikhailovich's son Mikhail in Pskov where he was welcomed heartily by the populace.[121] That same year Narimantas-Gleb took charge of his new patrimony. The archbishop also sought to retain the friendship of successive grand dukes of Moscow.[122]

Despite his failure to secure a bishopric for Pskov, Gediminas maintained his influence over Novgorod's 'younger brother' with his support of Aleksandr Mikhailovich and the promotion of a local cult of St Dovmont. Dovmont (sc. Daumantas) represented a local Pskovite prince of Lithuanian origin who appealed to the citizens' desire to break away from Novgorod and Gediminas' wish to dominate Pskovite political life. We have already noted how Daumantas fled Lithuania after the murder of Mindaugas.

During his life in Pskov (1265–99), Daumantas, whose baptismal name was Timofei, was renowned for his prowess in battles against the Teutonic Order. He built up the city's defences and founded several churches to commemorate his victories. These acts of what one might almost term self mythology were not in

118 *Ibid.* Briansk fluctuated within Lithuanian and Muscovite spheres of interest until Algirdas annexed it in the 1350s; it will be recalled that Feofil left a good deal of property in that city – see table 3.

119 *NL*, 344 – 'а в Новегороде печалне быша, занеже не бяша вести, нь сица весть промчеся, яко Владыку Литва яле, а детей его избиша' – 'and there was sorrow in Novgorod for there had been no news, but this news spread that Lithuania had attacked the Lord Archbishop and killed his people'.

120 *Ibid.*; *NL4*, 52–3; *Sof.*, 219–20. Kalita appears to have brought Moisei successfully out of retirement in 1335 – Fennell, *Emergence*, 148.

121 *NL4*, 53; *Sof.*, 220; *NL*, 345 – this was the first visit of an archbishop to Pskov since Moisei was consecrated in 1326.

122 Vasily sought peace with Moscow in 1333 and 1335 – *NL*, 345. On his later activities see Fennell, *Emergence*, 243f.

vain. After his death he was called upon to send aid from heaven.[123] The first military miracles of St Daumantas Timofei, as they are recorded in the Pskov chronicles s.a. 1323, 1341, 1407, coincide with the presence in Pskov of a Lithuanian prince.[124] The liturgical texts which are associated with Daumantas all concern the defence of Pskov from its internal and external enemies. Indeed the memory or cult of Daumantas appears to have been fostered by the princes of Pskov since a truly popular thaumaturgical cult developed only in the early sixteenth century.[125]

In recent work on the *Tale of Daumantas* (*Povest' o Dovmonte*), V. I. Okhotnikova has come to the conclusion that this tale which forms the basis of Daumantas' cult can be dated to the second quarter of the fourteenth century when Lithuanian influence in Pskov was very strong. Certainly Daumantas would have appealed to Gediminas. The story depicts the prince as an idol-worshipping Lithuanian who adopted Christianity and became a great patron of the Church. He is not depicted as a life-long opponent of Lithuania (which he was not) or the murderer of a heathen grand duke (which he was).[126] Lithuanian soldiers appear to have been buried around Daumantas' patronal church of St Timofei of Gaza within the Pskov kremlin.[127] He was acceptable as a hero to Pskovite and Lithuanian alike.

The cult remained very powerful in Pskov despite the fact that for political reasons the Russian Church refused to approve it for observance throughout Russia in the sixteenth century. The council which established the local Vladimir cult of Aleksandr Nevsky for veneration throughout Russia in 1547, suppressed the cult of this Pskovite hero. Pskov had been brutally incorporated into Muscovite Russia only in 1510.[128] Nevertheless Daumantas' legend was appropriated by Ivan IV and adapted by his propagandists to support the Muscovite claim to supremacy in Lithuania, whereby Moscow is the centre of Orthodoxy, the Lithuanian

[123] Rowell, 'Between Lithuania and Rus'', 23–4. [124] See below n. 130.

[125] Rowell, 'Between Lithuania and Rus'', 23–4. Liturgical texts run 'И ныне молимъ тя, моли пресвятую Троицу ... за благочестиваго царя нашего и за всехъ притекающихь кь раце мощей твоихъ' – 'And we pray thee, pray the most holy trinity for our blessed tsar and for all those who stream to the shrine of thy relics', *Kondak* for 20 May, feast of St Dovmont-Timofei, Pskov Museum, *Drevnekhranilishche*, 290/49, f.147v. [126] Okhotnikova, *Povest'*, 65–7, 188f.

[127] V. D. Beletskii, 'Dovmontov Gorod', *Drevnii Pskov. Istoria, Iskusstvo, Arkheologia. Novye issledovania* (Moscow, 1988), 107.

[128] Rowell, 'Between Lithuania and Rus'', 30.

Daumantas was Orthodox, therefore Lithuania was originally Orthodox and should submit to the new tsar. The different traditions of the Daumantas legend are discussed in closer detail elsewhere.[129] To the Pskovites he was a hero of local independence from Novgorod and a saint; to the Lithuanians he was a legendary soldier and to the Muscovites he was proof of Moscow's 'right' to govern in Vilnius.

Lithuanian princes ruled in Pskov for much of the fourteenth century by invitation rather than by right. If those sixteenth-century sources which call David of Grodno Daumantas' son were correct (and it is most probable that they are not), the interrelation of Daumantas, Lithuania and Pskov would be even more complex.[130] Pskov did not break away from the ecclesiastical domination of Novgorod until 1589 and it never fully escaped the political control of Novgorod or Moscow. An attempt to create a bishop of Pskov with Muscovite help similar to the fiasco of 1331 was made by the citizenry in 1463–64.[131] Nevertheless Pskovite churches were manned in the early fifteenth century by clergy who were trained in the Grand Duchy.[132] Gediminas' approach to ecclesiastical and political relations with north-west Rus' could be

[129] On the manipulation of Daumantas' cult see *ibid.*, 25–8, 30.

[130] Princes of Pskov, 1266–1400: *Daumantas* (1266–99) – *PL*, I, 3, 4, 5, 11, 13, 14; *David of Grodno* (1322–26) – *PL*, I, 15, 16; *Aleksandr Mikhailovich* (1330–37) – *PL*, I, 16, 17; Aleksandr Vsevolodovich (1341; 1342) *PL*, I, 18, *NL*, 354; *Algirdas* (1341) – *PL*, I, 18–19; *Andrei Algirdaitis* (1343, 1350, 1377) – *PL*, I, 20, 21, *PL*, II, 27, 105–6; *Yury Vitovtovich* (1341; 1349) – *PL*, I, 18, 20; Vasily Budivolna (1357) – *PL*, I, 22; Ostafei (1358–60) – *PL*, II, 102–3; Aleksandr (1368) – *PL*, II, 104; Matfei (1375) – *PL*, II, 105; Grigory Ostafevich (1397–99) – *PL*, II, 108–9; *NL*, 388; *Ivan Andreevich* (1400) – *PL*, II, 109. Names in italic indicate Lithuanian parentage or close alliance. On link between Daumantas and David see R. Heidenstein, *De Bello Muscovitico commentariorum libri sex* (Basle, 1588), 120 – 'ac postea filium eius [sc. Dovmonti] Davidum accepisse memorantur'. Heidenstein cites Russian annals from the royal library in Polotsk which was sacked in 1579 by Stephen Bathory. This tradition of David's origins was followed by nineteenth-century historians – N. I. Serebriansky, 'Ocherki po istorii pskovskogo monashestva', *ChOIDR*, 1908, No. 3, p. 220. It is possible that Heidenstein is translating an entry in *PL*, II s.a. 1407, p. 114 – только князь Домонтъ и по том князь Давыдъ со Псковичи воеваша' – 'only Prince Dovmont and after him Prince David fought alongside the Pskovites'. This of course implies no familial link.

[131] Misail was ordained the first bishop of Pskov in 1589 – Novgorod Third Chronicle, *Novgorodskie Letopisi*, ed. A. F. Bychkov (St Petersburg, 1879), 349 s.a. 7096. An attempt to create a bishopric there in 1463–64 failed – *PL*, II, 151–9.

[132] In 1426 Archbishop Evfimy of Novgorod wrote to the clergy of Pskov: 'И о томъ слышахъ отъ васъ, что приходятъ къ вамъ игумени или попы или дьяконы отъ иныхъ странъ, съ русской земли или изъ литовьской земли, что кои отъ васъ прежде сего ездели ставитися въ попы или в дьяконы на Русь или въ литовьскую землю' – 'And I have heard from you that there come to you abbots or priests or deacons from other countries, from the Rus'ian or the Lithuanian land, that

both heavy-handed and subtle. He managed to gain the support of the archbishop of Novgorod for a military presence on the northern borders of Novgorodia which was to last until Novgorod fell to Moscow.

Thus far we have considered the difficult relationships between the grand dukes of Lithuania and Rus'ian prelates in the context of the territorial expansion of the Grand Duchy. The history of the Church within the Grand Duchy is no less instructive for an understanding of the development of Lettovia. The Church flourished under Lithuanian hegemony. The claims of some modern scholars that in fourteenth-century Lithuanian Rus' the Church was weaker than it was in the rest of Rus' are not borne out by the data.[133] In Polotsk there were as many monasteries and churches built in the fourteenth century as in the previous three hundred years. Golubinsky and Danilevich record the building of two churches in the eleventh century, two monasteries in the twelfth and one monastery in the thirteenth century. In the fourteenth century, according to the slender surviving sources, four churches and three monasteries were built in the diocese of Polotsk and the patrons of these churches were Lithuanian princes.[134]

No doubt the importance of Polotsk as a commercial centre within the Grand Duchy strengthened the bishops of Polotsk in ways both financial and political. Like the bishops of Turov, they must have enjoyed considerable revenue from trade tariffs.[135] Polotsk was the lynch-pin of the Riga–Vilnius trade route and the city's bishop was ordinary in charge of the Rus'ian merchant church of St Nikolai in Riga.[136] In commercial matters the bishop of Polotsk worked very closely with the grand duke. As we have noted in the early years of the century, Bishop Iakov acted as

some of you before this went to Rus' or Lithuania to be ordained priest or deacon', *RIB*, no. 54, 473–4.

133 V. T. Pashuto, B. N. Floria and A. L. Khoroshkevich, *Drevnerusskoe nasledie i istoricheskie sud'by vostochnogo slavianstva* (Moscow, 1982), 131–2.

134 Golubinsky, *Istoria*, 566f.; V. E. Danilevich, *Ocherki istorii polotskoi zemli* (Kiev, 1896), 233f. Ul'iana of Tver' endowed the Uspenskaia Church in Ozeritskaia in 1377 (*AZR*, I, no. 5); Skirgaila gave Polotsk Cathedral three villages in 1380s (*AZR*, I, no. 174; *AZR*, II, no. 234); Andrei Algirdaitis granted a charter to the Monastery of St John the Baptist in Polotsk in 1399 (see below n. 141). See also A. Budilovich, 'Perechnevaia opis' nedvizhimym' imeniem' zapadno-russkoi tserkvi za X–XIXvv', *Kholmsko-Varshavskii Eparkhial'nyi Vestnik*, 1889, no. 2, Appendix p. 8.

135 Shchapov, 'Turovskie Ustavy', 271–2. On Polotsk trade see pp. 78, 257–8.

136 *RLA*, nos. 370, 374.

intermediary between 'his son' Vytenis and the archbishop of Riga.[137] When Gediminas made a trade treaty with the Livonian powers in 1338, it was done 'with the agreement of the bishop of Polotsk, the prince and the city of Polotsk'.[138] The bishop also collaborated with the local prince who was Gediminas' vassal. The seals of both Bishop Grigory and Prince Narimantas-Gleb hang side by side on a Polotsk treaty with Riga which dates from around the same time.[139] If we follow Khoroshkevich's interpretation of the use of the terms *poklon* and *blagoslovenie* by the bishop of Polotsk in his letter to Riga (*c.* 1309), it seems that in the absence of a local prince the bishop of Polotsk acted as head of state of the city. *Poklon* is a deferential term of address employed by the secular power in correspondence, whilst *blagoslovenie* or 'blessing' was bestowed by the clergy.[140] In return the princes enjoyed strong influence over the clerical courts in cases concerning their own foundations to the detriment of the local ordinary, as the *gramota* of Andrei Algirdaitis for the Polotsk monastery of St John the Baptist (1399) makes clear.[141] This close relationship of prince and bishop contrasts sharply with prince–metropolitan relations where the two princes (of state and Church) shared few local interests.

The bishop of Polotsk was the most senior prelate in the Grand Duchy after the metropolitan. When Metropolitan Kiprian of All Rus' died in 1406, Vytautas sent Archbishop Feodosy of Polotsk to Byzantium for ordination to the metropolitanate but the patriarch refused the grand duke's request. In 1415, when Vytautas desired to see Grigor Tsamblak made Metropolitan of Kiev for the Grand Duchy, it was Archbishop Feodosy who headed a local council of Lithuanian bishops in Novgorodok to elect Grigory.[142] Feodosy

[137] See above n. 7. One should beware placing *too* much emphasis on this clichéed reference to 'son'. For other evidence that the Lithuanians strengthened their grip on Polotsk *c.* 1307, see pp. 78, 83–4. [138] *GL*, 195.

[139] *PG*, no. 4, pp. 39–42 and A. L. Khoroshkevich, 'Pechati polotskikh gramot XIV–XVvv.', *Vspomogatel'nye istoricheskie distsipliny*, 4 (1972), 140–2.

[140] *Poklon* and *blagoslovenie* clearly distinguished in Novgorodian letters from 1270s to 1370s – *blagoslovenie ot vladyki ... poklon" ot posadnika*, *GVNiP*, nos. 1–4, 6–10, 14, 15. The same is true of Polotsk correspondence – *RLA*, no. 172, p. 138; no. 250, p. 203 and *PG*, I, no. 3 – *poklon" i blagoslovenie ot" Iakova episkupa*. See Khoroshkevich's discussion in *PG*, III, 126 and Kashtanov, 'Russkie', 112.

[141] 'А отъ кого будеть какая обида нашему монастырю, ино досмотрять и боронить намъ самимъ, а по насъ роду нашему ... а владыце не вступатися въ нашь монастырь', *AZR*, I, no. 14, p. 28.

[142] *Vitoldiana*, no. 207, p. 183. *NL*, 406; *PSRL*, XI, 227.

does not appear to have minded provoking the swift condemnation of Metropolitan Fotii, his superior, or the ire of the patriarch.[143] It is not known when the bishop of Polotsk was granted the title of archbishop but it appears to have been the gift of Vytautas in return for services rendered to the Grand Duchy. In one manuscript of the report of the Council of Novgorodok, Feodosy is styled *smirennyi arkhiepiskop Polotskii i Litovskii* ('serene archbishop of Polotsk and Lithuania') as if to underline his preeminence in the Grand Duchy.[144]

The Church in Turov was also very active, to judge from fourteenth-century recensions of canon law and regulations for the collection of tithes which survive from Gediminas' time.[145] The Pinsk monastery of Lashchinsky which functioned as the official residence of the bishops of Turov benefited from the generosity of the Gediminids.[146]

In Volyn' Liubartas-Dmitry continued the tradition of Lithuanian princely patronage of the Church. He built several churches including the cathedral of St Dmitry, his patron, in the eponymous town of Liubar and repaired the cathedral of St John the Baptist in Lutsk.[147] In this latter city, Armenian Orthodox merchants found

143 In a letter of 1415 Metropolitan Fotii refers to Feodosy as *прелещеный не-епископе полочьский* – 'the deceitful non-bishop of Polotsk' and accuses him of simony – *ты самъ окаанне, веси, елика еси пореклъ сребра и злата о томъ ставлении* – 'you know, most accursed one, how much silver and gold you paid for that appointment', *RIB*, no. 39, p. 329.

144 Three texts of Vytautas' letter of 15 November 1415 which discusses the council survive. The late fifteenth-century copy in the *Kormchaia Kniga* which used to be in the library of the Counts Tarnowski at Dzików (published in *AZR*, I, no. 24, p. 33) and is now in Kraków, Biblioteka Jagiellońska 71/52, p. 779–82 calls Feodosy simply *arkhiepiskop' polotskii*. The text given in the *Nikonovskaia Chronicle* (*PSRL*, XI, 227 s.a. 1416) calls him *smirennyi arkhiepiskop' Feodosii polotskii mitropolii kievskia* (i.e. archbishop belonging to the metropolitanate of Kiev). However the earliest copy which was probably used by the chronicler of *Nik.* refers to 'Polotsk and Lithuania' – *Drevnerossiiskaia Vivlioteka*, XIV (Moscow, 1790; reprinted The Hague 1970), 122. This used to be in the Iosifovskaia Biblioteka which has been placed in the State Historical Museum and the Lenin Library in Moscow. The text which uses the official style *smirennyi* – Gk. *tapeinotēs* – appears closer to the text of the original document.

145 Shchapov, 'Turovskie Ustavy', 255–6.

146 Gediminas' grandson Yury Narimantaitis endowed the monastery with an island at the confluence of the Pina, Strumen and Orlitsa rivers *c.* 1340 – Budilovich, 'Perechnevaia opis'', 8. On Ul'iana's gifts to the church in Pinsk, see *AZR*, I, no. 5.

147 N. I. Teodorovich, *Gorod Vladimir' Volvnskoi gubernii v sviazi s istoriei Volynskoi Ierarkhii* (Pochaev, 1893), 108, 109; and *Istoriko-statisticheskoe opisanie tserkovei i prikhodov Volynskoi eparkhii* (Pochaev, 1888), 271–87. O. Levitskii, 'Lutskaia starina', *Chtenia v istoricheskom obshchestve Nestora letopistsa*, 5 (1891), 78–9. *AIuZR*, I, 1, nos. 45, 46, p. 206.

a welcome home and built their own places of worship.[148] Like Bolesław-Yury II before him, Liubartas worked closely with his boiars and clergy in the conclusion of treaties. In 1366 Bishop Arseny of Lutsk witnessed the settlement Liubartas made with Casimir of Poland concerning the division of power in south-west Rus' between Lithuania and Kraków.[149] We recall that between 1342 and 1347, when grand-ducal power in Lithuania was in disarray, Liubartas maintained the metropolitanate of Galich.[150]

In Lithuania proper, Orthodoxy rarely spread outside the ducal towns of Trakai, Kaunas and Vilnius where there was some settlement of Rus'ian traders. In Gediminas' day Vilnius alone had an Orthodox church just as it provided a Catholic church for visitors from western Christendom. The areas which still supported Orthodox churches in the early seventeenth century, two hundred years after the grand dukes had prohibited the construction of new Russian churches, are all in the southern and eastern parts of the country in the old duchy of Nalšia and close to the borders with Black and White Rus': Vilnius, Kaunas, Rezeknė, Medilas and Merkinė (Merecz).[151] In Merkinė the Orthodox churches pre-date the foundation of the Catholic parish and in Nalšia in the thirteenth century Christianity had been imbibed from Rus'ian wetnurses.[152] Nalšia was the area closest to the Polotsk border, whence chattels, human or otherwise, were

[148] K. Stopka, 'Kościół ormiański na Rusi w wiekach srednich', *Nasza Przeszłość*, 64 (1984), 52. [149] Peshchak, *Pam'iatki ukrains'koi movi*, no. 19, p. 38.

[150] Disarray in Lithuania – see pp. 280f.

[151] Orthodox subjects not to build new churches – 'nec permittantur habere vel edificare absque diocesanorum ... licencia et consensu nova oratoria vel capellas', *Statuty synodalne Wieluńsko-Kaliskie Mikołaja Traby z r.* 1420 (Kraków, 1915–1920–1951), 96: *De scismaticis*. Despite this declaration which does not survive in a document of Jogaila himself, Jogaila, Vytautas (1392–1430), Kazimierz Jagiellończyk (1445–92) and Zygmunt Stary (1506–48) did grant permission to Orthodox nobles and clergy to build churches and monasteries – Chodynicki, *Kościół*, 70, 80, 84. Even given this relaxation of the rule it is valid to cite those churches which survived into the seventeenth century (especially after the Union of Brest 1596, when Lithuano-Polish Orthodoxy was reunited with Rome) as evidence of where Orthodoxy spread in Lithuania. A document dated 10 November 1632, the year of Piotr Mohyła's foundation of the Kiev Academy, notes 'Cerkwie naznaczone nieuniatom ... w Wielkim Xiestwie Litewskim: Wilno, Troki, Minsk, Lida, Nowogródek, Brześć, Słonim, Pinsk, Grodno, Wołkowysk, Kowno, Mozyrz, Rzeczyca, Kamieniec Litewski, Kobryn, Miadzioł, Merecz y inszych miastach y miasteczkach', *AIuZR*, I, 4 (Kiev, 1883), no. 266, pp. 656–8.

[152] On Merkinė (Merecz) parishes, see *Słównik geograficzny Królestwa Polskiego i innych krajów słowiańskich*, ed. F. Sulimierski *et al.*, VI (Warsaw, 1885; reprinted 1976), 258. On the Nalšians in the thirteenth century – 'Dicti Lectaui, Ietuesi et Nalsani de facili baptizantur eo quod a Christianis nutricibus ab ipsis cunabulis sunt enutriti', Colker, 'America', 723, §12.

plundered and traded. The acceptance of Catholicism in 1387 did not lead to the destruction of Lithuania's other Christian heritage; it merely curtailed its growth. In 1580 Vilnius still had more Orthodox churches than Catholic places of worship.[153] The *namestnik* of the Uniate metropolitan of Kiev still resided in the Lavrashev Monastery outside Novgorodok and in a Vilnius convent.[154] Meanwhile the Russians marvelled at the survival of the Greek faith among the Latins.[155] It is not surprising to find the survival of so many Russian words in Lithuanian religious terminology.

In pagan Vilnius Rus'ian merchants were joined in their worship by the kinsmen (more often the kinswomen) of the grand duke and various Lithuanian princes. Gediminas' sister-in-law and several of his daughters were baptised in the eastern rite, as were both of Algirdas' wives.[156] A number of pagans were converted but, like their Catholic counterparts, they risked their lives if they refused to conform publicly with heathen practices in obedience to the grand duke. Three convert courtiers were put to death by Algirdas *c.* 1370 after disobeying his commands to shave their beards and eat meat at a court banquet during Lent.[157]

When the Pope sent missionaries to Vilnius in 1324, he sent them spiritually armed to combat erroneous interpretations of the Mass, the primacy of Peter and the Holy Trinity. Clearly Lithuania already had a reputation for familiarity with Orthodoxy which the Chinese or the Tatars did not, if we are to judge by the letters

[153] Description of Vilnius in 1580 from a letter of J. Meletius to D. Chytraeus as cited in *Russkaia Vil'na: Prilozhenie k puteshestviiu po sviatym mestam russkim* (Vilnius, 1865), 35 n. 2 – '[Rutheni] Vilnae triginta templa habent omnia fere opere lateritio structa ... scholias semper templis adiunctas'. According to Sigismund Herberstein who visited Vilnius in 1526, the city had more Russian churches than Roman – *Sigizmund Gerberstein, Zapiski o Moskovii*, ed. V. L. Ianin *et al.* (Moscow, 1988), 187. Twelve churches and one monastery are named as providers of revenue to Mikhail Glinskii, the *namestnik* in 1506 – *AZR*, I, no. 224, p. 370.

[154] Chodynicki, *Kościół*, 146, 163.

[155] The *Stepennaia Kniga* records that 'въ державе литовскаго господарства мнози отъ семени его [sc. пути правовериа/Христа] вь величествии посреди латынства живуще и благочестие правоверно держаху' – 'in the power of the Lithuanian state many of His followers dwelt among the Latins and preserved their orthodox blessings' – P. G. Vasenko, 'Kniga Stepennaia tsarskogo rodoslovia i eia znachenie v drevnerusskoi istoricheskoi pis'mennosti', *Zapiski istoriko-filologicheskogo fakul'teta imperatorskogo S-Peterburgskogo Universiteta*, 73 (1904), 227–8, n. 4.

[156] See pp. 88, 90.

[157] R. Mažeika, 'The Relations of Grand Prince Algirdas with eastern and western Christians', *La Cristianizzazione*, 77–84. Kiprian claims to have baptised many unbelievers in Lithuania – see above n. 76.

and *symbola* which John XXII sent to Lithuania and China.[158] The missionaries were to ensure Gediminas entered the Church, having put aside completely the errors of the schismatics, *derelictis omnino scismaticorum erroribus*.[159] The Franciscans who served Catholic merchants in Novgorodok and Vilnius and the Court of Gediminas could hardly have been unaware of the presence and influence of Orthodox clergy and princes in the grand duchy. From the Orthodox point of view certain of the *ustavy* or canons of ecclesiastical law which were adapted for use in Lithuanian Rus' in the fourteenth century betray a deep suspicion of the Catholic influence in the Grand Duchy.[160] Nevertheless such dread competition did not prevent an Orthodox princess from preserving the bodies of two Franciscans who were martyred in Vilnius in 1341.[161] Lithuania straddled the frontier of eastern and western Christendom and could belong simultaneously to either and neither side. There is a certain balance between Algirdas' *rapprochements* with Constantinople and Avignon which Giedroyć has noted very succinctly, although it is not entirely clear that this balance was always intentional.[162]

In this analysis of Orthodoxy's role in Lithuania and Lithuania's role in Orthodoxy we have sought to discern three strands of the skein of Lithuano-Rus'ian and Russo-Byzantine ecclesiastical life. We have noted the contribution of prelates to the government of Church and state within the Grand Duchy. We have examined the influence of senior religious leaders on Gediminas' dealings with principalities which lay outside the borders of the Grand Duchy. Vilnius' competition with Moscow for the opportunity to

[158] The *credo* given to the Papal Envoys to Gediminas in June 1324 was the same as that sent to Stefan Uroš of Serbia in June 1323 – cf. *Acta Ioannis*, no. 72 with *VMPL*, no. 298, p. 197. The Pope stresses Petrine supremacy to Gediminas much more strongly than he did to the Chinese in Cambalic – cf. *VMPL*, no. 293, pp. 193–5 with *Acta Ioannis*, no. 138, pp. 255–8. On the use of unleavened bread in the Mass and the *Filioque* see *VMPL*, no. 293, pp. 193–5.

[159] *VMPL*, no. 293, p. 194.

[160] Stress on *nepravaia* and *pravaia vera* ('untrue' and 'true faith') in west Rus'ian redactions of *Ustav sviatogo Vladimira* and the importance of believing in 'святую Троицу по еуангельским проповеданиемь и по апостольскимъ оучением' shown in Shchapov, *Drevnerusskie*, 69.

[161] See below, p. 276.

[162] The alternation of Lithuanian dealings with the papacy and the patriarchate appears to fit very closely chronologically, but the agreements with Catholic powers in 1349–51 and 1357–58 were made only under the threat of imminent invasion. As soon as the western armies retreated the Lithuanians abandoned all pretence of wishing to become Catholic. For this 'dynamic balance' see Giedroyć, 'Arrival ... (1341–1387)', 48–52. In 1373 the baptism plans probably derive from the marriage alliance between Lithuania and Mazovia *c.* 1370 – Rowell, 'Pious princesses'.

influence the metropolitan of All Rus' and through him to control the Grand Duchy of All Rus' reveals the skill of the Gediminids in dealing with eastern Rus' and Byzantium.

We may safely conclude that Orthodoxy thrived in the Grand Duchy. As in eastern Rus' the local hierarchy lent support to, and in return received support from the political authorities. Gediminas was capable of both a subtle and a heavy-handed approach to the Church outside his undisputed domain as we have seen from his activities in the Archdiocese of Novgorod. Orthodoxy was the religion of the *status quo* in Lithuanian Rus' and as such it was accepted and protected by Gediminas and his sons. Nevertheless such acceptance and protection did not involve the wholesale proselytisation of the pagan hinterland. Outside Lithuania even after 1387, the old order was tolerated and upheld by the grand dukes although it was not actively propagated. As Vytautas told his Orthodox subjects in 1415, 'whoever wishes to remain under the power of the Metropolitan of Kiev, as of old, may do so, and whoever does not, may do as he wishes, but know this: we are not of your faith'.[163] He might have added 'but most of my married kin and my cousins are', but he did not.

In the fourteenth century, Orthodoxy was the unwilling handmaid of Lithuanian desires to gain control of Rus'. After the introduction of Catholicism in 1387, the rejection of the unionist metropolitan of All Rus', Isidore, by Moscow and his acceptance by Lithuania in 1439, and the Fall of Constantinople in 1453, Orthodoxy in the Grand Duchy became much more insular. Moscow became the centre of Orthodoxy and Lithuanian Kiev remained the seat of a unionist metropolitan. Gediminas is not known to have made any serious promise to convert to Orthodoxy, although he did appear willing to embrace Catholicism in 1323 in order to remove entirely the Teutonic threat from his western borders.[164] Algirdas, on the other hand, did make a promise to the patriarch of Constantinople that, if his monk Roman were made metropolitan of All Rus', he would become a Christian.[165] However where the important province of Rus' was

[163] *Vitoldiana*, no. 207, p. 184. In 1392 Vytautas made clear the fact that Orthodox Christians should not be forced to convert to Catholicism – *KDKDW*, no. 23, p. 39. Even so Catholic nobles enjoyed greater privileges – Chodynicki, *Kościół*, 76–107. Vytautas was closely connected through both his marriages with a convert Orthodox Lithuanian noble clan, the Alšeniškiai. His second wife Juliana was an Orthodox Christian – Rowell, 'Gediminid dynastic diplomacy'. [164] See pp. 225–6.
[165] See above n. 68.

concerned, the patriarch was unwilling to swap the Orthodox grand dukes of Moscow for potential convert Lithuanians as protectors of the Church's interests. Neither Algirdas nor the patriarch, neither the Pope nor Gediminas would risk surrendering all he held for all he might obtain.

The ambitions of Algirdas and perhaps his father Gediminas for dominion over a politically reunited Rus' were shared just as strongly by the princes of Moscow. The rulers of both rising nations faced two serious difficulties in these ecclesio-political ambitions. The metropolitans of the Rus'ian church(es) generally followed policies which benefited the Church throughout the theoretically united province without primary regard to the selfish ambitions of the divided political powers. Metropolitan Aleksei was the exception to this rule. His close spiritual and political ties with the grand duke of Moscow made him much more inclined to serve Moscow than Feognost had been or Kiprian would be. He was accepted by Constantinople in 1354 only after a whole year of careful scrutiny because Moscow had ready cash and Algirdas of Lithuania could not be trusted. The patriarch could not forget the Feodorit incident.[166] It must be noted that in 1359 when Ivan II Ivanovich died, Aleksei became regent of Rus' on behalf of Dmitry Ivanovich but Dmitry never became regent of the Church. The traditional conclusions of historians that the prelates of Rus' were always priested poodles in search of a prince must be challenged seriously. The metropolitans of Lithuania and All Rus' and indeed the archbishops of Novgorod were more akin to Thomas-à-Becket than Stalin's Patriarch Sergii.

The patriarch of Constantinople insisted under normal circumstances that the metropolitanate of All Rus' should remain united 'since the facts themselves have convinced us how great an evil is separation and division of that church in many parts and how great an advantage there is in having one metropolitan to govern that province'.[167] It should never be forgotten that the creation of a metropolitan was in the end a Byzantine, not a Rus'ian or a Lithuanian prerogative. Whatever the ambitions of a Gediminas or a Kalita and the services of a schismatic patriarch in

[166] On Aleksei's background and political life see above n. 66. Between 1359 and 1370 Aleksei ruled Rus' as regent for Dmitry Ivanovich who was only 9 years old when Ivan II died – Meyendorff, *Byzantium*, 184–8.

[167] So said Patriarch Antony in 1389 in response to Kiprian's success in being accepted in Moscow – *MM*, II, pp.116–19; tr. Meyendorff, *Byzantium*, 310.

the Balkan empires, the aims of a Feognost or a Glykys must not be overlooked. The appointment alternately of a Greek and Rus'ian hierarch in Rus' served to diminish the chances that a metropolitan could be appropriated by the political power.[168] Byzantium had already lost control of the Churches of Serbia and Bulgaria to the local *tsars* and did not wish to see Rus' follow the same path. As the political power in Rus' became splintered and then polarised around two grand dukes, one in Moscow and the other in Vilnius, the Church needed to maintain its political independence in order to be able to serve the whole flock and preserve its own unity. Ironically the more strong and united the metropolitanate appeared, the more attractive it became to the divided political powers, at first Vladimir and Galich–Volyn', then Moscow and Tver', and finally Lithuania and Moscow, as a means of uniting the whole people behind them. It is arguable, had the Lithuanian grand dukes not entertained ambitions to dominate Rus', whether they would have fought so persistently for the opportunity to control the Church. The rationale behind the struggle for the metropolitanate of Lithuania, after Feofil certainly, if not indeed *c.* 1316, was not so much the defence of the Grand Duchy from Muscovite ecclesiastical interference (there was none) as Lithuania's offensive urge to become lady of Rus'. Gediminas' skill in pushing Lithuania's borders ever eastwards is more than matched by his manipulation of the Orthodox Church. If Algirdas was the first grand duke to formulate the idea that 'all Rus' should belong to Lithuania', he could not have done so without the achievements of his father. The difference between Lithuania's stature in Rus' and Constantinople in 1315 and 1341 is enormous. Yet as Gediminas pushed eastwards he glowered at his western neighbours; it is to his manipulation of Catholic princes that we shall turn now.

[168] D. Obolensky, 'Byzantium, Kiev and Moscow: A study of ecclesiastical relations', *Dumbarton Oaks Papers*, 11 (1957), 45–75.

Chapter 7

PAGANS, PEACE AND THE POPE, 1322–24

Sometime in 1322 the grand duke of Lithuania wrote to Pope John XXII, announcing his readiness to make peace with his Christian neighbours and welcome the Catholic Faith into his realm. When the envoys of the papal legates reached Vilnius two years later to initiate the mission to Gediminas and his people, the grand duke unequivocally rejected baptism and declared his intention to live and die a pagan. Despite this thwarting of the Pope's carefully laid plans, the international peace which Gediminas had sought first in 1322, signed in Vilnius a year later and seen ratified by Rome in 1324 remained in force for four years. If Gediminas had truly wished to be baptised, why did he change his mind? Why did John XXII not change his mind about the peace treaty?

Between 1322 and 1328 when unrestrained war erupted once more in the Baltic lands, pagan Lithuania played an increasingly important role in the affairs of Christendom's eastern marches. It is manifestly unhelpful to view Lithuania simply as a passive appendix to the active ambitions of Poland, Rus' and the Teutonic Knights. To understand the complexity of Lithuanian interest in Catholicism between 1322 and 1324, which illumines the close interaction of Gediminas' religious diplomacy with his military and economic policies we must examine Lithuanian actions from a Lithuanian point of view within the broader European context.

It is essential to know what was happening in Catholic Christendom and Lithuania when Gediminas presented his proposals to John XXII. In 1322 the Pope was preoccupied by several major questions, the most serious of which by far was an unwelcome development in the competition between Louis of Bavaria and Frederick the Fair of Austria for the vacant imperial crown. Who was to become Holy Roman Emperor had been contested between these two German princes since 1314, but at Mühlsdorf in September 1322 Louis defeated Frederick in battle and declared himself king of the Romans without papal permission.[1] The imperial–papal conflict which had been sending tremors throughout Catholic Christendom for several years was about to erupt with a vengeance.

On the eastern borders of the Empire, the struggle between Władysław Łokietek and the Order over control of those Polish territories which lay under Teutonic dominion became increasingly bitter. In 1321 a papal Commission which had been summoned in Inowrocław by Łokietek found the Teutonic Order guilty of misappropriating the Polish territories of Gdańsk and eastern Pomorze. The Knights were instructed to return the disputed lands and pay compensation to Poland.[2] They did not comply and Łokietek turned from the courtroom to the battlefield to regain control of lost Polish lands.

Meanwhile the Avignon Curia investigated another complaint against the Order, brought this time by the archbishop of Riga, Frederick von Pernstein. Frederick, who had lain in exile in Avignon since the last papal Commission to visit Livonia (1312) had reported, continued to accuse the brethren of all manner of crime from the cremation of their dead to the desolation of Semigallia.[3] Frederick and the burghers of Riga were allies of Gediminas and the grand duke took a keen interest in the progress of the Rigan case.[4] The Order was so strongly pressed by these Polish and Rigan accusations that, according to the Chronicle of Oliwa, it took all the diplomatic skill of the Order's advocate, Grand Master Karl von Trier to save the Knights from destruction. The hapless fate of the Templars whose lives and property were forfeited in 1312 as a result of a papal court convened by the king of France was not one which the brethren sought to emulate.[5] In 1322 the archbishop summoned fresh evidence against the Knights from Riga to lay before the Curia.[6]

By 1322 both the Livonian and the Prussian branches of the

[1] See above pp. 2–3 and G. Benker, *Ludwig der Bayer. Ein Wittelsbacher auf dem Kaiserthron 1282–1347* (Munich, 1980), 78–117. For matters facing the Pope in 1322 and 1323, see *Annales ecclesiastici*, XXIV, 167–239. [2] Knoll, *Rise*, 44.

[3] Seraphim, *Das Zeugenverhör*, VII, 32–4; VI, 33, 37; XXII, 37, 183; XXIII, 32, 33, 37. The accusations were also discussed in a letter dated 13 June 1310 – see above p. 14, n. 44. See also Gidžiunas, 'De missionibus', 22f. [4] *GL*, 60–3.

[5] Chronicle of Oliwa, *MPH*, VI, 324. The fate of the Templars is noted above p. 10.

[6] Mollat, *Lettres Communes*, no. 18188. This report of Bishop James of Ösel, Vicar of the Archdiocese of Riga dated 1322 is recorded in Garampi's catalogue of manuscripts of the Vatican Secret Archive in the eighteenth century. It has since disappeared, probably misplaced.

Order were in a vulnerable position. In 1317 internal dissension over plans for the reform of the Order had resulted in the exile of the grand master to his home town of Trier, whence he continued nonetheless to defend his quarrelsome brethren against charges brought in Avignon.[7] In Prussia disputes concerning reform continued into the 1330s. Discord broke out among the Livonian brethren in 1322 when Johann von Hoenhorst and Johann Ungenade contested the leadership of the Livonian Order.[8] The Knights' war effort against Lithuania which was already strained was thus hampered further. To these self-inflicted burdens were added the hostility of Poland and Riga we have already noted and the growing isolation of the Order in international affairs. The Knights' only friend was Emperor Louis IV, himself the object of increasing papal suspicion. John of Bohemia, who later in the decade would use the northern crusades to further his own ambitions against Poland, was still not alienated from Łokietek.[9] The Knights' war with Lithuania[10] was dragging on, as we shall see, at a cost to both sides of much effort and many lives without any sustained advantage for either crusader or heathen.

The other major Christian power of the southern Baltic, Denmark, had taken the Order's side against Lithuania in 1318, when King Eric VI bade his vassals in Estonia aid the Knights in the crusade whilst maintaining strict neutrality in the conflict over Livonia. After his death in 1319, the 'mistress of Estonia', was in disarray under the weak rule of Christopher II (1320–32). The king's powers had been severely curtailed by his nobles and prelates who claimed to owe the king no service outside Denmark and often refused to pay him the taxes he demanded inside the peninsula.[11] Gediminas exploited this disarray to make peace with the Danish colonies in Estonia.

By 1322 Lithuania was in a strong position *vis-à-vis* the conflict with Christendom. Gediminas had won several allies and a good

[7] For the internal crisis of the Order see K. Górski, *Zakon krzyżacki a powstanie państwa pruskiego* (Wrocław-etc, 1977), 65–6. For the exile of Karl see 'Die Ältere Chronik von Oliva', *SRP*, I, 712–13 and *Wig.*, 457.

[8] *HW*, 60, and Niess, *Hochmeister Karl*, 157–62.

[9] For the relationship of the Order with Louis IV see J. von Pflugk-Harttung, *Der Johanniter und der Deutsche Orden im Kampfe Ludwigs des Bayern mit der Kurie* (Leipzig, 1900), 131. John of Bohemia's use of the crusade to attack Poland is mentioned below p. 241.

[10] *PD*, 146.

[11] For Eric VI Menved's charters of 1318 see *Diplomatarium Danicum*, ed. A. Afzelius *et al.*, II.8 (Copenhagen, 1953), nos. 72–3, pp. 66–8. A. Mohlin, *Kristoffer II av Danmark. Förra delen Välmakstiden* (Lund, 1960), 148–54, 195–300, 415–57.

deal of land in Rus'. Two of his sons had married Rus'ian princesses, his daughter Elżbieta had made a successful alliance in Mazovia and his best military commander was elected prince of Pskov in 1322.[12] In Novgorodok, which was a major commercial centre of Lithuanian Black Rus', the site of a Franciscan friary and formerly a political hub of the Grand Duchy, the Lithuanian Orthodox metropolitan see was established in 1315–16. The pagan grand duke was thus favoured by Constantinople with an Orthodox ecclesiastical hierarchy independent of the Metropolitan of Kiev, Vladimir and All Rus'.[13] Podlasie, the west Rus'ian land bordering Mazovia, fell under Lithuanian control near the beginning of Gediminas' reign and in the autumn of 1322 the grand duke directed his acquisitive sights towards the prosperous south Rus'ian principalities of Galich–Volyn' and Kiev.[14]

Besides his activity in Rus', Gediminas had allied himself with Wacław of Płock and had maintained the longstanding Lithuanian alliance with Riga.[15] Despite the decision forced on the Rigans by the Order and its allies at the Diet of Pernau in 1313 to break the 1298 Lithuano-Rigan concord, commercial intercourse (*antiqua mercatio*) between that city and the pagans was not discontinued.[16] In 1322 and 1323 the Rigans equipped envoys sent by Gediminas to Avignon and Denmark to discuss proposals for peace between Lithuania and the powers of the North.[17] A peace initiative was sorely needed in the Baltic lands.

Ever since Gediminas had assumed grand-ducal power in 1315–16, Lithuania continued to experience a vicious war of attrition with the Teutonic Order. The Knights attacked Žemaitija almost every year. Especially hard hit were the districts of Medininkai[18] and Vaikiai, Ariogala and Raseiniai which lay further east (see map 4).[19] These regions were closely associated with pagan worship and became habitual subjects of crusader zeal.[20] The Nemunas border forts of Junigeda and Pieštvė, Bisenė,

[12] See pp. 237–8. [13] See pp. 155–8. [14] See pp. 96–8.

[15] For Wacław see pp. 8–9, and Rigan alliance above pp. 76–7.

[16] See above, p. 77 and nn. 103, 104. The Peace of Pernau is given in *LU*, II, no. 645.

[17] *GL*, 147.

[18] January, February 1314 – *PD*, 180; 1316 – *PD*, 182, 183 and *EpG*, 286; 1320 – *PD*, 185 and *EpG*, 282, 286; not attacked again until 1329, see p. 240.

[19] 1317 – *PD*, 183. 1322 – *PD*, 186 and *EpG*, 287.

[20] See pp. 121, 240. They feature in the *Wegeberichte*, *SRP* II, 670, 672, 673, 677, 688 – Medininkai; *ibid.*, 676, 677, 686, 688 – Raseiniai; p. 688 – Vaikiai; pp. 676, 680, 685 – Ariogala. Raseiniai and Ariogala were supposedly donated to the Order by Mindaugas.

Gedimin-Burg and Paštuva also suffered frequent heavy assault.[21] In return the Žemaitijans and Lithuanians ravaged the Order's strongholds of Ragnit, Schalauenberg (Tilsit) and Christmemel from where many of the troops sent against Lithuania originated.[22] A Livonian wedding party was massacred by Gediminas' men at Kokenhusen in 1315 and in 1319 David of Grodno sacked Wohensdorf deep in eastern Prussia.[23] To these 'official' campaigns must be added countless raids by the irregular forces of both sides, the *latrunculi*.[24]

Despite *Reisen* directed early in 1322 against Vaikiai, Raseiniai, Ariogala and Pieštvė, the Knights could not gain the upper hand. As Długosz points out, the campaigns of this season brought more losses than gains.[25] That same year the pagans ravaged the see of Dorpat and capped their victory with an alliance with Pskov.[26] Thus the victims of two separate Livonian offensives formed a powerful alliance against both Danish and German settlements in Livonia and Prussia. In February 1323, a Pskovite army led by David of Grodno ravaged Danish Reval and the following months witnessed Lithuanian assaults on Memel and Wehlau (Wilow).[27] Because of the severe winters of 1322–23 and 1323–24, the Knights were unable to transport their armies to Lithuania to avenge these offensives.[28] In 1321 during another lull in the fighting which was most probably occasioned by the loss of the greatest of Livonian commanders, Heinrich von Plötzkau, whom the Lithuanians had

See W. Kętrzyński, 'O dokumentach Mendoga, króla litewskiego', *RAU*, 2nd series 25 (1907), 194f.

[21] Junigeda – 1315, *PD*, 182; 1317, *PD*, 184; 1318, *PD*, 184. Pieštvė – 1318, *PD*, 184; 1322 – Annalista Thorunensis, Dietmar von Lübeck, *SRP*, III, 64. Bisenė – 1315, *EpG*, 286; 1316 (twice), *PD*, 182–3. *Castrum Gedemini* – 1317, *PD*, 183; 1324, *PD*, 189–90. Paštuva – 1316 *PD*, 182.

[22] Ragnit and Schalauenberg – *PD*, 181; reflected in *L2*, *PSRL*, XXXV, 95, 152, 179, 200, 221. Christmemel – *PD*, 181. See map 4.

[23] Kokenhusen – *HW*, 58. Wohensdorf is in eastern Prussia half way between Allenburg and Friedland, *PD*, 185. See map 5.

[24] For a discussion of Lithuanian military techniques see pp. 243–6. The *latrunculi* ('bandits') supported themselves by raiding in the service of Lithuania and Prussia, see *GL*, 61 and *PD*, 190.

[25] 1322 *Reisen* – *EpG*, 287; *SRP*, III, 4. Długosz's remark is accurate for the whole war – *Długosz*, IX, 25.

[26] Dorpat – *PD*, 186; *EpG*, 284; *GL*, 77–9.

[27] Pskov like Lithuania was the victim of frequent Teutonic attack – see Rowell, 'Between Lithuania and Rus'', 11, 23. For Pskovite and Lithuanian campaigns in 1323 see *PD*, 187–8 and 'Annales Expeditiales Prussici 1233–1414', *SRP*, III, 9.

[28] *PD*, 186–7; 189. Crusaders came north in 1322 and 1323 but the poor weather conditions prevented a successful *Reise* – Paravicini, *Preussenreisen*, 147, 183.

slain in July 1320,[29] the Knights rebuilt the fort of Mezoten in Semigallia as a vantage point for future attacks on Lithuania.[30]

Control of Semigallia which was contested, as we have noted, by the archbishop of Riga too, formed a special focus of Gediminas' ambitions. The building of a Teutonic fort in that territory could hardly fail to interest him or the Rigans, for Semigallia divided Riga from Lithuania, and the Knights' allies in Courland from their other supporters in northern Livonia. At the end of the thirteenth century the Knights had made a concerted attempt to take charge of this territory in the course of which many neophyte Semigallians apostasised and fled south to Lithuania for refuge.[31] The Knights claimed that the tribesmen had abandoned their rights to their land when they fled and that therefore Semigallia was rightfully the property of the Order. The Knights realised that they could not maintain their garrisons there and so destroyed them in an attempt to make the territory uninhabitable. In the 1320s, however, the brethren began to rebuild their strongholds in Semigallia as part of their policy to settle the *Wildnis*.[32] The archbishop of Riga continued to pursue his claims to Semigallia in Avignon,[33] while in Lithuania the Semigallian refugees were put to work defending Lithuania's frontiers, where their experience of fighting the Knights was invaluable.[34] Although Lithuania had never controlled the territory (despite many attempts to do so), her grand duke regarded himself as *dux Semigalliae* since he was the lord of many thousands of Semigallian refugees. Gediminas styled himself in this way in his correspondence with western rulers and merchants. He did so in order to gain recognition of his claims.[35] He also intended to supervise the reconversion of the Semigallians to Catholicism, if this were necessary, to deny the Knights the opportunity of winning Semigallia for Christ and themselves.[36] Semigallia

[29] *PD*, 185; *EpG*, 282, 286. [30] *EpG*, 284; *HW*, 60. [31] *LR*, tr. p. 132f.

[32] For the destruction of the forts see *LR* lines 8015–71; 11595–11610; 11794–11808. The rebuilding of forts such as Mezoten (1321 – *HW*, 60), Terweten (1338 – *HW*, 67), Doblen (1335 – *HW*, 67) continued alongside the town building plans of the Knights, *Historia Pomorza*, ed. G. Labuda, I, part I (Poznań, 1969), 645–6. For details of Semigallia in the thirteenth century see W. L. Urban, 'The military occupation of Semigallia in the thirteenth century', in *Baltic History*, ed. A. Ziedonis, W. L. Winter, M. Valgemäe (Columbus, Ohio, 1974), 21–34. [33] See above n. 3.

[34] *PD*, 189 – *Campus Semigalliae* near Paštuva. [35] *GL*, 29, 37, 47, 51. See p. 64.

[36] On the disputed rights of a crusader to possess infidel land and the rights of pagans to *dominium* see J. Muldoon, *Popes, lawyers and infidels. The Church and the non-Christian world 1250–1550* (Liverpool, 1979), 109–14.

features in Gediminas' most original and daring plan to dish the Order.

Aware no doubt by 1322 that his victories over the Order were as pyrrhic as the Order's successes against him had proven, Gediminas sent out several letters to the Order and the Livonian colonies in 1322 suing for peace. Although these do not survive, their existence is known from references made to them in an excerpt from correspondence with Gediminas preserved in a Rigan register.[37] He also sent envoys to Denmark for the same purpose.[38] At the same time he wrote to Pope John XXII with details of his plans to make peace with Christendom, gain papal recognition of his borders and welcome Catholicism to Lithuania. No doubt he also hoped that by adding his voice to the cries of Riga against the Teutonic Order, he might neutralise with promises of peace what no amount of main force had been able to defeat: the power of the Knights.

In a very carefully drafted letter which he sent to Pope John XXII in 1322, Gediminas set down an explanation and a justification of Lithuania's past contacts with Catholic Christendom.[39] He begins by saying that he has known for a long time that the Christian Faith is governed by the Pope, to whom all Christians owe allegiance. He describes how King Mindaugas had been converted to Catholicism 'with the whole of his realm' (a pertinent exaggeration)[40] but the Teutonic Knights drove him to

[37] *GL*, 59–63. This text is often referred to as a letter. It is clear however from the manuscript which is preserved in the Latvian State Archive in Riga (LVVA, Fonds 673, apr. 4/K-18, no.17) that the text is a Register copy. It is referred to as *scripta* rather than *data* on 29 November (1322). The manuscript is small (77 mm x 175 mm) and is written on both sides, the second side having a different hand from the first and an inscription *Exemplum litterarum civitatis Rigensis ad Regem Lithuaniae Godemunde* ... gives the impression that the page was retained as a copy of Rigan correspondence with Gediminas when the rest of the register was destroyed. Dated from references within the letter to the Lithuanian Peace proposals having been made recently and without Rigan knowledge and a plea not to exclude Riga from any agreement struck with the Order. A date of *vigilia Andree* (29 November) is given at the end of one of the letters. This could not refer to November 1323 by when the Treaty of Vilnius had been signed for almost two months. Since the letters mention that Gediminas' lieutenant David [of Grodno] had become prince of Pskov (known from Pskovite sources to have been invited in Autumn 1322 although he led the city's armies first in March 1323 – *PL*, I, 15 and *SRP*, I, 284), the safest dating gives November 1322. For more details of the manuscripts of letters associated with Gediminas see Rowell, 'Letters'.

[38] 'Thi. de Soldwedele exposuit pro nunciis Leth[owinis] qui fuerunt in Dacia, xii marc., illas de consulibus recepit.' *LU*, III, no. 1054a.

[39] *GL*, 23–7.

[40] *GL*, 23. Mindaugas was converted with his queen and a small number of his followers but certainly not with his whole kingdom – Giedroyć, 'Arrival ... (thirteenth century)', 24–5.

apostasy (a twisting of the truth).[41] Crocodile tears over the fact that ever since those days the Lithuanians had abided in error would be [mis-]interpreted by the Pope as a sign of Gediminas' unwilling subjection to the errors of paganism.[42] Gediminas then details more recent events in the Baltic: Vytenis' alliance with Riga; Pope Boniface VIII's investigation of Rigan complaints against the Order; and the correspondence between Vytenis and Francis of Moliano, the envoy despatched from the Curia in 1312 to investigate a dispute between Riga and the Teutonic Knights.[43] He mentions how Vytenis asked for two Franciscans to serve a church he had built in Novgorodok and which the Knights destroyed in 1314. He lists other crimes committed by the Knights against Riga.[44] The Knights have turned Semigallia into a desert and call it the defence of Christendom. But Lithuania seeks not the destruction of Catholicism. Her grand duke only acts as other Christian princes act that he might defend his people.[45] He has welcomed Franciscans and Dominicans to his country and has granted them complete liberty to baptise, preach and minister the Faith. However he fails to specify to whom the friars may minister.[46] He is willing to obey the Pope as Christians must and *fidem catholicam recipere*, that is, 'welcome the Catholic Faith to Lithuania' or 'accept Catholicism', so long as the Knights have no part in the proceedings. John is implored to send envoys to Lithuania in company with Archbishop Frederick, not expressly to convert Gediminas but 'to make peace and determine borders': *pro facienda pace ac terminis disponendis*.[47]

[41] *Ibid*, 24. Gediminas speaks of 'atroces iniurias et innumerabiles proditiones magistri fratrum de domo Theutonica' – *GL*, 23.

[42] *GL*, 23 – 'sicut proh dolor et nos usque in hodiernum diem in errore... permanere' which the Pope interprets as '[Rex]..in eisdem litteris devote subnectens, quod ipse invitus in errore consistit' – *VMPL*, no. 290, p. 190.

[43] *GL*, 23–5. Seraphim, *Das Zeugenverhör*, VI, 52–5. See also Giedroyć, 'Arrival... (1281–1341)', 9–13.

[44] *GL*, 25–7. The whole of Novgorodok was razed by the Knights in 1314 and presumably the church was burned at this time – *PD*, 180–1.

[45] *GL*, 27.

[46] *Ibid.* In fact Gediminas granted full liberty to Catholic priests to minister to Catholics in his country. Those who attempted to convert the heathen were put to death for threatening the religious *status quo* which was intended to keep pagan, Catholic and Orthodox inhabitants of Lithuania content. This toleration was expressed by Gediminas to the papal legates' envoys in November 1324 – *GL*, 127–9. The punishment of priests who broke the rule is described below p. 276. The Pope interpreted Gediminas' words as meaning a mission to the pagans was welcome – *VMPL*, no. 293, p. 193.

[47] *Fidem recipere* – *GL*, 27. The plea to send Frederick to Lithuania to discuss terms for peace and the settlement of boundaries does not survive in the incomplete transcript of

In their gadarene rush to analyse whether or not Gediminas wished to be baptised, historians have overlooked the main purpose behind Gediminas' request for a papal legation as we read it here from his own letter: the cessation of hostilities in the Baltic region and international recognition of Lithuania's borders. Similarly the very careful phraseology of Gediminas' correspondence, which was recognised as ambiguous by the papal envoys in Vilnius, has been neglected.

The ambiguity of the phrase *fidem recipere* is surely deliberate. It gives the impression that the grand duke is asking for baptism and indeed it does mean this. However it is also so vague that it could simply mean that Catholics were welcome in Lithuania. This is the admittedly casuistical meaning Gediminas later chose to give to the periphrases his letters employ for conversion.[48] The portrait of the Knights here however is by no means ambiguous. They are described as wicked anti-Christian missionaries who have destroyed past faith and have no welcome contribution to make to the future conversion of Lithuania. Gediminas' accusations echo the Rigan complaints against the Order. However, this is not because the letter is a Rigan fabrication, as certain German scholars have claimed.[49] The grand duke is leaping on the Rigan bandwagon as though, by proving the futility of the Knights' crusade, he might corroborate the complaints of Christian princes and persuade the Pope to punish the Knights. Gediminas repeatedly expressed an interest in Archbishop Frederick's affairs in the Curia at this time and in his turn the exiled prelate stored letters from Gediminas among his personal effects.[50] News of the process against the Knights was one of the first items of information given to Gediminas by the envoys of the papal legates when they arrived at the grand-ducal court in November 1324.[51] Since Lithuania had been involved in several Rigan diplomatic offensives against the Order during the reigns of Gediminas'

Gediminas' letter in the Order's Archive (*GL*, no. 2). However it is recorded by the Pope in his letters to his legates and Gediminas – *VMPL*, nos. 290, 293, pp. 190, 193.

48 The meaning of the phrase was discussed by the legates' envoys and the friars who drafted the letter – *GL*, 135–45. See below p. 222 and n. 185.

49 Cf. *GL*, 23–7 with *PU*, II, no. 13, pp. 6–10. For the role of Rigan friars as scribes for Gediminas, see above p. 30 and J. Jakštas, 'Vokiečių Ordinas ir Lietuva Vytenio ir Gedimino metu, Gedimino Laiškai', *Senovė* 2 (1936), 32.

50 *GL*, 61–3, 173. The inventory of Frederick's possessions made in Lyons on 18 June 1324, presumably before the archbishop set off on the mission to Lithuania includes *litteris regis Letovie cum aliis litteris quam pluribus necessariis*, cited in Arbusow, 'Römischer Arbeitsbericht', 378.

51 *propter captandam suam benevolentiam* – *GL*, 123.

immediate predecessors, and Gediminas employed several Franciscan and Dominican friars as scribes and advisers, it is hardly surprising that the grand duke could initiate such a diplomatic *démarche*.[52] For his part, the Pope could eventually consider acting against the Order without endangering the Catholic provinces of Livonia since Gediminas himself, not merely the self-interested and optimistic archbishop of Riga, had provided evidence that the pagans might come peacefully to the font. In hindsight such an idea seems too naïve for Gediminas or John XXII to have considered it seriously. Nevertheless in the early 1320s, the weakness of the Order was far from imaginary. That later events, especially the hesitations of the Pope and Gediminas' adoption of a policy of military alliance with Poland against the Order in lieu of baptism, prevented such an idea from becoming reality, is not relevant to our argument based on the desiderata of 1322.

The making of peace and the demarcation of frontiers coupled with the constraint of the Teutonic Order were the main aims of Gediminas' approach to the Papacy. Conversion of the pagans was merely a (heavily) hinted incentive for papal compliance with Gediminas' offer. Since baptism was not mentioned *ipso verbo*, the grand duke left himself a means of escape from the proposal. To pay the soul-price Gediminas had to be sure that he would win. The conversion of his people to Christianity could only happen once even if he could promise it a thousand times to pope or patriarch. Throughout investigations into his letters carried out by Livonian ambassadors in 1323, Gediminas refused to commit himself openly to baptism.[53]

The connection between Lithuanian territorial aspirations and recourse to Catholicism is a familiar one. Mindaugas, with whose religious diplomacy Gediminas was clearly familiar, petitioned

[52] Traidenis had attempted a Rigan alliance against the Order in the 1280s but refused to be baptised because he feared he might suffer at the hands of the Knights as the Semigallians had – Giedroyć, 'Arrival ... (1281–1341)', 2. He eventually broke the peace with Riga in 1277 – see p. 77. For Vytenis' policy see Giedroyć, pp. 9–13. That Gediminas was conscious of renewing his brother's policy, see *GL*, 25, 59. Gediminas wrote directly to the curia, not to Riga. The nineteenth-century reading of *civitatem* for what is clearly *curiam* in both manuscripts of the legates' envoys report of November 1324 (*GL*, 123, 133) – Riga LVVA, Fonds 673, apr. 4/K-18, nos. 22 and 23. The suppression of the correct reading appears to be due to a rationalisation that the 'barbarian Lithuanians' could not have written to the Pope themselves. The translators of *GL* interpreted *civitatem* as a reference to Riga.

[53] Conversion of the pagans was Gediminas' 'principal negotiating asset' – Giedroyć, 'Arrival ... (1281–1341)', 28. Silence over plan to be christened, below p. 211.

Pope Alexander IV in 1254 to recognise his rule in any pagan or schismatic land he might conquer.[54] He seems to have abandoned Christianity in the forlorn hope of maintaining the loyalty of the pagan province of Žemaitija.[55] Gediminas' sons, Kestutis and Algirdas, in their dealings with Catholic princes in 1351 and 1358 both attached territorial claims to their proposals to accept Roman baptism. If the Knights were banished to the wastelands between Rus' and Tartary, conversion could be enforced in Lithuania. The Lithuanian price for becoming Christian was fixed as early as 1322 at the removal of the Knights from the Baltic.[56]

It is logical that Gediminas should take his international dispute to the international tribunal, the papal Curia. Gediminas was aware of this aspect of the Pope's role in Christian affairs from the Rigan litigation against the Knights and knowledge he claims to have had from childhood.[57] Perhaps even the approach made in 1317 by John XXII when he first ascended the throne of St Peter also influenced Gediminas. The Pope had sent him a very vague letter advising him that the 'door of grace' would be opened to him 'to the increase of your honour according to God's will'.[58] In 1322 Gediminas knocked on the Pope's door. The Pope promised to send envoys to Gediminas but the mission to Lithuania would not materialise for another year and a half.[59]

The usual military ravages of a forty years' war were not the only hardships to face Lithuania and her foes. It costs a good deal of money to wage war. The limited trade which continued between Lithuania, Riga and the Teutonic Order itself during the crusade was not helped by the economic depression and concomitant famine which affected most of Europe between 1315 and

54 As is clear from the reply of Alexander IV dated 19 December 1254 – *VMPL*, I, no. 123, pp. 60–1.

55 See above n. 40.

56 For the conversion attempts of 1351 and 1358 made in the face of impending military invasion (as was not the case in 1322–23) to the king of Hungary and the emperor, see Mažeika, 'Role', 113–14, 142–4.

57 W. Ullmann, 'The medieval papal court as an international tribunal', *Virginia Journal of International Law*, 11 (1971), reprinted in W. Ullmann, *The Papacy and political ideas in the Middle Ages* (London, 1976), 359. Gediminas used the loosing and binding motif of papal power to refer to his own power in Lithuania – *GL*, 37. For the claims of Gediminas to have known since childhood of the role of the Pope as international arbitrator see *GL*, 23 and *MPV*, no. 175, p. 232.

58 3 February 1317, 'ad tui honoris augmentum quantum cum Deo fieri poterit' – *Acta Ioannis*, no. 2, p. 3.

59 As is obvious from Gediminas' repeated references to his expecting the legates to arrive – *GL*, 29, 47.

1319.[60] In 1319 famine still affected Poland and Prussia to such a degree that mothers are alleged to have eaten their children and the carcasses of executed criminals were snatched down from the gibbet to feed a starving populace.[61] In Saxony, according to the Chronicle of Wigand Gerstenberg, householders abandoned their homes and moved to unspecified foreign lands.[62] How far Lithuania suffered from the effects of this general depression is difficult to gauge. The scarcity of coins from the early fourteenth century in Lithuanian hoards and the smaller number of Lithuanian entries in Rigan trade records between 1296 and 1327 are cited by some scholars as evidence for a decline in Lithuanian commerce.[63] Certainly the *Ronneburg Annals* mention famine in Lithuania in 1315 and it is known that several harsh winters and bad harvests were experienced in Prussia and the Grand Duchy in the early 1320s.[64]

One response to a crisis in food production and a general economic recession is to increase the number of farmers and craftsmen producing for the market by encouraging the immigration of skilled colonists. The famine seems to have coincided with a period in western European history when land usage had reached its upper limit. A combination of these three factors (depression, famine and land shortages) meant that settlement in a foreign country, where more land was available to farmers on terms more favourable than those prevalent in the west, and where new towns were being endowed with modern statutes, was a particularly attractive proposition for potential emigrants. In Prussia in the fourteenth century the colonisation of vast tracts of sparsely populated frontier land (the *Wildnis*) became more and

60 W. Abel, *Agricultural Fluctuations in Europe. From the thirteenth to the twentieth centuries*, tr. O. Ordish, foreword and bibliography J. Thirsk (London, 1980), 38–42. H. Lucas, 'The Great European Famine of 1315, 1316 and 1317', *Speculum*, 5 (1930), 343–77.

61 H. Lucas, 'Great European Famine', 376.

62 *Die Chroniken des Wigand Gerstenbergs von Frankenberg*, ed. H. Diemar (Marburg, 1909), 28.

63 M. Berezhkov, 'Drevnerusskaia torgovlia s Rigoi', *ZhMNP*, 189 (1877), 330–57. Berezhkov charts a decline in Lithuano-Rigan trade between 1296 and 1327 since in those years fewer than 100 entries were made in the Rigan Debt Register for merchants and rulers as compared with almost 200 entries for the ten years 1286–95. G. B. Fedorov, 'Topografia kladov s litovskimi slitkami i monetami', *KSIIMK*, 29 (1949), 64–75. Here Fedorov notes that fewer coins have been found in Lithuania which date from the early fourteenth century although the Belorussian trade route (also under Lithuanian control) seems to have been prosperous.

64 *Stryjkowski*, I, 283; bad weather and poor harvests are recorded in *PD*, 186, 187 and *SRP*, III, 65.

more common. Westphalian immigration into Prussia, especially to Elbing, Chełmno and Toruń is well attested from 1313 to 1341. The same settlement policies were adopted in Poland and south-west Rus' in the first decades of the century. This was a time of great migrations, as we have already seen.[65]

Between 1283 (the beginning of the *bellum lithuanicum*) and 1340 (a year before Gediminas' death), almost 500 grants of land and legal privileges (Culm or Magdeburg Law) were issued to settlers in Prussia by the Teutonic Knights. This is the number at least of those which survive in the Order's Archives.[66] Military service or the provision of weapons was required from many of the colonists who came from German principalities, Poland, Rus' and even Lithuania.[67] In some cases the Lithuanian crusades were stipulated as the reason for these requirements.[68] The Knights thus furnished themselves with direct military resources for their campaigns and the economic foundations necessary to pay for the conflict, at the same time as colonising the sparsely populated land they won from Baltic tribesmen during the crusade.

Lithuanian tribesmen dissatisfied with life in the Grand Duchy were among those granted land in Prussia in return for their betrayal of Lithuania. As an incentive to fight well, they were promised land in Lithuania in place of their Prussian fiefs, once the Knights had gained control of the pagan realm.[69] The policy of

[65] For the settlement of the *Wildnis*, see K. Abe, *Die Komturei Osterode des Deutschen Ordens in Preussen 1341–1525*, *Studien zur Geschichte Preussens*, XVI (Cologne, 1972), 28–9. The movements of population around northern Germany in the wake of the plagues of the fourteenth century are described in H. Reincke, 'Bevölkerungsprobleme der Hansestädte', *Hansische Geschichtsblätter*, 70 (1951), 11–19. On Westphalian immigration to Prussia see T. Jasiński, 'Imigracja westfalska do Prus w okresie późnego średniowiecza (XIII–XIVw.)', in *Niemcy-Polska w średniowieczu*, ed. J. Strzelczyk (Poznań, 1986), 105–18. For immigrants to Elbing, Chełmno and Toruń in the years 1313–41 see *Dortmunder Urkundenbuch*, ed. von Rübel, I.1 (Dortmund, 1881), nos. 329, 411, 431, 445, 449. Colonisation from Prussia and the west was encouraged by the south-west Rus'ian princes whom Gediminas fought in 1322–23. The economic wealth of Galich–Volyn' may have provoked the invasion. Settlement grants quite similar to those Gediminas made were issued in south-west Rus' in 1320 – see above p. 24. A general account of the migrations across Europe is given in B. Zientara, 'Les grandes migrations des XIII–XIV siècles en Europe du Centre-Est', *Studia Historiae Oeconomicae*, 18 (1983), 3–30.

[66] See *PU*, I.2–III.1 *passim*.

[67] For example see *PU*, II, nos. 30, 43, 77, 98, 125, 126, 130, 133, 142, 177, 331–3, 361, 485, 558, 615.

[68] As in *PU*, II, nos. 562, 781.

[69] It seems likely that the betrayal of Aukaimis to the Knights in 1302 and 1305 was connected with the settlement of Aukaimis men in Prussia in 1303 – *PD*, 166–7, 171 for fall of Aukaimis; *PU*, I.2, nos. 791, 792 for the settlement of Gegayle and Byenken in Pronitten (Labiau) with a promise of land in Aukaimis once Lithuania is under the

welcoming these settlers to the Order's lands was 'widely proclaimed' by the Knights and their chroniclers.[70]

Lithuania too needed a greater supply of skilled manpower in order to improve her economy which was vital to the continuation of the struggle against the Knights. Defection from Prussia was not unheard of but it was certainly not reliable as a basis for economic or military success.[71] The usual Lithuanian practice of settling land with slaves was also unsatisfactory. It lacked discrimination and, as Giedroyć has recently claimed, the number of potential slaves available to Gediminas may have declined by the 1320s.[72] He notes how the incorporation of more and more Rus'ian territories into the Grand Duchy had altered the position of Rus' as a rich source of captives for Lithuania. Even so, the economy of the Grand Duchy as a whole must have been improved immeasurably by the annexation of White Rus' and the alliance of the mercantile republic of Pskov with Lithuania.[73] Giedroyć also cites a growing friendship between Poland and Lithuania after 1307 as a similar reason for a decline in the number of captives taken by the pagans. He claims that after the Kalisz raid by Vytenis' men in 1306, which resulted in the capture of a *maximam multitudinem* of slaves, Lithuania and Poland embarked upon a period of alliance.[74] However, Vytenis did not make an alliance with Łokietek and as far as we can see, he continued his old policy of selective aggression towards Poland.[75] As for Gediminas, he attacked Polish territory inside the *Regnum* and the duchies of Cieszyń, Dobrzyń and Mazovia until 1325 when he made peace with Łokietek and married his daughter to Łokietek's heir.[76] It is always possible

control of the Order. Other Lithuanians were enfeoffed by the Order, see *PU*, I.2, nos. 529, 576, 838, 839; *PU*, II, nos. 30, 125, 126, 336, 781, 798; *PU*, III.1, nos. 249–51, 277, 321.

70 *LR*, lines 2794–2960, tr. pp. 39–41.

71 *Wig.*, 570; *HW*, 104–5.

72 Giedroyć, 'Arrival ... (1281–1341)', 22–3. On slavery see pp. 73–6.

73 For the gaining of the mercantile cities of Vitebsk and Polotsk and the alliance with Pskov, see pp. 83–5.

74 Giedroyć, 'Arrival ... (1281–1341)', 11.

75 Giedroyć cites Łowmiański who in his turn refers to a passage from the Chronicle of Oliwa (*MPH*, V1, 327) which speaks of 'contracta amicicia cum rege Litwinorum Vyten nomine, cuius filiam filius regis Polonie duxit in uxorem, incepit impetere terram Pomeranie'. This undated chronicle entry refers to the marriage of Gediminas' daughter Aldona with Łokietek's heir Casimir, see below pp. 232–3. The mistaking of Vytenis for Gediminas is not uncommon in fourteenth-century sources – *Wig.*, 459–60. Since Łokietek only had one son whose first bride was Aldona-Anna no earlier union is possible.

76 Attacks on Cieszyń-Oświęcim and Mazovia are recorded by allusion in a papal indulgence blessing the marriage of the duke of Cieszyń with the daughter of Trojden

however that the famine in Poland had led to a decline in population and hence in the number of potential slaves.

Whatever the number and quality of slaves available to Lithuanian raiders, a new source of colonists was clearly desirable. After the grand duke had sent out his peace proposals to Livonia and Prussia in 1322 and had corresponded on this matter and the question of Catholicism in Lithuania with the Pope, he issued invitations to western farmers, craftsmen, merchants, priests and soldiers to come and settle in Lithuania. The first of these invitations was promulgated on 25 January 1323.[77] This letter like its successors issued on 26 May (Corpus Christi) was not concerned primarily with the conversion of Lithuania although many historians have paid undue attention to Gediminas' religious pronouncements in these documents.[78]

Addressed to the burghers of Lübeck, Stralsund, Bremen, Magdeburg, Cologne and 'all cities as far as Rome', the letter announces that Gediminas has approached the Pope concerning the reception of Catholicism in Lithuania and that papal envoys are expected any day in Vilnius. He asks the recipients of the letter to assist the envoys as they make their way westwards. The letter serves a dual purpose: to illustrate the latest development in Lithuanian reaction to Catholicism and to encourage Catholics to move to Gediminas' realm where the Church was established.[79] Catholics who chose to settle in Lithuania would not be cut off from the sacraments. The grand duke describes how he has constructed three new churches; one for the Dominicans in Vilnius (built in 1320–22) and two for the Franciscans, one in Vilnius and the other in Novgorodok to replace Vytenis' church which the Knights had burned down.[80] It should be noted that these churches were built in the two main commercial centres of the Grand Duchy: Vilnius in Lithuania and Novgorodok in Lithuanian Rus'. A general invitation to come to Lithuania is

of Mazovia in 1324 – *VMPL*, no. 303, p. 200. For Dobrzyń see below n. 115. Raids on Miechów (north of Kraków) before 1318 – *Zbiór dokumentów*, no. 22, pp. 28–9. For attacks elsewhere in the *Regnum* see *Długosz*, IX, 103

77 *GL*, 29–37. On controversies surrounding the dating of this letter see Rowell, 'Letters'.

78 Rowell, 'Letters'.

79 'Tenore presencium significamus ... nostrum nuncium cum litteris nostris domino apostolico et patri nostro sanctissimo sub katholice fidei receptione direxisse ... Insuper terram dominium et regnum patefacimus' *GL*, 29–33.

80 *Ibid.*, 31. The Dominican house had been built *infra duos annos*. The whole of Novgorodok was razed in 1314 – *PD*, 180–1.

issued here to bishops, priests and all manner of religious except those who sell their monasteries to turn them into military outposts.[81] This exception refers to the Cistercians who sold their Dünamünde monastery to the Knights in 1305. The latter subsequently converted the former convent into a fortress guarding the Dvina river route to Riga and thereby enabled themselves to block the mouth of the Dvina river at will.[82]

Against this background of Lithuanian toleration and an implicit willingness to accept baptism, Gediminas called upon merchants and knights, apothecaries, men-at-arms and silversmiths; carpenters, cobblers, furriers and fishermen and all manner of artisans and farmers to come and settle in his land. Relief from the payment of taxes for ten years was offered to these newcomers along with land and the protection of Rigan Law which, as the statutes of his closest ally, was probably the code best known to Gediminas. However if a better law were to be found it could be adopted in lieu of this.[83] The invitation was to be spread throughout Christendom by the copying of its terms in each city it reached and the publication of these on church portals before the original letter was passed on to the next city.[84] It should go almost without saying, that Gediminas paid so much attention here to the condition of Christianity in Lithuania because he needed Church infrastructure to disseminate his letter. In May 1323 the grand duke would enlist the services of friars to preach his offer to the faithful.

The good offices of the Teutonic brethren were not available to Gediminas. The Knights were not pleased by his defamation of their character or his competition with them to attract settlers from the Hansa cities and the west to the Baltic wilderness. At Corpus Christi, five months after the issue of the first invitation, three very similar letters were distributed around northern Europe on the grand duke's behalf. This time the consuls of Riga assisted the dissemination of the correspondence to prevent its destruction by the Knights.[85] In these letters, the grand duke complains that the seals on his correspondence have been broken in an attempt to destroy its credibility. Since such a complaint is not a feature of the January letter, which in almost every other respect is the same as those sent in May, it is highly probable that that letter had been

[81] *GL*, 33.
[82] See above pp. 13–14.
[83] *GL*, 33–5. On Rigan Law see above p. 13, n. 41.
[84] *GL*, 35–7.
[85] *GL*, 37–57.

one of those intercepted by the Knights.[86] The three May invitations were much more selectively directed than the earlier one. This time a list of Saxon cities was specified as one addressee and the Provincials of the Franciscan and Dominican Orders in Saxony were sent their own letters.[87]

In the letter to the cities, Gediminas stresses the full extent of his power within Lithuania in terms which are familiar to Catholics as the claim of the Pope 'to teach and rule, lose and save, to close and to open'.[88] This is presumably intended to inspire confidence that what the grand duke says can be relied upon. He reviews how Germans have crossed his lands in safety to reach Novgorod and Pskov and how his predecessors have often invited Hansa citizens to come to Lithuania. No response had come to these invitations. However past events should not worry them.[89] He declares that he will double any offer made by anyone else. He can be trusted because he has already written to the Pope and he intends to make such a peace with Catholics as 'Christians have never known'.[90] The same conditions of settlement are granted to clergy and craftsmen who come to Lithuania here as in the January letter but greater emphasis is laid on the settlement of farmers. Gediminas wants grain production in Lithuania to exceed that in other countries.[91] He concludes with a statement that he has built churches in his lands to make newcomers feel more secure: *ut igitur securiores et magis certiores vos reddamus*.[92] This motivation behind his church building should not be dismissed lightly. It cannot be stressed too often that Catholicism was viewed politically by Gediminas as a means of comforting foreigners in Lithuania rather than as a religion to be imposed upon his unwilling pagan subjects. The final lines of the letter threaten those who despoil his correspondence and offer practical information about how best to reach Lithuania without travelling through the Order's territory.[93]

[86] Gediminas was well aware of the importance of seals for the validation of a document – *GL*, 35. The January letter is the only one of four letters sent out in 1323 not to mention the destruction of seals. For complaints about the breaking and burning of seals see *GL*, 45, 49–51, 57, 133–5.

[87] To the cities of Lübeck, Stralsund, Rostock, Greifswald, Stettin, Gotland – *GL*, 37–47; to the Franciscans of Saxony – *GL*, 51–7; to the Dominicans of Saxony – *GL*, 47–51.

[88] *GL*, 37. See above p. 59.

[89] *GL*, 39.

[90] *GL*, 39–41.

[91] 'quod nobiscum plus exuberabit granum, quam in aliis regnis est consuetum' – *GL*, 43.

[92] *Ibid.*, 45.

[93] That is via the lands of Wacław of Płock – *ibid.*, 45. For the textual reading *Subonislay* (Berlin, PKKA, Ms. LS XI.17) is clearly a scribal error in a copy of a copy of the

The other two letters sent at Corpus Christi were addressed to the Franciscans and Dominicans of Saxony who between them had houses in all the cities Gediminas approached for settlers and merchants.[94] Since Riga too belonged to the Saxon Province, the friars sought by Gediminas for Novgorodok and Vilnius (where Franciscans drafted Gediminas' correspondence and a Dominican acted as the grand duke's adviser on matters Catholic)[95] also fell under the authority of these two provincials.[96]

In the letter to the Dominicans, Gediminas announces that he has written to the Pope requesting investiture with the 'best robe' or *stola prima* which appears to be a periphrasis for baptism.[97] The grand duke remarks that he expects the Pope's envoys to arrive and proclaims his willingness to 'protect the laws of the Church, honour the clergy ... and promote the worship of God'.[98] Once more Gediminas says everything except the words 'baptism' or 'conversion'. He repeats the settlement conditions he made in other letters and requests the friars to speak of Gediminas'

original document. From the similarity of a Gothic W with the ligature sb the name should surely read *Wenceslay* (Wacław), as Prochaska supposed, see Rowell, 'Letters'.

94 For a list of Franciscan houses in Saxony, see J. B. Freed, 'Dzieje saskiej prowincji Franciszkanów w XIII wieku', in *Zakony Franciszkanskie w Polsce*, ed. J. Kłoczowski, I (Lublin, 1982), 218–25.

95 As is clear from *GL*, 119–21, 127, 131–5, 139–45. Brother Nicholas advised Gediminas on his alliance with Riga, see below p. 223. He was a Dominican – *de Ordine maiorum*. For other uses of this term to signify Dominican friars (in contrast with Franciscan *minores*) see *Der Stralsunder Liber Memorialis Teil I: Fol. 1–60, 1320–1410*, ed. H-D. Schroeder (Leipzig, 1964), no. 6, p. 25; no. 258, p. 57; no. 307, p. 63.

96 It is most probable that the Vilnius Franciscans came from Riga or Braunsberg, the houses where the Lithuanian or at least the Semigallian mission was prepared – *PU*, no. 13, p. 8 and *LU*, VI, no. 2769 (a letter of Pope Clement V dated 17 February 1311 commanding Archbishop Frederick of Riga to found Franciscan houses throughout his archdiocese). Some Polish historians have tended to exaggerate the role played by Polish mendicants in the Lithuanian Mission of the early fourteenth century. This seems to be based on the discovery by K. Kantak of a Polish *lector* in Riga in 1305 – K. Kantak, *Franciszkanie Polscy I (1237–1517)* (Kraków, 1937), 300. Polish friars arrived formally in Lithuania after the conversion of 1387 and the first bishop of Vilnius was a Polish Franciscan – Rowell, 'Lithuania', 313. The newcomers were suspicious of the German friars and restricted them to serving the Hansa missions – *KDKDW*, no. 159, p. 180.

97 *GL*, 47. *Stola prima* is a reference to St Luke XV, 22, the parable of the prodigal son. The phrase was used by John XXII in his letter to the king of the Georgians, dated 15 October 1321 – *Acta Ioannis*, no. 46, p. 92. The use of an allusion to this parable seems inappropriate here for unlike the Georgian, Gediminas was not a schismatic Christian. Perhaps it is used simply as a model of conversion. It appears not to be connected with the practice of *prima signatio* in earlier centuries by which pagans were admitted to intercourse with Christians after undergoing a ceremony of partial acceptance of Christianity.

98 *GL*, 49.

encouragement of trade and colonisation wherever they go to preach.[99]

The same requests are made of the Franciscans. Gediminas, they are to understand, is in communication with the Pope and wishes to welcome foreigners to his land.[100] The friars should make the grand duke's will known to their flock in all cities and places of habitation: 'Cupimus per vos et vestros fratres in omnibus civitatibus, locis seu villis nostrum pandere velle universis'.[101] This application to the Franciscans and Dominicans for help in publicising Gediminas' settlement plans is not merely the result of past familiarity with the mendicants but a well thought out use of an effective preaching machine. As J. B. Freed has noted, a list of houses in the custodies of the Franciscans and Dominicans in north-eastern Europe reads like a gazeteer of market places.[102]

These letters hint more at the work of Saxon friars among Catholic traders than the native pagan or schismatic population at large. We should note that Gediminas told the Franciscans he expected four friars to come to him in 1323 'knowing Polish, Semigallian and Prussian'.[103] This does not read like a prescription for ministry to the Lithuanians whose language is conspicuous here by its absence. Semigallian alone appears necessary for religious purposes. It seems that Gediminas was willing to baptise the Semigallians, who inhabited a region coveted by the Lithuanians and the Order alike, if by doing so he could deny the Knights the opportunity of exercising their rights as crusaders in that territory.[104] Polish was a language of Lithuanian slaves and, to a lesser degree, diplomacy and was relevant to commerce in Novgorodok and Vilnius. It seems no coincidence that both the earliest Catholic and Orthodox churches in Vilnius were dedicated to St Nicholas, the patron of merchants.[105]

99 'Idcirco petimus ut vos hec in civitatibus, locis et villis, ubi aliquem vestrum predicare contigerit, populo nuntietis' – *GL*, 49. For the settlement plans see *ibid.*, 49–51.

100 *GL*, 53.

101 *Ibid.*

102 Freed, 'Dzieje', 208, 212, 226. Given the Franciscan and Dominican presence at the time of urbanisation in central Europe it is tempting to see Gediminas' invitations to the mendicants as part of his plans for new towns in Lithuania. He had re-established Vilnius as the major political centre of the country – see pp. 69–73. For the role of the mendicants in the establishment of cities, see E. Fügedi, 'La formation des villes et les ordres mendiants en Hongrie', *Annales: Economies, Sociétés, Civilisations*, 25 (1970), 966–87.

103 *GL*, 55.

104 See above n. 36. For Semigallia, see above pp. 194–5. Lithuanian was not the Semigallian language.

105 The friars were destined for Vilnius and Novgorodok in particular not the Grand Duchy in general. Gediminas would not tolerate the alteration of the religious *status*

It may be apposite to recall how much was owed to the mercantile colonies of the north for the bringing of the Baltic peoples to Christ. Catholic merchants brought priests with them to their trade outposts to minister to them. The merchant church which also served as a storehouse was an important catalyst for the conversion of the Livonians and other northern pagans. This is why the mendicants followed the merchants to Tartary and Lithuania in the thirteenth and fourteenth centuries.[106]

Similar recourse to merchants and their mendicant pastors was a feature of Mindaugas' reign. He sent out invitations to merchants, settlers and friars in 1253, although it is difficult to tell how successful the policy was.[107] Friars were present at Mindaugas' coronation in 1253. Probably throughout almost the whole fourteenth century Franciscans were in Vilnius, as we can tell from evidence of their being martyred when they moved from serving merchants to preaching the Gospel to the pagans.[108] In 1382 the chief of the Livonian merchants, Hanul was a patron of the Vilnius Franciscans.[109] Gediminas stands at the centre of a Lithuanian tradition.

quo, see above n. 46. Wyrozumski considers these three languages to have been languages of diplomacy – J. Wyrozumski, 'Próba chrystianizacji Litwy w czasach Giedymina', *Analecta Cracoviensia*, 19 (1987), 77. However there was as yet little diplomatic contact with Poland. The reading *pruthenicum* is clear in the Berlin manuscript (see n. 93) and would involve Gediminas' taking responsibility for the Prussian tribesmen too. Some scholars, notably Prochaska, have suggested a reading of *ruthenicum*. Gediminas had no need of Russian-speaking Catholics for his nascent chancery. Catholic and Rus'ian merchants however did need help to communicate. The transcript betrays several other mistakes in copying – see Rowell, 'Letters'.

106 Archbishop John of Riga wrote in 1277 of how 'novella plantatio fidei catholice in partibus Livonie ... per strenuam honorabilium mercatorum industriam hactenus competenter profecerit' – *Lübeckisches Urkundenbuch*, I (Lübeck, 1843), no. 388, p. 357. See also A. Vööbus, *Studies in the History of the Estonian People*, I, *Papers of the Estonian Theological Society in Exile*, 18 (1969), 22–7 and P. Johansen, 'Die Kaufmannskirche in Ostseegebiet', *Studi in onore di Armando Sapore*, I (Milan, 1957), 311–26.

107 *LU*, I, no. 243, cols. 312–13. See K. Maleczyński, 'W sprawie autentyczności dokumentów Mendoga za lat 1253–61', *AW*, XI (1936), 5–6, 49–55. After Mindaugas' murder the friars ceased to function in Lithuania – 'in dicto regno cessaverunt esse episcopi, presbyteri, fratres minores et predicatores', Seraphim, *Das Zeugenverhör*, Appendix IX, 244, p. 202. They returned in Vytenis' reign – *GL*, 25.

108 Friars were present at the coronation for they have left an account of it – Colker, 'America', 712–26. For the martyrs see below p. 276.

109 W. Semkowicz, 'Hanul, namiestnik wileński (1382–87) i jego ród', *AW* VII (1930), 1–20. For his donation of the estate *Na Kyenny* to the Franciscans in Vilnius (St Mary *in arena*), see the Privilege of Zygmunt Stary to the Franciscans, dated 3 December 1522. Manuscript in the Library of the Polish Academy of Sciences, Kraków – Dok. 481: 'In primis exhibuit litteras quibus nobilis Hanul heres in Nakyenny namyesthnyk vilnen[sis] dedit hereditatem suam Nakÿenny nuncupatam cum omni iure et omnes areas suas ante, retro et ex latere Oratorii Sancti Nicolai eidem ecclesie

In response to Gediminas' *démarche*, the Franciscan provincial of Saxony applied to John XXII for permission to establish new houses in Prussia and Reval to serve the Lithuanian mission. Such permission for three houses, each containing up to a dozen friars, was granted by the Pope on 12 November 1324.[110]

Around the time that the Saxon letters were being drafted, Gediminas wrote again to the Pope affirming his belief in Father, Son and Holy Ghost and recognising the authority of the Holy See.[111] Still the grand duke awaited the arrival of the promised papal legates. However his period of waiting was not idle.

Between the autumn of 1322 and May 1323 the Lithuanians gained control of south-west Rus' and placed Kiev, the 'mother of Rus'ian cities' (and since 1320 the site of a new Catholic bishopric)[112] in the hands of a Lithuanian.[113] As a result of the campaign in Galich–Volyn', Gediminas came face to face with Łokietek and Polish ambitions in Rus' for the first time. A *modus vivendi* would have to be worked out between Gediminas and the king of Poland to satisfy their rival desires to control Rus'.

Gediminas' offensives against Catholic powers continued throughout 1323 too. A unilateral truce on Gediminas' part while he talked of peace was not countenanced by the heathen ruler. Attacks were launched against Reval in February (with Pskovite assistance), Memel in March and in August against Wehlau.[114] In September 'nine thousand' captives were taken in a joint

et oratorio sancti Nicolai quod tandem fratribus ordinis sancti Francisci monasterio vilnen[si] asscripsit.'

110 *MPV*, no. 177, pp. 235–6. Papal permission was required before any mendicant house could be established. This indulgence allowed the friars to build two houses in Prussia and one in Reval in addition to the Vilnius and Novgorodok foundations. Cf. the one granted in 1311 at Frederick's behest – above p. 58.

111 *VMPL*, no. 293, pp. 193–4. There is no date for the letter which John XXII cites here. However given that he wrote to Charles of France on 7 November 1323 announcing that Gediminas had written *nudius* (a more emphatic word for 'recently' than *nuper* which John used of letters which were eighteen months old – *VMPL*, no. 290, p. 190 and formed from the phrase *nunc dies*) it would seem that Gediminas' second letter had only recently arrived. It could take five or six months to get from Livonia to Avignon let alone from Lithuania to the curia when the route was blocked: cf. letter of James of Ösel to Pope, 6 February 1333, *LU*, VI, no. 2800, cols. 103–4. It should be noted that Forstreuter's interpretation of *nudius* as the comparative of *nude* ('nakedly' therefore 'undisguisedly false') is wrong. See also below n. 162.

112 *VMPL*, nos. 252, pp. 162–3 (15 December 1320) and 255, pp. 167–8 (18 February 1321). These documents appoint Henry, a Dominican friar as bishop of Kiev and authorise him to take up residence in his new see.

113 See above pp. 95f.

114 Reval – *PD*, 187, and *PL*, II, 22, 89. Memel – *PD*, 187; Wehlau – *PD*, 188.

Lithuano-Płock raid on Dobrzyń.[115] By way of a response to these attacks the Knights killed twelve Lithuanians during a harvest-time assault on the Semigallian settlement on the Nemunas near Paštuva.[116] The Livonians, the Knights and the Danes were neither politically nor militarily strong enough to win the war against Lithuania and Gediminas, whose emissaries had traversed Livonia and Prussia to Denmark, knew it.

The reaction of the northern Catholics to Gediminas' continued military activity and diplomatic initiatives for peace was at first very cautious. When the grand duke originally sent out his proposals to the Order and Livonia in 1322, the Rigans begged him not to make peace with the Knights without them.[117] We know little of the Knights' response, although it seems that, of the pretenders to the mastership of the Livonian Order, Johann Ungenade opposed the treaty.[118] However when the Saxon letters of May 1323 were copied in Lübeck on July 18 they were received well.[119] It was decided that despite other business the Knights would examine Gediminas' claims in detail without delay. Faced with such general enthusiasm for the proposals the Knights did not dare appear disdainful, although their approach to the proposals after the Lübeck meeting was more prevaricative than enthusiastic. The Rigans had made it plain that they were not willing to break their friendship with the Lithuanians despite Johann Ungenade's luckless attempts to persuade them to do so.[120]

On 10 August 1323 representatives of Riga (chapter and council), the Franciscans, Dominicans, Danes (from Reval) and the Livonian Order met in Ermes to discuss their response to the proposed treaty and examine the authenticity of Gediminas' letters.[121] It was decided to send messengers to Gediminas to question him about these missives. These envoys arrived in Vilnius

[115] *PD*, 188; *MPH*, III, 45, 229; *Długosz*, IX, 126–7. [116] *PD*, 189.

[117] *GL*, 59–63.

[118] 'In mutuo colloquio Dunemunde instituto magister ordinis teutonici Johannes Ungenade eximiis promissis sat egerunt ut a societate paganorum contra christianos inita Rigenses posset abducere, verum nihil apud eos profecisse' – cited from the Swedish Archives Register in F. G. von Bunge, *Die Stadt Riga im dreizehnten und vierzehnten Jahrhundert* (Leipzig, 1878), 62, n. 157. His men continued to attack Lithuania after the treaty had been signed – in 1324 they robbed Voinat of three horses – *GL*, 169.

[119] *volenti animo et hylari corde* according to the Stralsund and Lübeck transcriptions of the letters made on 15 and 18 July 1323. Raczyński, *Codex*, 31

[120] The Knights were willing to pay for an investigation of Gediminas' claims – *ibid.* On Ungenade see above n. 118. [121] *RLA*, no. 58, pp. 35–6.

on 8 September where they were well received.[122] They read the letters to the grand duke and asked if what the letters contained was accurate. Gediminas recognised the seals appended to the documents as his and acknowledged the proposals, adding that he was eager to meet the Pope's envoys. The measured caution of his response to questions about conversion ('God knows what is in my heart') contrasts sharply with his open enthusiasm for welcoming settlers to Lithuania and making peace with the Knights.[123] This is typical of the promissory but non-committal tone of his correspondence as a whole.

Gediminas' attitude to baptism might be summed up as one of 'wait and see'. He was astute enough not to make any unambiguous reference to baptism until he was sure that conversion was a completely effective way of neutralising the Teutonic threat to Lithuania. However he was fully prepared to sign a peace treaty with his Catholic enemies if terms were good.

On 2 October 1323, less than a month after Gediminas granted an audience to the Livonian envoys who came to discuss his proposals, a Lithuano-Livonian peace treaty was signed in Vilnius which was to last for four years.[124] The signatories to the treaty were the representatives of the archbishop and chapter of Riga and envoys from the bishops of Ösel and Dorpat. The lieutenant of the king of Denmark, the Dominican prior of Reval and several members of the Livonian branch of the Teutonic Order also added their names to the document.

The treaty guaranteed safe passage for Catholics in Lithuania (Aukštaitija and Žemaitija), Pskov and all the Rus'ian territories subject to the grand duke in return for free access for Lithuanians to the archdiocese of Riga, Memel, Courland, Livonia (including Ösel and Dorpat) and the territories of Harrien, Wirland and Alutaguse which Denmark controlled on the Gulf of Finland and the Novgorodian border (see map 5(b)).[125] It was agreed that should a serf flee from the lands of any party he would be repatriated.[126] Thus renegades were not to be granted asylum. Merchants were to enjoy Rigan Law (as Gediminas promised

[122] *Ibid.*; *GL*, 147–9.

[123] 'Wanne des paues boden der ych alle daghe wachtende byn to my komet wat ich an myme herten hebbe dat wet god wol unde ich suluen, wante ich dat ghe hort hebbe van minen olderen dat de paues user aller vader is', *RLA*, 36 and n.1.

[124] *GL*, 65–75.

[125] *Ibid.*, 65–71.

[126] *Ibid.*, 73. Is this a response to Lithuanian defections to the Order?

colonists in his 1323 letters) and the right to buy and sell all types of commodity.[127] It was stipulated that two months' warning of any intention to abandon the treaty should be given and agreed, although not written into the text of the treaty, that the Knights should surrender to Lithuania their newly rebuilt fort at Mezoten in Semigallia and their stronghold at Dünaburg which guarded the Dvina trade route between Rus', the Grand Duchy and Livonia.[128] Once signed and sealed, the treaty was sent to the Curia for papal ratification.[129]

By means of this agreement Gediminas managed to restrict the activities of his Livonian enemies at least officially. In the intervening year between his first approaches to the Order and the signing of the treaty Gediminas, by dint of his capture of Galich–Volyn', had deprived the Knights of yet another ally.[130] Nevertheless the Knights must have felt obliged rather than relieved to treat with Gediminas for only the Livonian branch of the Order was signatory to the treaty. This may be more than simply evidence of the Livonian brethren's more frequent contact, both mercantile and martial, with Lithuania. Although in theory the Livonians were removed from the conflict, the Prussians remained unbound by the agreement and unashamedly at war with Gediminas. The Knights could ill afford to allow Gediminas to prosper but they could not appear to the Pope and their enemies (Riga and Poland) who enjoyed his favour to be unwilling to make peace with a pagan prince who claimed he wanted to be a Catholic. Sending the Livonians to make peace was a clever compromise.

No sooner was the ink dry on the parchment than complaints began to be voiced in Prussia about Lithuanian perfidy. The Knights' reaction against the treaty has been described as naïve and

[127] Rigan Law – *ibid.* and *GL*, 35, 43. For trade, see *GL*, 75. There had previously been restrictions on the types of goods which could legally be sold to pagans, see Mažeika, 'Prekyba'. There was a tradition of truces between the pagans and the crusaders during which commerce flourished – Seraphim, *Das Zeugenverhör*, II, 46, p. 157 and *LR*, lines 4575f., tr. pp. 59–60.

[128] 'Item in ordinacione fuit, quod duo castra reddere debebant videlicet Duneborch et Medizota, quod non fecerunt', *GL*, 173. This comes from Gediminas' complaint of 1325.

[129] The papal transcripts of the Lithuanian document (*MPV*, no. 168, pp. 226–7) and the Livonian version of the treaty (*MPV*, no. 169, pp. 227–8) survive as do texts of the treaty in other papal letters intending to ratify the treaty – *MPV*, nos. 175, pp. 231–3; 176, pp. 233–5.

[130] In 1316 the Knights had concluded an alliance with Andrei and Lev Yurevich of Galich–Volyn' – see pp. 23–4.

reckless.[131] Comprehensive, concerted and desperate would better define a campaign aimed at undermining pagan and Christian confidence in the treaty. This included direct and indirect verbal and physical subversion of the agreement. The Knights did not relish being outmanoeuvred by Gediminas.

On 16 October, a practised apologist of the Order, Bishop Eberhard of Warmia, and his chapter issued an open letter in support of the Teutonic Knights which condemned Lithuanian atrocities.[132] The bishop listed Lithuania's most recent attacks on Christian lands. However he omitted to say, as is obvious from Prussian, Russian and Polish chronicles which also detail these attacks, that the campaigns were launched before the treaty was signed and in some cases with the connivance of Christian princes.[133] This letter was followed eight days later by another, composed 'at the behest of others'[134] by the bishop of Warmia in conjunction with the bishops of Sambia and Pomezania.[135] The prelates warned the Livonian signatories to the treaty that it was dangerous to make peace with the Devil's spawn.[136]

The war of words intensified in November 1323 when the custodian of the Prussian Franciscans, Brother Nicholas, wrote to the Pope in defence of the Knights who daily expose themselves to death on account of the Gospel.[137] He accused the king of Lithuania of sending out letters to various parts of the world proclaiming a desire to be baptised which, when messengers arrived at his court to corroborate the claim, was found to be false.[138] This letter was copied by the Knights for use as an exemplar and sent to the Pope in January 1324 by their allies, the Cistercian abbots of Pelplin and Oliwa.[139]

The Knights themselves spread disinformation in Lübeck about the sincerity of the intentions expressed in Gediminas' cor-

131 Giedroyć, 'Arrival ... (1281–1341)', 25, 26.

132 *GL*, 75. Eberhard's defence of the Order in 1310 is given in *PU*, II, no. 20, pp. 14–15.

133 *GL*, 77–81 – the attacks on Dorpat, Reval, Dobrzyń, Memel and Wehlau. Cf. above nn. 26, 27 and 114.

134 *CDP*, II, no. 105, pp. 136–7. *forte nutu aliorum* – *GL*, 157 – the 'others' are the Teutonic Knights.

135 Bishop Rudolf of Pomezania issued land grants to colonists in exchange for military assistance against the Lithuanians – *PU*, II, no. 562. A third of the area of the dioceses of Warmia, Sambia and Pomezania lay under the Knights' sway – *Chronicon de vitis episcoporum*, *Scriptores Rerum Warmiensium*, ed. K. P. Woelky and Y. M. Saage, I (Braunsberg, 1866), 47.

136 *CDP*, II, no. 105, 136–7.

137 *GL*, 87–91.

138 *Ibid.*, 89.

139 Exemplar – *CDP*, II, no. 106, pp. 138–9; Oliwa and Pelplin letter – *ibid.*, no. 108, p. 142.

respondence, presumably in an attempt to undermine the efficacy of Gediminas invitations to settlers.[140] The Livonian signatories to the treaty were also approached by the Knights and their clerical allies to renege on the agreement they had been encouraged to sign only three months earlier. Bishop James of Ösel was asked at the Diet of Pernau in December 1323 to renounce the treaty and send accusations against Gediminas to the Holy See.[141]

The Knights also approached Gediminas in a last attempt to persuade him (with a thousand silver marks) to accept baptism from them.[142] When the grand duke declined the offer – and he had always said that he would not accept baptism from the Order[143] – the brethren bribed his Žemaitijan tribesmen who were as venal as they were fiercely pagan to threaten Gediminas with dire consequences, should he accept baptism from anyone.[144] If Gediminas was to become a Christian and remove the Knights' *raison d'être*, only the Knights could be credited with the achievement. There certainly was opposition to Gediminas' conversion from the Žemaitijan and Rus'ian Orthodox subjects of the Grand Duchy.[145]

After bribery had failed to win Gediminas for the Teutonic font, the Knights embarked upon a systematic programme of disruption of the grand duke's communications with Christendom. His envoys were imprisoned and even on occasion hanged; his letters to the Curia were deprived of their seals and sometimes they were burned.[146] To all intents and purposes, the war continued in 1324 as before with Prussian and Livonian offensives, razzias by Prussian *latrunculi* and Lithuanian counter-attacks.[147]

[140] *GL*, 147.

[141] As the Ösel Archive Register shows in an entry dated to 1323–24: *LU*, VI, register p. 168: 'Ein bisschop van Curland heft gebeden Jacobum den bisscop van Ozell, dar he mit den Lettowen den bifrede wolde upseggen; krege her derwegen schaden, den wolde eme de orde upleggen, worde he vor dem stole to Rome verklaget, de bisscop van Curland wolde in siner eigener personen dar hen und eme vorantworden.' Cf. the report of this incident in the excommunication ban laid on the Order by Frederick of Riga at Easter 1325 – *CDP*, II, no. 111, p. 148. For the Diet of Pernau see *Akten und Recesse der Livländischen Ständetage mit Überstützung der Baltischen Ritterschaften und Städte*, ed. O. Stavenhagen, I (1304–1460) (Riga, 1907), no. 20, p. 16.

[142] The bribe was listed in the charges of the Easter Ban of 1325 – *CDP*, II, no. 111, p. 148.

[143] *GL*, 27.

[144] The *potenciores de Sameytis* were offered *multas tunicas et bona* along with details of Gediminas' alleged plans for conversion – *GL*, 138–9. The venality of the Žemaitijans was well known – *PSRL*, II, s.a. 1248, 1252, pp. 815–18.

[145] *GL*, 139–41.

[146] *GL*, 147–65, 167–73, 175–87.

[147] March 1324 – Grodno attacked, *PD*, 189; 22 May – Gedimin-Burg burned, *PD*, 189–90; Summer 1324 the Prussian bandit Mucko killed forty-five Lithuanians in the

The capture of men and goods, the murder of Gediminas' envoys and Teutonic raids in Lithuania were intended as *casus belli* to provoke Gediminas into abandoning the treaty which the Knights could not reject without incurring the wrath of the Pope.[148] In December 1323, the Knights concluded an alliance with Novgorod directed against Lithuania and Pskov. In 1323 and 1324 the Lithuanians were almost at war with the Novgorodians who objected to Lithuanian rule in Pskov.[149] Crude as these actions may seem, they almost succeeded. Gediminas complained to his co-signatories late in 1323 that he could not tolerate such conduct for much longer.[150]

It took the continued forbearance of Gediminas and the intervention of the Pope to bring the Knights to heel. On 31 August 1324, the Pope ratified the Vilnius Treaty and compelled the Prussian Brethren on pain of excommunication to abide by the agreement struck by the Livonians. When the papal legates reached Riga in October 1324, they repeated the commands of the Pope and, although the treaty was supposed to bind the whole Order only after Gediminas had been baptised, the Knights kept the peace.[151]

Gediminas achieved one of his diplomatic objectives in 1324: peace with the Order enforced by papal edict. How the Pope came to his decision to side with Riga and Lithuania against the Order after virtually ignoring Gediminas for two years is a question which deserves examination.

After the Pope received Gediminas' first letter, he indicated that

Wildnis and at another time robbed and enslaved Lithuanians who were travelling in that same area, *PD*, 190. The pagans attacked Christmemel, *PD*, 190 and on 22 November devastated Rositen in Livonia, *PD*, 192.

[148] *GL*, 179: 'in. eo videlicet nos predicte paci renunciaverimus', *GL*, 173: 'Insuper ubicunque possunt, hanc pacem nituntur destruere ... ita quod pax inter nos diu durare non potest'.

[149] *GVNiP*, no. 37, pp. 65–7. The dating of this treaty has caused much confusion despite the clear wording of the treaty: 'na den jare uses heren in dem dusendesten, in dem drehundersten, in deme dre und twintegesten, des lesten vridages vor des heiligen kerstes dage', *ibid.*, 67. That is, in 1323 on the last Friday before holy *kerstes dage*. *Kerstes dage* is the Middle Low German for Christmas Day, not Candlemas. The date of the treaty is 23 December 1323, not 28 January as Valk translated it and Fennell followed – *Emergence*, 98. Most recently an article by N. A. Kazakova has perpetuated the mistake – N. A. Kazakova, 'Novgorodsko-nemetskie dogovory ili Livonskie akty?' *Novgorodskii istoricheskii sbornik*, 3:13 (1989), 63–7. The treaty hurt Lithuania's ally Riga in her commerce with Novgorod – *GL*, 155. In 1323 and 1324 Lithuania met in skirmishes at Luki and on the Lovat' river route – *NL*, 97, 339.

[150] *GL*, 173.

[151] *MPV*, no. 175, pp. 231–3; *CDP*, II, no. 110, pp. 143–4.

he was willing to send envoys to Lithuania.[152] The grand duke continued to communicate with John XXII and Lithuanian couriers frequented the Curia. Later Rigan nuncios acting on Gediminas' behalf carried letters to the Pope, after the Knights successfully blockaded Lithuanian access to the papal court.[153] However progress was very slow, as the papal envoys confessed to Gediminas when they met him in November 1324. They claimed it had taken a long time to find suitable envoys, and judging by the care taken in these appointments, this is understandable and almost credible as an excuse. However, as with the Scottish case against England and Poland's struggle with Bohemia for recognition as a kingdom, John XXII waited in the vain hope that an international dispute would solve itself without his risking the alienation of one or other party.[154] With whom should he agree: the Lithuanians and Archbishop Frederick, or the Knights? The delay does not mean that the Pope was mistrustful of Gediminas or cool towards him as Forstreuter was wont to claim.[155] He exhibited his typical caution. John discussed Gediminas' letters with the College of Cardinals and the Lithuanian proposals were taken very seriously. The Pope was buying time.[156] In addition to examining recent episcopal appointments to the Livonian sees of Ösel, Dorpat, Reval and Courland where the interference of the Teutonic Knights might be suspected, the Pope was called upon to investigate the whole question of what to do with the Teutonic Order in the face of Polish, Rigan and now Lithuanian accusations against the Knights. The future of the Church in north-eastern Europe could not be decided in a day, or even in a year. The conversion of the last European pagans who happened to control vast tracts of schismatic Christian land was also not a prize to be squandered. The Lithuanian capture of south-west Rus', which John had long hoped to bring into the Catholic fold, and the seizure in May 1323, of Kiev, where John had appointed a

152 In January 1323 Gediminas expected the envoys to arrive at any moment – *GL*, 29.

153 'Hoc per nuntios suos, quos ad Sedem apostolicam propter hoc specialiter destinavit', *MPV*, no. 175, p. 231.

154 *GL*, 125. For choice of envoys, see below p. 219 and for events of 1322–23, above, n.1.

155 Forstreuter, 'Die Bekehrung Gedimins', 249.

156 *VMPL* no. 293, p. 193; *GL*, 125. In this referral to the Consistory we are reminded of the warning given to the Aragonese ambassador at the Curia by Cardinal Toscian in March 1323: 'per cert sapiats, quel papa no met res en Consistory, si no ço que no vol fer', *Acta Aragonensia, Quellen zur deutschen, italienischen, französischen, spanischen, zur Kirchen- und Kulturgeschichte aus der diplomatischen Korrespondenz Jaymes II* (1291–1327), ed. H. Finke, II (Berlin–Leipzig, 1908), no. 378, p. 586

Catholic bishop in 1320, made the conversion of Gediminas all the more attractive.[157]

The greatest spur to John's action was provided by the illegal appointment by Emperor Louis IV of his son Louis to the vacant Mark of Brandenburg in 1323 and the consequences of Louis IV's assumption of royal powers in Germany. The New Mark occupied what had been the Polish territory of Lubusz until it became an imperial possession in 1249.[158] As a former duchy of Poland, it formed part of Łokietek's ambition to reconstitute the *Regnum Poloniae* and the appointment of Louis' son to rule there angered the Pope because he considered it his privilege to nominate the next margrave.[159] Louis IV presumed to act openly as emperor before John had approved his election to the imperial throne. On 8 October 1323 John XXII began the process of excommunicating the emperor and drew up plans to remove Margrave Louis from Brandenburg. The Danes joined the fray by consenting to the marriage of King Christopher's daughter Margaret with Louis of Brandenburg.[160] Within a year the Lithuanian mission became entangled in this web of alliances and counteralliances until the Order appeared to support the emperor.

The Pope, who intended to replace Emperor Louis with Charles IV of France, began to consult the French king secretly on imperial matters including Brandenburg.[161] On 7 November 1323, in a letter to Charles, the Pope mentioned that he had very recently (*nudius*) received a letter from Gediminas requesting a papal legation be sent to Lithuania to discuss the union of Lithuania with the Catholic Church. The papal couriers would divulge more information about this to the king.[162] In view of Gediminas' later

[157] For the new bishop see above n. 112.

[158] The Ascanian family gained control of Lubusz in 1249 – 'Kronika Książąt Polskich', *MPH*, III, 491. The dynasty died out in 1320, see Walachowicz, *Geneza*, 22–3. For the appointment of Louis, see Benker, *Ludwig*, 115.

[159] *MGH. Legum sectio IV: Constitutiones et Acta Publica imperatorum et regum*, ed. J. Schwalm, V (Hanover–Leipzig, 1909–13), no. 792. p. 617, §2.

[160] Offler, 'Empire', 23. Danish marriage, the arrangements for which last through from 1323 to 1325, see *Diplomatarium Danicum*, II.9 (Copenhagen, 1946), nos. 51, pp. 34–8; 125, pp. 96–7; 163, pp. 121–2. See Mohlin, *Kristoffer*, 11 and R. Mažeika, 'The context of Pope John XXII's letters to Gediminas (1322–1324)' *Gedimino laikų Lietuva ir jos kaimynai* (Vilnius, forthcoming).

[161] G.Tobacco, *La casa di Francia nell'azione politica di papa Giovanni XXII* (Rome, 1953), 213–37. Finke, *Acta Aragonensia*, I (Berlin–Leipzig, 1908), no. 265, p. 400; no. 268, p. 406.

[162] *GL*, 55–85. Full text in Pope John XXII, *Lettres secrètes et curiales relatives à la France* ed. A. Coulon and S. Clemencet. *Bibliothèque des Ecoles françaises d'Athènes et de Rome*, 3rd

involvement in the Brandenburg question it seems likely that the Pope was already considering how support for Lithuania might put pressure on the Order to abstain from aiding the emperor further in this matter.[163]

Meanwhile the Pope continued his investigation of the charges levelled against the Order by Riga and Lithuania. As a result of this investigation, John sent a paternal reprimand to the grand master on 10 February 1324, chiding the Knights for their mistreatment of the clergy, their hindrance of messengers travelling across their lands and for acting in a manner which deterred pagans from accepting baptism. No specific mention of the Lithuanian case was made. Both sides were testing the waters of the Rubicon.[164]

In March of that year, the Pope formally excommunicated Louis in retaliation for the emperor's refusal to withdraw his declaration of imperial independence of the Papacy which he had made at Frankfurt in January. Each side suffered severe damage to the ego. On 22 May 1324 in the chapel of the Teutonic Order's house in Sachsenhusen, Louis cast his die. He openly espoused the cause of the 'Spiritual' Franciscans led by Michael of Cesena who held that Christ owned no property and that for the clergy to possess riches was sinful. John XXII was a heretic and therefore anti-pope, since he denied the absolute poverty of the apostles. An ecumenical council was demanded to replace John. Marsiglio of Padua, theoretician of the supremacy of imperial over papal authority completed his tract *Defensor Pacis* on 24 June.[165]

Within ten days of the Appeal of Sachsenhusen, on 1 June, when news of the furor probably had not yet reached Avignon, the long awaited papal legation left Avignon for Vilnius. This mission had been planned meticulously by John XXII. Since Gediminas had written to the Pope, all aspects of ecclesiastical government in Prussia and Livonia had been examined along with the Lithuanian proposals for peace and (as John thought) baptism.[166] The way was

series. 4 vols. (Paris, 1906–72), no. 1850. Where these texts read *nuper* the manuscript, *Registrum Vaticanum*, 112, f.156v. reads *nudius*.

[163] For details of the Brandenburg campaign and the papal involvement with it see pp. 234–7.

[164] *VMPL*, no. 279, p. 182.

[165] *MGH, Constitutiones*, V, nos. 909, 910, pp. 722–54. See also Mažeika, 'The context' for Sachsenhusen; for the Spiritual Franciscans and Marsiglio, see Black, *Political thought*, 72. Date of ms. given in J. Sullivan, 'The manuscripts and date of Marsiglio of Padua's 'Defensor pacis'', *English Historical Review*, 20 (1905), 293.

[166] From *LU*, VI come the following letters of John XXII which resulted from investigations into the Church in Livonia in 1322: 3 March 1322 – Election of James of Ösel confirmed no. 2778; 5 March 1322 – Investigation of the bishop of Courland

paved for two Benedictine missionaries to be sent to the grand duke.

It seems no accident that French Benedictines, Bishop Bartholomew of Alet and Abbot Bernard of St Chaffré du Puy, were chosen to lead the mission.[167] Bartholomew was renowned for his skill as a canon lawyer and his experience in dealing with heretics was especially relevant to converting a country where there was a large number of Orthodox Christians. In his instructions to the legates, the Pope stressed the need for emending Greek practices and laying aside schismatic errors.[168] In addition to commanding this skill, Bartholomew had only recently supervised the establishment of his new bishopric.[169] Being Benedictine, the legates had no obvious partiality for the Franciscans, Dominicans or Teutonic Knights who were already involved in the Lithuanian mission; being French, they were not pro-imperial and were more likely to favour Charles IV as emperor than Louis IV.

Arrangements were made for the safe passage of the legates across Europe, for their provisioning, for their religious practice and for the excommunication *ipso facto* of anyone who hindered them *en route*.[170] The Lithuanian Mission of 1324 became a model for future papal embassies to pagan nations.[171] The legates bore with them letters for both the grand duke and the grand master.

The Pope's letter to Gediminas, dated 1 June, is a paradigm of carefully measured exuberance. He had not quite abandoned the Knights' cause. John thanked the grand duke for his devotion to the Holy See and remarked on the joy which his letters had evoked

no. 2779; 14 March 1322 – Consecration of James of Ösel no. 2780, of Paul of Courland no. 2781; 26 November 1323 – Investigation of Engelbert, Bishop-elect of Dorpat no. 2782. In 1318 John had been made aware of the difficulties of choosing prelates in Riga and Ösel (*LU*, VI, no. 2774). That the peace treaty had been thoroughly examined is clear from the papal correspondence on this matter – see above n. 129.

167 *VMPL*, nos. 293, p. 194; 290, pp. 190–2. Details of the lives and careers of these monks are given in *Gallia Christiana*, II (Paris, 1720), 768; *Ibid.*, VI (1739), 273.

168 'Sit eciam vobis facultas eis, qui de scismaticis ad unitatem eiusdem fidei noviter sunt reversi ... dandi dispensacionem licentiamque' *VMPL*, no. 290, p. 191. To Gediminas he spoke of laying aside schismatical errors – *ibid.* no. 293, p. 194.

169 See above n. 167. The bishopric of Alet was formed in 1318.

170 *VMPL*, nos. 291, pp. 192–3; 292, p. 193; 294, p. 195; 295, pp. 195–6; 297, pp. 196–7; 299, pp. 198–9; 300, p. 199.

171 Many of the letters associated with this mission were collected together with other crusade material in Vatican Register 62. See J. Muldoon, 'The Avignon Papacy and the frontiers of Christendom: the evidence of Vatican Register 62', *Archivum Historiae Pontificiae*, 17 (1979), 125–95, esp. pp. 182–6. Also J. Richard, 'Les Papes d'Avignon et l'évangélisation du monde non-latin à la veille du Grand Schisme', *Genèse et débuts du Grand Schisme d'Occident 1362–1394* (Paris, 1980), 305–15, esp. p. 309 and n. 14.

in the Pope and the College of Cardinals. He reviewed in quotations from Gediminas' own letters the history of Christianity in Lithuania, including the troubles caused by the Order, and added a *credo* emphasising the Petrine Supremacy in the Church.[172] The letter also has resonances of those sent to the Orthodox princes of Rus' in 1317 and Uroš of Serbia in 1323 by John XXII.[173] He ended with a promise to help Lithuania against the Knights only after Gediminas had been baptised.[174] However the wholesale destruction of the Teutonic Order was not presaged.

The Pope's communication with the Order, also dated 1 June, was stern but amicable. The Knights were instructed to keep the peace with Lithuania after Gediminas had been baptised and were obliged not to hinder the mission in any way.[175] The Pope showed no hostility towards the Order. Indeed, he did not dare condemn them as perverters of the crusade for he needed to win their support in northern Europe. They had not yet taken Louis IV's side (as far as he knew) over the Brandenburg question and they acted as a check on the ambitions of the other powers of north-eastern Europe who coveted land in Livonia and Prussia and who had a habit of not paying papal taxes.[176] The Knights may have been an embarrassment to the Pope but they were also useful. The news that while the Order remained without a leader (Karl von Trier died in February 1324) the emperor had used one of its establishments as the pulpit to publish the Appeal of Sachsenhusen obviously had not percolated through to the Curia.[177]

Viewed from Avignon, the legation to Gediminas was a perfect

[172] Compare *VMPL*, no. 293, p. 193 with *GL*, 23–7. By means of this clever conceit John appeared to have confirmed Gediminas' interpretation of Lithuanian history without using his own words and making the condemnation of the Knights his own.

[173] 'derelictis omnino scismaticorum erroribus, in quorum observacione deviatur a via lucis', *VMPL*, no. 293, p. 194 is a quotation from John's letters to the princes of Rus' – *Acta Ioannis*, no.1, p.1. Compare the letter to Gediminas also with the letter of 12 June 1323 to Stefan Uroš III of Serbia, who had written earlier to the Pope on the question of reuniting Orthodox Serbia with Rome – *ibid*., no. 73, pp. 137f.

[174] *VMPL*, no. 293, pp. 194–5. Of course the treaty was eventually ratified without the baptism of Gediminas.

[175] *Ibid*., no. 296, p. 196.

[176] The Knights were a check on Swedish and Danish ambitions – Housley, *Avignon*, 271. See T. S. Nyberg, 'Skandinavien und die Christianisierung des sudöstlichen Baltikum', *La Cristianizzazione*, 248f. Giedroyć, 'Arrival ... (1281–1341)', 27 considers that the Pope wanted the Order and the Lithuanians to join forces against the Rus'ians. However the imperial crisis was more pressing in 1323–24 than the need to convert the Rus'ians, which given the expansion of Lithuania into Rus', could be more than satisfied by the conversion of the Lithuanians to Catholicism.

[177] Death of Karl von Trier – Mažeika, 'Context'.

example of balanced curial diplomacy, designed to please everyone and fated to please no one. The baptism of the last pagans in Europe, so eagerly hoped for by the Pope, was to be achieved without the assistance of any party favourable to the Empire. The baptism of Gediminas was the putative *sine qua non* which balanced assistance for Gediminas against the Order with the Knights' continued presence in the Baltic. The Order was obliged to observe the Treaty of Vilnius only after Gediminas had come to the font. The archbishop of Riga was given safe passage home from the Curia after twelve years of exile and endowed with the power to excommunicate the Knights should they ignore the commands of the Pope.[178] The legates and the bishop of Ösel were to ensure that all went according to papal plan.[179] The legates were to undertake another diplomatic *démarche* with regard to the emperor. They were commanded on 31 May 1324 to investigate the proposed Danish marriage of Louis of Brandenburg. The letter the legates bore from the Pope to King Christopher asks him to beware of the subplot beneath the planned marriage (*et videas occulta*) and the threat it poses to his own honour, his soul and the Church.[180]

After the full implications of events in Sachsenhusen had percolated through to the Curia by July and John had discovered the complicity of the Order with Louis' appeal, he wrote again to the grand master of Prussia on August 31. The gloves now were off. This time the Pope refers directly to the case of the Lithuanian pagans and stresses that even before they convert, they are not to be harmed in any way. The Knights must uphold the Treaty of Vilnius before any baptism and the Prussian brethren, not just the Livonian Order, must abide by the agreement. At last Rome had spoken, provoked by the emperor and the Order's perceived alliance with him, but the case was far from finished. Frederick of Riga too became more than simply the irritable victim of a power struggle in a northern land far away from France. He became an important Franciscan prelate whose loyalty to the Holy See and, judging from the inventories of his possessions, his opposition to the heretical Spiritual friars were assured. The text of the papal

[178] Safe conduct – *VMPL*, no. 301, p. 199; faculty of ecclesiastical censure – *Registrum Vaticanum*, 81, letter 2807; *Registrum Avenionense*, 25, f.596r.

[179] James of Ösel was given these instructions on 31 August 1324, the same date as John wrote to the Knights ratifying the treaty – *MPV*, no. 176, pp. 233–5.

[180] *Diplomatarium Danicum*, II.9, no. 114, p. 81.

letter of 31 August contains a verbatim translation of the latest Rigan accusations and the Livonian account of how the Treaty of Vilnius had come to be agreed.[181] However, by the time the missionaries reached Riga in September and the legates had bound the Order to abide by the terms of the Treaty of Vilnius on 20 October,[182] the situation in Lithuania had clarified also, but to the detriment of the mission.

When the legates' envoys arrived in Vilnius on 3 November to prepare the ground for their masters they discovered that Gediminas had decided against conversion. The day after their arrival the envoys were granted a public audience with Gediminas and around twenty of his *conciliarii* instead of the private interview they had expected. The advisers who had been absent from Gediminas' first brief meeting with the envoys on 3 November, were present the following day to observe what Gediminas would say to the Christians. Understandably, pagan and Rus'ian subjects of the grand duke objected strongly to his rumoured conversion to Catholicism.[183] As the envoys summed up the grand duke's letters as having expressed a desire to be baptised, Gediminas declared that he had never written of such a wish and that the Devil could christen him if he had. However he did acknowledge that he wished to respect the Pope as his father and make peace with Christendom. He then belched a diplomatic smoke screen of bitter tirade against the shameful conduct of Christian nations, describing how these Christians love one another and their neighbours to the point of war and destruction.[184] This outburst appears to have been intended to placate dissenting courtiers. Later when the air had cleared, during a private cross-examination of the Franciscan scribes who had drafted Gediminas' correspondence, it became clear that the periphrases which had always meant 'baptism' to the readers of Gediminas' letters did not now mean that to the grand duke.[185] The envoys also learned that during the previous year, the

181 Pope denounces Louis to Polish clergy, 15 July 1324 – *MPV*, no. 171, pp. 229–30. Letter to Order – *MPV*, no. 175, pp. 231–2; Rigan letter – *RLA*, no. 58, pp. 35–7. Frederick's property – see above n. 50 and below p. 279.

182 *CDP*, II, no. 110, pp. 143–4.

183 *GL*, 117–19, 123–5. For the role of royal advisers (*conciliarii*) in the conversion of a pagan king cf. St Bede, *Historia Ecclesiastica*, II, 13.

184 *Si unquam habui in proposito dyabolus me baptizet* – *GL*, 127, corrected from the Rigan manuscripts – Riga, LVVA, Fonds 673, apr. 4/K-18, nos. 22 and 23. See Rowell, 'Letters'. For tirade against Christian iniquity – *GL*, 129–31.

185 *GL*, 133–7. Brother Berthold was blamed for 'confusing' the grand duke.

grand duke's pagan Žemaitijan and Orthodox Rus'ian subjects had threatened Gediminas with death if he accepted Catholicism.[186] One of his mendicant advisers, Brother Nicholas, a Dominican private secretary had suggested to him that he abandon his alliance with Frederick of Riga (who could not even defend himself) and choose another more powerful prince as his protector and this he had done.[187] Such were the reasons given in Vilnius for Gediminas' change of heart. However the grand duke was anxious to preserve the Treaty of Vilnius and sent messengers to the Franciscan hospice to ask the envoys whether this was possible. Later what appears to be disinformation was spread among the Franciscans by 'one of the Queen's women' to the effect that Gediminas was grief-stricken to have been forced to give up his plans for baptism.[188]

The envoys left Vilnius with one of Gediminas' most senior advisers who was *quasi secundus post regem* and returned to Riga on 25 November to discuss the status of the Treaty of Vilnius.[189] The treaty did remain in force for four years until the *reisen* of 1328–29.[190] However, the legates never saw Gediminas. They spent the winter in Livonia and at Easter 1325 Abbot Bernard was present when Archbishop Frederick excommunicated the Order for its old crimes, including the capture of envoys sent to the legates by Gediminas in 1324.[191] Not until June 1325 did the legates make their return journey to Avignon at the Knights' expense.[192]

Gediminas had indeed chosen a new ally in the fight against the

[186] *Ibid.*, 139–41. See above p. 214 and n. 144.

[187] *GL*, 141. Brother Nicholas advised Gediminas to choose the king of Hungary or Bohemia. These princes however were more interested in fighting against Lithuania than for her. They were also strong enough to threaten to dominate a weaker Lithuanian ally. Gediminas chose Poland which was closer to Lithuania than the other two and Lithuania's equal in military strength.

[188] *GL*, 131. The day after the luckless interview with the envoys Gediminas again sent emissaries to the envoys to discuss *in camera* the peace which Gediminas had not been able to discuss fully either at the official audience on 4 November or subsequently in private – *ibid.*, 137. The story of Gediminas' weeping all night over his inability to accept baptism was told to a Franciscan by *una mulier de familia regine* – *ibid.*, 145. It is impossible to divine the wishes of Gediminas concerning his private religion. All indications point to greater considerations than personal piety lying behind the call to Rome.

[189] *PD*, 192. That the envoys agreed to fix a four years' duration for the Treaty see *CDP*, II, no. 114, p. 152.

[190] See pp. 239–41.

[191] *CDP*, II, no. 110, pp. 144–51. For the capture of Gediminas' Franciscan envoy to Frederick of Riga in 1324 see *ibid.*, p. 147. Captive envoys were released only after the intervention of the papal legates – *GL*, 183–5.

[192] The Knights gave the legates 380 gold gulden for their return journey on 29 May 1325 – *LU*, II, no. 712, col. 202.

Order as Brother Nicholas had advised: Łokietek of Poland. During the campaign against Galich–Volyn' in the autumn of 1322 and the following spring, Gediminas had been confronted by Łokietek for the first time. This confrontation was more than the clash of the slave-raider with the raided for the king of Poland also entertained hopes of ruling south-west Rus'.[193] Rather than replacing the slain Rus'ian princes with his own son Liubartas and risking war with Poland, Gediminas made a compromise with Łokietek. In Liubartas' place Bolesław of Mazovia, the son of Łokietek's cousin and the nephew of Gediminas' ally Wacław of Płock, was installed as Bolesław-Yury II of Galich–Volyn' in 1324. Bolesław, who was fourteen years old and scarcely politically aligned to any state, was betrothed to Gediminas' daughter Eufemia. Both were converted to Orthodoxy in order to reign in Rus'. In 1331 Bolesław married Eufemia in the Catholic cathedral in 'neutral' Płock. In this way the war over who was to control south-west Rus' was postponed until Bolesław died in 1340.[194] In 1325 another of Gediminas' daughters was married to Łokietek's heir Casimir and the first Lithuano-Polish alliance came into effect with an exchange of captives and a military contract between Lithuania and Poland for the continuation of the conflict with the Order.[195]

Łokietek needed an ally to continue his juridical struggle with the Knights on the field of battle. His daughter had married a Hungarian prince in 1320 as part of an alliance against the Order and the Empire but in 1322 the proposed marriage of Casimir and Jutta of Bohemia came to nought.[196] If Łokietek was to marry off his son as part of a military alliance against his enemies, only a daughter of Gediminas could be his bride.

From the Lithuanian point of view, Gediminas had come to realise by 1324 that a peace treaty with the Order, however desirable, was not enforcable. The blow he had hoped to deal the Knights by indicting them in a papal court had come to no satisfactory conclusion. While Hungary and Bohemia, the allies proposed by his friar-adviser, were not likely partners, Poland was the perfect ally. The kingdom was strong and firmly set against the

[193] For Polish interest in Rus' see Wyrozumski, *Kazimierz*, 76–86. Poles and Lithuanians usually came into contact when the pagans raided Polish towns and enslaved the population. [194] See below pp. 264f.

[195] For the baptism and marriage of Aldona-Anna see below p. 232.

[196] Wyrozumski, *Kazimierz*, 18–19.

Knights but it was not strong enough to overpower Lithuania.[197] It was also close to Lithuania's borders and an alliance there would stave off a war with Łokietek over control of disputed territory. To maintain Łokietek's war effort in the north, Gediminas agreed to provide mercenaries for the king's use on his Prussian campaigns.[198] Without accepting baptism, the grand duke was still able to participate in Christian policies against a common foe.

Having examined the events of 1322–24 in an economic and diplomatic context broader than the narrow confines of what has been generally misconceived as purely, or at least primarily, Lithuanian religious policy, we must come to the conclusion that, pressed by ineffectual war and economic depression, Gediminas wrote to Pope John XXII and the Catholic colonists of north-eastern Europe in 1322 and 1323 offering a special peace settlement, generous immigration rights and the opportunity to practise Catholicism within Lithuania. He communicated his willingness to the Pope himself in order to provide an acknowledged Catholic environment for merchants and settlers in his country and gain international recognition of his territorial claims. He also had a second, but no less important aim in his correspondence with John XXII, namely to corroborate Rigan accusations against the Order and persuade the Pope to take strong measures against the Knights. The price for the conversion of the Lithuanians was set at the destruction of the Order. This was hinted at only darkly in the grand duke's letters but he had no intention of selling his soul without winning the emasculation of his most dangerous enemy. The promises of a distant pope merely to keep the Knights at peace would not be good enough. The sword was pope enough for the Knights, as the Rigans knew to their cost.[199] While he awaited the papal decision Gediminas avoided all direct references to his

[197] *GL*, 141. On the strength of Poland see above pp. 4–7.

[198] For incidents of the 'phoney peace', 1325–28 see pp. 230–1. An indulgence for an anti-Lithuanian crusade was requested on the Order's behalf by Trojden and Siemowit of Mazovia in 1325 – *CDP*, II, no. 114, p. 153. The only indulgences given at this time were those sent to Łokietek in June, July and August 1325 – *VMPL*, nos. 316, 334, 338, pp. 205, 215–16. They had been requested for a war against Lithuania, Rus' and the Tatars before the Lithuano-Polish Treaty.

[199] When Frederick arrived in Livonia in 1305 to take up residence as archbishop of Riga the Knights are alleged to have greeted him with the news that: 'alios archiepiscopos captivavimus, de cetero magis valet interficere eum, ut saltem nobis non faciat verecundiam in Romana Curia ... ' *LU*, II, no. 616, col. 28. In 1309 the Knights threatened the Cistercians of Dünamünde into submission – 'gladius est papa noster et papa posset vobis nimis remotus esse', Seraphim, *Das Zeugenverhör*, VIII, 104, p. 151.

proposed 'baptism'. Even so he spoke readily of his peace proposals and willingness to welcome foreigners to Lithuania. He was working within a historical tradition which he understood well. He was reviewing the policies of his predecessors Mindaugas and Vytenis, but he did not intend to repeat the mistakes of Mindaugas who had fallen prey to the ambitions of the Order, which sponsored his conversion, and the enmity of his pagan rivals who eventually murdered him.

During 1323 and 1324, it became clear that the Pope would not (indeed he could not) destroy the Order for he had greater priorities. He needed the Knights to counter the emperor and the kings of Sweden and Denmark. Gediminas saw that the treaty of Vilnius which circumstances had compelled half the Knights to sign in October 1323 would be difficult for the Pope to safeguard effectively from Avignon. By the time John XXII had joined the Lithuano-Livonian camp as a result of the Order's perceived collaboration with the emperor, it was too late for the Lithuanian mission. Gediminas also discovered the extent of native opposition to Catholicism among the Žemaitijans and the Rus'ians of the Grand Duchy. When the envoys of the papal legates eventually arrived in Vilnius, they were publicly trounced for suggesting that Gediminas had ever wished to be baptised but were privately requested to save the treaty. Gediminas had also found a new potential ally during his invasion of south-west Rus', a campaign which had been aided by the slackening of the Teutonic offensive between 1320 and 1322. This new alliance with Poland enabled Gediminas to maintain military pressure on the Knights while a potentially damaging war on his south-western borders was avoided. The acquisition of Kiev, the Orthodox ecclesiastical heart of Rus' supported an already strong Lithuanian presence in Rus'. This presence would have been endangered by 'schismatic' opposition to a newly Catholic grand duke. Since 1322 therefore Gediminas had gained enough to make baptism an insane prodigality. It would have been both rash and unnecessary to give away his prized diplomatic asset, his soulprice, in 1324.

As for Gediminas' peace treaty and his invitations to settlers, lay and religious, to come to Lithuania, these appear to have borne modest rewards. The peace was maintained until 1328. The Knights, who were still relatively weak, faced the threat of papal censure and Lithuano-Polish arms if they broke the truce. The indulgence they requested of John XXII in 1325 to continue the

Lithuanian crusade came to nought and the years of 'phoney peace' were spent rebuilding fortresses and founding new settlements.

The effect of the immigration plans and the peace on the Lithuanian economy is difficult to gauge. What can be deduced from toponymical evidence is that foreign settlement did continue in Lithuania throughout the fourteenth century.[200] There are references in chronicles and other sources to the settlement of Rus'ians, Germans, Mazovians and Baltic pagans in Lithuania.[201] Although there are no surviving Hansa records of large-scale shipping in the Baltic in the 1320s which could have carried immigrants to Lithuania, there are records of Rigan craftsmen who were hindered by the Knights as they travelled between Riga and the Grand Duchy.[202] It is not impossible that some of those householders who deserted Saxon towns in the wake of the Great Famine made their way to Lithuania or Prussia.

The mercantile community in Vilnius continued to prosper. By 1382 the traders had their own chief who enjoyed the favour of the grand duke. The quality of shoemaking, iron working and carpentry in fourteenth-century Vilnius matched that in Poland, Rus' and Prussia.[203] Similarly Lithuanian agriculture seems to have enjoyed the same level of sophistication (or lack of it) as its counterparts in neighbouring Christian countries.[204] It may be that these developments merely ran parallel in Lithuania with the rest of Europe; alternatively they could be viewed as evidence of foreign influence in the pagan Grand Duchy.

Such were the benefits which Gediminas gained from his

[200] J. Ochmański, 'Inozemnye poselenia v Litve XIII–XIVvv. v svete etnonimicheskikh mestnikh nazvanii', *Balto-Slavianskie Issledovania* (1980), 112–31, esp. 115–21.

[201] *Wig.*, 552; *Wegeberichte*, nos. 63, 68, 81, 82 for villages bearing the names of foreign settlers. For the Mazovians Paweł and Rostko Nesitka in Lithuania, see a document of Siemowit II dated 4 April 1342 – E. Łuczycka, 'Trzy dokumenty książąt mazowieckich z pierwszej połowy XIV w.', *PH*, 64 (1973), 366.

[202] 'Hinrico dicto Lokesor, Kaykemele, Arnoldo, Thiderico Sutore, Toke et Kone et aliis pluribus quam triginta civibus Rigensibus' – *CDP*, II, no. 111, p. 147.

[203] For shoemaking in Vilnius in the fourteenth century see K. Navickas, 'Vilniaus gyventojų apavas XIII–XIVa.', *ILKI*, 4 (1964), 188–96. Lithuanian ironwork is discussed in J. Stankus, 'Geležiės dirbinių gamyba ir kalvystės lygis Lietuvoje XIV–XVI amžiais', *LMADA*, 52 (1975), 51–3. Wooden buildings in Vilnius in the fourteenth century were examined by archaeologists thirty years ago – A. Tautavičius, 'Archeologinai kasinėjimai Vilniaus žemutinės pilies teritorijoje 1960m.', *LMADA*, 11 (1961), 110–11.

[204] For the state of agriculture and cattle-breeding see R. Volkaitė-Kulikauskienė, 'Nauji duomenys', 51–65.

rapprochement with the Catholics of northern Europe and the Papacy. In their turn, the Christians gained a respite in a long war against the pagans and each other and better conditions for commerce. The Pope salvaged from his unrealised hopes of converting the Lithuanians another valuable ally in his own *Staatspolitik*. The Franciscans continued to maintain a presence in Vilnius, unmolested until they broke their code of practice by preaching publicly against the pagan cult.[205]

In their reaction to Gediminas' letters and events of 1322–24, historians, like John XXII, have been mesmerised by the grand duke's deliberately elusive hints and enigmatic references to conversion. Becoming a Catholic was never Gediminas' priority. He understood the advantages of belonging to Christendom but also he appreciated the benefits of living without its confines. In short Gediminas repudiated baptism because he came to realise how much he could gain without abandoning his trump card: his potential for conversion to Christianity, Roman Catholic or Greek Orthodox. The Pope, ever hopeful of baptising the grand duke, did not repudiate cooperation with the pagans because he needed their help in an arguably more important game – the one against the emperor.

[205] See below pp. 275–7.

Chapter 8

THE HARSHEST *REALPOLITIK*

From our analysis of Gediminas' dealings with the Orthodox Church throughout his reign and especially his approach to the Roman pontiff in 1322–24, it is clear that relations between pagan Lithuania and crusading Christendom are rather more complex than the traditional 'Wild East' adventure narratives of certain historians have led us to believe. The complexity of Lithuanian diplomacy is matched only by the sophistication of the military struggle which forms the backcloth to pagan relations with Christendom. The frequent *Litauen-* and *Litauerreisen* of the fourteenth century were well organised and carefully provisioned campaigns rather than the *ad hoc* scrimmages of chivalrous hoodlums.

In his military diplomacy with Christian powers Gediminas had resort to at least three kinds of agreement, foremost among which was the straightforward truce, as illustrated by the Treaty of Vilnius (1323). Here the grand duke and the Catholic powers of northern Europe ceased hostilities, recognised mutual rights in commerce and promised not to interfere in the internal affairs of their neighbours. The second type of agreement may be described as a damage limitation pact; this finds its representative in the treaty struck in November 1338 between Lithuania and the Livonian branch of the Teutonic Order. This guaranteed safe passage for all merchants across a strictly defined area within a continuing war zone. Thirdly we can delineate the contractual alliance whereby Lithuanian troops took part in campaigns which were planned by a Christian power against another Christian enemy. The latter, as in the case of the 1331 pact with Novgorod against Sweden, was not always a direct foe of Lithuania. Here we shall concentrate on the last two aspects of pagan diplomacy as part of Gediminas' attempt to maintain pressure on the Teutonic Order whilst safeguarding and funding Lithuanian interests in both the East and the West.

During the first five years of Gediminas' reign, Lithuania and the Teutonic Order were constantly at daggers drawn in a war which neither the pagans nor the Knights were capable of bringing to a successful conclusion. It reflects the stalemate which typifies most of Vytenis' conflicts with the Order when neither party could quite dominate the other. In 1320 the Knights were stunned into an unofficial ceasefire by the annihilation of a Livonian raiding party led by Marshal Heinrich von Plötzkau, who thitherto had been the most successful of the Teutonic warlords. Gediminas took charge of this impromptu armistice, during which he invaded south-west Rus', to exploit divisions within Catholic Christendom and make peace with the Order with papal blessing.[1]

The official cessation of hostilities which Gediminas won in November 1324 would better be termed the 'phoney peace'. Although large-scale attacks from either side did cease between that date, when the papal envoys to Lithuania ratified the Treaty of Vilnius, and 1328 when the Order marched against Grodno, Putenica and Aukaimis, minor but nonetheless vexatious raids into Lithuanian territory did continue.[2] In mid-1325, Gediminas complained to the co-signatories to the Treaty of Vilnius of attacks on his castles at Medilas and Polotsk and of the interruption of Lithuanian communications with Riga.[3] The following March, Gediminas' envoy, Lesse by name, who had been captured in Livonia in 1324–25 along with Lettovian merchants and released only after the intervention of the papal legates, was sent back to Livonia to establish whether the Order wished to maintain the peace.[4] Although neither side was satisfied with the truce, both parties recognised that some respite from forty years of conflict was necessary.

During this phoney peace the Order built more fortresses in central and north-eastern Prussia and transferred Memel from

[1] See pp. 191–4.

[2] *PD*, 192–4, 214–15.

[3] Gediminas complains of the murder of a huntsman at Upitė, the rustling of three horses which were subsequently retained by Ungenade (former Master of Livonia who opposed the treaty with Gediminas in 1323), and the assault on his castles. Lesse was assaulted and another envoy who had been sent to Riga was hanged. Dünaburg and Mezoten were not surrendered to Gediminas, although this had been promised – *GL*, 167–173. This letter bears the date of Trinity Day. A reference to the return of Archbishop Frederick to Riga (22 September 1324) encourages a date of 2 June 1325. The account of Lesse's tribulations is complemented by the nuncio's own testimony of 2 March 1326 which records Lettovian captives in Ascherad and Dünaburg and of the obstruction of the Dünaburg–Mitau trade route – *GL*, 175–87. On difficulties with Novgorod, see *GL*, 155–7.

[4] *GL*, 173, 175–87.

Livonian to Prussian control.[5] Western recruits for the crusade still came to Prussia in the hope of fighting alongside the Knights.[6] Meanwhile the Lithuanians rebuilt their castles which had been destroyed in the war and raided Mazovia and Brandenburg for plunder to support their martial economy. Both sides were busy attempting to attract settlers to their lands.[7]

Gediminas prepared for the inevitability of real war by contracting Lithuanian services to Christian powers which shared certain of his military objectives. In the early thirteenth century, according to Henricus Lettus, Lithuanian forces had accepted payment from the Semigallians to assess an invading Teutonic army.[8] By providing defence contracts for Poland and Riga, Pskov and Novgorod, Gediminas enabled himself to maintain pressure more easily on his Teutonic and, to a lesser degree, Muscovite enemies by waging war on several fronts simultaneously. The precedent for this cooperative policy was established in its barest form at the turn of the century when Vytenis supplied the citizens of Riga with a Lithuanian garrison.[9] After the conclusion of the Treaty of Vilnius, Gediminas came to realise that the threat posed to his realm by the Order could be countered

5 Gerdawen, Bartenburg, Bischopfswerder (founded by the bishop of Pomezania – *PU*, II, no. 651), Neumarkt – *PD*, 192–3; *EpG*, 280. For the transfer of Memel see *PU*, II, no. 617 and *HW*, 62–3. The Order also constructed Wartenburg in Galindia and Gutstat in Glottow. The Chełmno provincial built a new fort on the banks of the Drwęca, a site attacked by the Lithuanians and Poles in 1329–30 – see below pp. 241f. Lunenburg was built in 1326 and Morungen in 1327.

6 Like Thomas van Dyst who, in November 1325, settled his affairs in Utrecht *quando intendit ire ad Pruchiam – De Registers en vekeningen van Het Bisdom Utrecht 1325–1336*, ed. S. Muller, I, *Werken utgegeven door het Historisch Genootschap gevestigd te Utrecht*, n.s. 53 (Utrecht, 1889), no. 97, p. 106.

7 Grodno was repaired in 1325 – *PU*, II, no. 528; one may deduce that repairs were also made to the forts of Vaikiai and Gedimin-Burg which were destroyed in 1322 and 1324 respectively (*PD*, 186, 190) and again in 1330 (*PD*, 217). The Knights gave land to settlers throughout Prussia. For the period 1324–28 forty four such grants survive – *PU*, nos. 447, 457, 475, 476, 481, 485, 494, 496, 497, 505, 520, 521, 526, 527, 530, 532, 534, 543, 546, 555, 558–62, 568, 569, 571, 575, 580, 581, 587, 588, 595, 598, 601, 603, 608, 615, 616, 621, 624, 627, 630. The settlement of colonists brought the Knights *equis et armis in terra consuetis* (nos. 780–1), *armis prutenicalibus* (no. 775), *uno spadone et armis levibus, quod vulgariter dicitur eyn platendynst* (demanded by the bishop of Pomezania in 1326 – *PU*, II, no. 556) or *duabus toracibus aut duobus spadonibus* (no. 630 – two breastplates or two geldings). Most colonists were required to build new fortifications and repair ancient ones. The formulaic nature of these grants is such as to encourage a belief that more were issued than have survived. The practice was very common. The same requirements were demanded of Lithuanian settlers judging by the immunities granted to Vilnius Cathedral in 1387 – *KDKDW* no. 6, p. 14.

8 'mercedem a Semigallis', Henry, *Chronicon*, XXIII, 8, p. 244.

9 See pp. 57–8.

more effectively by military cooperation with Riga and Poland, than by the acceptance of Roman baptism. The enormous burden presented by the cost of maintaining armies in the northern war was thus spread more widely than on Lithuanian commerce and plunder alone.

Probably late in 1324 and certainly before 30 April 1325, some kind of agreement was reached between Gediminas and Łokietek of Poland. The treaty was sealed by the marriage of Aldona-Anna Gediminaitė to Prince Casimir in October 1325, after which the Lithuanians ceased their raids on Poland until after Anna died in 1339.[10] Casimir's new wife (who after 1333 was his crowned queen) played an important part in Polish life, as one might expect. The influence of this royal consort who acted as her husband's representative when he was away from Kraków has largely disappeared from historigraphy. In her lifetime she was adored for her piety among those who were not scandalised by her devotion to music. It may be that the cymbals which were played in procession before her represent some pagan Lithuanian tradition. They are described by several Polish chroniclers and interpreted as heathen ritual by Długosz. Queen Anna was a great patron of the Church and corresponded with the Papacy which indulged her remarkable piety. It is tempting to view the three Gediminaitės who married Polish princes as forming a Gediminid fifth column within the Piast political elite. Elżbieta's daughter was named Anna and Anna's, Elżbieta, although the names are too common among the Piasts to allow any certainty that the 'Lithuanian' courts were closely connected. Her sister Eufemia's marriage to Bolesław-Yury II was used by Casimir as an excuse for his invasion of Galich in 1340.[11]

Casimir's marriage was well chosen. He had been selected as the husband of Jutta, daughter of John of Bohemia, but this planned alliance was abandoned in 1322. His sister Elżbieta married King

[10] 30 April 1325, the date *ante quem* for the treaty, was the date of Aldona's baptism which was the prelude to her marriage – 'Rocznik Traski', *MPH*, II, 854. The date of baptism precludes the naming of Anna after the patron of that day. It is unclear whether she is named after the Mother of Our Lady for a specific reason or simply because her sister had taken the name Maria in 1320 – see p. 89.

[11] 'Calendarium Cracoviense', *MPH*, II, 934; 'Rocznik Kujawski', *MPH*, III, 209. *FRB*, IV, 315. For her piety and her love of music and games and the playing of cymbals before her see *MPH*, II, 860 and III, 199 and *Długosz*, IX, 213. Attacked by nobles opposing Casimir – *VMPL*, no. 533 (19.03.1338); papal dispensation granted in 1334, 1335, 1339 – *Bullarium Poloniae*, I, nos. 1736, 1773, 1877–79; for death of Eufemia see below p. 267.

Charles Robert to cement a Hungarian treaty in 1320. Gediminas' daughter was at least the equal of these two spouses. We must now return to the other practical aspect of this dynastic–military alliance.

The text of the treaty which accompanied this wedding does not survive. However we may extrapolate details of the agreement from what we know of Lithuano-Polish relations between 1325 and 1331, when the alliance appears to have disintegrated.[12] We should not imagine, as is the wont of Polish scholars, that the treaty was a mutual offence–defence pact.[13] It seems to me rather to have been a military contract of Lithuanian service to Poland based on shared objectives. It arose from the settlement of conflicting Polish and Lithuanian interests in southern Rus' in 1324.[14] Neither Gediminas nor Łokietek could easily afford to fight each other in the south and a common enemy in the north. Both rulers had recently lost confidence in diplomacy as an effective way of dealing with the Teutonic Knights.[15]

It is impossible to say with any certainty who proposed the alliance to whom. Each side gained as much as the other from the agreement. Zajączkowski argued that it was probably the suggestion of Łokietek since he, unlike Gediminas, had not made peace with the Order and hence his was the greater need of friendship.[16] However the contractual nature of Lithuano-Polish relations between 1325 and 1331 points to the hand of Gediminas, who made similar agreements with Pskov, Riga and Novgorod. Lithuania was in a good position to propose terms to Poland. A war with the Order or another of Poland's enemies would provide Gediminas with booty which was no longer available in Poland, whilst cooperation with that kingdom reduced the expense of launching such a campaign.[17] Lithuanian support for Łokietek would also sustain the Polish war effort and prevent Łokietek's having to come to terms with the Knights (or the emperor). For

[12] Marriage of Elżbieta – *Długosz*, IX, 113; planned marriage of Jutta and Casimir – *FRB*, IV, 314. Treaty of 1325 described in S. Zajączkowski, 'Przymierze polsko-litewskie 1325r', *KH*, 40 (1926), 575.

[13] Zajączkowski, 'Przymierze', 568, 612 or K. Tymieniecki, 'The Reunion of the Kingdom, 1295–1333', in *The Cambridge History of Poland: From the origins to Sobieski (to 1696)*, ed. W. F. Reddaway, J. H. Penson, O. Halecki and R. Dyboski (Cambridge, 1950), 121–2.

[14] See p. 224.

[15] See pp. 223f.

[16] Zajączkowski, 'Przymierze', 612.

[17] Captive Poles were released by Gediminas as part of his daughter's dowry – *Długosz*, IX, 131. Gediminas continued to take slaves from Brandenburg, Livonia (*PD*, 192) and Mazovia (*Długosz*, IX, 198). The expense of warfare is discussed below, p. 244.

his part, the Pole regarded the Lithuanians as forces *in servicio nostro* (as indeed did the Grand Master of Prussia), to be summoned and dismissed at will, who required payment in booty gained on campaign and compensation for the loss of any prize opportunity.[18] If there were no Teutons to maraud, the pagans were likely to attack Polish territory around their camp.[19] They were an army to be sent home should another ally, a Christian prince, take exception to fighting alongside heathens. There is no unambiguous evidence to show that Polish troops ever came to the relief of Lithuanian armies.

The most interesting result of this alliance during the phoney peace was a Lithuano-Polish assault on the Brandenburg city of Frankfurt in 1326. This attack led by David of Grodno benefited Lithuania which gained much plunder and many slaves from it.[20] However it was primarily a Polish campaign planned by Łokietek and supported by the Pope. By papal support, pontifical acquiescence to a Polish plan should be understood rather than a particular initiative of John XXII himself.

During 1325 John XXII had encouraged Polish princes and prelates to oppose Emperor Louis IV and his son Louis, whom the emperor had appointed illegally margrave of Brandenburg two years earlier.[21] Łokietek required no encouragement to attack the Mark which he regarded as rightfully the possession of the Polish crown. The Pope instructed Bishop Florian of Płock to pronounce Louis excommunicate on 6 August 1325[22] and four days later he commanded the Polish princes closest to Brandenburg, the dukes of western Pomorze and Głogów, who were already allied with Łokietek against Brandenburg, not to obey Margrave Louis and, if necessary, to oppose him actively.[23] In December 1325 and January 1326, the bishops of Kraków, Włocławek and Wrocław were commended by the Pope for their opposition to the

[18] Łokietek referred to Lithuanians *in servicio nostro* on 7 February 1326 – *PU*, II, no. 548, p. 368. Luder von Braunschweig complained to the Pope at the end of 1331 that Łokietek was maintaining pagan cohorts *penes se* for use in the Prussian War – *PU*, II, no. 747, p. 495. It is clear that Łokietek sent off to Lithuania for the troops which ravaged Brandenburg – *PD*, 193. For compensation for lost prizes see p. 247.

[19] *PD*, 193 and n. 92.

[20] *PD*, 193; Jeroschin, lines 26420–26637, pp. 608–11; *HW*, 62; *FRB*, IV, 399; *FRB*, V, 203; *MPH*, III, 703; *MPH*, III, 229.

[21] See p. 217.

[22] *VMPL*, no. 339, pp. 217–18.

[23] *Ibid.*, no. 340, p. 218. The western princes made an alliance with Łokietek on 18 June 1325 – *Lites ac res gestae* ..., ed. I. Zakrzewski and J. Karwasińska, *editio altera* I (Poznań–Warsaw, 1890–1935), Appendix XI, pp. 431–2.

margrave.[24] These commendations coincide with the Constitutions of Ulm whereby Louis IV was recognised as emperor by Frederick of Austria, his chief rival for the imperial throne.[25]

On 7 February 1326, Łokietek made a truce with the Knights and their recent allies, the three dukes of Mazovia, which was to last until Christmas.[26] It stipulated that the Mazovians and Prussians should grant the Lithuanian army safe passage across their territory while it was engaged on Polish service.[27] The exact nature of this 'Polish service' soon became clear. Between 10 February and 11 March, David of Grodno led a considerable force of Lettovian soldiers and Polish troops into Brandenburg.[28] The combined armies crossed the Oder and devastated Frankfurt, burning and looting its churches and monasteries and killing or enslaving allegedly six thousand men, women and children.[29] The Lithuanians returned home safely across Order lands laden with booty and slaves. The Knights' hands had been successfully tied by the 1324 treaty with Lithuania and the 1326 truce with Poland. It is difficult not to imagine that the bishop of Pomezania had this campaign in mind when in June 1326 he granted land to colonists in return for military aid against Lithuania.[30]

That the king of Poland employed pagan Lithuanian troops for a vicious attack on his Christian enemies is remarkable enough but by no means unusual. We shall see the same happen again as a result of Gediminas' military contracts with Novgorod and Riga. What is more remarkable is the involvement *in petto* of the Papacy in this anti-Brandenburg campaign. Several sources recall how the king of Poland planned this raid with the express permission of John XXII or at least with a view to pleasing the Pope. Dietmar of Lübeck even says that papal legates accompanied the army to ensure that the Knights did not attack the Lithuanians.[31] Louis IV's accusations against 'Herodian' John, made in April 1328, blame him for forcing the Knights to accept a peace with

[24] 18 December 1325 to Kraków – *VMPL*, no. 355, p. 227; 24 January 1326 to Wrocław – *ibid.*, no. 356; 29 January 1326 to Włocławek – *ibid.*, no. 357, p. 228.

[25] *Biblioteca classica italiana secolo XIV*, XXI: *Croniche di Giovanni, Matteo e Filippo Villani I: Cronica di Giovanni Villani* (Trieste, 1857), 291 (Book 9, chapter 316). *Reversales Frederici*, *MGH Constitutiones*, VI.1, no. 141, pp. 96–7.

[26] See above n. 18.

[27] *PU*, II, no. 548, p. 368 – *quousque ad propria revertantur* [*Lithuani*] *nobis serviciis exhibitis et peractis.*

[28] See above n. 20.

[29] *Ibid.*

[30] *PU*, II, no. 562, pp. 375–6.

[31] 'Do weren bi deme koninghe van Krakowe des paveses boden; de beden de Dudeschen brodere, dat se in ereme lande de heydene scholden nicht hinderen' – *SRP*, III, 66.

Lithuania which eventually led to the slaughter of Brandenburg innocents.[32] The Swiss chronicler John of Winterthur calls the campaign *Johannis Pape exsecrabile factum*,[33] while the Dutchman, William of Egmond, claims to have knowledge of a papal bull supporting the attack which would cause the Pope considerable embarrassment if it became common knowledge.[34] Bohemian and German chroniclers also claim that the assault was undertaken with papal permission or to please the Pope out of hatred for Louis IV.[35] Even the Polish 'Annales Cuiavienses' refer to papal favour for the Lithuanians which was inspired by loathing of the emperor.[36] Although it must be conceded that many of these sources share a bias for Louis IV in the papal–imperial conflict of the 1320s, it seems that the allegations of papal involvement in the 1326 campaign are not simply malicious rumour. Not all the sources which contain these allegations are consistently anti-papal. John XXII did actively encourage princes to oppose Louis IV and his son and he can hardly have been displeased by an attack which diverted the emperor's attention from his business in the West.[37] As for his use of the Lithuanians, whom he hoped soon to see baptised (for Mazovian reports said Gediminas would convert within four years), this is in keeping with his optimistic use of other non-Christians as part of his foreign policy. In 1322 he had enlisted the support of the Persian Il-Khan, Abu-Said, in the struggle to defend Cilician Armenia against the Mamluks. Abu-Said, like Gediminas, was a prince who was well-inclined towards the presence of Christian merchants and friars in his land but he had no intention of accepting baptism himself.[38]

[32] *MGH*, *Constitutiones*, VI.1, no. 436, p. 346.

[33] *Die Chronik Johanns von Winterthur*, ed. F. Baethgen, *MGH*, *SRG*, n.s. 3 (Berlin, 1924), 101–2, 183.

[34] Egmond, *Chronicon*, 148. On William's general bias in favour of the Empire see *ibid.*, xxxi–xxxii. For background to the chronicle and its author see M. Carasso-Kok, 'Willelmus fecit. Wilhelmus Jacobi over Friesland en de identiteit van Willelmus Procurator', *Ad Fontes*: *Opstellen aangeboden aan prof. dr. C. van de Kieft* (Amsterdam, 1984), 319–34. The bull Egmond claims to have seen does not survive.

[35] *Rex Polonie, volens Sedi Apostolice et pape conplacere* – *FRB*, IV, 279; Henry the Deaf, *Chronicon*, 39–40 – 'Rex Lichphonie cum multitudine paganorum marchionatum Brandenburgensem crudeliter depopulat ... in cuius odium [Louis IV] predicti pagani marchionatum depopulant permittente Johanne papa predicto'.

[36] *MPH*, V, 888. The chronicle mistakenly gives these events the date of 1315; it should of course be 1326.

[37] *Chronik Johanns*, 183.

[38] The dukes of Mazovia told John XXII in 1325 that Gediminas had promised *fallaciter* to be baptised during the four years of the 1323 truce – *CDP*, II, no. 114, p. 152. For John XXII's letter to Abu-Said, dated 4 July 1322 see *Acta Ioannis*, no. 58, pp. 115–17. Abu-

Even so such use of pagan *force majeure* was not contrary to canon law.[39]

During the march home from Brandenburg, David of Grodno was killed by a Polish Knight who was appalled by the slaughter of Christians at the hands of pagan marauders.[40] This murder was to be felt keenly in the Grand Duchy and is but one example (albeit unplanned) of the interaction of Gediminas' eastern and western policies. It is a feature of his reign that while he approached western powers to further his western concerns of trade and defence, Gediminas was busy expanding his empire into Rus'. Thus at the very time he was making overtures to Hansa cities and the mendicant orders associated with mercantile enterprise he was conquering a major part of south-west Rus'. This action in Galich–Volyn' in particular seems to have precipitated the Lithuano-Polish alliance of 1325 which led in turn to the Polish-sponsored raid into Brandenburg.

The Polish alliance of 1325 was the first 'contract' (as opposed to simple accord) that Gediminas made in the west. However a similar agreement with a Rus'ian power predates it by three years. In 1322–23, David of Grodno was invited by the citizens of Pskov to become their prince and supervise the defence of the city against the Teutonic Knights. In this way Pskov became so closely linked with Lithuania, that Gediminas came to regard the city as part of his dominion. This state of affairs persisted long after David's murder in 1326.[41]

The role of prince in Pskov was never that of hereditary ruler but of a military commandant hired by the City Council (*Veche*) for a limited and variable amount of time. The same was the case with Novgorod, Pskov's more powerful neighbour. No princely dynasty was permitted to establish itself in either city. David does not appear to have been resident in Pskov permanently. He continued to operate in Lithuania as is evident from the Pskovian

Said allowed Venetian *frari latini* to build chapels in his lands but had no intention of becoming a Catholic. Like Gediminas he wished to make conditions for western traders as attractive as possible – see J. Richard, *La Papauté et les missions d'Orient du Moyen Age (XIII–XV siècles). Collection de l'Ecole française de Rome*, XXXIII (1977), 175.

39 Later Cardinal Pierre d'Ailly judged that it was legal for a Catholic prince to employ pagans in a war against other Christians – E. Weise, *Die Staatsschriften des Deutschen Ordens in Preussen im 15 Jahrhundert, I: Die Traktate vor dem Konstanzer Konzil (1414–1418) über das Recht des Deutschen Ordens am Lande Preussen, Veröffentlichungen der niedersächsischen Archivverwaltung* XXVII (1970), 268–70. He records here not an innovation but old practice.

40 'Annalista Thorunensis', *SRP*, III, 66.

41 See p. 179, n. 130.

chronicle record for 1323, the only year of David's service which is recorded in Rus'ian sources. When David came in February to lead an army against Reval, the former prince, Yury, was still in Pskov. When the Livonian Order attacked Pskov in March of that year, David was not present. He was summoned to the city in May when another Livonian army could not be repulsed by local troops from Izborsk, the west Pskovian fort. Some time after this envoys came 'from all the *Nemtsy* (northern Catholic powers)' to make peace with Pskov. Given that in the late summer of 1323 Livonian envoys were despatched to investigate Gediminas' peace proposals (proposals which included Pskov, as is clear from the Treaty of Vilnius), it is tempting to view this Pskovo-Livonian agreement as part of the general Lithuanian Treaty. In the fourteenth century Lithuanian princes, including Algirdas and his son Andrei were approached on several occasions by the citizenry of Pskov with an offer to assume princely office. When Gediminas established his ally Aleksandr Mikhailovich in Pskov in 1331, the cooperation between that city and Lithuania was marked. Aleksandr appears even to have adopted on his seal the Lithuanian symbol, *vytis*. However the Pskovites were also quick to reject a Lithuanian prince and replace him with a local boiar if the Lithuanian failed to act according to Pskovite will. Being prince of Pskov was a job for which the precedents of Daumantas of Nalšia and David of Grodno made a Lithuanian a welcome candidate; nevertheless the provision of a leader for the city was never a Lithuanian prerogative.[42]

Gediminas' growing influence in north-west Rus' provoked the opposition of Pskov's superior, Novgorod. In December 1323 the Teutonic Knights and the Novgorodians allied themselves against a Lithuano-Pskovite axis. February 1323 had seen David lead the Pskovites against Reval a month before the Žemaitijans attacked Memel.[43] Gediminas' Rus'ian and Livonian policies were clearly working in tandem.

For three years Novgorod and Lithuania were in a state of virtual war.[44] However in February–March 1326, the very time that Lithuanian troops were marching against Brandenburg,

[42] The attacks on Pskov and the treaty are referred to in *PL*, I, 15–16; II, 22–3. For a list of Lithuanians in Pskov, see above pp. 173, 179 and nn. 94, 130. See also Pickhan, *Gospodin Pskov*, 155–170.

[43] Novgorodian alliance – *GVNiP*, no. 37, pp. 65–7. Lithuanian policy in Livonia and Rus' in tandem – *PD*, 187–8; *EpG*, 283.

[44] *NL*, 97; *GL* 15, 155; see also p. 215.

Lithuania, represented by the grand duke's Rus'ian princes, made peace with the Order and Novgorod.[45] A partial explanation for this reversal of Novgorodian policy may lie in the fact that both the prince of Novgorod (Yury Danilovich of Moscow) and the archbishop (David), who had overseen the 1323 anti-Lithuanian treaty, died in 1325. Gediminas' ally, Dmitry Mikhailovich of Tver' then also grand duke of Vladimir took charge of Novgorod in 1324.[46] In 1326 his *namestniki* probably enjoyed great influence in Novgorod during the absence of the new archbishop, Moisei, who did not return from his consecration in Moscow until after the new treaty had been agreed.[47] It does not appear rash to believe also that the peaceful relations between Lithuania and the Order since 1324, underscored by the Polono-Teutonic truce of February 1326 had made some impression on the Novgorodians.

The truce with Novgorod was barely two years old when the phoney peace ended and both Lithuania and the Order resumed the conflict. Although the Order was stronger than it had been in 1324, it had not yet emerged completely from internal disarray.[48] More fortresses had been built and the Order's allies were in a better position to aid the Knights. Their protector Louis IV was confirmed as emperor and John of Bohemia brought a large company of foreign knights to Prussia for the *Reise* along with bards to spread the word of the crusaders' glory abroad.[49]

The winter of 1328–29 witnessed the greatest *Reise* of the decade. In early December, John of Bohemia left Prague and travelled through Toruń and Königsberg on his way to crusade in Prussia for the first time.[50] He was joined by the flower of European chivalry. Knights came not only from Bohemia but also from Germany, England, France and the Low Countries to join the Teutonic brethren. Rather than fight that year in Granada with his wife's kinsman as he had planned to do, John decided to devote his energies to attacking the Lithuanians. His intention was to penetrate the Baltic pagan hinterland further than any Christian

[45] *NL*, 98. Gediminas was represented by his brother Voin of Polotsk, Vasily of Minsk and Fëdor Sviatoslavich – see above p. 84

[46] Fennell, *Emergence*, 103–4.

[47] On 18 March 1326 – *NL*, 97.

[48] Werner von Orseln was a more popular grand master than Karl von Trier. Nevertheless a disgruntled Knight murdered him on 18 November 1330 – *Wig.*, 476. See also the official report of the crime which was made on 21 November 1330 – *PU*, II, nos. 701, 702, pp. 464–6.

[49] Machaut, *Confort d'Ami*, 106–7; *FRB*, IV, 293–4.

[50] He left Prague on 6 December 1328 (*FRB*, V, 206), reached Toruń on New Year's Day 1329 (*EpG*, 287) and arrived at Königsberg on 20 January (*EpG*, 287).

prince had done before. He wished to assist the Knights whom he already patronised and to whom he had surrendered his wife's claim to the Polish territory of Pomorze.[51] The Order provided a large phalanx of Knights to fight alongside several thousand foot soldiers.[52] The attack was to be directed against Žemaitija where, in the space of little more than a week, four Lithuanian towns were razed and a fifth, Medvegalis, was reduced to capitulation.[53] After Medvegalis had fallen on 1 February, the occupants of the fort and their prince Margolis (Marger/Margiris)[54] were granted their lives in return for their souls. A good many Lithuanians (3,000 to 6,000 according to some sources) were baptised.[55] This act of clemency on the crusaders' part was attributed to John of Bohemia who thereby broke the Order's tradition of slaughtering or enslaving defeated pagans. As soon as the *Reise* ended the neophytes apostasised. Baptism in the hour of danger followed by a ready return to their vomit after that hour had passed was a Lithuanian tactic with which the Knights were familiar.[56]

On the same day as Medvegalis fell, Łokietek led his Polish army against Chełmno in an attempt to win it back from Bohemia

[51] *PD*, 215 and d'Outremeuse, *Chronique*, 412–16. The count of Hainault abandoned the Granadan Crusade to join John of Bohemia in Prussia – Finke, *Acta Aragonensia*, III, no. 256(2), p. 545. Paravicini, *Preussenreisen*, 178. Pomorze donated to Order – *PU*, II, nos. 688, 697, pp. 455, 462–3.

[52] Figures vary; *Wig.*, 463 gives 10,000; *PD*, 215 gives 18,000; 'Annales Expeditiales Prussici', *SRP*, III, 9 gives 200 Knights and 18,000 *armati*; Jeroschin, lines 26991–26994, p. 615 prefers 350 Knights and 18,000 *armati*. In all these figures it is unclear whether all the Knights are members of the Order. On medieval statistics see p. 246. See also Van D'Elden, *Peter Suchenwirt*, 179–80.

[53] *EpG*, 287. The campaign could not have lasted much more than a week since John left Königsberg for Lithuania on 20 January and was back there by 21 February, the date he left Königsberg to attack Dobrzyń. Machaut gives the names of the towns which were destroyed by the crusaders in Lithuania – Gegusë (Gegužkalnis, near Medvegalis); Aukahan (Aukaimis); Gedemine (Gedimin-Burg); Xedeyctain (Sisditen, near Medeninkai. The exact site of this fort remains unknown; it was attacked by the Knights in 1314 too – *PD*, 180) and Medouagle (Medvegalis) – Machaut, *Confort*, 3034, 3039–3040, p. 106. The modern versions of these names were given in A. Vaičiulaitis, 'Vidurinių amžių poetas Machaut Lietuvoje', *Lietuvių Katalikų Mokslo Akademijos Leidinys*, 3 (1939) (Rome, 1972), 318.

[54] Machaut, *Confort*, 107; *PD*, 215; *Wig.*, 463. The prince is named Margolis in d'Outremeuse, *Chronique*, 414. It is difficult to tell whether this Margolis is the Margiris whom Wigand mentions at Pilėnai in 1336 – see pp. 253–4. For Margolis and the merchants who *yroient tous marchans en sa terre*, see *Chronique*, 414. Medvegalis did lie in fact on a major trade route – see Map 3. On the castle at Ycône/Jūkainiai see above p. 33. Nikžentaitis, *Gediminas*, 10–11 considers Margiris to be a kinsman of Gediminas because he is called *rex*, but Latin authors use this title loosely and can intend merely 'duke' by it.

[55] *PD*, 215; *Wig.*, 463; Machaut, *Confort*, 107.

[56] Jeroschin, lines 27015–27052, p. 616; Henry, *Chronicon* I, 9 p. 6; II, 8 p. 11.

and the Order.[57] Some Polish historians have seen this attack as evidence of the Lithuano-Polish Treaty in action. Tymieniecki concluded that 'the bonds uniting Łokietek with Gedymin disposed the former to take up arms and attack the Order, which then turned against Poland in conjunction with the King of Bohemia'.[58] This interpretation of events seems to me to be not quite correct. Although Łokietek's Bohemian and Teutonic enemies refer to the Poles in their treaty of 12 March 1329 as *Lythowanorum fautores manifesti*,[59] it is surely over-romantic to view Łokietek's action as anything other than an opportunistic attempt to regain lost territory while its occupiers were busy elsewhere. There were no similar attacks by Poland on the Order at other times when the Lithuanians were under constant assault from Prussia and Livonia. It may appear that Łokietek's action drew the crusaders back from Lithuania but in fact, by mid-February the season for battle in Lithuania was already drawing to a close. Unfortunately for Łokietek, the combined armies of Bohemia and Prussia moved against Poland, capturing Dobrzyń outright and forcing the duke of Płock to become the vassal of King John.[60] Łokietek had let slip the dogs of war.

Throughout 1329 the Order was under pressure from Lithuanian and Polish attack. It comes as no surprise that colonists were required to provide military assistance to the Order and the bishop of Pomezania against Lithuania, according to land grants issued that year.[61] Historians who are rightfully impressed by the efficiency of the Order often fail to recognise the deadly pressure under which they strove against the heathen.

In September 1329 rumours arose that the Lithuanians were about to attack Bartenstein in east-central Prussia. The general chapter which was being held on 14 September at Marienburg had to draw up plans for the Order's defence.[62] In fact the main Lithuanian attack was to come in Livonia but while the chapter was in session Łokietek and his Hungarian allies crossed the

[57] *PD*, 215; Dietmar of Lübeck, *Chronik*, *SRP*, III, 67.

[58] Tymieniecki, 'Reunion', 121–2. The same view is taken by Knoll, *Rise*, 51; Housley, *Avignon Papacy*, 277–8. On these events, see also J. Powierski, 'Międzynarodowe tło konfliktu polsko-krzyżackiego przed kampanią wrześniowją 1331 roku', *Balticum* (Toruń, 1992), 269–84.

[59] *PU*, II, no. 637, pp. 423–4.

[60] *Wig.*, 463–83. The war is described in Knoll, *Rise*, 51–63. The act subjecting Płock to John of Bohemia is printed in *PU*, II, no. 642, pp. 428–9. John also seized Dobrzyń and donated half of the territory to the Order – *ibid.*, no. 643, pp. 429–30.

[61] *PU*, II, nos. 651, 659.

[62] *Wig.*, 466.

Drwęca river for a fourteen day *Reise* in Chełmno.[63] At the same time the Lithuanians attacked Livonia to help the Rigans.

During Gediminas' involvement in the Polono-Prussian war he was also caught up in Riga's struggle against the Order. Despite papal commands and the imposition of the interdict on Livonia in 1325, the Knights continued to hinder Rigan trade with Rus' and Lithuania and to demand territorial concessions from Riga.[64] The Dvina route to the city was blocked both at Dünamünde and upriver at Dünaburg. In 1328 the Livonian Knights surrendered Memel to their Prussian brethren who promptly declared the Minija river theirs far into Žemaitija.[65] The Lithuanians and Rigans had good reason to combine their efforts against the Order's two branches.

The Rigan war with the Order began in earnest on the night of 23 June 1328 when the Rigans attacked and razed Dünamünde. The next year they sought allies. In April 1329 four envoys, two each from the council and the community, were sent from Riga to Gediminas with the promise to hand over all the castles and fortifications of the archdiocese in return for the destruction of the Order.[66] This invitation to act as the city's garrison was, as we have seen, not a novel suggestion. Gediminas agreed to the terms of this military contract. However the Knights discovered the plan and seized five of the forts which had been promised to the grand duke.[67]

When the grand duke and his host arrived on the banks of the Dvina and realised that the Knights had already seized control of the cities which the Rigans had promised to Gediminas, the ambassadors accompanying the Lithuanians sought to console the grand duke and lift the siege of Riga by leading the pagan army 'whither it could do the Order most harm'.[68] Thus while the master of Livonia was at the general chapter discussing the defence of Prussia, the Lithuanians were ravaging four Livonian towns within a forty miles' radius in the diocese of Riga. Karkhus was attacked on 20 September 1329 before the pagans moved on two days later to Helmed (diocese of Dorpat) and on 23 September to Peysten (south of Fellin) where the troops bivouacked in the

63 *Wig.*, 467.

64 *GL*, 147–73.

65 *EpG*, 280. Prussian claims to Memel and the Minija river were made in a document of 19 May 1328 – *PU*, II, no. 617, pp. 407–9.

66 Rigan attack on Dünamünde – *HW*, 63; embassy to Gediminas – *HW*, 63–4.

67 *HW*, 64.

68 *Ibid.*

church. Around the Saccalian town of Tharwest 200 *unci* (*c.* 2,000 hectares) of land were destroyed and one Knight and two Dominicans were slain. In all in less than a week four hundred men were killed or led off into captivity.[69] On 4 March 1330 the Lithuanians returned with Rus'ian auxiliaries to take Pilten in Courland. Once more many slaves and much booty were captured.[70]

Despite all this activity, Gediminas could not take control of the promised Rigan fortresses, for on 21 March 1330 Riga capitulated to the Order. The city surrendered control of its trade to the master of Livonia along with St George's Monastery and several areas of disputed land. The citizens were compelled to break their links with Lithuania and accept a Teutonic garrison.[71] On 7 May John XXII repeated his 1317 instructions to the Order and Riga not to cause further scandal by fighting each other. It seemed that Riga and Lithuania had been put asunder. No one could tell that before the decade was out the Knights would be induced to reunite the erstwhile allies in order to maintain Livonian access to Rus'ian markets through the Grand Duchy.

Before proceeding further with our examination of the *Reisen*, we might do well to look more closely at Lithuanian military strategy and tactics. It is clear, for example, that Gediminas did not lead his men directly against the Order as its men lay encamped around the walls of Riga in 1329 because he preferred to avoid engaging in a pitched battle with the Knights. When the Lithuanians did engage the enemy in this way, as at Woplauken in 1311, Strėva in 1348 or Rudava in 1370, the result was either a heavy defeat for the pagans or a bloody slaughter hacked out *aequo marte*.[72] The Lithuanians relied on cavalry light brigades rather than heavy infantry.

[69] Karkhus had been attacked in 1298 when Vytenis had taken over the Rigan garrison – *PD*, 163. The raids of 1329 are described in *HW*, 64 and *Wig.*, 459. See also the analysis of tactics given in F. Benninghoven, 'Forschungsberichte zur Technik spätmittelalterlicher Feldzüge im Ostbaltikum', *ZfO*, 19 (1970), 644–6.

[70] *HW*, 65; *EpG*, 284.

[71] *LU*, II, no. 741; *Wig.*, 475–6; *PD*, 217–18; Hoeneke, *Liivimaa*, 58–60.

[72] Woplauken (6 April 1311) – *PD*, 176; Jeroschin, lines 23594–23653, pp. 575–6; *EpG*, 285; *Ronneburg Annals*, *Stryjkowski* I, 283; 'Annalista Thorunensis', *SRP*, III, 64; Strėva (2 February 1348) – *Wig.*, 511–13; *HW*, 75–6; Hoeneke, *Liivimaa*, 96–8; *TL*, 368–9; *PSRL*, IV (i), 276; *PSRL*, XV (i), 57; *PSRL*, XXV, 177; Rudava (17 February 1370) – *Wig.*, 565–7; *HW*, 96; Dietmar von Lübeck, *Chronik*, *SRP*, III, 89–90; Johann von Posilge, *Chronik*, *SRP*, III, 88–91; 'Annalista Thorunensis', *SRP*, III, 89–90. *PSRL*, XV (i), 91.

The method of combat best suited to Lithuanian conditions and skills was guerilla warfare directed against forts and isolated communities in the *Wildnis*. The only major difference between the pagan and Christian *ars bellandi* was reluctance on the pagan part to engage in pitched battles. The Teutonic tactic also was to harry the enemy *rapinis et incendiis*, burning his fields and homesteads and capturing booty in goods and human chattel.[73] The spoils of war were necessary to pay for the future defence of Lithuania (or Prussia) and the havoc wreaked in enemy lands weakened his potential to feed and arm his people and finance future raids. Men were slain and women and children tied to the back of the column of warriors to spend their lives in servitude. The price of the Hainault expedition to Prussia planned to last for seventy days in 1337, which consisted of only 157 knights and squires, cost Count William £943-4s-3d.[74] The cost to native princes of fighting in these wars may have been considerably less but it was still not insubstantial. It is not surprising that both the grand dukes and the grand masters made such efforts to increase the agricultural and technical wealth of their lands. To reduce the expense of military action Gediminas not only seized large quantities of booty, he also allied himself with Christian powers who were likewise at war with the Order or Moscow. The Lithuanians relied heavily for support upon the services of Rus'ian archers.[75] Similarly the Knights counted on the assistance of western cavaliers and *tyrunculi* in their battle with the heathen.[76]

The Lithuanian border against which all these costly assaults were directed was defended by a network of castles whose garrisons were changed regularly every month.[77] From these forts posted along the Nemunas and Jūra rivers, raiding parties sallied

[73] As in 1333, see p. 252. Jan Czarnkowski notes Casimir's discovery in 1350 that 'videns se eisdem Litwanis resistere non posse, quia cum ipso nunquam in proelium publicum convenire voluerunt, sed tamquam lupi rapaces terras suas furtive vastantes, raptis praediis fugiebant.' *MPH*, II, 630.

[74] L. Devilliers, 'Sur les expéditions des contes de Hainault et de la Hollande en Prusse', *Compte rendu des séances de la Commission Royale d'histoire ou Recueil de ses bulletins*, 4th series 5 (1878), 139. On the cost of later expeditions see W. Paravicini, 'Edelleute, Hausen, Brügger, Bürger: Die Finanzierung der westeuropäischen Preussenreisen im 14 Jahrhundert', *Hansische Geschichtsblätter*, 104 (1986), 5–20.

[75] For Rus'ian archers see *Wig*., 511 (at Strėva); in 1277 see *LR*, 8217, p. 188, tr. p. 101. Russian participation in the Strėva battle is clear from n. 72 above.

[76] As in 1329, 1336 and 1337, 1340 – see pp. 239, 253–4, 259. Western tyro knights used Prussia as a training ground *experiunde causa virtutis* – see letter of the bishop of Liège cited by *La Chronique de Jean de Hocsem*, ed. G. Kurth (Brussels, 1927), 257 s.a. 1337.

[77] *PD*, 174. On the Nemunas network of castles see above p. 56 and n. 26.

forth into Prussia. These bands were usually less than a hundred strong and their campaigns, which were carefully provisioned and preceded by scouting parties, usually lasted little more than a week or ten days.[78] The raid might encompass an area of between 20 and 40 kilometres a day.[79]

The raids were regular campaigns, not episodic skirmishes. Because of the difficulty of the terrain (marsh, river and forest), these attacks were launched only in the winter (from St Catherine's Day to Candlemas or perhaps early March) and mid-summer (from Trinity Sunday to Holy Cross) when the ground was firm enough for heavily armed horsemen and infantry to cross the quaggy *Wildnis* with their war machines and supplies and withdraw betimes with slaves and other booty. Both sides in the conflict used a network of spies to discover the enemy's whereabouts or disguise their own plans. In addition the Knights used their intelligence-gatherers to seek out fifth columnists within Lithuanian forts who were ill-disposed towards the grand-ducal régime. In 1337 the Knights' own new fort at Bayerburg was almost betrayed to Gediminas by Baltic soldiers in the Knights' service. The pagans familiarised themselves with the Knights' customs and time table. It is no coincidence that many autumn raids were launched around 14 September, the date fixed by the Order's statutes for the meeting of the general chapter.[80]

In addition to the well-planned official *reisen*, both sides were open to attack in the *Wildnis* and its borderlands by unofficial bandits, called in Latin sources *latrunculi*, *strutere* in German, who were allied to either major protagonist but most loyally to themselves. They preyed on isolated communities and unescorted merchants and emissaries as they traversed the trade routes.[81] One Prussian *struter*, Mucko ('the Gadfly') by name, was encouraged by the Order to molest Gediminas' people in 1324 when the Knights found themselves constrained to observe their treaty with

[78] *PD*, 185. Four-day *Reise* – *Wig.*, 514; Six-days – *SRP*, II, 8; a week – as in 1329. See also Benninghoven, 'Technik', 636.

[79] As in 1329 – Benninghoven, 'Technik', 644–6.

[80] Spies – *PD*, 152; fifth columnists – *PD*, 157, *Wig.*, 493; general chapter held on 14 September – J. Leuschner, *Deutschland im späten Mittelalter*, 3rd edn (Göttingen, 1983), 153.

[81] *PD*, 167; Jeroschin, lines 22264–22309, pp. 560–1. Robbers and pirates were a feature of Rus'ian life too, especially near the trade routes. The Novgorodians called them *ushkuyniki*, the Muscovites, *razboiniki*. These pirateers were sent on occasion by the Novgorodians to launch unofficial raids on their enemies – Fennell, *Emergence*, 243–4, n. 3.

Lithuania. These bandits could also work against official interests as did those Lithuanian *latrunculi* who robbed Rigan merchants en route for Lithuania in 1322–23.[82]

The number of participants in any *reise* is difficult to gauge with precision. The figures given by Peter of Dusburg, Wigand or even local bishops in their letters to the Pope represent an estimation of size rather than a precise head count. We read often of 200 Knights on a *Reise* when in the whole of the first half of the fourteenth century there were only 600 Knights in Prussia.[83] These set out against 6,000 or 1,200 heathen who were subsequently baptised or slain.[84] The modest numbers involved in certain campaigns are clear from the small number of casualties recorded; 6,000 is simply 'a large number' and 400, 'a small' one.[85] Large, medium or small are often the closest we can get to describing a campaign accurately. In 1337 the count of Hainault sent 157 knights and squires to Prussia *en chevauchée* with his son. However the young Hainault was not the only foreign lord to come east that winter.[86] If 10 such men came accompanied by as many knights and twice that number of foot-soldiers, and these were accompanied to Lithuania by 100 Knights and 1,000 Prussian men-at-arms, the total host would number barely 6,000. An obsession with statistics will not help our analysis of the crusades. Let us return to our examination of the war.

One of Wigand's figures cannot be denied; the Order faced three enemies in 1330–31: Poland, Hungary and Lithuania. Not least among this trinity was Lithuania.[87] Despite the Order's successes at Vaikiai and Gedimin-Burg in January and February 1330 and the capitulation of Riga in March,[88] Gediminas had his chances for retaliation.

[82] For Mucko see p. 214 and n. 147; for the Rigan complaints against Lithuanian *latrunculi* – *GL*, 61.

[83] 200 Knights in 1329 (*PD*, 215) and 1336 (*Wig.*, 488). On the numbers of Teutonic Knights see K. Scholz, *Beiträge zur Personengeschichte des Deutschen Ordens in der erste Hälfte des 14 Jahrhunderts. Untersuchungen zur Herkunft livländischer und preussischer Deutschordensbruder* (Munster, 1969), 6.

[84] 6,000 pagans – in 1329 (see above n. 57) and 1370 (or 5,500 – *HW*, 96). 1,200 in 1334 (*HW*, 67) and 1338 (*Wig.*, 495). Numbers given are usually uncannily round.

[85] As at Löbau in 1330 – see p. 247. This use of figures as expressions of quality rather than exact quantity is not peculiar to Baltic chroniclers – see R. C. Finucane, *Soldiers of the Faith: Crusaders and Moslems at war* (London–Melbourne, 1983), 103. On the exaggeration of heathen losses in Teutonic chronicles see P. Görlich, *Zur Frage des Nationalbewusstseins in östdeutschen Quellen des 12 bis 14 Jahrhunderts* (Marburg, 1964), 180–93.

[86] See below p. 254 and Paravicini, *Preussenreisen*, 147.

[87] *Wig.*, 471.

[88] *PD*, 217. For the capitulation of Riga see p. 243.

On 8 September 1330, Gediminas began a major onslaught against southern Prussia. He attacked Osterode and burned the city to the ground. The *Fischmeister* Brother Dietmar and nine others were murdered. The pagans then moved on to Löbau where they were intercepted by the bishop's advocate, Johann von Dyr and a small Löbavian force of forty men. This encounter deflected the Lithuanian attack to Kurnig where the town was burned before Gediminas crossed the Drwęca river into Michałowo. On 14 September, Werner von Orseln came to fight the Lithuanians at Strasburg but the Poles appeared and both sides withdrew from battle.[89]

The Lithuanians undertook the early part of this campaign alone. However it seems that they expected help from the Poles, to whom they later complained bitterly of having been left in the lurch.[90] The campaign was certainly most clearly in Poland's interest. Michałowo had been mortgaged to the Order in 1317 by Leszek, duke of Kujawy but Łokietek had not given up hope of regaining the territory for the kingdom.[91] The Lithuanians gained necessary spoils and revenge for past defeats from the attack.

The use of Lithuanian soldiers did not please Łokietek's other ally, Count William of Hungary, who threatened to return home rather then fight at the side of a pagan army. Thus the next time Lithuanian troops came to Poland on campaign, Łokietek had to pay the mercenaries off 'in gold, silver, cloth and horses ... each according to his merits'.[92] The grand master of Prussia, Luder von Braunschweig portrays this episode somewhat differently, as does Jeroschin. The latter sources claim that the winter of 1330–31 was too mild for a campaign in Prussia and the Lithuanian army which Łokietek had enlisted grew restless. Instead of ravaging Prussia, the pagans wrought havoc around their Polish encampment.[93]

89 *Wig.*, 471. A *Fischmeister* is an officer of the Order whose original duties were to look after the monks' fisheries. Chełmno and Löbau had been subject to Lithuanian attack earlier in the century – *PD*, 167–9.

90 Gediminas complained 'ego una vice condixi tecum ut in die Nativitatis Marie ibidem constitueremur, et ego veni, tu vero non', *Wig.*, 471.

91 Act of Mortgage dated 17 July 1317 – *PU*, II, no. 187, pp. 128–30. Casimir claimed the land back at the *Causa* of Warsaw, 4 February 1339 – *PU*, III.1, nos. 219, 220, pp. 157–61.

92 'salaria in auro, argento, panno et equis ... cuilibet secundum sua merita', *Wig.*, 471–2.

93 Luder complained to the Pope of Łokietek's use of *innumerabilem multitudinem Litwinorum* at the end of 1331 – *PU*, II, no. 747, p. 495. The account of the Lithuanian action against Poland is also given by Jeroschin, lines 27583–27624, pp. 622–3. This section of Jeroschin's verse translation of *PD* is not contained in Peter's original text.

Whichever account is the more accurate (and the latter is contemporary with the events described), the Lithuanian service contract with Poland fell into abeyance in early 1331. An armed peace seems to have been maintained between the allies until 1340, but there is no further evidence of Lithuanian involvement in Polish campaigns against the Order. In 1331 a second Lithuanian army inflicted heavy casualties on the Knights and their ally, John of Bohemia.[94]

Although the Polish and Rigan contracts were both void by early 1331, Gediminas went on to ally himself with Novgorod later that year. Whilst the Rigan and Polish alliances provided Lithuanian troops to continue the struggle against the Order, and the Pskov contract amounted to a very close relationship of mutual exploitation which sometimes appears as the virtual annexation of Pskov by Lithuania, the agreement struck between Gediminas and the archbishop of Novgorod in summer 1331 was more of a preventative measure than these. It seems to have been intended as a means of preventing Muscovite dominion in north-west Rus' rather than a way of incorporating the Novgorodian republic into the Grand Duchy.

In 1330 Moisei, the archbishop of Novgorod, who a year earlier had joined forces with Kalita and the Tatars to drive Aleksandr Mikhailovich from Pskov, resigned his see and retired to a monastery. Despite the claims of the Novgorod chronicles that Moisei took the *skhima* (the final stage of monastic profession in the Orthodox rite) of his own free will and to the dismay of the populace, it seems likely that tension between the Lithuanian and Muscovite factions within the city had forced his departure.[95] In early 1331, Vasily Kaleka replaced Moisei.[96] He was certainly a better friend to the Lithuanians and the Pskovites than Moisei had been.[97]

On 24 June 1331, Vasily set off for Vladimir Volynsky to be consecrated by Metropolitan Feognost. Before he left, Vasily built up Novgorod's stone defences from the Tower of St Vladimir via

[94] Egmond, *Chronicon*, 264.

[95] *NL*, 99.

[96] See p. 174. The adoption of the *skhima* amounts to the strictest withdrawal from the world. It expresses the prelate's free will to 'spend more time with his monastic family'. See also Powierski, 'Międzynarodowe tło', 276f.

[97] Fennell is correct to highlight the occasions Moisei is pro-Muscovite and Vasily pro-Lithuanian, in contrast with the general views of Russian scholarship – Fennell, *Emergence*, 137 and n. 3. It is probably even truer that Vasily was pro-Novgorodian and interested in any party which might benefit his city.

the Tower of the Mother of God to SS Boris and Gleb 'in the district across the river Volkov', *po toi storone ot Volkhova*, that is, on the side of the kremlin which faces the main route to Moscow.[98] It seems probable that Vasily expected some kind of trouble from Ivan Kalita who held the princely office in Novgorod at this time.

Vasily was accompanied on his journey by a diplomat and a military commander, the son of the *tysiatskii*. These were both important citizens and the sons of important citizens. The Novgorodian party travelled to Lithuania (not via Lithuania)[99] where they were met by Gediminas with whom they made an agreement to hand over to Narimantas Gediminaitis the northern defence outposts of Novgorod as his patrimony.[100] By the time Vasily reached home in early December, Kalita was in Novgorod attempting to persuade the citizens that since Vasily was obviously dead (rumours of his encounters with the Lithuanians on his way home had reached the city), they should bring Moisei out of retirement. Vasily arrived in time to put an end to these Muscovite dismal stories.[101]

Kalita was not pleased with Novgorod's change of allegiance – if such it was, for Novgorod was loyal to Novgorod and no one else. Vasily had approached Gediminas to help defend the city from the Swedes, a western foe whose methods the Lithuanians would know better than any Muscovite. However a Muscovite prince in Novgorod (Vasily had offered the border towns, not Novgorod to Lithuania) could hardly live with a Lithuanian army on the Republic's northern limits. Nevertheless Kalita was in no position to face Lithuania alone; he was still not in full possession of the Khan's *iarlyk*. In 1332 he contented himself with occupying Torzhok and Bezhetsky Verkh and, in January of the following year, he attacked Torzhok again before ravaging Novgorod territory for a month.[102] Vasily sent emissaries to Kalita to sue for peace but he received no answer. Meanwhile the archbishop went off to Pskov and christened the son of the excommunicate prince

[98] *PSRL*, VII (St Petersburg, 1856), 202, fuller than *NL*, 343. For the site of these fortifications see M. Kh. Aleshkovskii, 'Novgorodskii detinets 1044–1430gg. (po materialam novykh issledovanii)', *Arkhitekturnoe Nasledstvo*, 14 (1962), 20–1. The route of the *Bol'shaia Moskovskaia Doroga* on the Trade Side of Novgorod is depicted on a map of the city in the fifteenth century in Birnbaum, *Lord Novgorod* I, 69.

[99] *exaшa на литовскую землю* – *PSRL*, IV (i), 52.

[100] See p. 175.

[101] *NL*, 344; *PSRL*, IV (i), 52. See p. 177.

[102] *NL*, 344–5.

Aleksandr Mikhailovich.[103] In October 1333, Prince Narimantas was welcomed into his promised patrimony and baptised Gleb. By winter Kalita was seeking a marriage alliance with Lithuania.[104] The foundations of fifteenth-century factional disturbances within Novgorod were now firmly laid.

The Tatars, worried perhaps by Gediminas' success in taking up the Novgorod defence contract and by the alliance of Smolensk and Briansk with Lithuania in 1333,[105] not to mention the cosmetic settlement of Lithuano-Muscovite differences by the marriage of Semën Ivanovich and Aigusta Gediminaitė, now sought a subtler means of breaking the Lithuania–Novgorod connection. In 1334 with the likely connivance of the khan, Metropolitan Feognost acted as a go-between for Kalita and the Novgorodians. In June 1334, Vasily was summoned by Feognost to attend the consecration of a new bishop of Sarai and take advice.[106] By February 1335 Kalita had been recognised formally as prince of Novgorod. That year, at a date unspecified in *NL*, Narimantas left his new patrimony in the hands of his son Aleksandr and returned to Lithuania. Some historians have detected a connection between these two events.[107] They seem however to have been purely coincidental. It is possible that Narimantas left the Novgorodian marches simply to become prince of Polotsk, a much more valuable and stable position than that of mercenary captain of an unsure ally.[108]

A change in the emphasis of Novgorodian policy did come in 1335. Moisei re-appeared in public and was referred to by the chronicler as *vladyka*, a title of some reverence.[109] Kalita's desire of 1331 was thus realised. In the summer of 1335, it was the Lithuanians' turn to ravage Torzhok in dudgeon. The roles of 1331–33 were neatly reversed; Kalita was in and Gediminas, out of favour. Kalita avenged the attack on Torzhok by burning down the Lettovian forts of Osechen and Riasna along with 'many other strongholds'.[110]

[103] *NL*, 345. This was the first time in seven years that an archbishop of Novgorod had set foot in Pskov.

[104] Narimantas – *NL*, 346. The marriage of Semën – *TL*, 361; see above p. 90.

[105] See p. 113.

[106] *NL*, 346; Regel, *Analecta*, 54.

[107] Fennell, *Emergence*, 148–50.

[108] Fennell is wrong to think that Voin of Polotsk ruled until 1342, the date when we read of the death of his son Liubko – *ibid.*, 156. Liubko was killed in 1342 in a battle with the Order – *NL*, 355. The Lithuano-Livonian treaty of November 1338 shows that Narimantas was already prince of Polotsk in that year.

[109] *NL*, 346, 347.

[110] *Ibid.*, 347.

The Muscovite rising star soon fell to earth again. In 1337 the archimandrite of the Yuriev Monastery, Iosif, was removed during a popular uprising to be replaced by Lavrenty, the man from whom he had taken control of the monastery two years previously during the pro-Moscow *putsch*.[111] Gediminas seems to have been unwilling to build upon this situation. When the Novgorod marches were attacked by Sweden in 1337–38, the Lithuanians were slow to defend the Republic. Narimantas did not return from Polotsk to defend his patrimony and he even went as far as removing his son from the Orekhov garrison. Nevertheless he did leave his *namestniki* there.[112] Gediminas' family did not lose interest in the Novgorodian fortresses. Narimantas' sons Yury and Patrikii took charge of the border forts in 1379 and 1383, Semën Algirdaitis was similarly welcomed in Novgorod in 1407 and so was his son Yury in 1458.[113] Narimantas' reluctance to rush and fight the Swedes in 1337–38 was probably caused by the more pressing needs of Polotsk and the Baltic–Dvina trade route. In 1333 he had no patrimony; by 1337 he had two and of these Polotsk was undoubtedly the more important. Besides, it was late in 1337, a year which saw a major *Reise* against western Lithuania, that the emperor granted the Knights possession of Lithuania. Defence of the homeland counted more than a contract with the Novgorodians. Those historians who chide the Lithuanians for abandoning Novgorod in 1338 fail to examine Lithuanian politics from Lithuania's point of view. Gediminas no doubt did miss a good opportunity to press home his advantage over Moscow, as he did again in 1341 when he failed to rise from his death bed to secure a tighter hold on Novgorod.[114] However Lithuania, not Novgorod was his prime concern. The Lithuanian presence on the Novgorodian border was a dog in the Muscovite manger. Gediminas probably realised that Novgorod would not be amenable to Lithuanian domination in the same way as Pskov. Narimantas' presence in Novgorod helped keep Moscow at bay (as was the intention of the archbishop); it was not a discreet means of ruling the powerful Republic. Until Moscow annexed Novgorod by force in 1477 Lithuania had not lost the city nor had

[111] Fennell, *Emergence*, 148–149.

[112] *NL*, 349.

[113] Yury Narimantaitis – *NL*, 375; Patrikii – *NL*, 379; Semën (Lengvenis) Algirdaitis – *PSRL*, IV (i), 404; Yury Semënovich – *PSRL*, XVI, 198. See also V. L. Ianin, *Novgorodskaia Feodal'naia Votchina* (*Istoriko-genealogicheskoe issledovanie*) (Moscow, 1981), 216–23.

[114] Fennell, *Emergence*, 155, 247.

Moscow won it. The effects of the 1331 contract lasted a good 146 years.

Throughout the 1330s as Gediminas increased Lithuanian influence in Rus', the Prussian and Livonian Knights and their pilgrims concentrated their attacks on Žemaitija. These attacks were faced by Lithuania alone. The Order continued to build forts in north-east Prussia and Semigallia, the area hotly contested by Gediminas.[115] Forts were reconstructed at Mezoten, Terweten and Doblen.[116] Angirburg and Wehlau were founded in 1335 and Marienburg in 1336.[117] Nevertheless the overall impression we will gain from these military campaigns is one of continuous attrition wrought by both sides at considerable cost, interspersed with startling victories, usually on the German side when a large foreign army is present. Such victories are exceptional and occur once a decade (1328–29, 1336, 1348) but they are never consolidated for a variety of reasons including poor campaign conditions on the ground, lack of sufficient armament and fortification, and divisions within the leadership of the Order and the Grand Duchy (especially in the period 1340–45).

In August 1331, the master of the Livonian Order, Eberhard von Monheim, led his forces into Žemaitija to devastate Santholen (Santkore) where five hundred heathen were slain, according to Hermann of Wartberge, with the loss of but two brethren and forty Christian foot-soldiers.[118] Such modest losses encourage the belief that only modest forces were involved in the fray. The following year, Monheim reached the far eastern regions of Žemaitija where he destroyed noble castles in Mažeiken and Windeiken which lie to the north-north-west of Vilnius.[119] The Prussian brethren joined forces with the Livonians in 1333 to ravage Žemaitija *rapinis et incendiis*.[120] This was the year Monheim laid siege to Ukmergė, north-north-west of Vilnius, and sent a river-borne expedition against Polotsk in what was evidently an attempt to damage Lettovian trade along the Dvina route.[121] All in all, 1333 was a successful year for the Order, as in the east it was for Lithuania. Quite apart from the *Reisen*, the Order's policy of colonisation appears to have prospered. Sixteen land grants survive

[115] See p. 194.
[116] In 1338 and 1335 (Doblen) – *HW*, 67.
[117] *EpG*, 280; *Wig.*, 490.
[118] *HW*, 66; *Wig.*, 487. Hoeneke, *Liivimaa*, 60–2 records a Rus'ian contingent in the Lithuanian army.
[119] Hoeneke, *Liivimaa*, 62–4; *HW*, 66.
[120] *HW*, 67.
[121] 2 February 1333 – *HW*, 67; *Wig.*, 487.

mainly from north-east Prussia (Fischhausen, Königsberg, Holland) which mostly imposed conditions of military service upon the recipients.[122] Two such beneficiaries were Lithuanian tribesmen who took land in Bartenstein and Kremitten in return for promises to fight the Lithuanians. One of these colonists was absolved of the duty to keep Lithuanian prisoners on his land, while the other was promised land at Laukuva (Laygow) in Lithuania after the country was captured. Presumably this was the place he had lived in before his defection.[123]

The merchants' route east was followed again by Monheim in 1334. His troops attacked Dubingiai and Sicculen where a fair number of Lithuanians were killed before the army moved southwards to within four miles of Vilnius. From the capital the Livonians continued on to Polotsk for the second time in two years.[124]

There seems to have been a lull in the Order's attacks in 1335 when Luder von Braunschweig died. He was replaced by another good soldier and administrator, Dietrich von Altenburg. In that year, although no *Reise* was launched, a new fortress was built at Doblen in Semigallia and the Knights ravaged Pskov.[125]

The first substantial international *Litauenreise* since 1329 was led by Dietrich on 25 February 1336. He was accompanied by Louis, margrave of Brandenburg (Gediminas' enemy of 1326), the counts of Namur and Hainault (as in 1329) and many French and Austrian knights. In all the army was alleged to number 200 Knights and 6,000 footsoldiers – a traditional statistic.[126] This large force laid siege to the fortress of Pilėnai on the Lithuano-Prussian border in a district called Trapėnai. Some 4,000 pagans were alleged to have fled thither from four Lithuanian *terrae*. It was at Pilėnai that an old crone, probably a pagan priestess, slew 100 warriors with her axe to save them from captivity before she killed herself.[127] The princeling Margiris escaped from the fort with his wife whom he later killed and cremated to prevent her from

[122] *PU*, II, nos. 771, *775*, 780–2, *787*, *795–800*, *805*, *806*, 808, 813. (Italicised numbers refer to grants which specifically state military duties).

[123] Drowene received land at Wommen (Bartenstein) in the first instance – 23 May 1333, *PU*, II, no. 781; Leppe took land at Poernis – 29 August 1333, *ibid.*, no. 798.

[124] *HW*, 67.

[125] Hoeneke, *Liivimaa*, 62; for visit to Prussia in 1335–36, see Paravicini, *Preussenreisen*, 183.

[126] *Wig.*, 488–9; *EpG*, 283; 'Annales Expeditiales Prussici', *SRP*, III, 9.

[127] *Wig.*, 489. The figure of 100 pagans who killed themselves is hardly catastrophic when one considers that the fort was supposed to hold 4,000.

falling into enemy hands. Many captives were taken at Pilėnai and forcibly converted but it was the number of suicides which created the biggest impression on the Knights when they beheld the *schreckliche Specktakel*.[128] It is perhaps not without significance that one of the aims of a campaign against this prince in 1329 had been to force the Lithuanians to open up the trade route in Margiris' lands to Teutonic merchants.[129]

After this campaign, Dietrich went on to build a new fortification, called variously Marienburg and Georgenburg, on the island of Romayn in the Nemunas.[130] He did not manage to complete it before a Lithuanian army appeared and destroyed it. It would therefore seem clear that, despite local losses at Pilėnai, the pagans were not cowed by their defeat.

That year of 1336 brought the Order its last notable victory of the decade. Although another *Reise* was planned by John of Bohemia for the winter of 1336–37, it came to nothing. Princes of Burgundy, France, Spain and the Low Countries came to Prussia along with Henry of Bavaria, Wacław of Legnica and John of Bohemia's son, Charles of Moravia. However the unusually mild weather that winter made conditions for the *Reise* impossible. Early in 1337 John of Bohemia left Prussia behind him to go to Poland to treat with Casimir the Great.[131] The tide was beginning to turn against the Order and the Empire; Gediminas was in a position to exploit it.

In the spring of 1337, Duke Henry of Bavaria managed to take his army to Lithuania. In the space of three weeks a new fort was built on the banks of the Nemunas near the Lithuanian outpost of Veliuona. In honour of the Order's guest it was named Bayerburg.[132] The fortress was well-garrisoned with brethren and Prussian tribesmen (Wytingi) but in the summer of 1337 it almost fell to Gediminas' army after disaffected Wytingi attempted to betray the fort into Lithuanian hands. It was during this siege that a duke of Trakai was slain.[133]

The *Litauenreisen* of 1337 are dominated by a rather grandiose but ultimately insignificant parchment which some historians

[128] *Ibid.* [129] See above n. 54. [130] *Wig.*, 490; *EpG*, 280–1.

[131] *Wig.*, 490–1; Autobiography of Karl IV – *FRB*, III, 352, 382, 408; *FRB*, IV, 425; 'Kurze Preussische Annalen 1190–1337', *SRP*, III, 4. [132] *Wig.*, 493.

[133] The death of *dux Trocensis* (*Wig.*, 492–4) in 1337 was confused by Długosz with the death of *Gediminas*. This error, little regarded by historians relying on trustworthy Russian sources, was cleared up by Gudavičius in 1984. For a review of modern Lithuanian writing on the subject see Rowell, 'Lithuania', 303–26.

have regarded for too long as a threat to Lithuania: the imperial donation of Lithuania, Žemaitija (especially Karšuva) and Rus' to the Order. This bull was issued by Louis IV first on 15 November 1337.[134] By its decree Bayerburg was to become the new ecclesiastical and political centre of a Teutonic *Ordensstaat* stretching through Prussia, Livonia and the whole of Lithuania. However the parchment did not make Lithuania any easier to conquer and the Knights could already claim *qua* crusaders the land of the infidels as their own, as they did in Livonia.[135]

The background to the donation is rather complicated. In 1335 at the Congress of Visegrád in Hungary, John of Bohemia, fired by his ambition to win the imperial crown for his son Charles, formed an alliance with Casimir of Poland and Charles Robert of Hungary against the Wittelsbach emperor. At that time Louis had not incurred the enmity of the new Pope, Benedict XII, but by August 1337 negotiations with the Curia had broken down and Germany lay under the interdict.[136] The Teutonic Order was Louis' staunchest supporter.

The possibility of a rapprochement between the Order and Poland, orchestrated by King John and presaged by the Treaty of Inowrocław in January 1337, added to increasing imperial isolation in the west, may very well have prompted the emperor to grant Lithuania to the Order. In January Casimir agreed to surrender his rights to Pomorze in return for the Order's surrender of Kujawy and Dobrzyń to the Polish crown. The donation was intended to show the grand master that his truest friend was neither the Pope nor the king of Poland but the emperor. In July 1338 the same message was spelled out even more clearly when the emperor wrote to the grand master warning him not to join the 'self-styled king' of Poland or yield to papal pressure.[137]

As a result of the Second Congress of Visegrád in June 1338, when Galich–Volyn' joined Poland, Hungary and Bohemia in

[134] 15 November 1337 – *PU*, III.1, no. 134, pp. 96–100. Here the emperor gave the Knights control of *terram Lithwinorum cum omnibus pertinenciis ... Sameyten, Karsow vel Rusye*. Bayerburg was to be the capital of this new state and the ecclesiastical centre (with an archbishop and canons) too. Perhaps tact overcame Louis when he reissued the Bull on 12 December (*Ibid.*, no. 135, pp. 100–1) for he omitted the instructions concerning the creation of a new archbishopric (the Pope's undeniable prerogative). More probably this omission reflects the weakness of Louis' position in 1337.

[135] See p. 194 and n. 36. – the question of *dominium* and pagans was a vexed one.

[136] See Rowell, 'Lithuania', 314–15. On the interdict see Mollat, *The Popes*, 222–3.

[137] Inowrocław dealt with in Wyrozumski, *Kazimierz*, 59–60. Louis' letter is printed in *CDP*, III, no.8, pp. 12–13.

undisguised opposition to the emperor and the Knights, the Order's trade-routes to Rus' via Poland and Galich–Volyn' were cut. The south-west Rus'ian trade links which had previously been directed towards Toruń and Prussia now turned towards Poland.[138] In January 1339, Bolesław-Yury granted a charter to his new city of Sanok whose leading citizens were to be Poles, not Prussians or even Rus'ians.[139] Consequently the Knights had to turn to Lithuania to open up a trade route to Rus' through Prussia and the Grand Duchy as they would again before 1355, the date of a complaint that the Order had gone even as far as building new bridges in pagan territory to facilitate their merchants' journey east.[140] In 1338 Gediminas' daughter Elżbieta, the dowager duchess of Płock, arranged the marriage of her daughter Anna to a Silesian prince, Henry V of Żagań, thereby striking a balance for Mazovia (and possibly Lithuania) against the new alignment of powers in central Europe which favoured the king of Poland.[141] It is tempting to speculate on Gediminas' reaction to this union which created a distant connection between Lithuania and western Polish territories.

On 1 November 1338, the master of Livonia, the same Eberhard von Monheim who had been Lithuania's staunch enemy, his landmarshals and the citizenry of Riga concluded a commercial treaty with Gediminas and his sons Narimantas-Gleb and Algirdas who controlled the Lettovian cities of Polotsk and Vitebsk. Some scholars have tended to exaggerate the effect of this trade accord on general relations between the signatory powers.[142] The treaty did nothing to curtail the *Litauenreisen* or the settlement of colonists in Prussia under the obligation to provide arms against Lithuania or in defence of the *Ordensstaat*. Between 1338 and 1340 one hundred and sixteen settlement grants were issued, including six for Lithuanian renegades.[143] In the case of the village of Grondzaw in Strasburg, farmers were granted aid in paying their taxes in the event of general war, fire or devastation by the Lithuanians.[144] The Lithuanians continued to suffer attacks in Semigallia and Žemaitija (Veliuona, Pupillen, Medininkai), never-

[138] Rowell, 'Lithuania', 315.

[139] To judge from the Sanok Charter of 20 January 1339 according to which, the *advocatus* was to be Bartko of Sandomierz – *Boleslav'-Iurii*, 77–9. On the jealousy of the native boiars see below p. 266.

[140] See below n. 148.

[141] Jasiński, 'Małżeństwa', 70.

[142] *GL*, 187–95 and Rowell, 'Lithuania', 314.

[143] Grants to Lithuanians – *PU*, III.1, nos. 227, 249–51, 321. A grant for two Knights to be redeemed after the fall of Lithuania – *ibid.*, no. 261.

[144] *Ibid.*, no. 243.

theless they were still capable of taking war to Livonia.[145] What then was the purpose of the 1338 agreement if it was not to make peace? It was a damage-limitation pact of the type we signalled earlier.

In May 1338, the Knights oversaw the consolidation of the Lübeck–Novgorod trade route. The November agreement with Gediminas safeguarded the Riga–Polotsk traffic. The northern routes had increased in importance after the closure of the southern roads to Teutonic merchants. The Order no longer found it possible or practical to hinder Rigan commerce with the Grand Duchy. The treaty was not an armistice as the 1323 treaty had been. It was a clarification of the commercial realities of Prusso-Lithuanian life. Despite the war and the smashing of the Lithuano-Rigan alliance in 1330, Lettovian and Prussian merchants had continued to trade together. This agreement clarified past agreements and contemporary practice. Military action was to be forbidden for a decade within a strictly demarcated network of trade routes termed *vredelant* or 'zone of peace'. This term appears in other sources from other years as the *vredeweg*. It is reminiscent of the 'peace of the Fairs' common in Champagne in the twelfth century.[146] Christian and heathen merchants were to trade unimpeded and on equal terms along routes which stretched westwards to Nycevre from the mouth of the Ewest river and from Ewestmunde across the Dvina to Užpaliai and Stripayne (see map 3). The Šventoji river route from Užpaliai to Vilnius via Balninkai, Giedraičiai and Nemencinė provided a defensive arc of safe routes north of the capital. The Dvina and its tributaries north of the Ewest were also guaranteed as was the Ewest–Peden–Adzel route to Pskov which had previously been protected by *den olden vrede*.[147] The routes to Pskov and Polotsk and to Novgorod which was still allied to Lithuania, were thus open to commerce. Each side, Catholic, Orthodox and heathen confirmed the agreement in

145 Winter 1338 Medininkai was attacked – *Wig.*, 493, 494; the following winter Veliuona was assaulted, *Wig.*, 497, and the master *multas reysas fortes ordinavit* – *ibid.*; 'Kurze Reimchronik von Preussen', *SRP*, II, 8. Pupillen, 1339 – Hoeneke, *Liivimaa*, 64. In 1340 the new master of Livonia, Burchard von Dreynleven invaded Upitė – Hoeneke, *Liivimaa*, 60. For their part the Lithuanians and Zemaitijans led an unsuccessful attack on Galelauken (near Ragnit) in August 1338 – *Wig.*, 495; *EpG*, 283.

146 Describing the Okmiana river route from Ragnit to Medininkai and Kaltėnai, the Order's *Wegeberichte*, 12 (*SRP* II, 673) speaks of *czum erstin von Ragnit den* fredeweg *bis czu Pütinveld*.

147 *GL*, 189. Clearly the treaty of 1338 was no innovation, merely a consolidation and systematisation of previous agreements.

its own way. Obviously a conversion to Christianity was not envisaged on the Lithuanian part nor was it expected by the Christians just as when specific Baltic–Rus' river routes were established before 1355.[148] Again Gediminas' eastern and western policies complemented each other. It is unlikely that the bishop of Polotsk would have set his seal to a treaty involving a change in Gediminas' religious affiliation to the benefit of the Catholic Church nor would the prince of Smolensk have signed so readily an accord with the Order which complemented the 1338 treaty, had he supposed that Gediminas intended to convert. Nevertheless Bartholomäus Hoeneke records the opposition of the grand master to Russo-Rigan cooperation.[149] These events serve to highlight the complexity of Gediminas' position as he hovered between East and West: a conqueror in Rus', a fierce combatant in the West.

The route further eastwards into the Grand Duchy was safeguarded for Baltic merchants when Gediminas' ally, Ivan Aleksandrovich of Smolensk, signed a treaty, most probably in 1339, with the Livonian master and Riga 'according to that settlement which my senior brother Gediminas settled along with his sons, [Narimantas-] Gleb and Algirdas'.[150] By the time Ivan Aleksandrovich referred thus to Gediminas as his 'senior', the links between Smolensk and Lithuania had been firmly established. In the winter of 1339 the Khan sent a Russo-Tatar army against Smolensk to prise the city away from Lithuania and send a signal to Gediminas of Tatar disapprobation of Lithuanian meddling in eastern Rus' and Gediminas' truck with the West.[151] The expedition failed miserably. The Tatars were not averse to a reasonable degree of Lithuanian success for it was now their

[148] The 1355 complaint (*Regesta diplomatica necnon epistolaria Bohemiae et Moraviae*, VI (Prague, 1928), no. 167, p. 97) is discussed by K. Conrad in his article 'Litauen, der Deutschen Orden und Karl IV 1352–1366', *ZfO*, 21 (1972), 33f. On Lithuanian trade relations with the West see Varakauskas, *Lietuvos*, 255–64 and Mažeika, 'Prekyba'.

[149] Rowell, 'Lithuania', 315. The grand master's objections to Russo-Rigan cooperation (Hoeneke, *Liivimaa*, 66–8) led to war between Rus' and the Order in 1341–42 – *ibid.*, 68–76; *PL*, I, 18–20; II, 24–5, 92–7.

[150] 'по тому докончанью, како то брат мой стареиший Кедименъ и докончалъ и его дети Глебъ и Алкердъ', Avanesov, *Smolenskie*, 70. The treaty is undated but it is clear from its clauses that it is connected with the 1338 accord. Gleb and Alkerd (Algirdas) are the 'princes' who signed that agreement for Polotsk and Vitebsk. Since the archbishopric of Riga was vacant in 1340 it is likely that 1339 is more reliable than the traditional date of 1340. The Tatars attacked Smolensk in the winter of 1339–40, probably in response to this close cooperation between the Rus'ian city and Lithuania.

[151] *TL*, 363; *PSRL* X, 208.

apparent policy to balance Moscow and Vilnius, as earlier in the century it had been to play Tver' off against Moscow.[152] In 1338 the balance was swinging (too) heavily in Lithuania's favour.

In the West between 1338 and Gediminas' death in the winter of 1341–42 Lithuania's struggle with the Order continued. The heathens matched the crusaders blow for blow. In 1340 the grand master had to cut short a recruiting drive in Germany because of unspecified *arduis causis* which were presumably connected with the crusade.[153] The conflict did not sharpen considerably (on the Lithuanian side) until Algirdas' campaign of 1343. The Order lacked effective leadership until the election of Henry Dusemer in 1345.[154]

Lithuanian contacts with Christendom are much more complex than the generalisations of crusade historians lead us to believe. Concentration on the 'violent nature of relations between the Grand Principality and its Catholic neighbours'[155] belies the complicated network of Lithuanian alliances with Christian powers which led Gediminas to fight alongside as many of his Catholic neighbours as he battled against. It is true that regular, well-organised and expensive campaigns were launched in defence of Lithuania's western borders. Campaigns were also led against Catholic princes with the connivance of the king of Poland and the Pope. Indeed John XXII's response to Gediminas' overtures to the curia in 1322–23 seems to have been encouraged by hopes of Lithuanian support against the Wittelsbach Empire.

Rather than convert to Christianity, Gediminas used his western allies to maintain pressure on the Teutonic Order. This he chose to do primarily through contracts of Lithuanian service to Poland and Riga. By supplying troops to these two states Gediminas kept his men battle-ready in anticipation of future campaigns where Lithuania would have to fight alone (as after 1331). He diverted Teutonic attention away from the Lithuanian border by fuelling conflict in the Prussian and Livonian theatres of war. In addition such collaboration with Polish and Rigan armies cut both the cost and the risk of campaigning against the Knights. Meanwhile the Teutons had to rely heavily on the settlement of Prussia and the visits of western crusaders to maintain their war effort. If the documents preserved by the Knights and published in *Preussisches*

[152] See p. 114.
[153] *Wig.*, 497.
[154] *Wig.*, 501f.; *Długosz*, IX, 225; Matthias de Nuwenburg, *Chronica*, ed. A. Hofmeister *MGH, SRG*, n.s. 4(i) (Berlin, 1924), 171.
[155] Housley, *Avignon*, 66.

Urkundenbuch reflect accurately the pattern of settlement, it seems that more colonists were endowed with land during the periods when the Lithuanian War was particularly propitious for the Knights: 1311–15, 1333, 1338–41.[156] The pressing need to recruit foreigners for the campaigns of 1339–41 reveals a weakness in the Order which is ignored in general accounts of the crusade.

The contract made between Pskov and Lithuania was somewhat different from those made with Poland and Riga. It began as military collaboration against the Danish and German settlements in Livonia and ended with the virtual annexation of the Rus'ian city by Lithuania. This is best illustrated by Gediminas' reference to his dominion over Pskov in the peace treaty he signed with Denmark (and Livonia) in 1323.[157]

By contrast the Novgorodian agreement which Gediminas hammered out with the new archbishop in summer 1331 was not conceived in a spirit of acquisition. The defence of the Novgorodian marches against Sweden was intended by Gediminas to strengthen Lithuanian influence in the city rather than create conflict in the north or annex Novgorod. The city was too powerful to succumb to such an attempt. This influence assisted Lithuanian trade through Novgorod and safeguarded Pskov (which was technically still dependent upon Novgorod) from adverse archiepiscopal intervention. Most significantly of all, the agreement prevented the grand duke of Vladimir, that is the prince of Moscow, from gaining unrestricted control of the archiepiscopal Republic. The slowness of Lithuanian reaction to Swedish attacks on Novgorod's border in 1337 (the very kind of incursion Narimantas had been enlisted to counter) indicates that however interested Gediminas was in keeping the city's favour, he was more concerned with strictly Lithuanian than with Novgorodian affairs. Despite this apparent lackadaisical approach to the Republic's problems Lithuanian princes were to play a major role

[156] Settlers in Teutonic Lands: *Lithuanian settlers*; 1311–15 – *PU*, II, nos. 30, 125, 126; 1333 – *PU*, II, nos. 781, 798; 1338–40 – *PU*, III.1, nos. 249–51, 277, 321.
Non-Lithuanian settlers; 1311–15 – PU, II, nos. 27, 33, 34, 41–3, 49, 57, 58, 64–7, 74, 77, 98, 102–4, 127, 130, 131, 133, 142, 143; 1333 – see above n. 122; 1338–40 – *PU*, III.1, nos. 141, 150, 151, 153, 154, 159–61, 163, 164, 166, 172, 174–82, 185, 188, 189, 195, 196, 199, 200, 202, 214, 215, 224, 228–30, 236, 238, 239, 240, 242, 244, 247, 253, 254, 256, 258–67, 273, 278, 280, 282–5, 288, 290, 291, 293, 296, 298–302, 304–9, 311–18, 323, 326–34, 336–9, 341a-b, 342–4.

[157] 'Plessekowe unde alle der Russen, de under uns besethen sin' – *GL*, 69.

in Novgorodian politics for as long as the city remained independent.

Lithuanian armies were capable of fighting unaided on two major fronts. At the same time as he was facing the crusaders of Livonia and Prussia Gediminas spread his control over Rus'ian territories from Turov to Smolensk, from Kiev to Pskov. His Livonian and Rus'ian policies often complemented each other perfectly. In 1323 his Pskovite alliance helped Gediminas convince the Livonians that peace with the pagans was the better part of valour. Even if 1333 was an unsuccessful year for Lithuania in the west, in the east it witnessed the apogee of Lithuanian power in Rus'. In 1338 the strength of Lithuanian control over the eastern trade routes helped bring the Order to restore the Lithuano-Rigan association it had hoped to eradicate only eight years before. Trade was necessary to both sides to maintain the costly war. Gediminas and the Knights encouraged commerce at the very time they were embroiled in martial stalemate. The crusaders and the crusaded-against needed each other to survive. Gediminas was adept at switching deftly from the diplomatic to the martial plane, from east to west.

It is evident that Lithuania was by no means merely an unfortunate victim of Teutonic aggression. In 1326 the Knights stood by, helpless as the pagans ravaged Brandenburg from Prussia, as Dietmar of Lübeck laments, for Lithuanian diplomacy had foxed them into neutrality.[158] In September 1329, the Knights did not know which way to turn as Gediminas' allies ravaged southern Prussia, and Livonia was laid waste by the grand duke's army. It is not impossible to find some sympathy for the view of Weise (of the Order a little later in the century) that 'die unaufhörliche Kampf gegen Litauen war für den Orden härteste Realpolitik, nackter Kampf ums Dasein'.[159] The Order's victories at Medvegalis and Pilėnai were more than offset by Lithuanian successes in Prussia and Livonia.[160] Even the prematurely vaunted

[158] 'Do mochten de ghodesriddere wol hebben hindert in ereme lande de bosen ghodesviande, hedden se des ghuden willen hat' – Dietmar von Lübeck, *Chronik*, *SRP*, III, 66.

[159] E. Weise, 'Der Heidenkampf des Deutschen Ordens', *ZfO*, 12 (1963), 667. Weise exaggerates the vulnerability of the Order. Nevertheless the Knights were hard-pressed to survive their enemies in the 1340s.

[160] The statistics available for Lithuanian and Prussian losses in battles of the 1320s and 1330s, although they are not entirely reliable for the provision of an exact figure for war-dead, do give the impression that losses were similar on both sides. The Rigan

castle of Bayerburg almost fell to Lithuania within three months of its completion. Its predecessor, Georgenburg, which also stood opposite Veliuona was destroyed by the pagans in 1336 even before it was completed. It is easy to swallow a retrospective chauvinism which regards 'Prussian' always as 'best'. However until the second half of the fourteenth century, the Order's position in Prussia and Livonia was far from solid. The Knights remained dependent for military and agricultural strength on western European auxiliaries.

campaign of 1329 cost the Knights 449 men and five knights; the Santholen campaign of 1330 resulted in 500 Lithuanian deaths.

Chapter 9

1339–45: ENDINGS AND BEGINNINGS

The final years of Gediminas' reign, from the inconclusive attack on Bayerburg in 1337 and the trade agreement of November 1338 to his death in the winter of 1341/42, represent a period of relative calm on the western frontier, as the solutions which the grand duke had devised earlier to combat problems facing the eastern borderlands gradually broke down. The major protagonists of Gediminas' foreign policy, Bolesław-Yury II, Kalita, Frederick of Riga, John of Bohemia and Khan Uzbek all make another appearance before bowing out of the story. Trade continued with Riga and the Baltic Catholics and the war with the Knights was maintained as stalemate between two roughly equal forces. The Order relied on western knights to come on *Reise* in Prussia but the recruitment campaign, as we have seen, had lost momentum. The Order's pocket was suffering from a slackening in trade brought on by Polish opposition to German merchants. In 1340 the grand master was reduced to touring western Europe in order to gain support and complaining of a Tataro-Lithuanian assault on his lands. Meanwhile the Lithuanians prepared for conflict with Poland over Galich–Volyn'. Over the next few years Polish relations with Lithuania became increasingly more antagonistic.

With the beginning of a new decade, events on Lithuania's Rus'ian borders entered a new phase. On 31 March 1340, Ivan Kalita died and bequeathed the principality of Moscow to his sons under the leadership of the eldest, Semën. Kalita's cautious display of family unity and loyalty to the khan succeeded in persuading Uzbek to grant the *iarlyk* for Vladimir and all Rus' to Semën, Gediminas' son-in-law.[1] The political climate of Rus' was changing substantially, albeit very slowly for the first time in twenty years. Lithuania was faced with the prospect of dealing

[1] *PSRL*, XV (i), 52.

with a new prince of Moscow and re-establishing her gains in western Rus', both north and south. In Briansk Gleb Sviatoslavich, the pro-Lithuanian prince who had reigned there since 1333 was murdered by members of a local pro-Muscovite opposition faction on 6 December 1340.[2] It would be sixteen years before Algirdas could restore Lithuanian influence in the city.[3] In October 1341 this same prince led an unsuccessful assault on Mozhaisk which was the personal patrimony of his brother-in-law Semën Ivanovich, presumably in an attempt to punish the Muscovite for his active anti-Lithuanian policies.[4] The year before, Semën had imposed an agreement on the citizens of Novgorod which obliged them to recognise him as their prince. Although Fennell says that the Lithuanians did nothing to protect Novgorod from Semën, this does not appear to be completely accurate. It is not incredible to link the Lithuanian attack on Mozhaisk with dissatisfaction in Vilnius at Moscow's pressure on Novgorod.[5] Even so, Semën's gain was illusory, for the Lithuanians maintained their influence in Pskov and the archbishop of Novgorod undertook to educate Mikhail, the young prince of Tver' who was the son of Gediminas' late close ally Aleksandr Mikhailovich. The archbishop manipulated the rivalry between the princes of Lithuania and Moscow with considerable skill.[6]

In the south-west a more pressing problem arose when, towards the end of Lent 1340, Gediminas' son-in-law, Bolesław-Yury II of Galich–Volyn' was murdered, thereby undoing the settlement of 1324 between the boiars of south-west Rus', Gediminas, Łokietek and the dukes of Mazovia which had maintained peace in the region for nearly twenty years. How this tragedy came about and what were its consequences are questions which merit further investigation, for they are a hornets' nest of competing national

[2] *TL*, 364; *PSRL*, XV (i), 53.

[3] *PSRL*, XV (i), 65.

[4] *TL*, 365; *PSRL*, XV (i), 53–4.

[5] Fennell, *Emergence*, 247. Fennell is inclined to a rather simplistic interpretation of Novgorodian politics that seeks to determine which of Moscow and Vilnius is winning the big-power struggle for Novgorod. This loses sight of the manipulative skill of local factions and the local archbishop. Kaleka was particularly astute in his management of the tension in the north between the powers in Rus', Livonia and Lithuania.

[6] *PSRL*, XV (i), 54. Tigoshinov (Tishinov in *PSRL*, X, 213 s.a. 6849) was attacked by the Lithuanians in the summer of 1341. The location of this place is unknown. There are settlements of similar names in the Mozhaisk (i.e. Tishinskoe selishche) and Zvenigorod districts within the principality of Moscow. The battle is described after the attack on Mozhaisk and could well have been fought during the return march. For Pskov, see below p. 284; for Mikhail Aleksandrovich see *NL*, 354.

historiographies in Poland, Lithuania and the Ukraine. The achievements of the Galich ruler are worth exploring as an example of a non-Catholic power developing almost as a central European monarchy.[7]

Throughout his reign Bolesław maintained good relations with the Teutonic Order and with Poland. His conversion to Orthodoxy was a fundamental part of the agreement which established him as prince in 1324. However as early as 1327, it was bruited about that he was contemplating a return to the Catholic faith of his Mazovian father.[8] This western-looking policy, combined with dubious devotion to the Rus'ian Church came to a head in the late 1330s. In 1338 he joined the triple alliance of Poland, Hungary and Bohemia. At the Second Congress of Visegrád in June of that year, the fate of the *Regnum Ladomerie* after the death of a childless Bolesław was discussed between the rulers of the central kingdoms. The Congress intended to consolidate an anti-Teutonic policy and resolve the competition between Poland and Hungary (but not Lithuania) for control of south-west Rus'.[9] It may even be as a result of the 'increased friendship' forged at the Congress that Bolesław cooled his relations with the Order.[10] When he presented a charter to his new city of Sanok in January 1339, he appointed a Pole rather than a German or a Rus'ian as judge over *omnem hominem ... sive sit Theuthonicus, Polonus, Ungarus et Ruthenus*.[11] With the probable closure of the southern route to Rus'ian markets, the Order sought the alternative route via Lithuania which we have noted already.[12] The closure of such routes was not only an inconvenience and expense to merchants but it also entailed a severe loss of revenue to the towns which sheltered the merchants travelling to the markets, as contemporary tariff records make clear.[13]

[7] A. Nikžentaitis surveys the problem admirably in 'Lietuvos ir Lenkijos santykiai 1340–1345m. (Pietvakarių Rusios žemių prijungimo prie Lietuvos Didžiosios kunigaikštystės laiko problema)', *Iš Lietuvos istorijos tyrinėjimų* (Vilnius, 1991), 31–6. See especially Knoll, *Rise*, 129–42; Shabul'do, *Zemli*, 37–51 and Paszkiewicz, *Polityka ruska*, 42f.

[8] For relations with the Order see *PU*, II, nos. 537, pp. 361–2 (1325); 582, pp. 387–8 (9.03.1327); 826, pp. 554–5 (11.02.1334). In two letters dated 16 June 1327 John XXII hints to the king of Poland and to Bolesław that it is time for Bolesław to return to the fold with his new people – *VMPL*, nos. 383, 384, p. 299.

[9] *Chronicon Dubnicense*, 128; a letter of Louis the Great of Hungary, dated 4 April 1350 refers to the 1338 agreement against the *cruciferos de Pruscia*, see A. Prochaska, 'W sprawie zajęcia Rusi przez Kazimierza Wielkiego', *KH*, 6 (1892), 31.

[10] *Chronicon Dubnicense*, 128.

[11] *Boleslav'-Iurii*, 77.

[12] See above pp. 257f.

[13] *HU*, III, no. 559, pp. 312–14.

At the same time as political links with Bolesław's western neighbours improved, Bohemian, Polish and German settlers were invited to come to Rus' in company with their Catholic pastors. This situation is familiar from Gediminas' own policies in the 1320s.[14] As a direct result of Bolesław's actions, especially his confidence in officials of non-Rus'ian origin and the inevitable increase in Polish and Bohemian influence this brought to the prince's court – in sharp contrast with the diminished power of the local boiars who thitherto had held unrivalled sway – the Rus'ian nobles murdered Bolesław on 7 April 1340 with a dose of poison so strong that the prince's corpse is alleged to have disintegrated.[15] The boiars justified their crime by claiming that Bolesław had sought to change their religion and customs and even had violated their wives and their purses.[16] Independent attestation of details of Bolesław's activities and assassination is provided by a surprisingly large number of documents of undoubted integrity and annals from Poland, Bohemia and Hungary.[17]

The succession in Rus' became subject to intervention from Poland and Lithuania almost as soon as Bolesław's corpse was cold. Within ten days of the murder, Casimir of Poland invaded southern Rus', *circa festum pasche* (16 April), 1340.[18] This expedition, the first of two, seems to have been a small one intended to rescue Polish migrants from attack in Lviv and perhaps save Bolesław's widow from sharing her husband's fate. Eufemia was

[14] Bolesław invites foreigners – see *Boleslav'-Iurii*, 77–9. The effects of this was such that 'cum numerum et ritum Latinorum illic multiplicasset et hoc Ruthenis displicuisset' – *Chronik Johanns*, 184. On Gediminas' policy see above pp. 203f.

[15] 'Rocznik Traski' (*MPH* II, 860) records how Bolesław mistreated his subjects and introduced foreigners among them, including Bohemians and Germans. Jan Czarnkowski says that he was poisoned 'qui legem et fidem immutare nitebatur' – *MPH*, II, 620. A similar tale of the increase in Catholic settlers is told by John of Winterthur – *Chronik Johanns*, 184. Detail of the strength of poison, *ibid.*. Traska dates the murder to 1340 'circa festum annunciationis Beate Marie' and the 'Rocznik Poznański', *MPH*, n.s. VI (Warsaw, 1962), 130 gives 7 April. The independence of these two sources encourages belief in the April date. For the power of the boiars in Galich in the thirteenth century, see I. P. Krip'iakevich, *Galits'ko-Volins'kie kniazivstvo* (Kiev, 1984), 50–1, 111–15 and 124–5. Cf. the number of boiars who witnessed the charters cited above n. 8 and *PU*, II, no. 157, p. 108–9 (1316).

[16] *MPH*, II, 860; III, 199.

[17] 'Rocznik Traski'; Jan Czarnkowski; František of Prague and Beneš of Weitmile – see below; John of Winterthur; John of Victring – *Fontes rerum Germanicarum*, I, ed. J. F. Boehmer (Stuttgart, 1843); 'Spomniki Płockie', *MPH*, III, 119; 'Rodowód Xiążąt polskich', *MPH*, III, 284; 'Rocznik małopolski', *MPH*, III, 199; Benedict XII's Bull of 29 April, 1341 to the bishop of Kraków – *VMPL*, no. 566, p. 434.

[18] *MPH*, II, 860.

not only Gediminas' daughter, she was also Casimir's sister-in-law. Polish sources emphasise the family ties between Casimir and the dead prince and his wife.[19] Left to her own devices in Rus', Eufemia might have become the focus of loyalty for the leaderless boiars. She was murdered in 1342 in Poland, perhaps for a similar reason;[20] to the Rus'ians who murdered her, Eufemia may have appeared to be a Polish collaborator. Within a month of setting out from Kraków, Casimir returned to Poland with the Polish merchants, Catholic citizens and a large part of the Rus'ian treasury, including crowns and a throne, all of which the king had liberated from Lviv.[21] On 24 June he marched back to Rus' with a much larger army which included Mazovian soldiers who were sent presumably from Bolesław's father and uncle. Their participation in this campaign may have provoked a Lithuanian attack on Mazovia later in 1340.[22] The Polish army withdrew after four weeks, once Casimir had exchanged oaths of loyalty with the local boiars and their leader, Dmitry D'iadko. The exact nature of this mutually advantageous pact has not been preserved. Certainly within a few months Casimir was pleading for a dispensation from Pope Benedict XII to release him from his promises to D'iadko. From what we learn in the papal acknowledgement of Casimir's plea, the agreement with D'iadko was far from completely in Poland's favour. It reads more as a mutual alliance rather than a subjugation of Rus'. In return for 'certain services and duties', the Polish king promised to extend protection to D'iadko and his people, preserving their religion, laws and customs.[23]

Little is known of Dmitry D'iadko. He had been the most powerful Rus'ian boiar of Bolesław's court, appearing in major Rus'ian agreements with the Order in 1334 and 1335, but it is notable that in 1339 he does not appear to have retained this

[19] *Ibid.*, 626–7. Czarnkowski treats both attacks as one, but this is incorrect. Victring and Winterthur cite Eufemia as an excuse for the campaign. For Eufemia see above p. 224.

[20] Drowned by Rus'ians beneath the ice on the Vistula near Zawichost (in south-eastern Poland on the route from Lithuania/Rus' to Sandomierz) according to a tomb inscription described by Narbutt and cited by Hrushevsky, *Istoria*, III, 139.

[21] *MPH*, II, 860.

[22] *Ibid.* and 626–7; Lithuanian assault on Mazovia on 8 September 1340 in *Długosz*, IX, 217.

[23] *MPH*, II, 861; *VMPL*, no. 566, p. 434: 'rex et capitaneus atque gens certa conventiones et pacta cum certis servitiis et subjectionibus eidem regi exhibendis concorditer *invicem* inierunt. Inter que quidem conventiones et pacta prefatus rex prestito juramento promisit, quod capitaneum et gentem predictos in omnibus tueri debebat, ipsosque in eorum ritibus, juribus et consuetudinibus conservare'.

prominence at a court where Poles and Germans now dominated.[24] However Dmitry was powerful enough to pursue his own ambitions after Bolesław's death. He styles himself *provisor seu capitaneus terre Russie*,[25] a title which is rendered best by the English 'protector'. The usual Russian translation of *capitaneus*, *namestnik* implies subjection to a higher authority. In his dealings with Polish, Teutonic and Hungarian merchants in 1340 and 1344 D'iadko refers to his predecessors, by whom he clearly means recent princes of Galich–Volyn', and the *dominus* he cites is the dead Bolesław.[26] His main fort was Peremyshl', whence he controlled perhaps the whole of Galich.[27] Polish historians like to make him out as subject to Casimir, but this is not the case. The Polish king was right to mistrust the alliance (*unio*)[28] he had made with the Rus'ian.

In the winter of 1340/41, as a result of D'iadko's reporting the potential loss of tribute to the khan, the Tatars attacked Lublin in south-eastern Poland, probably with Lithuanian help.[29] Is it possible then that D'iadko was the representative of the Lithuanians? It is unclear how much of southern Rus' was seized by the Lithuanians at this time. It is known that Liubartas Gediminaitis gained Volyn' (and her chief city, Vladimir Volynsky) soon after Bolesław's death and in 1347 he was addressed by the emperor of Constantinople, John VI Kantakuzenos as *reks Volodimirou*.[30] However it is far from certain that the references to Galich in the emperor's discussion of the hierarchy of *Mikra Rhōsia* (Little Rus', that is Galich–Volyn') can be understood as pertaining to

[24] *PU*, II, no. 826, p. 555; III.1 no. 28, p. 19; Sanok – *Boleslav'-Iurii*, 77.

[25] *PU*, III.1, no. 415, pp. 284–5. The date of this charter for Torunian merchants to come to Lviv is unknown, but given references to recent killings in the city, it is probably from 1340 or 1341.

[26] He mentions charters given 'per nostros felicis recordacionis predecessores, reges et principes' in the Toruń document – *ibid.*, 285 and refers to the death of his *dominus*. When Louis the Great wrote to him on 20 April 1344, the Hungarian refers to *loca tributorum vestrorum*, implying that D'iadko is in a position to exact dues – *Boleslav'-Iurii*, 79.

[27] *MPH*, II, 627.

[28] *unio* used with reference to Poland and D'iadko's Rus' does not mean union but alliance – cf. *PU*, II, no. 826, p. 554 with III, no. 415, p. 284. Nikžentaitis points this out in 'Lietuvos ir Lenkijos', 33. See also Paszkiewicz, *Polityka ruska*, 71–88; Shabul'do, *Zemli*, 38f.

[29] *VMPL*, no. 566, p. 434; *MPH*, II, 627.

[30] *MPH*, II, 629; *MM*, I, 265. Nikžentaitis ('Lietuvos ir Lenkijos', 35) follows Shabul'do (*Zemli*, 40) in interpreting this Byzantine text as proof of Liubartas' control of all Galich–Volyn'. This is not clear since the text refers to the ecclesiastical province of Little Russia which covers the whole area and mentions Galich *nominatim* but carefully styles Liubartas as prince of Vladimir and not Galitzes. Note also the entry in *NL*, 361 for the Polish attack of 1349 which refers to Volyn', not Galich.

Liubartas' lands. After all, the boundaries of Byzantine ecclesiastical provinces frequently included several political entities. It may be that Liubartas enjoyed the support or alliance of D'iadko in Galich while D'iadko maintained his own policy between Poland and the Lithuanian.[31] There is no unambiguous evidence available for the history of southern Rus' at this time and almost all of our information is derived from foreign sources. The inscription on the bell in the Church of St George in Lviv in 1341 which refers to 'prince Dmitry' (Liubartas' Christian name too) may refer (flatteringly) to D'iadko.[32] The favourite quotation of Lithuanian historiography taken from Jan Czarnkowski to the effect that after Bolesław's murder, Liubartas 'eundem ducatum Russiae possidebat' is usually shorn of the qualifying phrase, 'quem rex Kazimirus anno domini MCCCXLIX cum exercitu forti ingrediens, obtinuit ex integro cum omnibus civitatibus et castris'.[33] This implies that in fact Liubartas held only Volyn' from his base in Lutsk, since Długosz, the only source for events of 1349, describes Casimir's conquest of Volynian cities in that year.[34] It was Vladimir Volynsky which was given as Liubartas' patrimony in the account of Gediminas' will of 1341/42 in the Lithuanian chronicles and Vladimir which the emperor uses in Liubartas' style.[35] D'iadko appears in the sources for the last time in 1344.[36]

Whether Poland or Lithuania or no one conquered Galich between 1344 and 1349 cannot be told. The best we can surmise is that after Bolesław was murdered, southern Rus' was invaded by the Poles and the Lithuanians and subsequently divided between Liubartas and D'iadko, of whom the latter made an alliance with Casimir. D'iadko managed to play off the Poles, Lithuanians and the Tatars for some time. When D'iadko disappears from the scene after 1344, the conflict between Casimir and Liubartas is renewed, ending in the Lithuanian control of Volyn' after two major campaigns in 1349 and 1351. The sources are too sparse to allow any safe embroidery upon this basic cloth.[37]

The Bohemian accounts of the death of Bolesław-Yury II have been the subject of heated debate in Lithuanian and western

[31] *MM*, I, 265–6. On D'iadko between Lithuania and Poland see Meyendorff, *Byzantium*, 64.

[32] *Boleslav'-Iurii*, 79, 121–2.

[33] 'he possessed the same duchy as King Casimir entered in 1349 with his strong army and gained in its entirety with all its towns and castles' – *MPH*, II, 629.

[34] *Długosz*, IX, 254–5.

[35] See below p. 280.

[36] Last noted in Louis of Hungary's letter – see above n. 26.

[37] Shabul'do, *Zemli*, 50 and *AZR*, I, no. 1, p. 1.

scholarship in recent years since the Vilnius scholar, Alvydas Nikžentaitis argued that the account of (the unnamed) Bolesław's violent death given by Beneš of Weitmile referred not to the Rus'ian, but to Gediminas.[38] Two main questions arise from this controversy: when did Gediminas die and what was the Bohemian contribution to the Franciscan mission to Lithuania?

Gediminas died in the winter of 1341/42 of causes unknown. This is all we learn of the event from reliable Rus'ian sources,[39] but even this brief notice contrasts sharply with the anonymity of Vytenis' death. By 1341 the fate of Lithuanian grand dukes was considered worthy of some note. The Novgorodian Chronicle informs us that Gediminas died in the year 6849, that is between 1 March 1341 and 28 February 1342. A closer date cannot be adduced with great certainty. However it is the case that in Rus'ian sources which mention the death of the grand duke, Gediminas is recorded after Khan Uzbek who died in the same year. If the order of events reflects actual chronology rather than hierarchical considerations (Uzbek being a more important figure in Rus'ian life than the Lithuanian ruler) then the winter (January–March) of 1342 is a more probable date for Gediminas' death. We know from Arabic chronicles that the Tatar khan died in (March) 1342.[40] As to the cause of the grand duke's demise, we may deduce from the silence of Prussian and Polish sources that Gediminas was not killed in battle with the crusaders; such an achievement would have been noted widely by the crusaders' annalists. In 1390 Grand Duke Vytautas noted what happened after his grandfather 'was lost' – *vorloren* – a euphemism for death which involves no hint of violence.[41] The report in *NL* uses the verb *umreti* ('to die') which

[38] E. Gudavičius, 'Kas žuvo 1337m. prie Bajerburgo?', *LMADA*, 89 (1984), 92–9; and 'Ką reiškė 'ugninė ietis' (*telum igneum*) Vygando kronikoje', *Lietuvos Istorijos Metraštis* (1984), 78–80; A. Nikžentaitis, 'Lietuvos diplomatinė kova su Vokiečių Ordinu 1337–1342m.', *Lietuvos Istorijos Metraštis* (1986), 5–20; and, 'Dar kartą', 31–43. Rowell, 'Lithuania', 303–11, 315–16.

[39] *NL*, 353; *PSRL*, XXV, 173. It is clear that Gediminas' death is always recorded in Rus'ian chronography after that of Uzbek, the Tatar khan.

[40] The historians Ibn Khaldun and Ibn Duqmaq record Uzbek as dying in AH 742, that is between AD 17.06.1341 and 05.06.1342 – Tiesenhausen, I, 388, 528. Al Melik en-Nasir cites the month of Shevval, 742, that is 10 March–7 April 1342 – *ibid.*, 254. B.Spuler, *Die Goldene Horde. Die Mongolen in Russland*, 2nd edn (Wiesbaden, 1965), 98 prefers late 1341. The chronology for the death in Nikžentaitis, 'Dar kartą', 34 is based on his reading of Beneš which we cannot hold.

[41] *Dis ist Witoldes sache wedir Jagaln und Skargaln*, *SRP*, II, 712. *Verlieren* means the same in modern German: to have no more because of death or accident – *Brockhaus Wahrig Deutsches Wörterbuch*, VI (Stuttgart, 1984), 517.

likewise has no overtones of violence. It is a bland word that provokes interest only by contrast with the euphemisms of 'passing over' which are employed in the same chronicle to denote the fate of Christians.[42] The Bohemian source which has been used with reference to Bolesław in historiography for more than eighty years deserves close scrutiny.

Beneš' *Chronicon ecclesie pragensis* was composed in Prague some time after 1355 and on the whole it is a reliable, albeit far from infallible, record of events concerning Bohemia and eastern Europe. It falls into two parts, the first of which deals with the years 1284–1346. The source which Beneš used in compiling this part of his chronicle was the Chronicle of František of Prague which is still extant, although the version available to Beneš is not identical with the redaction we have today; it was more expansive. On occasion Beneš copied František's text verbatim into his own work, although more often he provides a précis of his model. Details from personal knowledge of contemporary events sometimes find their way into the chronicle, for Beneš, far from being a cloistered scholar, was a trusted servant in the household of Emperor Charles IV, whose *Autobiography* is the major source behind the second half of Beneš' work.[43] In the case of events of 1341, just how heavily Beneš relies on František can be discerned by comparing the two authors:

František	*Beneš*
A. D. .MCCCXLI. [The Tatars invade Poland]... Alia causa est propter terram Rutenorum, quam pridem debellaverat et devastaverat rex Polonie propter ducem terre prefate qui erat de ipsius prosapia oriundus quem intoxi-	Anno Domini M° CCCXLI°. Kazymirus rex Polonie habuit gwerram cum Ruthenis et Lytwanis infidelibus qui venerant ad occupandum regnum et terras Polonie et deo propicio recesserunt post tempus breve.

42 Cf. accounts of Kalita's death (*prestavisia*) with those of Uzbek Khan the Mohammedan and Gediminas the Pagan – *NL*, 351, 353. On the use of the euphemism see G. D'iachenko, *Polny tserkovno-slovianskii slovar'*, I (Moscow, 1899), 491.

43 Beneš of Weitmile, *Chronicon ecclesie pragensis*, ed. J. Emler, *FRB*, IV, 490. For the date of composition see J. Loserth, 'Die Chronik des Benesch Krabice von Weitmühl. Beitrag zur Kritik derselben', *Archiv für österreichische Geschichte*, 53 (1875), 314. Further analysis is provided along with a modern Czech translation in *Kroniky Doby Karla IV* (Prague, 1987), 204, 567–71. Cf. with František of Prague, *Cronica pragensis*, *FRB*, IV, 430 and *Kroniky*, 131, 564–7. See also J. Zachová, *Die Chronik des Franz von Prag – Inhaltliche und stilistische Analyse*, *Acta Universitatis Carolinae*, *Philologica Monographia*, LIII (1974), 13–14 and L. P. Lapteva, *Pis'mennye istochniki po istorii Chekhii perioda feodalizma (do 1848 goda)* (Moscow, 1985), 63.

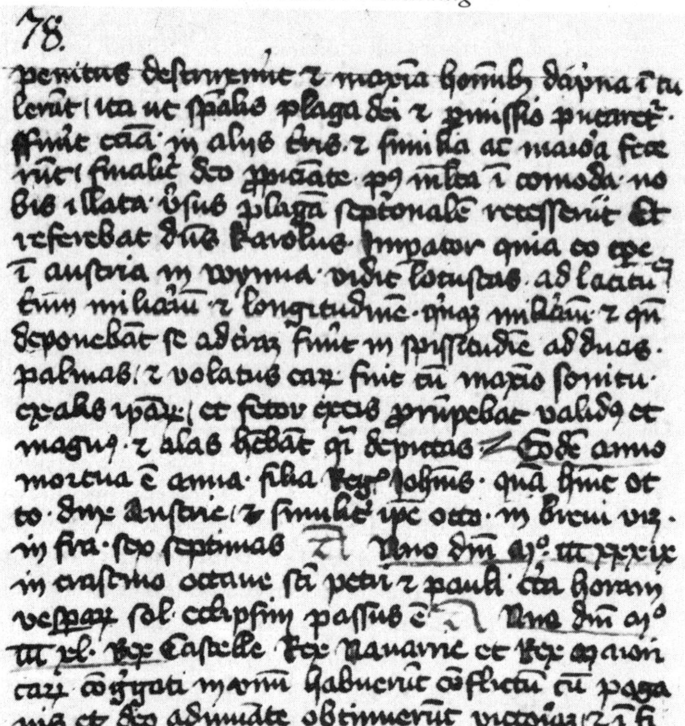

Fig. 5. Beneš of Weitmile, *Chronicon ecclesie pragensis*, AD 1340–41. Prague, Knihovna metropolitní Kapituly, MS. H6/3 fol. 39v. (22 × 15 cm, parchment, 1380–1410). Photo: Prague, Archiv Pražského Hradu.

catum nobiles dicte terre morti tradiderunt. Qui quidem dux zelo ductus fidei orthodoxe accersiri jussit fidei katholice sacerdotes et de diversis terris in sacra scriptura viros eruditos, volens germen vere fidei et vineam domini Sabaoth plantare et exstirpare scismaticum errorem Ruthenorum, qui nolentes relinquere sectam eorum ducem veneno necantes, Christianos ferro, igne, aqua aliisque modis variis extinxerunt.[44]

Eodem anno dux Luthwanorum accersiri fecerat ad se Christi sacerdotes et christianos plurimos, cupiens tandem christiana fide inbui.

Sui hoc considerantes ipsum ducem veneno intoxicarunt.[45]

Beneš' text is a clear condensing of the more detailed description given by František. There is nothing in Beneš which is not in his model except the reference to the Rus'ians and Lithuanians which fails to include the Tatars in the raid on Poland in 1341. The text of Beneš is given above from the sole surviving, but non-autograph manuscript which is kept in Prague Castle (see fig. 5). Emler, in his 1885 edition confuses the reader by printing the second half of Beneš' entry for 1341 in a different type from the rest, thus obscuring the reliance of the whole entry on František. He also gives an ambiguous reading of $\hat{X}$ *sacerdotes* which may be legitimately misinterpreted as *decem sacerdotes*, as it is by Nikžentaitis.[46] The abbreviation without the *due punti* which are added by this scribe when he gives a numeral has lent the impression that Beneš knew more about the 'Lithuanian' mission than František. $\hat{X}$ here is the normal abbreviation of *Christi*, as it is

[44] *FRB*, IV, 430, 'Another reason [for the Tatar invasion] is the land of the Rus'ians which the king of Poland had attacked and ravaged some good time before on account of the duke of the said land. The nobles poisoned him and he was of the king's line. For this duke, inspired by zeal for the true faith commanded priests of the Catholic faith and men from diverse lands learned in sacred writ to be summoned, wishing to plant the seed of true faith and the vineyard of the Lord, and root out the schismatic error of the Rus'ians. The latter, refusing to abandon their sect, killed the duke with poison and destroyed the Christians by the sword ['by iron'], fire, water and other various means.'

[45] 'In the year of the Lord 1341, King Casimir of Poland made war with the Rus'ians and pagan Lithuanians who had come to invade the kingdom and lands of Poland, and through God's favour they retreated after a short time ... That same year the duke of the Lus'ians had caused to be summoned to him priests of Christ and more Christians, for he wanted finally to be imbued with the Christian faith ... Considering this, his own men poisoned the duke himself with poison' – *FRB*, IV, 490 re-edited from the manuscript: Prague Castle, *Knihovna metropolitní Kapituly*, H 6/3, f.39v (= p. 78).

[46] Nikžentaitis, 'Lietuvos diplomatinė', 17.

on page 81 of the manuscript. As often is the case in central European descriptions of the East, Christian is taken as synonymous with Catholic and pagan with Orthodox. Further confusion is spread by the scribe's misunderstanding of the piece. He conflates *Ruthenorum* with *Lytwanorum* to produce *Luthwanorum*. The mistake is easily made. However elsewhere in the manuscript when the two forms do not appear within the same few lines, the form for Lithuanian is always *Lyt*wanus.[47] The linguistic coincidences of the two texts (especially *accersiri* which is much rarer than *vocari*) underline the connection. *Christianos plurimos* is a welcome shortening of the rather pompous reference in František to 'men from diverse lands, learned in sacred writ'. Several other Polish sources confirm the westernisation policy of Bolesław-Yury II and the ill-feeling this aroused in his Rus'ian boiars. There is no reason for believing that this murder of a Rus'ian by boiars fearing Catholic infiltration really refers to Gediminas. Indeed the year of the account adds to this. František alone of the other sources which deal with Bolesław's murder dates the event to 1341 rather than 1340. In fact František dates the Tatar invasion of Poland to 1341 (as do the others) and flashes back to its cause: Casimir's intervention in Rus' 'some good time earlier' (*pridem*) after the murder of the local prince. As he condenses the longer account, Beneš maintains the causation (the pluperfect of *fecerat* explains the earlier reference to war) but allows the date of the murder to be misconstrued. The apparent coincidence of the *annus Domini* date given here, 1341 (which refers to the war, not to the cause of it, a murder), with the *annus mundi* 6849 recorded for the death of Gediminas is not strong enough to require the changing of what is known for sure about the Rus'ian into a hypothesis relevant to Gediminas since Gediminas may well have died in the spring of AD 1342.

The alleged invitation to Catholic priests (known with respect to Bolesław) presents a problem to historians of Gediminian Lithuania. Far from wishing to attempt a conversion to Catholicism for the second time in his life, Gediminas in 1340 was faced with a problem posed by over-zealous Catholic clergy. The 1324 rejection of baptism was not overturned in the 1340s. Even so we must look again at the aftermath of that rejection. For some time scholars have presumed that silence means absence and that the

[47] *FRB*, IV, 480, 495, 505, 511. Dr Mažeika has drawn attention to the frequency of these forms.

odd whisper of a source is a mere hallucination. This at least is the case with the Franciscan mission in Lithuania after the débâcle of 1324 and before the restoration of 1387. In fact there is considerable evidence that the friars remained in Vilnius throughout the fourteenth century. They maintained their *hospitium* hard by the grand-ducal residence. Here the Franciscans preached to merchants and acted as state secretaries for relations with Catholic powers. We learn of their continued presence from occasional martyrdoms (1341, 1369). When the friars forgot their remit and began to preach against the pagan religion publicly in defiance of a grand-ducal command, they were punished severely. The same is true of Orthodox Christians who refused to support the *status quo*. We have in mind the martyrdoms of 1340, a time of stalemate in the Teutonic crusade and hardly a moment to threaten the peace of the multi-national community in Vilnius, and 1369–70 when five Franciscans and three Orthodox laymen were executed in separate incidents for public defiance of the pagan order during a critical phase in Algirdas' wars against Moscow and the Order when conformity was regarded as conducive to loyalty to the regime.[48]

Around 1339–40, as we learn from the Franciscan *Chronica XXIV Generalium*, two friars of the Bohemian province made their way to Vilnius fired with zeal to preach the Gospel.[49] We cannot discover where Martin de Ahd (or Alto) came from but his confrère Ulrich was from the village of Odlochovice to the south-south-east of Prague. Unfortunately the records of Bohemian Franciscan friaries are far from well preserved and thus far have offered no help with fourteenth-century prosopography.[50]

48 For martyrs of 1340 see below; for 1369–70 see Rowell, 'Lithuania', 311–13 where the *L3* Franciscans are linked with a martyrology of Bartholomew of Pisa. Nikžentaitis connected the *L3* account with 1340, in my view mistakenly – 'Lietuvos diplomatinė', 10–14. Both he and the present author seek a western source for *L3* but Bartholomew is the most convincing – see also A. Nikžentaitis, 'Legenda XIVv. o muchenichestve 14 frantsiskantsev v Vil'niuse i istoricheskaia istina', *Vspomogatel'nye istoricheskie distsipliny*, 21 (1990), 257–69. For the Orthodox martyrs of *c.* 1370 and a convincing redating from the convention of 1347 see Mažeika, 'The relations', 77–84.

49 'Passio Fratrum Ulrici de Adlechonvitz et Martini de Ahd', *Chronica XXIV Generalium*, *Analecta Franciscana* [*AF*], III (Quaracchi, 1910), 535–6. It was composed for the most part before 1369 (*ibid.*, viii).

50 A variant reading of *Alto* tempts an interpretation of Vyšehrad, Altum Castrum, in Prague but cannot be substantiated. Of Bohemian mss. one can say only that there are occasional letters in *Codex diplomaticus Moraviae* but these are no use in the identification of members of specific friaries. On the Order in Bohemia in general see J. Svátek, *Organisace reholních istitucí v českých zemích a péce o jejich archivy* (Prague, 1966) and J. Hájek, 'Bracia mnieszi w Czechach i na Morawach w XIII–XIV wieku', *Zakony franciszkańskie*, 263–6.

When the friars arrived in Vilnius, they lived at the Franciscan *hospitium*, a house with a long history dating back before the papal legation of 1324. It was while Martin was celebrating Mass *in loco fratrum* that Ulrich took up a cross and went out into the market place to preach against the heathens. The townsfolk were enraged, seized Ulrich and brought him before Gediminas. In the grand duke's presence the friar refused to apostasise in accordance with Gediminas' command, thereby causing the irate duke to sentence him to death. Gediminas then sent for Ulrich's companion and asked him why he had come to Vilnius. Martin replied that he had come to show Gediminas and his people the error of their ways and to preach to them the one true God. This frankness was rewarded with consignment to gaol. Meanwhile Ulrich was tortured and killed, his body being tossed into the river to float downstream to crusader territory *pour décourager les autres*, as it were. Gediminas now turned his attention to Martin and sought in vain to persuade him to abjure. The friar died under torture and his body was left for the dogs to devour. Gediminas' 'sister', however, 'a Christian nun albeit a schismatic', saved the body and buried it in her monastery.[51]

It is clear that the initiative for the mission lay at least with the friars themselves and not with Gediminas. Ulrich and Martin did not say that their mission was requested by Gediminas. This contrasts sharply with the avowal of the papal missionaries in a public audience with Gediminas in 1324 that the grand duke had summoned them.[52] Christians were not afraid to attribute a mission to the grand duke himself, if such were the case. Before Ulrich's public denunciation of the heathens, the Franciscans had practised their faith in private (and among foreign merchants) and unimpeded by Gediminas. The grand duke seems not to have been worried by their particular presence. After these two died the other Franciscans in Vilnius continued to man the *hospitium* – until the next outburst of rash preaching in 1369 when the same fate awaited five more friars.[53] Enflamed public preaching against

[51] *AF*, III, 536. Who this sister was is difficult to tell. She could be a daughter of Pukuveras who married a Rus'ian and spent her widowhood in Vilnius or even the wife of one of Gediminas' brothers.

[52] *GL*, 123–5.

[53] The existence of the 1369 martyrs should not be doubted for the story is to be found in a trustworthy, almost contemporary chronicle (Rowell, 'Lithuania', 312–13). Since we hear of the death of individual friars but never of the expulsion of the Order *en*

local tradition and the refusal of the monks to abjure publicly, in accordance with grand-ducal commands, led to their martyrdom. In this case Gediminas was not only involved with threats to his realm from southern Rus' and Prussia, he was also considering how best to hand power over to his heirs.

The case of Ulrich and Martin has aroused considerable interest in recent years not only as part of an alleged scenario where Gediminas attempts to introduce Catholicism into Lithuania in 1341–42 and is murdered as a result, but also because of the provenance of the martyrs of 1341. Noting the Bohemian origins of the friars in question, Nikžentaitis proposed an explanation of close links between Bohemia and Lithuania, probably from as early as the Bohemian crusade in Lithuania in 1329, which he interprets as evidence of John's desire to bring the pagan realm within the Bohemian sphere of influence.[54] After all, the friars we meet in Vilnius in 1324 are from Riga, that is the Saxon Province of the Franciscans. The change appears significant.

The theory that the Bohemians showed any interest in Lithuania other than as a place where Christian and, more especially, chivalric duty could find its expression in warfare is an interesting hypothesis. However surely King John fought in Lithuania as he did in Spain and no more sought hegemony for himself (rather than the Order) in Lithuania than he coveted the emirates of Cordoba and Granada. The Bohemian chronicler Petr Žitavski reports how John sought to go deeper into pagan lands than any other prince and took poets (the medieval equivalent of advertising agents) with him *ut communis omnium hominum preconizat fama.*[55] The discrete facts that in 1324 Gediminas' adviser Brother Nicholas suggested a Bohemian or Hungarian alliance to his master in lieu of the connection with Frederick of Riga and that the Franciscans of 1340–41 were of Bohemian provenance cannot alone or even with amplification support such an explanation. Gediminas did choose a more effective ally, but he was Łokietek of

masse, it seems justified to consider a small community to have been resident throughout the period. The Franciscans were well-liked by the pagans. Casimir of Poland informed Pope Innocent VI in a supplication of 27 July 1360 how 'ad Minorum predicationem infideles eis contigui maiorem devotionem habere videntur', Vatican, Archivio Segreto, *Reg. Suppl.*, 33 ff., 200^{r}-202^{v} (*MPV*, no. 393, pp. 371–2).

[54] A. Nikžentaitis, 'Dėl čekų feodalų vaidmens 1329m. Vokiečių ordino žygyje į Lietuvą', *LMADA*, 104 (1988), 52–5.

[55] *FRB*, III, 352, 364; IV, 480, 495, 505. Plan for Granada – see above p. 240, n. 51.

Poland. It would be more useful to examine the failure of 1324 more closely.

Despite King John's lack of a Lithuanian 'policy', Nikžentaitis is undoubtedly correct to smell a Bohemian rat behind the 'mission' of 1340. However the Bohemians themselves as monks chose to go to Lithuania and, while in a perfectly safe private *hospitium* connected with the royal castle, they chose to preach the Gospel to the unconverted. The *éminence grise* behind their enthusiasm was probably none other than the archbishop of Riga.

Historians usually lose interest in Frederick in 1325, after he returns from Livonia to the Curia, never to regain his archdiocese. Nevertheless Frederick did not wither away; he was not in fact the ecclesiastical has-been whom scholarship neglects. He continued an active but unsuccessful campaign against his old enemy, the Teutonic Order. Throughout the 1330s he still attempted to sway papal opinion against the Order. In 1335–36 a certain Brother Ulrich wrote a long 'letter' of 312 folios to Pope Benedict XII explaining how the Order was like unto Noah's ark and a very good thing. He prefaced this allegorical tract with a plea to the Pope to instruct the Rigan prelate to make peace with the Order and cease spreading tales against it.[56] The archbishop then was actively opposing the Order as he had in the 1320s.

Frederick von Pernstein is often disguised by the appearance of his name. He was not a Livonian and certainly not a German; his family came from Dubraunik in Moravia and his kinsmen included high-ranking officials in the cathedral in Prague.[57] Frederick was also a Franciscan of the Bohemian province. John XXII who had a horror of unemployed prelates, appears to have tired of the Rigan archbishop's fruitless presence in the curia and so posted him abroad. From 1319 to 1337 Frederick acted as executor of papal provisions for the Church in Bohemia, overseeing the appointment of his nephew Dirslaus to the Prague archdiaconate.[58] In

[56] Biblioteca Apostolica Vaticana, *Codex Ottobonus*, 528. For partial transcription of Ulrich's preface and discussion of the date of the MS, see Mažeika and Rowell '*Zelatores maximi*' Excursus §6. The author expressed his fear for the destruction of the Order: *interitum propter episcopatus inpedimentum* (fol. 5).

[57] *Codex diplomaticus et epistolaris Moraviae*, VI (Brünn, 1854), no. 451, p. 346 and K. Forstreuter, 'Erzbischof', 653. Nephew in Prague Cathedral – John XXII, *Lettres communes*, ed. Mollat, no. 8823. For details of Frederick's life and activity, see Mažeika and Rowell '*Zelatores maximi*'.

[58] In Bohemia: 1327 – John XXII, *Lettres communes*, ed. Mollat, nos. 28193, 29459, 30180, 30181 and *Regesta diplomatica Bohemiae et Moraviae*, ed. J. Emler, III (Prague, 1890) no. 1355, p. 531; in 1329 – John XXII, *Lettres communes*, ed. Mollat, nos. 43779, 47798; 1330 – nos. 49356, 50007; 1332–34 – nos. 58642, 61378, 61380, 62587; Benedict XII,

1337 he supervised the appointment of Hermann, warden of the diocese of Prague, to the bishopric of Warmia in Prussia, presumably in an attempt to restore balance to the chapter of a see which the Knights controlled.[59] The pieces of our Vilnius jigsaw are surely falling into place. The archbishop patronised the clergy of the sees of Prague and Olomouc and set about amassing lands and lordships in Bohemia to support him. In 1342 his successor in Livonia, Engelbert found it necessary to travel to Prague to redeem the revenues which were owed to the archbishopric there.[60]

Frederick always sought to regain his lost province and encouraged opposition to the Order. The best opponent of the Order remained Gediminas. Frederick was sincerely interested in the conversion of his erstwhile pagan allies and no doubt encouraged idealistic friars among his countrymen to take up the torch for Christ among the infidel. It was surely he or his example that inspired his zealous confrères from Bohemia to try their hand in the Lithuanian soul-harvest. As for Gediminas, he encouraged Franciscans in Vilnius to serve foreign trade missions and compose letters for him. It is understandable that he would not discourage his feckless ally although he had no doubt long given up on Frederick as a credible ally in the battle with the Order. We wonder whether it was the influence of Frederick on King John which led to an unusually mild treatment of the pagans during the *Reise* of 1328–29. It was at this time that Frederick first acted as papal representative in Prague.[61] After the troublemakers Ulrich and Martin were put to death, life in the Franciscan *hospitium* in Vilnius probably carried on much as before. The friars were put to death after a long investigation. We might even surmise that Gediminas finally executed the unrepentant troublemakers after he learned that their patron, his erstwhile ally, Frederick had died in France.[62]

Lettres communes, ed. J. M. Vidal, 3 vols. (Paris, 1903–11) nos. 281 (1335), 4100 (1337) and 6823 (1339).

59 For Hermann's appointment see *VMPL*, no. 526 dated 3 December 1337. In Riga he lent money to the Dominicans to maintain their preaching: Vatican, Archivio Segreto, RV 136, f.13^{v}, no. 25.

60 Letter of Bishop John of Olomouc concerning Archbishop Engelbert's quest for Frederick's dues – *Codex diplomaticus et epistolaris Moraviae*, VII.1, no. 586, p. 430, 7 February 1345. Frederick had also lent money to his nephew Dirslaus – *Regesta diplomatica Bohemiae et Moraviae*, ed. J. Emler, IV (Prague, 1892), no. 2205.

61 For Frederick and Bohemia at the time of the *Reise* see above n. 58.

62 Frederick died in 1341 – Forstreuter, 'Erzbischof', 661. For Avignon see Benedict XII's bull appointing Engelbert to Riga, 18 October 1341 – *VMPL*, no. 436.

Gediminas died a pagan, maintaining, as far as can be told, his established policies. In the hope of preserving the unity of the Grand Duchy, he divided his realm between his seven sons. To the eldest, Manvydas, he bequeathed Kernavė[63] and Slonim, to Narimantas, Pinsk and to Algirdas, Krėva and Vitebsk. Algirdas had gained Vitebsk many years earlier by dint of his marriage to the local heiress and it was here that he based his power in the late 1330s. Novgorodok was given to Karijotas-Mikhail. Vilnius and the title of grand duke of Lithuania was to be the lot of Gediminas' middle son Jaunutis, whilst Trakai and the 'grand' duchy of Žemaitija were reserved for Kestutis. Liubartas' hold on Vladimir Volynsky after the death of Bolesław and his rights to that territory which he had gained by marriage and main force were apparently so strong that Gediminas did not consider it necessary to grant this son any additional patrimony. Gediminas' daughters are not all recorded here and no portion is marked out for any of them. In their widowhood the Gediminaitės retained the *dotalicium* which they received on marriage.

The account of how Gediminas divided his realm between his sons finds its way into all redactions of the Lithuanian Chronicle and all genealogical treatises which deal with the Gediminids. From these, it is clear that Gediminas' hold on extra-Lithuanian lands within the Grand Duchy was strongest in Black and White Rus' and that Rus'ian cities provided most of his bequests.[64] Two sons were endowed with purely Lithuanian lands (Vilnius and Trakai) which bore the *de facto* title of grand duke, while two others received one Lithuanian and one Rus'ian city apiece. These

[63] The Lithuanian Chronicle and the Gediminid genealogies (see n. 64) give Karachev as Manvydas' patrimony. Lithuania did not control Karachev in 1341. Latin versions of this text which were based on an earlier text and translated from Russian for Długosz give Kiernow/Bernow, that is Kernavė. See *Długosz*, X, 92 and *PSRL*, XXXV, 115. For a general essay on Długosz's use of Lithuanian chronicles see J. Radziszewska, 'Przejątki Długosza z "Litewskiego Latopisu"', *Zeszyty Naukowe Uniwersytetu Jagiellońskiego: Prace Historyczne*, 65 (1985), 256–68.

[64] *PSRL*, XXXV, 61, 97, 110, 132–3, 153–4, 181, 201, 222. *PSRL*, XXXII, 138–9. For the genealogies see *PSRL*, XVII, 205, 573, 589, 605, 607–9, 613–14. Gediminas had seven sons (that is seven were alive in 1342) and six daughters (see genealogical table 2). There is no firm evidence, *pace* Nikžentaitis, 'Dar kartą', 35–6, that the father of Yury Vitovtovich who is recorded as prince of Pskov in 1341 and 1349 (*PL*, I, 18, 20) was a son of Gediminas named Vytautas (Vitovt). John of Winterthur, writing *c.* 1348, records that Gediminas had nine children (*novem filios*: *Chronik Johanns*, 203). This may be a mistake for the seven sons or even an accurate record of the nine Gediminaičiai still alive in 1348 – three daughters and one son died before 1348.

Lithuanian cities, Kernavė and Krėva, had previously been closely associated with grand-ducal power. Two of the Gediminids were granted a purely Rus'ian patrimony (Novgorodok and Pinsk). Narimantas' loss of Polotsk where he was prince from *c.* 1335 is not easily explicable. This arrangement of patrimonies is an indication of Gediminas' success in expanding Lithuania's borders so as to reduce the need to segment the original Lithuanian power-base out of viable existence. Such a necessity to provide their many sons with estates had sealed the fate of Gediminas' allies, the princes of Tver'.[65]

Jaunutis and Kestutis who shared out Lithuania proper and Žemaitija were not the oldest of Gediminas' sons. The eldest, as we have seen, inherited Kernavė which had once been Gediminas' own patrimony.[66] Clearly something more than primogeniture was used as a criterion for the succession to the grand-ducal throne. Adherence to paganism was essential, but so was the possession of the confidence of the sibling princes, the Lithuanian pagans and the Lettovian Orthodox. Exactly why Jaunutis was chosen as overlord of the Grand Duchy is unclear, although several unsubstantiated hypotheses have been mooted from 'Jaunutis the beloved son' to 'the compromise between the Lithuanian and Rus'ian Gediminids'.[67] The choice seems strange since during the last years of his reign Gediminas worked closely with his Rus'-based sons Narimantas-Gleb of Polotsk and Algirdas of Vitebsk. It is curious that he did not choose these sons as his successors. It is very probable that the fierce rivalry which existed between these two princes dissuaded Gediminas from risking his empire with them.[68] This is the most likely explanation of Narimantas' removal from the important duchy of Polotsk which had once been in control of Algirdas' city of Vitebsk. The grand duke realised that the prosperity of his realm depended on solid government which alone could dance the knife-edge between East and West, pagan, Catholic and Orthodox. The perils of disunity are evident from the days of Mindaugas and later, from the competition between Vytautas and Jogaila for control of the Grand Duchy in the 1380s.

[65] Fennell, *Emergence*, 225–6.

[66] *PSRL*, XXXV, 95, 151, 179, 199.

[67] Paszkiewicz, *Jagiellonowie*, 358–9.

[68] *Ibid.*, 362. The rivalry must have been deep-seated for Narimantas to have fled so swiftly to the Khan in 1345.

The special cooperation of Jaunutis (who was allied to Narimantas) and Kestutis, a pagan who was popular in Žemaitija (and inclined to favour Algirdas)[69] was an intelligent compromise to the succession problem. The compromise was not necessarily reckless but in the end it pleased no one. Jaunutis was a competent soldier and judging from his later achievements in international treaties as a minor prince, he was a capable service diplomat. However, even with the closest cooperation of Narimantas[70] he could not command the support of Algirdas and Kestutis which was essential to the smooth running of the Grand Duchy. In 1342 the succession game had been dealt out carefully, but it was far from played out. Fortunately for Lithuania, her main enemies, Moscow, the Order and Poland, were also in disarray. The Knights were governed for three years by a grand master who was as despised as he was ineffectual, Ludolf König.

While Vytenis is the successful prologue to Gediminas' greater success, the reign of Jaunutis is treated as a pathetic interlude between the strong national heroes: his father and his brother Algirdas. Even so, the short reign of Jaunutis does allow us to consider how Gediminas and Algirdas succeeded while the intermediary failed.

The abiding image of Jaunutis is of a feckless youth, caught by his brother Kestutis as he succumbed to cold feet, physically and metaphorically, on Vilnius castle hill during a bungled escape bid from a coup d'état. It is very tempting to view this just as history written (or rather, rewritten) by the victors, except that most sources are not Lithuanian and none mention Jaunutis before his removal from power. It is unclear whether Jaunutis ruled with the assistance of his uncles and his mother, the dowager grand-duchess. An interpolation in *L3* suggests that Gediminas' widow died *c.* 1345.[71] This would be an interesting example of the power of the queen mother in pagan Lithuania – the earliest we have, although of course there is the case of the widow of a duke who took part in the 1219 treaty with Galich–Volyn' which comes to mind as an example of local duchesses governing in their deceased

[69] See p. 144 and *PSRL*, XXXV, 61.

[70] 'Y po Hedemana seli na welikom kniazenii na litowskom (*wołynskom* by mistake in ms. following on from a description of Liubartas in Volyn') *dwa welikie kniazi Narymant y Iewnutey*' – *Rod welikich kniazey ruskich otkol rodiszasia*, Czartoryski 2211.iv, p. 64. This manuscript genealogy written in a cursive Polish hand of the sixteenth century is preserved in the Biblioteka Czartoryskich, Kraków. It measures 324 mm × 208 mm.

[71] *PSRL*, XXXII, 138. cf. Paszkiewicz, *Jagiellonowie*, 359.

spouse's stead.[72] After Algirdas died in 1377 his widow, Ul'iana Tverskaia exercised considerable political influence in the Grand Duchy, seeking out suitable marriages in Rus' for her son Jogaila in order to strengthen his claim to grand-ducal power in face of rivalry from his uncle Kestutis and cousin Vytautas. Ul'iana also granted her support to Jogaila's alliances with the Knights.[73]

The deepest impression one gains of east-central Europe in the late 1330s and early 1340s is one of stagnation. Most of the lands with which we have come into contact exhibit some positive features, but general weakness of leadership in politics, economics and religion is undeniable. Polish relations with Lithuania are complex. Apart from war in the south, Casimir seems to have preserved some alliance with the pagans. In 1343 he promised the Knights by the Treaty of Kalisz not to support the Lithuanians against the Order in the ways he and his father had done previously.[74] Casimir's enemies in the Curia reported his connivance with the Lithuanians to the Pope in order to discredit him in his legal battles with the Knights and the Silesian dukes. It seems that in 1344 Casimir employed Hungarian and Lithuanian troops against his kinsmen in Opava in order to remove a little of Silesia from increasing Bohemian influence.[75]

In relations with the Knights and Rus' between 1342 and 1345, Lithuania maintained the *status quo*. Much of this was achieved thanks to the weakness of the Order in the aftermath of Dietrich von Altenburg's death (1341) and the lacklustre grand magistracy of Ludolf König (1342–45). During the first years of the latter's ineffectual leadership, the Livonian natives in Ösel rose up against the Order (1343–45) whilst the Knights, led by the master of Livonia, Burchard von Dreynleven, were raiding Izborsk and Pskov.[76] This opposition was maintained despite several punitive

[72] *PSRL* II, 859 – widow of Plikas, referred to barely as *Plikosova*.

[73] Giedroyć, 'Lithuanian options', 94–8. The text of Jogaila's treaty with the Order concluded in 1382 *mit ... vulbort unser liben Muter Julianne der grossen koniginnen czu Littowen* is given in Raczyński, *Codex*, 58. Note *CDP*, VI, no. 2, p. 2.

[74] Treaty of Kalisz: *PU*, III.2, nos. 567–90, pp. 445–74, esp. no. 568, p. 449 and *VMPL*, no. 581, p. 453.

[75] *VMPL*, no. 604, p. 468; Opava in *FRB*, IV, 495.

[76] *HW*, 71; *Wig.*, 501–2. *PL*, II, 24–6, 93–8. After 1343 the Pskovites fought on without Lithuanian assistance. In 1341 the citizens approached Algirdas in Vitebsk – *PL*, II, 24, 93. Death of Liubko Voinaitis – *NL*, 355, *PL*, II, 96. It is clear that Algirdas undertook these campaigns with Kestutis and his own forces from Vitebsk-Polotsk without direct control from the grand duke. See also *NL*, 353–5. These attacks on the merchant cities of north-western Rus' harm German trade – *LU*, II, no. 809.

campaigns led from Prussia in February 1344 and 1345.[77] In 1342 and 1343 Pskov was defended from Teutonic assault by Algirdas and Kestutis who upheld the Lithuanian interest in the city which had been represented by the otherwise unknown prince, Yury Vitovtovich. Algirdas, although he refused to be baptised and accept the princeship of Pskov, succeeded temporarily in placing his own son, Andrei on the Rus'ian throne. For this purpose Andrei was baptised in 1342.[78] However it seems that Algirdas was more concerned in Lithuanian affairs. A Lithuanian army led by Algirdas and Kestutis made a three-pronged assault on Livonia during the early stages of the native uprising in Ösel (and throughout Estonia and Livonia) in August 1343, ravaging simultaneously Lenewaden, Üxküll and Rodepois (east of Riga).[79]

The Knights retaliated with a short attack on Veliuona and Pisten in the winter of 1344/45, but to little avail. This was the only part of a major *Reise* planned for William of Holland, John of Bohemia, his son Charles and many western knights to be realised. Unfortunately for Ludolf König the February campaign had to be curtailed due to several Lithuanian victories across Livonia. The crusaders blamed the grand master for the poor showing and Ludolf felt it necessary to resign his office.[80] It is clear that the Order was still in disarray. To add insult to injury, even when the pan-European *Reise* had ended in fiasco, news came through of a successful Lithuanian raid in Semigallia, Mitau and Riga.[81] It was here that a local noble, Segewald, proposed to Algirdas that they join forces. However the Lithuanian took exception to the man's presumption of royal status and had him killed. The pagans then marched on to Treiden and Kremun.[82]

From all these campaigns it is clear that the prime mover is not

[77] *HW*, 71, 72; *Wig.*, 504.

[78] *PL*, II, 25.

[79] *Wig.*, 501–2 – Algirdas and Kestutis raid Lenewaden, Üxküll and Rodepois. This attack is described too in Matthias de Nuwenburg, *Chronica*, I, 171. Both Nikžentaitis ('Lietuvos diplomatinė', 18) and the present author (Rowell, 'Lithuania', 310) mistake the leaders of this campaign for Jaunutis, the *rex paganus* which here means pagan prince (Algirdas) and not the pagan grand duke (Jaunutis).

[80] *HW*, 73; *Wig.*, 505–6; Dietmar of Lübeck, *SRP*, III, 74–6; Matthias, *Chronica*, I, 172; Oliwa Chronicle – *MPH*, VI, 338–9; Beneš, *FRB*, IV, 495; Autobiography of Charles IV, *FRB* III, 366. The last *Reise* of John of Bohemia is the subject of an essay by K. Conrad, 'Der dritte Litauerzug König Johanns von Böhmen und der Rücktritt des Hochmeisters Ludolf König', *Festschrift für Hermann Heimpel*, II (Göttingen, 1972), 382–401.

[81] *Wig.*, 505.

[82] *HW*, 72. Algirdas did not approve of the attempt of this 'peasant' to assume princely rank – *HW*, 74.

the grand duke, Jaunutis, but his more ambitious brothers Algirdas and Kestutis. It is hardly surprising that the more successful Gediminids began to wonder why they should accept a weaker brother as overlord. Algirdas and Kestutis who had long been allies plotted to remove Jaunutis from the scene and establish their own rule with Algirdas as grand duke.

How this coup came to pass can be reconstructed from two main source-groups: one Rus'ian, the entry for *annus mundi* 6853 in *NL* and cognate chronicles; and the other, the Lithuanian chronicle complex and its antecedents. After more than three years of waiting and the consolidation of their position in western Lithuania and the Rus'ian provinces of the Grand Duchy, the brothers carried out their coup sometime in the winter of 1344/45, the very time that the Knights were planning a major *Reise*.[83] Stryjkowski dates the deposition of Jaunutis to 22 November, but where he found this information remains unclear and it may well be a misunderstanding of the date of Jaunutis' baptism in Moscow, 23 September 1345.[84] The event seems to have taken place during cold weather, at a time when Algirdas was on campaign. All of this indicates the winter fighting season. In February 1345 Algirdas raided Livonia; neither group of sources records Algirdas' presence in Lithuania when the overthrow of the grand duke took place, although both note Algirdas' connivance with the plot.[85]

The use of the winter campaign season to launch a military *putsch* seems to be a Lithuanian tradition – we see the same in 1381. The technique reminds one strongly also of Daumantas' murder of Mindaugas in 1263.[86] Having imprisoned Jaunutis, Kestutis forced the citizenry to swear allegiance to the new regime.[87] Algirdas meanwhile was still on campaign and had to be summoned back to be acclaimed ruler by Kestutis who respected Algirdas' seniority. As for Jaunutis, he was imprisoned in Vilnius castle, but he managed to escape and flee to Moscow via Smolensk.

[83] *NL*, 358 and *PSRL*, IV(1), 224; XXIII, 107, XXV, 175. Lithuanian sources: *PSRL*, XXXV, 61, 85, 97, 110–11, 133, 154 with date of 6873 for ?6853, 181, 202, 222. Latin text, p. 115. Cf. *Dis ist Witoldes Sache wedir Jageln*, in *SRP*, II, 712. A third source would appear to be an undated Silesian account of an uprising in Vilnius led by Kestutis which is given in *CDP*, VI, no. 2, p. 2 under the wrong date of 1345. In fact it refers to Kestutis' overthrow of Jogaila in 1381 – cf. above pp. 141–2.

[84] Stryjkowski, *Kronika*, II, 2. Baptism – *TL*, 367; *NL*, 358.

[85] Cold weather – *PSRL*, XXV; campaign season – cf. *Wig.*, 505; *SRP*, II, 712.

[86] *CDP*, VI, no. 2, p. 2, cf. *PSRL*, II, 860.

[87] *SRP*, II, 712.

In Moscow he was baptised Ioann by his brother-in-law, Semën Ivanovich. Alas, his sister Aigusta had died earlier that year and no help was forthcoming from Moscow to restore Jaunutis to Vilnius. His ally, Narimantas took refuge swiftly with the Tatar khan, Jani-Beg in the hope of enlisting Tatar support against Algirdas.[88] It is perhaps a sign of the weakness of the Order at this time that neither brother chose to seek an ally among the Germans. Refuge in Marienburg became the most popular solution to the disputes between Jogaila and Vytautas in the 1380s.[89] The new ruler and his ally soon received the support of their other siblings.

By the time of the 1345 plot, Gediminas had been dead for three years. His legacy to his sons had worked itself out. Gediminas had recognised the divisions between his sons and had attempted to minimise their effects on the Grand Duchy by encouraging Kestutis (of the Algirdas camp) to work with Jaunutis (who enjoyed Narimantas' support). Within two years of being deposed, Jaunutis would return from his exile in Moscow and accept Zaslavl' from Algirdas.[90] Clearly Semën Ivanovich had no intention (or power) of assisting that brother-in-law to regain his throne. Narimantas returned from exile in the Horde – similarly the Tatars saw no convenience in denying Algirdas supremacy in Lithuania.[91] Both brothers fought in Algirdas' armies and witnessed his charters. Their sons became important dukes within Lithuanian Rus'.[92] The Gediminid clan was strong enough to survive fraternal disputes and maintain the delicate balance with neighbouring princes, most of whom were newly arrived in power.

Casimir continued in Kraków, the senior prince of central Europe, still seeking allies in the struggle to regain Chełmno and Pomorze from the Knights. The Polish king continued to seek an heir, marrying in 1365 for the fourth time. His last bride was a granddaughter of Gediminas, Jadwiga Henrykówna of Żagań.[93] In Bohemia, John (d. 1345) was succeeded by his son Charles who

88 *NL*, 358. This is taken up in later political tracts – see above pp. 109f. and 114.

89 *Wig.*, 592–3, 613–14, 617, 621–3.

90 In the principality of Minsk, held by Algirdas – *PSRL*, XXXV, 61; 115.

91 Fennell, *Emergence*, 259. Narimantas fought alongside Algirdas in February 1347 – *Wig.*, 508.

92 Narimantas died at the Battle of Strėva in 1348 – *HW*, 75–6; *PSRL*, V, 225. Jaunutis, the Narimantaičiai – *AZR*, I, no. 1, p. 1, *Iura Masoviae*, I, no. 16, pp. 19–20 (14 August 1358).

93 Jasiński, 'Małżeństwa', 68–76.

became eventually Holy Roman Emperor. The Hungarians, through judicious suspension of their claims to south-west Rus' in favour of Casimir gained rights of succession to the Polish throne for their king, Louis, should Casimir die without an heir. The Teutonic Order elected an effective grand master in December 1345, Henry Dusemer, who opened his mastership with a successful attack on Lithuania. Nevertheless success was not constant.[94] In Rus' Semën Ivanovich consolidated the gains of his father and the Golden Horde was ruled by a new khan after Uzbek's death in 1342: his son Jani-Beg.[95]

The pattern for central and eastern European history in the rest of the fourteenth century was now set. Algirdas expanded Lithuanian control of Rus' ever further eastwards to within a hundred miles of Moscow. Kestutis played an important role in the guarding of the western borders of Lithuania against the unwelcome attentions of the Order, the Poles and the Hungarians, to say nothing of Emperor Charles IV. Poland and Lithuania fought over the corpse of Galich–Volyn', dividing the realm between them in 1352.[96] Mazovia and Lithuania aided each other against the enemy in Marienburg. Trade continued across the war zone with the Knights building bridges in the Grand Duchy to facilitate their own merchants' passage via Lithuania to Rus'. The grand duke of Lithuania maintained a delicate balance between Rome and Constantinople, reopening the metropolitanate of Lithuania whilst seeming ready to promote the spread of Catholicism in his lands. His neighbours were only slowly regaining their strength, only slowly consolidating borders which by the 1380s would not bend so easily to Lithuanian pressure. At home the grand duke enjoyed the support of his whole family. The fissures in clan unity which strengthened Lithuania in the face of continued Teutonic pressure had been plastered, or rather, papered over. While Algirdas lived and enjoyed the support of his strongest sibling, Kestutis, the Grand Duchy was safe. Only after Algirdas' death when power was contested between uncle and nephew, cousin and cousin would a foothold be available for the Order to exploit its revived strength in the relentless but well-

[94] *HW*, 73 and *Wig.*, 507.
[95] Fennell, *Emergence*, 239–40.
[96] Shabul'do, *Zemli*, 50 and *AZR*, I, no. 1, p. 1.

matched struggle to dominate Lithuania. For another forty years the pagan realm had the chance to avoid an irrevocable decision to join the Christian club in Europe.[97]

[97] Z. Ivinskis, 'Jogailos santykiai su Kęstučiu ir Vytautu iki 1392m.', in *Jogaila*, ed. A. Šapoka (Kaunas, 1935; 2nd edn., 1991), 45–80; Giedroyć, 'Lithuanian options'; Paszkiewicz, *Jagiellonowie*, 409–46 and Mažeika, 'Role', *passim*.

Chapter 10

FACTORS CONTRIBUTING TO THE FORMATION OF THE GRAND DUCHY

Political entities do not spring full grown as Athene from the head of Zeus. They evolve over a longer or shorter period of time. In the case of Lithuania, the polity began to evolve out of a loose confederation of warrior duchies in the late twelfth and early thirteenth centuries and consolidated itself under the leadership of the House of Pukuveras after *c.* 1289. During the reign of Gediminas the poly-ethnic, multi-confessional character of the Grand Duchy of Lithuania was firmly established. When Gediminas died in the winter of 1341/42 he was able to hand on to his sons a politically stable, economically viable polity relatively free from serious internal division and capable of withstanding all that her neighbours could throw against her.

The development of Lithuania is best understood in the light of her position astride the geographical, commercial, political and confessional frontier between eastern and western Christendom. The wilderness which clad the western approaches to the lands irrigated by the watersheds of the Nevežis and Nemunas rivers marked, in the fourteenth century, the outer boundary of Catholic Europe. When the nations of the West wished to trade and converse with the cities of Byzantine Rus' and Tatary they found it convenient to traverse lands held by the Lithuanians. Along the Nemunas border Lithuanian grand-ducal forts and trading centres were established especially from the second half of the thirteenth century. There is archaeological evidence that Vilnius was a trading post long before this period.

The harsh terrain of forest, marsh and lake provided a fertile haven for the Lithuanians which their Teutonic, Tatar and Rus'ian enemies found difficult to penetrate and impossible to master. Chroniclers, apologists and rulers frequently complain of the difficulty of penetrating this area. The Knights found it necessary to bivouac in the *Wildnis* and plunder only the land around their encampments or *sowalks.*[1] By contrast the Baltic peoples of Prussia, Sudavia and Livonia, who farmed and traded in more easily accessible lands, were swiftly conquered by the Teutonic crusaders and their kinsmen deported to other regions or annihilated. Conditions in Lithuania may not have been radically different from the bogs and forests of Prussia, but yet more territory of that kind had to be traversed in order to reach Lithuanian outposts. At the same time the cities of Rus' were falling under Tatar occupation. Although the Lithuanians were as divided amongst themselves as their Livonian, Estonian and Courlandish neighbours in the twelfth century, their divisions could not be exploited so easily by the crusaders for their isolation protected them. This geographical advantage meant also that those neighbouring tribes which succumbed to the crusaders in battle often chose refuge with the Lithuanians rather than transportation at the hands of the Germans. Between 1270 and 1290 several bands of Sudavian, Barthian and Nadruvian tribesmen fled to Lithuania rather than submit to baptism. This influx, largely of skilled warriors, helped the Lithuanians in their own intensified war against the Teutonic Order. Similarly Rus'ian princes who had fallen from favour with their kinsmen or their Tatar overlords found respite in Lithuania. The example of Grand Duke Aleksandr Mikhailovich of Vladimir and Tver' springs immediately to mind. In 1329 he was compelled by Muscovite and Tatar force of arms to escape to Gediminas' court.

This secondary influence of foreign aggression as a factor in the development of Lithuania should not be exaggerated. Pashuto's theory that the prime factor in the formation of Lithuania was national unity in the face of the Teutonic threat to her existence says more of post-1945 Bolshevik fears than it does of fourteenth-century Lithuania.[2] Teutonic pressure did not directly unite the disparate tribes of Lithuania. The Žemaitijans frequently resisted the wishes of the grand duke and even threatened to join forces with the crusaders to depose their own ruler. In the 1380s the turnover of disaffected Lithuanian princes who went to Marienburg to enlist the aid of the grand master of the Order in their struggle to depose their kinsman, the grand duke, is remarkable.

[1] *HW*, 101–2 describes nine '*sowalk*, id est accubitum' during a *Reise* in August 1372. The name of Suvalkiai (the Lithuanophone region of western Lithuania and eastern Poland) may reflect the practice of such raids in this region.

[2] Pashuto, *Obrazovanie*, 365.

German pressure simply forced the Baltic enemies of the Lithuanians to choose between Marienburg and Vilnius.

Lithuania was able to develop at its own pace, unlike its less fortunate Baltic kindred, not merely thanks to its geography but even more importantly because it could defend itself efficiently and use main force to annex valuable territories from its weak Slav neighbours to the east. The military techniques of guerilla warfare which the Lithuanian terrain required could not be matched by either its German or its Slavonic foe. Furthermore the Lithuanian army was well ordered and well equipped. It was expert in cavalry warfare and stationed in garrisons which were regularly relieved. It benefited from excellent military intelligence which spied on the Knights, induced them to fall into ambushes by sending out *agents provocateurs* who pretended to be Polish or German in order to lure the enemy into the Lithuanian snare. Campaigns were correlated to times of the year when the Order was occupied with other business, especially its annual general chapter in September. Gediminas maintained his military machine by carefully contracting out Lithuanian arms to neighbouring Christian states. Thus the grand duke maintained his troops' war-readiness, supported other princes in wars against an enemy they had in common with Lithuania and won considerable booty which was necessary to the funding of an expensive war machine.

However, strength of arms was not sufficient unto itself; the military machine needed careful supervision and this was provided by the grand dukes. The wealth, diplomatic skill and greater military prowess of three particular Aukštaitijan clans led to the emergence of the grand-ducal office in the late twelfth century and more consistently after 1219. For most of the thirteenth century political unity within Lithuania was circumscribed by competition between the leaders of these families: the descendants of Ringaudas, Živinbudas and Dausprungas. It should be noted that these dynasties were all native to Lithuania. The foreign origin of the Rus'ian ruling class in Slavonic Kiev is not a feature of Lithuanian princes even though in the fifteenth century the Gediminids claimed descent variously from Nero and Attila.[3] None of the

[3] Certain scholars imagine foreign origins of the Lithuanian rulers – see, for example J. Puzyna, 'Początki państwowości i dynastii litewskiej według najnowszych badań', *Nauka i sztuka*, 6 (1947), 152–70 who asserts that the Lithuanian grand dukes are descended from defeated Englishmen who fled after Hastings. S. M. Kuczyński repeats the theory – *Jagiełło, ok.* 1351–1434 (Warsaw, 1985), 21. This is based on a complete

three grand-ducal clans succeeded in completely subjugating its rivals. Mindaugas murdered and married his way through many but not all of the kinsmen and peers who envied him his throne. He even adopted Christianity in 1251 as a means of gaining Teutonic support for his claims in Žemaitija. He dispossessed many dukes and even princes of their Lithuanian holdings and sent some out into western Rus' to carve out patrimonies for themselves where they could pose no direct threat to the Lithuanian regime. This is reminiscent of many warrior empires, even republican Rome. Nevertheless, Mindaugas' power as grand duke (or rather, king) was not pervasive enough to make a success of his conversion and land policies. The Teutonic alliance brought the prestige of a royal crown and the services of clerical scribes to Vilnius but it also incurred pressure from the Order to be given more territory within Lithuania and enmity from his Žemaitijan and eastern rivals who used the adoption of the new religion as a tool to stir up pagan discontent. Powerful political and dynastic rivals such as Tautvilas and Treniota were joined in opposition to Mindaugas by princes, such as Daumantas of Nalšia, whom the king had affronted personally. The early grand dukes did not enjoy the influence of a Géza of Hungary or Vladimir of Kiev who adopted Christianity as an ornament to their domestic power rather than a cornerstone of it. Géza had his enemies but those were few in number and inferior in clout.[4]

The blood-letting which destroyed Mindaugas' family in the 1260s and opened Lithuania up for a time to Rus'ian invasion was staunched by the careful policy and strong arm of Traidenis. This grand duke kept a tight rein on his Orthodox brothers and all his subjects. However Traidenis, who initiated the first Lithuano-

misunderstanding of the first entries in *L2* which refer to the coming of the Lithuanians from Italy. This is only a literary means of defining Lithuanian sovereignty in the face of Polish postures of superior ancestry in the 1440s. It is intended to show that the Lithuanian people too have a classical origin to match the Sarmatian fantasy of Polish ancestors. It derives Lithuania (*Lietuva*) from *Litus-tuba – PSRL*, XXXV, 129 and Kulicka, 'Legenda', 8f. For Polish–Lithuanian rivalry in 1447, see M. Biskup and K. Górski, *Kazimierz Jagiellończyk. Zbiór studiów o Polsce drugiej połowy XV wieku* (Warsaw, 1987), 10–14. The story is not an analogy with the non-Slav origins of the princes of Rus'.

[4] For the conversion plans of Géza and Stephen of Hungary, see J. P. Ripoche, 'La Hongrie entre Byzance et Rome: Problème du choix religieux', *Ungarn-Jahrbuch*, 6 (1974–75), 9–23; G. Adriányi, 'Der Eintritt Ungarns in die christlich-abendländische Völkergemeinschaft', *Ungarn-Jahrbuch*, 6 (1974–75), 24–37. For Vladimir of Kiev, see L. Müller, *Die Taufe Russlands. Die Frühgeschichte des russischen Christentums bis zum Jahre 988* (Munich, 1988).

Polish alliance and restored commercial links with Riga, left no heir to his power. The real consolidation of grand-ducal authority comes under the sons of Pukuveras, the founder of the dynasty which ruled Lithuania (and later, Poland) from *c.* 1289 until 1572.

Vytenis and his brother Gediminas not only controlled between them Lithuania, they also appropriated even the major Rus'ian territories of the Grand Duchy (Polotsk, Kiev, Novgorodok) from other princely lines by dint of marriage alliances and military intervention, mostly by the latter means. The power of this family of Octavians came to be acknowledged as august by the former princely and ducal families which it had rendered subservient. The clans of Gostautai, Alšeniškiai and the like, which had once been the equal of the Gediminids, served the grand dukes as *namestniki*, unambitious for royal estate outside any dynastic link with the Gediminids. Those nobles who presumed to seek royal dignity were put to death by the grand duke.

Although the Gediminid grand dukes did not establish full control of their own servitor kinsmen until the 1440s, when it was determined that the direct descendant of Jogaila, who was *de iure* king of Poland, should also hold the office of grand duke of Lithuania (rather than let that office fall to his cousins, the heirs of Vytautas or Skirgaila), the Gediminid clan was both small enough to share Rus'ian acquisitions among its members and large enough to spread its tentacles throughout the Grand Duchy.[5] In 1300 Gediminas and Vytenis had only two other brothers, Voin and Fëdor, and these were both willing to rule their Rus'ian lands under the overlordship of their eldest sibling. Only after the death of Gediminas' most powerful son, Grand Duke Algirdas (1345–77), did destructive discord between uncle and nephew, cousin and cousin bring dynastic strife to Lithuania. Even then alliances could be struck between the Gediminids to support the eldest son of Algirdas, Jogaila, as grand duke. The dynasty was too well established to be stripped of its authority. Much of Gediminas' diplomatic success was due to his careful grafting of Lithuanian spouses onto the dynastic trees of Poland and Rus', using his daughters as the most effective disseminators of Lithuanian princely status. After 1290 the only competitors for the Gediminid crown were fellow members of the clan. Indeed, the clannish

[5] The accession of Kazimierz Jagiellończyk in 1447 to the throne of Poland eventually ended the competition between the grandsons and great-grandsons of Gediminas for control of the grand-ducal office in Lithuania – see n. 3.

quality of grand-ducal rule should not be underestimated. The influence of the dowager grand duchesses and the brothers of a grand duke seems to have been considerable, judging by the admittedly sparse evidence available from the cases of Gediminas' brothers and Algirdas' wife and widow, Ul'iana Tver'skaia. When the clan was united, Lithuania was strong. When cousin took up arms against cousin, nephew against uncle, the Knights exploited these divisions. The clan system in government as in everyday life is reminiscent of Viking Scandinavia where the *aett* was the main social group.[6]

Given the importance of the collective rule of the Gediminid clan under the command of the ruler, the absolutism which certain scholars chose to detect in grand-ducal power during the 1930s never existed.[7] Individual members prospered as major trading princes and ruled their lands in accordance with local tradition. Like the Ottomans in Byzantine Asia Minor, the Tatars in Rus' and other warrior societies, the Lithuanians left their subject peoples in peace in return for armed service and payment of taxation.[8] We can speak of a *pax lithuanica* which safeguarded the commercial routes between the Baltic and the Tatar Black Sea, northern Germany and Rus'.

Expansion across the Lithuanian eastern frontier into White Rus' contributed immeasurably to the strength of the Lithuanian polity. It brought the skills of Orthodox Slavs into Lithuanian service. This military expansion into the trading heartland of Rus' was underpinned by Lithuanian manipulation of ecclesiastical structures to cut off the new territories from the spiritual influence of an east-Rus'ian hierarch, the metropolitan of Kiev, Vladimir and All Rus'. In Gediminas' day ecclesiastical patronage was used as a means of insinuating an acceptance of Lithuanian political suzerainty into Rus'ian society and making tangible the ambition that 'all Rus' should belong to Lithuania'. We must remain sensitive to the tensions of the several competing ambitions within Lithuania, Rus', Poland and every European state in the fourteenth century, even in exotic England and France.

6 L. H. Dommasnes, 'Women, kinship and the basis of power in the Norwegian Viking Age', in *Social approaches to Viking Studies*, ed. R. Samson (Glasgow, 1991), 70.

7 The theories of Avižonis and Kamieniecki concerning the absolute power of the grand dukes are noted conveniently in Pashuto, *Obrazovanie*, 342.

8 S. Shaw, *History of the Ottoman Empire and modern Turkey, I: Empire of the Gazis: the rise and decline of the Ottoman Empire, 1280–1808* (Cambridge, 1976), 12.

The influence of Rus' on Lithuania was important and remains undeniable. However the exaggerated claims made by the Polish historian Łowmiański for the Slavonic contribution to the formation of the Grand Duchy before 1282 should be tempered. The Rus'ian contribution to Lithuanian society began some six decades after the Grand Duchy had started to consolidate itself. That a west Rus'ian dialect eventually came to be used in grand-ducal documents (largely after 1385) reveals the origin of most Lettovian scribes who had to deal with Rus'ian leaders of Church and state. It certainly does not mean that the grand dukes were Rus'ian. It is clear that Vytautas and Jogaila spoke with each other in Lithuanian.[9] Terms such as *bajorai* were borrowed from Rus' for native institutions. What the Rus'ians brought to Lithuania were the important commodities of men and money for the Prussian wars and control of several of the major trading posts of Rus'.

As is commonly the case with nascent states – Kievan Rus' and Árpád Hungary are but two examples – military power and control of international commerce bolstered the Lithuanian polity.[10] Lithuania bestrode the Polotsk–Mazovia, Galich–Prussia, Prussia–Novgorod and Livonia–Polotsk trade routes. The pagans built cities along the land and river routes to defend access to the merchants. The income from trade in food, iron, horses and wax was essential for the maintenance of Lithuanian military campaigns. The valuable routes tempered foreign aggression towards the pagans and made Lithuania an attractive ally. Even the Teutonic Knights were willing to safeguard certain routes, *vredeweg*, from attack.

The importance of the confessional frontier which passed

[9] H. Łowmiański, *Studia nad początkami społeczeństwa i państwa litewskiego*, II (Vilnius, 1932), 142. Paszkiewicz, *Origin*, 205. J. Ochmanski, 'Uwagi o litewskim państwie wczesnofeudalnym', *Roczniki Historyczne*, 27 (1961), 155–7. Łowmiański decided that Lithuania was created before 1282 (the death of Traidenis) and probably as early as 1236 (the date he chose for the accession of Mindaugas). However neither Traidenis nor Mindaugas created a state ruled by an established dynasty or freed from boiar rivalry. As for the Slavonic influence in Mindaugas' realm, this is so minimal as to be non-existent. The Kievans attacked Lithuania for the first time in 1040 – *PVL*, II, 103. This campaign is given in some manuscripts of *NLk* s.a. 1044 – *NL*, 181. For Lithuano-Rus'ian relations from that date until the thirteenth century see Pashuto, *Obrazovanie*, 12–18. Permanent Lithuanian settlement in Rus' is described above, pp. 82–7. For use of Lithuanian by the grand dukes see *CEV*, no. 1345, p. 816.

[10] M. C. Webb, 'The flag follows trade: An essay on the necessary interaction of military and commercial factors in state formation', in *Ancient Civilisation and Trade*, ed. J. A. Sabloff and C. C. Lamberg-Karlovsky (Albuquerque, 1975), 155–209.

through Lithuania cannot be ignored. However in considering pagan–Christian relations in fourteenth-century eastern Europe it is not helpful to draw an iron curtain between pagan and Christian *tout court*. Pagans may have been outside the structures of Christendom but they were certainly not completely beyond the pale of the Church. What had been true of Scandinavia's intercourse with the Empire in the ninth century, or Emperor Henry II's use of the Slavonic Liutici in the eleventh was even more true of Lithuania and her relationships with Poland and Rus' in the fourteenth century.[11] Stark contrasts between 'pagan' Lithuania, 'Orthodox' Rus' and 'Catholic' Poland are misleading. Indeed the survival of pagan practices in Poland and Rus' well past 1300 may have made the differences between these peoples and Lithuania less sharp than they appear to historians who believe the dead to have lived within neat scholarly constraints. It is all too simple to regard the Middle Ages as a monolithic 'age of Faith' and the era of fundamentalism. We should be careful to remember we deal with the age of Catholicism – warts, heretics and all. What the canonists say and what the ordinary layman (or clerk) do can be plain different things. Rus'ian canon law of the thirteenth and fourteenth centuries refers to places 'where Christianity is' as if there were many areas where Christianity was not. The very repetition of canons against unblessed marriages, ancestor worship and praying in kilns and at the river-side indicates the prevalence of such heathen practices. The records of the synod called by Metropolitan Kirill in Kiev in 1274 are dominated by questions on pagan ritual. The adoration of fire, trees and the thunder god Perun survived among the eastern Slavs. Likewise in Poland pagan festivals involving the wearing of deer and horse masks flourished in Gniezno, the primatial metropolis, as late as 1326 when Archbishop Janisław promulgated the *Statutes of Uniejów* in an attempt to eradicate the practice.[12]

[11] I. Wood, 'Christian and pagan in ninth-century Scandinavia', in *The Christianization of Scandinavia*, ed. B. Sawyer, P. Sawyer and I. Wood (Alingsås, 1987), 36–67, esp. 51–2. The heathen Liutici, a Slavonic tribe, aided Henry II when he invaded Poland in 1005 – Thietmar of Merseburg, *Chronicon*, ed. J. Lappenberg, revised F. Kurze (Hanover, 1889), 146–9.

[12] Russian canon law (the *ustavy*) condemned ancestor worship and unblessed marriages throughout the fourteenth century. Serapion of Vladimir devotes two sermons to heathen rites and witchcraft whilst an anonymous author of *Slovo nekoego Khristoliubtsa* fulminates against belief in Perun and the worship of fire. See Ia. N. Shchapov, *Drevnerusskie kniazheskie ustavy XI–XVvv*. (Moscow, 1976), 23, 31; R. Bogert, 'On the rhetorical style of Serapion Vladimirskii', *Medieval Russian Culture, California Slavic*

More seriously there is a tendency to underestimate the presence of Christians within Lithuania. In our discussion of Christianity in Lithuania thus far we have considered mainly the institutionalised faith – its hierarchy and architecture, its use in affairs which are external to the pagan heartland of Lithuania; how Orthodoxy was a political tool in Lithuanian Rus'; how conversion to Catholicism was viewed by Gediminas as a political manoeuvre in his dealings with western Christendom. This is the traditional and accepted way of examining Christianity in Lithuania before the conversion of 1387. But what of the underground? It is just as enlightening to examine an association between Lithuania and the Church recumbent. It is easy to forget the secret missions of the Franciscans among the heathen did not end in 1324 but continued throughout the life of the pagan Grand Duchy, as is evident from the activities of Archbishop Frederick of Riga and the Franciscans of the Bohemian province in Lithuania before Gediminas' death. Here especially is history written about the victors, and the missions of 1324–87 are neither glamorous nor successful.

The history of Lithuanian Christianity as an institution is very quirky. The mad endeavours of Mindaugas are followed by a generation of silence. In 1298 Vytenis approaches Riga with a view to accepting Christianity but over the ensuing decade he changes his mind. Gediminas ignores a papal exhortation in 1317 but attempts to attract support in the West against the Teutonic Order by announcing his openness to the faith in 1322. This ends with 'let the devil baptise me' two years later. The next showdown comes in 1351, when Kestutis sacrifices an ox as proof of his willingness to accept baptism. He rejects the plan promptly as soon as news comes through that his brother Liubartas has been released from Polish captivity and the Hungaro-Polish army has left the borders of the Grand Duchy. Meanwhile the Orthodox Church is prevailed upon to establish a hierarchy for the Grand Duchy, based in Novgorodok outside pagan Lithuania. This lasts fourteen years or so, is liquidated in 1331 and re-appears openly in 1352. Grand-ducal patronage of the Orthodox within his Rus'ian territories continues apace without any sign of activity in Lithuania.

Studies, XII, ed. H. Birnbaum and M. S. Flier (Berkeley, Los Angeles–London, 1984), 280–310; T. V. Chertoritskoi, *Sokrovishchia drevnerusskoi literatury. Krasnorechie Drevnei Rusi (XI–XVIIvv.)* (Moscow, 1987), 123–5. The decisions of the Synod of Kiev are given in V. N. Beneshevich, *Drevnerusskaia kormchaia XIV titulov bez tolkovanii*, ed. Ia. N. Shchapov, II (Sofia, 1987), 182–5. On pagan survivals in fourteenth-century Gniezno, Burchardt, 'Dlaczego pogańscy', 33–40.

By sharp contrast, women's christianity has a continuous and steady history. It has few of the manic phases of the church-creation schemes. Women are the first native or permanently resident Christians known to be active in Lithuania. They are the wetnurses who, in the mid-thirteenth century, spread the faith with their milk, according to the Dublin *Descripciones terrarum*, with the result that it is safe for priests to preach their mission.[13] It is Queen Morta, Mindaugas' wife, who acts as patron of the mission clergy in Lithuania. She extends her protection to the priest Siebert in order to save him from Mindaugas' wrath after the decision has been taken to wipe Lithuania clean of Christianity in 1261.[14] The wives of later grand dukes and various princes support the building of Orthodox churches in Vilnius. It is an Orthodox princess, *soror regis*, who saves the relics of Franciscan martyrs in 1341. This woman acts to preserve the Catholic relics even though she is a schismatic (*licet schismatica*). This is even less of a surprise when we consider that it was the household of Gediminas' duchess which provided access to court for Franciscan missionaries in 1324.[15] Algirdas' mother-in-law took his daughter (unnamed in the source) to Tver' in 1364 to baptise her and train her for her future role as princely consort.[16] Algirdas' second wife, Ul'iana of Tver' built a monastery in Vilnius and patronised religious foundations throughout Lithuanian Rus'. It is through her that the metropolitan of Lithuania, her kinsman Roman was appointed in 1354.[17] This situation is not so different from the growth of Christianity elsewhere in northern Europe. In Sweden for example women were the most fervent Christians before the conversion.[18] The Gediminaitės took to the new religion with gusto when they married abroad, where they were renowned for their piety and patronage of the Church. Whether or not the new religion offered women a 'better deal' than the pagan cult is difficult to determine, given the sparse material available to us and the record of pagan priestesses, a vocation by which the Christian woman cannot be called.[19] Through this unofficial (or rather, non-grand-ducal)

[13] See above p. 183, n.152.

[14] *LR*, lines 3451–3608, 6427–6586, tr. p. 47–9, 79–81.

[15] *GL*, 145.

[16] *PSRL*, XV (i), 76; X, 13. See Mažeika, 'Role', 30 and n. 4. This incident may reflect Algirdas' use of male children in ecclesiastical politics. In 1364 he needed to regain the friendship of Metropolitan Aleksei who is asked to baptise the princess.

[17] Ul'iana as patroness – see above p. 180, n. 134.

[18] A. S. Gräslund, 'Some aspects of Christianisation in Central Sweden' *Social approaches*, 50–2.

[19] *Ibid.*; pagan priestesses in Lithuania noted above pp. 123–4.

patronage Christian clergy could hope for considerable favour in Vilnius.

The daughters of Gediminas highlight too another aspect of the grand duke's political success. Gediminas knew how to deal diplomatically with Christian princes. Through his many daughters he established a network of marriage alliances around his major rivals in Poland and Rus'. Gediminas took the advice of Catholic and Orthodox counsellors in foreign affairs. Orthodox monks brought scribal skills to the Vilnius court which probably made West-Russian the major written language of Lettovian government in the second half of the fourteenth century. Gediminas used the Orthodox Church to further his ambitions to rule the whole of Rus' and to bolster his control of cities which, like Pskov, were already under his sway. He was swift to exploit the political and religious antagonism between Moscow and Tver'. It seems that the establishment of an Orthodox metropolitanate in the Grand Duchy *c.* 1316 was connected with Tverite ecclesiastical politics. By 1342 Lithuania was a power to reckon with in the restoration of Rus'. Gediminas' death, unlike that of his brother Vytenis, does not go unmentioned in Rus'ian chronography. The Orthodox Church was manipulated by the grand duke as a tool for conducting Lettovian, not purely Lithuanian policy. Gediminas also exploited Catholicism to make military, political and commercial alliances with Catholic princes including, briefly, Pope John XXII, and to attract Catholic, that is German, technology to Lithuania. Franciscans copied correspondence for the grand duke, but Gediminas circumscribed the activity of Catholic friars so as to prevent them from preaching Christ to the infidel. The reason Catholic priests were invited to Lithuania was to comfort Christians who came to reside in Vilnius and Novgorodok and serve the grand duke. The role of Christianity in the pagan state, if it can be detected, was that of foreign adjunct to the foreign aspirations of the grand duke.

In his conduct of foreign affairs Gediminas was capable of taking both long and short shots. In 1322–24 he had two main aims: immediate peace with Christendom in order to encourage trade and settlement in Lithuania, and the removal of the Teutonic Order from the Baltic. Both hares were coursed but the huntsman kept a firm grip of his weapon, the potential to be baptised. When he realised that he could gain a peace without being baptised and that even baptism could not buy the emasculation of the Teutonic

Order, Gediminas accepted what he could take from the Pope and calmly set about bolstering Lithuanian security by hiring out his military expertise to troubled Christian princes. The grand duke knew how to take advantage of the infrastructure of Christendom, approaching the Papacy through his own messengers and exploiting the mendicant preaching machine to spread news of his 'new deal' throughout the mercantile cities of Saxony.

The military and diplomatic strategies which Gediminas developed in Lithuania should be appreciated fully. He dealt not only with potentially hostile Christian neighbours, he also balanced one foreign prince against another, dividing and defeating Christian princes, as the Knights had conquered the Prussian and Livonian tribes. His playing with papal and patriarchal ambitions for the churches of eastern and eastern-central Europe illustrates an impressive understanding of the politics of Christendom. His use of the Polish case against the Teutonic Order or the Pskovite battles with the Livonians to isolate his enemies forms the basis of Lithuanian foreign policy for the next sixty years. He understood the political nuances of imperial, Teutonic, Scandinavian and Rus'ian ambitions in the region.

Gediminas' capabilities in these areas owe much to the fact that he is the first Lithuanian ruler whom we know to have worked consciously within the historical tradition of his realm. He was familiar with the policies of his predecessors Mindaugas and Vytenis, as his letters make clear. He understood how Mindaugas had failed spectacularly through his alliance with the Knights and his abandonment of the cults which were dear to his subjects and his rivals. He was aware of the moderate gains in commerce and international (viz. Rigan) alliance made by his brother Vytenis. He claims to have learnt of papal authority during his youth. He recognised the weaknesses of his enemies and learned how to exploit them. He was not the originator of all his policies but built on the experience of past rulers. Gediminas' diplomatic skill and duplicity have been underestimated by past scholars who have been reluctant to acknowledge that a pagan Lithuanian could be a diplomat or that the 'innocently abused' pagans could outmanoeuvre the Teutonic Knights in craftiness.

Historical awareness was not the only key to Gediminas' political mastery. He was able to follow such policies of tolerant manipulation of all comers because of the Lithuanian attitude to political and religious tradition. The making of decisions by the grand duke in concert with other clan members and the non-Gediminid princely and boiar estates fostered a large degree of political plurality. The acknowledgement of local traditions which we encounter frequently in later centuries in the formula of *novin' ne uvodim', a starin' ne rukhaem*', 'we will introduce nothing new nor disturb what is old', contributed to the cohesion of ethnically, politically and religiously diverse elements within the Grand Duchy. This respect for Rus'ian traditions in Rus' is equalled by the armed support for pagan traditions in Lithuania. It is not a sign of fundamental Lithuanian political weakness, for local dynasties were apt to find themselves replaced by Lithuanian princes, and Lithuanian princes, by protégés of the grand duke, when need arose. This respect should not be mistaken for any modern concept of toleration. It is the exploitation of the desirable within the limits of the possible. Absolute power was never available to the grand duke (or later to the king of Poland). In Lithuanian Rus', as in Norman France in the tenth century, we see institutional continuity surviving in the new lands controlled by a military society whilst the ruling class is changed, sometimes drastically (as in Kiev), sometimes gradually (as with the annexation of Vitebsk through increasing military and economic pressure and eventual dynastic marriage). In fact the claim to respect the *status quo* is disingenuous, given that subjection to the grand duke of Lithuania was itself an innovation. In its turn, this tolerance of the *status quo* was fostered by the pagan religion which was decentralised and diverse of practice. It did not militate against the *ritus/mos* of the Christians who worship God in their own peculiar style so long as Christians did not offend the native divinities. This apparent tolerance continued even after the conversion, or rather, the Catholic Church never effected absolute control of Greater Lithuania any more than the pagan princes had. The pagan grand dukes appear to have shared the opinion expressed in the oft-quoted maxim of St Stephen of Hungary (997–1038) that 'the realm endowed with a single language and a single tradition is both weak and easily broken'.[20] It reflects a lack of a strong centralist authority but this surely is no weakness. The Grand Duchy and Poland survived as entities much longer than the Prussian Empire. In the sixteenth century Orthodox Russians,

[20] *Libellus de institutione morum*, ed. J. Balogh, in *Scriptores rerum hungaricarum*, II, ed. E. Szentpétery (Budapest, 1938), 625.

Uniate Catholics, Protestant Prussians and Mohammedan Tatars all felt themselves to be as Lettovian as immigrant Poles, Jews and native Catholic Lithuanians did. In Gediminas' day the use of the term *litovskii* in the sense of 'Lettovian' emerges for the first time.[21]

Qua religion, Christianity was not necessary to the political development of Lithuania, although the creation of an independent Orthodox metropolitanate in the Grand Duchy did contribute to Lithuanian control of her Rus'ian territories. Even the probable influence of Christian practice on the building of a temple in the lower castle in Vilnius had only a limited effect. A pagan papal system emanating from this central shrine never existed, *pace* Peter of Dusburg and the bevy of his admirers. Christianity's failure to attract Lithuania in the way it captured the heart of Vladimir, Mieszko and their like is not due only to the strength and fitness of the native cults. Unlike the tenth century, the fourteenth marks both the apogee of Christendom and a period of decline. Christendom provided culture which was too widespread to enjoy any truly exclusive appeal. Gediminas and his family could gain many of the advantages of 'Christian' civilisation by purchasing them with money or arms rather than with their souls. The last pagan state which was also a powerful political entity and the gateway to the other half of Christendom was a very attractive prize for both eastern and western patriarchs. Fourteenth-century Christendom found itself a seller in a buyer's market. Baptism was not the only means of winning the benefits of Christianity – written culture, ideological unity, the right of entry into the Christian trade community. The dangers which faced Gediminas' Lithuania were not great enough to require the close union which Jogaila later made with Poland and which demanded the adoption of Catholicism. Baptism was understood to be no guarantee of freedom from Christian aggression. Gediminas' control of the Grand Duchy never reached a stage where Vilnius was the undoubted centre of Orthodox Rus'. Union with another state, Muscovite or Catholic did not become an overriding military necessity until the Gediminid clan began to fight amongst itself and the defeat of the Teutonic threat required consistent reliable alliances rather than *ad hoc* agreements.

The 'frontier factors' which led to the power enjoyed by

[21] Riasna and Osechen are described in *NL*, 347 s.a.1335 as Lettovian towns. By 1380 a Smolensk scribe could call most cities of Black and White Rus' *litovskii* as he did Kaunas or Vilnius – see p. 81, n. 114.

Lithuania from before 1341–42 are best viewed not from Poland, Prussia or Rus' where historians of a particular Slavonic or Teutonic bent tend to regard those nations as the 'civilisers' of the Baltic pagans, but from another state on the Catholic–Orthodox frontier. Although there are obvious differences between fourteenth-century Lithuania and tenth-century Hungary, the experiences of the two peoples are similar in certain important respects. It need not concern us that the Magyars were a non-European nomadic people while the Lithuanians have been settled in the Baltic region for millennia. By 973, the Magyars governed a land on the Danube border between the Byzantine Commonwealth and the German Empire. They settled in royal forts and trading centres along this frontier and had commercial contact with Germany, Constantinople and Rus'. The concentration of towns and castles along the Danube, Rhine and Nemunas borders is very similar.[22] The Magyar cities such as Esztergóm, which until the twelfth century were of the same *castrum* and *suburbium* type as Gediminas' Vilnius, provided important staging posts for international trade. The *seniores* of the pagan Magyar royal *consilium* call to mind the *seniores* of Vytenis' *parlamentum*.[23] The Magyar horsemen sought to control the Slav populations of northern Bulgaria. At the end of the tenth century before St Stephen converted his people to Catholicism, the southern chieftain who was his bitterest rival, Ajtony of Morasvár welcomed Orthodox priests and traders from Vidin to strengthen his political position on the Bulgarian border.[24] Even after their official conversion to Catholicism in 1000, Magyar kings retained close links with the Church and state of Byzantium until the fourteenth century. It should be recalled that medieval Hungary controlled the Slav and Romanian areas of Croatia and Transylvania and, from time to time, northern Serbia and Bulgaria. St Stephen founded the Orthodox convent of the Theotokos in Veszprém and granted it a charter written in Byzantine Greek at his own court only a few years after his conversion to Catholicism. In 1401 the patriarch of Constantinople established a new metropolitanate of Ungrovlachia in Magyar territory.[25] The balance of the Árpádok, even

[22] On towns and trade see *Towns in medieval Hungary*, ed. L. Gerevich (Boulder, CO, 1990), 26–95. L. Gerevich, 'Hungary', in *European Towns. Their archaeology and early history*, ed. M. W. Barley (London–New York–San Francisco, 1977), 432–4.

[23] Vytenis' *parlamentum* above pp. 61–2; cf. D. Sinor, *History of Hungary* (London, 1959), 39.

[24] *Ibid.*, 36–8 and *Legenda s. Gerhardi episcopi Scriptores rerum hungaricarum*, II, 489.

[25] Expanse of medieval Hungary – see map 1. For Orthodoxy in Hungary see G.

when Catholic, between the Balkan Empire of the Byzantines and the ambitions of the western emperors reflects a little of Lithuanian policies. The princes of both realms, the one Christian, the other still pagan, were viewed as guardians of the western advance into Byzantium by the Pope and the German emperor; and by the Byzantine emperor and patriarch as defenders of the outer regions of the Orthodox *oikumene*. Both peoples were skilled warriors, the Magyars in conquering an alien land, the Lithuanians in defending their territory from alien Slavonic and German incursions. Trade, military expertise, diplomatic skill and the consolidation of a powerful ruling dynasty are features of Magyar life as the Hungarian state developed on the Germano-Byzantine frontier. The Magyars were the last people of central Europe to convert to Christianity. They converted when their princes, Géza (972–97) and his son Stephen (997–1038), already well established but still lacking total control, decided to quell German hostility by gaining a papal crown and a Catholic hierarchy. The same might be said of Lithuania in 1385–87.

Lithuania may be unfamiliar to western medievalists but it is far from being an alien land. Its development in the fourteenth century reflects the growth of pagan states in an earlier century on a similar Catholic--Byzantine frontier. The economic, religious and political growth of many states in central and eastern Europe in the late thirteenth and fourteenth centuries has its counterpart in Lithuania. The settlement of foreign artisans and farmers in Lithuania, which contributed to the national economy, has its counterpart in Poland, Hungary and Prussia. The restoration of past political institutions and the creation of new ones in post-Přemyslid Bohemia, Łokietek's Poland and Teutonic Prussia together with the 'collection of Rus'ian lands' around Moscow demonstrate how much Lithuania has in common with her Christian neighbours. We should do well to remember that when Lithuania emerges as a regular player in the affairs of Christendom in the 1320s her ruler employs the latest (Franco-German) political clichés, seeks the latest (German) technology and is taken seriously as a useful piece in the international great game between Pope and Emperor, Teuton and Slav, Catholic and Orthodox.

Moravcsik, *Byzantium and the Magyars* (Budapest, 1970), 77–102, 115–19; K. Mesterházy, 'Bizánci keresztemy nyomok Berettyóujfalu határában', *Archeologiai Értesitö*, 96 (1969), 91–8. See also F. Makk, *The Árpáds and the Comneni. Political relations between Hungary and Byzantium in the twelfth century* (Budapest, 1989).

Appendix 1

RUSSIAN SOURCES FOR THE FALL OF KIEV TO THE LITHUANIANS, 1322–23

L2, RACZYŃSKI CODEX, PSRL, XXXV, 152–3

И впокоившы землю от немцов Жомоитскую, и пошол на князи руские, и прыиде напервеи к городу Володымеру. И князь Володымер володымерскии, собравшыся з людми своими, и вчынить бои великии с князем великим Кгидимином. И поможеть бог князю великому Кгидимину, иж князя Володымера володымерского самого убил и воиско его все побил, и город Володымер озметь. И потом поидеть на князя Льва луцкого. И князь Лев услышал, што князя Володымера Литва убила и город Володымер узяли, и он не смел против его стати, и побежыть до князя Романа, до зятя своего, ко Бранску. А князи и бояре волынские били челом великому князю Кгидимину, жебы в них пановал и господарем в них был, а земли их не казил. И князь великии Кгидимин, укрепившы их прысягою и оставившы наместников своих в них, и там почнеть княжыти. А потом на зиму пошол до Берестя и з Берестя вси воиска свои роспустил, а сам у Берести зимовал. И скоро Велик день минул, и он, собравшы вси свои силы литовские, жмоитские и руские, и на другои недели по Велицэ дни поидеть на князя Станиславля киевъского и, прышодшы, возметь город Овручыи и город Жытомир. И князь Станиславль киевскии, обославшыся с князем Ольгом переяславским и с князем Романом бранским, и с князем волынским, которого князь великии Кгидимин выгнал з Луцька, и собралися вси у великом множестве людеи, и спотъкалися вси с князем великим Кгидимином на рецэ на Ръпени под Белым городом, в шести милях от Киева. И вчынили бои и сечу великую, и поможеть бог великому князю Кгидимину, побъеть всих князеи руских наголову, и воиско их все побито на пляцу зостало, и князя Льва луцъкого, и князя Ольга переяславского убили, и в малои дружыне Станиславль киевъскии и з Романом бранским утекуть до Бранска, а князь великии Кгидимин оступить Белъгород. И горожане видечы, иж господар их з воиска побег проч, а воиско все наголову побито, и они, не хотечы противитися воиску так великому литовскому, и передалися з городом князю Кгидимину, и прысягу вчынили служыти к Великому князству Литовскому. И затым князь великии Кгидимин пошол со всими силами своими до Киева и обляжеть город Киев, и кияне почалися ему боронити. И лежал князь великии Кгидимин под Киевом месец, а затым здумали межы собою горожане киевские, иж моцы великого князя не могли терпети и болш того без господара своего, великого князя Станиславля киевского. И въслышали тое, иж господар их Станиславль втек от Кгидимина и воиско господара их побито, а в них заставы князь их никоторое не зоставил. И они, змовившыся одноемыслне, и подалися великому князю Кгидимину, и пошодшы з города со кресты игумены, попы и дъяконы, и ворота городовые отворыли, и стретили великого князя честно, и вдарыли ему чолом, и поддалися служыти ему, и прысягу свою великому князю Кгидимину на том дали, и били чолом великому князю Кгидимину, штобы от них отчызны их не отнимал. И князь Кгидимин пры том их зоставил и сам честно у город Киев уехал. И въслышали тое прыгородки киевские, Вышегород, Черкасы, Канев, Путивль, Слеповрод, што кияне передалися з городом, а господаря своего слышали, иж втек до Бранска, а воиско его все побито, и вси прышли до великого князя Кгидимина, и с тыми вышеиречеными прыгородки киевъскими подалися служыти, и прысягу на том дали великому князю Кгидимину. И переяславлене слышали, иж Киев и прыгородки киевские подалися великому князю Кгидимину, а господар их, князь Олг, от великого князя Кгидимина убит, и они, прыехавши, и подалися з городом служыти великому князю Кгидимину, и прысягу свою на том дали. И князь велики Кгидимин, взявшы Киев и Переяславль и вси тые прыгородки, и посадил на них князя Миндовгова сына Олькгимонта, великого князя

Гольшанского, а сам з великим весэлем до Литвы прыехал.

Of Grand Duke Kgidimin and his battle with Prince Volodymer Volodymerskii

And once he had freed the land of Žemaitija from the Germans, he moved against the Rus'ian princes and came first of all to the town of Volodymer. Prince Volodymer Volodymerskii gathered his people together and waged a great battle with Grand Duke Kgidimin. And God aided Grand Duke Kgidimin, who killed Prince Volodymer Volodymerskii, destroyed his whole army and siezes the town of Volodymer. Next he goes against Prince Lev Lutskii. Prince Lev heard that the Lithuanians had killed Prince Volodymer and taken the town of Volodymer, and he dared not stand against them but fled to his brother-in-law to Prince Roman in Briansk. The princes and boiars of Volyn' paid homage to Grand Duke Kgidimin, that he might govern them and be lord over them and not punish their lands. Grand Duke Kgidimin bound them with an oath and left his own *namestniki* among them and he begins to be prince there. But then for the winter he goes to Brest. From Brest he disbanded all his army and wintered in Brest himself. Soon Easter day went by and he, having gathered all his Lithuanian, Žemaitijan and Rus'ian forces together, marched against Prince Stanislavl' Kievskii in the second week after Easter. Arriving [in the south] he takes the town of Ovruch and the town of Zhytomir'. Prince Stanislavl' Kievskii consulted Prince Oleg Pereiaslavskii, Prince Roman Brianskii and the prince of Volyn' whom Grand Duke Kgidimin had expelled from Lutsk and they all gathered their people in a great multitude and encountered Grand Duke Kgidimin on the river R'pen' below Belgorod, six miles from Kiev. They waged battle and a great slaughter and God aids Grand Duke Kgidimin. He smites all the Rus'ian princes on the head and on the shoulder all princes are smitten. The Lithuanians killed Prince Lev Lutskii and Prince Oleg Pereiaslavlskii and Stanislavl' Kievskii fled with his small retinue to Briansk along with Roman Brianskii. And Grand Duke Kgidimin encircles Belgorod. Seeing how their lord had fled from their army and that the whole army was smitten on the head, and they not wishing to stand against such a great Lithuanian host, the citizens surrendered their city to Prince Kgidimin and struck an oath to serve the Grand

Duchy of Lithuania. Then Grand Duke Kgidimin departed with all his forces to Kiev and laid siege to the city of Kiev and the Kievans began to defend their city against him. Grand Duke Kgidimin lay encamped below Kiev for a month and then the citizens of Kiev began to think to themselves how they could not withstand the might of the grand duke, especially [since they were] without their lord, Grand Duke Stanislavl' Kievskii. And they heard how their lord, Stanislavl' had fled from Kiev and how their lord's army was beaten and how their lord had left no rearguard with them. Having conferred unanimously, they surrendered to Grand Duke Kgidimin and the abbots, priests and deacons came out of the citadel carrying the cross. They opened the city gates and greeted the grand duke honourably. They paid him homage and gave themselves over to serve him. They gave their oath to Grand Duke Kgidimin to that effect and paid homage to Grand Duke Kgidimin, so that he would not deprive them of their homeland. After this Prince Kgidimin entered the city of Kiev with honour. The Kievan *prigorody*, Vyshgorod, Cherkasy, Kanev, Putivl' and Slepovrod, heard that the Kievans had surrendered their city and they heard of their lord how he had fled to Briansk, how all his army was beaten and so they all came to Grand Duke Kgidimin and gave themselves and the aforementioned Kievan *prigorody* over to his service and they gave their oath on this to Grand Duke Kgidimin. The Pereiaslavlians heard how Kiev and the Kievan *prigorody* had surrendered to Grand Duke Kgidimin and that their lord Prince Oleg had been killed by Grand Duke Kgidimin so they went and gave themselves and their city over to the service of Grand Duke Kgidimin and gave their oath on this. Grand Duke Kgidimin, having siezed Kiev, Pereiaslavl' and all these *prigorody*, installed over them Prince Ol'kgimont, son of Mindovg, grand prince of Golshany and with great joy he returned to Lithuania.

GUSTYNSKAIA CHRONICLE, *PSRL*, II (MOSCOW, 1843), 348

6812. Въ сие лето Гедиминъ князь литовский порази Лва Даниловича луцкаго и Володымера Василковича Волынскаго, и самаго уби, и Володимеръ градъ взятъ. Въ лето 6813. Паки Гедиминъ князь литовский Овруче и Житомиръ взятъ под княземъ Киевскимь Станиславомъ. Въ то же время и самаго князя Станислава Киевскаго и Лва луцкаго и Романа брянскаго и прочиихъ порази, и Киевъ под нимъ взяти и потомъ Каневъ, Черкасы, Путывль, Брянско и Волынъ. В сие лето Гедиминъ заложи место Троки и Вилно, брани же непрестанныя име зъ Ляхами, Крыжаками, Мазошани, пленяя ихъ землю.

6812 [AD 1304]. In this year the Lithuanian prince Gedimin" attacked Lev Danilovich of Lutsk and Volodymer Vasilkovich of Volyn', killing the latter and seizing the town of Volodimer'. In the year 6813 [AD 1305] the Lithuanian prince Gedimin" takes Ovruche and Zhitomir" from Prince Stanislav of Kiev. At the same time he attacked that Prince Stanislav of Kiev and Lev of Lutsk and Roman of Briansk and others and seized Kiev from them and then Kanev', Cherkasy, Putyvl', Briansko and Volyn'. In this year Gedimin" founded the city of Troki [Trakai] and Vilno and had unending battles with the Poles, Teutonic Knights, Mazovians and he took their lands captive.

MEZHIGORSKAIA CHRONICLE, DASHKEVICH, *ZAMETKI*, 56–7

Гедининъ князъ литовский посталъ на князя Киевскаго Станислава и победи его зъ киевскимъ и татарскимъ воиском над рекою Ирпеню, и Киевъ въ свою властъ взялъ, и зоставалъ Киевъ под литовскою властю.

The Lithuanian Prince Gedimin" stood against the Kievan Prince Stanislav and defeated him and his Kievan and Tatar army at the Irpen' river and he took Kiev into his control and Kiev remained under Lithuanian control.

POSLANIE SPIRIDONA-SAVVY IN DMITRIEVA, *SKAZANIE*, 167

Князь велики Александр Михайлович начят разсылати своя рядники по испаленым градом и местом от безбожнаго Батыя. Посла Бореика некоего на волынскую землю и на киевскую събирати оставшяа люди, бе бо муж храбр зело. Посла же и сего Гегиминика с седмию сыны его об сю страну Немиа такоже събирати люди по изпаленым градом и весем. Той же Гегиминик, преже бывши конюшец Витенев, начят съкровиша изискивати ливци некоими вълхвы страны тоя и сьбра богатства премнога. И прииди от Бореико от Волыня со многими данми. А сей Гегиминик, слободщик великого князя, от своея области, иже бе ему поручена от великого князя Александра Михаиловичя.

Grand Duke Aleksandr Mikhailovich begins to send out his officials around the towns and places burned down by the godless Baty. He sent a certain Boreiko to the Volynian and to the Kievan land to gather together the survivors, for he [Boreiko] was an exceedingly brave man. And he even sent this Gegiminik with his seven sons around the Nemunas land similarly to gather the people from the burned down cities and villages. This Gegiminik, having previously been Viten's groom, begins to seek out the treasuries of the Livs with the wizards of that country and he gathered a huge amount of wealth. And Boreiko comes from Volyn' with much tribute. But this Gegiminik was a subject (*slobodshchik*) of the grand duke in his domain which was granted to him by Grand Duke Aleksandr Mikhailovich.

SKAZANIE O KNIAZIAKH VLADIMIRSKIKH, DMITRIEVA, *SKAZANIE*, 179–80

Великий же князь (Юрий Данилович) начат разсылати по градом и местом собрати оставшаа люди. Посла убо сего Гегименика на *волоскую** землю и на киевьскую и обь сю страну Меньска наполняти плененыа грады и веси, у воставших имати дани царьскиа. И с ним посла некоего мужа славна именем Бореика и ины множайших. Сей же реченный Гегименик бе мужъ храбр зело и велика разума, начят брати дани на людех и съкровища изыскивати и обогатися зело. И собра к себе множество людей, дая им потребная нескудно, и начят владети многими землями. Назвася от них князь великий Гедиман литовъский первый великих государей русьских князей не съгласьем и междуусобными браньми.

* *волоскую* – *rectius*, *волынскую*; cf. above *Poslanie*

The Grand Duke [Yury Daniilovich] begins to send out around the towns and places to gather the survivors. So he sent this

Gegimenik to the Wallachian★ and Kievan land and around the land of Men'sk [Minsk] to capture the cities and villages and collect the tsar's tribute from the remnants. And with him he sent a certain renowned man named Boreiko and very many more. This so-called Gegimenik being an exceedingly brave man and of great understanding begins to take tribute from the people and seek out treasuries and he became exceedingly rich. And he gathered to himself a multitude of people, generously giving them what they required and he began to rule many lands. He was called by them the first Lithuanian grand duke, Gediman, without the consent of the great lord princes of Rus' and with internecine battles.

★ *rectius, Volynian.*

Appendix 2

LIST OF ORTHODOX HIERARCHS, 1283–1461

Metropolitans of Kiev (Vladimir) and All Rus'	Devolved Metropolitans of Galich/Lithuania within All Rus'	Metropolitans of Polish Galich (1371–98)
Maksim, 1283–1305 (Greek)	Nifon, 1303–05 GALICH **1592**[1]	
Pëtr, 1308–1326 (Rus'ian) **2008**	Feofil, *c.* 1316–30 LITHUANIA **2077, 2080** **2133, 2149**	
Feognost, 1327–53 (Greek) **2136, 2162** **2192, 2224** **2291, 2349** **2350**	?Gavriill, ?1331 GALICH **2163** ?Gavriill, 1336 **2172** Fëdor, 1342–47 GALICH **2224, 2291–92**	
	Feodorit, 1352–54 'RUS'' (A Lithuanian ordained in Bulgaria) **2336, 2363** **2368**	

<table>
<tr><th>Metropolitans of Kiev (Vladimir) and All Rus’</th><th>Devolved Metropolitans of Galich/Lithuania within All Rus’</th><th>Metropolitans of Polish Galich (1371–98)</th></tr>
<tr><td rowspan="3">Aleksei, 1354–78
(Rus’ian)
2363–64, 2366–68
2382, 2394, 2395
2406, 2434–35, 2445
2468, 2578–84, 2590
2592, 2625–26, 2635
2636–37, 2655–56,
2666</td><td rowspan="2">Roman, 1354–62
LITHUANIA–GALICH
2368, 2381–82, 2392
2394–95, 2406, 2434
2435, 2506, 2584</td><td></td></tr>
<tr><td rowspan="6">Antonii, (?) 1371–91
2616, 2622, 2635
2935, 3226, 3227</td></tr>
<tr><td rowspan="6">Kiprian, 1375–78
KIEV, LITHUANIA
AND RUS’
2690–91, 2693, 2701
2702, 2705–06, 2740
2789, 2796, 2820–22

Kiprian, metropolitan
of All Rus’, resident
in Lithuania, 1378–80,
1382–89

2847, 2849, 2852–54</td></tr>
<tr><td>Mikhail–Mitiai, 1378–79
(Muscovite pretender)
(PoM)</td></tr>
<tr><td>Kiprian accepted by
Dmitry Donskoi, 1381</td></tr>
<tr><td>Pimen, 1380; 1382–89
(Muscovite pretender)
(PoM)</td></tr>
<tr><td rowspan="2">Kiprian, metropolitan
of All Rus’, 1390–1406
2861, 2867, 2871,
2929–31, 2934–37, 3039,
3040, 3112</td></tr>
<tr><td rowspan="2">Ioann Baba, bishop
of Lutsk, 1391–98
First appointed, then
rejected by Jogaila
of Poland who recog-
nised Kiprian, 1398
2935, 3039, 3040</td></tr>
<tr><td rowspan="3">Fotii, 1408–31
(Greek)</td><td rowspan="2">Feodosy of Polotsk
Lithuanian pretender,
rejected in 1406
(Vitoldiana, 207)</td></tr>
<tr><td rowspan="2"></td></tr>
<tr><td></td></tr>
</table>

Metropolitans of Kiev (Vladimir) and All Rus'	Devolved Metropolitans of Galich/Lithuania within All Rus'	Metropolitans of Polish Galich (1371–98)
(Meyendorff, *Byzantium*, 256–8; 265–7)	Grigor Tsamblak Lithuanian pretender, rejected in 1415 (*Vitoldiana*, 207)	
Gerasim, 1434–35 (Lettovian) (*NL*, 417; *PL*, I, 40–3)		
Isidore, 1436–41 (Greek) (Golubinsky, *Istoria*, 426–68)	Isidore, 1441–58 Unionist metropolitan of Kiev	
Iona, 1448–61 First metropolitan appointed in Moscow (*PSRL*, XII, 74)	Grigory, 1458–70 Unionist metropolitan of Kiev (*RIB*, nos. 91–6)	

[1] Figures in bold face refer to documents in Darrouzès, *Regestes*, IV–VI.
PoM – *Povest' o Mitiae* (Prokhorov, *Povest'*, 218–24)

MANUSCRIPT SOURCES

BERLIN

Geheimes Staatsarchiv. Preussischer Kulturbesitz, Königsberg Archiv

Schlieblade 52 nr. 1–2; 54 nr. 3; 81 nr. 2

L. S. 10 nr. 38; 11 nr. 4, 17–21; 20; 26 nr. 1; 28 nr. 1; 30; 33; 34; 40 nr. 3

Papsturkunden 315

Ordens Folianten 1b; 11b; 12; 112; 271; 272; 293

CAMBRAI

Bibliothèque Municipale

538

CAMBRIDGE

University Library

Dd. II. 51

Ii. 2. 21

KRAKÓW

Biblioteka Czartoryskich

307

966

2211

3584/IV

IV/1180

Biblioteka Jagiellońska

2993

5887

Akc 34/52

Akc 71/52

Biblioteka Polskiej Akademii Nauk

Dok. 481; 1243

PRAGUE

Archiv Pražského Hradu, Knihovna metropolitní Kapituly

H 6/3

PSKOV

City Museum, *Drevnekhranilishche*

94/49;

90/49;

Shk. 23 n. 3 Mikhailov

RIGA

Central State Archive

LVVA, Fonds 673, 4/K-18, nos. 9, 17–25, 28, 30, 31

LVVA, Fonds 8, 3a, no. 41

LVVA, Fonds 8, 3b, no. 25a

ROME

Convento di Santa Sabina

XIII. 88350; 90520; 91540; 91800

XIV Lib R.513.

TALLINN

City Archives

Charters, Red Series, 44; 45; 67

VATICAN CITY

Archivio Segreto Vaticano

Registrum Vaticanum 22; 56; 62; 63; 76; 77; 78; 112; 136

Registrum Avenionense 2; 20; 21; 22; 53

Registra supplicationum 33

Archivium Arcis C. 1197; 1200; 1201

Instrumentum 1337

Biblioteca Apostolica Vaticana

Codex Vaticanus Graecus 840; 847

Codex Vaticanus Slavonicus 14

Codex Palatinus Graecus 226

Codex Ottobonus 528

VIENNA

Deutschordenszentralarchiv

Urkunden *c.* 1332

781

VILNIUS

Central Library of the Lithuanian Academy of Sciences

F6–132

F6–180

F43–210/1

F43–210/2
F43–20393

WARSAW
Biblioteka Narodowa
Biblioteka Ordynacji Zamojskiej 124; 201; 1108; cim 78; cim 154

BIBLIOGRAPHY

SOURCES

Acta aragonensia: Quellen zur deutschen, italienischen, französischen, spanischen, zur Kirchen- und Kulturgeschichte aus der diplomatischen Korrespondenz Jaymes II (1291–1327), ed. H. Finke, 3 vols. (Leipzig–Berlin, 1908–22).

Acta Clementis PP V, ed. A. L. Tautu (Vatican City, 1955).

Acta Ioannis PP XXII (1317–1334), ed. A. L. Tautu (Vatican City, 1952).

Acta Patriarchatus Constantinopolitani, ed. F. Miklosich and J. Müller, 2 vols. (Vienna, 1862).

Adamus Bremensis, *Gesta Hammaburgiensis ecclesiae pontificum*, ed. B. Schmeidler (Hanover–Leipzig, 1917).

Aelnothus monachus Cantuarensis, De vita et passione S. Canuti regis Daniae. Item anonymus, De passione S. Caroli comitis Flandriae eius filius, ed. J. Meursius (Copenhagen, 1631).

Aeneas Silvius Piccolomineus Senensis [Pope Pius II], *Opera quae extant omnia* (Basle, 1551).

Akta Grodzkie i ziemskie z czasów Rzeczypospolitej Polskiej z Archiwum tak zwanego Bernardyńskiego we Lwowie, ed. A. Stadnicki, VII (Lwow, 1878).

Akten und Recesse der livländischen Ständetage mit Überstützung der Baltischen Ritterschaften und Städte I (1304–1460), ed. O. Stavenhagen (Riga, 1907).

Akty Grodnenskogo Zemskogo Suda (Vilnius, 1865).

Akty i pechati Moskovskoi Rusi, ed. V. L. Ianin, 2 vols. (Leningrad, 1970).

Akty, otnosiashchiesia k istorii iuzhnoi i zapadnoi Rossii, I (1361–1598), ed. N. Kostomarov (St Petersburg, 1863).

Akty, otnosiashchiesia k istorii zapadnoi Rossii, ed. I. Grigorovich, I–II (St Petersburg, 1846–48).

Akty sotsial'no-ekonomicheskoi istorii severo-vostochnoi Rusi kontsa XIV–nachala XVI (Moscow, 1964).

Albert von Bardewik, 'Aufzeichnungen', *Chroniken der deutschen Städte*, XXVI (Leipzig, 1899), 285–316.

Analecta Byzantino-Russica, ed. W. Regel (St Petersburg–Leipzig, 1891).

Analecta Vaticana 1202–1366, ed. J. Ptaśnik, *Monumenta Poloniae Vaticana*, III (Kraków, 1914).

'Annales Cuiavienses', *MPH*, V, 885–9.

Annales Danici Medii Aevi, ed. E. Jørgensen (Copenhagen, 1920).

Annales Ecclesiastici, ed. C. Baronius *et al.*, 37 vols. (Paris–Freiburg–Bar le Duc, 1864–87).

'Annales Expeditiales Prussici (1233–1414)', *SRP*, III, 6–12.

'Annales Poloniae Maioris', *MPH*, n.s. VI (Warsaw, 1962).

'Annales Posnanienses', *MPH*, V, 874–84.

'Annalista Thorunensis', *SRP*, III, 57–316.

Annuae Litterae Societatis Jesu, 1604 (Douai, 1618).

Annuae Litterae Societatis Jesu, 1605 (Douai, 1618).

Arkhiv iugo-zapadnoi Rossii, V.1 (Kiev, 1869).

Bacon, Roger, *Opus Maius*, ed. J. H. Bridges, 3 vols. (Oxford–London–Edinburgh, 1897–1900).

Bartholomaeus Hoeneke, *Die Jüngere Livländische Reimchronik*, ed. K. Hohlbaum (Leipzig, 1872).

Liivimaa noorem riimkroonika (1315–1348) (Tallinn, 1960).

Bede, *Historia Ecclesiastica*, ed. C. Plummer (Oxford, 1896).

Benedict XII, *Lettres communes du pape Benoît XII*, ed. J. M. Vidal, *Bibliothèque des Ecoles françaises d'Athènes et de Rome*, 3rd series, 3 vols. (Paris, 1903–11).

Beneš of Weitmile, *Chronicon ecclesie pragensis*, *FRB*, IV, 459–548.

Beowulf edited with an introduction, notes and new prose translation by M. Swanton (Manchester, 1978).

Die Berichte der General Prokuratoren des Deutschen Ordens an der Kurie, ed. K. Forstreuter, I (Göttingen, 1961).

Blumenau, Laurenz, 'Historia de Ordine Theutonicorum Cruciferorum', *SRP*, IV, 35–75.

von Braun, F., *Civitates Orbis Terrarum*, III (Cologne, 1593).

'Breve Chronicon Silesiae', *SRP*, I, 249.

Brockhaus Wahrig Deutsches Wörterbuch, VI (Stuttgart, 1984).

Bündner Urkundenbuch, ed. E. Meyer-Marthaler and F. Perret, III (Chur, 1985).

Bullarium Franciscanum, ed. K. Eubel, 7 vols. (Rome, 1759–1904).

Bullarium Ordinis fratrum praedicatorum, ed. T. Ripoll, 8 vols. (Rome, 1729–40).

Bullarium Poloniae, ed. I. Sułkowska-Kuraś and S. Kuraś, 3 vols. (Rome, 1982–).

'Calendarium Cracoviense', *MPH*, II, 905–41.

La Chanson de Roland, ed. F. Whitehead (Oxford, 1965).

Chartularium Sangallense, ed. O. P. Clavadetscher (St Gallen, 1985).

Chronica XXIV Generalium, *Analecta Franciscana*, III (Quaracchi, 1897).

Chronicon de vitis episcoporum, *Scriptores Rerum Warmiensium*, ed. K. P. Woelky and Y. M. Saage, I (Braunsberg, 1886).

Chronicon Dubnicense, *Historiae Hungariae Fontes Domestici*, ed. M. Florianus, III (Leipzig, 1884).

'Chronik von Dünamünde', *SRP*, II, 139–42.

Chronik Johanns von Winterthur, ed. F. Baethgen, *MGH*, *SRG*, n.s. III (Berlin, 1924).

Die Chroniken des Wigand Gerstenbergs von Frankenberg, ed. H. Diemar (Marburg, 1909).

La Chronique de Jean de Hocsem, ed. G. Kurth (Brussels, 1927).

Codex diplomaticus et epistolaris Moraviae, ed. A. Boczek *et al.*, 15 vols. (Olomouc and Brünn, 1836–1903).

Codex Diplomaticus Lithuaniae, ed. E. Raczyński (Wrocław, 1845).

Codex Diplomaticus Prussicus, ed. J. Voigt, 6 vols. (Königsberg, 1836–61).
Codex Diplomaticus regni Poloniae et Magni Ducatus Lithuaniae, ed. M. Dogiel, I, IV, V (Vilnius, 1758–64).
Codex Diplomaticus Warmiensis, ed. H. Schmauch, I (Braunsberg, 1927).
Codex Epistolaris Saeculi Decimi Quinti, ed. A. Lewicki, 3 vols. (Kraków, 1876–94).
Codex Epistolaris Vitoldi magni ducis Lithuaniae, 1376–1430, ed. A. Prochaska, *Monumenta medii aevi historica*, VI (Kraków, 1882).
Colker, M. L., 'America rediscovered in the thirteenth century?', *Speculum*, 54 (1979), 712–26.
Corpus Historicum Medii Aevi, ed. J. G. Eccardus, 2 vols. (Leipzig, 1723–24).
Corpus Iuris Canonici, ed. E. L. Richter and E. Friedberg, II (Leipzig, 1881).
'Cronica di Giovanni Villani': *Biblioteca Classica italiana secolo XIV*, XXI, *Croniche di Giovanni, Matteo e Filippo Villani* (Trieste, 1857).
'Die Danziger Ordenschronik', *SRP*, IV, 357–65.
David, Lucas, *Preussische Chronik*, 8 vols. (Königsberg, 1812–17).
Decius, J. L., *De vetustatibus Polonorum*, *Poloniae Historicae Corpus*, ed. Pistorius (Basle, 1582).
Descripciones terrarum – see above Colker, 'America'.
Dietmar von Lübeck, *Chronik SRP*, III, 57–237.
Diplomatarium Danicum, ed. Danske Sprogog Litteraturselskab (Copenhagen, 1938–).
Długosz, Jan [Dlugossius, Johannes], *Annales seu cronicae incliti regni Poloniae*, ed. J. Dąbrowski, D. Turkowska *et al.* (Warsaw, 1964–).
Drevnerusskaia kormchaia XIV titulov bez tolkovania, ed. V. N. Beneshevich, re-ed. Ia. N. Shchapov (Sofia, 1987).
Drevnerusskie kniazheskie ustavy XI–XVvv., ed. Ia. N. Shchapov (Moscow, 1976).
Dubrawius, Johannes, *Historia Bohemica*, I (Frankfurt, 1687).
Dudo of St Quentin, *De moribus et actis primorum Normanniae ducum*, ed. J. Lair (Caen, 1865).
Epifany Premudry, 'Povest' o Stefane episkope Permskom', *Sokrovishche drevnerusskoi literatury: Drevnerusskie predania (XI–XVIvv)*, ed. V. V. Kuskov *et al.* (Moscow, 1982), 161–94.
'Epitome Gestorum Prussiae (Canonici Sambiensis)', *SRP*, I, 272–90.
'Epitome principum Lithuaniae', J. Jakubowski, *Studya nad stosunkami narodowościowemi na Litwie przed Unią Lubelską* (Warsaw, 1912).
Die Erste Novgoroder Chronik nach ihrer ältesten Redaktion (Synodalhandschrift) 1016–1333/1352, ed. J. Dietze (Leipzig, 1971).
Eulogium Historiarum, ed. F. Scott-Haydon, 3 vols. (London, 1858–63).
'Fontes Olivenses', *MPH*, VI, 257–382.
Fontes Rerum Bohemicarum, ed. F. Palacký, J. Emler *et al.*, 8 vols. (Prague, 1873–92).
František of Prague, *Chronica pragensis*, *FRB*, IV, 347–456.
Gedimino Laiškai, ed. V. T. Pashuto and I. Štal (Vilnius, 1966).
Germaniae historicorum illustrium, ed. C. Wurstisen, II (Frankfurt, 1670).

Oeuvres de Ghillebert de Lannoy, voyageur, diplomate et moraliste, ed. C. Potvin and J-C. Houzeau (Louvain, 1878).

Golubtsev, S. T., 'Drevnii pomiannik Kievo-Pecherskoi Lavry (kontsa XV–nachala XVIvv)', *Chtenia v istoricheskom obshchestve Nestora Letopistsa*, VI (1892).

Gramoty Velikogo Novgoroda i Pskova, ed. S. N. Valk (Moscow–Leningrad, 1949).

Gregory of Tours, *The History of the Franks*, tr. L. Thorpe (Harmondsworth, 1974).

Guillaume de Machaut, *Oeuvres Complètes*, ed. E. Hoepffner, 3 vols. (Paris, 1921).

Hansisches Urkundenbuch, ed. K. Höhlbaum, II (Halle, 1879).

Heidenstein, R., *De Bello Moscovitico commentariorum libri sex* (Kraków, 1588).

Heinrich Truchsess von Diessenhoffen, 'Chronica', *SRP*, III, 420

(Henry the Latvian) Henricus Lettus, *Chronicon Livoniae*, ed. L. Arbusow and A. Bauer (Darmstadt, 1959).

(Henry the Deaf) Henricus Surdus de Selbach, *Chronicon*, ed. H. Bresslau, *MGH, SRG*, n.s. I (Berlin, 1922).

Henrikas Latvis, Hermanas Vartbergė, *Livonijos Kronikos*, ed. and tr. J. Jurginis (Vilnius, 1991).

Henryk z Gore, 'Tractatulus contra Cruciferos regni Poloniae invasores', *MPH*, IV, 143–91.

Hermann of Wartberge, *Chronicon Livoniae*, *SRP*, II, 21–116.

Ibn Battuta, *Travels in Asia and Africa 1325–1354* (London, 1929; 2nd edn 1983).

In Cornelii Taciti equitis Romani Germaniam commentaria, D. Iodocus Vuillichius Resellianus (Frankfurt, 1551).

Iura Masoviae Terrestria. Pomniki dawnego prawa mazowieckiego ziemskiego, ed. J. Sawicki, 3 vols. (Warsaw, 1972–74).

Jean d'Outremeuse des Preïs, *Chronique et geste*, ed. A. Borgnet and S. Bormans, 7 vols. (Brussels, 1864–87).

Johann von Posilge, 'Chronik', *SRP*, III, 79–388.

Johann von Wurzburg, *Wilhelm von Österreich aus der Gothaer Handschrift*, ed. E. Regel, *Deutsche texte des Mittelalters*, III (1906).

John XXII, *Lettres communes du pape Jean XXII analysées d'après les régistres dits d'Avignon et du Vatican*, ed. G. Mollat, *Bibliothèque des Ecoles françaises d'Athènes et de Rome*, 3rd series, 16 vols. (Paris, 1904–47).

Lettres secrètes et curiales relatives à la France, ed. A. Coulon and S. Clémencet, *Bibliothèque des Ecoles françaises d'Athènes et de Rome*, 3rd series, 4 vols. (Paris, 1906–72).

John of Salisbury, *Polycraticus*, PL, CXCIX (Paris, 1855).

(John of Victring) *Johannes Victoriensis und andere Geschichtsquellen Deutschlands im vierzehnten Jahrhundert*, ed. J. F. Boehmer, *Fontes Rerum Germanicarum*, I (Stuttgart, 1843).

Jüngere Hochmeisterchronik, *SRP*, V, 1–148.

Kammerei-Register der Stadt Riga 1348–1361 und 1405–1474, ed. A. von Bulmerincq, I (Leipzig, 1909).

Karskii, E.Th., *Zapadno-russkii sbornik XVogo veka prinadlezhashchii imperatorskoi publichnoi biblioteke Q.1. no.391* (St Petersburg, 1897).

Kodeks dyplomatyczny katedry i diecezji wileńskiej, ed. J. Fijałek and W. Semkowicz (Kraków, 1948).
Kodeks dyplomatyczny Księstwa Mazowieckiego (Warsaw, 1863).
Kodeks dyplomatyczny Małopolski, ed. F. Piekosiński, 4 vols. (Kraków, 1876–1905).
Komorowski, J., 'Memoriale Ordinis Fratrum Minorum', *MPH*, V, 1–418.
Kraštas ir žmonės. Lietuvos geografiniai ir etnografiniai aprašymai (XIV–XIXa.), ed. J. Jurginis and A. Šidlauskas (Vilnius, 1983).
'Kronika Pulkavová', *FRB*, V, 3–326.
Kronika Jana z Czarnkowa, *MPH*, II, 601–756.
'Kronika Książąt Polskich', *MPH*, III, 423–578.
'Kronika Wielkopolska', *MPH*, II, 454–600.
Kroniky doby Karla IV (Prague, 1987).
'Kurze Preussische Annalen 1190–1337', *SRP*, III, 1–4.
'Kurze Reimchronik von Preussen', *SRP*, II, 1–8.
Lampros, S., 'Duo anaforai mētropolitou Monemvasios pros ton patriarkhēn', *Nēos Hellēnomēnōn*, 12 (1915), 257–318.
Laonici Chalcocondylae Athenensis Historiarum Libri X, ed. I. Bekker (Bonn, 1843).
Der Russland Exkurs des Laonikos Chalkokondyles. Berliner Byzantische Arbeiten, XXXIX (1968).
Legenda sancti Gerhardi episcopi, ed. E. Szentpétery, *Scriptores rerum hungaricarum*, ed. E. Szentpétery, II (Budapest, 1938), 461–506.
Legum Iustiniani imperatoris vocabularium. Novellae pars graeca, ed. G. G. Archi, IV (Milan, 1988).
Libellus de institutione morum, ed. J. Balogh, *Scriptores rerum hungaricarum*, II (Budapest, 1938), 611–27.
Libro des conoscimiento de todos los reynos ..., ed. and tr. C. Markham *Hakluyt Society*, 2nd series, XXIX (London, 1912).
'Life of St Euphrosyne of Polack', tr. A. Nadson, *Journal of Byelorussian Studies*, 2:1 (1969), 3–24.
Litauische und Lettische Drucke des 16 Jahrhunderts I: Der litauische Katechismus vom Jahre 1547, ed. A. Bezzenberger (Göttingen, 1874).
Litauische Wegeberichte, *SRP*, II, 662–711.
Lites ac res gestae inter Polonos Ordinemque cruciferorum, ed. T. Działyński, I.1 (Poznań, 1855).
Lites ..., ed. I. Zakrzewski and J. Karwasińska, *editio altera*, I (Poznań–Warsaw, 1890–1935).
Lites ..., ed. H. Chłopocka, I (Wrocław–Warsaw–Kraków, 1970).
Liv- Esth- und Kurländisches Urkundenbuch, nebst Regesten, ed. F. G. von Bunge, 6 vols. (Riga–Reval, 1853–71; 2nd edn Aalen, 1967–74)
Die Livländische Reimchronik, ed. L. Meyer (Paderborn, 1876).
The Livonian Rhymed Chronicle, translated with an historical introduction, maps and appendices by J. C. Smith and W. L. Urban [*Indiana University Publications: Uralic and Altaic series*, CXXVIII (1977)].
Lübeckisches Urkundenbuch, I (Lübeck, 1843).

Łuczyca, E., 'Trzy dokumenty książąt mazowieckich z pierwszej połowy XIVw.', *PH*, 64 (1973), 345–66.

Maciej z Miechowa, *Opis Sarmacji azjatyckiej i europejskiej*, ed. H. Barycz and T. Bieńkowski, *Źródła do Dziejów Nauki i Techniki*, XIV (1972).

Magistri P. Belae Regis notarii Gesta Hungarorum, *Historiae hungaricae fontes domestici*, ed. M. Florianus, II (Leipzig, 1863), 1–51.

Mannhardt, W., *Letto-Preussische Götterlehre*, *Magazin der Lettisch Litterärischen Gesellschaft*, XXI (Riga, 1936; reprinted Hanover–Döhren, 1971).

Marino Sanudo Torsello the Elder, *Secretum Fidelium Crucis* and *Epistolae* in: *Gesta Dei per Francos*, ed. J. Bongars, II (Hanover, 1611).

Marsiglio of Padua, *Defensor pacis*, *Fontes iuris germanici antiqui*, ed. R. Scholz (Hanover, 1932).

Matthias de Nuwenburg, *Chronica*, ed. A. Hofmeister, *MGH*, *SRG*, n.s. IV(1) (Berlin, 1924).

de Mézières, Philippe, *Songe du Vieil Pelerin*, ed. G. W. Coopland, 2 vols. (Cambridge, 1969).

Miscellanea rerum ad statum ecclesiasticum in Magno Lithuaniae Ducatu pertinentium, ed. A. W. Koialowicz SJ (Vilnius, 1650).

Monumenta Germaniae Historica. Legum Sectio IV: *Constitutiones et Acta Publica imperatorum et regum*, ed. J. Schwalm, V–VI (Hanover–Leipzig, 1909–27).

Monumenta Poloniae Historica, ed. Akademia Umiejętności, 6 vols. (Lwów–Kraków, 1864–93).

Mykolas Lietuvis, *Apie Totorių, Lietuvių ir Maskvenių Papročius*, ed. K. Korsakas *et al.* (Vilnius, 1966).

Nicephoras Gregoras, *Historiae Byzantinae*, PG, CXLVIII–CXLIX (Paris, 1855).

Parisot, V., 'Notice sur le livre XXXVII de Nicéphore Grégoras avec une traduction française et des notes', *Notices et Extraits des manuscrits*, 17:2 (1851), 1–406.

Nicolaus von Jeroschin, *Di Kronike von Pruzinlant*, *SRP*, I, 291–624.

Notitiae Episcopatuum ecclesiae constantinopolitanae. Texte critique, introduction et notes, ed. J. Darrouzès (Paris, 1981).

Nova Alamanniae, ed. E. F. Stengel, I (Berlin, 1921).

Novgorodskaia Kharateinaia Letopis', ed. M. N. Tikhomirov (Moscow, 1964).

Novgorodskaia Pervaia Letopis' starshego i mladshego izvodov, ed. A. N. Nasonov (Moscow–Leningrad, 1950).

Novgorodskie Letopisi, ed. A. F. Bychkov (St Petersburg, 1879).

Novgorodskie Pistsovskie Knigi, I–II (St Petersburg, 1859).

Nowy kodeks dyplomatyczny Mazowsza. Część druga, ed. I. Sułkowska-Kuraś, S. Kuraś *et al.* (Wrocław–Warsaw–etc, 1989).

Obolensky, M. A., *Iarlyk' khana Zolotoi Ordy Tokhtamysha k pol'skomu koroliu Iagailu 1392–1393 goda* (Kazan', 1850).

On the properties of things. John Trevisa's translation of Bartholomaeus Anglicus, De proprietatibus rerum. A critical text, ed. M. C. Seymour, 2 vols. (Oxford, 1975).

Origines Livoniae sacrae, ed. J. D. Gruber (Frankfurt, 1740).

d'Orville, Jean Cabaret, *La chronique du bon duc Loys de Bourbon*, ed. M. Chazaud (Paris, 1876).

'Otryvki V. N. Beneshevicha po istorii russkoi tserkvi XIV veka', ed. M. D. Priselkov and M. R. Vasmer, *IORIaS*, 21 (1916), 48–67.

Pam'iatki ukrains'koi movi – Gramoty XIV stoletia, ed. M. M. Peshchak (Kiev, 1974).

Pavlov, A. S., *Pamiatniki drevnerusskogo kanonicheskogo prava, Russkaia Istoricheskaia Biblioteka*, VI (St Petersburg, 1880).

Pavstos Bouzand, *Pamut'yun Hayoc – Istoria Armenii Favstosa Buzanda*, ed. M. A. Gevorgian (Erevan, 1953).

Peter of Dusburg, *Chronica Terrae Prussiae*, *SRP*, I, 3–219.

Petras Dusburgietis Prūsijos žemės Kronika, ed. R. Batūra (Vilnius, 1985).

Die Peters von Dusburg Chronik des Preussenlandes, ed. and tr. K. Scholz and D. Wojtecki, *Ausgewählte Quellen zur deutschen Geschichte des Mittelalters*, XXV (Darmstadt, 1984).

Peter von Suchenwirt, *Werke*, *SRP*, II, 155–69.

Petra Žitavského Kronika Zbraslavska, *FRB*, IV, 3–337.

Francesci Petrarcae Vergilianus Codex, ed. G. Galbiati (Milan, 1930).

Polnoe Sobranie Russkikh Letopisei:

1 *Lavrent'evskaia Letopis' i Suzdal'skaia Letopis' po akademicheskomu spisku* (Moscow, 1962).

2 *Ipat'evskaia Letopis'*; *Gustynskaia Letopis'* (Moscow, 1843).
Ipatev'skaia Letopis' (Moscow, 1962).

4 *Novgorodskaia IVaia Letopis'* (St Petersburg, 1848).

5–6 *Pskovskaia i Sofiiskie Letopisi* (St Petersburg, 1851–53).

7–8 *Letopis' po Voskresenskomu Spisku* (St Petersburg, 1856–59).

9–14 *Patriarshaia ili Nikonovskaia Letopis'* (Moscow, 1965).

15 *Rogozhskii Letopisets* and *Tverskoi Sbornik* (Moscow, 1965).

16 *Letopisnyi Sbornik, imenuemyi Letopis'iu Avraamki* (St Petersburg, 1889).

17 *Zapadno-Russkie Letopisi* (St Petersburg, 1907).

18 *Semeonovskaia Letopis'* (St Petersburg, 1913).

20 *L'vovskaia Letopis'* (St Petersburg, 1910).

21 *Stepennaia Kniga* (St Petersburg, 1913).

23 *Ermolinskaia Letopis'* (St Petersburg, 1910).

24 *Tipografskaia Letopis'* (Petrograd, 1921).

25 *Moskovskii Letopisnyi Svod kontsa XV veka* (Moscow–Leningrad, 1949).

26 *Vologodsko-Permskaia Letopis'* (Moscow–Leningrad, 1954).

27 *Nikanorovskaia Letopis'*; *Sokrashchennye Letopisnye Svody kontsa XV veka* (Moscow–Leningrad, 1962).

28 *Letopisnyi Svod 1497g.*; *Uvarovskaia Letopis'* (Moscow–Leningrad, 1963).

30 *Vladimirskii Letopisets*; *Novgorodskaia Vtoraia* (*Arkhivskaia*) *Letopis'* (Moscow, 1965).

31 *Letopistsy poslednei chetverti XVIIv.* (Moscow, 1968).

32 *Khroniki Litovskaia i zhmoitskaia*; *Bykhovtsa* (Moscow, 1975).

33 *Kholmogorskaia Letopis'*; *Dvinskoi Letopisets* (Leningrad, 1977).

34 *Postnikovskii, Piskarevskii, Moskovskii i Bel'skii Letopistsy* (Moscow, 1978).
35 *Letopisi Belorussko-Litovskie* (Moscow, 1980).

Polotskie Gramoty XIII–nachalo XVIvv., ed. A. L. Khoroshkevich, 3 vols. (Moscow, 1977–80).

Poslanie Spiridona-Savvy, Skazanie o Kniaziakh Vladimirskikh, 159–70.

Povesti o Kulikovskoi bitve, ed. M. N. Tikhomirov (Moscow, 1959).

'Povest' o vodvorenii Khristianstva v Murome', *Pamiatniki Starinnoi russkoi literatury*, ed. N. Kostomarov (St Petersburg, 1860).

Povest' Vremennykh Let, ed. D. S. Likhachev, 2 vols. (Moscow–Leningrad, 1950).

Preussisches Urkundenbuch (Politisches Abtheilung), ed. K. P. Woelky, M. Hein, E. Maschke *et al.*, 6 vols. (Königsberg–Marburg, 1882–1986).

Priselkov, M. D., *Khanskie Iarlyki russkim mitropolitam, Zapiski istoriko-filologicheskogo fakul'teta Imperatorskogo S Peterburgskogo Universiteta*, CXXXIII (1916).

Prochaska, A., 'Z Archiwum Zakonu niemieckiego. Analecta z wieku XIV i XV', *Archiwum Komisyi historycznej Akademii Umiejętnosci w Krakowie*, 11 (1911), 217–56.

Pskovskie Letopisi, ed. A. N. Nasonov, 2 vols. (Moscow–Leningrad, 1941–55).

Rashid-ad-Din, *Chronicle*, ed. V. G. Tiesenhausen, *Sbornik Materialov*, II, 27–9.

'Rasskaz o Aleksei Mitropolite', G. M. Prokhorov, *Povest' o Mitiae: Rus' i Vizantia v epokhu Kulikovskoi bitvy* (Leningrad, 1978), 216–24.

Regesta diplomatica necnon epistolaria Bohemiae et Moraviae, ed. J. Emler, B. Mendl *et al.*, III–VI (Prague, 1890–1928).

Regesta historico-diplomatica Ordinis S. Mariae Theutonicorum 1198–1525, ed. W. Hubatsch and E. Joachim, I (Göttingen, 1948).

Regesta Lithuaniae ab origine usque ad Magni Ducatus cum regno Poloniae unionem, I: Tempora usque ad annum 1315 complectens, ed. H. Paszkiewicz (Warsaw, 1930).

Les Regestes du patriarchat de Constantinople, I: Les actes des patriarches, ed. J. Darrouzès, IV–VI (Paris, 1977–79).

Das Register des Patriarchats von Konstantinopel, II: Edition und Übersetzung der Urkunden aus den Jahren 1315–1331, ed. H. Hunger and O. Kresten (Vienna, 1981).

De Registers en vekeningen van Het Bisdom Utrecht 1325–1336, ed. S. Muller, I, *Werken utgegeven door het Historisch Genootschap gevestigd te Utrecht*, n.s. LIII (Utrecht, 1889).

Relationes status diocesium in Magno Ducatu Lithuaniae, I: Diocesis Vilnensis et Samogitiae, ed. P. Rabikauskas (Rome, 1971).

Reversales Frederici – MGH Constitutiones et Acta Publica imperatorum et regum, ed. J. Schwalm, VI.1 (Hanover, 1914–27).

Das Rigische Schuldbuch (1285–1352), ed. H. Hildebrand (St Petersburg, 1872).

'Rocznik Cystersów Henrykowskich', *MPH*, III, 699–704.

'Rocznik Kujawski', *MPH*, III, 204–12.

'Rocznik Małopolski', *MPH*, III, 135–202.

'Rocznik Miechowski', *MPH*, II, 880–96.

'Rocznik Poznański', *MPH*, n.s. VI, 127–41.
'Rocznik Swietokrzyski', *MPH*, III, 53–87.
'Rocznik Traski', *MPH*, II, 826–61.
'Rodowód Xiążąt polskich', *MPH*, III, 280–4.
Ronneburg Annals, *Stryjkowski*, I, 282–4.
Rozmowa Polaka z Litwinem 1564, ed. J. Korzeniowski (Kraków, 1890).
Russkaia Pravda – prostrannaia redaktsia, Pamiatniki Russkogo Prava, I: Pamiatniki prava kievskogo gosudarstva X–XIIvv., ed. A. A. Zimin (Moscow, 1952).
Russkii feodal'nyi arkhiv XIV–pervoi treti XVI veka (Moscow, 1986).
Russko-Livonskie Akty, ed. K. E. Napiersky (St Petersburg, 1868).
Saxo Grammaticus, *Historia Danica*, ed. P. Müller and J. M. Velochow, II (Copenhagen, 1839).
Danorum Regum Heroumque Historia Books X–XVI. The text of the first edition with translation and commentary in three volumes by E. Christiansen. II: *Books XIV, XV, XVI, British Archaeological Reports*, International Series CXVIII(ii) (1981)
Sbornik letopisei otnosiashchikhsia k istorii Iuzhnoi i Zapadnoi Rossii, izdannyi Kommissiciu dla razbora drcvnikh aktov sostoiashchci pri Kievskom, Podolskom i Volynskom General'-Gubernatore, ed. V. Antonovich (Kiev, 1888).
Schäfer, K. H., *Die Ausgaben der Apostolischen Kammer unter Johann XXII* (Paderborn, 1911).
Schondochs Gedichte, ed. H. Heintz, *Germanistische Abhandlungen*, 30 (Breslau, 1908), 42–55.
Scriptores Rerum Livonicarum, II (Riga–Leipzig, 1848).
Scriptores Rerum Prussicarum, ed. F. Hirsch, M. Töppen and E. Strehlke, 5 vols. (Leipzig, 1861–74; 2nd edn Frankfurt-am-Main, 1965, vol. VI added).
Sigizmund Gerbershtein, *Zapiski o Moskovii*, ed. A. L. Khoroshkevich and V. L. Ianin (Moscow, 1988).
Sinopsis, Kiev 1681. Facsimile mit einer Einleitung, ed. H. Rothe, *Bausteine zur Geschichte der Literatur bei den Slaven*, XVII (Cologne–Vienna, 1983).
Skazanie o Kniaziakh Vladimirskikh, ed. R. P. Dmitrieva (Moscow–Leningrad, 1955).
Smolenskaia Starina, I, part 2 (Smolensk, 1911).
Smolenskie Gramoty XIII–XIV vekov, ed. R. I. Avanesov (Moscow, 1963).
Sobranie gosudarstvennykh gramot i dogovorov khraniashchikhsia v gosudarstvennoi kollegii inostrannykh del', I (Moscow, 1813).
Sokrovishchia drevnerusskoi literatury. Krasnorechie Drevnei Rusi (XI–XVIIvv), ed. T. V. Chertoritskoi (Moscow, 1987).
Speranskii, M. N., *Serbskoe Zhitie litovskikh muchenikov*, *ChOIDR* (1909/4), 1–47.
Spisok Russkikh gorodov dal'nikh ĭ blizhnikh, ed. M. N. Tikhomirov, *Istoricheskie Zapiski*, 40 (1952), 236–42.
'Spomniki Gnieźnieńskie', *MPH*, III, 42–5.
'Spomniki Mieszane', *MPH*, III, 228–31.
'Spomniki Płockie i Sochaczewskie', *MPH*, III, 118–24.

Statuty synodalne Wieluńsko-Kaliskie Mikolaja Traby z r.1420 (Kraków, 1915–1920–1951).

Der Stralsunder Liber Memorialis, I., Fol. 1–60, 1320–1410, ed. H-D. Schroeder (Leipzig, 1964).

Stryjkowski, M., *O początkach, wywodach, dzielnościach, sprawach rycerskich i domowych sławnego narodu litewskiego, źemojdzkiego, i ruskiego, przedtym nigdy od żadnego ani kuszone, ani opisane, z natchnienia Bożego a uprzejmie pilnego doświadczenia*, ed. J. Radziszewska (Warsaw, 1978).

Kronika polska, litewska, zmódźka i wszystkiej Rusi, 2 vols. (Warsaw, 1846; reprinted 1985).

Tacitus, *Opera Minora*, ed. M. Winterbottom and R. M. Ogilvie (Oxford, 1975).

Thietmar of Merseburg, *Chronicon*, ed. J. Lappenberg and F. Kurze (Hanover, 1889).

Tiesenhausen, V. G., *Sbornik materialov, otnosiashchikhsia k istorii Zolotoi Ordy*, I (St Petersburg, 1884); II, ed. A. A. Romashkevich and S. L. Volin (Moscow–Leningrad, 1941).

Treaty Rolls preserved in the Public Record Office, ed. P. Chaplais, I (1234–1325) (London, 1955).

Troitskaia Letopis': rekonstruktsia teksta, ed. M. D. Priselkov (Moscow, 1950).

'Turovskie ustavy XIV veka o desiatine', ed. Ia. N. Shchapov, *AE* (1964), 252–73.

Tyc, T., 'Inwekty na Litwinów i Polaków z XV wieku – *Opusculum contra canciones adversum regem Albertum confictas*', *AW*, 4 (1927), 459–62.

Vetera Monumenta Poloniae et Lithuaniae gentiumque finitimarum historiam illustrantia, ed. A. Theiner, I (Rome, 1860).

Vita S. Adalberti, *MGH*, *Scriptores*, IV (Hanover, 1841), 574–616.

Vitae paparum avenionensium, ed. E. Baluze and G. Mollat, I (Paris, 1914).

Vitoldiana: Codex privilegiorum Vitoldi Magni Ducis Lithuaniae 1386–1430, ed. J. Ochmáski (Warsaw–Poznań, 1986).

Wadding, Luke, *Annales Minorum*, 6 vols. (Lyons, 1625–48); 25 vols. (Rome, 1731–1933).

Weise, E., *Die Staatsscriften des Deutschen Ordens in Preussen im 15 Jahrhundert, I: Die Traktate vor dem Konstanzer Konzil (1414–1418) über das Recht des Deutschen Ordens am Lande Preussen, Veröffentlichungen der niedersächsischen Archiv-verwaltung*, XXVII (1970).

Wigand of Marburg, *Cronica nova Prutenica*, *SRP*, II, 429–662.

Willelmi Capellani in Brederode postea monachi et procuratoris Egmondensis Chronicon ed. C. Pijnacker Hordijk, *Werken utgegeven door het Historisch Genootschap gevestigd te Utrecht*, 3rd series, XX (Amsterdam, 1904).

Zbiór dokumentów małopolskich, ed. S. Kuraś *et al.*, I, IV (Wrocław–Warsaw–Kraków–Łódź, 1962, 1969).

Zbiór praw litewskich, ed. V. Działynski (Poznań, 1849).

Das Zeugenverhör des Franciscus de Moliano (1312). *Quellen zur Geschichte des Deutschen Ordens*, ed. A. Seraphim (Königsberg, 1912).

Zhitie Mitropolita Petra (Prokhor version), Makary, *Istoria russkoi tserkvi*, IV, 1 (St Petersburg, 1866), 311–13.

(Metropolitan Kiprian's version), B. S. Angelov, *Iz starata b''lgarska, ruska i s'rbska literatura* (Sofia, 1958), 166–9.
Život česaře Karla IV, FRB, III, 325–417.
Źródła do mytologii litewskiej, ed. A. Mierzyński, 2 vols. (Warsaw, 1892–96).

STUDIES

Abbot, T. K., *Catalogue of the manuscripts in the library of Trinity College Dublin* (Dublin–London, 1900).
Abe, K., *Die Komturei Osterode des Deutschen Ordens in Preussen 1341–1525*, *Studien zur Geschichte Preussens*, XVI (Cologne, 1972).
Abel, W., *Agricultural fluctuations in Europe. From the thirteenth to the twentieth centuries*, tr. O. Ordish, foreword and bibliography J. Thirsk (London, 1980).
Abraham, W., 'Stanowisko kurii papieskiej wobec koronacji Łokietka', *Księga pamiątkowa wydana przez Uniwersytet lwowski ku uczczeniu 500-letniego jubileusza Uniwersytetu krakowskiego* (Lwów, 1900), 1–34.
Powstanie organizacyi kościoła łacińskiego na Rusi (Lwów, 1904).
Abramowicz, A., 'Maciej Stryjkowski o pobojowiskach', *Studia nad kulturą materialną wieków od XIV do XVI*, ed. T. Poklewski (Wrocław–Warsaw–Kraków–Gdańsk–Łódź, 1986), 61–74.
Adamus, J., 'O tytule panującego i państwa litewskiego parę spostrzeżeń', *KH*, 44 (1930), 313–32.
Adriányi, G., 'Der Eintritt Ungarns in die Chrsitlich-abendländlische Völkergemeinschaft', *Ungarn-Jahrbuch*, 6 (1974–75), 24–37.
Agapkina, T. A. and Toporkov, A. L., 'Materialy po slavian'skomu iazychestvu (drevnerusskie svidetel'stva o pochitanii derev'ev)', *Literatura Drevnei Rusi. Istochnikovedenie, Sbornik nauchnykh trudov*, ed. D. S. Likhachev (Leningrad, 1988), 224–35.
Akinian, P. N., 'Johannes Nasredinean Erzbischof der Armener Galiziens und der Walachei (1380–1415)', *Handes Amsorya*, 61 (1947), 299–318.
Aleksandrowicz, S., *Rozwój kartografii Wielkiego Księstwa Litewskiego od XV do połowy XVIII wieku*, 2 vols. (Poznań, 1989).
Alekseev, L. V., *Smolenskaia zemlia v IX–XIIIvv. Ocherki istorii Smolenshchiny i vostochnoi Belorussii* (Moscow, 1980).
Aleshkovskii, M. Kh., 'Novgorodskii detinets 1044–1430gg. (po materialam novykh issledovanii)', *Arkhitekturnoe Nasledstvo*, 14 (1962), 3–26.
Alessio, G. C., Billanovich, G. and De Angelis, V., 'L'Alba del Petrarca filologo. Il Virgilio Ambrosiano', *Studi Petrarcheschi*, n.s. 2 (1985), 15–33.
Alssen, L., 'Peter Suchenwirt and the *Drang nach Osten*', *Lituanus*, 22:4 (1978), 5–16.
Andriiashov, A. M., *Ocherki istorii Volynskoi zemli do kontsa XIV stoletia* (Kiev, 1887).
Andriūlis, V., 'Gedimino diplomatijos dokumentai kaip šaltinis teisės istorijai pažinti', *Teisinių Institutų raida Lietuvoje XVI–XIXa.*, ed. P. Dičius *et al.* (Vilnius, 1981), 33–43.

Bibliography

Angenendt, A., 'The conversion of the Anglo-Saxons considered against the background of the early medieval mission', *Settimane di Studio del Centro Italiano di Studi sull'alto medioevo XXXII: Angli e sassoni al di qua e al di là del mare*, 2 (Spoleto, 1986), 747–81.

Antanavičius, J., 'Balno kilpos Lietuvoje X–XIVa.', *LMADA*, 54 (1976), 69–81.

Antonova, V. I. and Mneva, N. E., *Katalog drevnerusskoi zhivopisi – Opyt istoriko-khudozhestvennoi klassifikatsii*, II (Moscow, 1963).

Antonovich, V. B., *Monografii po istorii zapadnoi i iugo-zapadnoi Rossii*, I (Kiev, 1885).

Antonovich, V. B. and Ilovaiskii, D., *Istoria Velikogo Kniazhestva Litovskogo* (Ternopol', 1887).

Apanovich, E. M., *Rukopisnaia svetskaia kniga XVIIIv. na Ukraine. Istoricheskie Sborniki* (Kiev, 1983).

Arbusow, L., 'Römischer Arbeitsbericht', *Latvijas Ūniversitātes Raksti*, 17 (1928), 285–422 and 20 (1929), 445–656.

Arnold, U., 'Deutschordenshistoriographie in Deutschen Reich', in *Die Rolle der Ritterorden in der mittelalterlichen Kultur*, ed. Z. H. Nowak (Toruń, 1985), 65–87.

Arquillière, H-X., *Le plus ancien traité de l'Eglise. Jacques de Viterbe, De Regimine Christiano (1301–1302). Etude des sources et édition critique* (Paris, 1926).

Aścik, K., 'O pochodzeniu rodu Ościków (legendy i rzeczywistość)', *Acta Baltico-Slavica* 11 (1977), 317–29.

Avižonis, K., *Die Entstehung und Entwicklung des litauischen Adels bis zur litauisch-polnischen Union 1385* (Berlin, 1932).

Balard, M., 'Gênes et la Mer noire (XIII–XV siècles)', *Revue Historique*, 547 (1983), 31–54.

Balticum. Studia z dziejów polityki, gospodarki i kultury XII–XVII wieku ofiarowane Marianowi Biskupowi w siedemdziesiątą rocznicę urodzin. ed. Z. H. Nowak (Toruń, 1992).

Baltramaitis, S., *Sbornik bibliograficheskikh materialov dlia geografii, etnografii i statistiki Litvy s prilozheniem spiska litovskikh i drevnerusskikh knig s 1553 po 1891* (St Petersburg, 1891).

Balzer, O., *Genealogia Piastów* (Kraków, 1895).

Sądownictwo ormiańskie w średniowiecznym Lwowie – Studya nad historyą prawa polskiego, IV (Lwów, 1909).

Bardach, J., *Studia z ustroju i prawa Wielkiego Księstwa Litewskiego XIV–XVIIw* (Warsaw, 1970).

O dawnej i niedawnej Litwie (Poznań, 1988).

Bates, D., *Normandy before 1066* (London, 1982).

Batūra, R., 'XIIIa. Lietuvos sostinės klausimų', *LMADA*, 20 (1966), 141–65.

'Lietuvos metraščių legendinės dalies ir M. Stryjkovskio "Kronikos" istoriškumo klausimo', *LMADA*, 21 (1966), 265–83.

Lietuva tautų kovoje prieš Aukso Ordą: Nuo Batu antplūdžio iki mūšio prie Mėlynųjų Vandenų (Vilnius, 1975).

'Oborona pravoberezh'ia Nizhnego Nemana protiv agressii Tevtonskogo

Ordena (XIII–nachalo XIVv.)', *Drevneishie gosudarstva na territorii SSSR* (1985), 184–93.
Bektineev, Sh. I., 'Prazhskii grosh v denezhnom obrashchenii Velikogo Kniazhestva Litovskogo (XIVv)', in *Drevnosti Litvy i Belorussii*, ed. L. D. Pobol' and A. Z. Tautavičius (Vilnius, 1988), 130–4.
Beletskii, S. V., 'Pechati "Kniazha Oleksandrova"', *Sovetskaia Arkheologia* (1985), 231–40.
Beletskii, V. D., 'Pechat' posadnikov pskovskikh', *Soobshchenia Gosudarstvennogo Ermitazha*, 38 (1974), 28–30.
'Dovmontov gorod', *Drevnii Pskov. Istoria, Iskusstvo, Arkheologia. Novye Issledovania* (Moscow, 1988), 99–112.
Beliamuk, M., *Vytoki Belaruskikh Piachatkaŭ* (Cleveland, OH, 1986).
Benker, G., *Ludwig der Bayer. Ein Wittelsbacher auf dem Kaiserthron 1282–1347* (Munich, 1980).
Benninghoven, F., *Rigas Entstehung und der Frühhansische Kaufmann* (Hamburg, 1961).
Der Orden der Schwertbruder. Fratres milicie Christi de Livonia (Cologne, 1965).
'Forschungsberichte zur Technik spätmittelalterliche Feldzüge im Ostbaltikum', *Zeitschrift für Ostforschung*, 19 (1970), 631–51.
Beresnevičius, G., *Dausos. Pomirtinio gyvenimo samprata senojoje Lietuvių pasaulėžiūroje* (Klaipėda, 1990).
Berezhkov, M., 'Drevnerusskaia torgovlia s Rigoi', *ZhMNP*, 189 (1877), 330–37.
Berta, T. M., *Monety v arkheologicheskikh pamiatnikakh Latvii IX–XIIvv.* (Riga, 1988).
Bieniak, J., *Wielkopolska, Kujawy, ziemie Łęczycka i Sieradzka wobec problemu zjednoczenia państwowego w latach 1300–1306* (Toruń, 1969).
Biernacki, K., *Speculum Minorum* (Kraków, 1688).
Biezais, H., 'Dzieje badań nad religią Bałtów', *Euhemer*, 99 (1976/1), 19–35.
Birkhan, H., 'Les croisades contre les paiens de Lituanie et de Prusse. Idéologie et réalité', in *La Croisade: réalités et fictions. Actes du colloque d'Amiens 18–22 mars 1987*, ed. D. Buschinger (Göppingen, 1989), 31–50.
Birnbaum, H., *Lord Novgorod the Great. Essays in the history and culture of a medieval city-state. Part One: the historical background* (Los Angeles, CA, 1981).
Biskup, M. and Labuda, G., *Dzieje zakonu Krzyżackiego w Prusach* (Gdańsk, 1986).
Black, A., *Political thought in Europe 1250–1450* (Cambridge, 1992).
Blaschke, K., 'Nikolaikirchen und Stadtentstehung im pommerschen Raum', *Greifswald-Stralsunder Jahrbuch*, 9 (1970), 21–40.
Błaszczyk, W., 'Location of main Dominican convents in Poland in relation to settlements developing before the Magdeburgian urban reform and to towns founded on this law as shown by the development of Old City in Poznań until the thirteenth century', *Rapports du IIIe Congrès international de l'archéologie slave. Bratislava 7–14 septembre 1975*, II, 51–63.
Bogert, R., 'On the rhetorical style of Serapion Vladimirskii', *Medieval Russian*

Culture, California Slavic Studies, ed. H. Birnbaum and M. S. Flier, XII (Berkeley, CA–London, 1984), 280–310.

Boko-Slijepchevich, D., *Istorija srpske pravoslavne tsrkve*, I (Munich, 1962).

Boleslav'-Iurii II kniaz' vsei Maloi Rusi. Sbornik materialov i issledovanii (St Petersburg, 1907).

Bolina, P., 'K problematice kolonizace a počátků hradů na severovýchodni Moravě ve 13 století', *Československý Časopis Historický*, 34 (1986), 565–84.

Bol'shakova, S. A., 'Papskie poslania galitskomu kniaziu kak istoricheskii istochnik', *Drevneishie gosudarstva na territorii SSSR* (1976), 122–9.

Bonnell, E., *Russisch-Livländische Chronologie* (St Petersburg, 1862).

Boockmann, H., *Der Deutsche Orden* (Munich, 1981).

Boojamra, J. L., *Church reform in the late Byzantine Empire: A study for the patriarchate of Athanasios of Constantinople* (Thessaloniki, 1982).

'The Affair of Alexis and Roman', *Greek Orthodox Theological Review*, 28 (1983), 173–94.

Borawksi, P., 'Za dziejów kolonizacji tatarskiej w Wielkim Księstwie Litewskim i w Polsce (XIV–XVIIw)', *Przegląd Orientalistyczny*, 104 (1977/4), 291–304.

Tatarzy w dawnej Rzeczypospolitej (Warsaw, 1986).

Borisov, N. S., *Russkaia tserkov' v politicheskoi bor'be XIV–XV vekov* (Moscow, 1986).

Tserkovnye deiateli srednevekovoi Rusi XIII–XVIIvv. (Moscow, 1988).

Borovskii, P., 'Istoricheskaia monografia goroda Grodny', *Vestnik Zapadnoi Rossii*, 14 (1865–66), kn. 7, t. 3, otd. 2, pp. 28–43.

Borowska, N., 'Wpływy słowianskie na litewską terminologię kościelną', *Studia z filologii polskiej i słowianskiej*, II (Warsaw, 1957), 320–65.

Borzakovskii, V. S., *Istoria Tverskogo Kniazhestva* (St Petersburg, 1876; 2nd edn The Hague, 1969).

Bosley, R. D., 'The Saints of Novgorod: à propos of A. S. Chorošev's *Book on the Church in mediaeval Novgorod*', *Jahrbücher fur Geschichte Osteuropas*, 32 (1984), 1–15.

Böthführ, H-J., *Die Rigische Rathslinie von 1226 bis 1876* (Riga–Moscow–Odessa, 1877; 2nd edn Hanover–Döhren, 1969).

de Bray, Comte, *Essai critique sur l'Histoire de la Livonie*, 3 vols. (Dorpat, 1817).

Briantsev, P. D., *Istoria Litovskogo gosudarstva s drevneishikh vremen* (Vilnius, 1889).

Brønsted, J., *The Vikings* (London, 1980).

Brückner, A., *Starożytna Litwa. Ludy i Bogi. Szkice historyczne i mitologiczne*, ed. J. Jaskanis (Olsztyn, 1979).

Mitologia słowiańska i polska, ed. S. Urbańczyk (Warsaw, 1985).

Bruns, F. and Weczerka, H., *Hansische Handelstrassen: Atlas und Darstellungen zur Hansischen Geschichte*, n.s. XIII (1962).

Budilovich, A., 'Perechnavaia opis' nedvizhimym imeniem zapadno-russkoi tserkvi za X–XIXvv.', *Kholmsko-Varshavskii Eparkhial'nyi Vestnik* (1889/2).

Budovnits, I. V., 'Otrazhenie politicheskoi bor'by Moskvy i Tveri v XIVv.', *TODRL*, 12 (1956), 79–104.

Budreika, E., *Vil'niusskii Zamok* (Vilnius, 1980).
Buga, K. K., 'Lituanica', *IORIaS*, 17 (1912), 1–52.
von Bunge, F. G., *Die Stadt Riga im dreizehnten und vierzehnten Jahrhundert* (Leipzig, 1878).
Burchardt, J., 'Dlaczego pogańscy Polanie w XIw nie zniszczyli katedry Gnieźnieńskiej?', *Literatura Ludowa* (1986/1), 33–40.
Burleigh, M., 'The Knights, nationalists and the historians: Images of medieval Prussia from the Enlightenment to 1945', *European History Quarterly*, 17 (1987), 35–55.
Burmov, A., *Istoria na B'lgaria prez vremeto na Shishmanovtsi (1323–1396), Izbrani Proizvedenia*, I (Sofia, 1968).
Bychkova, M. E., 'Obzor spiskov rodoslovnykh knig XVI–XIXvv.', *AE* (1966), 254–75.
'Otdel'nye momenty istorii Litvy v interpretatsii russkikh genealogicheskikh istochnikov', *Pol'sha i Rus'*, ed. B. A. Rybakov (Moscow, 1974), 365–72.
Byrne, F. J., *Irish Kings and High-Kings* (London, 1973).
Carasso-Kok, M., 'Willelmus fecit. Wilhelmus Jacobi over Friesland en de identiteit van Willelmus Procurator', *Ad Fontes: Opstellen aangeboden aan prof. dr. C. van de Kieft* (Amsterdam, 1984), 319–34.
Chadwick, N. K., *The Beginnings of Russian History. An enquiry into sources* (Cambridge, 1946).
Chamiarytski, V. A., *Belaruskia letapisy iak pomniki literatury* (Minsk, 1969).
Chanturia, V. A., *Istoria arkhitektury Belorussii: Dooktiabr'skii period* (Minsk, 1969).
Charles-Edwards, T., 'Early medieval kingships in the British Isles', *The origins of Anglo-Saxon kingdoms*, ed. S. Bassett (Leicester, 1989), 28–39.
Cherepnin, L. V., *Obrazovanie russkogo tsentralizovannogo gosudarstva v XIV–XV vekakh* (Moscow, 1960).
Chłopocka, H., *Procesy Polski z Zakonem krzyżackim w XIV wieku. Studium źródłoznawcze* (Poznań, 1967).
Chodynicki, K., 'Próby zaprowadzenia Chrześcijaństwa na Litwie przed r. 1386', *PH*, 18 (1914), 215–319.
'Stosunek Rzeczypospolitej do wyznania grecko-wschódniego', *PH*, 23 (1921/1922), 122–34.
'Geneza dynastji Giedymina', *KH*, 40 (1926), 541–66.
'Tradycja jako źródło historyczne. Studia staropolskie', *Księga ku czci A. Brücknera* (Kraków, 1928), 173–90.
Kościół prawosławny a Rzeczpospolita Polska. Zarys historyczny 1370–1632 (Warsaw, 1934).
Christiansen, E., *The northern crusades: The Baltic and the Catholic frontier 1100–1525* (London, 1980).
Chrystianizacja Litwy, ed. J. Kłoczowski (Kraków, 1987).
Chubatii, M., 'Derzhavno-pravne stanovishche ukrains'kikh zemel' litovskoi derzhavy pid kinets' XIVv.', *Zapiski Naukovago Tovaristva imeni Shevchenka*, 154–5 (1926), 1–108.
Chubaty, M. D., *Istoria Khristianstva na Rusi-Ukraine*, I (Rome, 1965).

The Cilician Kingdom of Armenia, ed. T. S. R. Boase (Edinburgh–London, 1978).
Clanchy, M. T., *From memory to written record. England 1066–1307* (London, 1979).
Conrad, K., 'Litauen, der Deutschen Orden und Karl IV 1352–1360', *ZfO*, 21 (1972), 20–41.
'Der dritte Litauerzug König Johanns von Böhmen und der Rücktritt des Hochmeisters Ludolf König', *Festschrift für Hermann Heimpel*, II (Göttingen, 1972), 382–401.
La Cristianizzazione della Lituania, Atti e Documenti, II (1989).
Czołowski, A., 'Lwów za ruskich czasów', *KH*, 5 (1891), 779–812.
Pomniki dziejowe Lwowa z Archiwum miasta, 4 vols. (Lwow, 1892–1921).
Dąbrowski, J., 'Z czasów Łokietka. Studya nad stosunkami polsko-węgierskimi w XIVw. Część I', *RAU*, 2nd series 24 (1916), 278–326.
Dawne Dziejopisarstwo polskie (do roku 1480) (Wrocław–Warsaw–Kraków, 1964).
Danilevich, V. E., *Ocherk istorii Polotskoi zemli do kontsa XIV stoletia* (Kiev, 1896).
Dashkevich, N., *Zametki po istorii litovsko-russkogo gosudarstva* (Kiev, 1885).
Daukantas, S., *Darbay senuju Lituwiu yr Zemayczíu, 1822*, ed. V. and M. Biržiškai, *Lietuvos Universiteto Bibliotekos Leidinys*, I (Kaunas, 1929).
Dawna świadomość historyczna w Polsce, Czechach i Słowacji. Prace polsko-czechosłowackiej komisji historycznej, ed. R. Heck (Wrocław–Warsaw–Kraków–Gdańsk, 1978).
Dergacheva, I. V., 'K literaturnoi istorii drevnerusskogo sinodika XV–XVIIvv.', in *Literatura drevnei Rusi. Istochnikovedenie*, ed. D. S. Likhachev (Leningrad, 1988), 63–73.
Deveike, J., 'The Lithuanian Diarchies', *Slavonic and East European Review*, 28 (1949–50), 392–405.
Devilliers, L., 'Sur les expéditions des comtes de Hainault et de la Hollande en Prusse', *Compte rendu des séances de la Commission Royale d'histoire ou Recueil de ses bulletins*, 4th series 5 (1878), 130–42.
Długopolski, E., *Władysław Łokietek na tle swoich czasów* (Wrocław, 1951).
Dmitrieva, R. P., 'O nekotorykh istochnikakh 'Poslania' Spiridona-Savvy', *TODRL*, 13 (1959), 440–5.
Dobrianskii, F., *Staraia i novaia Vil'na*, 3rd edn (Vilnius, 1904).
Dogiel, M., *Limites regni Poloniae et Magni ducatus Lithuaniae ex originalibus et authenticis exemplis descripti et in lucem editi* (Vilnius, 1758).
Dommasnes, L. H., 'Women, kinship and the basis of power in the Norwegian Viking Age', in *Social approaches to Viking Studies*, ed. R. Samson (Glasgow, 1991), 65–73.
Drevnerossiiskaia Vivlioteka, XIV (Moscow, 1790; The Hague, 1970).
Drevnerusskie Kniazhestva X–XIIIvv., ed. L. G. Bezkrovnyi *et al.* (Moscow, 1975).
Drevnerusskoe nasledie i istoricheskie sud'by vostochnogo slavianstva, ed. V. T. Pashuto, B. N. Floria and A. L. Khoroshkevich (Moscow, 1982).
Drevnosti Belorussii i Litvy, ed. L. D. Pobol' and A. Z. Tautavičius (Minsk, 1982).
Drevnosti Litvy i Belorussii, ed. L. D. Pobol' and A. Z. Tautavičius (Vilnius, 1988).

Drevnosti slavian' i Rusi, ed. B. A. Timoshchuk (Moscow, 1988).
Dumville, D. N., 'Kingship, genealogies and regnal lists', *Early Medieval Kingship* (*qv*), 72–104.
'Essex, Middle Anglia and the expansion of Mercia in the south-east Midlands', in *The origins of Anglo-Saxon kingdoms*, ed. S. Basset (*qv*), 123–40.
Dundulienė, P., 'Arklys Lietuvių liaudies pasaulėjautoje', *LAMMDI*, 17:1 (1977), 83–102.
Early medieval kingship, ed. P. H. Sawyer and I. N. Wood (Leeds, 1977).
Ellis-Davidson, H. R., *Myths and symbols in pagan Europe. Early Scandinavian and Celtic religions* (Manchester, 1988).
Encyclopedia Lituanica, 6 vols. (Boston, 1970–78).
Engel'man, A. E., *Khronologicheskie issledovania v oblasti russkoi i livonskoi istorii v XIII i XIV stoletiakh* (St Petersburg, 1858).
Fedorov, G. B., 'Topografia kladov s litovskimi slitkami i monetami', *KSIIMK*, 29 (1949), 64–75.
Fennell, J. L. I., *The emergence of Moscow, 1304–1359* (London, 1968).
The crisis of medieval Russia 1200–1304 (London–New York, 1983).
Fijałek, J., 'Średniowieczne biskupstwa kościoła wschodniego na Rusi i Litwie', *KH*, 10 (1896), 487–521.
Filevich, P., *Bor'ba Pol'shi i Litvy-Rusi za Galitsko-Vladimirskoe nasledie* (St Petersburg, 1890).
Filimonov, G. D., *Ikonopisnyi podlinnik svodnoi redaktsii XVIII veka* (Moscow, 1876).
Fine jun., J. V. A., *The late medieval Balkans: A critical survey from the late twelfth century to the Ottoman Conquest* (Ann Arbor, MI, 1987).
Finucane, R. C., *Soldiers of the Faith: Crusaders and Moslems at war* (London, 1983).
Floria, B. N., 'Rodoslovie litovskikh kniazei v russkoi politicheskoi mysli XVIv.', *Vostochnaia Evropa* (*qv*), 320–8.
'Litva i Rus' pered bitvoi na Kulikovskom Pole', *Kulikovskaia Bitva: Sbornik statei* (Moscow, 1980), 142–73.
Follieri, E., *Codices graeci Bibliothecae Vaticanae selecti temporum locorumque ordine digesti, commentariis et transcriptionibus instructi* (Vatican City, 1969).
Fonkich, B. L., *Grechesko-russkie kul'turnye sviazi v XV–XVIIv* (Moscow, 1977).
'Paleograficheskie zametki o grecheskikh rukopisiakh ital'ianskikh bibliotek', *Vizantiiskie Ocherki. Trudy sovetskikh uchenykh k XVI mezhdunarodnomu kongressu vizantinistov* (Moscow, 1982), 254–62.
Forey, A., *The Military Orders. From the twelfth to the early fourteenth centuries* (London, 1992).
Forstreuter, K., 'Die Bekehrung Gedimins und der Deutsche Orden', *Altpreussische Forschungen*, 5:2 (1928), 239–61.
Preussen und Russland im Mittelalter. Die Entwicklung ihrer Beziehungen vom 13 bis 17 Jahrhundert. Osteuropäische Forschungen, n.s. XXV (1938).
'Die Bekehrung des Litauerkönigs Gedimin; eine Streitfrage', *Jahrbuch der Albertus Universität Königsberg*, 6 (1955), 142–58, reprinted in Forstreuter, *Deutschland und Litauen im Mittelalter* (Cologne–Graz, 1962), 43–60.

Der Deutsche Orden am Mittelmeer (Bonn, 1967).
'Erzbischof Friedrich von Riga (1304–1341). Ein Beitrag zu seiner Charakteristik', *ZfO*, 19 (1970), 652–65.
Foster, K., *Petrarch. Poet and humanist* (Edinburgh, 1984).
Fraenkel, E., *Litauisches Etymologisches Wörterbuch*, 2 vols. (Heidelberg–Göttingen, 1962–65).
Franklin, S., 'Malalas in Slavonic', *Studies in John Malalas*, ed. E. Jeffreys, B. Croke and R. Scott (*Byzantina Australiensia*, 6 (1990)), 276–87.
'Diplomacy and ideology: Byzantium and the Russian Church in the mid twelfth century', in *Byzantine Diplomacy*, ed. J. Shepard and S. Franklin (London, 1992), 145–50.
Freed, J. B., 'Dzieje saskiej prowincji Franciszkanów w XIII wieku', *Zakony Franciszkańskie w Polsce* (*qv*), 218–25.
Fügedi, E., 'La formation des villes et les ordres mendiants en Hongrie', *Annales: Economies, Sociétés, Civilisations*, 25 (1970), 966–87.
'Das mittelalterliche Königreich Ungarn als Gastland', *Vorträge und Forschungen*, 18 (1974), 471–507.
Kings, bishops and burghers in medieval Hungary (London, 1986).
Fugelstad, F., 'Earth-priests, 'priest-chiefs' and sacred kings in Ancient Norway, Iceland and West Africa. A comparative study', *Scandinavian Journal of History*, 4 (1979), 47–74.
Gallen, J., *Nöteborgsfreden och Finlands medeltide östgräns* (Helsingfors, 1968).
Gallia Christiana, 16 vols. (Paris, 1715–1865).
Garnett, G. S., 'Coronation and propaganda: Some implications of the Norman claim to the throne of England in 1066', *TrRHS*, 5th series, 36 (1986), 91–116.
Gąsiorowski, A., *Itinerarium króla Władysława-Jagiełły 1386–1434* (Kraków, 1972).
Gaudemet, J., 'Le rôle de la papauté dans le règlement des conflits entre états aux XIIIe et XIVe siècles', *Recueil de la Société Jean Bodin*, XV: *La Paix* (Brussels, 1961), 79–106.
Geary, P. J., *Before France and Germany. The creation and transformation of the Merovingian world* (Oxford–New York, 1988).
Gedimin, V., *Proshloe goroda Pskova v ego istoricheskikh pamiatnikakh* (*Putevoditel' po drevnostiam goroda Pskova i ego okrestnostei*), 2nd edn (Pskov, 1903).
Gedimino laikų Lietuva ir jos kaimynai (Vilnius, forthcoming).
Gen'sors'ky, A. I., *Halyts'ko-Volyns'kyi Litopys: Protses skladannia redaktsii i redaktory* (Kiev, 1958).
Geremek, B., 'Poland and the cultural geography of medieval Europe', *Republic of Nobles* (*qv*), 10–27.
Gerevich, L., 'Hungary', in *European towns. Their archaeology and early history*, ed. M. W. Barley (London–New York–San Francisco, 1977), 431–54. (ed.), *Towns in medieval Hungary* (Boulder, CO, 1990).
Gerlich, A., *Habsburg–Luxemburg–Wittelsbach in Kampf um die deutsche Königskrone. Studium zur Vorgeschichte des Königtums Ruprechts von der Pfalz* (Wiesbaden, 1960).

Die Geschichte der Deutschen Literatur von dem Anfängen bis zur Gegenwart, ed. H. de Boor *et al.* III/1 (Munich, 1962).

Gidžiunas, V., 'De missionibus fratrum minorum in Lituania', *Archivum Franciscanum Historicum*, 42 (1949), 1–36.

'Legendariškieji Pranciškonų kankiniai Vilniuje', *Aidai*, 69 (1954/3), 105–10; 70 (1954/4), 175–80.

Giedroyć, M., 'The rulers of thirteenth-century Lithuania: a search for the origins of Grand Duke Traidenis and his kin', *OSP*, n.s. 17 (1984), 1–22.

'The arrival of Christianity in Lithuania: early contacts (thirteenth century)', *OSP*, n.s. 18 (1985), 1–30.

'The arrival of Christianity in Lithuania: between Rome and Byzantium (1281–1341)', *OSP*, n.s. 20 (1987), 1–33.

'The arrival of Christianity in Lithuania: baptism and survival (1341–1387)', *OSP*, n.s. 22 (1989), 34–57.

'Lithuanian options prior to Kreva (1385)', *La Cristianizzazione*, 85–103.

'The Ruthenian–Lithuanian metropolitanates and the progress of Christianisation (1300–1458)', *Nuovi studi storici*, 17 (1992), 315–42.

Gierlach, B., 'Wczesnośredniowieczne ośrodki kultu pogańskiego w Polsce', *Euhemer-Przegląd Religioznawczy*, 112 (1979/2), 19–24.

Gieysztor, A., 'Początki misji ruskiej biskupstwa Lubuskiego', *Nasza Przeszłość*, 4 (1948), 83–102.

'Polska w "El Libro des Conoscimiento" z połowy XIV wieku', *PH*, 56 (1965), 397–412.

'In cronicis fratrum domus Teutonice. Nieznany fragment dziejopisarstwa krzyżackiego z XIV wieku', *Studia i materiały z dziejów nauki polskiej, Seria A: Historia nauk społecznych*, 12 (1968), 44–54.

Gimbutas, M., *Ancient symbolism in Lithuanian folk art, Memoirs of the American Folklore Society*, XLIX (1958).

The Balts (London, 1963).

Gli inizi del cristianesimo in Livonia-Lettonia, Atti e documenti, I (Vatican City, 1989).

Gol'dberg, A. L., 'K istorii rasskaza o potomkakh Avgusta i o darakh Monomakha', *TODRL*, 30 (1976), 204–16.

Goldfrank, D. M., 'The Lithuanian Prince-Monk Vojšelk: A study in competing legends', *Harvard Ukrainian Studies*, 11:1–2 (1987), 44–76.

Golubinskii, E. E., 'Mitropolit' vseia Rossii sv. Petr'' *Bogoslovskii Vestnik*, 2 (January 1893), 18–67.

Kratkii ocherk istorii pravoslavennykh tserkvei Bolgarskoi, Serbskoi i Rumynskoi ili Moldo-valashskoi (Moscow, 1871).

Istoria Russkoi Tserkvi, II.1 (Moscow, 1900).

Golubovich, E. and V., 'Krìvoi Gorod-Vil'no', *KSIIMK*, 11 (1945), 114–25.

Golubovskii, P. V., *Istoria Smolenskoi zemli do nachala XVst.* (Kiev, 1895).

Görlich, P., *Zur Frage des Nationalbewusstseins in Ost-deutschen Quellen des 12 bis 14 Jahrhunderts* (Marburg, 1964).

Górski, K., *Zakon krzyżacki a powstanie państwa pruskiego* (Wrocław–Warsaw–Kraków–Gdańsk, 1977).

'Descriptiones terrarum, nowe źródło do dziejów Prus w XIII wieku', *ZH*, 46 (1981), 7–16.

Studia i szkice z dziejów państwa krzyżackiego (Olsztyn, 1986).

Grabmüller, H-J., *Die Pskover Chroniken. Untersuchungen zur russischen Regionalchronistik im 13–15 Jahrhundert* (Wiesbaden, 1975).

Grabski, A. F., *Polska w opiniach Europy zachodniej XIV–XVw.* (Warsaw, 1968).

Gräslund, A. S., 'Some aspects of Christianisation in Central Sweden', *Social Approches* (*qv*), 45–52.

Greek Lexicon of the Roman and Byzantine periods (*From B.C. 146 to A.D. 1100*), ed. E. A. Sophocles (New York, 1900).

Greimas, J., *Apie Dievus ir žmonės* (Chicago, 1979).

Des dieux et des hommes. Etudes de mythologie lithuanienne (Paris, 1985).

Grimm, J., *Teutonic Mythology*, tr. J. S. Stallybrass, III (London, 1883).

Grimsted, P. J. K., 'The Archival legacy of the Grand Duchy of Lithuania: The fate of early historical archives in Vilnius', *Slavonic and East European Review*, 57 (1979), 552–71.

'Czym jest i czym była Metryka Litewska?', *KH*, 92:1 (1985), 55–85.

Grimsted, P. J. K. and Sułkowska-Kurasiowa, I., *The 'Lithuanian Metrica' in Moscow and Warsaw: Reconstructing the Archives of the Grand Duchy of Lithuania. Including an annotated edition of the 1887 Inventory compiled by Stanisław Ptaszycki* (Cambridge, MA., 1984).

Gritsak, P., *Galits'ko-Volins'ka Derzhava* (New York, 1958).

Grumel, V., *La Chronologie* (Paris, 1958).

Gudavičius, E., '1219 metų sutarties dalyviai ir jų vaidmuo suvienyjant Lietuvą', *LAMMDI*, 22 (1982), 33–46.

'Aukščiausia žemės nuosavybė 'barbarinėje' Lietuvoje', *LAMMDI*, 23 (1983), 3–11.

'Dėl Lietuvos valstybės kūrimosi centro ir laiko', *LMADA*, 83 (1983/2), 61–70.

'Lietuvos vardas XIa–XIIa I pusės šaltinuose', *LMADA*, 84 (1983/3), 79–88.

'Kas žuvo 1337m. prie Bajerburgo?', *LMADA*, 89 (1984/4), 92–9.

'Po povodu taknazyvaemoi 'diarkhii' v Velikom Kniazhestve Litovskom', *Feodālisms Baltijas reģionā. Zinātisko Rakstu krājums* (Riga, 1985), 35–44.

'Ryges recht ir ius civile Rigensis civitatis Gedimino aktuose', *Lietuvos Istorijos Metraštis* (1986), 79–85.

'Gedimino pilies (Žemaitijoje), Pagraudės srities ir Paragaudžio vietovės problematika', *LMADA*, 100 (1987/3), 59–66; 101 (1987/4), 82–91.

Kryžiaus karai Pabaltijyje ir Lietuva XIII amžiuje (Vilnius, 1989).

Miestų atsiradimas Lietuvoje (Vilnius, 1991).

Guldon, Z. and Powierski, J., *Podziały administracyjne Kujaw i ziemi dobrzyńskiej w XIII i XIV wieku* (Warsaw–Poznań, 1974).

Gumowski, M., 'Pieczęcie książąt litewskich', *AW*, 7:3–4 (1930), 684–725.

'Uzbrojenie i ubiór rycerski w czasach piastowskich', *Broń i Barwa*, 3:3 (1936), 51–71.

Gurevich, F. D., *Drevnosti belorusskogo Poneman'ia* (Moscow–Leningrad, 1962).

'Detinets i okol'nyi gorod drevnerusskogo Novogrudka v svete arkheologicheskikh rabot 1956–1977gg.', *Sovetskaia Arkheologia* (1980/4), 87–101.
'Zapadnaia Rus' i Vizantia v XII i XIIIvv.', *Sovetskaia Arkheologia* (1988/3), 130–44.
Halperin, C. J., *Russia and the Golden Horde. The Mongol impact on Russian history* (London, 1987).
Hájek, J., 'Bracia mniejszi w Czechach i na Morawach w XIII–XIV wieku', *Zakony Franciszkańskie (qv)*, 263–6.
Halecki, O., *The borderlands of western civilisation: A history of East Central Europe* (New York, 1952).
Haney, J. A. V., 'Moscow – second Constantinople, third Rome or second Kiev? (The tale of the princes of Vladimir)', *Canadian Slavic Studies*, 3:2 (1968), 354–67.
Heisenberg, A., *Aus der Geschichte und Literatur der Paläologenzeit* I (Munich, 1920).
Hellmann, M., 'Der Deutsche Orden und die Königskrönung des Mindaugas', *ZfO*, 3 (1954), 387–96.
Studien über die Anfänge der Mission in Livland, Vorträge und Forschungen. Sonnerband, XXXVII (1989).
Helm, K. and Ziesemer, W., *Die Literatur des Deutschen Ritterordens, Giessener Beiträge zur deutschen Philologie*, 94 (1951).
Hendy, M. F., *Studies in the Byzantine monetary economy c. 300–1450* (Cambridge, 1985).
Higounet, C., *Die deutsche Ostsiedlung im Mittelalter* (Munich, 1990).
Historia dyplomacji polskiej, ed. M. Biskup, I (Warsaw, 1982).
Hodges, R., *Dark Age economics. The origins of towns and trade AD 600–1000* (London, 1982).
Housley, N., 'The Franco-Papal crusade negotiations of 1322–1323', *Papers of the British School at Rome*, 48 (1980), 166–85.
The Italian crusades. The papal-Angevin alliances and the Crusades against Christian lay powers, 1254–1343 (Oxford, 1982).
The Avignon Papacy and the Crusades 1305–1378 (Oxford, 1986).
Hrushevsky, M., *Istoria Ukraini-Rusi*, 10 vols. in 11 (New York, 1954–58).
Ianin, V. L., *Novgorodskaia Feodal'naia Votchina (Istoriko-genealogicheskoe issledovanie)* (Moscow, 1981).
Novgorodskie Akty XII–XVvv. Khronologicheskie kommentarii (Moscow, 1991).
Ilovaiskii, D. I., *Istoria riazanskogo kniazhestva* (Moscow, 1858).
Iš kur atėjome, ed. A. Nekrošienė (Kaunas, 1988).
Istoria Litovskoi SSR (s drevneishikh vremen do nashikh dnei) (Vilnius, 1978).
Istoria mist i sil ukrains'koi SSR XX: Zhitomirs'ka Oblast' (Kiev, 1973).
Istoricheskie razgovory o drevnostiakh Velikogo Novgoroda (Moscow, 1808).
Istoricheskie traditsii dukhovnoi kul'tury narodov SSSR i sovremennost'. Sbornik nauchnykh trudov, ed. V. N. Rusanovskii *et al.* (Kiev, 1987).
Istoricheskoe opisanie nakhodiashchikhsia v Rossii Eparkhii, monastyrei i tserkvei s pokazaniem nachala i postroenia onykh; krestnykh khodov; khramovykh prazdnikov v Sanktpeterburge i Moskve; paskhalii na 50 let; i dostopamiatneishikh

v Rossii proizshestvii khronologicheskim poriadkom, 2nd edn (St Petersburg, 1825).
Ivakin, G. Iu., *Kiev v XIII–XV vekakh* (Kiev, 1982).
Ivinskis, Z., *Geschichte des Bauernstandes in Litauen. Von den ältesten Zeiten bis zum Anfang des 16 Jahrhunderts. Beiträge zur sozialen und wirtschaftlichen Entwicklung des Bauernstandes in Litauen im Mittelalter, Historische Studien*, CCXXXVI (1933).
'Jogailos santykiai su Kęstučiu ir Vytautu iki 1392m.', in *Jogaila*, ed. A. Šapoka (Kaunas, 1935; 2nd edn 1991), 45–80.
'Die Handelsbeziehungen Litauens mit Riga im 14 Jahrhundert', *Conventus primus historicorum balticorum. Acta et relata* (Riga, 1938), 276–85.
'A Contribution to the history of the conversion of Lithuania', *Baltic Countries*, 5 (1939), 12–21.
'Mindaugas und seine Kröne', *ZfO*, 3 (1954), 360–86.
Lietuvos istorija iki Vytauto Didžiojo mirties (Rome, 1978; 2nd edn Vilnius, 1991).
'Litwa w dobie Chrztu i unii z Polska', in *Chrystianizacja Litwy*, ed. J. Kłoczowski (Kraków, 1987), 15–126.
Iwańczyk, W., *Tropem rycerskiej przygody. Wzorzec rycerski w piśmiennictwie czeskim XIV wieku* (Warsaw, 1985).
Jacob, L., *Traicté des plus belles bibliothèques publiques et particulières* (Paris, 1644).
Jakštas, J., 'Vokiečių Ordinas ir Lietuva Vytenio ir Gedimino metų, Gedimino Laiškai', *Senovė*, 2 (1936), 3–59.
'Naujausi Gedimino dinastijos kilmės tyrinėjimai', *Lietuvos Praeitis* (1940/1), 29–56.
Jakubowski, J., 'Opis księstwa trockiego z roku 1387', *PH*, 5 (1907), 22–48.
James, E., 'The origins of barbarian kingdoms: the continental evidence', in S. Basset (ed.), *The origins of Anglo-Saxon kingdoms* (*qv*), 40–52.
Jaroszewicz, J., *Obraz Litwy pod względem jej cywilizacyi od czasów najdawniejszych do końca wieku XVIII. Część II: Litwa w pierwszych trzech wiekach po przyjęciu wiary chrześcijańskiej* (Vilnius, 1844)
Jasiński, K., 'Małżeństwa i kolegacje polityczne Kazimerza Wielkiego', *Studia Źródłoznawcze*, 32–33 (1990), 67–76.
Jasiński, T., 'Imigracja westfalska do Prus w okresie późnego średniowiecza (XIII–XIVw.)', in *Niemcy-polska w średniowieczu*, ed. J. Strzelczyk (Poznań, 1986), 105–18.
Jaskiewicz, W. C., 'A study in Lithuanian mythology: Jan Lasicki's Samogithian Gods', in *Accademia Toscana di scienze e lettere 'La Columbiana' Studi II: Studi Baltici*, ed. G. Devoto (Florence, 1952).
Johansen, P., 'Die Kaufmannskirche in Ostseegebiet', *Studi in onore di Armando Sapore*, I (Milan, 1957), 311–26.
Jorga, N., *Philippe de Mézières 1327–1405* (Paris, 1896; 2nd edn London, 1973).
Jučas, M., 'Lietuvos didžiųjų kunigaikščių metraštis', *LMADA*, 2 (1957/2), 111–21.
'Russkie letopisi XIV–XVvv. kak istochnik po istorii Litvy', *LMADA*, 5 (1958/2), 69–83.

Lietuvos metraščiai (Vilnius, 1968).
Jurginis, J., 'Valstečių bendruomenė ir feodalinė tėvonija Lietuvoje XIII–XIV amžiais', *LMADA*, 1 (1957/1), 51–67.
'Lietuvių šeima XIII–XIV amžiais', *ILKI*, 1 (1958), 248–59.
'Vilniaus miesto ikurimo klausimų', *LMADA*, 6 (1959/1), 103–13.
'Prichiny pozdnego rasprostranenia Khristianstva v Pribaltike', *XIII Mezhdunarodnyi Kongress istoricheskikh nauk, Moskva 16–13 avgusta 1970g.* (Moscow, 1973), 139–51.
Pagonybės ir krikščionybės santykiai Lietuvoje (Vilnius, 1976).
'Boiare i shlakhta v Litovskom gosudarstve', *Vostochnaia Evropa (qv)*, 124–30.
Jurginis, J. and Lukšaitė, I., *Lietuvos kultūros istorijos bruožai (Feodalizmo epocha. Iki aštuonioliktojo amžiaus)* (Vilnius, 1981).
Kaeppeli, R. P. T., 'Deux nouveaux ouvrages de Philippe de Péra', *Archivum fratrum praedicatorum*, 23 (1953), 163–83.
Kajačkas, A., 'History and recent archaeological investigations of Vilnius Cathedral', *La Cristianizzazione*, 263–84.
Kalligas, H. A., *Byzantine Monemvasia. The Sources* (Monemvasia, 1990).
Kamieniecki, W., *Społeczeństwo litewskie w XV wieku* (Warsaw, 1947).
Kamieński, P., *Antiquitas praedicatorum ordinis in Magno Ducatu Lithuaniae eiusque a provincia Poloniae independentia* (Vilnius, 1642).
Kantak, K., *Dzieje kościoła polskiego, II: Wieki XIII, XIV. Kościół ostaja państwa* (Gdańsk, 1914).
Franciszkanie polscy I (1237–1517) (Kraków, 1937).
Karamzin, N. M., *Istoria gosudarstva rossiiskogo*, Kn. 1. t. IV (St Petersburg, 1842; Moscow, 1988).
Karlsson, G., '*Goþar* and *höfþingar* in Iceland', *Saga Book of the Viking Society*, 19:4 (1977), 358–70.
Karpov, General, 'Ocherk iz istorii rossiiskoi tserkovnoi ierarkhii', *ChOIDR* (1864/3).
Kashprovskii, E. N., *Uchrezhdenie Smolenskoi Episkopii* (Kiev, 1896).
Kashtanov, S. M., *Finansy srednevekovoi Rusi* (Moscow, 1988).
Kasiske, K., *Die Siedlungstätigkeit des Deutschen Ordens im Östlichen Preussen bis zum Jahre 1410* (Königsberg, 1934).
Kazakova, N. A., 'Novgorodsko-nemetskie dogovory ili livonskie akty?', *Novgorodskii Istoricheskii Sbornik*, 3:13 (1989), 63–7.
Kazakova, N. A. and Lur'e, Ia. S., *Antifeodal'nye ereticheskie dvizhenia na Rusi XIV–nachala XVI veka* (Moscow–Leningrad, 1955).
Kazimierz Jagiellończyk. Zbiór studiów o Polsce drugiej połowy XV wieku ed. M. Biskup and K. Górski (Warsaw, 1987).
Kerbelytė, B., *Lietuvių liaudies padavimai* (Vilnius, 1970).
Kętrzyński, W., 'O dokumentach Mendoga króla litewskiego', *RAU*, 2nd series 25 (1907), 180–222.
Khachikian, L. S., *Novye materialy o drevnei armianskoi kolonii Kieva* (Erevan, 1961).
Khoroshev, A. S., *Tserkov' v sotsial'no-politicheskoi sisteme Novgorodskoi feodal'noi respubliki* (Moscow, 1980).

Politicheskaia istoria russkoi kanonizatsii (XI–XVIvv) (Moscow, 1986).
Khoroshkevich, A. L., 'Pechati Polotskikh gramot XIV–XVvv', *Vspomogatel'nye istoricheskie distsipliny*, 4 (1972), 128–46.
Kiaupa, Z., 'Svečių (pirklių) teisė Vilniuje XVa–XVIa pradžioje', *LMADA*, 85 (1983/4), 35–45.
Kiparskii, V., 'Philippe de Mézières sur les rives de la Baltique', *Neuphilologischen Mitteilungen*, 41 (1940), 61–7.
Kirpichnikov, A. N., *Drevnerusskoe oruzhie*, I (Moscow–Leningrad, 1966).
Kamennye kreposti Novgorodskoi zemli (Leningrad, 1984).
Kitkauskas, N., *Vilniaus pilys. Statyba ir architektūra* (Vilnius, 1989).
Kitkauskas, N. and Lisanka, A., 'Nauji duomenys apie viduramžių Vilniaus katedrą', *Kultūros Barai* (1986/4), 59–63; (1986/5), 57–61; (1986/6), 47–51.
Kitkauskas, N. and Dzikas, L., 'Žemutinės pilies karalių rūmai', *Kultūros Barai* (1988/6), 50–6.
Kitkauskas, N., Lisanka, A. and Lasavickas, S., 'Perkūno šventyklos liekanos Vilniaus žemutinėje pilyje', *Kultūros Barai* (1986/12), 51–5; (1987/1), 60–3; (1987/2), 53–7.
Klepatskii, P. G., *Ocherki po istorii Kievskoi zemli I: Litovskii period* (Odessa, 1912).
Klibanov, A. I., 'K istorii russkoi reformatsionnoi mysli (Tver'skaia "raspria o rae") v seredine XIV veka', *Voprosy istorii religii i ateizma*, 5 (1958), 233–63.
Klimas, P., *Litwa starożytna* (Vilnius, 1921).
Kłoczowski, J., 'The mendicant orders between the Baltic and the Adriatic Seas in the Middle Ages', in *La Pologne au XVe Congrès international des sciences historiques à Bucarest. Etudes sur l'histoire de la culture de l'Europe centrale-orientale* ed. S. Bylina (Wrocław–Warsaw–Kraków–Gdańsk, 1980), 95–110.
Europa Słowiańska w XIV–XV wieku (Warsaw, 1984).
Kloss, V. I., *Nikonovskii svod i russkie letopisi XVI–XVII vekov* (Moscow, 1980).
Knoll. P. W., *The rise of the Polish monarchy: Piast Poland in East Central Europe, 1320–1370* (Chicago–London, 1972).
Koczerska, M., *Rodzina szlachecka w Polsce późnego średniowiecza* (Warsaw, 1975).
Koialovich, M. I., *Lektsii po istorii Zapadnoi Rossii* (Moscow, 1864).
Kolankowski, L., *Dzieje Wielkiego Księstwa Litewskiego za Jagiellonów, I: (1377–1499)* (Warsaw, 1930).
Kolotilova, S. I., 'K voprosu o polozhenii Pskova v sostave Novgorodskoi feodal'noi respubliki', *Istoria SSSR* (1975/2), 145–52.
Kosman, M., 'Forma umów międzynarodowych Litwy w pierwszej ćwierci XIII wieku', *PH*, 57 (1966), 213–34.
'Średniowieczna dyplomatyka litewska – stań i potrzeby badawcze', *Zeszyty Naukowe Uniwersytetu im. Adama Mickiewicza, Historia*, 7 (1967), 179–93.
'Rzekoma działalność pisarka Hanula', *Studia Źródłoznawcze*, 12 (1967), 149–53.
'Pogaństwo, chrześcijaństwo i synkretizm na Litwie w dobie przedreformacyjnej', *Komunikaty Mazursko-Warmińskie*, 115 (1972/1), 103–36.
'Podniesienie książąt litewskich', *Acta Baltico-Slavica*, 10 (1976), 15–36.
Drogi zaniku pogaństwa u Bałtów (Wrocław–Warsaw–Kraków–Gdańsk, 1976).

'Przenikanie Katolicyzmu do Europy połnowschodniej', in *Katolicyzm Średniowieczny*, ed. J. Keller (Warsaw, 1977), 107–32.
Zmierzch Perkuna czyli ostatni poganie nad Bałtykiem (Warsaw, 1981).
'Myśl zachodnia w polityce Jagiellonów', *Przegląd Zachodni* (1984/3), 1–24.
'Polacy o Litwinach (do połowy XVI wieku)', in *Społeczeństwo Polski średniowiecznej*, ed. S. K. Kuczyński, III (Warsaw, 1985), 387–428.
'Między Zakonem krzyżackim, Rusią i Polską (Początki Chrystianizacji Litwy', *Przegląd Zachodni* (1987/5–6), 73–94.
Litwa pierwotna: mity, legendy, fakty (Warsaw, 1989).
Kourouses, S. I., *Manouēl Gabalas eita Matthaios Mētropolitēs Efesou* (1271/2–1355/60) *A-ta biografika* (Athens, 1972).
Kowalenko, W., 'Bałtyk i Pomorze w historii kartografii (VII–XVIw.)', *Przegląd Zachodni*, 10 (1953), 353–89.
Krikščionybė ir jos socialnis vaidmuo Lietuvoje, ed. V. Lazutka (Vilnius, 1976).
Krip'iakevich, I. P., *Galits'ko-Volins'skie Kniazivstvo* (Kiev, 1984).
Kryczyński, S., *Tatarzy litewscy: Próba monografii historyczno-etnograficznej*, *Rocznik Tatarski-Tatar Yili*, III (Warsaw, 1938).
Kubinyi, A., 'Urbanisation in the east-central part of medieval Hungary', in *Towns in medieval Hungary*, ed. L. Gerevich (Boulder, CO, 1990), 103–49.
Kuchkin, V. A., 'Istochniki 'Napisania' mnikha Akindina', *AE* (1962), 60–8.
'Skazanie o smerti mitropolita Petra', *TODRL*, 18 (1962), 59–79.
Povesti o Mikhaile Tverskom. Istoriko-tekstologicheskoe issledovanie (Moscow, 1974).
Kučinskas, A., *Kęstutis* (Marijampolė, 1938; 2nd edn Vilnius, 1988).
Kuczyński, S., *Ziemie Czernihowsko-Siewierskie pod rządami Litwy* (Warsaw, 1936).
Kuczyński, S. K., *Pieczęcie książąt mazowieckich* (Wrocław–Warsaw–Kraków–Gdańsk, 1978).
Kuczyński, S. M., *Jagiełło, ok. 1351–1434* (Warsaw, 1985).
Kulicka, E., 'Legenda o pochodzeniu Litwinów', *PH*, 71 (1980), 1–21.
Kulikauskas, P., 'Badania archeologiczne na Litwie w latach 1955–1961', *Acta Baltico-Slavica*, 2 (1965), 203–59.
'Sudargo piliakalniai', *LAMMDI*, 15:2 (1975), 105–24.
Kuncienė, O., 'XIII–XV amžių rytų Lietuvos moterų galvos papuošalai', *LMADA*, 48 (1974/3), 67–75.
Kurczewski, J., *Opowiadania o dziejach chrześcijaństwa na Litwie i Rusi* (Vilnius, 1914).
Kuza, A. V. and Solov'eva, G. F., 'Iazycheskoe sviatilishche v zemli Radimichei', *Sovetskaia Arkheologia* (1972/1), 146–53.
Kuz'min, A. G., *Riazanskoe Letopisanie. Svedenie letopisei o Riazani i Murome do serediny XVI veka* (Moscow, 1965).
Labuda, G., *Historia Pomorza*, I.1 (Poznań, 1969).
'Zu den Quellen der "Preussische Chronik" Peters von Dusburg', in *Der Deutschordensstaat Preussen in der Polnischen Geschichtsschreibung der Gegenwart*, ed. U. Arnold and M. Biskup – *Quellen und Studien zur Geschichte des Deutschen Ordens*, XXX (1982), 133–64.

Labutina, I. K., *Istoricheskaia topografia Pskova v XIV–XVvv.* (Moscow, 1985).

Ładogorski, T., *Studia nad zaludnieniem Polski XIV wieku* (Wrocław, 1958).

Laiou, A. E., *Constantinople and the Latins. The foreign policy of Andronicus II 1282–1328* (Cambridge, MA, 1972).

Lapis, B., *Rex utilis. Kryteria oceny władców germańskich we wczesnym średniowieczu (od połowy V do początku VIII wieku)* (Poznań, 1986).

Lapteva, L. P., *Pis'mennye istochniki po istorii chekhii perioda feodalizma (do 1848g.)* (Moscow, 1985).

Laurent, V., 'La chronologie des patriarches de Constantinople de la première moitié du XIVe siècle (1294–1350)', *Revue des études byzantines*, 7 (1949), 145–55.

'Isidore de Kiev et la métropole de Monembasie', *Revue des études byzantines*, 17 (1959), 150–7.

'Notes de chronologie et d'histoire byzantine de la fin du XIIIe siècle', *Revue des études byzantines*, 27 (1969), 209–28.

von Lehe, E., 'Die Schuldbücher von Lübeck, Riga und Hamburg', in *Städtwesen und Bürgertum als geschichtliche Kräfte. Gedächtnisschrift Fritz Rörig*, ed. A. von Brandt and W. Koppe (Lübeck, 1953), 165–77.

Lesnikov, M. P., 'Lübeck als Handelsplatz für osteuropawaren im 14 Jahrhundert', *Hansische studien: Heinrich Sproemberg zum 70 Geburtstag* (Berlin, 1961), 273–92.

Leuscher, J., *Deutschland im späten Mittelalter*, 3rd edn (Göttingen, 1983).

Levitskii, O., 'Lutskaia Starina', *Chtenia v istoricheskom obshchestve Nestora letopistsa*, V (Kiev, 1891), 54–90.

Leyser, K., *Rule and conflict in an early medieval society. Ottonian Saxony* (London, 1979).

Liden, H. E., 'From pagan sanctuary to Christian church. The excavations of Maere Church in Trøndelag', *Norwegian Archaeological review*, 2 (1969), 3–32.

Liedtke, A., 'Stanowisko papieża Jana XXII wobec koronacji Władysława Łokietka', *Nasza Przeszłość*, 36 (1971), 91–107.

Lietuvos gyventojų prekybiniai ryšiai I–XIIIa, ed. M. Michelbertas (Vilnius, 1972)

Lietuvos TSR Archeologijos Atlasas, III: I–XIIIa. pilkapynai ir senkapiai, ed. R. Rimantienė (Vilnius, 1977).

Likhachev, N. P., *Razriadnye d'iaki XVI veka: Opyt istoricheskogo issledovania* (St Petersburg, 1888).

Materialy dla istorii Vizantiiskoi i russkoi sfragistiki, I (Leningrad, 1928).

Likhachev, D. S., 'Obshchie printsipy rekonstruktsii literaturno-khudozhestvennykh tekstov', in *Tekstologia Slavianskikh Literatur. Sbornik statei*, ed. D. S. Likhachev (Leningrad, 1973), 131–7.

Little, A. G., *Franciscan papers, lists and documents* (Manchester, 1943).

Liubavskii, M. K., *Oblastnoe delenie i mestnoe upravlenie litovsko-russkogo gosudarstva ko vremeni izdania pervogo litovskogo statuta* (Moscow, 1893).

Ljungberg, H., *Tor: Undersökningar i Indoeuropeisk och Nordisk religionshistoria*, *Uppsala Universitets Årsskrift* (1947/9).

Loserth, J., 'Die Chronik des Benesch Krabice von Weitmühl. Beitrag zur Kritik derselben', *Archiv für österreichische Geschichte*, 53 (1875), 301–33.
Łowmiańska, M., *Wilno przed najazdem Moskowskim 1655r.* (Vilnius, 1929).
Łowmiański, H., *Studia nad początkami społeczeństwa litewskiego*, 2 vols. (Vilnius, 1931–32).
'Z zagadnień spornych społeczeństwa litewskiego w wiekach średnich', *PH*, 40 (1950), 96–127.
'Agresja Zakonu krzyżackiego na Litwę w wiekach XIII–XV', *PH*, 45 (1954), 338–71.
'Elementy indoeuropejskie w religii Bałtów', *Ars Historica. Prace z dziejów powszechnych i Polski* (*Księga pamiątkowa G. Labudy*) (Poznań, 1976), 145–53.
Studia nad dziejami wielkiego księstwa litewskiego (Poznań, 1983).
Religia slowiań i jej upadek (*w VI-XII*) (Warsaw, 1986).
Prusy–Litwa–Krzyżacy, ed. M. Kosman (Warsaw, 1989).
Lukhtan, A. B. and Ušinskas, V. A., 'K voprosu o stolitse Litvy do 1323g.', *Trudy V mezhdunarodnogo kongressa slavianskoi arkheologii* (*Kiev 18–25 sentiabria 1985*), *III.1b Sektsia V*: *Goroda, ikh kulturnye i torgovye sviazi* (Moscow, 1987), 5–13.
'Ranee srednevekov'e i epokha feodalizma. K probleme stanovlenia litovskoi zemli v svete arkheologicheskich dannykh', in *Drevnosti Litvy i Belorussii*, ed. L. D. Pobol' and A. Z. Tautavičius (Vilnius, 1988), 89–104.
Lur'e, Ia.S., Review of Dmitrieva's *Skazanie* in *Izvestia Akademii Nauk SSSR. Otdelenie literatury i iazyka*, 15 (1956), 176.
Ideologicheskaia bor'ba v russkoi publitsistike kontsa XV–nachala XVI veka (Moscow–Leningrad, 1960).
Obshcherusskie letopisi XIV–XVvv (Leningrad, 1976).
Makary, *Istoria russkoi tserkvi*, 3 vols. in 12, 3rd edn (St Petersburg, 1886–91; The Hague–Vaduz, 1969).
Makk, F., *The Árpáds and the Comneni. Political relations between Hungary and Byzantium in the twelfth century* (Budapest, 1989).
Maleczyński, K., 'W sprawie autentyczności dokumentów Mendoga za lat 1253–61', *AW*, 11 (1936), 1–56.
Malevskaia, M. V. and Sholokhova, E. V., 'Raskopi tserkovnykh postroek na detintse Novogrudka', *AO* (1974), 391–2.
Małowist, M., *Wschód a zachód Europy w XIII–XVI wieku* (Warsaw 1973).
Marchenko, M. I., *Ukrains'ka istoriografia* (*z davnikh chasiv do seredini XIXst.*) (Kiev, 1959).
Maschke, E., *Der Peterspfenning in Polen und dem Deutschen Orden* (Leipzig, 1933).
Matusas, J., *Švitrigaila Lietuvos didysis kunigaikštis* (Kaunas, 1938; 2nd edn Vilnius, 1991).
Matuzova, V. I., 'Vostochnaia Pribaltika v sochinenii Bartolomeia Angliiskogo 'O svoistvakh veshchei'', *Vostochnaia Evropa* (*qv*), 49–55.
'Ideino-teologicheskaia osnova "Khroniki zemli prusskoi" Petra iz Dusberga', *Drevneishie gosudarstva na territorii SSSR* (1982), 152–69.
'"Khronika zemli prusskoi" Petra iz Dusberga v kul'turno-istoricheskim kontekste', *Balto-Slavianskie Issledovania* (1985), 102–18.

Maxime de Sardes, *Le Patriarchat oecuménique dans l'église orthodoxe* (Paris, 1975).
Mažeika, R., 'The role of pagan Lithuania in Roman Catholic and Greek Orthodox religious diplomacy in east-central Europe (1345–1377)', Unpublished doctoral dissertation, Fordham, New York, 1987, revised. (University Microfilms International, Ann Arbor, MI, 1987).
'Was Grand Prince Algirdas a Greek Orthodox Christian?', *Lituanus*, 33:4 (1987), 35–55.
'The relations of Grand Prince Algirdas with eastern and western Christians', *La Cristianizzazione*, 63–84.
'"Nenorim kad jus kovotų prieš mus mūsų pačių ginklais..." Popiežių bandymai reguliuoti prekybą su pabaltyjo pagonimis', *Lituanistica* (1990/4), 11–18.
'Prekyba ir taika mirties zonoje: Prekybinės taikos sutartys tarp kryžuočių ir Lietuvių XIVa.', *Lietuvių katalikų Mokslo Akademijos suvažiavimo darbai*, XIV (Rome, forthcoming).
'The context of Pope John XXII's letters to Gediminas (1322–1324)', *Gedimino laikų Lietuva ir jos kaimynai* (Vilnius, forthcoming).
'Of cabbages and knights: Trade and trade treaties with the Infidel on the Northern Frontier, 1200–1390', *Journal of Medieval History* (forthcoming).
Mažeika, R. and Rowell, S. C., '*Zelatores maximi*: Pope John XXII, Archbishop Frederick of Riga and the Baltic Mission, 1305–1340', *Archivum Historiae Pontificiae* 31 (1993).
Mel'nikova, A. S., 'Pskovskie monety XVv.', *Numizmatika i Epigrafika*, 4 (1963), 222–44.
Melzer, F., *Die Ostraumpolitik König Johanns von Böhmen* (Jena, 1940).
Merzhinskii, A. T., 'Romove', *Trudy desiatoi arkheologicheskogo s"ezda v Rige, 1896*, I (Moscow, 1899), 350–455.
Mesterházy, K., 'Bizánci keresztemy nyomok Berettyóujfalu határában', *Aecheologiai Értesitö*, 96 (1969), 91–8.
Meyendorff, J., 'Alexis and Roman: A study on Byzantino-Russian relations (1352–1354)', *Byzantinoslavica*, 28 (1967), 278–88.
Byzantium and the rise of Russia. A study of Byzantino-Russian relations in the fourteenth century (Cambridge, 1981; 2nd edn New York, 1989).
Michelbertas, M., 'Bizantiška moneta iš Daukšaičių, Klaipėdos raj.', *LAMMDI*, 18:2 (1978), 101–4.
Mikucki, S., 'Etudes sur la diplomatie russe la plus ancienne', *Bulletin international de l'Académie polonaise des sciences et des lettres. Classe de philologie–Classe d'histoire et de philosophie. Numéro supplémentaire*, 7 (1953).
Milovidov, A., 'O polozhenii pravoslavia v Pinske', *Chtenia v obshchestve liubitelei dukhovnoi prosveshchenia*, 31 (April, 1894).
Misiunas, R. J., 'Algirdo tikėjimas', *Lietuvių katalikų Mokslo Akademijos Suvažiavimo Darbai*, VIII (Rome, 1974), 241–52.
The modern encyclopedia of Russian and Soviet history, ed. J. L. Wieczyński, 53 vols. (Gulf Breeze, 1976–).
Mohlin, A., *Kristoffer II av Danmark. Förra delen Välmakstiden* (Lund, 1960).

Mokslinės konferencijos Vilniaus pilys naujausių mokslinių tyrinėjimų šviesoje tezės (1983m. gruodžio 20d.) (Vilnius, 1983).
Mollat, G., *The Popes at Avignon*, tr. J. Love (London, 1963).
Moltke, E., *Runerne i Danmark og deres oprindelse* (Copenhagen, 1976).
Moravcsik, G., *Byzantium and the Magyars* (Budapest, 1970).
Mortensen, G., *Beiträge zu Nationalitäten und Siedlungsverhältnissen von Pr. Litauen* (Königsberg, 1927).
Mukhlinskii, A., 'Zadanie sprawy o Tatarach litewskich przez jednego z tych Tatarów złozone sułtanowi Sulejmanowi w r. 1558', *Teka Wileńska*, 4 (1858), 241–72.
Issledovanie o proiskhozhdenii i sostoianii litovskikh Tatar' (Odessa, 1902).
Muldoon, J., 'The Avignon Papacy and the frontiers of Christendom: the evidence of Vatican Register 62', *Archivum Historiae Pontificiae*, 17 (1979), 125–95.
Popes, lawyers and infidels. The Church and the non-Christian world 1250–1550 (Liverpool, 1979).
Müller, L., *Die Taufe Russlands. Die Frühgeschichte des russischen Christentums bis zum Jahre 988* (Munich, 1988).
Murav'eva, L. L., 'Novgorodskie izvestia Vladimirskogo letopistsa', *AE* (1966), 37–40.
Letopisanie severo-vostochnoi Rusi XIII–XV vekov (Moscow, 1983).
Murgurevich, E. S., *Vostochnaia Latvia i sosednie zemli v X–XIIIvv. Ekonomicheskie sviazi s Rus'iu i drugimi territoriami. Puti soobshchenia* (Riga, 1965).
'The culture of inhabitants of mediaeval settlements in Latvia in the Livonian period (the end of the 12th to the 16th century)', *Fasciculi Archaeologiae Historicae*, 2 (Wrocław–Warsaw–Kraków–Gdańsk–Łódź, 1988), 57–70.
Nakaitė, L., 'Auksakalystės Lietuvoje iki XIIIa klausimu (1. Technika, ornamentika)', *LMADA*, 22 (1966/3), 67–84.
Napiersky, K.E, *Rigas ältere Geschichte* (Riga–Leipzig, 1844).
Narbutt, T., *Dzieje Narodu Litewskiego*, IV (Vilnius, 1838).
Nasonov, A. N., *Mongoly i Rus'* (Moscow–Leningrad, 1940).
Istoria russkogo letopisania XI–nachalo XVIII veka: Ocherki i issledovania (Moscow, 1969).
Navickaitė-Kuncienė, O., 'Senosios Rusios importas X–XIII amžių Lietuvoje', *LMADA*, XVI (1964/1), 115–34.
'Seniausios (X–XIII amžių) svorio matų sistemos Lietuvoje klausimų', *LMADA*, 16 (1966/2), 143–59.
'Vakarų Europos importas Lietuvoje IX–XII amžiais', *LMADA*, 22 (1966/3), 85–103.
Navickas, K., 'Vilniaus gyventojų apavas XIII–XIVa', *ILKI*, 4 (1964), 188–96.
Nazarova, E. L., 'Pravoslavie i sotsial'naia struktura obshchestva v Latvii (XI–XIIIvv)', in *Feodalizm v Rossii. Sbornik statei i vospominanii posviashchennykh pamiati Akademika L. V. Cherepnina*, ed. V. L. Ianin (Moscow, 1987), 201–10.
Neandrus, M., *Orbis terrae partium succincta explicatio* (Leipzig, 1586).
Nicol, D. M., *The last centuries of Byzantium 1261–1453* (London, 1979).

Niesiecki, K., *Herbarz Polski* VIII (Leipzig, 1841; 2nd edn Warsaw, 1979).
Niess, U., *Hochmeister Karl von Trier (1311–1324). Stationen einer Karriere im Deutschen Orden (Quellen und Studien zur Geschichte des Deutschen Ordens*, XLVII) (Marburg, 1992)
Nikžentaitis, A., 'Lietuvos diplomatinė kova su Vokiečių ordinu 1337–1342m.', *Lietuvos Istorijos Metraštis* (1986), 5–21.
'1324m. Lietuvos paliaubos su Vokiečių ordinu ir jų reikšmė', *LMADA*, 95 (1986/2), 61–70.
'Rašytiniai šaltiniai apie Lietuvių pilių systemą XIIIa. pabaigoje–XIVa. pradžioje', *LMADA*, 96 (1986/3), 51–62.
'Dar kartą apie tai "Kas žuvo prie Bajerburgo?'", *LMADA*, 98 (1987/1), 31–43.
'Dėl Gedimino laiškų autentiškumo (1. Gedimino laiškai Hanzos miestams)', *LMADA*, 101 (1987/4), 92–9.
'Dėl Gedimino laiškų autentiškumo (2. Gedimino laiškai popiežiui ir krikščionybės įvedimo Lietuvoje klausimas 1323–1324m.)', *LMADA*, 103 (1988/2), 66–76.
'Dėl čekų feodalų vaidmens 1329m. vokiečių ordino žygyje į Lietuvą', *LMADA*, 104 (1988/3), 52–7.
Gediminas (Vilnius, 1989).
'Legenda XIVv. o muchenistve 14 frantsiskantsev v Vil'niuse i istoricheskaia istina', *Vspomogatel'nye istoricheskie distsipliny*, 21 (1990), 257–69.
'Trapėnų žemė', *Žemaičių praeitis*, 1 (1990), 93–9.
'Lietuvos ir Lenkijos santykiai 1340–1345m. (Pietvakarių Rusios žemių prijungimo prie Lietuvos Didžiosios Kunigaikštystės laiko problema)', *Iš Lietuvos istorijos turinėjimų* (Vilnius, 1991), 31–6.
Nock, A. D., *Conversion: the Old and the New in religion from Alexander the Great to Augustine of Hippo* (Oxford, 1933).
Nohejlová-Prátová, E., 'A propos de la période du gros pragois', *Nummus et historia. Pieniądz Europy średniowiecznej* (Warsaw, 1985), 237–44.
de Nolhac, P., *Petrarque et l'humanisme*, 2 vols. (Paris, 1907).
Nowacki. B., *Czeskie roszczenia do korony w Polsce w latach 1290–1335* (Poznań, 1987).
Nyberg, T. S., 'Skandinavien und die Christianisierung des südöstlichen Baltikum', *La Cristianizzazione*, 235–61.
Obolensky, D., 'Byzantium, Kiev and Moscow: A study of ecclesiastical relations', *Dumbarton Oaks Papers*, 11 (1957), 23–78.
Ochmański, J., 'Uwagi o litewskim państwie wczesnofeudalnym', *Roczniki Historyczne*, 27 (1961), 143–60.
'Noms des terres lithuaniennes au XIII siècle', *Lingua posnaniensia*, 9 (1962), 169–74.
'Nad kroniką Bychowca', *Studia Źródłoznawcze*, 12 (1967), 155–63.
'Przyczyny opóźnienia Chrystianizacji Litwy', *KH*, 78 (1971), 870–1.
'Gediminovichi – "Pravnuki Skolomendovye"', *Pol'sha i Rus'*, 358–64.
'Krzywy gród wileński. Próba lokalizacji', *ZH*, 36 (1979), 57–66.
'Mikhalon Litvin i ego Traktat o nravakh Tatar, litovtsev i moskvitian

serediny XVIv.', in *Rossia, Pol'sha i Prichernomor'e v XV–XVIIIvv.*, ed. B. A. Rybakov (Moscow, 1979), 97–117.
'Inozemnye poselenia v Litve XIII–XIVvv. v svete etnonimicheskikh mestnikh nazvanii', *Balto-Slavianskie Issledovania* (1980), 112–31.
Historia Litwy, 2nd edn (Wrocław–Warsaw–Kraków–Gdańsk–Łódź, 1982).
'Neizvestny avtor "Opisania zemel'" vtoroi poloviny XIIIv. i ego svedenia o Baltakh', *Balto-Slavianskie Issledovania* (1985), 89–95.
Dawna Litwa. Studia Historyczne (Olsztyn, 1986).
Offler, H. S., 'Empire and Papacy: the last struggle', *TrRHS*, 5th series 6 (1956), 21–47.
Ogizki, D., 'Blutzeugenisse für Christus im Litauen des 14 Jahrhunderts: Legende und wirklichkeit der drei Märtyrer von Wilna', *Stimme der Orthodoxie*, 8 (1984), 39–48.
Okhotnikova, V. I., *Povest' o Dovmonte* (Leningrad, 1985).
Okolski, S., *Chioviensium et Czernichoviensium episcoporum sanctae catholicae ecclesiae Romanae ordo et numerus* (Lwów, 1646; reprinted Kraków, 1853).
Olsen, O., *Hørg, Hov og Kirke. Historiske og Arkaeologiske Vikingetidsstudier* (Copenhagen, 1966).
'Vorchristliche Heiligtümer in Nordeuropa', *Abhandlungen der Akademie der Wissenschaften in Göttingen, Phil.-Hist. Klasse* 74 (1970), 259–78.
The origins of Anglo-Saxon kingdoms, ed. S. Bassett (Leicester, 1989).
Pacuski, K., 'Mazowsze wobec walk o władze w Polsce na przełomie XIII/XIVw.', *KH*, 85 (1978), 585–603.
Państwo, naród, stany w świadomości wieków średnich. Pamięci Benedykta Zientary (Warsaw, 1991).
Paravicini, W., 'Die Preussenreisen des europäischen Adels', *Historische Zeitschrift*, 232 (1981), 25–38.
'Edelleute, Hansen, Brügger, Bürger: Die Finanzierung der westeuropäischen Preussenreisen im 14 Jahrhundert', *Hansische Geschichtsblätter*, 104 (1986), 5–20.
Die Preussenreisen des europäischen Adels, I, *Beihefte der Francia* XVII/1 (Sigmaringen, 1989).
Pashuto, V. T., *Ocherki po istorii galitsko-volynskoi Rusi* (Moscow, 1950).
Obrazovanie Litovskogo Gosudarstva (Moscow, 1959).
'Poslania Gedimina kak istoricheskii istochnik', *Issledovania po otechestvennomu istochnikovedeniu. Sbornik statei posviashchennykh 75-letiu professora S. N. Valka* (Moscow, 1964), 463–73.
Paszkiewicz, H., 'Ze studiów nad polityką polską, litewską i krzyżacką Bolesława Jerzego, ostatniego księcia Rusi Halicko-Włodimierskiej', *AW*, 2 (1924), 31–67.
Polityka ruska Kazimerza Wielkiego (Warsaw, 1925).
'Z dziejów Podlasia w XIV wieku', *KH*, 42 (1928), 229–45.
Jagiellonowie a Moskwa I: Litwa a Moskwa w XIII i XIV wieku (Warsaw, 1933).
O genezie i wartości Krewa (Warsaw, 1938).
The origin of Russia (London, 1954).
Pavlov, A. S., 'O nachale galitskoi i litovskoi mitropolii po vizantiiskim

dokumental'nym istochnikam XIV veka', *Russkoe Obozrenie*, 27 (May, 1894), 214–51.

Pāvulāns, V. V., 'Khoziaistvennoe i politicheskoe znachenie daugavskogo torgovogo puti v XIII–XVIIvv.', in *Ekonomicheskie sviazi Pribaltiki s Rossiei. Sbornik statei*, ed. Ia. P. Krastyn' *et al.* (Riga, 1968), 75–94.

Satiksmes celi Latvijā XIII–XVII gs. (Riga, 1971).

Perlbach, M., 'Urkunden des Rigischen Capitel-Archivs in der fürstlich Czartoryskischen Bibliothek zu Krakau', *Mitteilungen aus dem Gebiete der Geschichte Liv-Est und Kurlands*, 13 (1886), 1–23.

Perogovskii, *Materialy dla istorii Volyni* (Zhitomir, 1879).

Petrowicz, G., *La Chiesa armena in Polonia. Parte prima 1350–1624* (Rome, 1971).

Petrushevich, A. S., *Arkhieratikon Kievskoi mitropolii s poloviny XIV stoletia* (Lwów, 1901).

Pflugk-Harttung, J., *Der Johanniter und der Deutsche Orden im Kampfe Ludwigs des Bayerns mit der Kurie* (Leipzig, 1900).

Pickhan, G., *Gospodin Pskov. Entstehung und Entwicklung eines städtischen Herrschaftszentrums in Altrussland, Forschungen zur osteuropäische Geschichte*, XLVII (Berlin, 1992).

Piech, Z., 'Mitra książęca w swietle przekazów ikonograficznych od czasów rozbica dzielnicowego do końca epoki Jagiellońskiej', *Kwartalnik Historii Kultury Materialnej*, 35 (1987/1), 3–48.

Piekarczyk, S., *Studia z dziejów miast polskich w XIII–XIVw.* (Warsaw, 1955).

Platon, Mitropolit, *Kratkaia tserkovnaia Rossiiskaia istoria*, I, 2nd edn (Moscow, 1823).

Pliguzov, A., 'On the title "Metropolitan of Kiev and all Rus'"', *Harvard Ukrainian Studies* 15:3–4 (1991), 340–53.

Plitz, E., *Trois sakkoi byzantins: analyse iconographique*, *Acta Universitatis Upsaliensis*, n.s. 17 (1976).

Podosinov, A. V., 'O printsipakh postroenia i mesta sozdania 'Spiska russkikh gorodov dal'nikh i blizhnikh", *Vostochnaia Evropa (qv)*, 40–8.

Pollakówna, M., *Osadnictwo Warmii w okresie krzyżackim*, *Prace Instytutu Zachodniego*, XVII (1953).

Kronika Piotra z Dusburga (Wrocław–Warsaw–Kraków, 1968).

Polny tserkovno-slovianskii slovar', ed. G. D'iachenko, I (Moscow, 1899).

Pol'sha i Rus'; cherty obshchnosti i svoeobrazia v istoricheskom razvitii Rusi i Pol'shi XII–XIVxx, (*Sbornik statei*), ed. B. A. Rybakov (Moscow, 1974).

Poppe, A., 'Words that serve the authority. On the title of "grand prince" in Kievan Rus'', *Acta Poloniae Historica*, 60 (1989), 159–84.

Poschmann, B., 'Bistümer und Deutsche Orden in Preussen 1243–1525', *Zeitschrift für die Geschichte und Altertumskunde Ermlands*, 30 (1962), 227–354.

Powierski, J., *Podziały administracyjne Kujaw i ziemi dobrzyńskiej w XIII i XIV wieku* (Poznań, 1974).

'Międzynarodowe tło konfliktu polsko-krzyżackiego przed kampanią wrześniową 1331 roku' *Balticum* (q.v.), 269–84.

Preobrazhenski, S., 'Vil'na v nachale XVI stoletia: po Braunu i drugim istochnikam', in *Vilenskii Sbornik*, ed. V. Kulin', I (Vilnius 1869), 244–65.

Prochaska, A., 'W sprawie zajęcia Rusi przez Kazimierza Wielkiego', *KH*, 6 (1892), 1–33.

'Stosunki krzyzaków z Giedyminem i Łokietkiem', *KH*, 10 (1896), 1–66.

'Od Mendoga do Jagiełły', *Litwa i Ruś*, 4:1 (1912).

Prokhorov, G. M., *Povest' o Mitiae: Rus' i Vizantia v epokhu kulikovskoi bitvy* (Leningrad, 1978).

Pustejovsky, O., *Schlesiens Übergang an die Böhmische Krone* (Cologne–Vienna, 1975).

Puti razvitia feodalizma (*Zakavkaz'e, Sredniaia Azia, Rus', Pribaltika*) (Moscow, 1972).

Puzyna, J., 'Kim był i jak się naprawdę nazywał Pukuwer, ojciec Gedymina', *AW*, 10 (1935), 1–43.

'Sukcesorowie Trojdena' *AW*, 13 (1938), 1–31.

'Początki państwowości i dynastii litewskiej według najnowszych badań', *Nauka i sztuka*, 6 (1947), 152–70.

Raba, J., 'Evfimij II Erzbischof von Gross Novgorod und Pskov. Ein Kirchenfürst als Leiter einer weltlichen Republik', *Jahrbücher für Geschichte Osteuropas*, n.s. 25 (1977), 161–73.

Rabikauskas, P., 'La cristianizzazione della Samogizia'. *La Cristianizzazione della Lituania, Atti e Document*: II (Vatican City, 1989) , 219–33.

Radzimiński, Z. L., 'Sprawa odrębnego pochodzenia Chodkiewiczów litewskich i białoruskich (z tablicami genealogicznymi)', *Rocznik polskiego Towarzystwa heraldycznego we Lwowie*, 8 (1926–27), 109–32.

Radziszewska, J., *Maciej Stryjkowski: Historyk-poetarz epoki Odrodzenia* (Katowice, 1978).

'Przejątki Długosza z "Litewskiego Latopisu"', *Zeszyty Naukowe Uniwersytetu Jagiellońskiego: Prace Historyczne*, 65 (1985), 256–68.

Rajewski, Z. A., 'Pogańscy kapłani-czarodzieje w walce klasowej słowiań we wczesnym średniowieczu', *Wiadomości Archeologiczne*, 39:4 (1975), 503–9.

'Koń w wierzeniach u słowiań wczesnośredniowiecznych', *Wiadomości Archeologiczne*, 39:4 (1975), 516–21.

Rebane, P. P., 'The Danish bishops of Tallinn, 1260–1346', *JBS*, 5 (1974), 315–28.

'Denmark, the Papacy and the christianization of Estonia', *Gli inizi* (*qv*), 171–201.

Reincke, H., 'Bevölkerungsprobleme der Hansestädte', *Hansische Geschichtsblätter*, 70 (1951), 1–33.

Renouard, Y., 'Comment les papes d'Avignon expédiaient leur courrier', *Revue Historique*, 180 (1937), 1–29.

A republic of nobles. Studies in Polish history to 1864, ed. J. K. Fedorowicz (Cambridge, 1984).

Reuter, T., 'Plunder and tribute in the Carolingian Empire', *TrRHS*, 5th series 35 (1985), 75–94.

Reynolds, S., 'Medieval *origines gentium* and the community of the realm', *History*, 68 (1983), 375–90.

Řežabek, J., 'Jiři II, posledni kniže veškevé Malé Rusi', *Časopis Musea Království Českého*, 57 (1883), 120–41.

Richard, J., *La Papauté et les missions d'Orient du Moyen Age (XIII–XV siècles), Collection de l'Ecole française de Rome*, XXXIII (1977).

'Les Papes d'Avignon et l'évangélisation du monde non-latin à la veille du Grand Schisme', *Genèse et débuts du Grand Schisme d'Occident 1362–1394* (Paris, 1980), 305–15.

Rickievičiutė, K., 'Raskopi mogil'nika Šulaičiai', *AO* (1985), 485–6.

Rimantienė, R. and Urbanavičius V., 'Iazycheskoe sviatilishche v Zhemaitii', *AO* (1970), 330.

Ripoche, J. P., 'La Hongrie entre Byzance et Rome: problème du choix religieux', *Ungarn-Jahrbuch*, 6 (1974–75), 9–23.

Rituals of royalty. Power and ceremonial in traditional societies, ed. D. Cannadine and S. Price (Cambridge, 1987).

Roesdahl, E., *Viking Age Denmark*, tr. S. Margeson and K. Williams (London, 1982).

Rogov, A. I., *Russko-pol'skie kul'turnye sviazi v epokhu Vozrozhdenia (Stryikovskii i ego Khronika)* (Moscow, 1966).

'Kirillicheskie rukopisi v knigokhranilishchakh Pol'shi', *Studia Źródłoznawcze*, 14 (1969), 153–67.

Roman, S., 'Stanowisko majątkowe wdowy w średniowiecznym prawie polskim', *Czasopismo prawno-historyczne*, 5 (1953), 80–108.

Roth, W., *Die Dominikaner und Franziskaner im Deutsch-Ordensland Preussen bis zum Jahre* 1466 (Königsberg, 1918).

Roux, J-P., 'Tängri, Essai sur le Ciel-dieu des peuples altaïques', *Revue de l'Histoire des religions*, 149 (1956), 49–82, 197–230 and 150 (1956), 27–54, 173–212.

Rowell, S. C., 'Lithuania and the West 1337–1341: A question of sources', *JBS*, 20:4 (1989), 303–26.

'Pagans, peace and the Pope 1322–1324: Lithuania in the centre of European diplomacy', *Archivum Historiae Pontificiae*, 28 (1990), 63–98.

'A pagan's word: Lithuanian diplomatic procedure 1200–1385', *Journal of Medieval History*, 18 (1992), 145–60.

'Between Lithuania and Rus': Dovmont-Timofey of Pskov, his life and cult', *OSP*, n.s. 25 (1992), 1–33.

'Of men and monsters: Sources for the history of Lithuania in the time of Gediminas (ca. 1315–1342)', *JBS*, 24:1 (1993), 73–112.

'Gediminid dynastic diplomacy in Žemaitija 1350–1430', *Žemaičių Praeitis*, 3 (1993).

'The Letters of Gediminas: *Gemachte Lüge*? Notes on a controversy', *Jahrbücher für Geschichte Osteuropas* 41: 3 (1993).

'Swords for sale? An aspect of Lithuanian diplomacy 1326–1342', *Gedimino laikų Lietuva ir jos kaimynai* (Vilnius, forthcoming).

'Pious princesses or the daughters of Belial: Pagan Lithuanian dynastic diplomacy 1279–1423', *Medieval Prosopography*, 15: 1 (1994).

Rozov, N. N., *Kniga v Rossii v XV veke* (Leningrad, 1981).

Runciman, S., *A history of the First Bulgarian Empire* (London, 1930).
Russkaia sfragistika i geral'dika, ed. E. I. Kamentseva and N. V. Ustiugov, 2nd edn (Moscow, 1974).
Russkaia Vil'na. Prilozhenie k puteshestviu po sviatym mestam russkim (Vilnius, 1865).
Rybina, E. A., *Inozemnye dvory v Novgorode XII–XVIIvv.* (Moscow, 1986).
Sadauskaitė, I., 'Dėl mirusiųjų deginimo papročio', *ILKI*, 3 (1961), 125–31.
Safargaliev, M. G., *Raspad zolotoi ordy* (Saransk, 1960).
Sakharov, A. M., 'O termine 'gorod' v istochnikakh XVIv.', *Obshchestvo i Gosudarstvo feodal'noi Rossii. Sbornik statei posviashchennykh 70-letiiu Akademika L. V. Cherepnina* (Moscow, 1975), 62–6.
Sakharov, A. N., *Diplomatia Drevnei Rusi IX–pervaia polovina Xv.* (Moscow, 1980).
Samoilo, N., 'Litovskaia legenda ob osnovanii goroda Vil'no', *Russkaia Starina* (1895/4), 94–5.
Samsonowicz, H., 'Przemiany strefy bałtyckiej w XIII–XVIw', *Roczniki dziejów społecznych i gospodarczych*, 37 (1976), 47–61.
Sapunov, A. R., *Istoricheskie sud'by polotskoi eparkhii s dreveishikh vremen do poloviny XIX veka* (Vitebsk, 1889).
Sarnicius, S., *Annales sive de origine et rebus gestis Polonorum et Lituanorum, Libri octo* (Kraków, 1587).
Sbornik materialov i statei po istorii pribaltiiskogo kraia II (Riga, 1879).
Schmidt, R., *Die Deutschordenskommenden Trier und Beckingen 1242–1794* (Marburg, 1979).
Schmutz, R. A., 'Medieval papal representatives: legates, nuncios and judges-delegate', *Studia Gratiana*, 15 (1972), 441–63.
Scholz, K., *Beiträge zur Personengeschichte des Deutschen Ordens in der erste Hälfte des 14 Jahrhunderts. Untersuchungen zur Herkunft livländischer und preussischer Deutschordensbrüder* (Münster, 1969).
Schreiner, P., *Die Byzantischen Kleinchroniken, I: Einleitung und Text* (Vienna, 1975).
Sedov, V. V., 'Pagan sanctuaries and idols of the Eastern Slavs', *Slavica Gandensia*, 7–8 (1980–81), 69–85.
Semenov, P., *Geograficheskii staticheskii slovar' rossiiskoi imperii* II (St Petersburg, 1865).
Semkowicz, W., 'O litewskich rodach bojarskich zbratanych ze szlachtą polską w Horodle r.1413', *Rocznik polskiego towarzystwa heraldycznego we Lwowie*, 5 (1920), 39–57; 6 (1921–23), 116–28; 7 (1924–25), 210–20; 8 (1926–27), 133–43; 9 (1928–29), 251–60. Reprinted in *Lituano-Slavica Posnaniensia Studia Historica*, 3 (1989), 7–139.
'Tradycja o kniaziowskim pochodzeniu Radziwiłłów w świetle krytyki historycznej', *KH*, 34 (1920), 88–108.
'Hanul, namiestnik wileński (1382–87) i jego ród', *AW*, 7 (1930), 1–20.
Senga, T., 'Béla királyfi Bolgár, halicsi és osztrák Hadjárataihoz', *Századok*, 122 (1988), 36–51.

Serebrianskii, N. I., 'Ocherki po istorii Pskovskogo monashestva', *ChOIDR* (1908/3).

Setsinskii, E., 'Istoricheskie svedenia o prikhodakh i tserkvakh Podol'skoi eparkhii', *Trudy podol'skogo eparkhial'nogo istoriko-statisticheskogo komiteta*, VII (Kamenets–Podol'skoi, 1895).

Ševchenko, I., 'Nicolas Cabasilas' "anti-zealot" discourse: A reinterpretation', *Dumbarton Oaks Papers*, 11 (1957), 81–171.

Shabul'do, F. M., *Zemli iugo-zapadnoi Rusi v sostave velikogo kniazhestva litovskogo* (Kiev, 1987).

Shaw, S. J., *History of the Ottoman Empire and modern Turkey, I : Empire of the Gazis: The rise and decline of the Ottoman Empire 1280–1808* (Cambridge, 1976).

Shchapov, Ia. N., 'Iuzhno-slavianskii politicheskii opyt na sluzhbe u russkikh ideologov XVv.', *Byzantino-Bulgarica*, 2 (1966), 199–214.

Kniazheskie ustavy i tserkov' v Drevnei Rusi XI–XIVvv (Moscow, 1972).

'Biblioteka Polotskogo Sofiiskogo sobora i biblioteka Akademii Zamoiskoi', in *Kul'turnye sviazi narodov vostochnoi evropy v XVIv. Problemy vzaimootnoshenii Pol'shi, Rossii, Ukrainy, Belorussii i Litvy v epokhu Vozrozhdenia*, ed. B. A. Rybakov (Moscow, 1976), 262–82.

Drevnerusskie ... – see Sources section.

Gosudarstvo i tserkov' drevnei Rusi X–XIIIvv. (Moscow, 1989).

Shennikov, A. A., *Chervlenyi Iar. Issledovanie po istorii i geografii srednego Podon'ia v XIV–XVIvv*. (Leningrad, 1987).

Sholokhova, E. V., 'Raskopi tserkovnykh postroek na detintse Novogrudka', *AO* (1974), 391–2.

Sielecki, F., 'Kronikarze polscy w latopisarstwie i dawnej historiografii ruskiej', *Slavia Orientalis*, 14 (1965), 143–78.

Sinitskii, A., 'Kharakter' tserkovnogo upravlenia v iugo-zapadnoi i zapadnoi Rossii pred' Brestkoiu Unieiu', *Vestnik iugo-zapadnoi i zapadnoi Rossii*, 1 (1862), kn. 4, otd. 2.

Sinor, D., *History of Hungary* (London, 1959).

Skardžius, P., *Die slavische Lehnwörter im Altlitauischen* (Kaunas, 1931).

Skibniewski, M., 'Stefan II biskup Lubuski 1316–45', *Przegląd Powszechny* (1914), 3–24.

Skyum-Nielsen, N., 'Estonia under Danish rule', in *Danish medieval history. New currents*, ed. N. Skyum-Nielsen and N. Lund (Copenhagen, 1981), 112–35.

Šležas, P., 'Ar Gediminaičiai kilė iš Žemaičių?', *Atheneum*, 6 (1935), 1–12.

Sliwiński, B., 'Kształtowanie się własności rycerskiej w pólnocnej części ziemi dobrzyńskiej w XIII i XIVw.', *ZH*, 50 (1985/4), 5–24.

Slovar' istoricheskii o sviatykh proslavennykh v Rossiiskoi tserkvi i o nekotorykh podvizhnikakh blagochestia mestnochtimykh (St Petersburg, 1836).

Slovar' knizhnikov i knizhnosti Drevnei Rusi. ed. D. S. Likhachev 3 vols. (Leningrad, 1987–89).

Słównik geograficzny Królestwa polskiego i innych krajów słowiańskich ed. F. Sulimierski *et al.* 15 vols. in 16 (Warsaw, 1880–1902; reprinted 1975–77).

Smith, J. and Urban, W. L., 'Peter von Suchenwirt', *Lituanus*, 31:2 (1985), 5–26.

Soboleva, N. A., 'K voprosu o monetakh Vladimira Ol'gerdovicha', *Numizmatika i Epigrafika*, 8 (1970), 81–7.
'O denezhnykh sistemakh Velikogo Kniazhestva Litovskogo v XIV–XVvv.', *Nummus et Historia. Pieniądz Europy średniowiecznej* (Warsaw, 1985), 205–12.
Sobolevskii, A., 'Russkoe izvestie o poslednikh galitskikh Riurikovichakh', *Sbornik statei v chest' Matveia Kuz'micha Liubavskogo* (Petrograd, 1917), 214–15.
Social approaches to Viking studies, ed. R. Samson (Glasgow, 1991).
Sokolov, P., *Russkii arkhierei iz Vizantii i pravo ego naznachenia do nachala XV veka* (Kiev, 1913; Gregg International, 1970).
Solov'ev, M., 'Krestonostsy i Litva', *Otechestvennye Zapiski*, 82 (May–June, 1852), 43–62.
Sotnikova, M. P., 'Riazanskii klad serebrianykh litovskikh slitkov iz sobrania Ermitazha', *Soobshchenia Gosudarstvennoi Ermitazha*, 12 (1957), 15–18.
Soulis, G. C., *The Serbs and Byzantium during the reign of Tsar Stephen Dušan (1331–1355) and his successors* (Washington, 1984).
Spěváček, J., *Král diplomat/ Jan Lucemburský 1296–1346* (Prague, 1982).
Spitsyn, A., 'Litovskie drevnosti', *Tauta ir žodis humanitarinių Mokslo Fakulteto leidinys*, 3 (1925), 112–71.
Spliet, H., *Eine Quellenkritische Übersicht zu den Gediminbriefen in Erwiderung auf Kurt Forstreuters Forschungsergebnisse* (Sinsheim, 1959).
Sprogis, M. V., *Geograficheskii slovar' drevnei zhomoitskoi zemli XVI stoletia, sostavlennyi po 40 aktovym knigam Rossieiskogo zemskogo suda* (Vilnius, 1888).
Spuler, B., *Die Goldene Horde. Die Mongolen in Russland*, 2nd edn (Wiesbaden, 1965).
Staich, W., *Chrzciciele Litwy: udział polskich Franciszkanów w nawracaniu ludu litewskiego. Pamiątka rekoncyliacji i otwarcia kościoła OO. Franciszkanów w Wilnie 1864–1934* (Vilnius, 1935).
Staniewicz, W., 'Dzieje agrarne na ziemiach litewskich', *AW*, 2 (1924), 103–21.
Stankus, J., 'Geležies dirbinių gamyba ir kalvystės lygis Lietuvoje XIV–XVI amžiais', *LMADA*, 52 (1975/3), 51–63.
Stasiw, M., *Metropolia Haliciensis – eius historia et iuridica forma* (Rome, 1960).
Stebelski, I., *Dwa wielkie swiatła na horyzoncie połockim z cieniów zakonnych powstajace, czyli Zywoty SS Panien y matek Eufrozyny y Parascewi*, I (Vilnius, 1781).
Steinsland, G., 'Kvinner og kult in Vikingtid', in *Kvinnearbeid i Norden fra Vikingtiden til Reformasjonen*, ed. Andersen, Randi *et al.* (Bergen, 1985), 31–42.
Stein-Wilkeshuis, M., 'Laws in mediaeval Iceland', *Journal of Medieval History*, 12:1 (1986), 37–53.
Stopka, K., 'Kościół ormiański na Rusi w wiekach średnich', *Nasza Przeszłość*, 62 (1984), 27–95.
'Misja wewnętrzna na Litwie w czasach Mendoga a zagadnienie autorstwa "Descriptiones Terrarum"', *Nasza Przeszłość*, 68 (1987), 247–62.

'Próby Chrystianizacji Litwy w latach 1248–1263', *Analecta Cracoviensia*, 19 (1987), 1–65.

Straub, V., *Entstehung und Entwicklung des frühneuhochdeutschen Prosaromans*, *Amsterdamer Publikationen zur Sprache und Literatur*, XVI (1974).

Sturms, E., 'Baltische Alkhügel', *Conventus primus historicorum balticorum. Acta et relata* (Riga, 1938), 116–32 and 23 plates.

Suchocki, J., 'Formowanie się i skład narodu politycznego w Wielkim Księstwie Litewskim późnego średniowiecza', *ZH*, 48:1–2 (1983), 31–76.

'Geneza litewskiej legendy etnogenetycznej', *ZH*, 52 (1987), 27–66.

Suchodolska, E., *Kancelarie na Mazowszu w latach 1248–1348. Ośrodki zarządzania i kultury* (Warsaw, 1977).

Regesty dokumentów mazowieckich z lat 1248–1345 (Warsaw – Łódź, 1980).

Sullivan, J., 'The manuscripts and date of Marsiglio of Padua's "Defensor Pacis"', *English Historical Review*, 20 (1905), 293–307.

Suvorov, N. S., *Sledy zapadno-katolicheskoi tserkovnogo prava v pamiatnikakh drevnerusskogo prava* (Yaroslavl', 1888).

Svátek, J., *Organisace reholních istitucí v českých zemích a péce o jejich archivy* (Prague, 1966).

Szacherska, S. M., 'The political role of the Danish monasteries in Pomerania 1171–1223', *Mediaeval Scandinavia*, 10 (1976), 122–55.

Szaraniewicz, I., *Istoria galitsko-volodimerskoi Rusi. Ot naidavneishikh vremen do roku 1453* (Lwow, 1863).

Szeftel, M., 'The title of the Muscovite monarch up to the end of the seventeenth century', *Canadian–American Slavic Studies*, 13:1–2 (1979), 59–81.

Szymczak, J., 'Genealogia Przemyślidów z przełomu XIII i XIV wieku spokrewnionych z Piastami', *Acta Universitatis Nicolai Copernici. Historia*, 8 (1973), 39–54.

Tautavičius, A., 'Iš XIVa. Vilniaus gyventojų buities', *ILKI*, 1 (1958), 94–103.

'Archeologinai kasinėjimai Vilniaus žemutinės piliės teritorijoje 1960m', *LMADA*, 11 (1961/2), 103–24.

'Vilniaus žemutinės piliės mediniai pastatai XIII–XIV amžiais', *ILKI*, 4 (1964), 171–87.

'Papildomi duomenys apie naujas sidabro lydinių ir XIVa. II pusės–XVa. pradžios Lietuvos monetų radinius Lietuvos TSR teritorijoje', *LMADA*, 18 (1965/1), 67–84.

Teodorovich, N. I., *Istoriko-statisticheskoe opisanie tserkvei i prikhodov Volynskoi eparkhii* (Pochaev, 1888).

Gorod Vladimir-Volynskoi gubernii v sviazi s istoriei Volynskoi Ierarkhii (Pochaev, 1893).

Tikhomirov, M. N., 'Puti iz Rossii v Vizantiu v XIV–XVvv.', *Vizantiiskie Ocherki* (Moscow, 1961), 3–33.

Tikhomirov, N. D., *Galitskaia mitropolia i tserkovno-istoricheskoe issledovanie* (St Petersburg, 1896).

'Galitskie i litovskie metropolity XIV i XVvv. i otnoshenie k nim episkopov Polotskoi i Turovskoi eparkhii', *Trudy Vitebskoi Uchenoi Arkhivnoi Komissii*, I (Vitebsk, 1910).

T(itov), Th., 'Postavlenie v diakona i sviashchennika i izbranie episkopa v drevnei zapadno-russkoi tserkvi ili kievskoi mitropolii v XIV–XVIvv.', *Trudy Kievskoi Dukhovnoi Akademii* (1902, May), 134–45.
Tobacco, G., *La Casa di Francia nell'azione politica di Papa Giovanni XXII* (Rome, 1953).
Toporov, V. N., 'Zametki po baltiiskoi mifologii', *Balto-Slavianskii Sbornik* (1972), 289–314.
Prusskii Iazyk. Slovar' (Moscow, 1975–).
'Vilnius, Wilno, Vil'na. Gorod i mif', in *Balto-Slavianskie Etnoiazykovye kontakty*, ed. T. M. Sudnik (Moscow, 1980), 3–71.
'Zametki po pokhoronnoi obriadnosti', *Balto-Slavianskie Issledovania* (1985), 10–52.
Trajdos, T. M., *Kościół katolicki na ziemiach ruskich Korony i Litwy za panowanie Władysława II Jagiełły (1386–1434)*, I (Wrocław–Warsaw–Kraków–Gdańsk–Łódź, 1983).
'Metropolicy kijowscy Cyprian i Grzegorz Camblak (Bulgarscy duchowni prawosławni) a problemy cerkwi prawosławnej w państwie polsko-litewskim u schyłku XIV i w pierwszej ćwierci XVw.', *Balcanica Posnaniensia*, 2 (1985), 211–34.
Trudy Pskovskogo tserkovnogo istoriko-arkheologicheskogo komiteta – Pskovskaia Starina, I (1910).
Tymieniecki, K., 'The Reunion of the kingdom 1295–1333', in *The Cambridge History of Poland: From the origins to Sobieski (to 1696)*, ed. W. F. Reddaway, J. H. Penson, O. Halecki and R. Dyboski (Cambridge, 1950), 108–24.
Tyrtov, A., *O pravoslavnykh Vilenskikh khramakh prezhde byvshikh i nyne sushchestvuiushchikh* (Vilnius, 1892).
Tyszkiewicz, J., *Tatarzy na Litwie i w Polsce. Studia z dziejów XIII–XVIIIw.* (Warsaw, 1989).
Ulanowski, B., 'O dacie przywileju Bolesława Mazowieckiego rzekomo z r. 1278 wydanego dla klasztoru w Jeżowie', *RAU*, 1st series 17 (1884), 64–91.
Ulashchik, N. N., 'Podgotovka k pechati i izdanii Toma XVII "Polnogo Sobrania Russkikh Letopisei"', *Letopisi i Khroniki* (1973), 360–8.
Vvedenie v izuchenie Belorussko-Litovskogo letopisania (Moscow, 1985).
Ullmann, W., 'The medieval papal court as an international tribunal', *Virginia Journal of International Law*, 11 (1971), 356–71.
The papacy and political ideas in the Middle Ages (London, 1976).
Urban, W. L., 'The military occupation of Semigallia in the thirteenth century', in *Baltic History*, ed. A. Ziedonis, W. L. Winter and M. Valgemaë (Columbus, OH, 1974), 21–34.
'The correct translation of "Ruce"', *JBS*, 13:1 (1982), 12–18.
'Roger Bacon and the Teutonic Knights', *JBS*, 19 (1988), 363–70.
Urbanavičius, V., 'K voprosu o pogrebeniakh s trupopolozheniem XIVv. v Litve', *LMADA*, 21 (1966/2), 183–90.
'Laidosena Lietuvoje XIV–XVII amžiais', *LMADA*, 22 (1966/3), 105–19.
'XIV–XVII amžių monetas Lietuvos kapinynuose', *LMADA*, 24 (1967/2), 61–74.

'Issledovania mogil'nikov XIV–XVIIvv v Piktagalise i v Skrebinai', *AO* (1970), 328–30.
'Iazycheskie sviatilishcha XVI–XVIIvv v Litve', *AO* (1971), 420–1.
'Senųjų tikėjimų reliktai Lietuvoje XV–XVII amžiais (1. Pagoniškųjų laidojimo papročio nykimas rytų Lietuvoje)', *LMADA*, 48 (1974/3), 77–91.
'—— (3. Laidojimo papročiai Uliūnuose XVI–XVII amž.)', *LMADA*, 50 (1975/1), 51–62.
'—— (4. Pagoniškos šventvietės XVI–XVII amž.)', *LMADA*, 60 (1977/3), 79–89.
'Relikty iazychestva v pamiatnikakh 14–16vv v Litve', in *Novoe v arkheologii Pribaltiki i sosednikh territorii*, ed. J. Selirand (Tallinn, 1985), 161–7.
Ustrialov, N., *Issledovanie voprosa, kakoe mesto v russkoi istorii dolzhno zanimat' Velikoe Kniazhestvo Litovskoe?* (St Petersburg, 1839).
Vaičiulaitis, A., 'Vidurinių amžių poetas Machaut Lietuvoje', *Lietuvių Katalikų Mokslo Akademijos Leidinys*, III (1939) (Rome, 1972), 315–19.
Van D'Elden, S. C., *Peter Suchenwirt and Heraldic Poetry, Wiener Arbeiten zur Germanistischen Altertumskunde und Philologie*, IX (Vienna, 1976).
Varakauskas, R., 'Lietuvos valstybės pergalių prieš Livonijos ordiną XIIIa. pabaigoje–XIVa. pradžioje klausimų', *LAMMDI*, 7 (1965), 129–39.
'Lietuvos ir Livonijos santykiai Gedimino valdymo laikotarpių', *LAMMDI*, 11 (1970), 179–97.
'Lietuvos ir Livonijos prekybiniai santykiai XIII–XIVa primojoje pusėje', *LAMMDI*, 12:2 (1972), 127–42.
Lietuvos ir Livonijos santykiai XIII–XVIa. (Vilnius, 1982).
Vasenko, P. G., 'Kniga stepennaia tsarskogo rodoslovia i eia znachenie v drevnerusskoi istoricheskoi pis'mennosti', *Zapiski istoriko-filologicheskogo fakul'teta imperatorskogo SanktPeterburgskogo Universiteta*, 73 (1904).
Vasil'evskii, V. G., 'Obrashchenie Gedimina v katolichestvo', *ZhMNP*, 159:2 (1872), 65–196.
'Zapisi o postavlenii russkikh episkopov', *ZhMNP* (1888/2), 445–63.
Vėlius, N., *The world outlook of the Ancient Balts* (Vilnius, 1989).
Veselovskii, S. B., *Feodal'noe zemlevladenie v severo-vostochnoi Rusi*, I (Leningrad, 1947).
Vestergaard, E., 'A note on Viking Age inaugurations', in *Coronations. Medieval and early modern monarchic ritual*, ed. J. M. Bak (Berkeley–Los Angeles–Oxford, 1990), 119–24.
Vladimirovas, L., 'Kokia kalba buvo kalbama ir rašoma Lietuvos Didžiojoje Kunigaikštystėje XIV–XVIIa.?', *LAMMDI*, 22 (1982), 103–18.
Vodoff, W., 'La titulature princière en Russie du XIe au début du XVIe siècle', *Jahrbücher für Geschichte Osteuropas*, 35 (1987), 1–35.
Volkaitė-Kulikauskienė, R., 'Uspekhi arkheologicheskoi nauki v Litovskoi SSR', *Sovetskaia Arkheologia* (1967/3), 91–105.
'Nauji duomenys apie žemdirbystę ir gyvulininkystę rytų Lietuvoje', *LMADA*, 48 (1974/3), 51–65.
Vööbus, A., *Studies in the history of the Estonian people, I: Papers of the Estonian Theological Society in Exile*, XVIII (1969).

Voronin, N. N., 'Tverskoe zodchestvo XIII–XIV vekov', *Izvestia Akademii Nauk. Seria istorii i filosofii*, 5 (1945), 373–86.
'Andrei Bogoliubskii i Luka Khrizoverg (iz istorii russko-vizantiiskikh otnoshenii XIIv.)', *Vizantiiskii Vremennik*, 21 (1962), 29–50.
Vostochnaia Evropa v drevnosti i srednevekov'e. Sbornik statei, ed. L. V. Cherepnin (Moscow, 1978).
Vysotskii, S. A., *Drevnerusskie nadpisi Sofii kievskoi XI–XIV vv.* (Kiev, 1966).
Walachowicz, J., *Geneza i ustrój polityczny Nowej Marchii do początku XIV wieku, Poznańskie Towarzystwo Przyjaćiół nauk – Wydźiał Historii i nauk społecznych. Prace komisji historycznej*, XXXI (1980).
Wallace-Hadrill, J. M., *The long-haired kings* (London, 1962).
Early Germanic kingship in England and on the Continent (Oxford, 1971).
Walter, C., *Art and ritual of the Byzantine Church* (London, 1982).
Wasilewski, T., 'Prawosławne imiona Jagiełły i Witolda', *Analecta Cracoviensia*, 19 (1987), 105–16.
'Trzy małżeństwa wielkiego księcia Litwy Olgierda. Przyczynek do genealogii Giedyminowiczów', *Kultura średniowieczna i staropolska. Studia ofiarowane Aleksandrowi Gieysztorowi w pięćdziesięciolecie pracy naukowej* (Warsaw, 1991), 673–82.
'Daty urodzin Jagiełły i Witolda', *Przegląd Wschodni*, 1:1 (1991), 15–34.
Wdowiszewski, Z., *Genealogia Jagiellonów* (Warsaw, 1968).
Webb, M. C., 'The flag follows trade: An essay on the necessary interaction of military and commercial factors in state formation', in *Ancient Civilisation and Trade*, ed. J. A. Sabloff and C. C. Lamberg-Karlovsky (Albuquerque, 1975), 155–209.
Weise, E., 'Der Heidenkampf des Deutschen Ordens', *ZfO*, 12 (1963), 420–73, 622–72.
Wenskus, R., 'Der Deutsche Orden und die nichtdeutsche Bevölkerung des Preussenlandes', *Studien zum Deutschtum im Osten*, 8 (1971), 86–106.
Wiesiołowski, J., *Kolekcje historyczne w Polsce średniowiecznej XIV–XV wieku* (Wrocław–Warsaw–Kraków, 1967).
Winowski, L., *Innowiercy w poglądach uczonych Zachodniego Chrześcijaństwa XIII–XIV wieku. Prace Wrocławskiego Towarzystwa naukowego*, Series A CCXXXVI (1985).
Włodarski, B., 'Wołyń pod rządami Rurykowiczów i Bolesława Jerzego Trojdenowicza', *Rocznik Wołyński*, 3 (1934), 105–48.
Polska i Ruś 1194–1340 (Warsaw, 1966).
Wojtkowiak, Z., 'Chrystianizacja Litwy w historiografii polskiej ostatniego czterdziestolecia', in *Chrystianizacja Litwy*, ed. J. Kłoczowski (Kraków, 1987), 321–39.
Wolff, J., *Ród Gedymina. Dodatki i poprawki do dzieł Hr. K. Stadnickiego 'Synowie Gedymina, Olgierd i Kiejstut' i 'Bracia Władysława-Jagiełły'* (Kraków, 1886).
Wolter, E., 'Mythologische Skizzen', *Archiv für slavische Philologie*, 9 (1887), 635–42.
'Perkunastempel und litauische Opfer oder Deivensteine', *Mitteilungen der litauischen literarischen Gesellschaft*, 4: 22 (1897), 393–5.

Wood, I. N., 'Kings, kingdoms and consent', *Early medieval kingship* (*qv*), 6–29.
'Christian and pagan in ninth-century Scandinavia', in *The Christianization of Scandinavia*, ed. B. Sawyer, P. Sawyer and I. N. Wood (Alingsås, 1987), 36–67.
Wos, J. W., 'Prolegomeni allo studio di Paulus Wladimiri di Brudzen, canonista polacco', *Rivista di Letteratura e di Storia ecclesiastica* (1973/1), 3–24.
Wunder, H., 'Siedlung und Bevölkerung im Ordensstaat, Herzogtum und Königreich Preussen 13–18 Jahrhundert', *Studien zum Deutschtum im Osten*, 19:2 (1987), 67–98.
Wyrozumski, J., *Kazimierz Wielki*, 2nd edn (Wrocław–Warsaw–Kraków–Gdańsk–Łódź, 1986).
'Próba Chrystianizacji Litwy w czasach Giedymina', *Analecta Cracoviensia*, 19 (1987), 69–90.
Zabiela, G., 'Pozdnesrednevekovyi mogil'nik Biačiai', *AO* (1985), 480.
Zachara-Wawrzyńczyk, M., 'Geneza legendy o Rzymskim pochodzeniu Litwinów', *Zeszyty Historyczne Uniwersytetu Warszawskiego*, 3 (1963), 5–35.
Zachová, J., *Die Chronik des Franz von Prag. Inhaltliche und stilistische Analyse*, *Acta Universitatis Carolinae, Philologica Monographia*, LIII (1974).
Zajączkowski, S., 'Przymierze polsko-litewskie 1325r.', *KH*, 40 (1926), 567–617.
'Przyczynki do hipotezy o pochodzeniu dynastji Giedymina ze Źmudzi', *AW*, 4: 13 (1927), 392–416.
Zakony Franciszkańskie w Polsce średniowiecznej I: Franciszkanie na ziemiach polskich, ed. J. Kłoczowski (Lublin, 1983).
Zakrzewska-Dubasowa, M., *Historia Armenii* (Wrocław–Warsaw–Kraków–Gdańsk, 1977).
Ormianie w dawnej Polsce (Lublin, 1982).
Zakrzewski, S., 'Wpływ sprawy ruskiej na państwo polskie w XIVw.', *PH*, 23 (1921–22), 86–121.
Zhidkov, G. V., *Moskovskaia zhivopis' srediny XIV veka* (Moscow, 1928).
Zientara, B., '*Melioratio terrae*: the thirteenth-century breakthrough in Polish history', *Republic of nobles* (*qv*.), 28–48.
'Les grandes migrations des XII-XIV siècles en Europe du Centre-Est', *Studia Historiae Oeconomicae*, 18 (1983), 3–30.
Zimin, A. A., 'Antichnye momenty v russkoi publitsistike kontsa XV veka', *Feodal'naia Rossia v vsemirno-istoricheskom protsesse. Sbornik statei posviashchennykh L'vu Vladimirovichu Cherepninu* (Moscow, 1972), 128–38.
Kholopy na Rusi (*s drevneishikh vremen do kontsa XVv.*) (Moscow, 1973).
Rossia na rubezhe XV–XVIst. (Moscow, 1982).
Formirovanie boiarskoi aristokratii v Rossii vo vtoroi polovine XV-pervoi treti XVIv. (Moscow, 1988).
Zinkiavičius, Z., 'K istorii litovskoi khristianskoi terminologii vostochno-slavianskogo proiskhozhdenia', *Balto-Slavianskie Issledovania* (1980), 131–9.
Znosko, A., *Mały słownik wyrazów starocerkiewno-słowiańskich i terminologii cerkiewno-teologicznej* (Warsaw, 1983).

Zotov, R. V., *O chernigovskikh kniaziakh po Liubetskomu Sinodiku i o Chernigovskom Kniazhestve v tatarskoe vremia* (St Petersburg, 1892).
Žulkus, V., 'Birutės kalnas ir gyvenvietė Palangoje', *Lietuvos Istorijos Metraštis* (1985), 21–35.

INDEX

The following abbreviations have been used: (a)bp – (arch)bishop; Cple – Constantinople; GDL – G[rand] D[uke] of Lithuania; GDV – Grand Duke of Vladimir (later, of Moscow) and All Rus'; GM – Grand Master of the T[eutonic] O[rder]; grd – granddaughter, gr-grd – great granddaughter; k. – king; pr. – prince

Index

Cambridge studies in medieval life and thought
Fourth series

Titles in the series

1 The Beaumont Twins: The Roots and Branches of Power in the Twelfth Century
D. B. CROUCH

2 The Thought of Gregory the Great*
G. R. EVANS

3 The Government of England under Henry I*
JUDITH A. GREEN

4 Charity and Community in Medieval Cambridge
MIRI RUBIN

5 Autonomy and Community: The Royal Manor of Havering, 1200–1500
MARJORIE KENISTON MCINTOSH

6 The Political Thought of Baldus de Ubaldis
JOSEPH CANNING

7 Land and Power in Late Medieval Ferrara: The Rule of the Este, 1350–1450
TREVOR DEAN

8 William of Tyre: Historian of the Latin East*
PETER W. EDBURY AND JOHN GORDON ROWE

9 The Royal Saints of Anglo-Saxon England: A Study of West Saxon and East Anglian Cults
SUSAN J. RIDYARD

10 John of Wales: A Study of the Works and Ideas of a Thirteenth-Century Friar
JENNY SWANSON

11 Richard III: A Study of Service*
ROSEMARY HORROX

12 A Marginal Economy? East Anglian Breckland in the Later Middle Ages
MARK BAILEY

13 Clement VI: The Pontificate and Ideas of an Avignon Pope
DIANA WOOD

14 Hagiography and the Cult of Saints: The Diocese of Orléans, 800–1200
THOMAS HEAD

15 Kings and Lords in Conquest England
ROBIN FLEMING

16 Council and Hierarchy: The Political Thought of William Durant the Younger
CONSTANTIN FASOLT

17 Warfare in the Latin East, 1192–1291
CHRISTOPHER MARSHALL

* Also published as a paperback

18 Province and Empire: Brittany and the Carolingians
JULIA M. H. SMITH

19 A Gentry Community: Leicestershire in the Fifteenth Century, *c.* 1422–*c.* 1485
ERIC ACHESON

20 Baptism and Change in the Early Middle Ages, *c.* 200–1150
PETER CRAMER

21 Royal Monasteries and Itinerant Kingship in Early Medieval Germany, *c.* 936–1075
JOHN W. BERNHARDT

22 Caesarius of Arles: The Making of a Christian Community in Late Antique Gaul
WILLIAM E. KLINGSHIRN

23 Bishop and Chapter in Twelfth-Century England: A Study of the *Mensa Episcopalis*
EVERETT U. CROSBY

24 Trade and Traders in Muslim Spain: The Commercial Realignment of the Iberian Peninsula, 900–1500
OLIVIA REMIE CONSTABLE

25 Lithuania Ascending: A Pagan Empire within East-Central Europe, 1295–1345
S. C. ROWELL